Real-Time Data Analysis Exercises

Up-to-date macro data is a great way to engage in and understand the usefulness of macro variables and their impact on the economy. Real-Time Data Analysis exercises communicate directly with the Federal Reserve Bank of St. Louis's FRED® site, so every time FRED posts new data, students see new data.

End-of-chapter exercises accompanied by the Real-Time Data Analysis icon  include Real-Time Data versions in **MyEconLab**.

Select in-text figures labeled **MyEconLab** Real-Time Data update in the electronic version of the text using FRED data.

Current News Exercises

Posted weekly, we find the latest microeconomic and macroeconomic news stories, post them, and write auto-graded multi-part exercises that illustrate the economic way of thinking about the news.

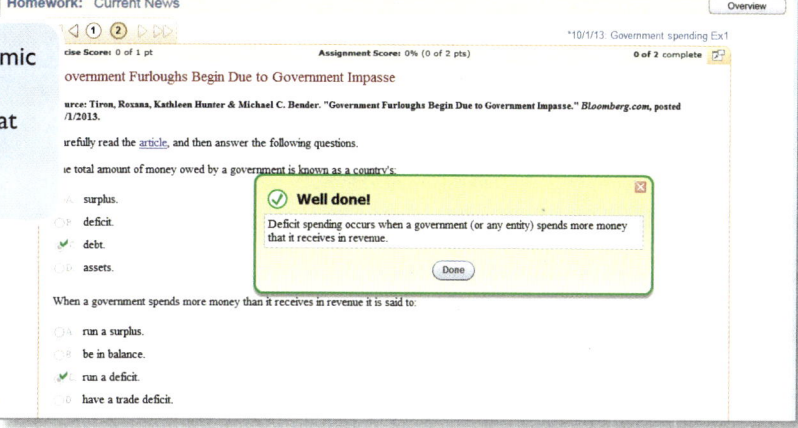

Interactive Homework Exercises

Participate in a fun and engaging activity that helps promote active learning and mastery of important economic concepts.

Pearson's experiments program is flexible and easy for instructors and students to use. For a complete list of available experiments, visit *www.myeconlab.com*.

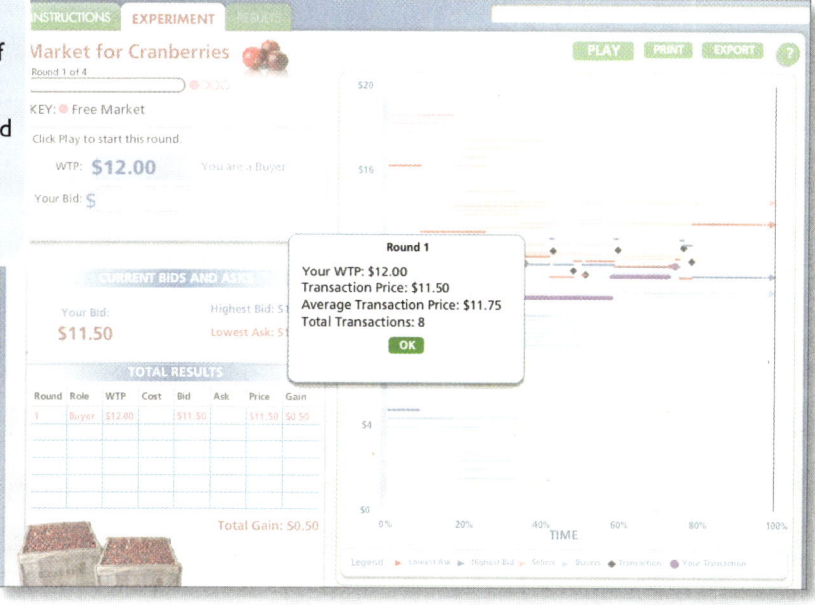

THE PEARSON SERIES IN ECONOMICS

Abel/Bernanke/Croushore
*Macroeconomics**

Bade/Parkin
*Foundations of Economics**

Berck/Helfand
*The Economics of the
Environment*

Bierman/Fernandez
*Game Theory with
Economic Applications*

Blanchard
*Macroeconomics**

Blau/Ferber/Winkler
*The Economics of Women,
Men, and Work*

Boardman/Greenberg/
Vining/Weimer
Cost-Benefit Analysis

Boyer
*Principles of
Transportation Economics*

Branson
*Macroeconomic Theory
and Policy*

Bruce
*Public Finance and the
American Economy*

Carlton/Perloff
*Modern Industrial
Organization*

Case/Fair/Oster
*Principles of Economics**

Chapman
*Environmental Economics:
Theory, Application, and
Policy*

Cooter/Ulen
Law & Economics

Daniels/VanHoose
*International Monetary &
Financial Economics*

Downs
*An Economic Theory of
Democracy*

Ehrenberg/Smith
Modern Labor Economics

Farnham
Economics for Managers

Folland/Goodman/Stano
*The Economics of Health
and Health Care*

Fort
Sports Economics

Froyen
Macroeconomics

Fusfeld
The Age of the Economist

Gerber
*International Economics**

González-Rivera
*Forecasting for Economics
and Business*

Gordon
*Macroeconomics**

Greene
Econometric Analysis

Gregory
*Essentials of
Economics*

Gregory/Stuart
*Russian and Soviet
Economic Performance
and Structure*

Hartwick/Olewiler
*The Economics of Natural
Resource Use*

Heilbroner/Milberg
*The Making of the Economic
Society*

Heyne/Boettke/Prychitko
*The Economic Way of
Thinking*

Holt
*Markets, Games, and
Strategic Behavior*

Hubbard/O'Brien
*Economics**

*Money, Banking, and the
Financial System**

Hubbard/O'Brien/Rafferty
*Macroeconomics**

Hughes/Cain
*American Economic
History*

Husted/Melvin
*International
Economics*

Jehle/Reny
*Advanced Microeconomic
Theory*

Johnson-Lans
*A Health Economics
Primer*

Keat/Young/Erfle
Managerial Economics

Klein
*Mathematical Methods for
Economics*

Krugman/Obstfeld/Melitz
*International Economics:
Theory & Policy**

Laidler
The Demand for Money

Leeds/von Allmen
The Economics of Sports

Leeds/von Allmen/Schiming
*Economics**

Lynn
*Economic Development:
Theory and Practice for a
Divided World*

Miller
*Economics Today**

*Understanding Modern
Economics*

Miller/Benjamin
*The Economics of Macro
Issues*

Miller/Benjamin/North
*The Economics of Public
Issues*

Mills/Hamilton
Urban Economics

Mishkin
*The Economics of Money,
Banking, and Financial
Markets**

*The Economics of Money,
Banking, and Financial
Markets, Business School
Edition**

*Macroeconomics: Policy
and Practice**

Murray
*Econometrics: A Modern
Introduction*

O'Sullivan/Sheffrin/Perez
*Economics: Principles,
Applications and Tools**

Parkin
*Economics**

Perloff
*Microeconomics**

*Microeconomics: Theory
and Applications with
Calculus**

Perloff/Brander
*Managerial Economics
and Strategy**

Phelps
Health Economics

Pindyck/Rubinfeld
*Microeconomics**

Riddell/Shackelford/Stamos/
Schneider
*Economics: A Tool for
Critically Understanding
Society*

Roberts
*The Choice: A Fable of
Free Trade and Protection*

Rohlf
*Introduction to Economic
Reasoning*

Roland
Development Economics

Scherer
*Industry Structure,
Strategy, and Public
Policy*

Schiller
*The Economics of Poverty
and Discrimination*

Sherman
Market Regulation

Stock/Watson
*Introduction to
Econometrics*

Studenmund
*Using Econometrics: A
Practical Guide*

Tietenberg/Lewis
*Environmental and
Natural Resource
Economics*

*Environmental Economics
and Policy*

Todaro/Smith
Economic Development

Waldman/Jensen
*Industrial Organization:
Theory and Practice*

Walters/Walters/Appel/
Callahan/Centanni/Maex/
O'Neill
*Econversations: Today's
Students Discuss Today's
Issues*

Weil
Economic Growth

Williamson
Macroeconomics

*denotes 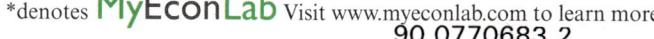 MyEconLab Visit www.myeconlab.com to learn more.

MyEconLab® Provides the Power of Practice

Optimize your study time with **MyEconLab**, the online assessment and tutorial system. When you take a sample test online, **MyEconLab** gives you targeted feedback and a personalized Study Plan to identify the topics you need to review.

Study Plan

The Study Plan shows you the sections you should study next, gives easy access to practice problems, and provides you with an automatically generated quiz to prove mastery of the course material.

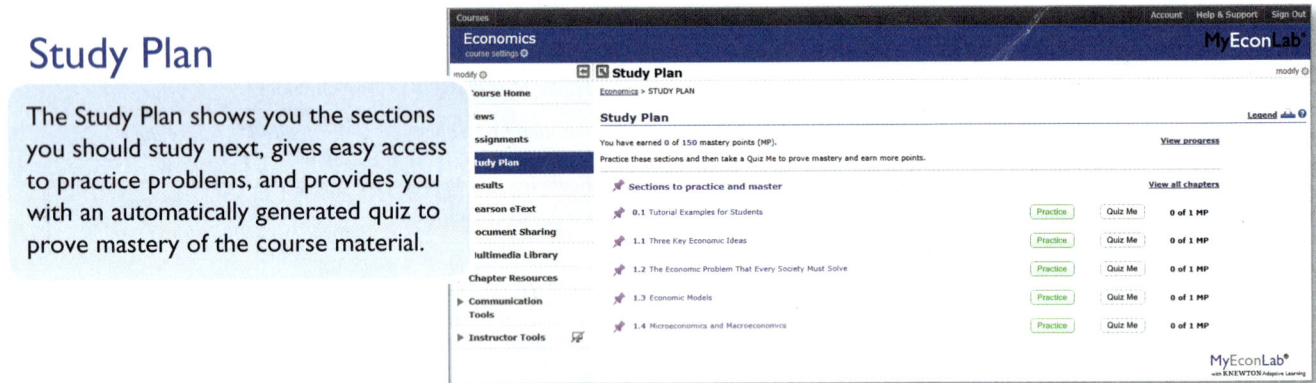

Unlimited Practice

As you work each exercise, instant feedback helps you understand and apply the concepts. Many Study Plan exercises contain algorithmically generated values to ensure that you get as much practice as you need.

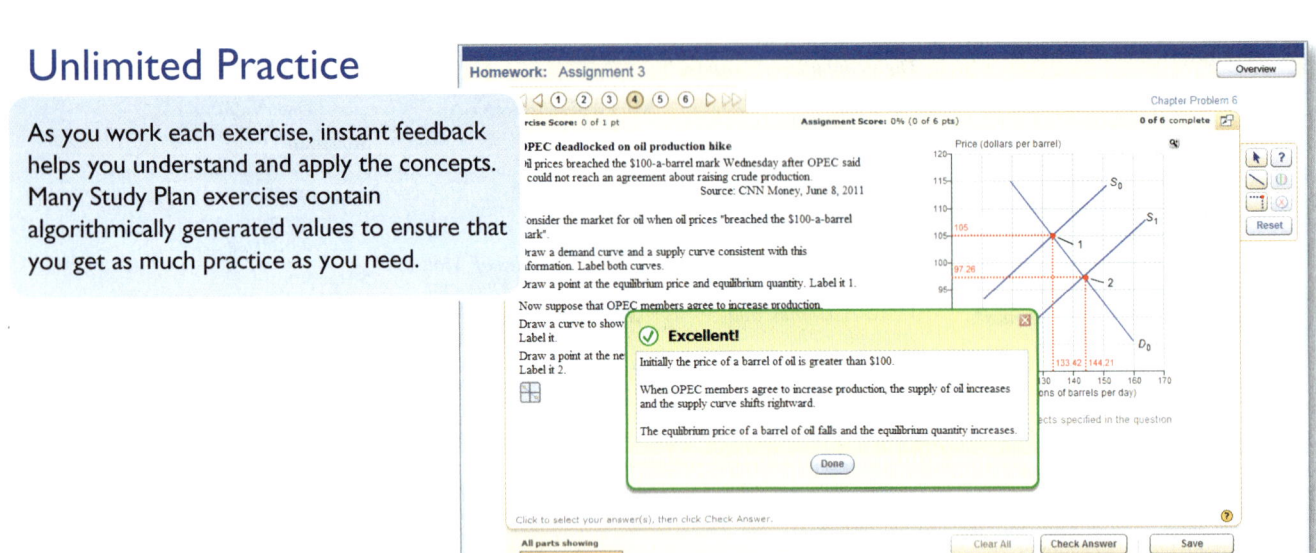

Learning Resources

Study Plan problems link to learning resources that further reinforce concepts you need to master.

- **Help Me Solve This** learning aids help you break down a problem much the same way as an instructor would do during office hours. Help Me Solve This is available for select problems.

- **eText links** are specific to the problem at hand so that related concepts are easy to review just when they are needed.

- A **graphing tool** enables you to build and manipulate graphs to better understand how concepts, numbers, and graphs connect.

Find out more at www.myeconlab.com

International Trade

THEORY AND POLICY

TENTH EDITION

GLOBAL EDITION

Paul R. Krugman
Princeton University

Maurice Obstfeld
University of California, Berkeley

Marc J. Melitz
Harvard University

PEARSON

Boston   Columbus   Indianapolis   New York   San Francisco   Upper Saddle River
Amsterdam   Cape Town   Dubai   London   Madrid   Milan   Munich   Paris   Montréal   Toronto
Delhi   Mexico City   São Paulo   Sydney   Hong Kong   Seoul   Singapore   Taipei   Tokyo

For Robin—P.K.
For my family—M.O.
For Clair, Benjamin, and Max—M.M.

Editor in Chief: Donna Battista
Managing Editor: Jeff Holcomb
Head of Learning Asset Acquisition, Global Editions:
    Laura Dent
Associate Editor, Global Editions: Toril Cooper
Program Manager: Carolyn Philips
International Marketing Manager: Kristin Schneider
Production Project Manager: Carla Thompson
Assistant Project Editor, Global Editions: Paromita Banerjee
Procurement Specialist: Carol Melville
Senior Operations Supervisor: Arnold Vila
Operations Specialist: Michelle Klein
Senior Art Director: Jonathan Boylan
Text Permissions Associate Project Manager:
    Samantha Graham

Interior Design: Integra-Chicago
Image Manager: Rachel Youdelman
Photo Research: Aptara, Inc.
Director of Media: Susan Schoenberg
Content Leads, MyEconLab: Courtney Kamauf and
    Noel Lotz
Senior Media Producer: Melissa Honig
Senior Production Manufacturing Controller, Global Editions:
    Trudy Kimber
Full-Service Project Management and Composition:
    Integra Software Services, Inc.
Media Producer, Global Editions: Vikram Kumar
Cover Image Credit: © Denis Vrublevski/Shutterstock
Cover Designer: PreMedia Global USA, Inc.

Pearson Education Limited
Edinburgh Gate
Harlow
Essex CM20 2JE
England

and Associated Companies throughout the world

Visit us on the World Wide Web at:
www.pearsonglobaleditions.com

© Pearson Education Limited 2015

*Authorized adaptation from the United States edition, entitled International Economics: Theory and Policy, 10th Edition
ISBN 978-0-13-342364-8 by Paul R. Krugman, Maurice Obstfeld, and Marc J. Melitz, published by Pearson Education © 2015.*

ISBN 10: 1-292-06043-3
ISBN 13: 978-1-292-06043-9

British Library Cataloguing-in-Publication Data
A catalogue record for this book is available from the British Library

10 9 8 7 6 5 4 3 2 1
15 14

Typeset in 10/12 Times New Roman, Integra Software Services, Inc.

Printed and bound by Courier Kendallville in The United States of America

ECON

Brief Contents

Contents

9

MATHEMATICAL POSTSCRIPTS   337

INDEX   351

CREDITS   360

ONLINE APPENDICES (*www.pearsonglobaleditions.com/krugman*)

Preface

Years after the global financial crisis that broke out in 2007–2008, the industrial world's economies are still growing too slowly to restore full employment. Emerging markets, despite impressive income gains in many cases, remain vulnerable to the ebb and flow of global capital. And finally, an acute economic crisis in the euro area has lasted since 2009, bringing the future of Europe's common currency into question. This tenth edition therefore comes out at a time when we are more aware than ever before of how events in the global economy influence each country's economic fortunes, policies, and political debates. The world that emerged from World War II was one in which trade, financial, and even communication links between countries were limited. More than a decade into the 21st century, however, the picture is very different. Globalization has arrived, big time. International trade in goods and services has expanded steadily over the past six decades thanks to declines in shipping and communication costs, globally negotiated reductions in government trade barriers, the widespread outsourcing of production activities, and a greater awareness of foreign cultures and products. New and better communications technologies, notably the Internet, have revolutionized the way people in all countries obtain and exchange information. International trade in financial assets such as currencies, stocks, and bonds has expanded at a much faster pace even than international product trade. This process brings benefits for owners of wealth but also creates risks of contagious financial instability. Those risks were realized during the recent global financial crisis, which spread quickly across national borders and has played out at huge cost to the world economy. Of all the changes on the international scene in recent decades, however, perhaps the biggest one remains the emergence of China—a development that is already redefining the international balance of economic and political power in the coming century.

Imagine the astonishment of the generation that lived through the depressed 1930s as adults, had its members been able to foresee the shape of today's world economy! Nonetheless, the economic concerns that continue to cause international debate have not changed that much from those that dominated the 1930s, nor indeed since they were first analyzed by economists more than two centuries ago. What are the merits of free trade among nations compared with protectionism? What causes countries to run trade surpluses or deficits with their trading partners, and how are such imbalances resolved over time? What causes banking and currency crises in open economies, what causes financial contagion between economies, and how should governments handle international financial instability? How can governments avoid unemployment and inflation, what role do exchange rates play in their efforts, and how can countries best cooperate to achieve their economic goals? As always in international economics, the interplay of events and ideas has led to new modes of analysis. In turn, these analytical advances, however abstruse they may seem at first, ultimately do end up playing a major role in governmental policies, in international negotiations, and in people's everyday lives. Globalization has made citizens of all countries much more aware than ever before of the worldwide economic forces that influence their fortunes, and globalization is here to stay.

New to the Tenth Edition

For this edition, we are offering an Economics volume as well as Trade and Finance splits. The goal with these distinct volumes is to allow professors to use the book that best suits their needs based on the topics they cover in their International Economics course. In the Economics volume for a two-semester course, we follow the standard practice of dividing the book into two halves, devoted to trade and to monetary questions. Although the trade and monetary portions of international economics are often treated as unrelated subjects, even within one textbook, similar themes and methods recur in both subfields. We have made it a point to illuminate connections between the trade and monetary areas when they arise. At the same time, we have made sure that the book's two halves are completely self-contained. Thus, a one-semester course on trade theory can be based on Chapters 2 through 12, and a one-semester course on international monetary economics can be based on Chapters 13 through 22. For professors' and students' convenience, however, they can now opt to use either the Trade or the Finance volume, depending on the length and scope of their course.

We have thoroughly updated the content and extensively revised several chapters. These revisions respond both to users' suggestions and to some important developments on the theoretical and practical sides of international economics. The most far-reaching changes in the Trade volume are the following:

- **Chapter 5, Resources and Trade: The Heckscher-Ohlin Model** This edition offers expanded coverage of the effects on wage inequality of North-South trade, technological change, and outsourcing. The section describing the empirical evidence on the Heckscher-Ohlin model has been rewritten, emphasizing new research. That section also incorporates some new data showing how China's pattern of exports has changed over time in a way that is consistent with the predictions of the Heckscher-Olhin model.
- **Chapter 6, The Standard Trade Model** This chapter has been updated with some new data documenting how the terms of trade for the U.S. and Chinese economies have evolved over time.
- **Chapter 8, Firms in the Global Economy: Export Decisions, Outsourcing, and Multinational Enterprises** The coverage emphasizing the role of firms in international trade has been revised. There is also a new Case Study analyzing the impact of offshoring in the United States on U.S. unemployment.
- **Chapter 9, The Instruments of Trade Policy** This chapter features an updated treatment of the effects of trade restrictions on United States firms. This chapter now describes the recent trade policy dispute between the European Union and China regarding solar panels and the effects of the "Buy American" restrictions that were written into the American Recovery and Re-Investment Act of 2009.
- **Chapter 12, Controversies in Trade Policy** A new case study discusses the recent garment factory collapse in Bangladesh (in April 2013) and the tension between the costs and benefits of Bangladesh's rapid growth as a clothing exporter.

In addition to these structural changes, we have updated the book in other ways to maintain current relevance. Thus, in the Trade volume, we examine the educational profile of foreign born workers in the United States and how it differs from the overall population (Chapter 4); we review recent anti-dumping disputes involving China (Chapter 8).

About the Book

The idea of writing this book came out of our experience in teaching international economics to undergraduates and business students since the late 1970s. We perceived two main challenges in teaching. The first was to communicate to students the exciting intellectual advances in this dynamic field. The second was to show how the development of international economic theory has traditionally been shaped by the need to understand the changing world economy and analyze actual problems in international economic policy.

We found that published textbooks did not adequately meet these challenges. Too often, international economics textbooks confront students with a bewildering array of special models and assumptions from which basic lessons are difficult to extract. Because many of these special models are outmoded, students are left puzzled about the real-world relevance of the analysis. As a result, many textbooks often leave a gap between the somewhat antiquated material to be covered in class and the exciting issues that dominate current research and policy debates. That gap has widened dramatically as the importance of international economic problems—and enrollments in international economics courses—have grown.

This book is our attempt to provide an up-to-date and understandable analytical framework for illuminating current events and bringing the excitement of international economics into the classroom. In analyzing both the real and monetary sides of the subject, our approach has been to build up, step by step, a simple, unified framework for communicating the grand traditional insights as well as the newest findings and approaches. To help the student grasp and retain the underlying logic of international economics, we motivate the theoretical development at each stage by pertinent data and policy questions.

The Place of This Book in the Economics Curriculum

Students assimilate international economics most readily when it is presented as a method of analysis vitally linked to events in the world economy, rather than as a body of abstract theorems about abstract models. Our goal has therefore been to stress concepts and their application rather than theoretical formalism. Accordingly, the book does not presuppose an extensive background in economics. Students who have had a course in economic principles will find the book accessible, but students who have taken further courses in microeconomics or macroeconomics will find an abundant supply of new material. Specialized appendices and mathematical postscripts have been included to challenge the most advanced students.

Some Distinctive Features

This book covers the most important recent developments in international economics without shortchanging the enduring theoretical and historical insights that have traditionally formed the core of the subject. We have achieved this comprehensiveness by stressing how recent theories have evolved from earlier findings in response to an evolving world economy. The text is divided into a core of chapters focused on theory, followed by chapters applying the theory to major policy questions, past and current.

In Chapter 1, we describe in some detail how this book addresses the major themes of international economics. Here we emphasize several of the topics that previous authors failed to treat in a systematic way.

Increasing Returns and Market Structure

Even before discussing the role of comparative advantage in promoting international exchange and the associated welfare gains, we visit the forefront of theoretical and empirical research by setting out the gravity model of trade (Chapter 2). We return to the research frontier (in Chapters 7 and 8) by explaining how increasing returns and product differentiation affect trade and welfare. The models explored in this discussion capture significant aspects of reality, such as intraindustry trade and shifts in trade patterns due to dynamic scale economies. The models show, too, that mutually beneficial trade need not be based on comparative advantage.

Firms in International Trade

Chapter 8 also summarizes exciting new research focused on the role of firms in international trade. The chapter emphasizes that different firms may fare differently in the face of globalization. The expansion of some and the contraction of others shift overall production toward more efficient producers within industrial sectors, raising overall productivity and thereby generating gains from trade. Those firms that expand in an environment of freer trade may have incentives to outsource some of their production activities abroad or take up multinational production, as we describe in the chapter.

Politics and Theory of Trade Policy

Starting in Chapter 4, we stress the effect of trade on income distribution as the key political factor behind restrictions on free trade. This emphasis makes it clear to students why the prescriptions of the standard welfare analysis of trade policy seldom prevail in practice. Chapter 12 explores the popular notion that governments should adopt activist trade policies aimed at encouraging sectors of the economy seen as crucial. The chapter includes a theoretical discussion of such trade policy based on simple ideas from game theory.

Learning Features

This book incorporates a number of special learning features that will maintain students' interest in the presentation and help them master its lessons.

Case Studies

Case studies that perform the threefold role of reinforcing material covered earlier, illustrating its applicability in the real world, and providing important historical information often accompany theoretical discussions.

Special Boxes

Less central topics that nonetheless offer particularly vivid illustrations of points made in the text are treated in boxes. Among these are U.S. President Thomas Jefferson's trade embargo of 1807–1809 (Chapter 3); the astonishing ability of disputes over banana trade to generate acrimony among countries far too cold to grow any of their own bananas (Chapter 10).

Captioned Diagrams

More than 200 diagrams are accompanied by descriptive captions that reinforce the discussion in the text and help the student in reviewing the material.

Learning Goals

A list of essential concepts sets the stage for each chapter in the book. These learning goals help students assess their mastery of the material.

Summary and Key Terms

Each chapter closes with a summary recapitulating the major points. Key terms and phrases appear in boldface type when they are introduced in the chapter and are listed at the end of each chapter. To further aid student review of the material, key terms are italicized when they appear in the chapter summary.

Problems

Each chapter is followed by problems intended to test and solidify students' comprehension. The problems range from routine computational drills to "big picture" questions suitable for classroom discussion. In many problems we ask students to apply what they have learned to real-world data or policy questions.

Further Readings

For instructors who prefer to supplement the textbook with outside readings, and for students who wish to probe more deeply on their own, each chapter has an annotated bibliography that includes established classics as well as up-to-date examinations of recent issues.

MyEconLab

MyEconLab

MyEconLab is the premier online assessment and tutorial system, pairing rich online content with innovative learning tools. MyEconLab includes comprehensive homework, quiz, test, and tutorial options, allowing instructors to manage all assessment needs in one program. Key innovations in the MyEconLab course for the tenth edition of *International Trade: Theory & Policy* include the following:

- *Real-Time Data Analysis Exercises,* marked with , allow students and instructors to use the latest data from FRED, the online macroeconomic data bank from the Federal Reserve Bank of St. Louis. By completing the exercises, students become familiar with a key data source, learn how to locate data, and develop skills to interpret data.
- In the *enhanced eText* available in MyEconLab, figures labeled MyEconLab Real-Time Data allow students to display a pop-up graph updated with real-time data from FRED.
- *Current News Exercises,* new to this edition of the MyEconLab course, provide a turnkey way to assign gradable news-based exercises in MyEconLab. Every week, Pearson scours the news, finds a current article appropriate for an economics course, creates an exercise around the news article, and then automatically adds it to MyEconLab. Assigning and grading current news-based exercises that deal with the latest economic events has never been more convenient.

Students and MyEconLab

This online homework and tutorial system puts students in control of their own learning through a suite of study and practice tools correlated with the online, interactive version of the textbook and learning aids such as animated figures. Within MyEconLab's structured environment, students practice what they learn, test their understanding, and then pursue a study plan that MyEconLab generates for them based on their performance.

Instructors and MyEconLab

MyEconLab provides flexible tools that allow instructors easily and effectively to customize online course materials to suit their needs. Instructors can create and assign tests, quizzes, or homework assignments. MyEconLab saves time by automatically grading all questions and tracking results in an online gradebook. MyEconLab can even grade assignments that require students to draw a graph.

After registering for MyEconLab instructors have access to downloadable supplements such as an instructor's manual, PowerPoint lecture notes, and a test bank. The test bank can also be used within MyEconLab, giving instructors ample material from which they can create assignments—or the Custom Exercise Builder makes it easy for instructors to create their own questions.

Weekly news articles, video, and RSS feeds help keep students updated on current events and make it easy for instructors to incorporate relevant news in lectures and homework.

For more information about MyEconLab or to request an instructor access code, visit www.myeconlab.com.

Additional Supplementary Resources

A full range of additional supplementary materials to support teaching and learning accompanies this book.

- The Online Instructor's Manual—updated by Hisham Foad of San Diego State University—includes chapter overviews and answers to the end-of-chapter problems.
- The Online Test Bank offers a rich array of multiple-choice and essay questions, including some mathematical and graphing problems, for each textbook chapter. It is available in Word, PDF, and TestGen formats. This Test Bank was carefully revised and updated by Robert F. Brooker of Gannon University.
- The Computerized Test Bank reproduces the Test Bank material in the TestGen software that is available for Windows and Macintosh. With TestGen, instructors can easily edit existing questions, add questions, generate tests, and print the tests in variety of formats.
- The Online PowerPoint Presentation with Tables, Figures, & Lecture Notes was revised by Amy Glass of Texas A&M University. This resource contains all text figures and tables and can be used for in-class presentations.
- The Companion Web Site at www.pearsonglobaleditions.com/Krugman contains additional appendices. (See page 14 of the Contents for a detailed list of the Online Appendices.)

Instructors can download supplements from our secure Instructor's Resource Center. Please visit www.pearsonglobaleditions.com/Krugman.

Acknowledgments

Our primary debt is to Christina Masturzo, the Acquisitions Editor in charge of the project. We also are grateful to the Program Manager, Carolyn Philips, and the Project Manager, Carla Thompson. Heather Johnson's efforts as Project Manager with Integra-Chicago were essential and efficient. We would also like to thank the media team at Pearson—Denise Clinton, Noel Lotz, Courtney Kamauf, and Melissa Honig—for all their hard work on the MyEconLab course for the tenth edition. Last, we thank the other editors who helped make the first nine editions of this book as good as they were.

We also wish to acknowledge the sterling research assistance of Tatjana Kleineberg and Sandile Hlatshwayo. Camille Fernandez provided superb logistical support, as usual. For helpful suggestions and moral support, we thank Jennifer Cobb, Gita Gopinath, Vladimir Hlasny, and Phillip Swagel.

We thank the following reviewers, past and present, for their recommendations and insights:

Jaleel Ahmad, *Concordia University*
Lian An, *University of North Florida*
Anthony Paul Andrews, *Governors State University*
Myrvin Anthony, *University of Strathclyde, U.K.*
Michael Arghyrou, *Cardiff University*
Richard Ault, *Auburn University*
Amitrajeet Batabyal, *Rochester Institute of Technology*
Tibor Besedes, *Georgia Tech*
George H. Borts, *Brown University*
Robert F. Brooker, *Gannon University*
Francisco Carrada-Bravo, *W.P. Carey School of Business, ASU*
Debajyoti Chakrabarty, *University of Sydney*
Adhip Chaudhuri, *Georgetown University*
Jay Pil Choi, *Michigan State University*
Jaiho Chung, *National University of Singapore*
Jonathan Conning, *Hunter College and The Graduate Center, The City University of New York*
Brian Copeland, *University of British Columbia*
Kevin Cotter, *Wayne State University*
Barbara Craig, *Oberlin College*
Susan Dadres, *University of North Texas*
Ronald B. Davies, *University College Dublin*
Ann Davis, *Marist College*
Gopal C. Dorai, *William Paterson University*
Robert Driskill, *Vanderbilt University*
Gerald Epstein, *University of Massachusetts at Amherst*
JoAnne Feeney, *State University of New York at Albany*

Robert Foster, *American Graduate School of International Management*
Patrice Franko, *Colby College*
Diana Fuguitt, *Eckerd College*
Byron Gangnes, *University of Hawaii at Manoa*
Ranjeeta Ghiara, *California State University, San Marcos*
Neil Gilfedder, *Stanford University*
Amy Glass, *Texas A&M University*
Patrick Gormely, *Kansas State University*
Thomas Grennes, *North Carolina State University*
Bodil Olai Hansen, *Copenhagen Business School*
Michael Hoffman, *U.S. Government Accountability Office*
Henk Jager, *University of Amsterdam*
Arvind Jaggi, *Franklin & Marshall College*
Mark Jelavich, *Northwest Missouri State University*
Philip R. Jones, *University of Bath and University of Bristol, U.K.*
Tsvetanka Karagyozova, *Lawrence University*
Hugh Kelley, *Indiana University*
Michael Kevane, *Santa Clara University*
Maureen Kilkenny, *University of Nevada*
Hyeongwoo Kim, *Auburn University*
Stephen A. King, *San Diego State University, Imperial Valley*
Faik Koray, *Louisiana State University*
Corinne Krupp, *Duke University*
Bun Song Lee, *University of Nebraska, Omaha*
Daniel Lee, *Shippensburg University*
Francis A. Lees, *St. Johns University*
Jamus Jerome Lim, *World Bank Group*
Rodney Ludema, *Georgetown University*

Stephen V. Marks, *Pomona College*
Michael L. McPherson, *University of North Texas*
Marcel Mérette, *University of Ottawa*
Shannon Mitchell, *Virginia Commonwealth University*
Kaz Miyagiwa, *Emory University*
Shannon Mudd, *Ursinus College*
Marc-Andreas Muendler, *University of California, San Diego*
Ton M. Mulder, *Erasmus University, Rotterdam*
Robert G. Murphy, *Boston College*
E. Wayne Nafziger, *Kansas State University*
Steen Nielsen, *University of Aarhus*
Dmitri Nizovtsev, *Washburn University*
Terutomo Ozawa, *Colorado State University*
Arvind Panagariya, *Columbia University*
Nina Pavcnik, *Dartmouth College*
Iordanis Petsas, *University of Scranton*
Thitima Puttitanun, *San Diego State University*
Peter Rangazas, *Indiana University-Purdue University Indianapolis*
James E. Rauch, *University of California, San Diego*
Michael Ryan, *Western Michigan University*

Donald Schilling, *University of Missouri, Columbia*
Patricia Higino Schneider, *Mount Holyoke College*
Ronald M. Schramm, *Columbia University*
Craig Schulman, *Texas A&M University*
Yochanan Shachmurove, *University of Pennsylvania*
Margaret Simpson, *The College of William and Mary*
Enrico Spolaore, *Tufts University*
Robert Staiger, *University of Wisconsin-Madison*
Jeffrey Steagall, *University of North Florida*
Robert M. Stern, *University of Michigan*
Abdulhamid Sukar, *Cameron University*
Rebecca Taylor, *University of Portsmouth, U.K.*
Scott Taylor, *University of British Columbia*
Aileen Thompson, *Carleton University*
Sarah Tinkler, *Portland State University*
Arja H. Turunen-Red, *University of New Orleans*
Dick vander Wal, *Free University of Amsterdam*
Gerald Willmann, *University of Kiel*
Rossitza Wooster, *California State University, Sacramento*
Bruce Wydick, *University of San Francisco*
Jiawen Yang, *The George Washington University*
Kevin H. Zhang, *Illinois State University*

Although we have not been able to make each and every suggested change, we found reviewers' observations invaluable in revising the book. Obviously, we bear sole responsibility for its remaining shortcomings.

Paul R. Krugman
Maurice Obstfeld
Marc J. Melitz
October 2013

Pearson would like to thank and acknowledge the following people for their work on the Global Edition:

Contributors:

Stefania Paladini, *Coventry University*

Pritish Kumar Sahu, *Multimedia University*

Reviewers:

Lap-kei Chow, *CUHK Business School*
Timo Korkeamäki, *Hanken School of Economics*
Joyce Chai Hui Ming, *Temasek Polytechnic*

Erkan Ilgün, *International Burch University*
Yue (Lucy) Liu, *University of Edinburgh*
Özlem Olgu, *Koç University*

CHAPTER 1

INTRODUCTION

You could say that the study of international trade and finance is where the discipline of economics as we know it began. Historians of economic thought often describe the essay "Of the Balance of Trade" by the Scottish philosopher David Hume as the first real exposition of an economic model. Hume published his essay in 1758, almost 20 years before his friend Adam Smith published *The Wealth of Nations*. And the debates over British trade policy in the early 19th century did much to convert economics from a discursive, informal field to the model-oriented subject it has been ever since.

Yet the study of international economics has never been as important as it is now. In the early 21st century, nations are more closely linked than ever before through trade in goods and services, flows of money, and investment in each other's economies. And the global economy created by these linkages is a turbulent place: Both policy makers and business leaders in every country, including the United States, must now pay attention to what are sometimes rapidly changing economic fortunes halfway around the world.

A look at some basic trade statistics gives us a sense of the unprecedented importance of international economic relations. Figure 1-1 shows the levels of U.S. exports and imports as shares of gross domestic product from 1960 to 2012. The most obvious feature of the figure is the long-term upward trend in both shares: International trade has roughly tripled in importance compared with the economy as a whole.

Almost as obvious is that, while both imports and exports have increased, imports have grown more, leading to a large excess of imports over exports. How is the United States able to pay for all those imported goods? The answer is that the money is supplied by large inflows of capital—money invested by foreigners willing to take a stake in the U.S. economy. Inflows of capital on that scale would once have been inconceivable; now they are taken for granted. And so the gap between imports and exports is an indicator of another aspect of growing international linkages—in this case the growing linkages between national capital markets.

Finally, notice that both imports and exports took a plunge in 2009. This decline reflected the global economic crisis that began in 2008 and is a reminder of the close links between world trade and the overall state of the world economy.

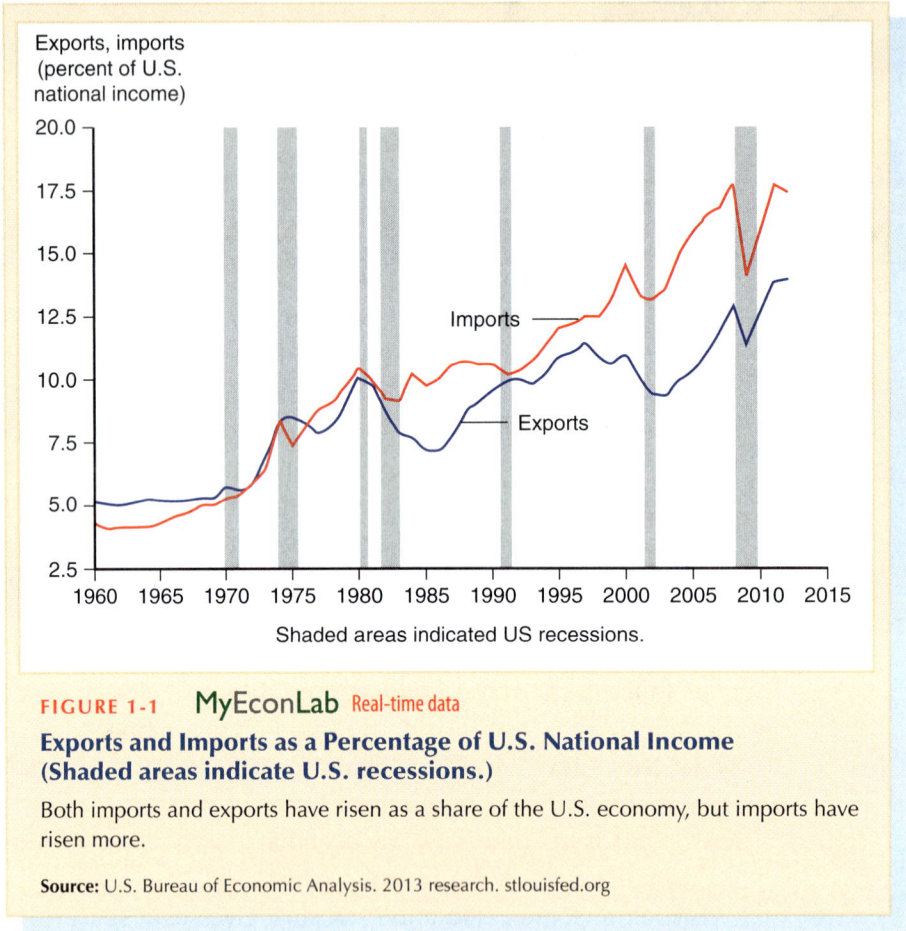

FIGURE 1-1   MyEconLab Real-time data

Exports and Imports as a Percentage of U.S. National Income (Shaded areas indicate U.S. recessions.)

Both imports and exports have risen as a share of the U.S. economy, but imports have risen more.

Source: U.S. Bureau of Economic Analysis. 2013 research. stlouisfed.org

If international economic relations have become crucial to the United States, they are even more crucial to other nations. Figure 1-2 shows the average of imports and exports as a share of GDP for a sample of countries. The United States, by virtue of its size and the diversity of its resources, relies less on international trade than almost any other country.

This text introduces the main concepts and methods of international economics and illustrates them with applications drawn from the real world. Much of the text is devoted to old ideas that are still as valid as ever: The 19th-century trade theory of David Ricardo and even the 18th-century monetary analysis of David Hume remain highly relevant to the 21st-century world economy. At the same time, we have made a special effort to bring the analysis up to date. In particular, the economic crisis that began in 2007 threw up major new challenges for the global economy. Economists were able to apply existing analyses to some of these challenges, but they were also forced to rethink some important concepts. Furthermore, new approaches have emerged to old questions, such as the impacts of changes in monetary and fiscal policy. We have attempted to convey the key ideas that have emerged in recent research while stressing the continuing usefulness of old ideas.

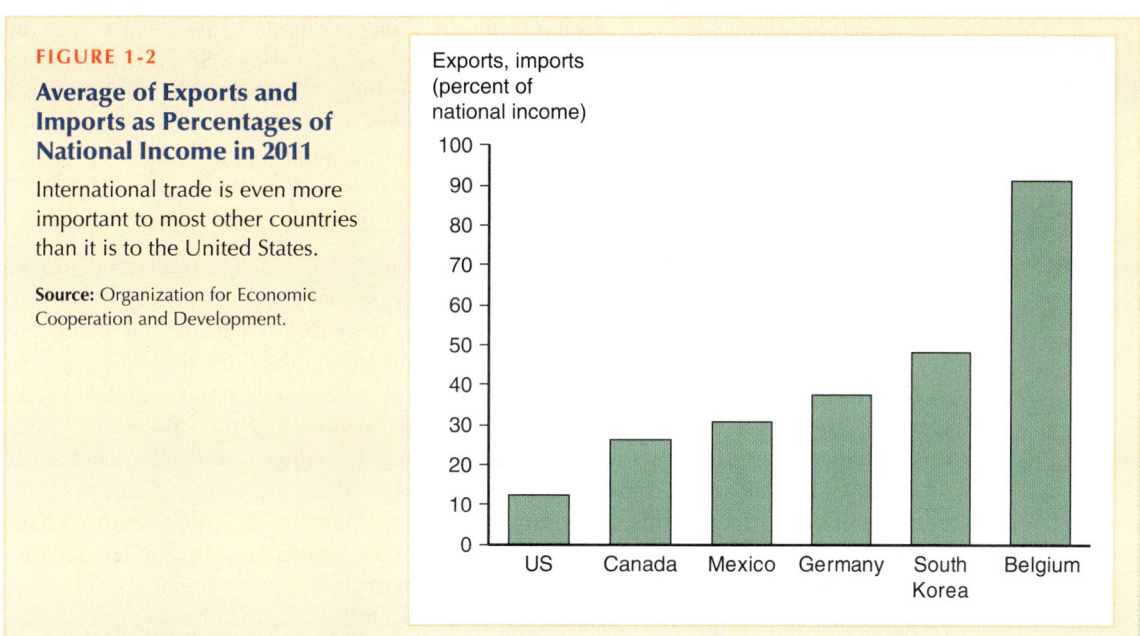

FIGURE 1-2

Average of Exports and Imports as Percentages of National Income in 2011

International trade is even more important to most other countries than it is to the United States.

Source: Organization for Economic Cooperation and Development.

LEARNING GOALS

After reading this chapter, you will be able to:

- Distinguish between international and domestic economic issues.
- Explain why seven themes recur in international economics, and discuss their significance.
- Distinguish between the trade and monetary aspects of international economics.

What Is International Economics About?

International economics uses the same fundamental methods of analysis as other branches of economics because the motives and behavior of individuals are the same in international trade as they are in domestic transactions. Gourmet food shops in Florida sell coffee beans from both Mexico and Hawaii; the sequence of events that brought those beans to the shop is not very different, and the imported beans traveled a much shorter distance than the beans shipped within the United States! Yet international economics involves new and different concerns because international trade and investment occur between independent nations. The United States and Mexico are sovereign states; Florida and Hawaii are not. Mexico's coffee shipments to Florida could be disrupted if the U.S. government imposed a quota that limits imports; Mexican coffee could suddenly become cheaper to U.S. buyers if the peso were to fall in value against the dollar. By contrast, neither of those events can happen in commerce within the United States because the Constitution forbids restraints on interstate trade and all U.S. states use the same currency.

The subject matter of international economics, then, consists of issues raised by the special problems of economic interaction between sovereign states. Seven themes recur throughout the study of international economics: (1) the gains from trade, (2) the pattern of trade, (3) protectionism, (4) the balance of payments, (5) exchange rate determination, (6) international policy coordination, and (7) the international capital market.

The Gains from Trade

Everybody knows that some international trade is beneficial—for example, nobody thinks that Norway should grow its own oranges. Many people are skeptical, however, about the benefits of trading for goods that a country could produce for itself. Shouldn't Americans buy American goods whenever possible to help create jobs in the United States?

Probably the most important single insight in all of international economics is that there are *gains from trade*—that is, when countries sell goods and services to each other, this exchange is almost always to their mutual benefit. The range of circumstances under which international trade is beneficial is much wider than most people imagine. For example, it is a common misconception that trade is harmful if large disparities exist between countries in productivity or wages. On one side, businesspeople in less technologically advanced countries, such as India, often worry that opening their economies to international trade will lead to disaster because their industries won't be able to compete. On the other side, people in technologically advanced nations where workers earn high wages often fear that trading with less advanced, lower-wage countries will drag their standard of living down—one presidential candidate memorably warned of a "giant sucking sound" if the United States were to conclude a free trade agreement with Mexico.

Yet the first model this text presents of the causes of trade (*International Trade* Chapter 3) demonstrates that two countries can trade to their mutual benefit even when one of them is more efficient than the other at producing everything and when producers in the less efficient country can compete only by paying lower wages. We'll also see that trade provides benefits by allowing countries to export goods whose production makes relatively heavy use of resources that are locally abundant while importing goods whose production makes heavy use of resources that are locally scarce (*International Trade* Chapter 5). International trade also allows countries to specialize in producing narrower ranges of goods, giving them greater efficiencies of large-scale production.

Nor are the benefits of international trade limited to trade in tangible goods. International migration and international borrowing and lending are also forms of mutually beneficial trade—the first a trade of labor for goods and services (*International Trade* Chapter 4), the second a trade of current goods for the promise of future goods (*International Trade* Chapter 6). Finally, international exchanges of risky assets such as stocks and bonds can benefit all countries by allowing each country to diversify its wealth and reduce the variability of its income (*International Finance* Chapter 9). These invisible forms of trade yield gains as real as the trade that puts fresh fruit from Latin America in Toronto markets in February.

Although nations generally gain from international trade, it is quite possible that international trade may hurt particular groups *within* nations—in other words, that international trade will have strong effects on the distribution of income. The effects of trade on income distribution have long been a concern of international trade theorists who have pointed out that:

International trade can adversely affect the owners of resources that are "specific" to industries that compete with imports, that is, cannot find alternative employment in other industries. Examples would include specialized machinery, such as power looms made less valuable by textile imports, and workers with specialized skills, like fishermen who find the value of their catch reduced by imported seafood.

Trade can also alter the distribution of income between broad groups, such as workers and the owners of capital.

These concerns have moved from the classroom into the center of real-world policy debate as it has become increasingly clear that the real wages of less-skilled workers in the United States have been declining—even though the country as a whole is continuing to grow richer. Many commentators attribute this development to growing international trade, especially the rapidly growing exports of manufactured goods from low-wage countries. Assessing this claim has become an important task for international economists and is a major theme of *International Trade* Chapters 4 through 6.

The Pattern of Trade

Economists cannot discuss the effects of international trade or recommend changes in government policies toward trade with any confidence unless they know their theory is good enough to explain the international trade that is actually observed. As a result, attempts to explain the pattern of international trade—who sells what to whom—have been a major preoccupation of international economists.

Some aspects of the pattern of trade are easy to understand. Climate and resources clearly explain why Brazil exports coffee and Saudi Arabia exports oil. Much of the pattern of trade is more subtle, however. Why does Japan export automobiles, while the United States exports aircraft? In the early 19th century, English economist David Ricardo offered an explanation of trade in terms of international differences in labor productivity, an explanation that remains a powerful insight (*International Trade* Chapter 3). In the 20th century, however, alternative explanations also were proposed. One of the most influential, explanations links trade patterns to an interaction between the relative supplies of national resources such as capital, labor, and land on one side and the relative use of these factors in the production of different goods on the other. We present this theory in *International Trade* Chapter 5. We then discuss how this basic model must be extended in order to generate accurate empirical predictions for the volume and pattern of trade. Also, some international economists have proposed theories that suggest a substantial random component, along with economies of scale, in the pattern of international trade, theories that are developed in *International Trade* Chapters 7 and 8.

How Much Trade?

If the idea of gains from trade is the most important theoretical concept in international economics, the seemingly eternal debate over how much trade to allow is its most important policy theme. Since the emergence of modern nation-states in the 16th century, governments have worried about the effect of international competition on the prosperity of domestic industries and have tried either to shield industries from foreign competition by placing limits on imports or to help them in world competition by subsidizing exports. The single most consistent mission of international economics has been to analyze the effects of these so-called protectionist policies—and usually, though not always, to criticize protectionism and show the advantages of freer international trade.

The debate over how much trade to allow took a new direction in the 1990s. After World War II the advanced democracies, led by the United States, pursued a broad policy of removing barriers to international trade; this policy reflected the view that free trade was a force not only for prosperity but also for promoting world peace.

In the first half of the 1990s, several major free trade agreements were negotiated. The most notable were the North American Free Trade Agreement (NAFTA) between the United States, Canada, and Mexico, approved in 1993, and the so-called Uruguay Round agreement, which established the World Trade Organization in 1994.

Since that time, however, an international political movement opposing "globalization" has gained many adherents. The movement achieved notoriety in 1999, when demonstrators representing a mix of traditional protectionists and new ideologies disrupted a major international trade meeting in Seattle. If nothing else, the anti-globalization movement has forced advocates of free trade to seek new ways to explain their views.

As befits both the historical importance and the current relevance of the protectionist issue, roughly a quarter of this text is devoted to this subject. Over the years, international economists have developed a simple yet powerful analytical framework for determining the effects of government policies that affect international trade. This framework helps predict the effects of trade policies, while also allowing for cost-benefit analysis and defining criteria for determining when government intervention is good for the economy. We present this framework in *International Trade* Chapters 9 and 10 and use it to discuss a number of policy issues in those chapters and in the two that follow.

In the real world, however, governments do not necessarily do what the cost-benefit analysis of economists tells them they should. This does not mean that analysis is useless. Economic analysis can help make sense of the politics of international trade policy by showing who benefits and who loses from such government actions as quotas on imports and subsidies to exports. The key insight of this analysis is that conflicts of interest *within* nations are usually more important in determining trade policy than conflicts of interest *between* nations. *International Trade* Chapters 4 and 5 show that trade usually has very strong effects on income distribution within countries, while *International Trade* Chapters 10 through 12 reveal that the relative power of different interest groups within countries, rather than some measure of overall national interest, is often the main determining factor in government policies toward international trade.

Balance of Payments

In 1998, both China and South Korea ran large trade surpluses of about $40 billion each. In China's case, the trade surplus was not out of the ordinary—the country had been running large surpluses for several years, prompting complaints from other countries, including the United States, that China was not playing by the rules. So is it good to run a trade surplus and bad to run a trade deficit? Not according to the South Koreans: Their trade surplus was forced on them by an economic and financial crisis, and they bitterly resented the necessity of running that surplus.

This comparison highlights the fact that a country's *balance of payments* must be placed in the context of an economic analysis to understand what it means. It emerges in a variety of specific contexts: in discussing foreign direct investment by multinational corporations (*International Trade* Chapter 8), in relating international transactions to national income accounting (*International Finance* Chapter 2), and in discussing virtually every aspect of international monetary policy (*International Finance* Chapters 6 through 11). Like the problem of protectionism, the balance of payments has become a central issue for the United States because the nation has run huge trade deficits every year since 1982.

Exchange Rate Determination

In September 2010, Brazil's finance minister, Guido Mantegna, made headlines by declaring that the world was "in the midst of an international currency war." The occasion for his remarks was a sharp rise in the value of Brazil's currency, the *real*, which was worth less than 45 cents at the beginning of 2009 but had risen to almost 60 cents when he spoke (and would rise to 65 cents over the next few months). Mantegna accused wealthy countries—the United States in particular—of engineering this rise, which was devastating to Brazilian exporters. However, the surge in the *real* proved short-lived; the currency began dropping in mid-2011, and by the summer of 2013 it was back down to only 45 cents.

A key difference between international economics and other areas of economics is that countries usually have their own currencies—the euro, which is shared by a number of European countries, being the exception that proves the rule. And as the example of the *real* illustrates, the relative values of currencies can change over time, sometimes drastically.

For historical reasons, the study of exchange rate determination is a relatively new part of international economics. For much of modern economic history, exchange rates were fixed by government action rather than determined in the marketplace. Before World War I, the values of the world's major currencies were fixed in terms of gold; for a generation after World War II, the values of most currencies were fixed in terms of the U.S. dollar. The analysis of international monetary systems that fix exchange rates remains an important subject. *International Finance* Chapter 7 is devoted to the working of fixed-rate systems, *International Finance* Chapter 8 to the historical performance of alternative exchange-rate systems, and *International Finance* Chapter 10 to the economics of currency areas such as the European monetary union. For the time being, however, some of the world's most important exchange rates fluctuate minute by minute and the role of changing exchange rates remains at the center of the international economics story. *International Finance* Chapters 3 through 6 focus on the modern theory of floating exchange rates.

International Policy Coordination

The international economy comprises sovereign nations, each free to choose its own economic policies. Unfortunately, in an integrated world economy, one country's economic policies usually affect other countries as well. For example, when Germany's Bundesbank raised interest rates in 1990—a step it took to control the possible inflationary impact of the reunification of West and East Germany—it helped precipitate a recession in the rest of Western Europe. Differences in goals among countries often lead to conflicts of interest. Even when countries have similar goals, they may suffer losses if they fail to coordinate their policies. A fundamental problem in international economics is determining how to produce an acceptable degree of harmony among the international trade and monetary policies of different countries in the absence of a world government that tells countries what to do.

For almost 70 years, international trade policies have been governed by an international agreement known as the General Agreement on Tariffs and Trade (GATT). Since 1994, trade rules have been enforced by an international organization, the World Trade Organization, that can tell countries, including the United States, that their policies violate prior agreements. We discuss the rationale for this system in *International Trade* Chapter 9 and look at whether the current rules of the game for international trade in the world economy can or should survive.

While cooperation on international trade policies is a well-established tradition, coordination of international macroeconomic policies is a newer and more uncertain topic. Attempts to formulate principles for international macroeconomic coordination date to the 1980s and 1990s and remain controversial to this day. Nonetheless, attempts at international macroeconomic coordination are occurring with growing frequency in the real world. Both the theory of international macroeconomic coordination and the developing experience are reviewed in *International Finance* Chapter 8.

The International Capital Market

In 2007, investors who had bought U.S. mortgage-backed securities—claims on the income from large pools of home mortgages—received a rude shock: as home prices began to fall, mortgage defaults soared, and investments they had been assured were safe turned out to be highly risky. Since many of these claims were owned by financial institutions, the housing bust soon turned into a banking crisis. And here's the thing: it wasn't just a U.S. banking crisis, because banks in other countries, especially in Europe, had also bought many of these securities.

The story didn't end there: Europe soon had its own housing bust. And while the bust mainly took place in southern Europe, it soon became apparent that many northern European banks—such as German banks that had lent money to their Spanish counterparts—were also very exposed to the financial consequences.

In any sophisticated economy, there is an extensive capital market: a set of arrangements by which individuals and firms exchange money now for promises to pay in the future. The growing importance of international trade since the 1960s has been accompanied by a growth in the *international* capital market, which links the capital markets of individual countries. Thus in the 1970s, oil-rich Middle Eastern nations placed their oil revenues in banks in London or New York, and these banks in turn lent money to governments and corporations in Asia and Latin America. During the 1980s, Japan converted much of the money it earned from its booming exports into investments in the United States, including the establishment of a growing number of U.S. subsidiaries of Japanese corporations. Nowadays, China is funneling its own export earnings into a range of foreign assets, including dollars that its government holds as international reserves.

International capital markets differ in important ways from domestic capital markets. They must cope with special regulations that many countries impose on foreign investment; they also sometimes offer opportunities to evade regulations placed on domestic markets. Since the 1960s, huge international capital markets have arisen, most notably the remarkable London Eurodollar market, in which billions of dollars are exchanged each day without ever touching the United States.

Some special risks are associated with international capital markets. One risk is currency fluctuations: If the euro falls against the dollar, U.S. investors who bought euro bonds suffer a capital loss. Another risk is national default: A nation may simply refuse to pay its debts (perhaps because it cannot), and there may be no effective way for its creditors to bring it to court. Fears of default by highly indebted European nations have been a major concern in recent years.

The growing importance of international capital markets and their new problems demand greater attention than ever before. The *International Finance* volume of this text devotes two chapters to issues arising from international capital markets: one on the functioning of global asset markets (*International Finance* Chapter 9) and one on foreign borrowing by developing countries (*International Finance* Chapter 11).

International Economics: Trade and Money

The economics of the international economy can be divided into two broad subfields: the study of *international trade* and the study of *international money*. International trade analysis focuses primarily on the *real* transactions in the international economy, that is, transactions involving a physical movement of goods or a tangible commitment of economic resources. International monetary analysis focuses on the *monetary* side of the international economy, that is, on financial transactions such as foreign purchases of U.S. dollars. An example of an international trade issue is the conflict between the United States and Europe over Europe's subsidized exports of agricultural products; an example of an international monetary issue is the dispute over whether the foreign exchange value of the dollar should be allowed to float freely or be stabilized by government action.

In the real world, there is no simple dividing line between trade and monetary issues. Most international trade involves monetary transactions, while, as the examples in this chapter already suggest, many monetary events have important consequences for trade. Nonetheless, the distinction between international trade and international money is useful. The first volume of *International Economics* covers international trade issues. *International Trade* Part One (Chapters 2 through 8) develops the analytical theory of international trade, and *International Trade* Part Two (Chapters 9 through 12) applies trade theory to the analysis of government policies toward trade. The second volume, *International Finance*, is devoted to international monetary issues. *International Finance* Part One (Chapters 2 through 7) develops international monetary theory, and *International Finance* Part Two (Chapters 8 through 11) applies this analysis to international monetary policy.

MyEconLab Can Help You Get a Better Grade

MyEconLab   If your exam were tomorrow, would you be ready? For each chapter, MyEconLab Practice Tests and Study Plans pinpoint sections you have mastered and those you need to study. That way, you are more efficient with your study time, and you are better prepared for your exams.

Here's how it works:

1. Make sure you have a Course ID from your instructor. Register and log in at www.myeconlab.com
2. Click on "Study Plan" and select the "Practice" button for the first section in this chapter.
3. Work the Practice questions. MyEconLab will grade your work automatically.
4. The Study Plan will serve up additional Practice Problems and tutorials to help you master the specific areas where you need to focus. By practicing online, you can track your progress in the Study Plan.
5. If you do well on the practice questions, the "Quiz Me" button will become highlighted. Work the Quiz questions.
6. Once you have mastered a section via the "Quiz Me" test, you will receive a Mastery Point and be directed to work on the next section.

CHAPTER | 2 |

WORLD TRADE: AN OVERVIEW

In 2013, the world as a whole produced goods and services worth about $74 trillion at current prices. Of this total, more than 30 percent was sold across national borders: World trade in goods and services exceeded $23 trillion. That's a whole lot of exporting and importing.

In later chapters, we'll analyze why countries sell much of what they produce to other countries and why they purchase much of what they consume from other countries. We'll also examine the benefits and costs of international trade and the motivations for and effects of government policies that restrict or encourage trade.

Before we get to all that, however, let's begin by describing who trades with whom. An empirical relationship known as the *gravity model* helps to make sense of the value of trade between any pair of countries and sheds light on the impediments that continue to limit international trade even in today's global economy.

We'll then turn to the changing structure of world trade. As we'll see, recent decades have been marked by a large increase in the share of world output sold internationally by a shift in the world's economic center of gravity toward Asia and by major changes in the types of goods that make up that trade.

LEARNING GOALS

After reading this chapter, you will be able to:

- Describe how the value of trade between any two countries depends on the size of these countries' economies and explain the reasons for that relationship.
- Discuss how distance and borders reduce trade.
- Describe how the share of international production that is traded has fluctuated over time and why there have been two ages of globalization.
- Explain how the mix of goods and services that are traded internationally has changed over time.

Who Trades with Whom?

Figure 2-1 shows the total value of trade in goods—exports plus imports—between the United States and its top 15 trading partners in 2012. (Data on trade in services are less well broken down by trading partner; we'll talk about the rising importance of trade in

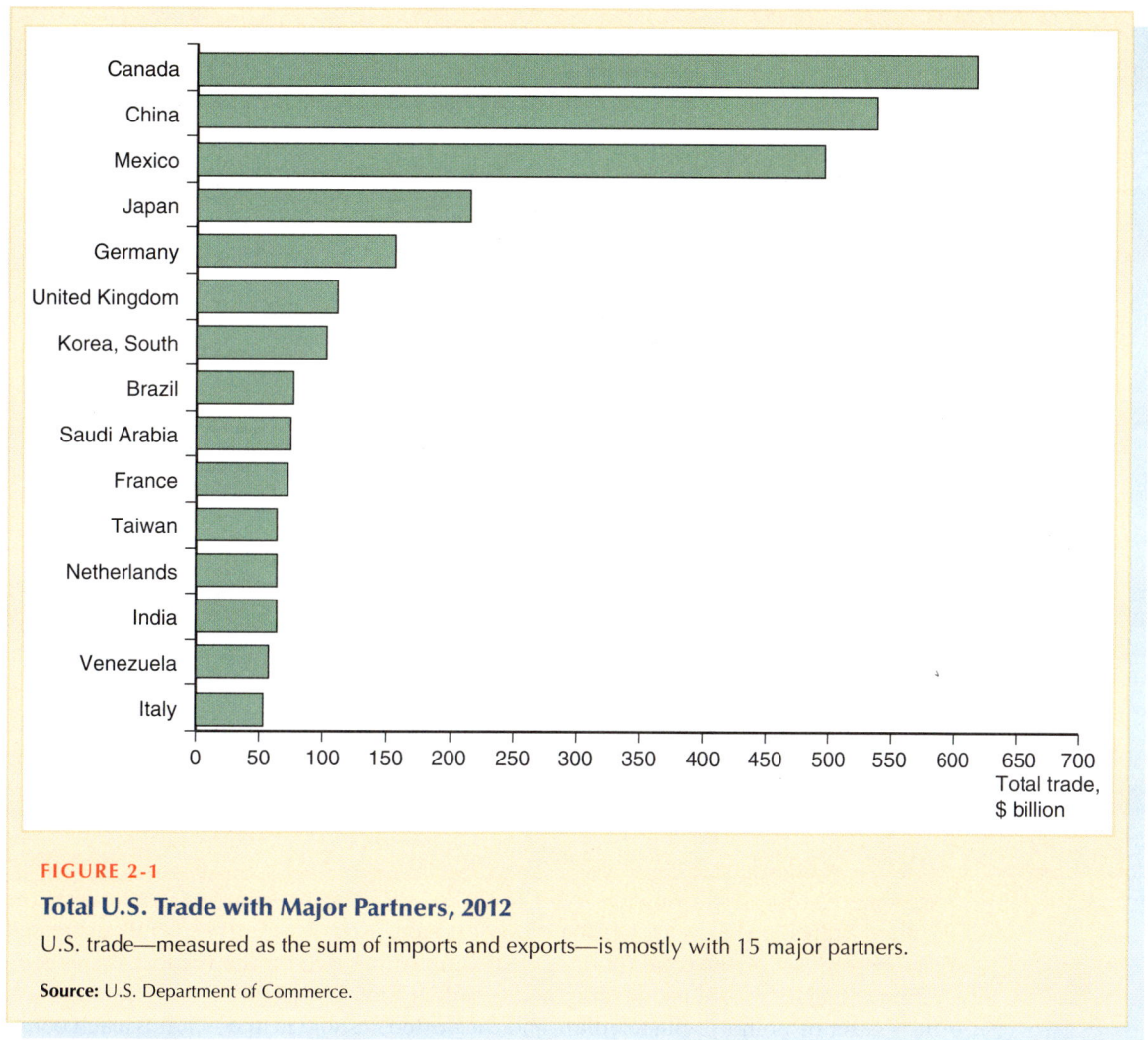

FIGURE 2-1

Total U.S. Trade with Major Partners, 2012

U.S. trade—measured as the sum of imports and exports—is mostly with 15 major partners.

Source: U.S. Department of Commerce.

services, and the issues raised by that trade, later in this chapter.) Taken together, these 15 countries accounted for 69 percent of the value of U.S. trade in that year.

Why did the United States trade so much with these countries? Let's look at the factors that, in practice, determine who trades with whom.

Size Matters: The Gravity Model

Three of the top 15 U.S. trading partners are European nations: Germany, the United Kingdom, and France. Why does the United States trade more heavily with these three European countries than with others? The answer is that these are the three largest European economies. That is, they have the highest values of **gross domestic product (GDP),** which measures the total value of all goods and services produced in an economy. There is a strong empirical relationship between the size of a country's economy and the volume of both its imports and its exports.

Figure 2-2 illustrates this relationship by showing the correspondence between the size of different European economies—specifically, America's 15 most important

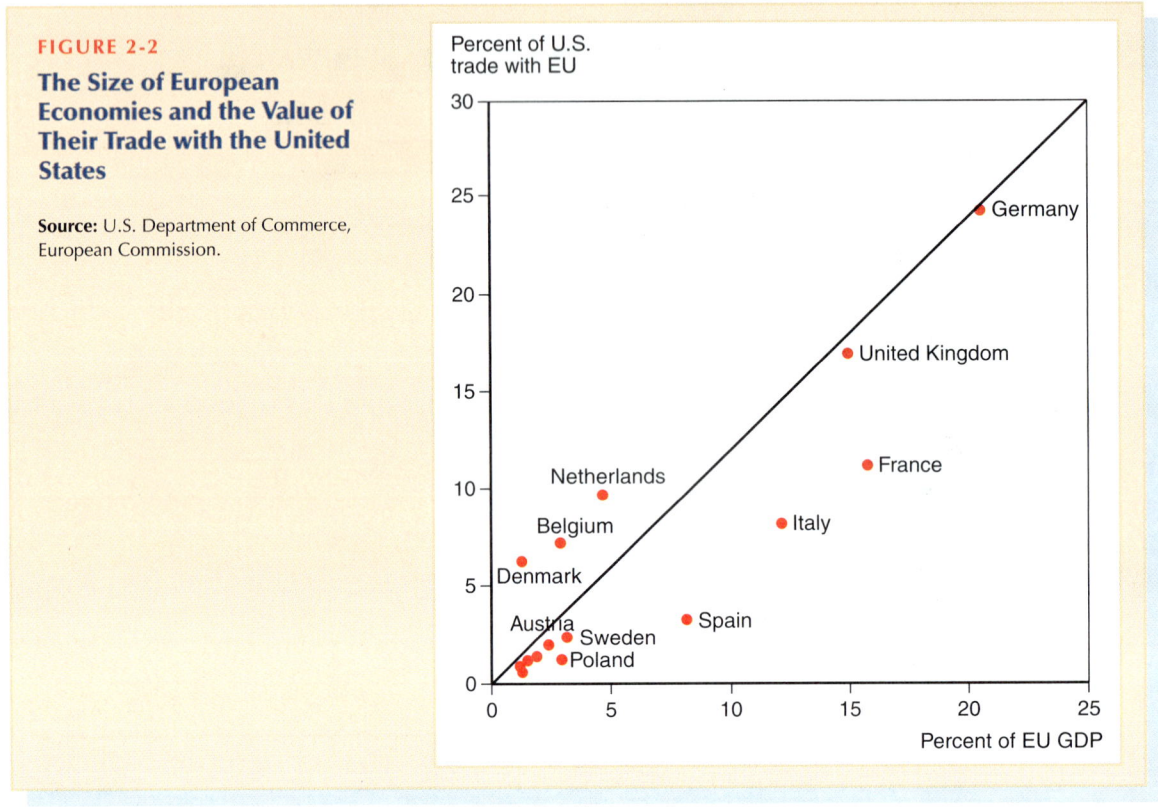

FIGURE 2-2

The Size of European Economies and the Value of Their Trade with the United States

Source: U.S. Department of Commerce, European Commission.

Western European trading partners in 2012—and those countries' trade with the United States in that year. On the horizontal axis is each country's GDP, expressed as a percentage of the total GDP of the European Union; on the vertical axis is each country's share of the total trade of the United States with the EU. As you can see, the scatter of points is clustered around the dotted 45-degree line—that is, each country's share of U.S. trade with Europe was roughly equal to that country's share of Western European GDP. Germany has a large economy, accounting for 20 percent of Western European GDP; it also accounts for 24 percent of U.S. trade with the region. Sweden has a much smaller economy, accounting for only 3.2 percent of European GDP; correspondingly, it accounts for only 2.3 percent of U.S.–Europe trade.

Looking at world trade as a whole, economists have found that an equation of the following form predicts the volume of trade between any two countries fairly accurately,

$$T_{ij} = A \times Y_i \times Y_j/D_{ij}, \tag{2-1}$$

where A is a constant term, T_{ij} is the value of trade between country i and country j, Y_i is country i's GDP, Y_j is country j's GDP, and D_{ij} is the distance between the two countries. That is, the value of trade between any two countries is proportional, other things equal, to the *product* of the two countries' GDPs and diminishes with the distance between the two countries.

An equation such as (2-1) is known as a **gravity model** of world trade. The reason for the name is the analogy to Newton's law of gravity: Just as the gravitational attraction between any two objects is proportional to the product of their masses and diminishes with distance, the trade between any two countries is, other things equal, proportional to the product of their GDPs and diminishes with distance.

Economists often estimate a somewhat more general gravity model of the following form:

$$T_{ij} = A \times Y_i^a \times Y_j^b / D_{ij}^c. \qquad (2\text{-}2)$$

This equation says that the three things that determine the volume of trade between two countries are the size of the two countries' GDPs and the distance between the countries, without specifically assuming that trade is proportional to the product of the two GDPs and inversely proportional to distance. Instead, a, b, and c are chosen to fit the actual data as closely as possible. If a, b, and c were all equal to 1, Equation (2-2) would be the same as Equation (2-1). In fact, estimates often find that (2-1) is a pretty good approximation.

Why does the gravity model work? Broadly speaking, large economies tend to spend large amounts on imports because they have large incomes. They also tend to attract large shares of other countries' spending because they produce a wide range of products. So, other things equal, the trade between any two economies is larger—the larger is *either* economy.

What other things *aren't* equal? As we have already noted, in practice countries spend much or most of their income at home. The United States and the European Union each account for about 25 percent of the world's GDP, but each attracts only about 2 percent of the other's spending. To make sense of actual trade flows, we need to consider the factors limiting international trade. Before we get there, however, let's look at an important reason why the gravity model is useful.

Using the Gravity Model: Looking for Anomalies

It's clear from Figure 2-2 that a gravity model fits the data on U.S. trade with European countries pretty well—but not perfectly. In fact, one of the principal uses of gravity models is that they help us to identify anomalies in trade. Indeed, when trade between two countries is either much more or much less than a gravity model predicts, economists search for the explanation.

Looking again at Figure 2-2, we see that the Netherlands, Belgium, and Ireland trade considerably more with the United States than a gravity model would have predicted. Why might this be the case?

For Ireland, the answer lies partly in cultural affinity: Not only does Ireland share a language with the United States, but tens of millions of Americans are descended from Irish immigrants. Beyond this consideration, Ireland plays a special role as host to many U.S.-based corporations; we'll discuss the role of such *multinational corporations* in Chapter 8.

In the case of both the Netherlands and Belgium, geography and transport costs probably explain their large trade with the United States. Both countries are located near the mouth of the Rhine, Western Europe's longest river, which runs past the Ruhr, Germany's industrial heartland. So the Netherlands and Belgium have traditionally been the point of entry to much of northwestern Europe; Rotterdam in the Netherlands is the most important port in Europe, as measured by the tonnage handled, and Antwerp in Belgium ranks second. The large trade of Belgium and the Netherlands suggests, in other words, an important role of transport costs and geography in determining the volume of trade. The importance of these factors is clear when we turn to a broader example of trade data.

Impediments to Trade: Distance, Barriers, and Borders

Figure 2-3 shows the same data as Figure 2-2—U.S. trade as a percentage of total trade with Western Europe in 2012 versus GDP as a percentage of the region's total GDP—but adds two more countries: Canada and Mexico. As you can see, the two neighbors of the United States do a lot more trade with the United States than European economies of equal size. In fact, Canada, whose economy is roughly the same size as Spain's, trades as much with the United States as all of Europe does.

Why does the United States do so much more trade with its North American neighbors than with its European partners? One main reason is the simple fact that Canada and Mexico are much closer.

All estimated gravity models show a strong negative effect of distance on international trade; typical estimates say that a 1 percent increase in the distance between two countries is associated with a fall of 0.7 to 1 percent in the trade between those countries. This drop partly reflects increased costs of transporting goods and services. Economists also believe that less tangible factors play a crucial role: Trade tends to be intense when countries have close personal contact, and this contact tends to diminish when distances are large. For example, it's easy for a U.S. sales representative to pay a quick visit to Toronto, but it's a much bigger project for that representative to go to Paris. Unless the company is based on the West Coast, it's an even bigger project to visit Tokyo.

In addition to being U.S. neighbors, Canada and Mexico are part of a **trade agreement** with the United States, the North American Free Trade Agreement, or NAFTA, which ensures that most goods shipped among the three countries are not subject to tariffs or

FIGURE 2-3

Economic Size and Trade with the United States

The United States does markedly more trade with its neighbors than it does with European economies of the same size.

Source: U.S. Department of Commerce, European Commission.

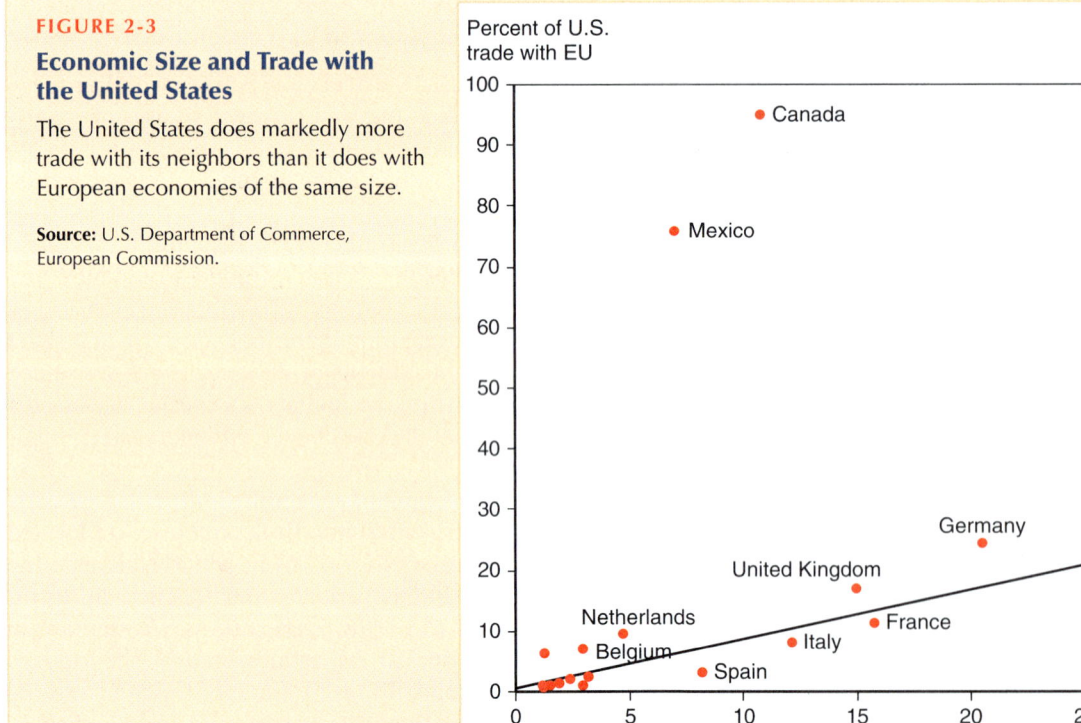

other barriers to international trade. We'll analyze the effects of barriers to international trade in Chapters 8–9, and the role of trade agreements such as NAFTA in Chapter 10. For now, let's notice that economists use gravity models as a way of assessing the impact of trade agreements on actual international trade: If a trade agreement is effective, it should lead to significantly more trade among its partners than one would otherwise predict given their GDPs and distances from one another.

It's important to note, however, that although trade agreements often end all formal barriers to trade between countries, they rarely make national borders irrelevant. Even when most goods and services shipped across a national border pay no tariffs and face few legal restrictions, there is much more trade between regions of the same country than between equivalently situated regions in different countries. The Canadian–U.S. border is a case in point. The two countries are part of a free trade agreement (indeed, there was a Canadian–U.S. free trade agreement even before NAFTA); most Canadians speak English; and the citizens of either country are free to cross the border with a minimum of formalities. Yet data on the trade of individual Canadian provinces both with each other and with U.S. states show that, other things equal, there is much more trade between provinces than between provinces and U.S. states.

Table 2-1 illustrates the extent of the difference. It shows the total trade (exports plus imports) of the Canadian province of British Columbia, just north of the state of Washington, with other Canadian provinces and with U.S. states, measured as a percentage of each province or state's GDP. Figure 2-4 shows the location of these provinces and states. Each Canadian province is paired with a U.S. state that is roughly the same distance from British Columbia: Washington State and Alberta both border British Columbia; Ontario and Ohio are both in the Midwest; and so on. With the exception of trade with the far eastern Canadian province of New Brunswick, intra-Canadian trade drops off steadily with distance. But in each case, the trade between British Columbia and a Canadian province is much larger than trade with an equally distant U.S. state.

Economists have used data like those shown in Table 2-1, together with estimates of the effect of distance in gravity models, to calculate that the Canadian–U.S. border, although it is one of the most open borders in the world, has as much effect in deterring trade as if the countries were between 1,500 and 2,500 miles apart.

Why do borders have such a large negative effect on trade? That is a topic of ongoing research. Chapter 21 describes one recent focus of that research: an effort to determine how much effect the existence of separate national currencies has on international trade in goods and services.

TABLE 2-1	**Trade with British Columbia, as Percent of GDP, 2009**		
Canadian Province	**Trade as Percent of GDP**	**Trade as Percent of GDP**	**U.S. State at Similar Distance from British Columbia**
Alberta	6.9	2.6	Washington
Saskatchewan	2.4	1.0	Montana
Manitoba	2.0	0.3	California
Ontario	1.9	0.2	Ohio
Quebec	1.4	0.1	New York
New Brunswick	2.3	0.2	Maine

Source: Statistics Canada, US Department of Commerce

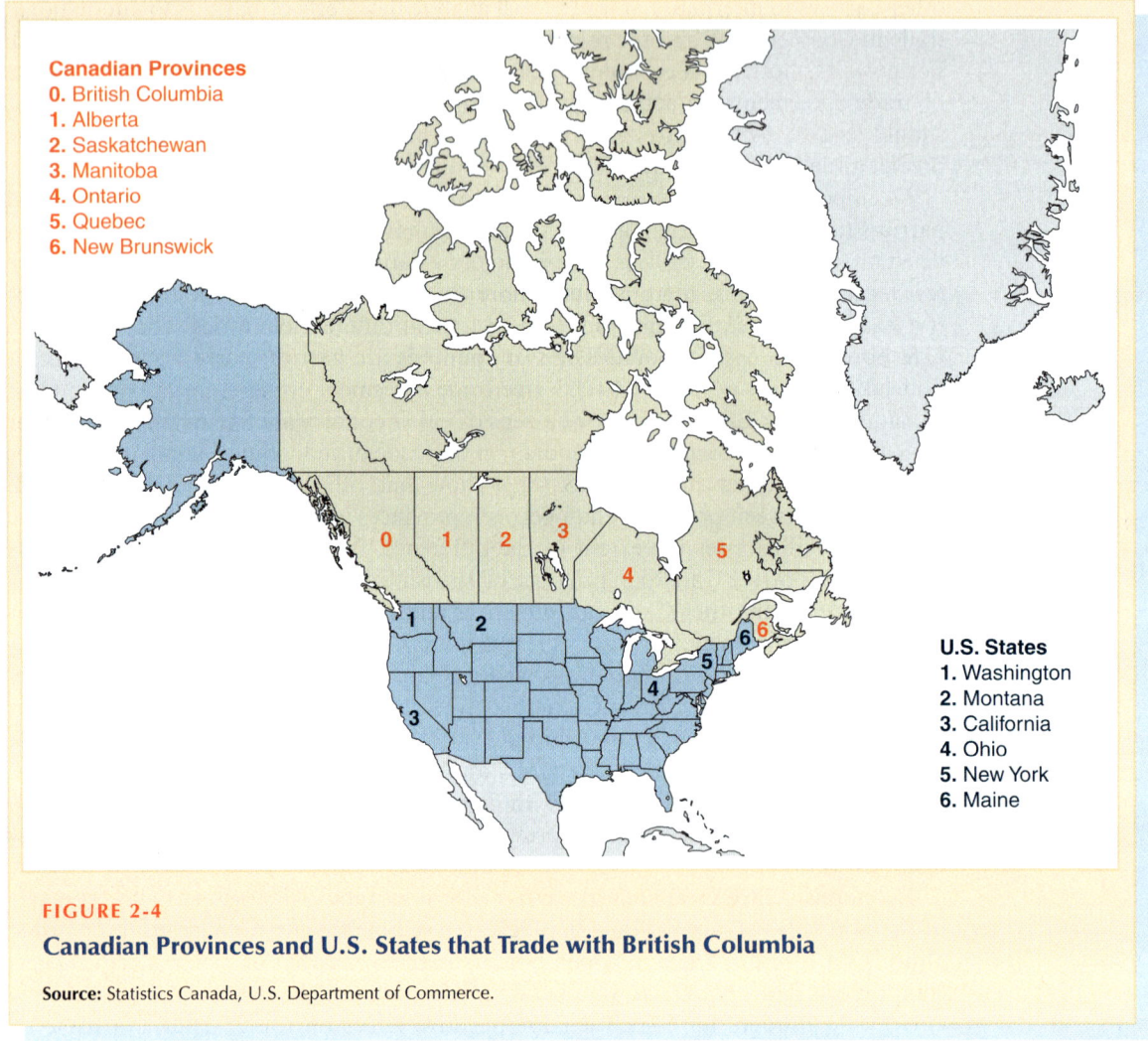

Canadian Provinces
0. British Columbia
1. Alberta
2. Saskatchewan
3. Manitoba
4. Ontario
5. Quebec
6. New Brunswick

U.S. States
1. Washington
2. Montana
3. California
4. Ohio
5. New York
6. Maine

FIGURE 2-4

Canadian Provinces and U.S. States that Trade with British Columbia

Source: Statistics Canada, U.S. Department of Commerce.

The Changing Pattern of World Trade

World trade is a moving target. The direction and composition of world trade is quite different today from what it was a generation ago and even more different from what it was a century ago. Let's look at some of the main trends.

Has the World Gotten Smaller?

In popular discussions of the world economy, one often encounters statements that modern transportation and communications have abolished distance, so that the world has become a small place. There's clearly some truth to these statements: The Internet makes instant and almost free communication possible between people thousands of miles apart, while jet transport allows quick physical access to all parts of the globe. On the other hand, gravity models continue to show a strong negative relationship between distance and international trade. But have such effects grown weaker over time? Has the progress of transportation and communication made the world smaller?

The answer is yes—but history also shows that political forces can outweigh the effects of technology. The world got smaller between 1840 and 1914, but it got bigger again for much of the 20th century.

Economic historians tell us that a global economy, with strong economic linkages between even distant nations, is not new. In fact, there have been two great waves of globalization with the first wave relying not on jets and the Internet but on railroads, steamships, and the telegraph. In 1919, the great economist John Maynard Keynes described the results of that surge of globalization:

> What an extraordinary episode in the economic progress of man that age was which came to an end in August 1914!...The inhabitant of London could order by telephone, sipping his morning tea in bed, the various products of the whole earth, in such quantity as he might see fit, and reasonably expect their early delivery upon his doorstep.

Notice, however, Keynes's statement that the age "came to an end" in 1914. In fact, two subsequent world wars, the Great Depression of the 1930s and widespread protectionism, did a great deal to depress world trade. Figure 2-5 shows one measure of international trade: the ratio of an index of world exports of manufactured goods

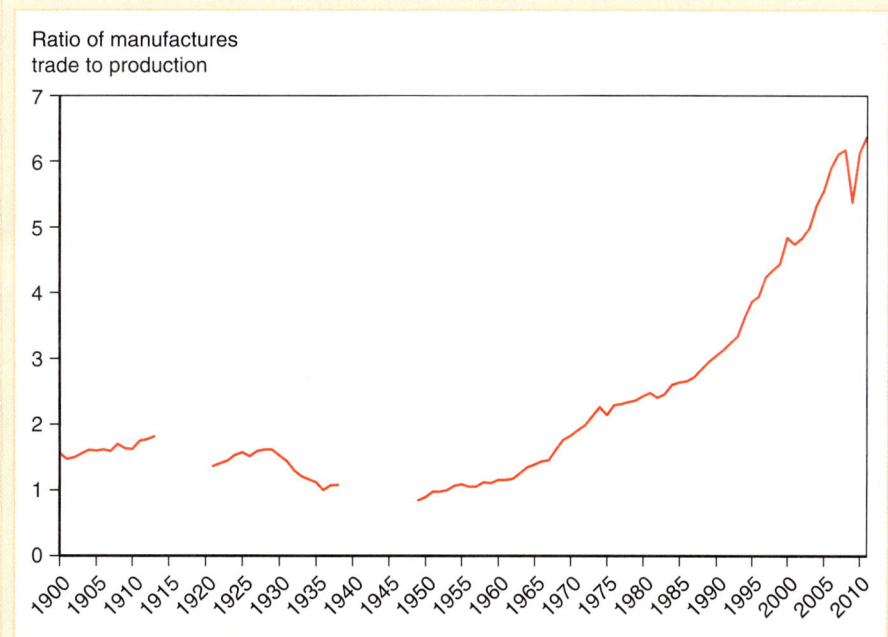

FIGURE 2-5

The Fall and Rise of World Trade

The ratio of world exports of manufactured goods to world industrial production—shown here as an index with 1953=1—rose in the decades before World War I but fell sharply in the face of wars and protectionism. It didn't return to 1913 levels until the 1970s but has since reached new heights.

Source: UN Monthly Bulletin of Statistics, World Trade Organization

to an index of world industrial production. World trade grew rapidly in the decades leading up to World War I but then fell significantly. As you can see, by this measure globalization didn't return to pre-World-War-I levels until the early 1970s.

Since then, however, world trade as a share of world production has risen to unprecedented heights. Much of this rise in the value of world trade reflects the so-called "vertical disintegration" of production: Before a product reaches the hands of consumers, it often goes through many production stages in different countries. For example, consumer electronic products—cell phones, iPods, and so on—are often assembled in low-wage nations such as China from components produced in higher-wage nations like Japan. Because of the extensive cross-shipping of components, a $100 product can give rise to $200 or $300 worth of international trade flows.

What Do We Trade?

When countries trade, what do they trade? For the world as a whole, the main answer is that they ship manufactured goods such as automobiles, computers, and clothing to each other. However, trade in mineral products—a category that includes everything from copper ore to coal, but whose main component in the modern world is oil—remains an important part of world trade. Agricultural products such as wheat, soybeans, and cotton are another key piece of the picture, and services of various kinds play an important role and are widely expected to become more important in the future.

Figure 2-6 shows the percentage breakdown of world exports in 2011. Manufactured goods of all kinds make up the lion's share of world trade. Most of the value of mining goods consists of oil and other fuels. Trade in agricultural products, although crucial in feeding many countries, accounts for only a small fraction of the value of modern world trade.

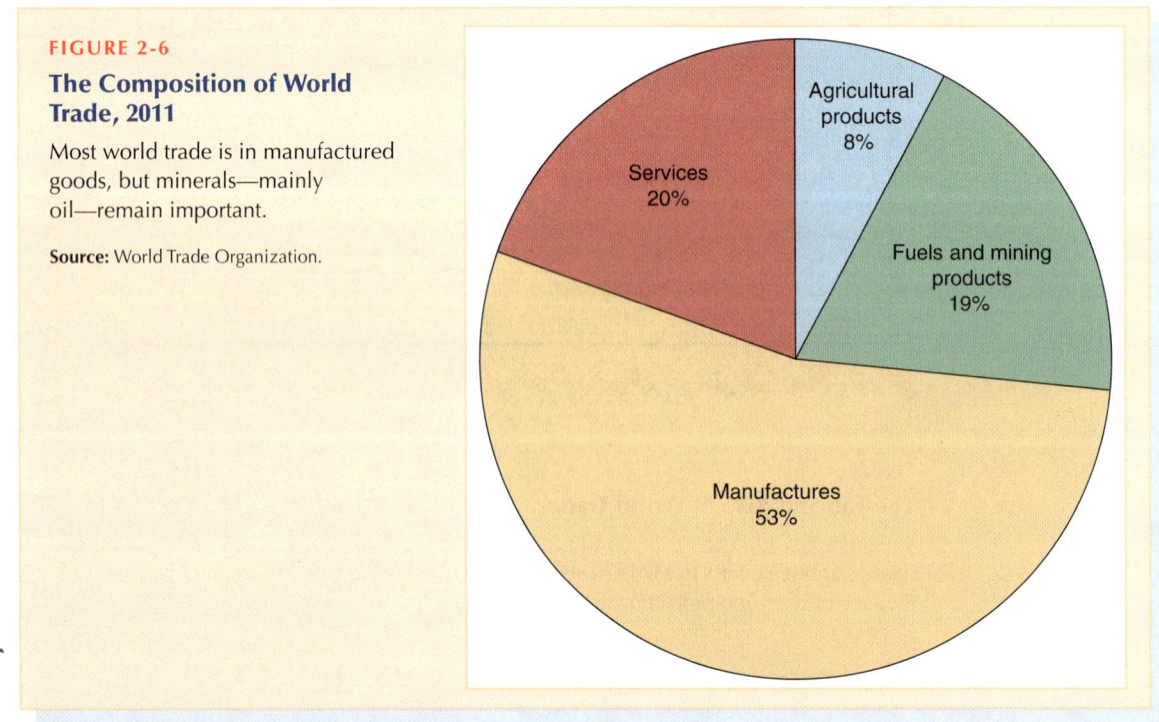

FIGURE 2-6

The Composition of World Trade, 2011

Most world trade is in manufactured goods, but minerals—mainly oil—remain important.

Source: World Trade Organization.

Meanwhile, service exports include traditional transportation fees charged by airlines and shipping companies, insurance fees received from foreigners, and spending by foreign tourists. In recent years, new types of service trade, made possible by modern telecommunications, have drawn a great deal of media attention. The most famous example is the rise of overseas call and help centers: If you call an 800 number for information or technical help, the person on the other end of the line may well be in a remote country (the Indian city of Bangalore is a particularly popular location). So far, these exotic new forms of trade are still a relatively small part of the overall trade picture, but as explained below, that may change in the years ahead.

The current picture, in which manufactured goods dominate world trade, is relatively new. In the past, primary products—agricultural and mining goods—played a much more important role in world trade. Table 2-2 shows the share of manufactured goods in the exports and imports of the United Kingdom and the United States in 1910 and 2011. In the early 20th century Britain, while it overwhelmingly exported manufactured goods (manufactures), mainly imported primary products. Today, manufactured goods dominate both sides of its trade. Meanwhile, the United States has gone from a trade pattern in which primary products were more important than manufactured goods on both sides to one in which manufactured goods dominate.

A more recent transformation has been the rise of third world exports of manufactured goods. The terms **third world** and **developing countries** are applied to the world's poorer nations, many of which were European colonies before World War II. As recently as the 1970s, these countries mainly exported primary products. Since then, however, they have moved rapidly into exports of manufactured goods. Figure 2-7 shows the shares of agricultural products and manufactured goods in developing-country exports since 1960. There has been an almost complete reversal of relative importance. For example, more than 90 percent of the exports of China, the largest developing economy and a rapidly growing force in world trade, consists of manufactured goods.

Service Offshoring

One of the hottest disputes in international economics right now is whether modern information technology, which makes it possible to perform some economic functions at long range, will lead to a dramatic increase in new forms of international trade. We've already mentioned the example of call centers, where the person answering your request for information may be 8,000 miles away. Many other services can also be done in a remote location. When a service previously done within a country is shifted to a foreign location, the change is known as **service offshoring** (sometimes known as **service outsourcing**). In addition, producers must decide whether they should set up a foreign subsidiary to provide those services (and operate as a multinational firm) or

TABLE 2-2	Manufactured Goods as Percent of Merchandise Trade			
	United Kingdom		United States	
	Exports	Imports	Exports	Imports
1910	75.4	24.5	47.5	40.7
2011	72.1	69.1	65.3	67.2

Source: 1910 data from Simon Kuznets, *Modern Economic Growth: Rate, Structure and Speed.* New Haven: Yale Univ. Press, 1966. 2011 data from World Trade Organization.

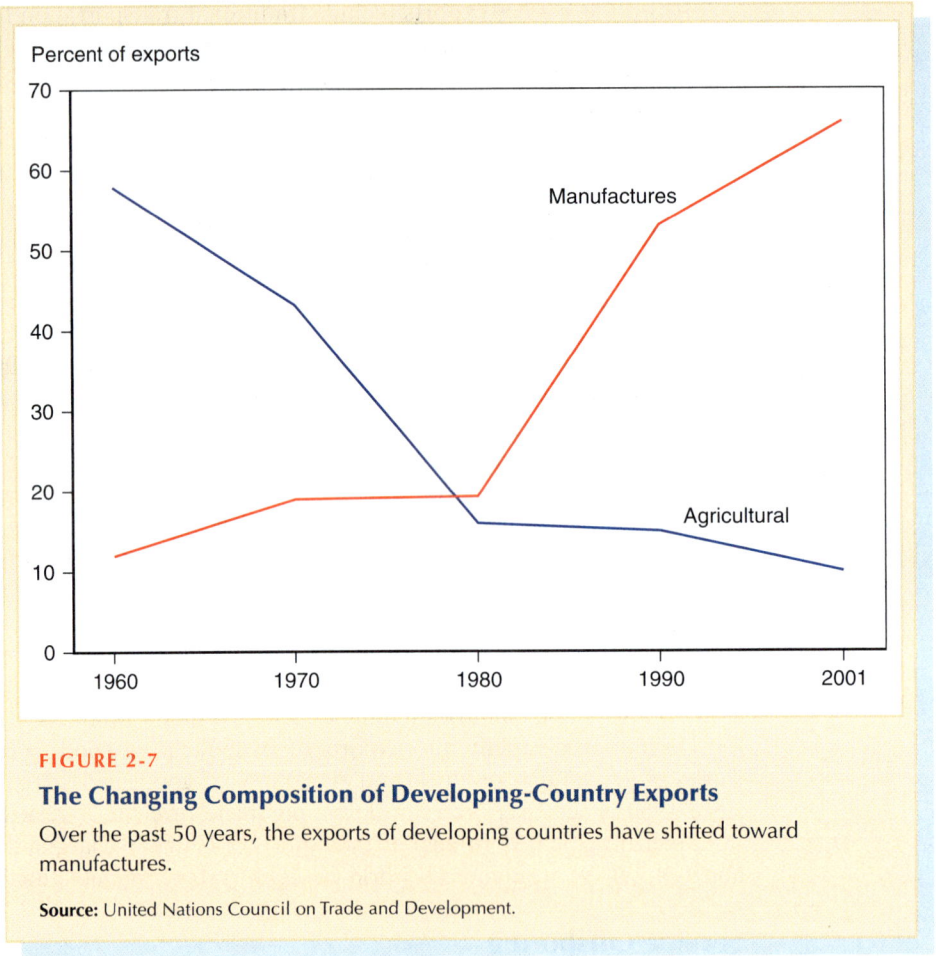

FIGURE 2-7

The Changing Composition of Developing-Country Exports

Over the past 50 years, the exports of developing countries have shifted toward manufactures.

Source: United Nations Council on Trade and Development.

outsource those services to another firm. In Chapter 8, we describe in more detail how firms make these important decisions.

In a famous *Foreign Affairs* article published in 2006, Alan Blinder, an economist at Princeton University, argued that "in the future, and to a great extent already in the present, the key distinction for international trade will no longer be between things that can be put in a box and things that cannot. It will, instead, be between services that can be delivered electronically over long distances with little or no degradation of quality, and those that cannot." For example, the worker who restocks the shelves at your local grocery has to be on site, but the accountant who keeps the grocery's books could be in another country, keeping in touch over the Internet. The nurse who takes your pulse has to be nearby, but the radiologist who reads your X-ray could receive the images electronically anywhere that has a high-speed connection.

At this point, service outsourcing gets a great deal of attention precisely because it's still fairly rare. The question is how big it might become, and how many workers who currently face no international competition might see that change in the future. One way economists have tried to answer this question is by looking at which services are traded at long distances *within* the United States. For example, many financial services are provided to the nation from New York, the country's financial capital; much of the country's software publishing takes place in Seattle, home of Microsoft; much

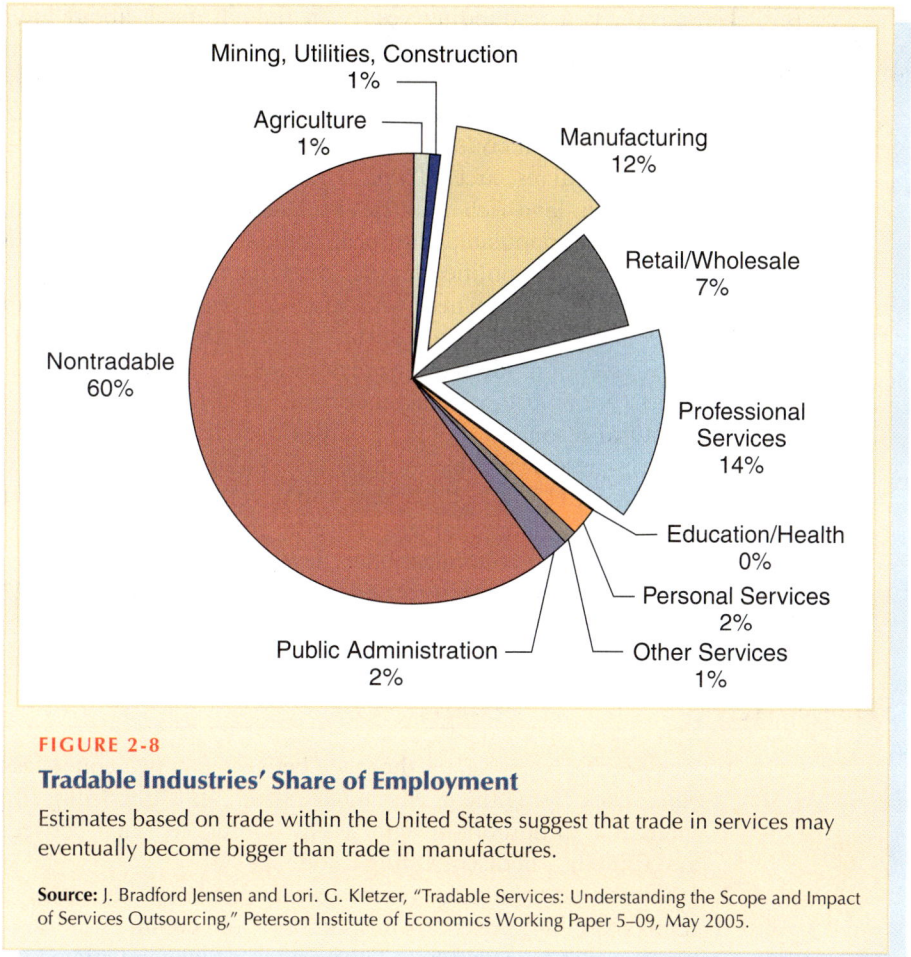

FIGURE 2-8

Tradable Industries' Share of Employment

Estimates based on trade within the United States suggest that trade in services may eventually become bigger than trade in manufactures.

Source: J. Bradford Jensen and Lori. G. Kletzer, "Tradable Services: Understanding the Scope and Impact of Services Outsourcing," Peterson Institute of Economics Working Paper 5–09, May 2005.

of America's (and the world's) Internet search services are provided from the Googleplex in Mountain View, California, and so on.

Figure 2-8 shows the results of one study that systematically used data on the location of industries within the United States to determine which services are and are not tradable at long distances. As the figure shows, the study concluded that about 60 percent of total U.S. employment consists of jobs that must be done close to the customer, making them nontradable. But the 40 percent of employment that is in tradable activities includes more service than manufacturing jobs. This suggests that the current dominance of world trade by manufactures, shown in Figure 2-6, may be only temporary. In the long run, trade in services, delivered electronically, may become the most important component of world trade. We discuss the implication of these trends for U.S. employment in Chapter 8.

Do Old Rules Still Apply?

We begin our discussion of the causes of world trade in Chapter 3 with an analysis of a model originally put forth by the British economist David Ricardo in 1819. Given all the changes in world trade since Ricardo's time, can old ideas still be relevant?

The answer is a resounding yes. Even though much about international trade has changed, the fundamental principles discovered by economists at the dawn of a global economy still apply.

It's true that world trade has become harder to characterize in simple terms. A century ago, each country's exports were obviously shaped in large part by its climate and natural resources. Tropical countries exported tropical products such as coffee and cotton; land-rich countries such as the United States and Australia exported food to densely populated European nations. Disputes over trade were also easy to explain: The classic political battles over free trade versus protectionism were waged between English landowners who wanted protection from cheap food imports and English manufacturers who exported much of their output.

The sources of modern trade are more subtle. Human resources and human-created resources (in the form of machinery and other types of capital) are more important than natural resources. Political battles over trade typically involve workers whose skills are made less valuable by imports—clothing workers who face competition from imported apparel and tech workers who now face competition from Bangalore.

As we'll see in later chapters, however, the underlying logic of international trade remains the same. Economic models developed long before the invention of jet planes or the Internet remain key to understanding the essentials of 21st-century international trade.

SUMMARY

1. The *gravity model* relates the trade between any two countries to the sizes of their economies. Using the gravity model also reveals the strong effects of distance and international borders—even friendly borders like that between the United States and Canada—in discouraging trade.

2. International trade is at record levels relative to the size of the world economy, thanks to falling costs of transportation and communications. However, trade has not grown in a straight line: The world was highly integrated in 1914, but trade was greatly reduced by economic depression, protectionism, and war, and took decades to recover.

3. Manufactured goods dominate modern trade today. In the past, however, primary products were much more important than they are now; recently, trade in services has become increasingly important.

4. *Developing countries*, in particular, have shifted from being mainly exporters of primary products to being mainly exporters of manufactured goods.

KEY TERMS

developing countries, p. 43
gravity model, p. 36
gross domestic product (GDP), p. 35

service offshoring (service outsourcing), p. 43

third world, p. 43
trade agreement, p. 38

PROBLEMS

MyEconLab

1. Explain why Canada and South Korea are similar in terms of population and GDP but differ in trade—the US arguably Canada's largest trading partner, whilst Korea divides 60 percent of its exports among China, ASEAN, the US and the EU.

2. The gravity model is often used to not only explain trade between two countries, but also to investigate the reasons why they don't. Illustrate this anomaly with suitable examples and reasons.

3. Equation (2.1) says that trade between any two countries is proportional to the product of their GDPs. Docs this mean that if the GDP of every country in the world doubled, world trade would quadruple?

4. Over the past few decades, East Asian economies have increased their share of world GDP. Similarly, intra–East Asian trade—that is, trade among East Asian nations—has grown as a share of world trade. More than that, East Asian countries do an increasing share of their trade with each other. Explain why, using the gravity model.

5. A century ago, most British imports came from relatively distant locations: North America, Latin America, and Asia. Today, most British imports come from other European countries. How does this fit in with the changing types of goods that make up world trade?

FURTHER READINGS

Paul Bairoch. *Economics and World History*. London: Harvester, 1993. A grand survey of the world economy over time.

Alan S. Blinder. "Offshoring: The Next Industrial Revolution?" *Foreign Affairs*, March/April 2006. An influential article by a well-known economist warning that the growth of trade in services may expose tens of millions of previously "safe" jobs to international competition. The article created a huge stir when it was published.

Frances Cairncross. *The Death of Distance*. London: Orion, 1997. A look at how technology has made the world smaller.

Keith Head. "Gravity for Beginners." A useful guide to the gravity model, available at http:// pacific. commerce.ubc.ca/keith/gravity.pdf

Harold James. *The End of Globalization: Lessons from the Great Depression*. Cambridge: Harvard University Press, 2001. A survey of how the first great wave of globalization ended.

J. Bradford Jensen and Lori G. Kletzer. "Tradable Services: Understanding the Scope and Impact of Services Outsourcing." Peterson Institute Working Paper 5–09, May 2005. A systematic look at which services are traded within the United States, with implications about the future of international trade in services.

World Bank. *World Development Report 1995*. Each year the World Bank spotlights an important global issue; the 1995 report focused on the effects of growing world trade.

World Trade Organization. *World Trade Report*. An annual report on the state of world trade. Each year's report has a theme; for example, the 2004 report focused on the effects on world trade of domestic policies such as spending on infrastructure.

MyEconLab Can Help You Get a Better Grade

MyEconLab If your exam were tomorrow, would you be ready? For each chapter, MyEconLab Practice Tests and Study Plans pinpoint sections you have mastered and those you need to study. That way, you are more efficient with your study time, and you are better prepared for your exams.

To see how it works, turn to page 33 and then go to

www.myeconlab.com

CHAPTER 3

LABOR PRODUCTIVITY AND COMPARATIVE ADVANTAGE: THE RICARDIAN MODEL

Countries engage in international trade for two basic reasons, each of which contributes to their gains from trade. First, countries trade because they are different from each other. Nations, like individuals, can benefit from their differences by reaching an arrangement in which each does the things it does relatively well. Second, countries trade to achieve economies of scale in production. That is, if each country produces only a limited range of goods, it can produce each of these goods at a larger scale and hence more efficiently than if it tried to produce everything. In the real world, patterns of international trade reflect the interaction of both these motives. As a first step toward understanding the causes and effects of trade, however, it is useful to look at simplified models in which only one of these motives is present.

The next four chapters develop tools to help us to understand how differences between countries give rise to trade between them and why this trade is mutually beneficial. The essential concept in this analysis is that of comparative advantage.

Although comparative advantage is a simple concept, experience shows that it is a surprisingly hard concept for many people to understand (or accept). Indeed, the late Paul Samuelson—the Nobel laureate economist who did much to develop the models of international trade discussed in Chapters 4 and 5—once described comparative advantage as the best example he knows of an economic principle that is undeniably true yet not obvious to intelligent people.

In this chapter, we begin with a general introduction to the concept of comparative advantage, then proceed to develop a specific model of how comparative advantage determines the pattern of international trade.

LEARNING GOALS

After reading this chapter, you will be able to:

- Explain how the *Ricardian model*, the most basic model of international trade, works and how it illustrates the principle of *comparative advantage*.

- Demonstrate *gains from trade* and refute common fallacies about international trade.
- Describe the empirical evidence that wages reflect productivity and that trade patterns reflect relative productivity.

The Concept of Comparative Advantage

On Valentine's Day, 1996, which happened to fall less than a week before the crucial February 20 primary in New Hampshire, Republican presidential candidate Patrick Buchanan stopped at a nursery to buy a dozen roses for his wife. He took the occasion to make a speech denouncing the growing imports of flowers into the United States, which he claimed were putting American flower growers out of business. And it is indeed true that a growing share of the market for winter roses in the United States is supplied by imports flown in from South American countries, Colombia in particular. But is that a bad thing?

The case of winter roses offers an excellent example of the reasons why international trade can be beneficial. Consider first how hard it is to supply American sweethearts with fresh roses in February. The flowers must be grown in heated greenhouses, at great expense in terms of energy, capital investment, and other scarce resources. Those resources could be used to produce other goods. Inevitably, there is a trade-off. In order to produce winter roses, the U.S. economy must produce fewer of other things, such as computers. Economists use the term **opportunity cost** to describe such trade-offs: The opportunity cost of roses in terms of computers is the number of computers that could have been produced with the resources used to produce a given number of roses.

Suppose, for example, that the United States currently grows 10 million roses for sale on Valentine's Day and that the resources used to grow those roses could have produced 100,000 computers instead. Then the opportunity cost of those 10 million roses is 100,000 computers. (Conversely, if the computers were produced instead, the opportunity cost of those 100,000 computers would be 10 million roses.)

Those 10 million Valentine's Day roses could instead have been grown in Colombia. It seems extremely likely that the opportunity cost of those roses in terms of computers would be less than it would be in the United States. For one thing, it is a lot easier to grow February roses in the Southern Hemisphere, where it is summer in February rather than winter. Furthermore, Colombian workers are less efficient than their U.S. counterparts at making sophisticated goods such as computers, which means that a given amount of resources used in computer production yields fewer computers in Colombia than in the United States. So the trade-off in Colombia might be something like 10 million winter roses for only 30,000 computers.

This difference in opportunity costs offers the possibility of a mutually beneficial rearrangement of world production. Let the United States stop growing winter roses and devote the resources this frees up to producing computers; meanwhile, let Colombia grow those roses instead, shifting the necessary resources out of its computer industry. The resulting changes in production would look like Table 3-1.

Look what has happened: The world is producing just as many roses as before, but it is now producing more computers. So this rearrangement of production, with the United States concentrating on computers and Colombia concentrating on roses, increases the size of the world's economic pie. Because the world as a whole is producing more, it is possible in principle to raise everyone's standard of living.

TABLE 3-1	Hypothetical Changes in Production	
	Million Roses	**Thousand Computers**
United States	−10	+100
Colombia	+10	−30
Total	0	+70

The reason that international trade produces this increase in world output is that it allows each country to specialize in producing the good in which it has a comparative advantage. A country has a **comparative advantage** in producing a good if the opportunity cost of producing that good in terms of other goods is lower in that country than it is in other countries.

In this example, Colombia has a comparative advantage in winter roses and the United States has a comparative advantage in computers. The standard of living can be increased in both places if Colombia produces roses for the U.S. market, while the United States produces computers for the Colombian market. We therefore have an essential insight about comparative advantage and international trade: *Trade between two countries can benefit both countries if each country exports the goods in which it has a comparative advantage.*

This is a statement about possibilities—not about what will actually happen. In the real world, there is no central authority deciding which country should produce roses and which should produce computers. Nor is there anyone handing out roses and computers to consumers in both places. Instead, international production and trade are determined in the marketplace, where supply and demand rule. Is there any reason to suppose that the potential for mutual gains from trade will be realized? Will the United States and Colombia actually end up producing the goods in which each has a comparative advantage? Will the trade between them actually make both countries better off?

To answer these questions, we must be much more explicit in our analysis. In this chapter, we will develop a model of international trade originally proposed by British economist David Ricardo, who introduced the concept of comparative advantage in the early 19th century.[1] This approach, in which international trade is solely due to international differences in the productivity of labor, is known as the **Ricardian model**.

A One-Factor Economy

To introduce the role of comparative advantage in determining the pattern of international trade, we begin by imagining that we are dealing with an economy—which we call Home—that has only one factor of production. (In Chapter 4 we extend the analysis to models in which there are several factors.) We imagine that only two goods, wine and cheese, are produced. The technology of Home's economy can be summarized by labor productivity in each industry, expressed in terms of the **unit labor requirement,** the number of hours of labor required to produce a pound of cheese or a gallon of wine. For example, it might require one hour of labor to produce a pound of cheese and two hours to produce a gallon of wine. Notice, by the way, that we're defining unit

---

[1]The classic reference is David Ricardo, *The Principles of Political Economy and Taxation*, first published in 1817.

labor requirements as the *inverse* of productivity—the more cheese or wine a worker can produce in an hour, the *lower* the unit labor requirement. For future reference, we define a_{LW} and a_{LC} as the unit labor requirements in wine and cheese production, respectively. The economy's total resources are defined as L, the total labor supply.

Production Possibilities Because any economy has limited resources, there are limits on what it can produce, and there are always trade-offs; to produce more of one good, the economy must sacrifice some production of another good. These trade-offs are illustrated graphically by a **production possibility frontier** (line *PF* in Figure 3-1), which shows the maximum amount of wine that can be produced once the decision has been made to produce any given amount of cheese, and vice versa.

When there is only one factor of production, the production possibility frontier of an economy is simply a straight line. We can derive this line as follows: If Q_W is the economy's production of wine and Q_C its production of cheese, then the labor used in producing wine will be $a_{LW}Q_W$, and the labor used in producing cheese will be $a_{LC}Q_C$. The production possibility frontier is determined by the limits on the economy's resources—in this case, labor. Because the economy's total labor supply is L, the limits on production are defined by the inequality

$$a_{LC}Q_C + a_{LW}Q_W \leq L. \tag{3-1}$$

Suppose, for example, that the economy's total labor supply is 1,000 hours, and that it takes 1 hour of labor to produce a pound of cheese and 2 hours of labor to produce a gallon of wine. Then the total labor used in production is (1 × pounds of cheese produced) + (2 × gallons of wine produced), and this total must be no more than the 1,000 hours of labor available. If the economy devoted all its labor to cheese production, it could, as shown in Figure 3-1, produce L/a_{LC} pounds of cheese (1,000 pounds). If it devoted all its labor to wine production instead, it could produce L/a_{LW} gallons—1000/2 = 500 gallons—of wine. And it can produce any mix of wine and cheese that lies on the straight line connecting those two extremes.

FIGURE 3-1

Home's Production Possibility Frontier

The line *PF* shows the maximum amount of cheese Home can produce given any production of wine, and vice versa.

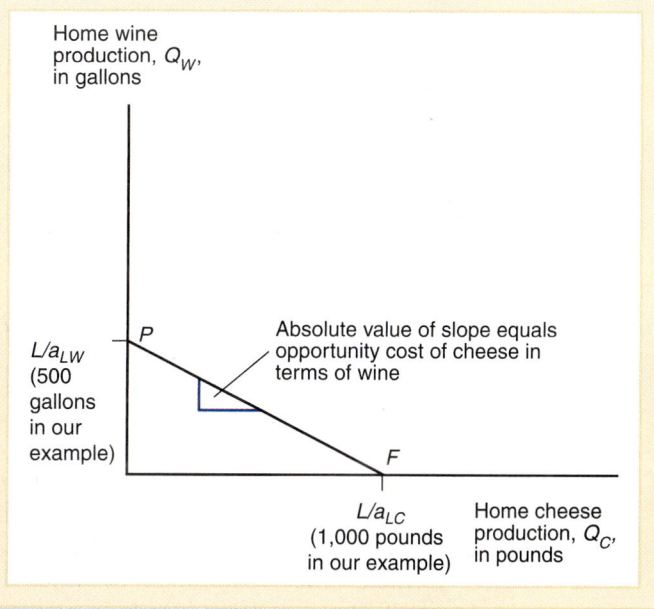

Home wine production, Q_W, in gallons

L/a_{LW} (500 gallons in our example)

P

Absolute value of slope equals opportunity cost of cheese in terms of wine

F

L/a_{LC} (1,000 pounds in our example)

Home cheese production, Q_C, in pounds

When the production possibility frontier is a straight line, the *opportunity cost* of a pound of cheese in terms of wine is constant. As we saw in the previous section, this opportunity cost is defined as the number of gallons of wine the economy would have to give up in order to produce an extra pound of cheese. In this case, to produce another pound would require a_{LC} person-hours. Each of these person-hours could in turn have been used to produce $1/a_{LW}$ gallons of wine. Thus, the opportunity cost of cheese in terms of wine is a_{LC}/a_{LW}. For example, if it takes one person-hour to make a pound of cheese and two hours to produce a gallon of wine, the opportunity cost of each pound of cheese is half a gallon of wine. As Figure 3-1 shows, this opportunity cost is equal to the absolute value of the slope of the production possibility frontier.

Relative Prices and Supply

The production possibility frontier illustrates the different mixes of goods the economy *can* produce. To determine what the economy will actually produce, however, we need to look at prices. Specifically, we need to know the relative price of the economy's two goods, that is, the price of one good in terms of the other.

In a competitive economy, supply decisions are determined by the attempts of individuals to maximize their earnings. In our simplified economy, since labor is the only factor of production, the supply of cheese and wine will be determined by the movement of labor to whichever sector pays the higher wage.

Suppose, once again, that it takes one hour of labor to produce a pound of cheese and two hours to produce a gallon of wine. Now suppose further that cheese sells for $4 a pound, while wine sells for $7 a gallon. What will workers produce? Well, if they produce cheese, they can earn $4 an hour. (Bear in mind that since labor is the only input into production here, there are no profits, so workers receive the full value of their output.) On the other hand, if workers produce wine, they will earn only $3.50 an hour, because a $7 gallon of wine takes two hours to produce. So if cheese sells for $4 a pound while wine sells for $7 a gallon, workers will do better by producing cheese—and the economy as a whole will specialize in cheese production.

But what if cheese prices drop to $3 a pound? In that case, workers can earn more by producing wine, and the economy will specialize in wine production instead.

More generally, let P_C and P_W be the prices of cheese and wine, respectively. It takes a_{LC} person-hours to produce a pound of cheese; since there are no profits in our one-factor model, the hourly wage in the cheese sector will equal the value of what a worker can produce in an hour, P_C/a_{LC}. Since it takes a_{LW} person-hours to produce a gallon of wine, the hourly wage rate in the wine sector will be P_W/a_{LW}. Wages in the cheese sector will be higher if $P_C/P_W > a_{LC}/a_{LW}$; wages in the wine sector will be higher if $P_C/P_W < a_{LC}/a_{LW}$. Because everyone will want to work in whichever industry offers the higher wage, the economy will specialize in the production of cheese if $P_C/P_W > a_{LC}/a_{LW}$. On the other hand, it will specialize in the production of wine if $P_C/P_W < a_{LC}/a_{LW}$. Only when P_C/P_W is equal to a_{LC}/a_{LW} will both goods be produced.

What is the significance of the number a_{LC}/a_{LW}? We saw in the previous section that it is the opportunity cost of cheese in terms of wine. We have therefore just derived a crucial proposition about the relationship between prices and production: *The economy will specialize in the production of cheese if the relative price of cheese exceeds its opportunity cost in terms of wine; it will specialize in the production of wine if the relative price of cheese is less than its opportunity cost in terms of wine.*

In the absence of international trade, Home would have to produce both goods for itself. But it will produce both goods only if the relative price of cheese is just equal to its opportunity cost. Since opportunity cost equals the ratio of unit labor requirements in cheese and wine, we can summarize the determination of prices in the absence of international trade with a simple labor theory of value: *In the absence of international trade, the relative prices of goods are equal to their relative unit labor requirements.*

Trade in a One-Factor World

To describe the pattern and effects of trade between two countries when each country has only one factor of production is simple. Yet the implications of this analysis can be surprising. Indeed, to those who have not thought about international trade, many of these implications seem to conflict with common sense. Even this simplest of trade models can offer some important guidance on real-world issues, such as what constitutes fair international competition and fair international exchange.

Before we get to these issues, however, let us get the model stated. Suppose there are two countries. One of them we again call Home and the other we call Foreign. Each of these countries has one factor of production (labor) and can produce two goods, wine and cheese. As before, we denote Home's labor force by L and Home's unit labor requirements in wine and cheese production by a_{LW} and a_{LC}, respectively. For Foreign, we will use a convenient notation throughout this text: When we refer to some aspect of Foreign, we will use the same symbol that we use for Home, but with an asterisk. Thus Foreign's labor force will be denoted by L^*, Foreign's unit labor requirements in wine and cheese will be denoted by a_{LW}^* and a_{LC}^*, respectively, and so on.

In general, the unit labor requirements can follow any pattern. For example, Home could be less productive than Foreign in wine but more productive in cheese, or vice versa. For the moment, we make only one arbitrary assumption: that

$$a_{LC}/a_{LW} < a_{LC}^*/a_{LW}^* \tag{3-2}$$

or, equivalently, that

$$a_{LC}/a_{LC}^* < a_{LW}/a_{LW}^*. \tag{3-3}$$

In words, we are assuming that the ratio of the labor required to produce a pound of cheese to that required to produce a gallon of wine is lower in Home than it is in Foreign. More briefly still, we are saying that Home's relative productivity in cheese is higher than it is in wine.

But remember that the ratio of unit labor requirements is equal to the opportunity cost of cheese in terms of wine; and remember also that we defined comparative advantage precisely in terms of such opportunity costs. So the assumption about relative productivities embodied in equations (3-2) and (3-3) amounts to saying that *Home has a comparative advantage in cheese.*

One point should be noted immediately: The condition under which Home has this comparative advantage involves all four unit labor requirements, not just two. You might think that to determine who will produce cheese, all you need to do is compare the two countries' unit labor requirements in cheese production, a_{LC} and a_{LC}^*. If $a_{LC} < a_{LC}^*$, Home labor is more efficient than Foreign in producing cheese. When one country can produce a unit of a good with less labor than another country, we say that the first country has an **absolute advantage** in producing that good. In our example, Home has an absolute advantage in producing cheese.

What we will see in a moment, however, is that we cannot determine the pattern of trade from absolute advantage alone. One of the most important sources of error

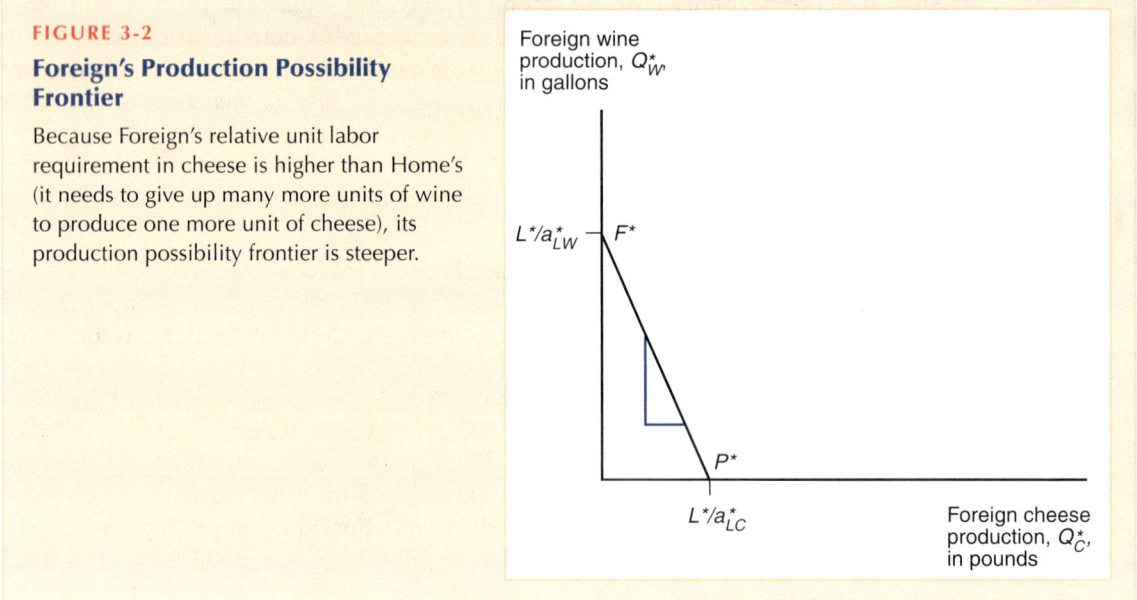

FIGURE 3-2

Foreign's Production Possibility Frontier

Because Foreign's relative unit labor requirement in cheese is higher than Home's (it needs to give up many more units of wine to produce one more unit of cheese), its production possibility frontier is steeper.

Foreign wine production, Q_W^*, in gallons

L^*/a_{LW}^* — F^*

P^*

L^*/a_{LC}^*

Foreign cheese production, Q_C^*, in pounds

[handwritten in margin: THE different mix that country can produce]

in discussing international trade is to confuse comparative advantage with absolute advantage.

Given the labor forces and the unit labor requirements in the two countries, we can draw the production possibility frontier for each country. We have already done this for Home, by drawing *PF* in Figure 3-1. The production possibility frontier for Foreign is shown as *P*F** in Figure 3-2. Since the slope of the production possibility frontier equals the opportunity cost of cheese in terms of wine, Foreign's frontier is steeper than Home's.

In the absence of trade, the relative prices of cheese and wine in each country would be determined by the relative unit labor requirements. Thus, in Home the relative price of cheese would be a_{LC}/a_{LW}; in Foreign it would be a_{LC}^*/a_{LW}^*.

Once we allow for the possibility of international trade, however, prices will no longer be determined purely by domestic considerations. If the relative price of cheese is higher in Foreign than in Home, it will be profitable to ship cheese from Home to Foreign and to ship wine from Foreign to Home. This cannot go on indefinitely, however. Eventually, Home will export enough cheese and Foreign enough wine to equalize the relative price. But what determines the level at which that price settles?

Determining the Relative Price after Trade

Prices of internationally traded goods, like other prices, are determined by supply and demand. In discussing comparative advantage, however, we must apply supply-and-demand analysis carefully. In some contexts, such as some of the trade policy analysis in Chapters 9 through 12, it is acceptable to focus only on supply and demand in a single market. In assessing the effects of U.S. import quotas on sugar, for example, it is reasonable to use **partial equilibrium analysis,** that is, to study a single market, the sugar market. When we study comparative advantage, however, it is crucial to keep track of the relationships between markets (in our example, the markets for wine and cheese). Since Home exports cheese only in return for imports of wine, and Foreign

FIGURE 3-3

World Relative Supply and Demand

The *RD* and *RD'* curves show that the demand for cheese relative to wine is a decreasing function of the price of cheese relative to that of wine, while the *RS* curve shows that the supply of cheese relative to wine is an increasing function of the same relative price.

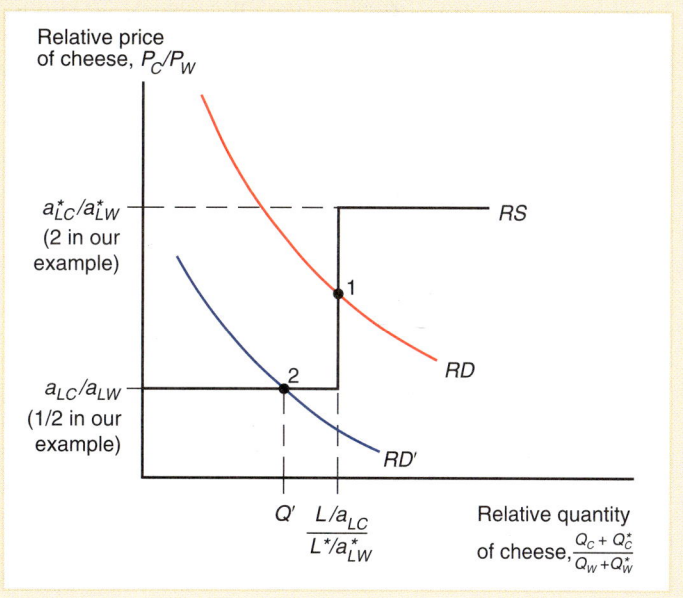

exports wine in return for cheese, it can be misleading to look at the cheese and wine markets in isolation. What is needed is **general equilibrium analysis,** which takes account of the linkages between the two markets.

One useful way to keep track of two markets at once is to focus not just on the quantities of cheese and wine supplied and demanded but also on the *relative* supply and demand, that is, on the number of pounds of cheese supplied or demanded divided by the number of gallons of wine supplied or demanded.

Figure 3-3 shows world supply and demand for cheese relative to wine as functions of the price of cheese relative to that of wine. The **relative demand curve** is indicated by *RD*; the **relative supply curve** is indicated by *RS*. World general equilibrium requires that relative supply equal relative demand, and thus the world relative price is determined by the intersection of *RD* and *RS*.

The striking feature of Figure 3-3 is the funny shape of the relative supply curve *RS*: It's a "step" with flat sections linked by a vertical section. Once we understand the derivation of the *RS* curve, we will be almost home-free in understanding the whole model.

First, as drawn, the *RS* curve shows that there would be *no* supply of cheese if the world price dropped below a_{LC}/a_{LW}. To see why, recall that we showed that Home will specialize in the production of wine whenever $P_C/P_W < a_{LC}/a_{LW}$. Similarly, Foreign will specialize in wine production whenever $P_C/P_W < a_{LC}^*/a_{LW}^*$. At the start of our discussion of equation (3-2), we made the assumption that $a_{LC}/a_{LW} < a_{LC}^*/a_{LW}^*$. So at relative prices of cheese below a_{LC}/a_{LW}, there would be no world cheese production.

Next, when the relative price of cheese P_C/P_W is exactly a_{LC}/a_{LW}, we know that workers in Home can earn exactly the same amount making either cheese or wine. So Home will be willing to supply any relative amount of the two goods, producing a flat section to the supply curve.

We have already seen that if P_C/P_W is above a_{LC}/a_{LW}, Home will specialize in the production of cheese. As long as $P_C/P_W < a_{LC}^*/a_{LW}^*$, however, Foreign will continue to specialize in producing wine. When Home specializes in cheese production, it produces L/a_{LC} pounds. Similarly, when Foreign specializes in wine, it produces L^*/a_{LW}^* gallons. So for any relative price of cheese between a_{LC}/a_{LW} and a_{LC}^*/a_{LW}^*, the relative supply of cheese is

$$(L/a_{LC})/(L^*/a_{LW}^*). \tag{3-4}$$

At $P_C/P_W = a_{LC}^*/a_{LW}^*$, we know that Foreign workers are indifferent between producing cheese and wine. Thus, here we again have a flat section of the supply curve.

Finally, for $P_C/P_W > a_{LC}^*/a_{LW}^*$, both Home and Foreign will specialize in cheese production. There will be no wine production, so that the relative supply of cheese will become infinite.

A numerical example may help at this point. Let's assume, as we did before, that in Home it takes one hour of labor to produce a pound of cheese and two hours to produce a gallon of wine. Meanwhile, let's assume that in Foreign it takes six hours to produce a pound of cheese—Foreign workers are much less productive than Home workers when it comes to cheesemaking—but only three hours to produce a gallon of wine.

In this case, the opportunity cost of cheese production in terms of wine is $1/2$ in Home—that is, the labor used to produce a pound of cheese could have produced half a gallon of wine. So the lower flat section of RS corresponds to a relative price of $1/2$.

Meanwhile, in Foreign the opportunity cost of cheese in terms of wine is 2: The six hours of labor required to produce a pound of cheese could have produced two gallons of wine. So the upper flat section of RS corresponds to a relative price of 2.

The relative demand curve RD does not require such exhaustive analysis. The downward slope of RD reflects substitution effects. As the relative price of cheese rises, consumers will tend to purchase less cheese and more wine, so the relative demand for cheese falls.

The equilibrium relative price of cheese is determined by the intersection of the relative supply and relative demand curves. Figure 3-3 shows a relative demand curve RD that intersects the RS curve at point 1, where the relative price of cheese is between the two countries' pretrade prices—say, at a relative price of 1, in between the pretrade prices of $1/2$ and 2. In this case, each country specializes in the production of the good in which it has a comparative advantage: Home produces only cheese, while Foreign produces only wine.

This is not, however, the only possible outcome. If the relevant RD curve were RD', for example, relative supply and relative demand would intersect on one of the horizontal sections of RS. At point 2, the world relative price of cheese after trade is a_{LC}/a_{LW}, the same as the opportunity cost of cheese in terms of wine in Home.

What is the significance of this outcome? If the relative price of cheese is equal to its opportunity cost in Home, the Home economy need not specialize in producing either cheese or wine. In fact, at point 2 Home must be producing both some wine and some cheese; we can infer this from the fact that the relative supply of cheese (point Q' on the horizontal axis) is less than it would be if Home were in fact completely specialized. Since P_C/P_W is below the opportunity cost of cheese in terms of wine in Foreign, however, Foreign does specialize completely in producing wine. It therefore remains true that if a country does specialize, it will do so in the good in which it has a comparative advantage.

For the moment, let's leave aside the possibility that one of the two countries does not completely specialize. Except in this case, the normal result of trade is that the price of a traded good (e.g., cheese) relative to that of another good (wine) ends up somewhere in between its pretrade levels in the two countries.

COMPARATIVE ADVANTAGE IN PRACTICE: THE CASE OF BABE RUTH

Everyone knows that Babe Ruth was the greatest slugger in the history of baseball. Only true fans of the sport know, however, that Ruth also was one of the greatest *pitchers* of all time. Because Ruth stopped pitching after 1918 and played outfield during all the time he set his famous batting records, most people don't realize that he even could pitch. What explains Ruth's lopsided reputation as a batter? The answer is provided by the principle of comparative advantage.

As a player with the Boston Red Sox early in his career, Ruth certainly had an *absolute* advantage in pitching. According to historian Geoffrey C. Ward and filmmaker Ken Burns:

In the Red Sox's greatest years, he was their greatest player, the best left-handed pitcher in the American League, winning 89 games in six seasons. In 1916 he got his first chance to pitch in the World Series and made the most of it. After giving up a run in the first, he drove in the tying run himself, after which he held the Brooklyn Dodgers scoreless for eleven innings until his teammates could score the winning run .... In the 1918 series, he would show that he could still handle them, stretching his series record to 29²/₃ scoreless innings, a mark that stood for forty-three years.*

The Babe's World Series pitching record was broken by New York Yankee Whitey Ford in the same year, 1961, that his teammate Roger Maris shattered Ruth's 1927 record of 60 home runs in a single season.

Although Ruth had an absolute advantage in pitching, his skill as a batter relative to his teammates' abilities was even greater: His *comparative* advantage was at the plate. As a pitcher, however, Ruth had to rest his arm between appearances and therefore could not bat in every game. To exploit Ruth's *comparative* advantage, the Red Sox moved him to center field in 1919 so that he could bat more frequently.

The payoff to having Ruth specialize in batting was huge. In 1919, he hit 29 home runs, "more than any player had ever hit in a single season," according to Ward and Burns. The Yankees kept Ruth in the outfield (and at the plate) after they acquired him in 1920. They knew a good thing when they saw it. That year, Ruth hit 54 home runs, set a slugging record (bases divided by at bats) that remains untouched to this day, and turned the Yankees into baseball's most renowned franchise.

*See Geoffrey C. Ward and Ken Burns, *Baseball: An Illustrated History* (New York: Knopf, 1994), p. 155. Ruth's career preceded the designated hitter rule, so American League pitchers, like National League pitchers today, took their turns at bat. For a more extensive discussion of Babe Ruth's relation to the comparative advantage principle, see Edward Scahill, "Did Babe Ruth Have a Comparative Advantage as a Pitcher?" *Journal of Economic Education* 21(4), Fall 1990, pp. 402–410.

The effect of this convergence in relative prices is that each country specializes in the production of that good in which it has the relatively lower unit labor requirement. The rise in the relative price of cheese in Home will lead Home to specialize in the production of cheese, producing at point *F* in Figure 3-4a. The fall in the relative price of cheese in Foreign will lead Foreign to specialize in the production of wine, producing at point *F** in Figure 3-4b.

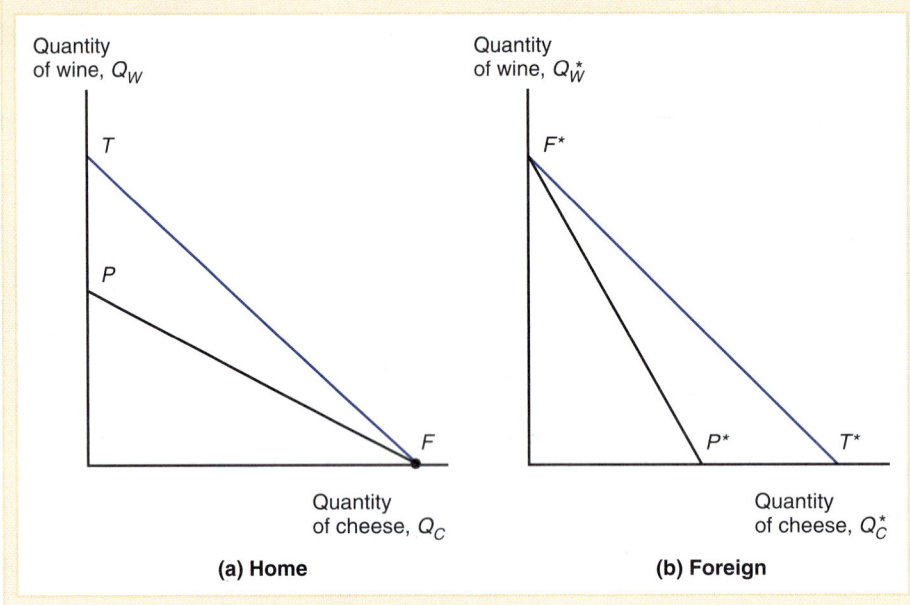

Quantity of wine, Q_W

Quantity of wine, Q_W^*

T

P

F

Quantity of cheese, Q_C

(a) Home

F^*

P^*

T^*

Quantity of cheese, Q_C^*

(b) Foreign

FIGURE 3-4

Trade Expands Consumption Possibilities

International trade allows Home and Foreign to consume anywhere within the colored lines, which lie outside the countries' production frontiers.

The Gains from Trade

We have now seen that countries whose relative labor productivities differ across industries will specialize in the production of different goods. We next show that both countries derive **gains from trade** from this specialization. This mutual gain can be demonstrated in two alternative ways.

The first way to show that specialization and trade are beneficial is to think of trade as an indirect method of production. Home could produce wine directly, but trade with Foreign allows it to "produce" wine by producing cheese and then trading the cheese for wine. This indirect method of "producing" a gallon of wine is a more efficient method than direct production.

Consider our numerical example yet again: In Home, we assume that it takes one hour to produce a pound of cheese and two hours to produce a gallon of wine. This means that the opportunity cost of cheese in terms of wine is $^1/_2$. But we know that the relative price of cheese after trade will be higher than this, say 1. So here's one way to see the gains from trade for Home: Instead of using two hours of labor to produce a gallon of wine, it can use that labor to produce two pounds of cheese, and trade that cheese for *two* gallons of wine.

More generally, consider two alternative ways of using an hour of labor. On one side, Home could use the hour directly to produce $1/a_{LW}$ gallons of wine. Alternatively, Home could use the hour to produce $1/a_{LC}$ pounds of cheese. This cheese could then be traded for wine, with each pound trading for P_C/P_W gallons, so our original hour of labor yields $(1/a_{LC})(P_C/P_W)$ gallons of wine. This will be more wine than the hour could have produced directly as long as

$$(1/a_{LC})(P_C/P_W) > 1/a_{LW}, \tag{3-5}$$

or

$$P_C/P_W > a_{LC}/a_{LW}.$$

But we just saw that in international equilibrium, if neither country produces both goods, we must have $P_C/P_W > a_{LC}/a_{LW}$. This shows that Home can "produce" wine more efficiently by making cheese and trading it than by producing wine directly for itself. Similarly, Foreign can "produce" cheese more efficiently by making wine and trading it. This is one way of seeing that both countries gain.

Another way to see the mutual gains from trade is to examine how trade affects each country's possibilities for consumption. In the absence of trade, consumption possibilities are the same as production possibilities (the solid lines PF and P^*F^* in Figure 3-4). Once trade is allowed, however, each economy can consume a different mix of cheese and wine from the mix it produces. Home's consumption possibilities are indicated by the colored line TF in Figure 3-4a, while Foreign's consumption possibilities are indicated by T^*F^* in Figure 3-4b. In each case, trade has enlarged the range of choice, and therefore it must make residents of each country better off.

A Note on Relative Wages

Political discussions of international trade often focus on comparisons of wage rates in different countries. For example, opponents of trade between the United States and Mexico often emphasize the point that workers in Mexico are paid only about $6.50 per hour, compared with more than $35 per hour for the typical worker in the United States. Our discussion of international trade up to this point has not explicitly compared wages in the two countries, but it is possible in the context of our numerical example to determine how the wage rates in the two countries compare.

In our example, once the countries have specialized, all Home workers are employed producing cheese. Since it takes one hour of labor to produce one pound of cheese, workers in Home earn the value of one pound of cheese per hour of their labor. Similarly, Foreign workers produce only wine; since it takes three hours for them to produce each gallon, they earn the value of $1/3$ of a gallon of wine per hour.

To convert these numbers into dollar figures, we need to know the prices of cheese and wine. Suppose that a pound of cheese and a gallon of wine both sell for $12; then Home workers will earn $12 per hour, while Foreign workers will earn $4 per hour. The **relative wage** of a country's workers is the amount they are paid per hour, compared with the amount workers in another country are paid per hour. The relative wage of Home workers will therefore be 3.

Clearly, this relative wage does not depend on whether the price of a pound of cheese is $12 or $20, as long as a gallon of wine sells for the same price. As long as the relative price of cheese—the price of a pound of cheese divided by the price of a gallon of wine—is 1, the wage of Home workers will be three times that of Foreign workers.

Notice that this wage rate lies between the ratios of the two countries' productivities in the two industries. Home is six times as productive as Foreign in cheese, but only one-and-a-half times as productive in wine, and it ends up with a wage rate three times as high as Foreign's. It is precisely because the relative wage is between the relative productivities that each country ends up with a *cost* advantage in one good. Because of its lower wage rate, Foreign has a cost advantage in wine even though it

THE LOSSES FROM NONTRADE

Our discussion of the gains from trade took the form of a "thought experiment" in which we compared two situations: one in which countries do not trade at all and another in which they have free trade. It's a hypothetical case that helps us to understand the principles of international economics, but it does not have much to do with actual events. After all, countries don't suddenly go from no trade to free trade or vice versa. Or do they?

As economic historian Douglas Irwin* has pointed out, in the early history of the United States the country actually did carry out something very close to the thought experiment of moving from free trade to no trade. The historical context was as follows: In the early 19th century Britain and France were engaged in a

massive military struggle, the Napoleonic Wars. Both countries endeavored to bring economic pressures to bear: France tried to keep European countries from trading with Britain, while Britain imposed a blockade on France. The young United States was neutral in the conflict but suffered considerably. In particular, the British navy often seized U.S. merchant ships and, on occasion, forcibly recruited their crews into its service.

In an effort to pressure Britain into ceasing these practices, President Thomas Jefferson declared a complete ban on overseas shipping. This embargo would deprive both the United States and Britain of the gains from trade, but Jefferson hoped that Britain would be hurt more and would agree to stop its depredations.

Irwin presents evidence suggesting that the embargo was quite effective: Although some smuggling took place, trade between the United States and the rest of the world was drastically reduced. In effect, the United States gave up international trade for a while.

The costs were substantial. Although quite a lot of guesswork is involved, Irwin suggests that real income in the United States may have fallen by about 8 percent as a result of the embargo. When you bear in mind that in the early 19th century only a fraction of output could be traded—transport costs were still too high, for example, to allow large-scale shipments of commodities like wheat across the Atlantic—that's a pretty substantial sum.

Unfortunately for Jefferson's plan, Britain did not seem to feel equal pain and showed no inclination to give in to U.S. demands. Fourteen months after the embargo was imposed, it was repealed. Britain continued its practices of seizing American cargoes and sailors; three years later the two countries went to war.

*Douglas Irwin, "The Welfare Cost of Autarky: Evidence from the Jeffersonian Trade Embargo, 1807–1809," *Review of International Economics* 13 (September 2005), pp. 631–645.

has lower productivity. Home has a cost advantage in cheese, despite its higher wage rate, because the higher wage is more than offset by its higher productivity.

We have now developed the simplest of all models of international trade. Even though the Ricardian one-factor model is far too simple to be a complete analysis of either the causes or the effects of international trade, a focus on relative labor productivities can be a very useful tool for thinking about trade issues. In particular, the simple one-factor model is a good way to deal with several common misconceptions about the meaning of comparative advantage and the nature of the gains from free trade. These misconceptions appear so frequently in public debate about international economic policy, and even in statements by those who regard themselves as experts, that in the next section we take time out to discuss some of the most common misunderstandings about comparative advantage in light of our model.

Misconceptions about Comparative Advantage

There is no shortage of muddled ideas in economics. Politicians, business leaders, and even economists frequently make statements that do not stand up to careful economic analysis. For some reason this seems to be especially true in international economics. Open the business section of any Sunday newspaper or weekly news magazine and you will probably find at least one article that makes foolish statements about international trade. Three misconceptions in particular have proved highly persistent. In this section we will use our simple model of comparative advantage to see why they are incorrect.

Productivity and Competitiveness

Myth 1: Free trade is beneficial only if your country is strong enough to stand up to foreign competition. This argument seems extremely plausible to many people. For example, a well-known historian once criticized the case for free trade by asserting that it may fail to hold in reality: "What if there is nothing you can produce more cheaply or efficiently than anywhere else, except by constantly cutting labor costs?" he worried.[2]

The problem with this commentator's view is that he failed to understand the essential point of Ricardo's model—that gains from trade depend on *comparative* rather than *absolute* advantage. He is concerned that your country may turn out not to have anything it produces more efficiently than anyone else—that is, that you may not have an absolute advantage in anything. Yet why is that such a terrible thing? In our simple numerical example of trade, Home has lower unit labor requirements and hence higher productivity in both the cheese and wine sectors. Yet, as we saw, both countries gain from trade.

It is always tempting to suppose that the ability to export a good depends on your country having an absolute advantage in productivity. But an absolute productivity advantage over other countries in producing a good is neither a necessary nor a sufficient condition for having a *comparative* advantage in that good. In our one-factor model, the reason that an absolute productivity advantage in an industry is neither necessary nor sufficient to yield competitive advantage is clear: *The competitive advantage of an industry depends not only on its productivity relative to the foreign industry, but also on the domestic wage rate relative to the foreign wage rate.* A country's wage rate, in turn, depends on relative productivity in its other industries. In our numerical example, Foreign is less efficient than Home in the manufacture of wine, but it is at an even greater relative productivity disadvantage in cheese. Because of its overall lower productivity, Foreign must pay lower wages than Home, sufficiently lower that it ends up with lower costs in wine production. Similarly, in the real world, Portugal has low productivity in producing, say, clothing as compared with the United States, but because Portugal's productivity disadvantage is even greater in other industries, it pays low enough wages to have a comparative advantage in clothing over the United States all the same.

But isn't a competitive advantage based on low wages somehow unfair? Many people think so; their beliefs are summarized by our second misconception.

---

[2]Paul Kennedy, "The Threat of Modernization," *New Perspectives Quarterly* (Winter 1995), pp. 31–33. Used by permission of John Wiley & Sons, Ltd.

DO WAGES REFLECT PRODUCTIVITY?

In the numerical example that we use to puncture common misconceptions about comparative advantage, we assume the relative wage of the two countries reflects their relative productivity—specifically, that the ratio of Home to Foreign wages is in a range that gives each country a cost advantage in one of the two goods. This is a necessary implication of our theoretical model. But many people are unconvinced by that model. In particular, rapid increases in productivity in "emerging" economies like China have worried some Western observers, who argue that these countries will continue to pay low wages even as their productivity increases—putting high-wage countries at a cost disadvantage—and dismiss the contrary predictions of orthodox economists as unrealistic theoretical speculation. Leaving aside the logic of this position, what is the evidence?

The answer is that in the real world, national wage rates do, in fact, reflect differences in productivity. The accompanying figure compares estimates of productivity with estimates of wage rates for a selection of countries in 2011 (except for China, where the data are for 2009). Both measures are expressed as percentages of U.S. levels. Our estimate of productivity is GDP per worker measured in U.S. dollars. As we'll see in the second

half of this text, that basis should indicate productivity in the production of traded goods. Wage rates are measured by wages in manufacturing.

If wages were exactly proportional to productivity, all the points in this chart would lie along the indicated 45-degree line. In reality, the fit isn't bad. In particular, low wage rates in China and India reflect low productivity.

The low estimate of overall Chinese productivity may seem surprising, given all the stories one hears about Americans who find themselves competing with Chinese exports. The Chinese workers producing those exports don't seem to have extremely low productivity. But remember what the theory of comparative advantage says: Countries export the goods in which they have relatively high productivity. So it's only to be expected that China's overall relative productivity is far below the level of its export industries.

The figure that follows tells us that the orthodox economists' view that national wage rates reflect national productivity is, in fact, verified by the data at a point in time. It's also true that in the past, rising relative productivity led to rising wages. Consider, for example, the case of South Korea. In 2011, South Korea's labor productivity was a bit less than half of the U.S. level, and its

The Pauper Labor Argument

Myth 2: Foreign competition is unfair and hurts other countries when it is based on low wages. This argument, sometimes referred to as the **pauper labor argument,** is a particular favorite of labor unions seeking protection from foreign competition. People who adhere to this belief argue that industries should not have to cope with foreign industries that are less efficient but pay lower wages. This view is widespread and has acquired considerable political influence. In 1993, Ross Perot, a self-made billionaire and former presidential candidate, warned that free trade between the United States and Mexico, with the latter's much lower wages, would lead to a "giant sucking sound" as U.S. industry moved south. In the same year, another self-made billionaire, Sir James Goldsmith, who was an influential member of the European Parliament, offered similar if less picturesquely expressed views in his book *The Trap*, which became a best seller in France.

Again, our simple example reveals the fallacy of this argument. In the example, Home is more productive than Foreign in both industries, and Foreign's lower cost of wine production is entirely due to its much lower wage rate. Foreign's lower wage rate, however, is irrelevant to the question of whether Home gains from trade. Whether the lower cost

wage rate was actually slightly higher than that. But it wasn't always that way: In the not too distant past, South Korea was a low-productivity, low-wage economy. As recently as 1975, South Korean wages were only 5 percent those of the United States. But when South Korea's productivity rose, so did its wage rate.

In short, the evidence strongly supports the view, based on economic models, that productivity increases are reflected in wage increases.

Productivity and Wages

A country's wage rate is roughly proportional to the country's productivity

Source: International Monetary Fund, Bureau of Labor Statistics, and The Conference Board.

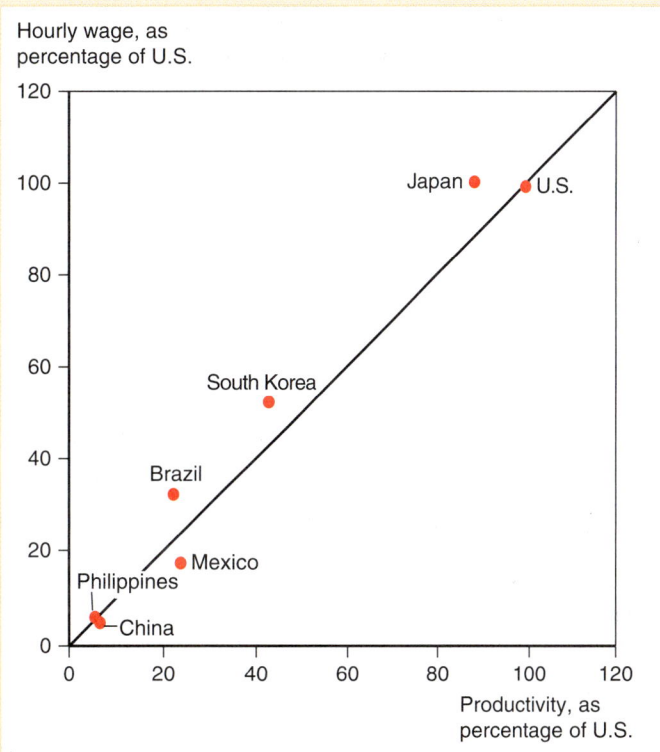

of wine produced in Foreign is due to high productivity or low wages does not matter. All that matters to Home is that it is cheaper *in terms of its own labor* for Home to produce cheese and trade it for wine than to produce wine for itself.

This is fine for Home, but what about Foreign? Isn't there something wrong with basing one's exports on low wages? Certainly it is not an attractive position to be in, but the idea that trade is good only if you receive high wages is our final fallacy.

Exploitation

Myth 3: Trade exploits a country and makes it worse off if its workers receive much lower wages than workers in other nations. This argument is often expressed in emotional terms. For example, one columnist contrasted the multimillion-dollar income of the chief executive officer of the clothing chain The Gap with the low wages—often less than $1 an hour—paid to the Central American workers who produce some of its merchandise.[3]

---

[3]Bob Herbert, "Sweatshop Beneficiaries: How to Get Rich on 56 Cents an Hour," *New York Times* (July 24, 1995), p. A13.

It can seem hard-hearted to try to justify the terrifyingly low wages paid to many of the world's workers.

If one is asking about the desirability of free trade, however, the point is not to ask whether low-wage workers deserve to be paid more but to ask whether they and their country are worse off exporting goods based on low wages than they would be if they refused to enter into such demeaning trade. And in asking this question, one must also ask, *What is the alternative?*

Abstract though it is, our numerical example makes the point that one cannot declare that a low wage represents exploitation unless one knows what the alternative is. In that example, Foreign workers are paid much less than Home workers, and one could easily imagine a columnist writing angrily about their exploitation. Yet if Foreign refused to let itself be "exploited" by refusing to trade with Home (or by insisting on much higher wages in its export sector, which would have the same effect), real wages would be even lower: The purchasing power of a worker's hourly wage would fall from $1/3$ to $1/6$ pound of cheese.

The columnist who pointed out the contrast in incomes between the executive at The Gap and the workers who make its clothes was angry at the poverty of Central American workers. But to deny them the opportunity to export and trade might well be to condemn them to even deeper poverty.

Comparative Advantage with Many Goods

In our discussion so far, we have relied on a model in which only two goods are produced and consumed. This simplified analysis allows us to capture many essential points about comparative advantage and trade and, as we saw in the last section, gives us a surprising amount of mileage as a tool for discussing policy issues. To move closer to reality, however, it is necessary to understand how comparative advantage functions in a model with a larger number of goods.

Setting Up the Model

Again, imagine a world of two countries, Home and Foreign. As before, each country has only one factor of production, labor. However, let's assume that each of these countries consumes and is able to produce a large number of goods—say, N different goods altogether. We assign each of the goods a number from 1 to N.

The technology of each country can be described by its unit labor requirement for each good, that is, the number of hours of labor it takes to produce one unit of each good. We label Home's unit labor requirement for a particular good as a_{Li}, where i is the number we have assigned to that good. If cheese is assigned the number 7, a_{L7} will mean the unit labor requirement in cheese production. Following our usual rule, we label the corresponding Foreign unit labor requirement a_{Li}^*.

To analyze trade, we next pull one more trick. For any good, we can calculate a_{Li}/a_{Li}^*, the ratio of Home's unit labor requirement to Foreign's. The trick is to relabel the goods so that the lower the number, the lower this ratio. That is, we reshuffle the order in which we number goods in such a way that

$$a_{L1}/a_{L1}^* < a_{L2}/a_{L2}^* < a_{L3}/a_{L13}^* < \ldots < a_{LN}/a_{LN}^*. \tag{3-6}$$

Relative Wages and Specialization

We are now prepared to look at the pattern of trade. This pattern depends on only one thing: the ratio of Home to Foreign wages. Once we know this ratio, we can determine who produces what.

Let w be the wage rate per hour in Home and w^* be the wage rate in Foreign. The ratio of wage rates is then w/w^*. The rule for allocating world production, then, is simply this: Goods will always be produced where it is cheapest to make them. The cost of making some good, say good i, is the unit labor requirement times the wage rate. To produce good i in Home will cost wa_{Li}. To produce the same good in Foreign will cost $w^*a_{Li}^*$. It will be cheaper to produce the good in Home if

$$wa_{Li} < w^*a_{Li}^*,$$

which can be rearranged to yield

$$a_{Li}^*/a_{Li} > w/w^*.$$

On the other hand, it will be cheaper to produce the good in Foreign if

$$wa_{Li} > w^*a_{Li}^*,$$

which can be rearranged to yield

$$a_{Li}^*/a_{Li} < w/w^*.$$

Thus, we can restate the allocation rule: Any good for which $a_{Li}^*/a_{Li} > w/w^*$ will be produced in Home, while any good for which $a_{Li}^*/a_{Li} < w/w^*$ will be produced in Foreign.

We have already lined up the goods in increasing order of a_{Li}/a_{Li}^* (equation (3-6)). This criterion for specialization tells us that there is a "cut" in the lineup determined by the ratio of the two countries' wage rates, w/w^*. All the goods to the left of that point end up being produced in Home; all the goods to the right end up being produced in Foreign. (It is possible, as we will see in a moment, that the ratio of wage rates is exactly equal to the ratio of unit labor requirements for one good. In that case, this borderline good may be produced in both countries.)

Table 3-2 offers a numerical example in which Home and Foreign both consume and are able to produce *five* goods: apples, bananas, caviar, dates, and enchiladas.

The first two columns of this table are self-explanatory. The third column is the ratio of the Foreign unit labor requirement to the Home unit labor requirement for each good—or, stated differently, the relative Home productivity advantage in each good. We have labeled the goods in order of Home productivity advantage, with the Home advantage greatest for apples and least for enchiladas.

Which country produces which goods depends on the ratio of Home and Foreign wage rates. Home will have a cost advantage in any good for which its relative productivity is

TABLE 3-2	Home and Foreign Unit Labor Requirements		
Good	Home Unit Labor Requirement a_{Li}	Foreign Unit Labor Requirement (a_{Li}^*)	Relative Home Productivity Advantage (a_{Li}^*/a_{Li})
Apples	1	10	10
Bananas	5	40	8
Caviar	3	12	4
Dates	6	12	2
Enchiladas	12	9	0.75

higher than its relative wage, and Foreign will have the advantage in the others. If, for example, the Home wage rate is five times that of Foreign (a ratio of Home wage to Foreign wage of five to one), apples and bananas will be produced in Home and caviar, dates, and enchiladas in Foreign. If the Home wage rate is only three times that of Foreign, Home will produce apples, bananas, and caviar, while Foreign will produce only dates and enchiladas.

Is such a pattern of specialization beneficial to both countries? We can see that it is by using the same method we used earlier: comparing the labor cost of producing a good directly in a country with that of indirectly "producing" it by producing another good and trading for the desired good. If the Home wage rate is three times the Foreign wage (put another way, Foreign's wage rate is one-third that of Home), Home will import dates and enchiladas. A unit of dates requires 12 units of Foreign labor to produce, but its cost in terms of Home labor, given the three-to-one wage ratio, is only 4 person-hours (12/4 = 3). This cost of 4 person-hours is less than the 6 person-hours it would take to produce the unit of dates in Home. For enchiladas, Foreign actually has higher productivity along with lower wages; it will cost Home only 3 person-hours to acquire a unit of enchiladas through trade, compared with the 12 person-hours it would take to produce it domestically. A similar calculation will show that Foreign also gains; for each of the goods Foreign imports, it turns out to be cheaper in terms of domestic labor to trade for the good rather than produce the good domestically. For example, it would take 10 hours of Foreign labor to produce a unit of apples; even with a wage rate only one-third that of Home workers, it will require only 3 hours of labor to earn enough to buy that unit of apples from Home.

In making these calculations, however, we have simply assumed that the relative wage rate is 3. How does this relative wage rate actually get determined?

Determining the Relative Wage in the Multigood Model

In the two-good model, we determined relative wages by first calculating Home wages in terms of cheese and Foreign wages in terms of wine. We then used the price of cheese relative to that of wine to deduce the ratio of the two countries' wage rates. We could do this because we knew that Home would produce cheese and Foreign wine. In the many-good case, who produces what can be determined only after we know the relative wage rate, so we need a new procedure. To determine relative wages in a multigood economy, we must look behind the relative demand for goods to the implied relative demand for labor. This is not a direct demand on the part of consumers; rather, it is a **derived demand** that results from the demand for goods produced with each country's labor.

The relative derived demand for Home labor will fall when the ratio of Home to Foreign wages rises, for two reasons. First, as Home labor becomes more expensive relative to Foreign labor, goods produced in Home also become relatively more expensive, and world demand for these goods falls. Second, as Home wages rise, fewer goods will be produced in Home and more in Foreign, further reducing the demand for Home labor.

We can illustrate these two effects using our numerical example as illustrated in Table 3-2. Suppose we start with the following situation: The Home wage is initially 3.5 times the Foreign wage. At that level, Home would produce apples, bananas, and caviar while Foreign would produce dates and enchiladas. If the relative Home wage were to increase from 3.5 to 3.99, the pattern of specialization would not change. However, as the goods produced in Home became relatively more expensive, the relative demand for these goods would decline and the relative demand for Home labor would decline with it.

Suppose now that the relative wage increased slightly from 3.99 to 4.01. This small further growth in the relative Home wage would bring about a shift in the pattern of specialization. Because it is now cheaper to produce caviar in Foreign than in Home, the production of caviar shifts from Home to Foreign. What does this imply for the relative demand for Home labor? Clearly it implies that as the relative wage rises from a little less than 4 to a little more than 4, there is an abrupt drop-off in the relative demand, as Home production of caviar falls to zero and Foreign acquires a new industry. If the relative wage continues to rise, relative demand for Home labor will gradually decline, then drop off abruptly at a relative wage of 8, at which point production of bananas shifts to Foreign.

We can illustrate the determination of relative wages with a diagram like Figure 3-5. Unlike Figure 3-3, this diagram does not have relative quantities of goods or relative prices of goods on its axes. Instead it shows the relative quantity of labor and the relative wage rate. The world demand for Home labor relative to its demand for Foreign labor is shown by the curve *RD*. The world supply of Home labor relative to Foreign labor is shown by the line *RS*.

The relative supply of labor is determined by the relative sizes of Home's and Foreign's labor forces. Assuming the number of person-hours available does not vary with the wage, the relative wage has no effect on relative labor supply and *RS* is a vertical line.

Our discussion of the relative demand for labor explains the "stepped" shape of *RD*. Whenever we increase the wage rate of Home workers relative to that of Foreign workers, the relative demand for goods produced in Home will decline and the demand for Home labor will decline with it. In addition, the relative demand for Home labor will drop off abruptly whenever an increase in the relative Home wage makes a good cheaper to produce in Foreign. So the curve alternates between smoothly

FIGURE 3-5

Determination of Relative Wages

In a many-good Ricardian model, relative wages are determined by the intersection of the derived relative demand curve for labor, *RD*, with the relative supply, *RS*.

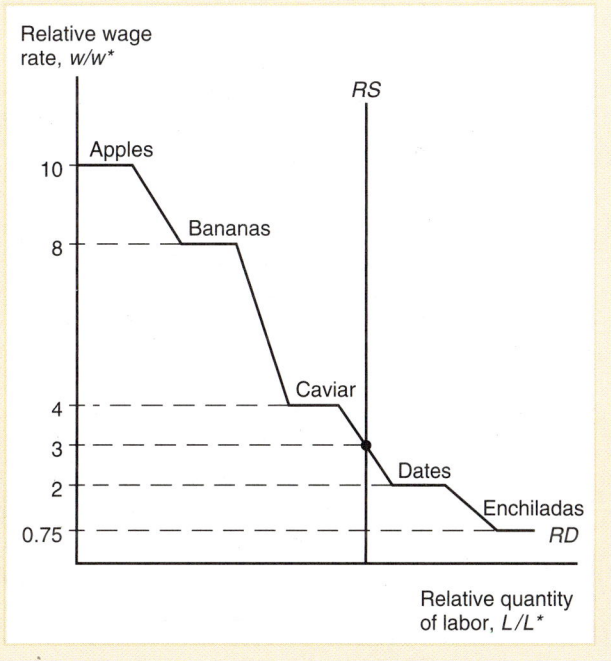

downward-sloping sections where the pattern of specialization does not change and "flats" where the relative demand shifts abruptly because of shifts in the pattern of specialization. As shown in the figure, these "flats" correspond to relative wages that equal the ratio of Home to Foreign productivity for each of the five goods.

The equilibrium relative wage is determined by the intersection of *RD* and *RS*. As drawn, the equilibrium relative wage is 3. At this wage, Home produces apples, bananas, and caviar while Foreign produces dates and enchiladas. The outcome depends on the relative size of the countries (which determines the position of *RS*) and the relative demand for the goods (which determines the shape and position of *RD*).

If the intersection of *RD* and *RS* happens to lie on one of the flats, both countries produce the good to which the flat applies.

Adding Transport Costs and Nontraded Goods

We now extend our model another step closer to reality by considering the effects of transport costs. Transportation costs do not change the fundamental principles of comparative advantage or the gains from trade. Because transport costs pose obstacles to the movement of goods and services, however, they have important implications for the way a trading world economy is affected by a variety of factors such as foreign aid, international investment, and balance of payments problems. While we will not deal with the effects of these factors yet, the multigood one-factor model is a good place to introduce the effects of transport costs.

First, notice that the world economy described by the model of the last section is marked by very extreme international specialization. At most, there is one good that both countries produce; all other goods are produced either in Home or in Foreign, but not in both.

There are three main reasons why specialization in the real international economy is not this extreme:

1. The existence of more than one factor of production reduces the tendency toward specialization (as we will see in the next two chapters).
2. Countries sometimes protect industries from foreign competition (discussed at length in Chapters 9 through 12).
3. It is costly to transport goods and services; in some cases the cost of transportation is enough to lead countries into self-sufficiency in certain sectors.

In the multigood example of the last section, we found that at a relative Home wage of 3, Home could produce apples, bananas, and caviar more cheaply than Foreign, while Foreign could produce dates and enchiladas more cheaply than Home. *In the absence of transport costs*, then, Home will export the first three goods and import the last two.

Now suppose there is a cost to transport goods, and that this transport cost is a uniform fraction of production cost, say 100 percent. This transportation cost will discourage trade. Consider dates, for example. One unit of this good requires 6 hours of Home labor or 12 hours of Foreign labor to produce. At a relative wage of 3, 12 hours of Foreign labor costs only as much as 4 hours of Home labor; so in the absence of transport costs, Home imports dates. With a 100 percent transport cost, however, importing dates would cost the equivalent of 8 hours of Home labor (4 hours of labor plus the equivalent of 4 hours for the transportation costs), so Home will produce the good for itself instead.

A similar cost comparison shows that Foreign will find it cheaper to produce its own caviar than to import it. A unit of caviar requires 3 hours of Home labor to produce. Even at a relative Home wage of 3, which makes this the equivalent of 9 hours of Foreign labor, this is cheaper than the 12 hours Foreign would need to produce caviar for itself. In the absence of transport costs, then, Foreign would find it cheaper to import caviar than to make it domestically. With a 100 percent cost of transportation, however, imported caviar would cost the equivalent of 18 hours of Foreign labor and would therefore be produced locally instead.

The result of introducing transport costs in this example, then, is that Home will still export apples and bananas and import enchiladas, but caviar and dates will become **nontraded goods,** which each country will produce for itself.

In this example, we have assumed that transport costs are the same fraction of production cost in all sectors. In practice there is a wide range of transportation costs. In some cases transportation is virtually impossible: Services such as haircuts and auto repair cannot be traded internationally (except where there is a metropolitan area that straddles a border, like Detroit, Michigan–Windsor, Ontario). There is also little international trade in goods with high weight-to-value ratios, like cement. (It is simply not worth the transport cost of importing cement, even if it can be produced much more cheaply abroad.) Many goods end up being nontraded either because of the absence of strong national cost advantages or because of high transportation costs.

The important point is that nations spend a large share of their income on nontraded goods. This observation is of surprising importance in our later discussion of international monetary economics.

Empirical Evidence on the Ricardian Model

The Ricardian model of international trade is an extremely useful tool for thinking about the reasons why trade may happen and about the effects of international trade on national welfare. But is the model a good fit to the real world? Does the Ricardian model make accurate predictions about actual international trade flows?

The answer is a heavily qualified yes. Clearly there are a number of ways in which the Ricardian model makes misleading predictions. First, as mentioned in our discussion of nontraded goods, the simple Ricardian model predicts an extreme degree of specialization that we do not observe in the real world. Second, the Ricardian model assumes away effects of international trade on the distribution of income *within* countries, and thus predicts that countries as a whole will always gain from trade; in practice, international trade has strong effects on income distribution. Third, the Ricardian model allows no role for differences in resources among countries as a cause of trade, thus missing an important aspect of the trading system (the focus of Chapters 4 and 5). Finally, the Ricardian model neglects the possible role of economies of scale as a cause of trade, which leaves it unable to explain the large trade flows between apparently similar nations—an issue discussed in Chapters 7 and 8.

In spite of these failings, however, the basic prediction of the Ricardian model— that countries should tend to export those goods in which their productivity is relatively high—has been strongly confirmed by a number of studies over the years.

Several classic tests of the Ricardian model, performed using data from the early post-World War II period, compared British with American productivity and trade.[4]

---

[4]The pioneering study by G. D. A. MacDougall is listed in Further Readings at the end of the chapter. A well-known follow-up study, on which we draw here, was Bela Balassa, "An Empirical Demonstration of Classical Comparative Cost Theory," *Review of Economics and Statistics* 45 (August 1963), pp. 231–238; we use Balassa's numbers as an illustration.

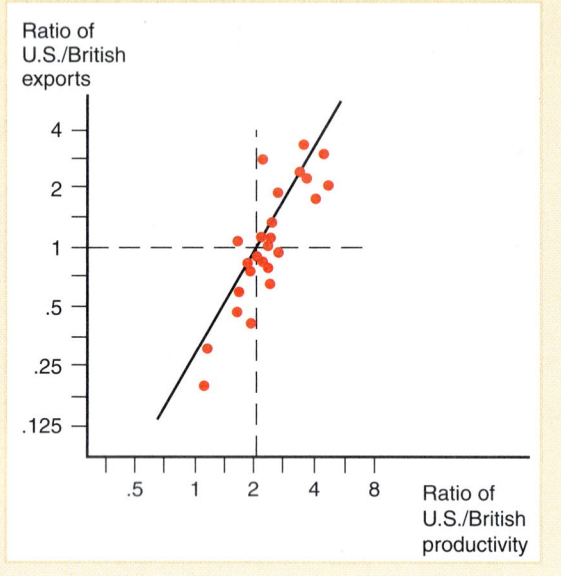

FIGURE 3-6

Productivity and Exports

A comparative study showed that U.S. exports were high relative to British exports in industries in which the United States had high relative labor productivity. Each dot represents a different industry.

This was an unusually illuminating comparison, because it revealed that British labor productivity was lower than American productivity in almost every sector. As a result, the United States had an absolute advantage in everything. Nonetheless, the amount of overall British exports was about as large as the amount of American exports at the time. Despite its lower absolute productivity, there must have been some sectors in which Britain had a comparative advantage. The Ricardian model would predict that these would be the sectors in which the United States' productivity advantage was smaller.

Figure 3-6 illustrates the evidence in favor of the Ricardian model, using data presented in a paper by the Hungarian economist Bela Balassa in 1963. The figure compares the ratio of U.S. to British exports in 1951 with the ratio of U.S. to British labor productivity for 26 manufacturing industries. The productivity ratio is measured on the horizontal axis, the export ratio on the vertical axis. Both axes are given a logarithmic scale, which turns out to produce a clearer picture.

Ricardian theory would lead us broadly to expect that the higher the relative productivity in the U.S. industry, the more likely U.S. rather than U.K. firms would export in that industry. And that is what Figure 3-6 shows. In fact, the scatterplot lies quite close to an upward-sloping line, also shown in the figure. Bearing in mind that the data used for this comparison are, like all economic data, subject to substantial measurement errors, the fit is remarkably close.

As expected, the evidence in Figure 3-6 confirms the basic insight that trade depends on *comparative*, not *absolute* advantage. At the time to which the data refer, U.S. industry had much higher labor productivity than British industry—on average about twice as high. The commonly held misconception that a country can be competitive only if it can match other countries' productivity, which we discussed earlier in this chapter, would have led one to predict a U.S. export advantage across the board. The Ricardian model tells us, however, that having high productivity in an industry compared with that of foreigners is not enough to ensure that a country will export that industry's products; the relative productivity must be high compared with relative productivity in other sectors. As it happened, U.S. productivity exceeded British productivity in all 26 sectors (indicated by dots) shown in Figure 3-6, by margins ranging from 11 to 366 percent. In 12 of the sectors, however, Britain actually had larger exports than the United States. A glance at the figure shows that, in general, U.S. exports were larger than U.K. exports only in industries where the U.S. productivity advantage was somewhat more than two to one.

More recent evidence on the Ricardian model has been less clear-cut. In part, this is because the growth of world trade and the resulting specialization of national economies means that we do not get a chance to see what countries do badly! In the world economy of the 21st century, countries often do not produce goods for which they are at a comparative disadvantage, so there is no way to measure their productivity in those sectors. For example, most countries do not produce airplanes, so there are no data on what their unit labor requirements would be if they did. Nonetheless, several pieces of evidence suggest that differences in labor productivity continue to play an important role in determining world trade patterns.

Perhaps the most striking demonstration of the continuing usefulness of the Ricardian theory of comparative advantage is the way it explains the emergence of countries with very low overall productivity as export powerhouses in some industries. Consider, for example, the case of clothing exports from Bangladesh. The Bangladeshi clothing industry received the worst kind of publicity in April 2013, when a building housing five garment factories collapsed, killing more than a thousand people. The backstory to this tragedy, however, was the growth of Bangladesh's clothing exports, which were rapidly gaining on those of China, previously the dominant supplier. This rapid growth took place even though Bangladesh is a very, very poor country, with extremely low overall productivity even compared with China, which as we have already seen is still low-productivity compared with the U.S.

What was the secret of Bangladesh's success? It has fairly low productivity even in the production of clothing – but its productivity disadvantage there is much smaller than in other industries, so that the nation has a comparative advantage in clothing. Table 3-3 illustrates this point with some estimates based on 2011 data.

Compared with China, Bangladesh still has an *absolute* disadvantage in clothing production, with significantly lower productivity. But because its relative productivity in apparel is so much higher than in other industries, Bangladesh has a strong comparative advantage in apparel—and its apparel industry is giving China a run for the money.

In sum, while few economists believe that the Ricardian model is a fully adequate description of the causes and consequences of world trade, its two principal implications—that productivity differences play an important role in international trade and that it is comparative rather than absolute advantage that matters—do seem to be supported by the evidence.

TABLE 3-3	Bangladesh versus China, 2011	
	Bangladeshi Output per Worker as % of China	**Bangladeshi exports as % of China**
All industries	28.5	1.0
Apparel	77	15.5

Source: McKinsey and Company, "Bangladesh's ready-made garments industry: The challenge of growth," 2012; UN Monthly Bulletin of Statistics.

SUMMARY

1. We examined the Ricardian model, the simplest model that shows how differences between countries give rise to trade and gains from trade. In this model, labor is the only factor of production, and countries differ only in the productivity of labor in different industries.

2. In the Ricardian model, countries will export goods that their labor produces relatively efficiently and will import goods that their labor produces relatively inefficiently. In other words, a country's production pattern is determined by comparative advantage.

3. We can show that trade benefits a country in either of two ways. First, we can think of trade as an indirect method of production. Instead of producing a good for itself, a country can produce another good and trade it for the desired good. The simple model shows that whenever a good is imported, it must be true that this indirect "production" requires less labor than direct production. Second, we can show that trade enlarges a country's consumption possibilities, which implies gains from trade.

4. The distribution of the gains from trade depends on the relative prices of the goods countries produce. To determine these relative prices, it is necessary to look at the relative world supply and demand for goods. The relative price implies a relative wage rate as well.

5. The proposition that trade is beneficial is unqualified. That is, there is no requirement that a country be "competitive" or that the trade be "fair." In particular, we can show that three commonly held beliefs about trade are wrong. First, a country gains from trade even if it has lower productivity than its trading partner in all industries. Second, trade is beneficial even if foreign industries are competitive only because of low wages. Third, trade is beneficial even if a country's exports embody more labor than its imports.

6. Extending the one-factor, two-good model to a world of many commodities does not alter these conclusions. The only difference is that it becomes necessary to focus directly on the relative demand for labor to determine relative wages rather than to work via relative demand for goods. Also, a many-commodity model can be used to illustrate the important point that transportation costs can give rise to a situation in which some goods are nontraded.

7. While some of the predictions of the Ricardian model are clearly unrealistic, its basic prediction—that countries will tend to export goods in which they have relatively high productivity—has been confirmed by a number of studies.

KEY TERMS

absolute advantage, p. 53
comparative advantage, p. 50
derived demand, p. 66
gains from trade, p. 58
general equilibrium analysis, p. 55
nontraded goods, p. 69

opportunity cost, p. 49
partial equilibrium analysis, p. 54
pauper labor argument, p. 62
production possibility frontier, p. 51
relative demand curve, p. 55

relative supply curve, p. 55
relative wage, p. 59
Ricardian model, p. 50
unit labor requirement, p. 50

PROBLEMS

1. Home has 1,200 units of labor available. It can produce two goods, apples and bananas. The unit labor requirement in apple production is 3, while in banana production it is 2.
   a. Graph Home's production possibility frontier.
   b. What is the opportunity cost of apples in terms of bananas?
   c. In the absence of trade, what would be the price of apples in terms of bananas? Why?

2. Home is as described in problem 1. There is now also another country, Foreign, with a labor force of 800. Foreign's unit labor requirement in apple production is 5, while in banana production it is 1.
   a. Graph Foreign's production possibility frontier.
   b. Construct the world relative supply curve.

3. Now suppose world relative demand takes the following form: Demand for apples/demand for bananas = price of bananas/price of apples.
   a. Graph the relative demand curve along with the relative supply curve.
   b. What is the equilibrium relative price of apples?
   c. Describe the pattern of trade.
   d. Show that both Home and Foreign gain from trade.

4. Suppose an hour's labor produces 10 kg of rice and 5 meter of cloth in India, and 5 kg and 2 meter in Thailand. Using opportunity costs, explain which country will export cloth and which will export paddy in trade.

5. Suppose Mike and Johnson produce two products—hamburgers and T-shirts. Mike produces 10 hamburgers or 3 T-shirts a day and Johnson produces 7 hamburgers or 4 T-shirts. Assuming they can devote time in making either hamburgers or T-shirts.
   a. Draw the production possibility curve.
   b. Who enjoys the absolute advantage of producing both?
   c. Who has a higher opportunity cost of making T-shirts?
   d. Who has a comparative advantage in producing hamburgers?

6. "Chinese workers earn only $.75 an hour; if we allow China to export as much as it likes, our workers will be forced down to the same level. You can't import a $10 shirt without importing the $.75 wage that goes with it." Discuss.

7. Japanese labor productivity is roughly the same as that of the United States in the manufacturing sector (higher in some industries, lower in others), while the United States is still considerably more productive in the service sector. But most services are nontraded. Some analysts have argued that this poses a problem for the United States, because our comparative advantage lies in things we cannot sell on world markets. What is wrong with this argument?

8. Anyone who has visited Japan knows it is an incredibly expensive place; although Japanese workers earn about the same as their U.S. counterparts, the purchasing power of their incomes is about one-third less. Extend your discussion from question 7 to explain this observation. (Hint: Think about wages and the implied prices of nontraded goods.)

9. International immobility of resources is compensated by the international flow of goods—justify.

10. We have focused on the case of trade involving only two countries. Suppose that there are many countries capable of producing two goods, and that each country has only one factor of production, labor. What could we say about the pattern of production and trade in this case? (Hint: Try constructing the world relative supply curve.)

FURTHER READINGS

Donald Davis. "Intraindustry Trade: A Heckscher-Ohlin-Ricardo Approach." *Journal of International Economics* 39 (November 1995), pp. 201–226. A recent revival of the Ricardian approach to explain trade between countries with similar resources.

Rudiger Dornbusch, Stanley Fischer, and Paul Samuelson. "Comparative Advantage, Trade and Payments in a Ricardian Model with a Continuum of Goods." *American Economic Review* 67 (December 1977), pp. 823–839. More recent theoretical modeling in the Ricardian mode, developing the idea of simplifying the many-good Ricardian model by assuming that the number of goods is so large as to form a smooth continuum.

Giovanni Dosi, Keith Pavitt, and Luc Soete. *The Economics of Technical Change and International Trade.* Brighton: Wheatsheaf, 1988. An empirical examination that suggests that international trade in manufactured goods is largely driven by differences in national technological competencies.

Stephen Golub and Chang-Tai Hsieh. "Classical Ricardian Theory of Comparative Advantage Revisited." *Review of International Economics* 8(2), 2000, pp. 221–234. A modern statistical analysis of the relationship between relative productivity and trade patterns, which finds reasonably strong correlations.

G. D. A. MacDougall. "British and American Exports: A Study Suggested by the Theory of Comparative Costs." *Economic Journal* 61 (December 1951), pp. 697–724; 62 (September 1952), pp. 487–521. In this famous study, MacDougall used comparative data on U.S. and U.K. productivity to test the predictions of the Ricardian model.

John Stuart Mill. *Principles of Political Economy.* London: Longmans, Green, 1917. Mill's 1848 treatise extended Ricardo's work into a full-fledged model of international trade.

David Ricardo. *The Principles of Political Economy and Taxation.* Homewood, IL: Irwin, 1963. The basic source for the Ricardian model is Ricardo himself in this book, first published in 1817.

CHAPTER 4

SPECIFIC FACTORS AND INCOME DISTRIBUTION

As we saw in Chapter 3, international trade can be mutually beneficial to the nations engaged in it. Yet throughout history, governments have protected sectors of the economy from import competition. For example, despite its commitment in principle to free trade, the United States limits imports of apparel, textiles, sugar, ethanol, and dairy products, among many other commodities. During presidential re-election cycles, punitive tariffs are often imposed on import of goods produced in key political swing states.[1] If trade is such a good thing for the economy, why is there opposition to its effects? To understand the politics of trade, it is necessary to look at the effects of trade not just on a country as a whole, but on the distribution of income within that country.

The Ricardian model of international trade developed in Chapter 3 illustrates the potential benefits from trade. In that model, trade leads to international specialization, with each country shifting its labor force from industries in which that labor is relatively inefficient to industries in which it is relatively more efficient. Because labor is the only factor of production in that model, and it is assumed that labor can move freely from one industry to another, there is no possibility that individuals will be hurt by trade. The Ricardian model thus suggests not only that all *countries* gain from trade, but also that every *individual* is made better off as a result of international trade, because trade does not affect the distribution of income. In the real world, however, trade has substantial effects on the income distribution within each trading nation, so that in practice the benefits of trade are often distributed very unevenly.

There are two main reasons why international trade has strong effects on the distribution of income. First, resources cannot move immediately or without cost from one industry to another—a short-run consequence of trade. Second, industries differ in the factors of production they demand. A shift in the mix of goods a country produces will ordinarily reduce the demand for some factors of production, while raising the demand for others—a long-run consequence of trade. For

---

[1]The latest examples are the 35 percent tariff imposed on tires (imported from China) during Barack Obama's first term and a 30 percent tariff on steel imports during Georges W. Bush's first term. Production of both steel and tires is concentrated in Ohio, a key swing state in the past several U.S. presidential elections.

both of these reasons, international trade is not as unambiguously beneficial as it appeared to be in Chapter 3. While trade may benefit a nation as a whole, it often hurts significant groups within the country in the short run, and potentially, but to a lesser extent, in the long run.

Consider the effects of Japan's rice policy. Japan allows very little rice to be imported, even though the scarcity of land means that rice is much more expensive to produce in Japan than in other countries (including the United States). There is little question that Japan as a whole would have a higher standard of living if free imports of rice were allowed. Japanese rice farmers, however, would be hurt by free trade. While the farmers displaced by imports could probably find jobs in manufacturing or services, they would find changing employment costly and inconvenient: The special skills they developed for rice farming would be useless in those other jobs. Furthermore, the value of the land that the farmers own would fall along with the price of rice. Not surprisingly, Japanese rice farmers are vehemently opposed to free trade in rice, and their organized political opposition has counted for more than the potential gains from trade for the nation as a whole.

A realistic analysis of trade must go beyond the Ricardian model to models in which trade can affect income distribution. In this chapter, we focus on the short-run consequences of trade on the income distribution when factors of production cannot move without cost between sectors. To keep our model simple, we assume that the sector-switching cost for some factors is high enough that such a switch is impossible in the short run. Those factors are *specific* to a particular sector.

LEARNING GOALS

After reading this chapter, you will be able to:

- Understand how a mobile factor will respond to price changes by moving across sectors.
- Explain why trade will generate both winners and losers in the short run.
- Understand the meaning of gains from trade when there are losers.
- Discuss the reasons why trade is a politically contentious issue.
- Explain the arguments in favor of free trade despite the existence of losers.

The Specific Factors Model

The **specific factors model** was developed by Paul Samuelson and Ronald Jones.[2] Like the simple Ricardian model, it assumes an economy that produces two goods and that can allocate its labor supply between the two sectors. Unlike the Ricardian model, however, the specific factors model allows for the existence of factors of production

---

[2]Paul Samuelson, "Ohlin Was Right," *Swedish Journal of Economics* 73 (1971), pp. 365–384; and Ronald W. Jones, "A Three-Factor Model in Theory, Trade, and History," in Jagdish Bhagwati et al., eds., *Trade, Balance of Payments, and Growth* (Amsterdam: North-Holland, 1971), pp. 3–21.

WHAT IS A SPECIFIC FACTOR?

In the model developed in this chapter, we assume two factors of production—land and capital—are permanently tied to particular sectors of the economy. In advanced economies, however, agricultural land receives only a small part of national income. When economists apply the specific factors model to economies like those of the United States or France, they typically think of factor specificity not as a permanent condition but as a matter of time. For example, the vats used to brew beer and the stamping presses used to build auto bodies cannot be substituted for each other, and so these different kinds of equipment are industry-specific. Given time, however, it would be possible to redirect investment from auto factories to breweries or vice versa. As a result, in a long-term sense both vats and stamping presses can be considered two manifestations of a single, mobile factor called capital.

In practice, then, the distinction between specific and mobile factors is not a sharp line. Rather, it is a question of the speed of adjustment, with factors being more specific the longer it takes to redeploy them between industries. So how specific are the factors of production in the real economy?

Worker mobility varies greatly with the characteristics of the worker (such as age) and the job occupation (whether it requires general or job-specific skills). Nevertheless, one can measure an average rate of mobility by looking at the duration of unemployment following a worker's displacement. After four years, a displaced worker in the United States has the same probability of being employed as a similar worker who was not displaced.* This four-year time-span compares with a lifetime of 15 or 20 years for a typical specialized machine, and 30 to 50 years for structures (a shopping mall, office building, or production plant). So labor is certainly a less specific factor than most kinds of capital. However, even though most workers can find new employment in other sectors within a four-year time-span, switching occupations entails additional costs: A displaced worker who is re-employed in a different occupation suffers an 18 percent permanent drop in wages (on average). This compares with a 6 percent drop if the worker does not switch occupations.† Thus, labor is truly flexible only before a worker has invested in any occupation-specific skills.

*See Bruce Fallick, "The Industrial Mobility of Displaced Workers," *Journal of Labor Economics* 11 (April 1993), pp. 302–323.
†See Gueorgui Kambourov and Iourii Manovskii, "Occupational Specificity of Human Capital," *International Economic Review* 50 (February 2009), pp. 63–115.

besides labor. Whereas labor is a **mobile factor** that can move between sectors, these other factors are assumed to be **specific.** That is, they can be used only in the production of particular goods.

Assumptions of the Model

Imagine an economy that can produce two goods, cloth and food. Instead of one factor of production, however, the country has *three*: labor (L), capital (K), and land (T for *terrain*). Cloth is produced using capital and labor (but not land), while food is produced using land and labor (but not capital). Labor is therefore a *mobile* factor that can be used in either sector, while land and capital are both *specific* factors that can be used only in the production of one good. Land can also be thought of as a different type of capital, one that is specific to the food sector (see box above).

How much of each good does the economy produce? The economy's output of cloth depends on how much capital and labor are used in that sector. This relationship is summarized by a **production function** that tells us the quantity of cloth that can be produced given any input of capital and labor. The production function for cloth can be summarized algebraically as

$$Q_C = Q_C(K, L_C), \tag{4-1}$$

where Q_C is the economy's output of cloth, K is the economy's capital stock, and L_C is the labor force employed in cloth. Similarly, for food we can write the production function

$$Q_F = Q_F(T, L_F), \tag{4-2}$$

where Q_F is the economy's output of food, T is the economy's supply of land, and L_F is the labor force devoted to food production. For the economy as a whole, the labor employed must equal the total labor supply L:

$$L_C + L_F = L. \tag{4-3}$$

Production Possibilities

The specific factors model assumes that each of the specific factors, capital and land, can be used in only one sector, cloth and food, respectively. Only labor can be used in either sector. Thus, to analyze the economy's production possibilities, we need only to ask how the economy's mix of output changes as labor is shifted from one sector to the other. This can be done graphically, first by representing the production functions (4-1) and (4-2), and then by putting them together to derive the **production possibility frontier**.

Figure 4-1 illustrates the relationship between labor input and output of cloth. The larger the input of labor for a given capital supply, the larger the output. In Figure 4-1, the slope of $Q_C(K, L_C)$ represents the **marginal product of labor**, that is, the addition to output generated by adding one more person-hour. However, if labor input is increased without increasing capital, there will normally be **diminishing returns**: Because adding a worker means that each worker has less capital to work with, each successive increment of labor will add less to production than the last. Diminishing returns are reflected in the shape of the production function: $Q_C(K, L_C)$ gets flatter as we move to

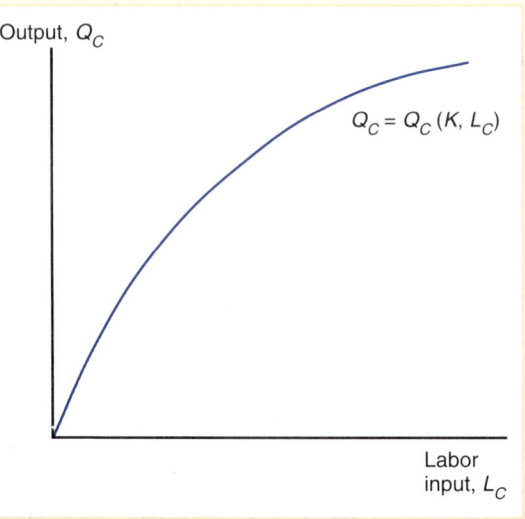

FIGURE 4-1

The Production Function for Cloth

The more labor employed in the production of cloth, the larger the output. As a result of diminishing returns, however, each successive person-hour increases output by less than the previous one; this is shown by the fact that the curve relating labor input to output gets flatter at higher levels of employment.

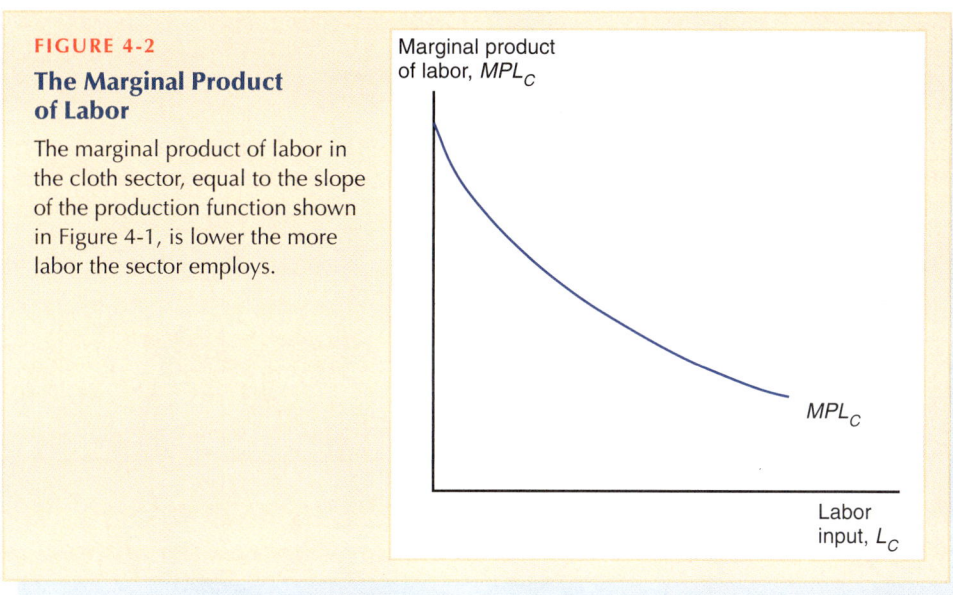

FIGURE 4-2

The Marginal Product of Labor

The marginal product of labor in the cloth sector, equal to the slope of the production function shown in Figure 4-1, is lower the more labor the sector employs.

the right, indicating that the marginal product of labor declines as more labor is used.[3] Figure 4-2 shows the same information a different way. In this figure, we directly plot the marginal product of labor as a function of the labor employed. (In the appendix to this chapter, we show that the area under the marginal product curve represents the total output of cloth.)

A similar pair of diagrams can represent the production function for food. These diagrams can then be combined to derive the production possibility frontier for the economy, as illustrated in Figure 4-3. As we saw in Chapter 3, the production possibility frontier shows what the economy is capable of producing; in this case, it shows how much food it can produce for any given output of cloth and vice versa.

Figure 4-3 is a four-quadrant diagram. In the lower-right quadrant, we show the production function for cloth illustrated in Figure 4-1. This time, however, we turn the figure on its side: A movement downward along the vertical axis represents an increase in the labor input to the cloth sector, while a movement to the right along the horizontal axis represents an increase in the output of cloth. In the upper-left quadrant, we show the corresponding production function for food; this part of the figure is also flipped around, so that a movement to the left along the horizontal axis indicates an increase in labor input to the food sector, while an upward movement along the vertical axis indicates an increase in food output.

The lower-left quadrant represents the economy's allocation of labor. Both quantities are measured in the reverse of the usual direction. A downward movement along the vertical axis indicates an increase in the labor employed in cloth; a leftward movement along the horizontal axis indicates an increase in labor employed in food. Since an increase in employment in one sector must mean that less labor is available for the other, the possible allocations are indicated by a downward-sloping line. This line, labeled AA, slopes downward at a 45-degree angle, that is, it has a slope of -1.

---

[3]Diminishing returns to a single factor does not imply diminishing returns to scale when all factors of production are adjusted. Thus, diminishing returns to labor is entirely consistent with constant returns to scale in both labor and capital.

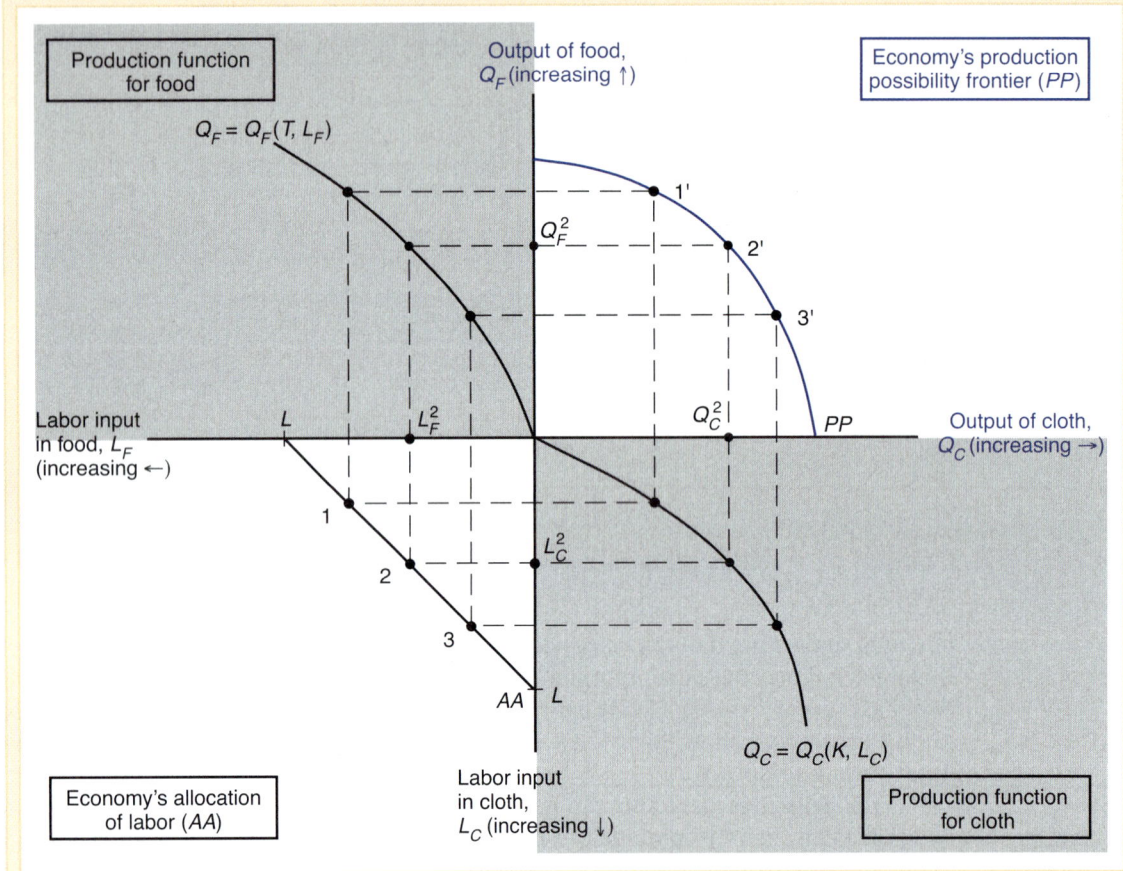

FIGURE 4-3

The Production Possibility Frontier in the Specific Factors Model

Production of cloth and food is determined by the allocation of labor. In the lower-left quadrant, the allocation of labor between sectors can be illustrated by a point on line AA, which represents all combinations of labor input to cloth and food that sum up to the total labor supply L. Corresponding to any particular point on AA, such as point 2, is a labor input to cloth (L_C^2) and a labor input to food (L_F^2). The curves in the lower-right and upper-left quadrants represent the production functions for cloth and food, respectively; these allow determination of output (Q_C^2, Q_F^2) given labor input. Then in the upper-right quadrant, the curve PP shows how the output of the two goods varies as the allocation of labor is shifted from food to cloth, with the output points 1', 2', 3' corresponding to the labor allocations 1, 2, 3. Because of diminishing returns, PP is a bowed-out curve instead of a straight line.

To see why this line represents the possible labor allocations, notice that if all labor were employed in food production, L_F would equal L, while L_C would equal 0. If one were then to move labor gradually into the cloth sector, each person-hour moved would increase L_C by one unit while reducing L_F by one unit, tracing a line with a slope of -1, until the entire labor supply L is employed in the cloth sector. Any particular allocation of labor between the two sectors can then be represented by a point on AA, such as point 2.

We can now see how to determine production given any particular allocation of labor between the two sectors. Suppose the allocation of labor were represented by point 2 in the lower-left quadrant, that is, with L_C^2 hours in cloth and L_F^2 hours in food. Then we can use the production function for each sector to determine output: Q_C^2 units of cloth, Q_F^2 units of food. Using coordinates Q_C^2, Q_F^2, point 2′ in the upper-right quadrant of Figure 4-3 shows the resulting outputs of cloth and food.

To trace the whole production possibility frontier, we simply imagine repeating this exercise for many alternative allocations of labor. We might start with most of the labor allocated to food production, as at point 1 in the lower-left quadrant, then gradually increase the amount of labor used in cloth until very few workers are employed in food, as at point 3; the corresponding points in the upper-right quadrant will trace out the curve running from 1′ to 3′. Thus, PP in the upper-right quadrant shows the economy's production possibilities for given supplies of land, labor, and capital.

In the Ricardian model, where labor is the only factor of production, the production possibility frontier is a straight line because the opportunity cost of cloth in terms of food is constant. In the specific factors model, however, the addition of other factors of production changes the shape of the production possibility frontier PP to a curve. The curvature of PP reflects diminishing returns to labor in each sector; these diminishing returns are the crucial difference between the specific factors and the Ricardian models.

Notice that when tracing PP, we shift labor from the food to the cloth sector. If we shift one person-hour of labor from food to cloth, however, this extra input will increase output in that sector by the marginal product of labor in cloth, MPL_C. To increase cloth output by one unit, then, we must increase labor input by $1/MPL_C$ hours. Meanwhile, each unit of labor input shifted out of food production will lower output in that sector by the marginal product of labor in food, MPL_F. To increase output of cloth by one unit, then, the economy must reduce output of food by MPL_F/MPL_C units. The slope of PP, which measures the opportunity cost of cloth in terms of food—that is, the number of units of food output that must be sacrificed to increase cloth output by one unit—is therefore

$$\text{Slope of production possibilities curve} = -MPL_F/MPL_C.$$

We can now see why PP has the bowed shape it does. As we move from 1′ to 3′, L_C rises and L_F falls. We saw in Figure 4-2, however, that as L_C rises, the marginal product of labor in cloth falls; correspondingly, as L_F falls, the marginal product of labor in food rises. As more and more labor is moved to the cloth sector, each additional unit of labor becomes less valuable in the cloth sector and more valuable in the food sector: The opportunity cost (foregone food production) of each additional cloth unit rises, and PP thus gets steeper as we move down it to the right.

We have shown how output is determined, given the allocation of labor. The next step is to ask how a market economy determines what the allocation of labor should be.

Prices, Wages, and Labor Allocation

How much labor will be employed in each sector? To answer this, we need to look at supply and demand in the labor market. The demand for labor in each sector depends on the price of output and the wage rate. In turn, the wage rate depends on the combined demand for labor by food and cloth producers. Given the prices of cloth and food together with the wage rate, we can determine each sector's employment and output.

First, let's focus on the demand for labor. In each sector, profit-maximizing employers will demand labor up to the point where the value produced by an additional person-hour equals the cost of employing that hour. In the cloth sector, for example, the value of an additional person-hour is the marginal product of labor in cloth multiplied by the price of one unit of cloth: $MPL_C \times P_C$. If w is the wage rate of labor, employers will therefore hire workers up to the point where

$$MPL_C \times P_C = w. \qquad (4\text{-}4)$$

But the marginal product of labor in cloth, already illustrated in Figure 4-2, slopes downward because of diminishing returns. So for any given price of cloth P_C, the value of that marginal product, $MPL_C \times P_C$, will also slope down. We can therefore think of equation (4-4) as defining the demand curve for labor in the cloth sector: If the wage rate falls, other things equal, employers in the cloth sector will want to hire more workers.

Similarly, the value of an additional person-hour in food is $MPL_F \times P_F$. The demand curve for labor in the food sector may therefore be written

$$MPL_F \times P_F = w. \qquad (4\text{-}5)$$

The wage rate w must be the same in both sectors because of the assumption that labor is freely mobile between sectors. That is, because labor is a mobile factor, it will move from the low-wage sector to the high-wage sector until wages are equalized. The wage rate, in turn, is determined by the requirement that total labor demand (total employment) equals total labor supply. This equilibrium condition for labor is represented in equation (4-3).

By representing these two labor demand curves in a diagram (Figure 4-4), we can see how the wage rate and employment in each sector are determined given the prices of food and cloth. Along the horizontal axis of Figure 4-4, we show the total labor supply L. Measuring from the left of the diagram, we show the value of the marginal

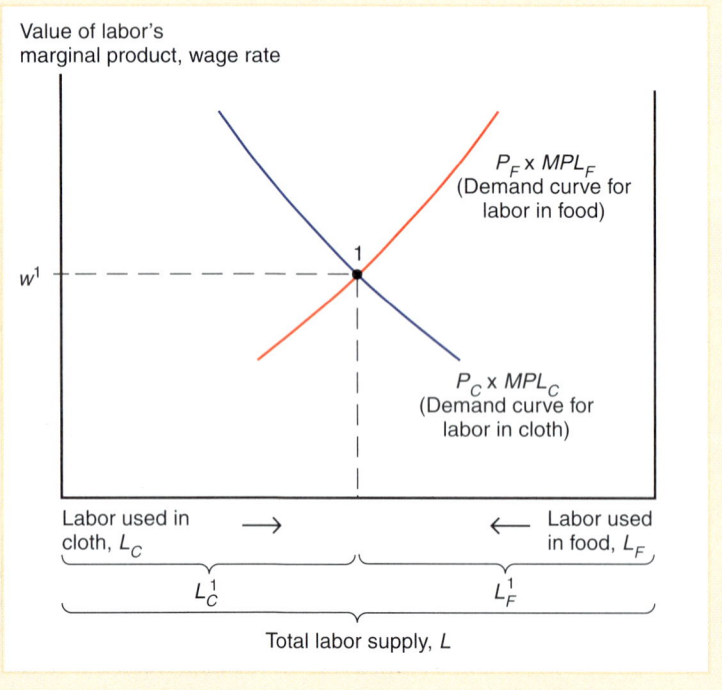

FIGURE 4-4

The Allocation of Labor

Labor is allocated so that the value of its marginal product ($P \times MPL$) is the same in the cloth and food sectors. In equilibrium, the wage rate is equal to the value of labor's marginal product.

product of labor in cloth, which is simply the MPL_C curve from Figure 4-2 multiplied by P_C. This is the demand curve for labor in the cloth sector. Measuring from the right, we show the value of the marginal product of labor in food, which is the demand for labor in food. The equilibrium wage rate and allocation of labor between the two sectors is represented by point 1. At the wage rate w^1, the sum of labor demanded in the cloth (L_C^1) and food (L_F^1) sectors just equals the total labor supply L.

A useful relationship between relative prices and output emerges clearly from this analysis of labor allocation; this relationship applies to more general situations than that described by the specific factors model. Equations (4-4) and (4-5) imply that

$$MPL_C \times P_C = MPL_F \times P_F = w$$

or, rearranging, that

$$-MPL_F/MPL_C = -P_C/P_F. \tag{4-6}$$

The left side of equation (4-6) is the slope of the production possibility frontier at the actual production point; the right side is minus the relative price of cloth. This result tells us that *at the production point, the production possibility frontier must be tangent to a line whose slope is minus the price of cloth divided by that of food.* As we will see in the following chapters, this is a very general result that characterizes production responses to changes in relative prices along a production possibility frontier. It is illustrated in Figure 4-5: If the relative price of cloth is $(P_C/P_F)^1$, the economy produces at point 1.

What happens to the allocation of labor and the distribution of income when the prices of food and cloth change? Notice that any price change can be broken into two parts: an equal-proportional change in both P_C and P_F and a change in only one price. For example, suppose the price of cloth rises 17 percent and the price of food rises 10 percent. We can analyze the effects of this by first asking what happens if cloth and food prices both rise by 10 percent and then by finding out what happens if only cloth prices rise by 7 percent. This allows us to separate the effect of changes in the overall price level from the effect of changes in relative prices.

FIGURE 4-5

Production in the Specific Factors Model

The economy produces at the point on its production possibility frontier (*PP*) where the slope of that frontier equals minus the relative price of cloth.

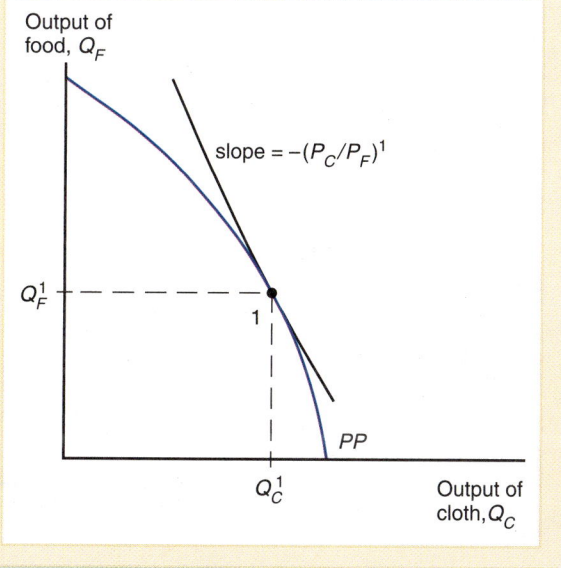

An Equal-Proportional Change in Prices Figure 4-6 shows the effect of an equal-pro-portional increase in P_C and P_F. P_C rises from P_C^1 to P_C^2; P_F rises from P_F^1 to P_F^2. If the prices of both goods increase by 10 percent, the labor demand curves will also shift up by 10 percent. As you can see from the diagram, these shifts lead to a 10 percent increase in the wage rate from w^1 (point 1) to w^2 (point 2). However, the allocation of labor between the sectors and the outputs of the two goods does not change.

In fact, when P_C and P_F change in the same proportion, no real changes occur. The wage rate rises in the same proportion as the prices, so *real* wage rates, the ratios of the wage rate to the prices of goods, are unaffected. *With the same amount of labor employed in each sector, receiving the same real wage rate, the real incomes of capital owners and landowners also remain the same. So everyone is in exactly the same position as before.* This illustrates a general principle: Changes in the overall price level have no real effects, that is, do not change any physical quantities in the economy. Only changes in relative prices—which in this case means the price of cloth relative to the price of food, P_C/P_F—affect welfare or the allocation of resources.

A Change in Relative Prices Consider the effect of a price change that *does* affect relative prices. Figure 4-7 shows the effect of a change in the price of only one good, in this case a 7 percent rise in P_C from P_C^1 to P_C^2. The increase in P_C shifts the cloth labor demand curve in the same proportion as the price increase and shifts the equilibrium from point 1 to point 2. Notice two important facts about the results of this shift. First, although the wage rate rises, it rises by *less* than the increase in the price of cloth. If wages had risen in the same proportion as the price of cloth (7 percent increase), then wages would have risen from w^1 to $w^{2\prime}$. Instead, wages rise by a smaller proportion, from w^1 to w^2.

FIGURE 4-6

An Equal-Proportional Increase in the Prices of Cloth and Food

The labor demand curves in cloth and food both shift up in proportion to the rise in P_C from P_C^1 to P_C^2 and the rise in P_F from P_F^1 to P_F^2. The wage rate rises in the same proportion, from w^1 to w^2, but the allocation of labor between the two sectors does not change.

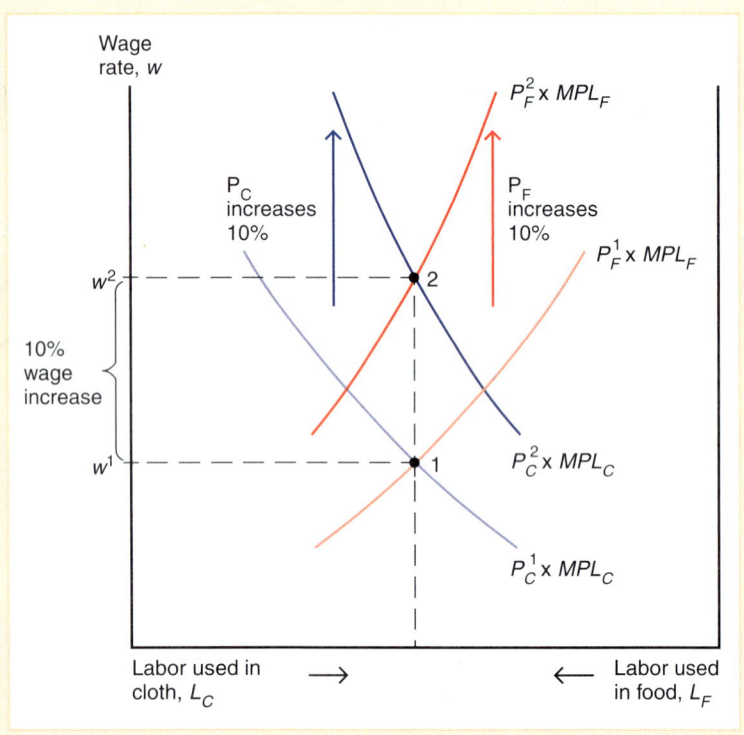

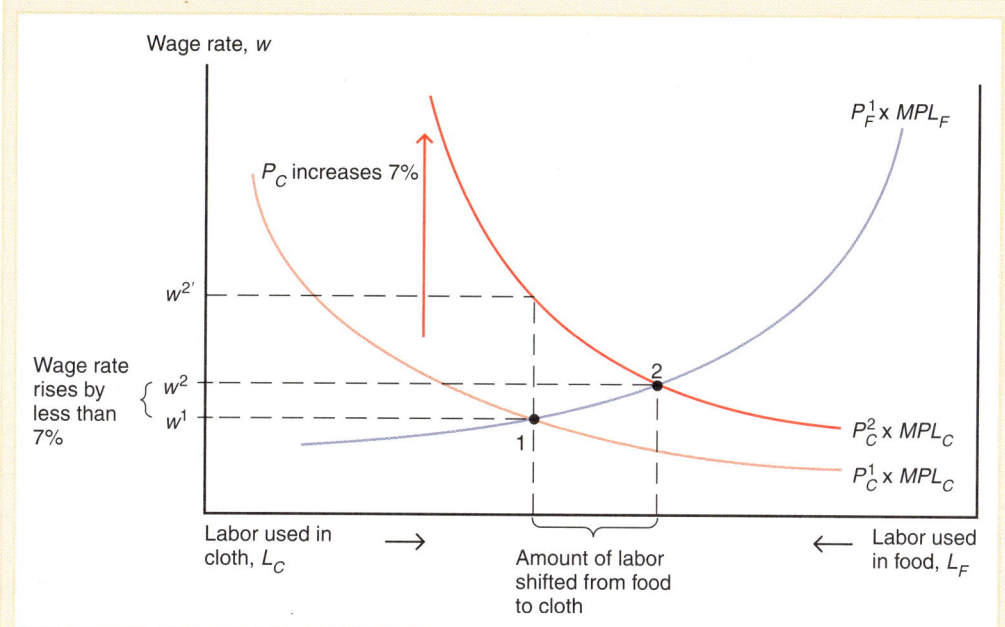

FIGURE 4-7

A Rise in the Price of Cloth

The cloth labor demand curve rises in proportion to the 7 percent increase in P_C, but the wage rate rises less than proportionately. Labor moves from the food sector to the cloth sector. Output of cloth rises; output of food falls.

Second, when only P_C rises, in contrast to a simultaneous rise in P_C and P_F, labor shifts from the food sector to the cloth sector and the output of cloth rises while that of food falls. (This is why w does not rise as much as P_C: Because cloth employment rises, the marginal product of labor in that sector falls.)

The effect of a rise in the relative price of cloth can also be seen directly by looking at the production possibility curve. In Figure 4-8, we show the effects of the same rise in the price of cloth, which raises the *relative* price of cloth from $(P_C/P_F)^1$ to $(P_C/P_F)^2$. The production point, which is always located where the slope of PP equals minus the relative price, shifts from 1 to 2. Food output falls and cloth output rises as a result of the rise in the relative price of cloth.

Since higher relative prices of cloth lead to a higher output of cloth relative to that of food, we can draw a relative supply curve showing Q_C/Q_F as a function of P_C/P_F. This relative supply curve is shown as RS in Figure 4-9. As we showed in Chapter 3, we can also draw a relative demand curve, which is illustrated by the downward-sloping line RD. In the absence of international trade, the equilibrium relative price $(P_C/P_F)^1$ and output $(Q_C/Q_F)^1$ are determined by the intersection of relative supply and demand.

Relative Prices and the Distribution of Income

So far, we have examined the following aspects of the specific factors model: (1) the determination of production possibilities given an economy's resources and technology and (2) the determination of resource allocation, production, and relative prices

FIGURE 4-8

The Response of Output to a Change in the Relative Price of Cloth

The economy always produces at the point on its production possibility frontier (PP) where the slope of PP equals minus the relative price of cloth. Thus, an increase in P_C/P_F causes production to move down and to the right along the production possibility frontier corresponding to higher output of cloth and lower output of food.

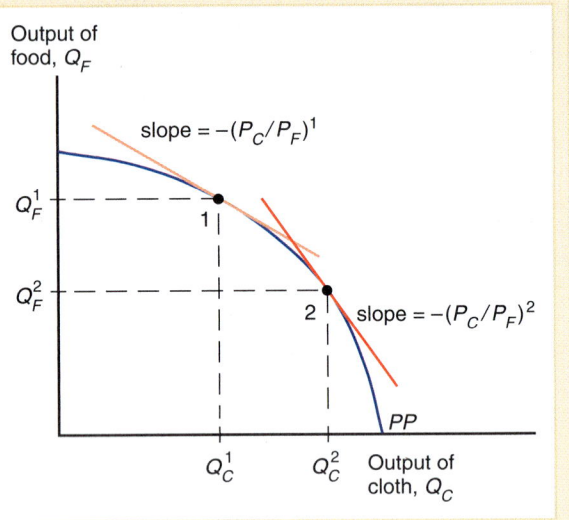

in a market economy. Before turning to the effects of international trade, we must consider the effect of changes in relative prices on the distribution of income.

Look again at Figure 4-7, which shows the effect of a rise in the price of cloth. We have already noted that the demand curve for labor in the cloth sector will shift upward in proportion to the rise in P_C, so that if P_C rises by 7 percent, the curve defined by $P_C \times MPL_C$ also rises by 7 percent. We have also seen that unless the price of food also rises by at least 7 percent, w will rise by *less* than P_C. Thus, if only cloth prices rise by 7 percent, we would expect the wage rate to rise by only, say, 3 percent.

Let's look at what this outcome implies for the incomes of three groups: workers, owners of capital, and owners of land. Workers find that their wage rate has risen, but less than in proportion to the rise in P_C. Thus, their real wage in terms of cloth (the

FIGURE 4-9

Determination of Relative Prices

In the specific factors model, a higher relative price of cloth will lead to an increase in the output of cloth relative to that of food. Thus, the relative supply curve RS is upward sloping. Equilibrium relative quantities and prices are determined by the intersection of RS with the relative demand curve RD.

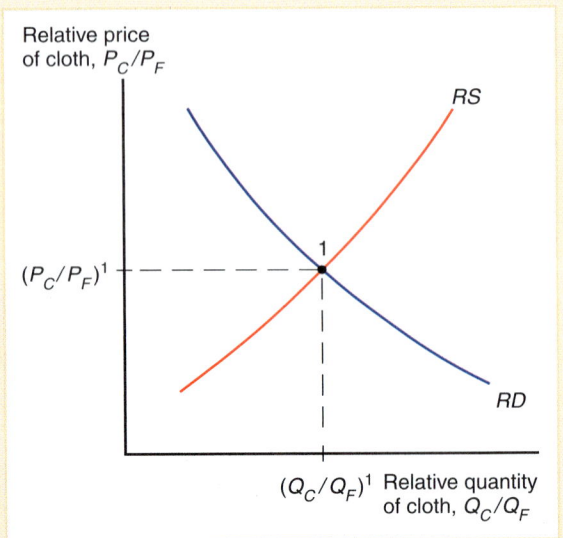

amount of cloth they can buy with their wage income), w/P_C, falls, while their real wage in terms of food, w/P_F, rises. Given this information, we cannot say whether workers are better or worse off; this depends on the relative importance of cloth and food in workers' consumption (determined by the workers' preferences), a question we will not pursue further.

Owners of capital, however, are definitely better off. The real wage rate in terms of cloth has fallen, so the profits of capital owners in terms of what they produce (cloth) rises. That is, the income of capital owners will rise more than proportionately with the rise in P_C. Since P_C in turn rises relative to P_F, the income of capitalists clearly goes up in terms of both goods. Conversely, landowners are definitely worse off. They lose for two reasons: The real wage in terms of food (the good they produce) rises, squeezing their income, and the rise in cloth price reduces the purchasing power of any given income. (The chapter appendix describes the welfare changes of capitalists and landowners in further detail.)

If the relative price had moved in the opposite direction and the relative price of cloth had *decreased*, then the predictions would be reversed: Capital owners would be worse off, and landowners would be better off. The change in the welfare of workers would again be ambiguous because their real wage in terms of cloth would rise, but their real wage in terms of food would fall. The effect of a relative price change on the distribution of income can be summarized as follows:

- The factor specific to the sector whose relative price increases is definitely better off.
- The factor specific to the sector whose relative price decreases is definitely worse off.
- The change in welfare for the mobile factor is ambiguous.

International Trade in the Specific Factors Model

We just saw how changes in relative prices have strong repercussions for the distribution of income, creating both winners and losers. We now want to link this relative price change with international trade and match up the predictions for winners and losers with the trade orientation of a sector.

For trade to take place, a country must face a world relative price that differs from the relative price that would prevail in the absence of trade. Figure 4-9 shows how this relative price was determined for our specific factors economy. In Figure 4-10, we also add a relative supply curve for the world.

Why might the relative supply curve for the world be different from that for our specific factors economy? The other countries in the world could have different technologies, as in the Ricardian model. Now that our model has more than one factor of production, however, the other countries could also differ in their resources: the total amounts of land, capital, and labor available. What is important here is that the economy faces a different relative price when it is open to international trade.

The change in relative price is shown in Figure 4-10. When the economy is open to trade, the relative price of cloth is determined by the relative supply and demand for the world; this corresponds to the relative price $(P_C/P_F)^2$. If the economy could not trade, then the relative price would be lower, at $(P_C/P_F)^1$.[4] The increase in the relative price from $(P_C/P_F)^1$ to $(P_C/P_F)^2$ induces the economy to produce relatively more cloth. (This is also shown as the move from point 1 to point 2 along the economy's

---

[4]In the figure, we assumed there were no differences in preferences across countries, so we have a single relative demand curve for each country and the world as a whole.

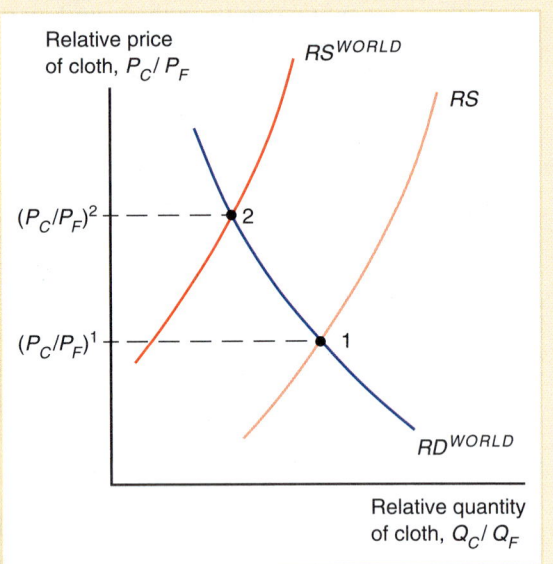

FIGURE 4-10

Trade and Relative Prices

The figure shows the relative supply curve for the specific factors economy along with the world relative supply curve. The differences between the two relative supply curves can be due to either technology or resource differences across countries. There are no differences in relative demand across countries. Opening up to trade induces an increase in the relative price from $(P_C/P_F)^1$ to $(P_C/P_F)^2$.

production possibility frontier in Figure 4-8.) At the same time, consumers respond to the higher relative price of cloth by demanding relatively more food. At the higher relative price $(P_C/P_F)^2$, the economy thus exports cloth and imports food.

If opening up to trade had been associated with a decrease in the relative price of cloth, then the changes in relative supply and demand would be reversed, and the economy would become a food exporter and a cloth importer. We can summarize both cases with the intuitive prediction that—when opening up to trade—an economy exports the good whose relative price has increased and imports the good whose relative price has decreased.[5]

Income Distribution and the Gains from Trade

We have seen how production possibilities are determined by resources and technology; how the choice of what to produce is determined by the relative price of cloth; how changes in the relative price of cloth affect the real incomes of different factors of production; and how trade affects both relative prices and the economy's response to those price changes. Now we can ask the crucial question: Who gains and who loses from international trade? We begin by asking how the welfare of particular groups is affected, and then how trade affects the welfare of the country as a whole.

To assess the effects of trade on particular groups, the key point is that international trade shifts the relative price of the goods traded. We just saw in the previous section that opening to trade will increase the relative price of the good in the new export sector. We can link this prediction with our results regarding how relative price changes translate into changes in the distribution of income. More specifically, we saw that the specific factor in the sector whose relative price increases will gain and that the specific factor in the other sector (whose relative price decreases) will lose. We also saw that the welfare changes for the mobile factor are ambiguous.

[5]We describe how changes in relative prices affect a country's pattern of trade in more detail in Chapter 6.

The general outcome, then, is simple: *Trade benefits the factor specific to the export sector of each country but hurts the factor specific to the import-competing sectors, with ambiguous effects on mobile factors.*

Do the gains from trade outweigh the losses? One way to try to answer this question would be to sum up the gains of the winners and the losses of the losers and compare them. The problem with this procedure is that we are comparing welfare, which is inherently subjective. A better way to assess the overall gains from trade is to ask a different question: Could those who gain from trade compensate those who lose and still be better off themselves? If so, then trade is *potentially* a source of gain to everyone.

In order to show aggregate gains from trade, we need to state some basic relationships among prices, production, and consumption. In a country that cannot trade, the output of a good must equal its consumption. If D_C is consumption of cloth and D_F consumption of food, then in a closed economy, $D_C = Q_C$ and $D_F = Q_F$. International trade makes it possible for the mix of cloth and food consumed to differ from the mix produced. While the amounts of each good that a country consumes and produces may differ, however, a country cannot spend more than it earns: The *value* of consumption must be equal to the value of production. That is,

$$P_C \times D_C + P_F \times D_F = P_C \times Q_C + P_F \times Q_F. \qquad (4\text{-}7)$$

Equation (4-7) can be rearranged to yield the following:

$$D_F - Q_F = (P_C/P_F) \times (Q_C - D_C). \qquad (4\text{-}8)$$

$D_F - Q_F$ is the economy's food *imports*, the amount by which its consumption of food exceeds its production. The right-hand side of the equation is the product of the relative price of cloth and the amount by which production of cloth exceeds consumption, that is, the economy's *exports* of cloth. The equation, then, states that imports of food equal exports of cloth times the relative price of cloth. While it does not tell us how much the economy will import or export, the equation does show that the amount the economy can afford to import is limited, or constrained, by the amount it exports. Equation (4-8) is therefore known as a **budget constraint.**[6]

Figure 4-11 illustrates two important features of the budget constraint for a trading economy. First, the slope of the budget constraint is minus P_C/P_F, the relative price of cloth . The reason is that consuming one less unit of cloth saves the economy P_C; this is enough to purchase P_C/P_F extra units of food. In other words, one unit of cloth can be exchanged on world markets for P_C/P_F units of food. Second, the budget constraint is tangent to the production possibility frontier at the chosen production point (shown as point 1 here and in Figure 4-5). Thus, the economy can always afford to consume what it produces.

To illustrate that trade is a source of potential gain for everyone, we proceed in three steps:

1. First, we notice that in the absence of trade, the economy would have to produce what it consumed, and vice versa. Thus, the *consumption* of the economy in the absence of trade would have to be a point on the *production* possibility frontier. In Figure 4-11, a typical pretrade consumption point is shown as point 2.

---

[6]The constraint that the value of consumption equals that of production (or, equivalently, that imports equal exports in value) may not hold when countries can borrow from other countries or lend to them. For now, we assume that these possibilities are not available and that the budget constraint (equation (4-8)) therefore holds. International borrowing and lending are examined in Chapter 6, which shows that an economy's consumption *over time* is still constrained by the necessity of paying its debts to foreign lenders.

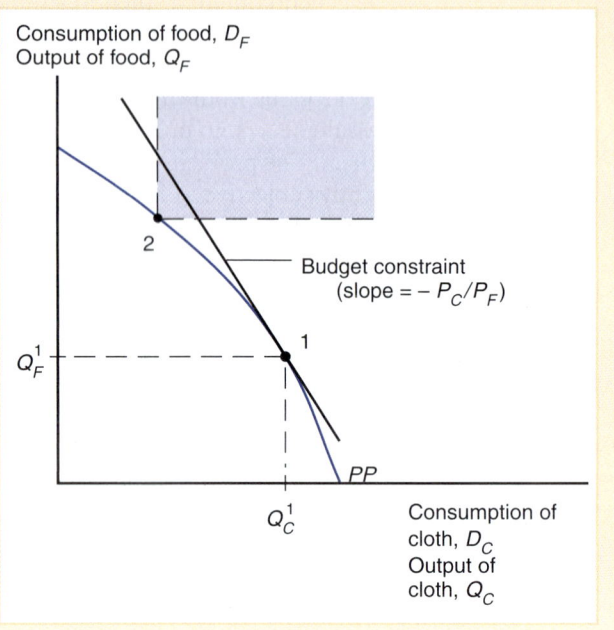

FIGURE 4-11

Budget Constraint for a Trading Economy and Gains from Trade

Point 1 represents the economy's production. The economy can choose its consumption point along its budget constraint (a line that passes through point 1 and has a slope equal to minus the relative price of cloth). Before trade, the economy must consume what it produces, such as point 2 on the production possibility frontier (*PP*). The portion of the budget constraint in the colored region consists of feasible post-trade consumption choices, with consumption of both goods higher than at pretrade point 2.

2. Next, we notice that it is possible for a trading economy to consume more of *both* goods than it would have in the absence of trade. The budget constraint in Figure 4-11 represents all the possible combinations of food and cloth that the country could consume given the world relative price of cloth. Part of that budget constraint—the part in the colored region—represents situations in which the economy consumes more of both cloth and food than it could in the absence of trade. Notice that this result does not depend on the assumption that pretrade production and consumption is at point 2; unless pretrade production is at point 1, so that trade has no effect on production at all, there is always a part of the budget constraint that allows the consumption of more of both goods.

3. Finally, observe that if the economy as a whole consumes more of both goods, then it is possible in principle to give each *individual* more of both goods. This would make everyone better off. This shows, then, that it is possible to ensure that everyone is better off as a result of trade. Of course, everyone might be even better off if they had less of one good and more of the other, but this only reinforces the conclusion that everyone has the potential to gain from trade.

The fundamental reason why trade potentially benefits a country is that it *expands the economy's choices*. This expansion of choice means that it is always possible to redistribute income in such a way that everyone gains from trade.[7]

That everyone *could* gain from trade unfortunately does not mean that everyone actually does. In the real world, the presence of losers as well as winners from trade is one of the most important reasons why trade is not free.

---

[7]The argument that trade is beneficial because it enlarges an economy's choices is much more general than this specific example. For a thorough discussion, see Paul Samuelson, "The Gains from International Trade Once Again," *Economic Journal* 72 (1962), pp. 820–829.

The Political Economy of Trade: A Preliminary View

Trade often produces losers as well as winners. This insight is crucial to understanding the considerations that actually determine trade policy in the modern world economy. Our specific factors model informs us that those who stand to lose most from trade (at least in the short run) are the immobile factors in the import-competing sector. In the real world, this includes not only the owners of capital but also a portion of the labor force in those importing-competing sectors. Some of those workers (especially lower-skilled workers) have a hard time transitioning from the import-competing sectors (where trade induces reductions in employment) to export sectors (where trade induces increases in employment). Some suffer unemployment spells as a result. In the United States, workers in the import-competing sectors earn wages substantially below the average wage, and those workers earning the lowest wage face the highest risk of separation from their current employer due to import competition. (For example, the average wage of production workers in the apparel sector in 2012 was 35 percent below the average wage for all production workers.) One result of this disparity in wages is widespread sympathy for the plight of those workers and, consequently, for restrictions on apparel imports. The gains that more affluent consumers would realize if more imports were allowed and the associated increases in employment in the export sectors (which hire, on average, relatively higher-skilled workers) do not matter as much.

Does this mean that trade should be allowed only if it doesn't hurt lower-income people? Few international economists would agree. In spite of the real importance of income distribution, most economists remain strongly in favor of more or less free trade. There are three main reasons why economists do *not* generally stress the income distribution effects of trade:

1. Income distribution effects are not specific to international trade. Every change in a nation's economy—including technological progress, shifting consumer preferences, exhaustion of old resources and discovery of new ones, and so on—affects income distribution. Why should an apparel worker, who suffers an unemployment spell due to increased import competition, be treated differently from an unemployed printing machine operator (whose newspaper employer shuts down due to competition from Internet news providers) or an unemployed construction worker laid off due to a housing slump?

2. It is always better to allow trade and compensate those who are hurt by it than to prohibit the trade. All modern industrial countries provide some sort of "safety net" of income support programs (such as unemployment benefits and subsidized retraining and relocation programs) that can cushion the losses of groups hurt by trade. Economists would argue that if this cushion is felt to be inadequate, more support rather than less trade is the answer. (This support can also be extended to all those in need, instead of indirectly assisting only those workers affected by trade.)[8]

3. Those who stand to lose from increased trade are typically better organized than those who stand to gain (because the former are more concentrated within regions and industries). This imbalance creates a bias in the political process that requires a counterweight, especially given the aggregate gains from trade. Many trade restrictions tend to favor the most organized groups, which are often not the most in need of income support (in many cases, quite the contrary).

---

[8]An op-ed by Robert Z. Lawrence and Matthew J. Slaughter in the *New York Times*, "More Trade and More Aid," argues this point (June 8, 2011).

Most economists, while acknowledging the effects of international trade on income distribution, believe it is more important to stress the overall potential gains from trade than the possible losses to some groups in a country. Economists do not, however, often have the deciding voice in economic policy, especially when conflicting interests are at stake. Any realistic understanding of how trade policy is determined must look at the actual motivations of that policy.

Income Distribution and Trade Politics

It is easy to see why groups that lose from trade lobby their governments to restrict trade and protect their incomes. You might expect those who gain from trade would lobby as strongly as those who lose from it, but this is rarely the case. In the United States and most other countries, those who want trade limited are more effective politically than those who want it extended. Typically, those who gain from trade in any particular product are a much less concentrated, informed, and organized group than those who lose.

A good example of this contrast between the two sides is the U.S. sugar industry. The United States has limited imports of sugar for many years; over the past 25 years,

---

CASE STUDY

Trade and Unemployment

Opening to trade shifts jobs from import-competing sectors to export sectors. As we have discussed, this process is not instantaneous and imposes some very real costs: Some workers in the import-competing sectors become unemployed and have difficulty finding new jobs in the growing export sectors. We have argued in this chapter that the best policy response to this serious concern is to provide an adequate safety net to unemployed workers, without discriminating based on the economic force that induced their involuntary unemployment (whether due to trade or, say, technological change). Here, we quantify the extent of unemployment that can be traced back to trade. Plant closures due to import competition or overseas plant relocations are highly publicized, but they account for a very small proportion of involuntary worker displacements. The U.S. Bureau of Labor Statistics tracks the primary cause of all extended mass layoffs, defined as an unemployment spell lasting more than 30 days and affecting more than 50 workers from the same employer. During 2001–2010, unemployment spells caused by either import competition or overseas relocations accounted for less than 2 percent of total involuntary displacements associated with extended mass layoffs.

Figure 4-12 shows that, over the last 50 years in the United States, there is no evidence of a positive correlation between the unemployment rate and imports (relative to U.S. GDP). (In fact, the correlation between changes in unemployment and imports is significantly negative.) On the other hand, the figure clearly shows how unemployment is a macroeconomic phenomenon that responds to overall economic conditions: Unemployment peaks during the highlighted recession years. Thus, economists recommend the use of macroeconomic policy, rather than trade policy, to address concerns regarding unemployment.

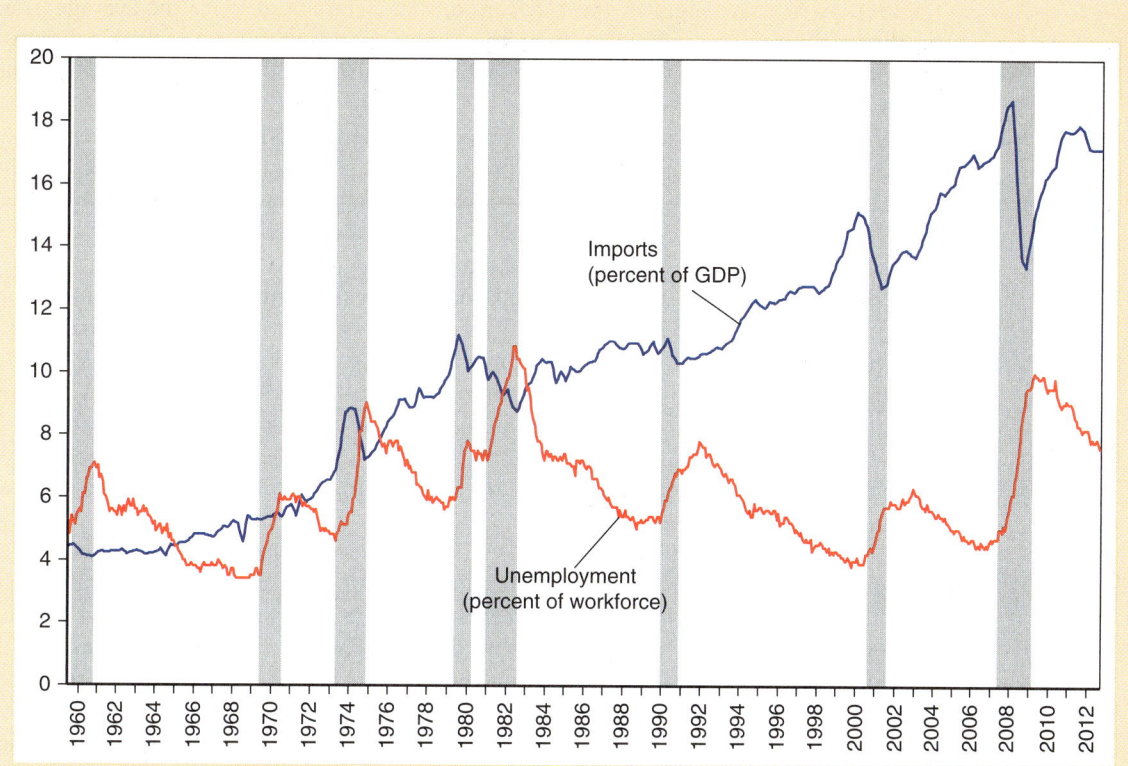

FIGURE 4-12   MyEconLab Real-time data

Unemployment and Import Penetration in the United States

The highlighted years are recession years, as determined by the National Bureau of Economic Research.

Source: U.S. Bureau of Economic Analysis for imports and U.S. Bureau of Labor Studies for unemployment.

Still, because changes in trade regimes—as opposed to other forces affecting the income distribution—are driven by policy decisions, there is also substantial pressure to bundle those decisions with special programs that benefit those adversely affected by trade. The **U.S. Trade Adjustment Assistance program** provides extended unemployment coverage (for an additional year) to workers who are displaced by a plant closure due to import competition or an overseas relocation to a country receiving preferential access to the United States. While this program is important, to the extent that it can influence political decisions regarding trade, it unfairly discriminates against workers who are displaced due to economic forces other than trade.[9]

---

[9]See Lori G. Kletzer, "Trade-related Job Loss and Wage Insurance: A Synthetic Review," *Review of International Economics* 12 (November 2004), pp. 724–748; and Grant D. Aldonas, Robert Z. Lawrence, and Matthew J. Slaughter, *Succeeding in the Global Economy: A New Policy Agenda for the American Worker* (Washington, D.C.: Financial Services Forum, 2007) for additional details on the U.S. TAA program and proposals to extend the same type of insurance coverage to all workers.

the average price of sugar in the U.S. market has been about twice the average price on the world market. A 2000 study by the U.S. General Accounting Office estimated that those import restrictions and the associated higher sugar prices generated annual losses of $2 billion for U.S. consumers. This study was recently updated in 2013, and this cost has now risen above $3 billon, representing $10 a year for every man, woman, and child. The gains to sugar producers are substantially smaller because the import restrictions also generate distortions in the sugar market and foreign producers assigned the rights to sell sugar to the United States keep the differential between the higher U.S. price and the lower world price.

If producers and consumers were equally able to get their interests represented, this policy would never have been enacted. In absolute terms, however, each consumer suffers very little. Ten dollars a year is not much; furthermore, most of the cost is hidden, because most sugar is consumed as an ingredient in other foods rather than purchased directly. As a result, most consumers are unaware that the import quota even exists, let alone that it reduces their standard of living. Even if they were aware, $10 is not a large enough sum to provoke people into organizing protests and writing letters to their congressional representatives.

The situation of the sugar producers (those who would lose from increased trade) is quite different. The higher profits from the import quota are highly concentrated in a small number of producers. (Seventeen sugar cane farms generate more than half of the profits for the whole sugar cane industry.) Those producers are organized in trade associations that actively lobby on their members' behalf, and make large campaign contributions. (The American Sugar Alliance spent nearly $3 million in lobbying expenses in a single 12-month period leading up to the 2013 congressional vote on the U.S. Farm Bill, which reauthorizes the restrictions on U.S. imports of sugar.)

As one would expect, most of the gains from the sugar import restrictions go to that small group of sugar cane farm owners and not to their employees. Of course, the trade restrictions do prevent job losses for those workers, but the consumer cost per job saved is astronomically high: over $3 million per job saved. In addition, the sugar import restrictions also reduce employment in other sectors that rely on large quantities of sugar in their production processes. In response to the high sugar prices in the United States, for example, candy-making firms have shifted their production sites to Canada, where sugar prices are substantially lower. (There are no sugar farmers in Canada, and hence no political pressure for restrictions on sugar imports.) On net, the sugar restrictions thus generate employment *losses* for U.S. workers.

As we will see in Chapters 9 through 12, the politics of import restriction in the sugar industry is an extreme example of a kind of political process that is common in international trade. That world trade in general became steadily freer from 1945 to 1980 depended, as we will see in Chapter 10, on a special set of circumstances that controlled what is probably an inherent political bias against international trade.

International Labor Mobility

In this section, we will show how the specific factors model can be adapted to analyze the effects of labor mobility. In the modern world, restrictions on the flow of labor are legion—just about every country imposes restrictions on immigration. Thus, labor mobility is less prevalent in practice than capital mobility. However, the analysis of physical capital movements is more complex, as it is embedded along with other factors in a multinational's decision to invest abroad (see Chapter 8). Still, it is important to understand the international economic forces that drive *desired* migration of workers across borders and the short-run consequences of those migration flows whenever they are realized. We will also explore the long-run consequences of changes in a country's labor and capital endowments in the next chapter.

In the previous sections, we saw how workers move between the cloth and food sectors within one country until the wages in the two sectors are equalized. Whenever international migration is possible, workers will also want to move from the low-wage to the high-wage country.[10] To keep things simple and to focus on international migration, let's assume that two countries produce a single good with labor and an immobile factor, land. Since there is only a single good, there is no reason to trade it; however, there will be "trade" in labor services when workers move in search of higher wages. In the absence of migration, wage differences across countries can be driven by technology differences, or alternatively, by differences in the availability of land relative to labor.

Figure 4-13 illustrates the causes and effects of international labor mobility. It is very similar to Figure 4-4, except that the horizontal axis now represents the total world labor force (instead of the labor force in a given country). The two marginal product curves now represent production of the same good in different countries (instead of the production of two different goods in the same country). We do not multiply those curves by the prices of the good; instead, we assume the wages measured on the vertical axis represent real wages (the wage divided by the price of the unique good in each country). Initially, we assume there are OL^1 workers in Home and L^1O^* workers in Foreign. Given those employment levels, technology and land endowment differences are such that real wages are higher in Foreign (point B) than in Home (point C).

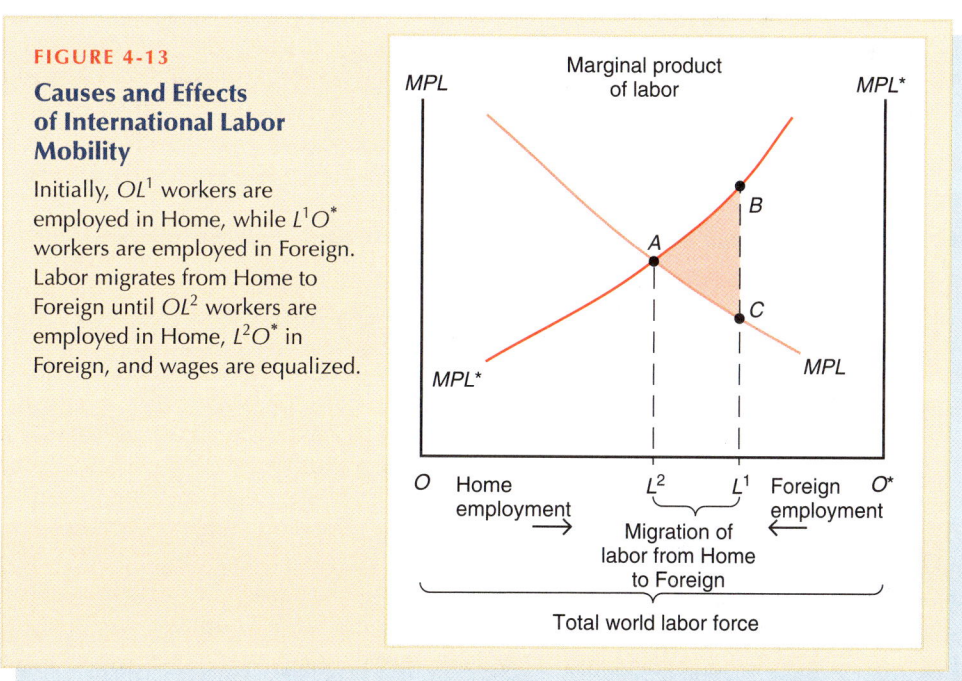

FIGURE 4-13

Causes and Effects of International Labor Mobility

Initially, OL^1 workers are employed in Home, while L^1O^* workers are employed in Foreign. Labor migrates from Home to Foreign until OL^2 workers are employed in Home, L^2O^* in Foreign, and wages are equalized.

[10]We assume workers' tastes are similar so location decisions are based on wage differentials. Actual wage differentials across countries are very large—large enough that, for many workers, they outweigh personal tastes for particular countries.

Now suppose that workers are able to move between these two countries. Workers will move from Home to Foreign. This movement will reduce the Home labor force and thus raise the real wage in Home, while increasing the labor force and reducing the real wage in Foreign. If there are no obstacles to labor movement, this process will continue until the real wage rates are equalized. The eventual distribution of the world's labor force will be one with OL^2 workers in Home and L^2O* workers in Foreign (point A).

Three points should be noted about this redistribution of the world's labor force.

1. It leads to a convergence of real wage rates. Real wages rise in Home and fall in Foreign.
2. It increases the world's output as a whole. Foreign's output rises by the area under its marginal product curve from L^1 to L^2, while Home's falls by the corresponding area under its marginal product curve. (See appendix for details.) We see from the figure that Foreign's gain is larger than Home's loss, by an amount equal to the colored area ABC in the figure.
3. Despite this gain, some people are hurt by the change. Those who would originally have worked in Home receive higher real wages, but those who would originally have worked in Foreign receive lower real wages. Landowners in Foreign benefit from the larger labor supply, but landowners in Home are made worse off.

As in the case of the gains from international trade, then, international labor mobility, while allowing everyone to be made better off in principle, leaves some groups worse off in practice. This main result would not change in a more complex model where countries produce and trade different goods, so long as some factors of production are immobile in the short run. However, we will see in the following chapter that this result need not hold in the long run when all factors are mobile across sectors. Changes in a country's labor endowment, so long as the country is integrated into world markets through trade, can leave the welfare of all factors unchanged. This has very important implications for immigration in the long run and has been shown to be empirically relevant in cases where countries experience large immigration increases.

CASE STUDY

Wage Convergence in the Age of Mass Migration

Although there are substantial movements of people between countries in the modern world, the truly heroic age of labor mobility—when immigration was a major source of population growth in some countries, while emigration caused population in other countries to decline—was in the late 19th and early 20th centuries. In a global economy newly integrated by railroads, steamships, and telegraph cables, and not yet subject to many legal restrictions on migration, tens of millions of people moved long distances in search of a better life. Chinese people moved to Southeast Asia and California, while Indian people moved to Africa and the Caribbean; in addition, a substantial number of Japanese people moved to Brazil. However, the greatest migration involved people from the periphery of Europe—from Scandinavia, Ireland, Italy, and Eastern Europe—who moved to places where land was abundant and wages were high: the United States, Canada, Argentina, and Australia.

TABLE 4-1		
	Real Wage, 1870 (U.S. = 100)	Percentage Increase in Real Wage, 1870–1913
Destination Countries		
Argentina	53	51
Australia	110	1
Canada	86	121
United States	100	47
Origin Countries		
Ireland	43	84
Italy	23	112
Norway	24	193
Sweden	24	250

Source: Jeffrey G. Williamson, "The Evolution of Global Labor Markets Since 1830: Background Evidence and Hypotheses," *Explorations in Economic History* 32 (1995), pp. 141–196.

Did this process cause the kind of real wage convergence that our model predicts? Indeed, it did. Table 4-1 shows real wages in 1870, and the change in these wages up to the eve of World War I, for four major "destination" countries and for four important "origin" countries. As the table shows, at the beginning of the period, real wages were much higher in the destination than in the origin countries. Over the next four decades real wages rose in all countries, but (except for a surprisingly large increase in Canada) they increased much more rapidly in the origin than in the destination countries, suggesting that migration actually did move the world toward (although not by any means all the way to) wage equalization.

As documented in the case study on the U.S. economy, legal restrictions put an end to the age of mass migration after World War I. For that and other reasons (notably a decline in world trade and the direct effects of two world wars), convergence in real wages came to a halt and even reversed itself for several decades, only to resume in the postwar years.

CASE STUDY   Foreign Workers: The Story of the GCC

Following the discovery of large oil and natural gas reserves in the mid-1900s, the Gulf Cooperation Council (GCC) countries' economies have relied heavily on foreign workers.[11] As Figure 4-14 shows, the mean share of foreign workers in the GCC countries has steadily increased, and made up

[11]See GCC countries: Bahrain, Kuwait, Oman, Qatar, Saudi Arabia, and United Arab Emirates.

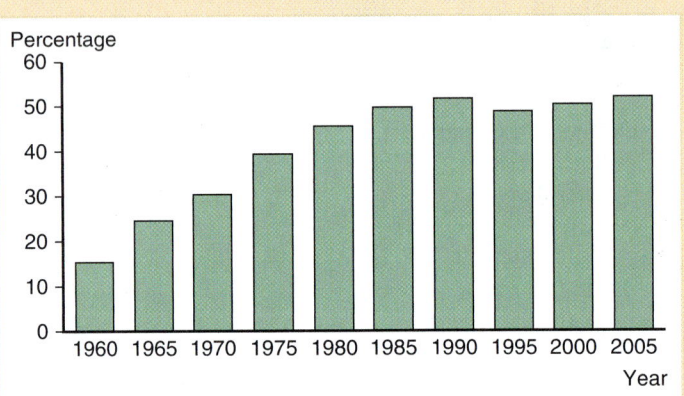

FIGURE 4-14

Mean Migrant Stock as a Percentage of the GCC Population

Source: World Development Indicators Online database.

50 percent of the population in 2005. While the influx of workers to the Gulf has been mainly from Arab and Indian subcontinent countries, recently there has been a significant inflow of people from Europe and North America.[12] The Gulf has become home to the regional headquarters of many multinational corporations (for instance, Oracle, Microsoft, and IBM) generating demand for highly skilled foreign workers mainly from the West with professional and technical skills needed to run these companies in sync with their home country operations. With such a large presence, one has to wonder about the implications for the GCC economies of large numbers of expatriates. First of all, the standards of living reflected in Gross Domestic Product (GDP) per capita have increased tremendously in the last three decades. Kuwait, Qatar and the United Arab Emirates (UAE) consistently rank in the top 15 countries in terms of standards of living.

The large number of foreigners puts serious pressures on the GCC economies. The proportion of foreign workers to the total population is even higher when one looks only at the labor force.[13] This fact results in severe competition for local workers, which prompted all GCC governments to issue labor protective policies that have their own share of consequences.[14] Furthermore, foreigners are separated into two types of accommodations based on their skill level.[15] While no foreign

[12]See G. Naufal and C. Vargas-Silva. "Migrant Transfers in the MENA Region: A Two Way Street in Which Traffic Is Changing." *Migration Letters* 7(2), 2010, pp. 168–178.

[13]See N. Ann Colton. "The International Political Economy of Gulf Migration." *Viewpoints* Special Edition Migration and the Gulf. *Middle East Institute Viewpoints* (February 2010), pp. 34–36.

[14]For example, in the United Arab Emirates, the government has introduced Emiratization as a policy aimed at securing jobs for the local labor force.

[15]Low-skilled workers are housed in labor camps (similar to army barracks), and high-skilled workers are housed in regular accommodations.

worker can become a citizen or own property, low-skilled workers cannot even sponsor their families to join them. These restrictions have turned migration to the Gulf into a temporary guest worker program. The nature of the foreign labor market in the Gulf has installed a sense of unease among foreign workers, which is explicitly expressed in the size of remittances. The official remittances from the GCC economies in 2007 surpassed US$37 billion, making the Gulf one of the most active remitting regions in the world.

Thus, the GCC countries present a unique and interesting case of migration. While the large share of foreigners in the population has subjected the local economies to certain complications, foreign workers have also helped the local population achieve one of the highest standards of living in the world. This is the story of the GCC; a story of trade-offs.

SUMMARY

1. International trade often has strong effects on the distribution of income within countries, so that it often produces losers as well as winners. Income distribution effects arise for two reasons: Factors of production cannot move instantaneously and costlessly from one industry to another, and changes in an economy's output mix have differential effects on the demand for different factors of production.

2. A useful model of income distribution effects of international trade is the *specific factors* model, which allows for a distinction between general-purpose factors that can move between sectors and factors specific to particular uses. In this model, differences in resources can cause countries to have different relative supply curves and thus cause international trade.

3. In the specific factors model, factors specific to export sectors in each country gain from trade, while factors specific to import-competing sectors lose. Mobile factors that can work in either sector may either gain or lose.

4. Trade nonetheless produces overall gains in the limited sense that those who gain could in principle compensate those who lose while still remaining better off than before.

5. Most economists do not regard the effects of international trade on income distribution a good reason to limit this trade. In its distributional effects, trade is no different from many other forms of economic change, which are not normally regulated. Furthermore, economists would prefer to address the problem of income distribution directly, rather than by interfering with trade flows.

6. Nonetheless, in the actual politics of trade policy, income distribution is of crucial importance. This is true in particular because those who lose from trade are usually a much more informed, cohesive, and organized group than those who gain.

7. International factor movements can sometimes substitute for trade, so it is not surprising that international migration of labor is similar in its causes and effects to international trade. Labor moves from countries where it is abundant to countries where it is scarce. This movement raises total world output, but it also generates strong income distribution effects, so that some groups are hurt as a result.

KEY TERMS

budget constraint, p. 89
diminishing returns, p. 78
marginal product of labor,
    p. 78

mobile factor, p. 77
production function, p. 78
production possibility frontier,
    p. 78

specific factor, p. 77
specific factors model, p. 76
U.S. Trade Adjustment
    Assistance program, p. 93

| PROBLEMS | MyEconLab |

1. A country opts for free trade while some workers remain unemployed in the import-competing sector. Why? Given real wage rate in Thailand is higher than Bangladesh, how would international trade affect real wages between them under perfectly mobile labor movement?

2. An economy can produce good 1 using labor and capital and good 2 using labor and land. The total supply of labor is 100 units. Given the supply of capital, the outputs of the two goods depend on labor input as follows:

Labor Input to Good 1	Output of Good 1	Labor Input to Good 2	Output of Good 2
0	0.0	0	0.0
10	25.1	10	39.8
20	38.1	20	52.5
30	48.6	30	61.8
40	57.7	40	69.3
50	66.0	50	75.8
60	73.6	60	81.5
70	80.7	70	86.7
80	87.4	80	91.4
90	93.9	90	95.9
100	100	100	100

   a. Graph the production functions for good 1 and good 2.
   b. Graph the production possibility frontier. Why is it curved?

3. The marginal product of labor curves corresponding to the production functions in problem 2 are as follows:

Workers Employed	MPL in Sector 1	MPL in Sector 2
10	1.51	1.59
20	1.14	1.05
30	1.00	.82
40	.87	.69
50	.78	.60
60	.74	.54
70	.69	.50
80	.66	.46
90	.63	.43
100	.60	.40

   a. Suppose the price of good 2 relative to that of good 1 is 2. Determine graphically the wage rate and the allocation of labor between the two sectors.
   b. Using the graph drawn for problem 2, determine the output of each sector. Then confirm graphically that the slope of the production possibility frontier at that point equals the relative price.
   c. Suppose the relative price of good 2 falls to 1.3. Repeat (a) and (b).
   d. Calculate the effects of the price change from 2 to 1.3 on the income of the specific factors in sectors 1 and 2.

4. Consider two countries (Home and Foreign) that produce goods 1 (with labor and capital) and 2 (with labor and land) according to the production functions described in problems 2 and 3. Initially, both countries have the same supply of labor (100 units each), capital, and land. The capital stock in Home then grows. This change shifts out both the production curve for good 1 as a function of labor employed (described in problem 2) and the associated marginal product of labor curve (described in problem 3). Nothing happens to the production and marginal product curves for good 2.
   a. Show how the increase in the supply of capital for Home affects its production possibility frontier.
   b. On the same graph, draw the relative supply curve for both the Home and the Foreign economy.
   c. If those two economies open up to trade, what will be the pattern of trade (i.e., which country exports which good)?
   d. Describe how opening up to trade affects all three factors (labor, capital, land) in both countries.

5. In Home and Foreign, there are two factors each of production, land, and labor used to produce only one good. The land supply in each country and the technology of production are exactly the same. The marginal product of labor in each country depends on employment as follows:

Number of Workers Employed	Marginal Product of Last Worker
1	20
2	19
3	18
4	17
5	16
6	15
7	14
8	13
9	12
10	11
11	10

Initially, there are 11 workers employed in Home, but only 3 workers in Foreign. Find the effect of free movement of labor from Home to Foreign on employment, production, real wages, and the income of landowners in each country.

6. Using the numerical example in problem 5, assume now that Foreign limits immigration so that only 2 workers can move there from Home. Calculate how the movement of these two workers affects the income of five different groups:
   a. Workers who were originally in Foreign
   b. Foreign landowners
   c. Workers who stay in Home
   d. Home landowners
   e. The workers who do move

7. A country produces two crops—paddy and wheat. Given the price of paddy (Pp) and wheat (Pw), the relationship of labor allocation is shown as $MPLp \times Pp = MPLw \times Pw = w$, where $MPLp$ and $MPLw$ are marginal products of labor for the two. If wheat's price increases by 10 percent with no changes in paddy prices, what will happen to labor demand for wheat production, and the market wage rate?

FURTHER READINGS

Avinash Dixit and Victor Norman. *Theory of International Trade.* Cambridge: Cambridge University Press, 1980. The problem of establishing gains from trade when some people may be made worse off has been the subject of a long debate. Dixit and Norman show it is always possible in principle for a country's government to use taxes and subsidies to redistribute income in such a way that everyone is better off with free trade than with no trade.

Lawrence Edwards and Robert Z. Lawrence. 2013. *Rising Tide: Is Growth in Emerging Economies Good for the United States?* Peterson Institute for International Economics. An accessible book that examines how increased trade with emerging economies (such as China and India) has affected the United States and its workers.

Hanson, Gordon H. 2009. "The Economic Consequences of the International Migration of Labor." *Annual Review of Economics* 1 (1): 179–208. A survey paper reviewing how increased migration has affected both sending and recipient countries.

Douglas A. Irwin, *Free Trade under Fire,* 3rd edition. Princeton, NJ: Princeton University Press, 2009. An accessible book that provides numerous details and supporting data for the argument that freer trade generates overall welfare gains. Chapter 4 discusses the connection between trade and unemployment in detail (an issue that was briefly discussed in this chapter).

Charles P. Kindleberger. *Europe's Postwar Growth: The Role of Labor Supply.* Cambridge: Harvard University Press, 1967. A good account of the role of labor migration during its height in Europe.

Robert A. Mundell. "International Trade and Factor Mobility." *American Economic Review* 47 (1957), pp. 321–335. The paper that first laid out the argument that trade and factor movement can substitute for each other.

Michael Mussa. "Tariffs and the Distribution of Income: The Importance of Factor Specificity, Substitutability, and Intensity in the Short and Long Run." *Journal of Political Economy* 82 (1974), pp. 1191–1204. An extension of the specific factors model that relates it to the factor proportions model of Chapter 5.

J. Peter Neary. "Short-Run Capital Specificity and the Pure Theory of International Trade." *Economic Journal* 88 (1978), pp. 488–510. A further treatment of the specific factors model that stresses how differing assumptions about mobility of factors between sectors affect the model's conclusions.

Mancur Olson. *The Logic of Collective Action.* Cambridge: Harvard University Press, 1965. A highly influential book that argues the proposition that in practice, government policies favor small, concentrated groups over large ones.

David Ricardo. *The Principles of Political Economy and Taxation.* Homewood, IL: Irwin, 1963. While Ricardo's *Principles* emphasizes the national gains from trade at one point, elsewhere in his book the conflict of interest between landowners and capitalists is a central issue.

MyEconLab Can Help You Get a Better Grade

MyEconLab   If your exam were tomorrow, would you be ready? For each chapter, MyEconLab Practice Tests and Study Plans pinpoint sections you have mastered and those you need to study. That way, you are more efficient with your study time, and you are better prepared for your exams.

To see how it works, turn to page 33 and then go to

www.myeconlab.com

Further Details on Specific Factors

The specific factors model developed in this chapter is such a convenient tool of analysis that we take the time here to spell out some of its details more fully. We give a fuller treatment of two related issues: (1) the relationship between marginal and total product within each sector and (2) the income distribution effects of relative price changes.

Marginal and Total Product

In the text, we illustrated the production function of cloth in two different ways. In Figure 4-1, we showed total output as a function of labor input, holding capital constant. We then observed that the slope of that curve is the marginal product of labor and illustrated that marginal product in Figure 4-2. We now want to demonstrate that the total output is measured by the area under the marginal product curve. (Students familiar with calculus will find this obvious: Marginal product is the derivative of total, so total is the integral of marginal. Even for these students, however, an intuitive approach can be helpful.)

In Figure 4A-1, we show once again the marginal product curve in cloth production. Suppose we employ L_C person-hours. How can we show the total output of cloth? Let's approximate this using the marginal product curve. First, let's ask what would happen if we used slightly fewer person-hours, say dL_C fewer. Then output would be less. The fall in output would be approximately

$$dL_C \times MPL_C,$$

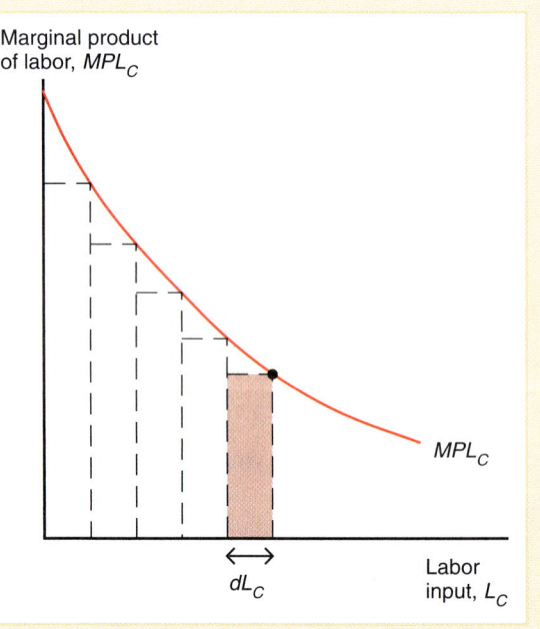

FIGURE 4A-1

Showing that Output Is Equal to the Area under the Marginal Product Curve

By approximating the marginal product curve with a series of thin rectangles, one can show that the total output of cloth is equal to the area under the curve.

that is, the reduction in the work force times the marginal product of labor at the initial level of employment. This reduction in output is represented by the area of the colored rectangle in Figure 4A-1. Now subtract another few person-hours; the output loss will be another rectangle. This time the rectangle will be taller because the marginal product of labor rises as the quantity of labor falls. If we continue this process until all the labor is gone, our approximation of the total output loss will be the sum of all the rectangles shown in the figure. When no labor is employed, however, output will fall to zero. So we can approximate the total output of the cloth sector by the sum of the areas of all the rectangles under the marginal product curve.

This is, however, only an approximation because we used the marginal product of only the first person-hour in each batch of labor removed. We can get a better approximation if we take smaller groups—the smaller the better. As the groups of labor removed get infinitesimally small, however, the rectangles get thinner and thinner, and we approximate ever more closely the total area under the marginal product curve. In the end, then, we find the total output of cloth produced with labor L_C, Q_C is equal to the area under the marginal product of labor curve MPL_C up to L_C.

Relative Prices and the Distribution of Income

Figure 4A-2 uses the result we just found to show the distribution of income within the cloth sector. We saw that cloth employers hire labor L_C until the value of the workers' marginal product, $P_C \times MPL_C$, is equal to the wage w. We can rewrite this in terms of the real wage of cloth as $MPL_C = w/P_C$. Thus, at a given real wage, say $(w/P_C)^1$, the marginal product curve in Figure 4A-2 tells us that L_C^1 worker-hours will be employed. The total output produced with those workers is given by the area under the marginal product curve up to L_C^1. This output is divided into the real income (in terms of cloth) of workers and capital owners. The portion paid to workers is the real wage $(w/P_C)^1$ times the employment level L_C^1, which is the area of the rectangle shown. The remainder is the real income of the capital owners. We can determine the

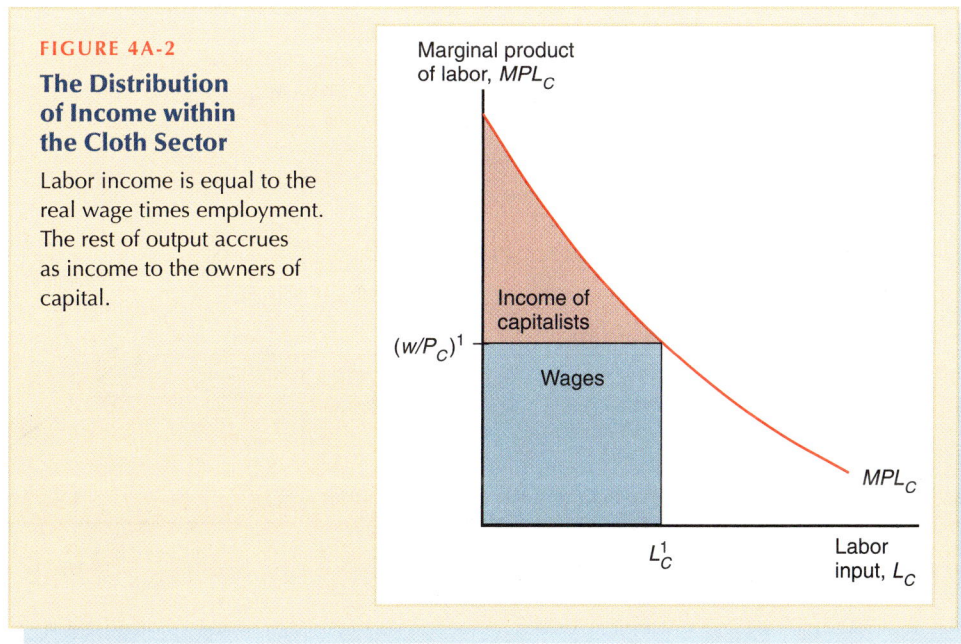

FIGURE 4A-2

The Distribution of Income within the Cloth Sector

Labor income is equal to the real wage times employment. The rest of output accrues as income to the owners of capital.

distribution of food production between labor and landowners in the same way, as a function of the real wage in terms of food, w/P_F.

Suppose the relative price of cloth now rises. We saw in Figure 4-7 that a rise in P_C/P_F lowers the real wage in terms of cloth (because the wage rises by less than P_C) while raising it in terms of food. The effects of this on the income of capitalists and landowners can be seen in Figures 4A-3 and 4A-4. In the cloth sector, the real wage falls from $(w/P_C)^1$ to $(w/P_C)^2$; as a result, capitalists receive increased real income in

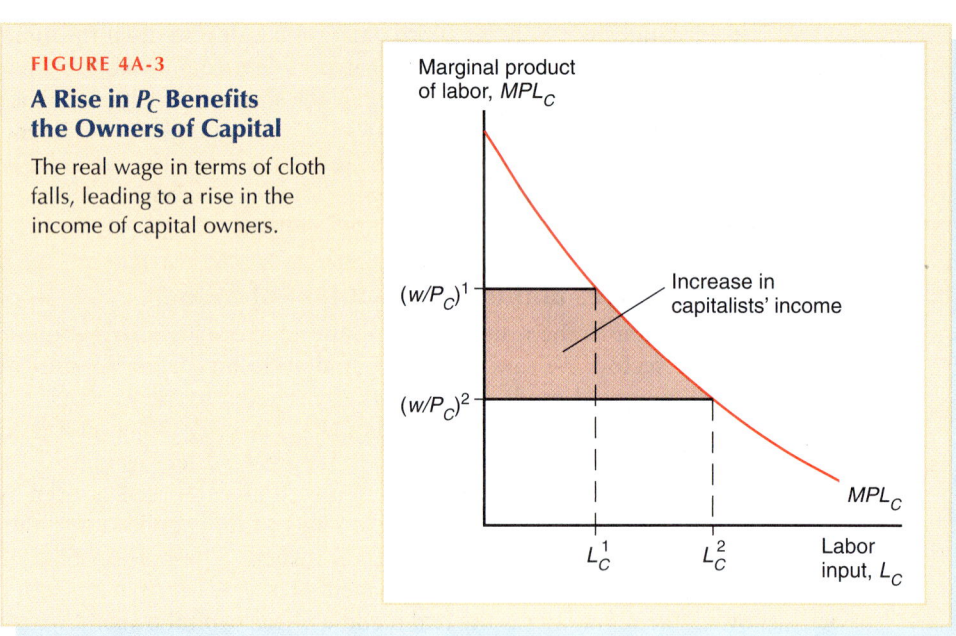

FIGURE 4A-3

A Rise in P_C Benefits the Owners of Capital

The real wage in terms of cloth falls, leading to a rise in the income of capital owners.

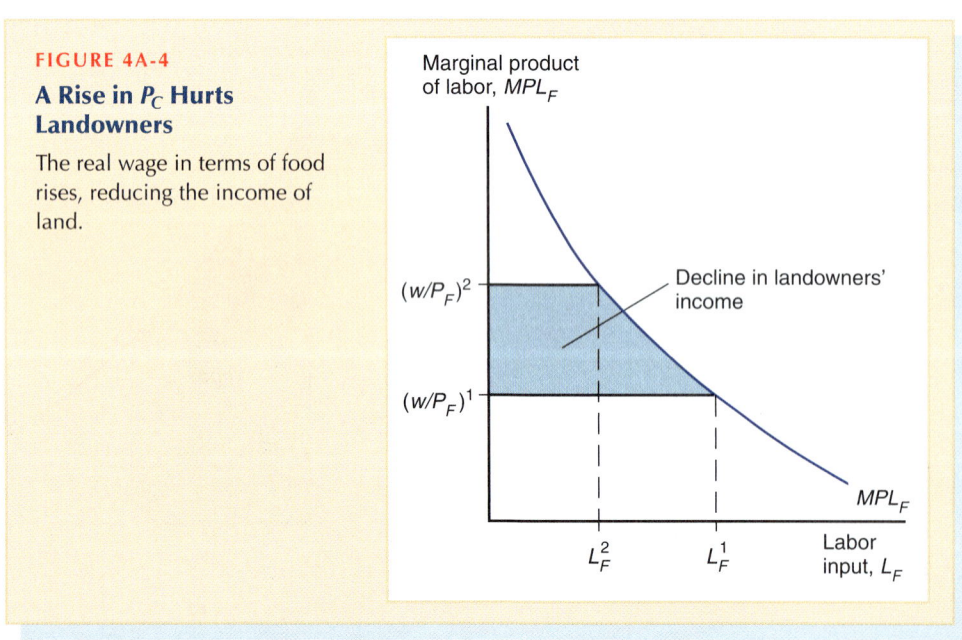

FIGURE 4A-4

A Rise in P_C Hurts Landowners

The real wage in terms of food rises, reducing the income of land.

terms of cloth. In the food sector, the real wage rises from $(w/P_F)^1$ to $(w/P_F)^2$, and landowners receive less real income in terms of food.

This effect on real income is reinforced by the change in P_C/P_F itself. The real income of capital owners in terms of food rises by more than their real income in terms of cloth—because food is now relatively cheaper than cloth. Conversely, the real income of landowners in terms of cloth drops by more than their real income in terms of food—because cloth is now relatively more expensive.

CHAPTER 5

RESOURCES AND TRADE: THE HECKSCHER-OHLIN MODEL

If labor were the only factor of production, as the Ricardian model assumes, comparative advantage could arise only because of international differences in labor productivity. In the real world, however, while trade is partly explained by differences in labor productivity, it also reflects differences in countries' resources. Canada exports forest products to the United States not because its lumberjacks are more productive relative to their U.S. counterparts but because sparsely populated Canada has more forested land per capita than the United States. Thus, a realistic view of trade must allow for the importance not just of labor but also of other factors of production such as land, capital, and mineral resources.

To explain the role of resource differences in trade, this chapter examines a model in which resource differences are the *only* source of trade. This model shows that comparative advantage is influenced by the interaction between nations' resources (the relative **abundance of factors** of production) and the technology of production (which influences the relative **intensity** with which different **factors** of production are used in the production of different goods). Some of these ideas were presented in the specific factors model of Chapter 4, but the model we study in this chapter puts the interaction between abundance and intensity in sharper relief by looking at long-run outcomes when all factors of production are mobile across sectors.

That international trade is largely driven by differences in countries' resources is one of the most influential theories in international economics. Developed by two Swedish economists, Eli Heckscher and Bertil Ohlin (Ohlin received the Nobel Prize in economics in 1977), the theory is often referred to as the **Heckscher-Ohlin theory**. Because the theory emphasizes the interplay between the proportions in which different factors of production are available in different countries and the proportions in which they are used in producing different goods, it is also referred to as the **factor-proportions theory**.

To develop the factor-proportions theory, we begin by describing an economy that does not trade and then ask what happens when two such economies trade with each other. We will see that as opposed to the Ricardian model with a single factor of production, trade can affect the distribution of income across factors, even in the long run. We discuss the extent to which trade may be contributing to increases in wage inequality in developed countries. We then conclude with a further review of the empirical evidence for (and against) the predictions of the factor-proportions theory of trade.

LEARNING GOALS

After reading this chapter, you will be able to:

- Explain how differences in resources generate a specific pattern of trade.
- Discuss why the gains from trade will not be equally spread even in the long run and identify the likely winners and losers.
- Understand the possible links between increased trade and rising wage inequality in the developed world.
- See how empirical patterns of trade and factor prices support some (but not all) of the predictions of the factor-proportions theory.

Model of a Two-Factor Economy

In this chapter, we'll focus on the simplest version of the factor-proportions model, sometimes referred to as "2 by 2 by 2": two countries, two goods, two factors of production. In our example, we'll call the two countries Home and Foreign. We will stick with the same two goods, cloth (measured in yards) and food (measured in calories), that we used in the specific factors model of Chapter 4. The key difference is that in this chapter, we assume that the immobile factors that were specific to each sector (capital in cloth, land in food) are now mobile in the long run. Thus, land used for farming can be used to build a textile plant; conversely, the capital used to pay for a power loom can be used to pay for a tractor. To keep things simple, we model a single additional factor that we call capital, which is used in conjunction with labor to produce either cloth or food. In the long run, both capital and labor can move across sectors, thus equalizing their returns (rental rate and wage) in both sectors.

Prices and Production

Both cloth and food are produced using capital and labor. The amount of each good produced, given how much capital and labor are employed in each sector, is determined by a production function for each good:

$$Q_C = Q_C(K_C, L_C),$$
$$Q_F = Q_F(K_F, L_F),$$

where Q_C and Q_F are the output levels of cloth and food, K_C and L_C are the amounts of capital and labor employed in cloth production, and K_F and L_F are the amounts of capital and labor employed in food production. Overall, the economy has a fixed supply of capital K and labor L that is divided between employment in the two sectors.

We define the following expressions that are related to the two production technologies:

$$a_{KC} = \text{capital used to produce one yard of cloth}$$
$$a_{LC} = \text{labor used to produce one yard of cloth}$$
$$a_{KF} = \text{capital used to produce one calorie of food}$$
$$a_{LF} = \text{labor used to produce one calorie of food}$$

These unit input requirements are very similar to the ones defined in the Ricardian model (for labor only). However, there is one crucial difference: In these definitions, we speak of the quantity of capital or labor *used* to produce a given amount of cloth or food, rather than the quantity *required* to produce that amount. The reason for this change from the Ricardian model is that when there are two factors of production, there may be some room for choice in the use of inputs.

In general, those choices will depend on the factor prices for labor and capital. However, let's first look at a special case in which there is only one way to produce each good. Consider the following numerical example: Production of one yard of cloth requires a combination of two work-hours and two machine-hours. The production of food is more automated; as a result, production of one calorie of food requires only one work-hour along with three machine-hours. Thus, all the unit input requirements are fixed at $a_{KC} = 2$; $a_{LC} = 2$; $a_{KF} = 3$; $a_{LF} = 1$; and there is no possibility of substituting labor for capital or vice versa. Assume that an economy is endowed with 3,000 units of machine-hours along with 2,000 units of work-hours. In this special case of no factor substitution in production, the economy's production possibility frontier can be derived using those two resource constraints for capital and labor. Production of Q_C yards of cloth requires $2Q_C = a_{KC} \times Q_C$ machine-hours and $2Q_C = a_{LC} \times Q_C$ work-hours. Similarly, production of Q_F calories of food requires $3Q_F = a_{KF} \times Q_F$ machine-hours and $1Q_F = a_{LF} \times Q_F$ work-hours. The total machine-hours used for both cloth and food production cannot exceed the total supply of capital:

$$a_{KC} \times Q_C + a_{KF} \times Q_F \le K, \text{ or } 2Q_C + 3Q_F \le 3,000 \qquad (5\text{-}1)$$

This is the resource constraint for capital. Similarly, the resource constraint for labor states that the total work-hours used in production cannot exceed the total supply of labor:

$$a_{LC} \times Q_C + a_{LF} \times Q_F \le L, \text{ or } 2Q_C + Q_F \le 2,000 \qquad (5\text{-}2)$$

Figure 5-1 shows the implications of (5-1) and (5-2) for the production possibilities in our numerical example. Each resource constraint is drawn in the same way we drew the production possibility line for the Ricardian case in Figure 3-1. In this case, however, the economy must produce subject to *both* constraints, so the production possibility frontier is the kinked line shown in red. If the economy specializes in food production (point 1), then it can produce 1,000 calories of food. At that production point, there is spare labor capacity: Only 1,000 work-hours out of 2,000 are employed. Conversely, if the economy specializes in cloth production (point 2), then it can produce 1,000 yards of cloth. At that production point, there is spare capital capacity: Only 2,000 machine-hours out of 3,000 are employed. At production point 3, the economy is employing all of its labor and capital resources (1,500 machine-hours and

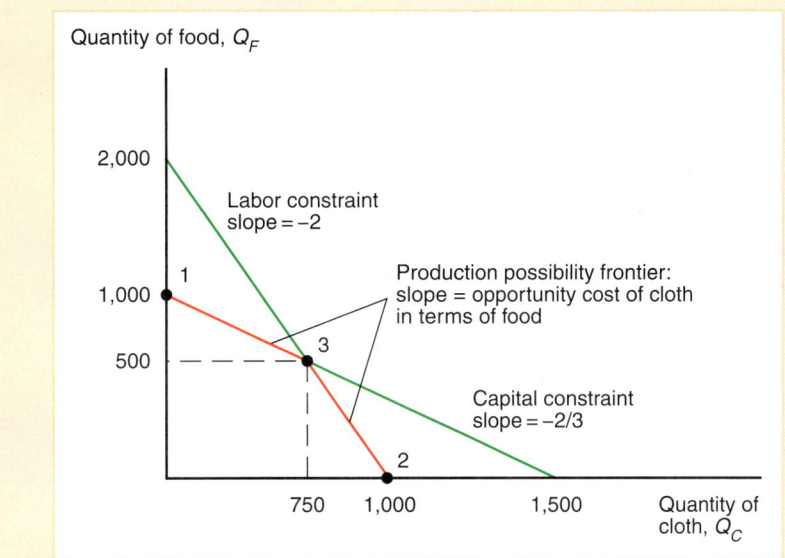

FIGURE 5-1

The Production Possibility Frontier Without Factor Substitution: Numerical Example

If capital cannot be substituted for labor or vice versa, the production possibility frontier in the factor-proportions model would be defined by two resource constraints: The economy can't use more than the available supply of labor (2,000 work-hours) or capital (3,000 machine-hours). So the production possibility frontier is defined by the red line in this figure. At point 1, the economy specializes in food production, and not all available work-hours are employed. At point 2, the economy specializes in cloth, and not all available machine-hours are employed. At production point 3, the economy employs all of its labor and capital resources. The important feature of the production possibility frontier is that the opportunity cost of cloth in terms of food isn't constant: It rises from $2/3$ to 2 when the economy's mix of production shifts toward cloth.

1,500 work-hours in cloth production, and 1,500 machine-hours along with 500 work-hours in food production).[1]

The important feature of this production possibility frontier is that the opportunity cost of producing an extra yard of cloth in terms of food is not constant. When the economy is producing mostly food (to the left of point 3), then there is spare labor capacity. Producing two fewer units of food releases six machine-hours that can be used to produce three yards of cloth: The opportunity cost of cloth is $2/3$. When the economy is producing mostly cloth (to the right of point 3), then there is spare capital capacity. Producing two fewer units of food releases two work-hours that can be used to produce one yard of cloth: The opportunity cost of cloth is 2. Thus, the opportunity cost of cloth is higher when more units of cloth are being produced.

---

[1]The case of no factor substitution is a special one in which there is only a single production point that fully employs both factors; some factors are left unemployed at all the other production points on the production possibilities frontier. In the more general case below with factor substitution, this peculiarity disappears, and both factors are fully employed along the entire production possibility frontier.

FIGURE 5-2

The Production Possibility Frontier with Factor Substitution

If capital can be substituted for labor and vice versa, the production possibility frontier no longer has a kink. But it remains true that the opportunity cost of cloth in terms of food rises as the economy's production mix shifts toward cloth and away from food.

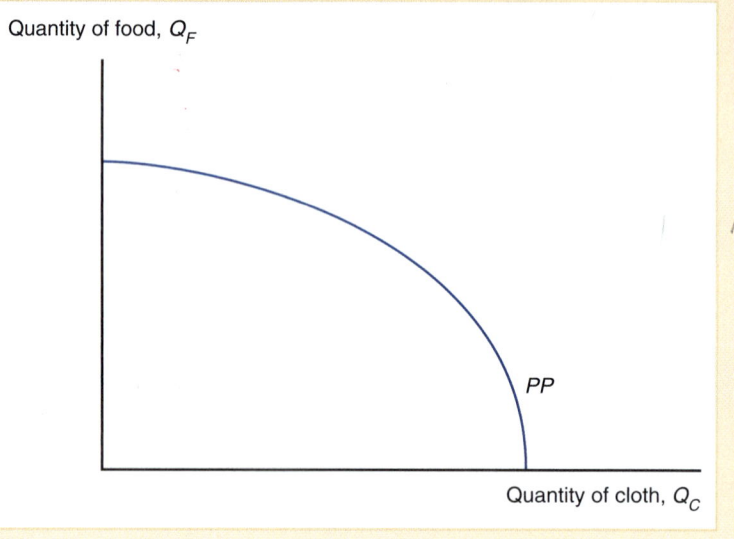

Now let's make the model more realistic and allow the possibility of substituting capital for labor and vice versa in production. This substitution removes the kink in the production possibility frontier; instead, the frontier *PP* has the bowed shape shown in Figure 5-2. The bowed shape tells us that the opportunity cost in terms of food of producing one more unit of cloth rises as the economy produces more cloth and less food. That is, our basic insight about how opportunity costs change with the mix of production remains valid.

Where on the production possibility frontier does the economy produce? It depends on prices. Specifically, the economy produces at the point that maximizes the value of production. Figure 5-3 shows what this implies. The value of the economy's production is

$$V = P_C \times Q_C + P_F \times Q_F,$$

FIGURE 5-3

Prices and Production

The economy produces at the point that maximizes the value of production given the prices it faces; this is the point on the highest possible isovalue line. At that point, the opportunity cost of cloth in terms of food is equal to the relative price of cloth, P_C/P_F.

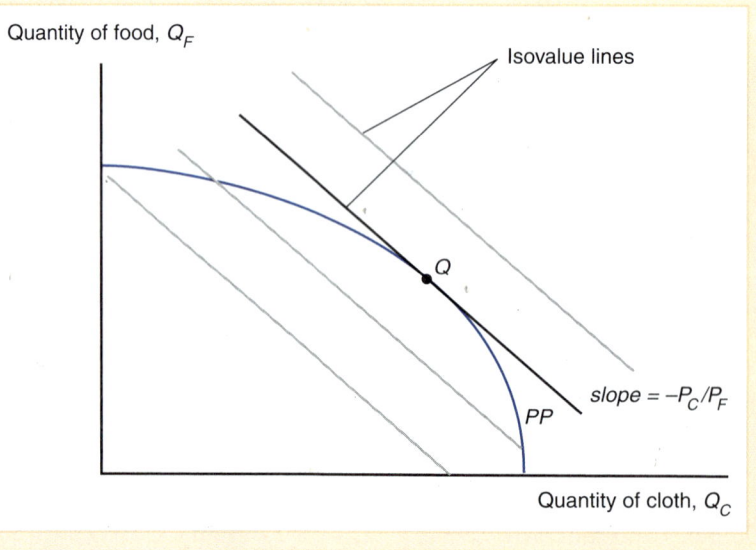

where P_C and P_F are the prices of cloth and food, respectively. An isovalue line—a line along which the value of output is constant—has a slope of $-P_C/P_F$. The economy produces at the point Q, the point on the production possibility frontier that touches the highest possible isovalue line. At that point, the slope of the production possibility frontier is equal to $-P_C/P_F$. So the opportunity cost in terms of food of producing another unit of cloth is equal to the relative price of cloth.

Choosing the Mix of Inputs

As we have noted, in a two-factor model producers may have room for choice in the use of inputs. A farmer, for example, can choose between using relatively more mechanized equipment (capital) and fewer workers, or vice versa. Thus, the farmer can choose how much labor and capital to use per unit of output produced. In each sector, then, producers will face not fixed input requirements (as in the Ricardian model) but trade-offs like the one illustrated by curve II in Figure 5-4, which shows alternative input combinations that can be used to produce one calorie of food.

What input choice will producers actually make? It depends on the relative costs of capital and labor. If capital rental rates are high and wages low, farmers will choose to produce using relatively little capital and a lot of labor; on the other hand, if the rental rates are low and wages high, they will save on labor and use a lot more capital. If w is the wage rate and r the rental cost of capital, then the input choice will depend on the ratio of these two **factor prices**, w/r.[2] The relationship between factor prices and the ratio of labor to capital use in production of food is shown in Figure 5-5 as the curve FF.

There is a corresponding relationship between w/r and the labor-capital ratio in cloth production. This relationship is shown in Figure 5-5 as the curve CC. As drawn, CC is shifted out relative to FF, indicating that at any given factor prices, production of cloth will always use more labor relative to capital than will production of food. When this is true, we say that production of cloth is *labor-intensive*, while production of food is *capital-intensive*. Notice that the definition of intensity depends on the ratio of labor to capital used in production, not the ratio of labor or capital to output. Thus a good cannot be both capital- and labor-intensive.

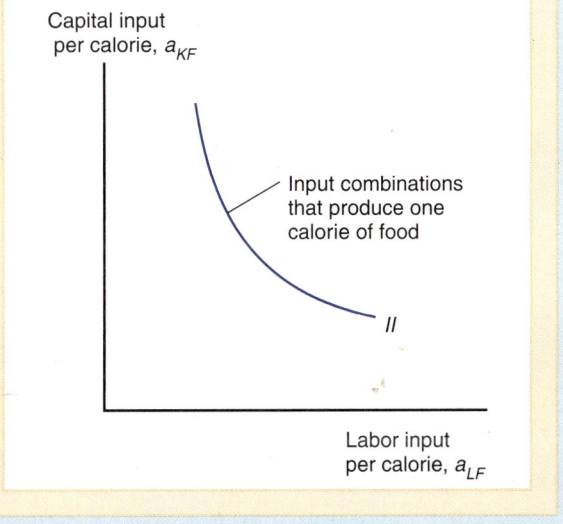

FIGURE 5-4

Input Possibilities in Food Production

A farmer can produce a calorie of food with less capital if he or she uses more labor, and vice versa.

Capital input per calorie, a_{KF}

Input combinations that produce one calorie of food

II

Labor input per calorie, a_{LF}

---

[2] The optimal choice of the labor-capital ratio is explored at greater length in the appendix to this chapter.

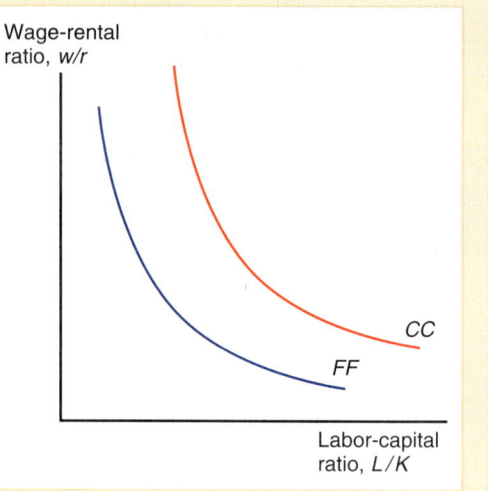

FIGURE 5-5

Factor Prices and Input Choices

In each sector, the ratio of labor to capital used in production depends on the cost of labor relative to the cost of capital, w/r. The curve FF shows the labor-capital ratio choices in food production, while the curve CC shows the corresponding choices in cloth production. At any given wage-rental ratio, cloth production uses a higher labor-capital ratio; when this is the case, we say that cloth production is *labor-intensive* and that food production is *capital-intensive*.

The CC and FF curves in Figure 5-5 are called relative factor demand curves; they are very similar to the relative demand curve for goods. Their downward slope characterizes the substitution effect in the producers' factor demand. As the wage w rises relative to the rental rate r, producers substitute capital for labor in their production decisions. The previous case we considered with no factor substitution is a limiting case, where the relative demand curve is a vertical line: The ratio of labor to capital demanded is fixed and does not vary with changes in the wage-rental ratio w/r. In the remainder of this chapter, we consider the more general case with factor substitution, where the relative factor demand curves are downward sloping.

Factor Prices and Goods Prices

Suppose for a moment the economy produces both cloth and food. (This need not be the case if the economy engages in international trade because it might specialize completely in producing one good or the other; but let us temporarily ignore this possibility.) Then competition among producers in each sector will ensure that the price of each good equals its cost of production. The cost of producing a good depends on factor prices: If wages rise—other things equal—the price of any good whose production uses labor will also rise.

The importance of a particular factor's price to the cost of producing a good depends, however, on how much of that factor the good's production involves. If food production makes use of very little labor, for example, then a rise in the wage will not have much effect on the price of food, whereas if cloth production uses a great deal of labor, a rise in the wage *will* have a large effect on the price. We can therefore conclude that there is a one-to-one relationship between the ratio of the wage rate to the rental rate, w/r, and the ratio of the price of cloth to that of food, P_C/P_F. This relationship is illustrated by the upward-sloping curve SS in Figure 5-6.[3]

Let's look at Figures 5-5 and 5-6 together. In Figure 5-7, the left panel is Figure 5-6 (of the SS curve) turned counterclockwise 90 degrees, while the right panel reproduces

---

[3]This relationship holds only when the economy produces both cloth and food, which is associated with a given range for the relative price of cloth. If the relative price rises beyond a given upper-bound level, then the economy specializes in cloth production; conversely, if the relative price drops below a lower-bound level, then the economy specializes in food production.

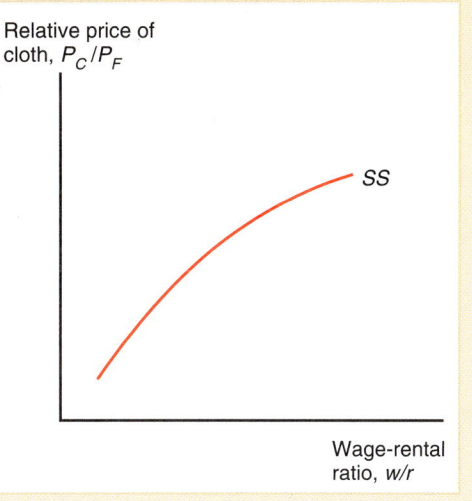

FIGURE 5-6

Factor Prices and Goods Prices

Because cloth production is labor-intensive while food production is capital-intensive, there is a one-to-one relationship between the factor price ratio w/r and the relative price of cloth P_C/P_F; the higher the relative cost of labor, the higher must be the relative price of the labor-intensive good. The relationship is illustrated by the curve SS.

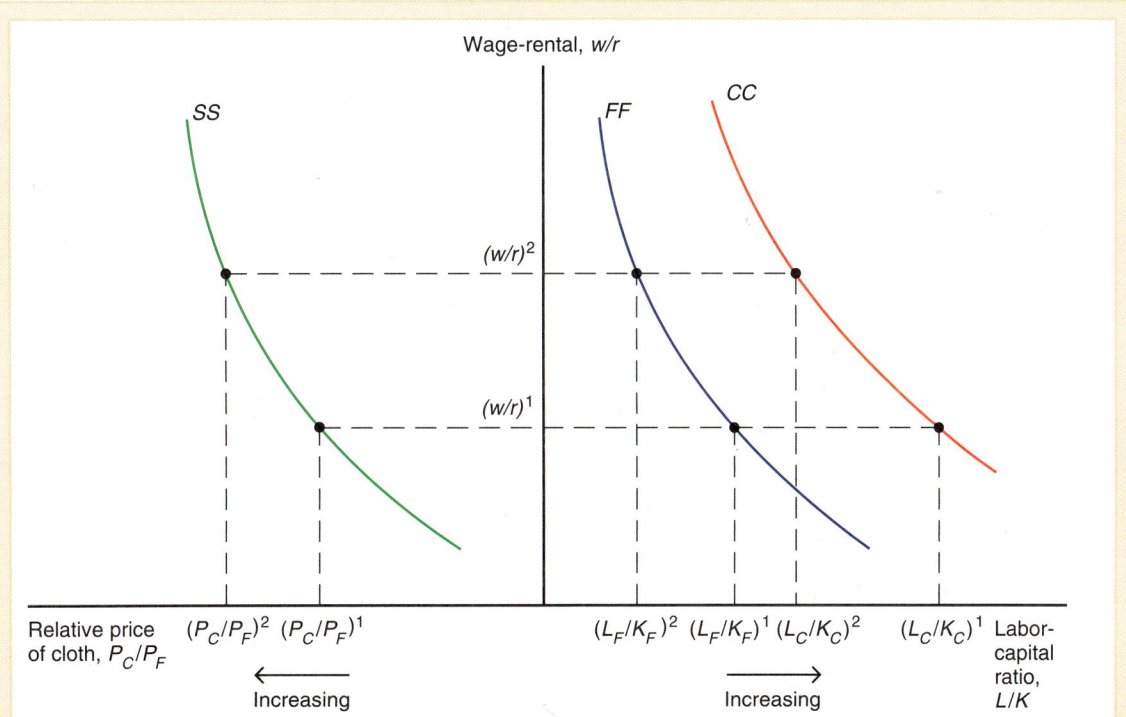

FIGURE 5-7

From Goods Prices to Input Choices

Given the relative price of cloth $(P_C/P_F)^1$, the ratio of the wage rate to the capital rental rate must equal $(w/r)^1$. This wage-rental ratio then implies that the ratios of labor to capital employed in the production of cloth and food must be $(L_C/K_C)^1$ and $(L_F/K_F)^1$. If the relative price of cloth rises to $(P_C/P_F)^2$, the wage-rental ratio must rise to $(w/r)^2$. This will cause the labor-capital ratio used in the production of both goods to drop.

Figure 5-5. By putting these two diagrams together, we see what may seem at first to be a surprising linkage of the prices of goods to the ratio of labor to capital used in the production of each good. Suppose the relative price of cloth is $(P_C/P_F)^1$ (left panel of Figure 5-7); if the economy produces both goods, the ratio of the wage rate to the capital rental rate must equal $(w/r)^1$. This ratio then implies that the ratios of labor to capital employed in the production of cloth and food must be $(L_C/K_C)^1$ and $(L_F/K_F)^1$, respectively (right panel of Figure 5-7). If the relative price of cloth were to rise to the level indicated by $(P_C/P_F)^2$, the ratio of the wage rate to the capital rental rate would rise to $(w/r)^2$. Because labor is now relatively more expensive, the ratios of labor to capital employed in the production of cloth and food would therefore drop to $(L_C/K_C)^2$ and $(L_F/K_F)^2$.

We can learn one more important lesson from this diagram. The left panel already tells us that an increase in the price of cloth relative to that of food will raise the income of workers relative to that of capital owners. But it is possible to make a stronger statement: Such a change in relative prices will unambiguously raise the purchasing power of workers and lower the purchasing power of capital owners by raising real wages and lowering real rents in terms of *both* goods.

How do we know this? When P_C/P_F increases, the ratio of labor to capital falls in both cloth and food production. But in a competitive economy, factors of production are paid their marginal product—the real wage of workers in terms of cloth is equal to the marginal productivity of labor in cloth production, and so on. When the ratio of labor to capital falls in producing either good, the marginal product of labor in terms of that good increases—so workers find their real wage higher in terms of both goods. On the other hand, the marginal product of capital falls in both industries, so capital owners find their real incomes lower in terms of both goods.

In this model, then, as in the specific factors model, changes in relative prices have strong effects on income distribution. Not only does a change in the prices of goods change the distribution of income; it always changes it so much that owners of one factor of production gain while owners of the other are made worse off.[4]

Resources and Output

We can now complete the description of a two-factor economy by describing the relationship between goods prices, factor supplies, and output. In particular, we investigate how changes in resources (the total supply of a factor) affect the allocation of factors across sectors and the associated changes in output produced.

Suppose we take the relative price of cloth as given. We know from Figure 5-7 that a given relative price of cloth, say $(P_C/P_F)^1$, is associated with a fixed wage-rental ratio $(w/r)^1$ (so long as both cloth and food are produced). That ratio, in turn, determines the ratios of labor to capital employed in both the cloth and the food sectors: $(L_C/K_C)^1$ and $(L_F/K_F)^1$, respectively. Now we assume that the economy's labor force grows, which implies that the economy's aggregate labor to capital ratio, L/K, increases. At the given relative price of cloth $(P_C/P_F)^1$, we just saw that the ratios of labor to capital employed in both sectors remain constant. How can the economy accommodate the increase in the aggregate relative supply of labor

---

[4] This relationship between goods prices and factor prices (and the associated welfare effects) was clarified in a classic paper by Wolfgang Stolper and Paul Samuelson, "Protection and Real Wages," *Review of Economic Studies* 9 (November 1941), pp. 58–73, and is therefore known as the *Stolper-Samuelson effect.*

FIGURE 5-8

Resources and Production Possibilities

An increase in the supply of labor shifts the economy's production possibility frontier outward from TT^1 to TT^2, but does so disproportionately in the direction of cloth production. The result is that at an unchanged relative price of cloth (indicated by the slope $-P_C/P_F$), food production actually declines from Q_F^1 to Q_F^2.

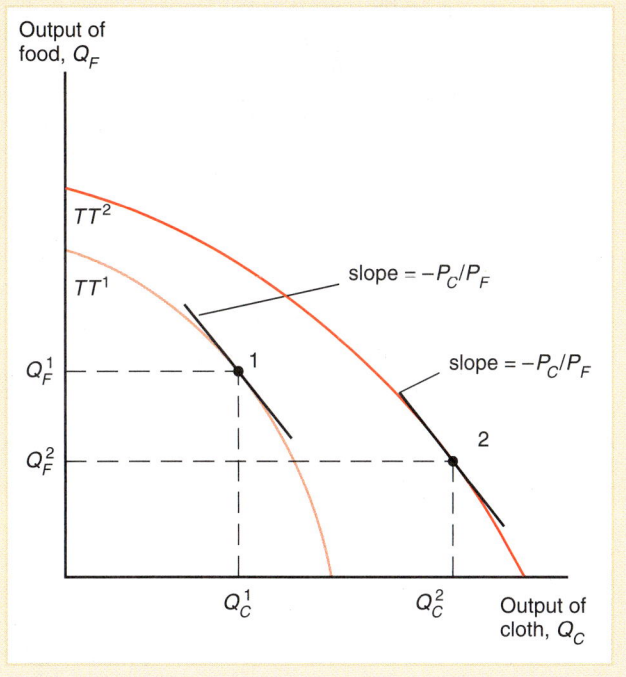

L/K if the relative labor demanded in each sector remains constant at $(L_C/K_C)^1$ and $(L_F/K_F)^1$? In other words, how does the economy employ the additional labor hours? The answer lies in the allocation of labor and capital across sectors: The labor-capital ratio in the cloth sector is higher than that in the food sector, so the economy can increase the employment of labor to capital (holding the labor-capital ratio fixed in each sector) by allocating more labor and capital to the production of cloth (which is labor-intensive).[5] As labor and capital move from the food sector to the cloth sector, the economy produces more cloth and less food.

The best way to think about this result is in terms of how resources affect the economy's production possibilities. In Figure 5-8, the curve TT^1 represents the economy's production possibilities before the increase in labor supply. Output is at point 1, where the slope of the production possibility frontier equals minus the relative price of cloth, $-P_C/P_F$, and the economy produces Q_C^1 and Q_F^1 of cloth and food. The curve TT^2 shows the production possibility frontier after an increase in the labor supply. The production possibility frontier shifts out to TT^2. After this increase, the economy can produce more of both cloth and food than before. The outward shift of the frontier is, however, much larger in the direction of cloth than of food—that is, there is a **biased expansion of production possibilities,** which occurs when the production possibility frontier shifts out much more in one direction than in the other. In this case, the expansion is so strongly biased toward cloth production that at unchanged relative prices, production moves from point 1 to point 2, which involves an actual fall in food output from Q_F^1 to Q_F^2 and a large increase in cloth output from Q_C^1 to Q_C^2.

---

[5]See the appendix for a more formal derivation of this result and additional details.

The biased effect of increases in resources on production possibilities is the key to understanding how differences in resources give rise to international trade.[6] An increase in the supply of labor expands production possibilities disproportionately in the direction of cloth production, while an increase in the supply of capital expands them disproportionately in the direction of food production. Thus, an economy with a high relative supply of labor to capital will be relatively better at producing cloth than an economy with a low relative supply of labor to capital. *Generally, an economy will tend to be relatively effective at producing goods that are intensive in the factors with which the country is relatively well endowed.*

We will further see below some empirical evidence confirming that changes in a country's resources lead to growth that is biased toward the sectors that intensively use the factor whose supply has increased. We document this for the Chinese economy, which has recently experienced substantial growth in its supply of skilled labor.

Effects of International Trade between Two-Factor Economies

Having outlined the production structure of a two-factor economy, we can now look at what happens when two such economies, Home and Foreign, trade. As always, Home and Foreign are similar along many dimensions. They have the same tastes and therefore have identical relative demands for food and cloth when faced with the same relative prices of the two goods. They also have the same technology: A given amount of labor and capital yields the same output of either cloth or food in the two countries. The only difference between the countries is in their resources: Home has a higher ratio of labor to capital than Foreign does.

Relative Prices and the Pattern of Trade

Since Home has a higher ratio of labor to capital than Foreign, Home is *labor-abundant* and Foreign is *capital-abundant*. Note that abundance is defined in terms of a ratio and not in absolute quantities. For example, the total number of workers in the United States is roughly three times higher than that in Mexico, but Mexico would still be considered labor-abundant relative to the United States since the U.S. capital stock is more than three times higher than the capital stock in Mexico. "Abundance" is always defined in relative terms, by comparing the ratio of labor to capital in the two countries; thus no country is abundant in everything.

Since cloth is the labor-intensive good, Home's production possibility frontier relative to Foreign's is shifted out more in the direction of cloth than in the direction of food. Thus, other things equal, Home tends to produce a higher ratio of cloth to food.

Because trade leads to a convergence of relative prices, one of the other things that will be equal is the price of cloth relative to that of food. Because the countries differ in their factor abundances, however, for any given ratio of the price of cloth to that of food, Home will produce a higher ratio of cloth to food than Foreign will: Home will have a larger *relative supply* of cloth. Home's relative supply curve, then, lies to the right of Foreign's.

---

[6] The biased effect of resource changes on production was pointed out in a paper by the Polish economist T. M. Rybczynski, "Factor Endowments and Relative Commodity Prices," *Economica* 22 (November 1955), pp. 336–341. It is therefore known as the *Rybczynski effect.*

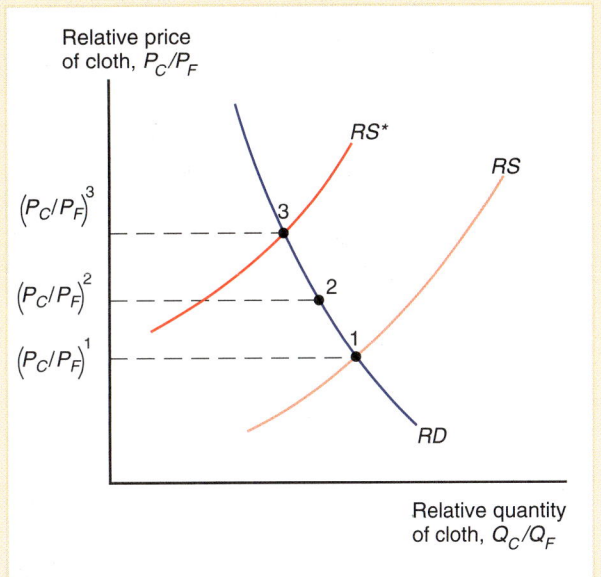

FIGURE 5-9

Trade Leads to a Convergence of Relative Prices

In the absence of trade, Home's equilibrium would be at point 1, where domestic relative supply *RS* intersects the relative demand curve *RD*. Similarly, Foreign's equilibrium would be at point 3. Trade leads to a world relative price that lies between the pretrade prices $(P_C/P_F)^1$ and $(P_C/P_F)^3$, such as $(P_C/P_F)^2$ at point 2.

The relative supply schedules of Home (*RS*) and Foreign (*RS**) are illustrated in Figure 5-9. The relative demand curve, which we have assumed to be the same for both countries, is shown as *RD*. If there were no international trade, the equilibrium for Home would be at point 1, and the relative price of cloth would be $(P_C/P_F)^1$. The equilibrium for Foreign would be at point 3, with a relative price of cloth given by $(P_C/P_F)^3$. Thus, in the absence of trade, the relative price of cloth would be lower in Home than in Foreign.

When Home and Foreign trade with each other, their relative prices converge. The relative price of cloth rises in Home and declines in Foreign, and a new world relative price of cloth is established at a point somewhere between the pretrade relative prices, say at $(P_C/P_F)^2$. In Chapter 4, we discussed how an economy responds to trade based on the direction of the change in the relative price of the goods: The economy exports the good whose relative price increases. Thus, Home will export cloth (the relative price of cloth rises in Home), while Foreign will export food. (The relative price of cloth declines in Foreign, which means that the relative price of food rises there).

Home becomes an exporter of cloth because it is labor-abundant (relative to Foreign) and because the production of cloth is labor-intensive (relative to food production). Similarly, Foreign becomes an exporter of food because it is capital-abundant and because the production of food is capital-intensive. These predictions for the pattern of trade (in the two-good, two-factor, two-country version that we have studied) can be generalized as the following theorem, named after the original developers of this model of trade:

Hecksher-Ohlin Theorem: *The country that is abundant in a factor exports the good whose production is intensive in that factor.*

In the more realistic case with multiple countries, factors of production, and numbers of goods, we can generalize this result as a correlation between a country's abundance in a factor and its exports of goods that use that factor intensively: *Countries tend to export goods whose production is intensive in factors with which the countries are abundantly endowed.*[7]

Trade and the Distribution of Income

We have just discussed how trade induces a convergence of relative prices. Previously, we saw that changes in relative prices, in turn, have strong effects on the relative earnings of labor and capital. A rise in the price of cloth raises the purchasing power of labor in terms of both goods while lowering the purchasing power of capital in terms of both goods. A rise in the price of food has the reverse effect. Thus, international trade can have a powerful effect on the distribution of income, even in the long run. In Home, where the relative price of cloth rises, people who get their incomes from labor gain from trade, but those who derive their incomes from capital are made worse off. In Foreign, where the relative price of cloth falls, the opposite happens: Laborers are made worse off and capital owners are made better off.

The resource of which a country has a relatively large supply (labor in Home, capital in Foreign) is the **abundant factor** in that country, and the resource of which it has a relatively small supply (capital in Home, labor in Foreign) is the **scarce factor.** The general conclusion about the income distribution effects of international trade in the long run is: *Owners of a country's abundant factors gain from trade, but owners of a country's scarce factors lose.*

In our analysis of the specific factors case, we found that factors of production that are "stuck" in an import-competing industry lose from the opening of trade. Here, we find that factors of production that are used intensively by the import-competing industry are hurt by the opening of trade—regardless of the industry in which they are employed. Still, the theoretical argument regarding the aggregate gains from trade is identical to the specific factors case: Opening to trade expands an economy's consumption possibilities (see Figure 4-11), so there is a way to make everybody better off. However, one crucial difference exists regarding the income distribution effects in these two models. The specificity of factors to particular industries is often only a temporary problem: Garment makers cannot become computer manufacturers overnight, but given time the U.S. economy can shift its manufacturing employment from declining sectors to expanding ones. Thus, income distribution effects that arise because labor and other factors of production are immobile represent a temporary, transitional problem (which is not to say that such effects are not painful to those who lose). In contrast, effects of trade on the distribution of income among land, labor, and capital are more or less permanent.

Compared with the rest of the world, the United States is abundantly endowed with highly skilled labor while low-skilled labor is correspondingly scarce. This means that international trade has the potential to make low-skilled workers in the United States worse off—not just temporarily, but on a sustained basis. The negative effect of trade on low-skilled workers poses a persistent political problem, one that cannot be remedied by policies that provide temporary relief (such as unemployment insurance). Consequently, the potential effect of increased trade on income inequality in advanced economies such as the United States has been the subject of a large amount of empirical research. We review some of that evidence in the case study that follows, and conclude that trade has been, at most, a contributing factor to the measured increases in income inequality in the United States.

---

[7]See Alan Deardorff, "The General Validity of the Heckscher-Ohlin Theorem," *American Economic Review* 72 (September 1982), pp. 683–694, for a formal derivation of this extension to multiple goods, factors, and countries.

North-South Trade and Income Inequality

The distribution of wages in the United States has become considerably more unequal since the 1970s. In 1970, a male worker with a wage at the 90th percentile of the wage distribution (earning more than the bottom 90 percent but less than the top 10 percent of wage earners) earned 3.2 times the wage of a male worker at the bottom 10th percentile of the distribution. By 2010, that worker at the 90th percentile earned more than 5.2 times the wage of the worker at the bottom 10th percentile. Wage inequality for female workers has increased at a similar rate over that same timespan. Much of this increase in wage inequality was associated with a rise in the premium attached to education, especially since the 1980s. In 1980, a worker with a college degree earned 40 percent more than a worker with just a high school education. This education premium rose steadily through the 1980s and 1990s to 80 percent. Since then, it has been roughly flat (though wage disparities among college graduates continued rising).

Why has wage inequality increased? Many observers attribute the change to the growth of world trade and in particular to the growing exports of manufactured goods from newly industrializing economies (NIEs) such as South Korea and China. Until the 1970s, trade between advanced industrial nations and less-developed economies—often referred to as "North-South" trade because most advanced nations are still in the temperate zone of the Northern Hemisphere—consisted overwhelmingly of an exchange of Northern manufactures for Southern raw materials and agricultural goods, such as oil and coffee. From 1970 onward, however, former raw material exporters increasingly began to sell manufactured goods to high-wage countries like the United States. As we learned in Chapter 2, developing countries have dramatically changed the kinds of goods they export, moving away from their traditional reliance on agricultural and mineral products to a focus on manufactured goods. While NIEs also provided a rapidly growing market for exports from the high-wage nations, the exports of the newly industrializing economies obviously differed greatly in factor intensity from their imports. Overwhelmingly, NIE exports to advanced nations consisted of clothing, shoes, and other relatively unsophisticated products ("low-tech goods") whose production is intensive in unskilled labor, while advanced-country exports to the NIEs consisted of capital- or skill-intensive goods such as chemicals and aircraft ("high-tech goods").

To many observers, the conclusion seemed straightforward: What was happening was a move toward factor-price equalization. Trade between advanced countries that are abundant in capital and skill and NIEs with their abundant supply of unskilled labor was raising the wages of highly skilled workers and lowering the wages of less-skilled workers in the skill- and capital-abundant countries, just as the factor-proportions model predicts.

This is an argument with much more than purely academic significance. If one regards the growing inequality of income in advanced nations as a serious problem, as many people do, and if one also believes that growing world trade is the main cause of that problem, it becomes difficult to maintain economists' traditional support for free trade. (As we have previously argued, in principle, taxes and government payments can offset the effect of trade on income distribution, but one may argue that this is unlikely to happen in practice.) Some influential commentators have argued that advanced nations will have to restrict their trade with low-wage countries if they want to remain basically middle-class societies.

While some economists believe that growing trade with low-wage countries has been the main cause of rising income inequality in the United States, most empirical researchers believed at the time of this writing that international trade has been at most a contributing factor to that growth, and that the main causes lie elsewhere.[8] This skepticism rests on three main observations.

First, the factor-proportions model says that international trade affects income distribution via a change in relative prices of goods. So if international trade was the main driving force behind growing income inequality, there ought to be clear evidence of a rise in the prices of skill-intensive products compared with those of unskilled-labor-intensive goods. Studies of international price data, however, have failed to find clear evidence of such a change in relative prices.

Second, the model predicts that relative factor prices should converge: If wages of skilled workers are rising and those of unskilled workers are falling in the skill-abundant country, the reverse should be happening in the labor-abundant country. Studies of income distribution in developing countries that have opened themselves to trade have shown that at least in some cases, the reverse is true. In Mexico, in particular, careful studies have shown that the transformation of the country's trade in the late 1980s—when Mexico opened itself to imports and became a major exporter of manufactured goods—was accompanied by rising wages for skilled workers and growing overall wage inequality, closely paralleling developments in the United States.

Third, although trade between advanced countries and NIEs has grown rapidly, it still constitutes only a small percentage of total spending in the advanced nations. As a result, estimates of the "factor content" of this trade—the skilled labor exported, in effect, by advanced countries embodied in skill-intensive exports and the unskilled labor, in effect, imported in labor-intensive imports—are still only a small fraction of the total supplies of skilled and unskilled labor. This suggests that these trade flows couldn't have had a very large impact on income distribution.

What, then, *is* responsible for the growing gap between skilled and unskilled workers in the United States? The view of the majority is that the villain is not trade but rather new production technologies that put a greater emphasis on worker skills (such as the widespread introduction of computers and other advanced technologies in the workplace). This is often referred to as a technology-skill complementarity or **skill-biased technological change**.[9]

We discuss the links between this type of technological change and rising wage inequality in the following case study.

---

[8]Among the important entries in the discussion of the impact of trade on income distribution have been Robert Lawrence and Matthew Slaughter, "Trade and U.S. Wages: Giant Sucking Sound or Small Hiccup?" *Brookings Papers on Economic Activity: Microeconomic* 2 (1993), pp. 161–226; Jeffrey D. Sachs and Howard Shatz, "Trade and Jobs in U.S. Manufacturing," *Brookings Papers on Economic Activity* 1 (1994), pp. 1–84; and Adrian Wood, *North-South Trade, Employment, and Income Inequality* (Oxford: Oxford University Press, 1994). For a survey of this debate and related issues, see Chapter 9 in Lawrence Edwards and Robert Z. Lawrence, *Rising Tide: Is Growth in Emerging Economies Good for the United States?* (Peterson Institute for International Economics, 2013).

[9]See Claudia Goldin and Lawrence F. Katz, "The Origins of Technology-Skill Complementarity," *The Quarterly Journal of Economics* (1998), pp. 693–732.

CASE STUDY Skill-Biased Technological Change and Income Inequality

In this case study, we extend our two-factor production model to incorporate technological change that is skill-biased. We discuss how this provides a much better fit for the empirical patterns associated with rising wage inequality in the United States. We also describe some new research that links back portions of this technological change to trade and outsourcing.

Consider the variant of our two good, two factor model where skilled and unskilled labor are used to produce "high-tech" and "low-tech" goods. Figure 5-10 shows the relative factor demands for producers in both sectors: the ratio of skilled-unskilled workers employed as a function of the skilled-unskilled wage ratio (*LL* curve for low-tech and *HH* for high-tech).

We have assumed that production of high-tech goods is skilled-labor intensive, so the HH curve is shifted out relative to the LL curve. In the background, an SS curve

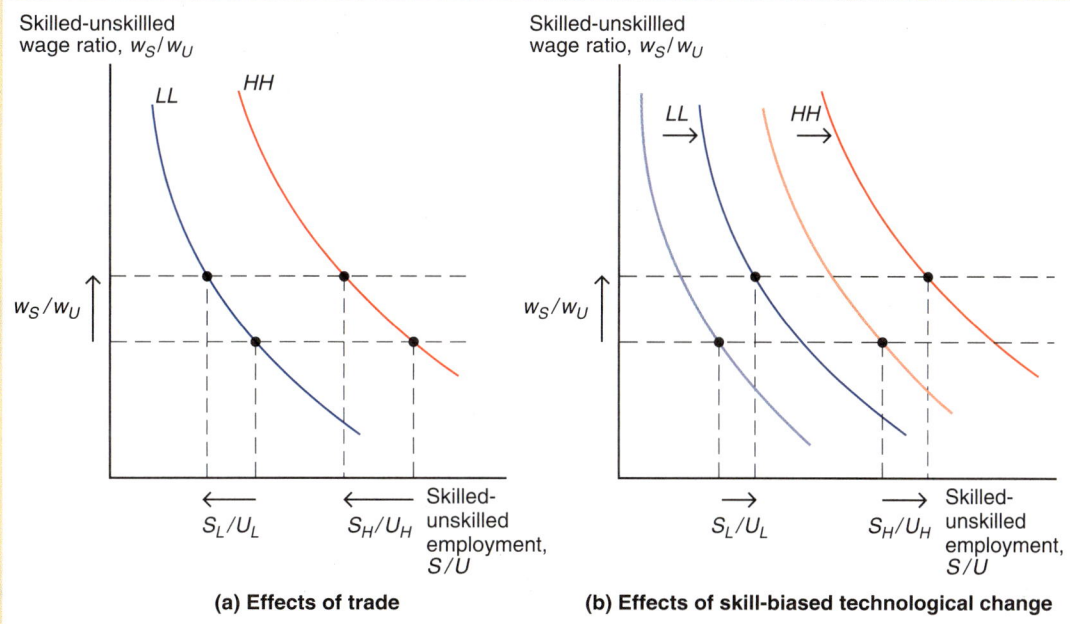

FIGURE 5-10

Increased Wage Inequality: Trade- or Skill-Biased Technological Change?

The *LL* and *HH* curves show the skilled-unskilled employment ratio, S/U, as a function of the skilled-unskilled wage ratio, w_S/w_U, in the low-tech and high-tech sectors. The high-tech sector is more skill-intensive than the low-tech sector, so the *HH* curve is shifted out relative to the *LL* curve. Panel (a) shows the case where increased trade with developing countries leads to a higher skilled-unskilled wage ratio. Producers in both sectors respond by *decreasing* their relative employment of skilled workers: S_L/U_L and S_H/U_H both decrease. Panel (b) shows the case where skill-biased technological change leads to a higher skilled-unskilled wage ratio. The *LL* and *HH* curves shift out (increased relative demand for skilled workers in both sectors). However, in this case producers in both sectors respond by *increasing* their relative employment of skilled workers: S_L/U_L and S_H/U_H both increase.

(see Figures 5-6 and 5-7) determines the skilled-unskilled wage ratio as an increasing function of the relative price of high-tech goods (with respect to low-tech goods).

In panel (a), we show the case where increased trade with developing countries generates an increase in wage inequality (the skilled-unskilled wage ratio) in those countries (via an increase in the relative price of high-tech goods). The increase in the relative cost of skilled workers induces producers in both sectors to *reduce* their employment of skilled workers relative to unskilled workers.

In panel (b), we show the case where technological change in both sectors generates an increase in wage inequality. This technology change is classified as "skill-biased" because it shifts out the relative demand for skilled workers in both sectors (both the *LL* and the *HH* curves shift out). It also induces larger productivity gains in the high-tech sector due to its complementarity with skilled workers. Thus, for any given relative price of high-tech goods, the technology change is associated with a higher skilled-unskilled wage ratio (the SS curve shifts). Even though skilled labor is relatively more expensive, producers in both sectors respond to the technological change by *increasing* their employment of skilled workers relative to unskilled workers. (Note that the trade explanation in panel (a) predicts an opposite response for employment in both sectors.)

We can now examine the relative merits of the trade versus skill-biased technological change explanations for the increase in wage inequality by looking at the changes in the skilled-unskilled employment ratio within sectors in the United States. A widespread increase in these employment ratios for all different kinds of sectors (both skilled-labor-intensive and unskilled-labor-intensive sectors) in the U.S. economy points to the skill-biased technological explanation. This is exactly what has been observed in the United States over the last half-century.

In Figure 5-11, sectors are separated into four groups based on their skill intensity. U.S. firms do not report their employment in terms of skill but use a related categorization of production and non-production workers. With a few exceptions, non-production positions require higher levels of education—and so we measure the skilled-unskilled employment ratio in a sector as the ratio of non-production employment to production employment.[10] Sectors with the highest non-production to production employment ratios are classified as most skill-intensive. Each quadrant of Figure 5-11 shows the evolution of this employment ratio over time for each group of sectors (the average employment ratio across all sectors in the group). Although there are big differences in average skill intensity across the groups, we clearly see that the employment ratios are increasing over time for all four groups. This widespread increase across most sectors of the U.S. economy is one of the main pieces of evidence pointing to the technology explanation for the increases in U.S. wage inequality.

Yet, even though most economists agree that skill-biased technological change has occurred, recent research has uncovered some new ways in which trade has been an indirect contributor to the associated increases in wage inequality, by accelerating this process of technological change. These explanations are based on the principle that firms have a choice of production methods that is influenced by openness to trade and foreign investment. For example, some studies show that firms that begin to export also upgrade to more skill-intensive production

---

[10]On average, the wage of a non-production worker is 60 percent higher than that of a production worker.

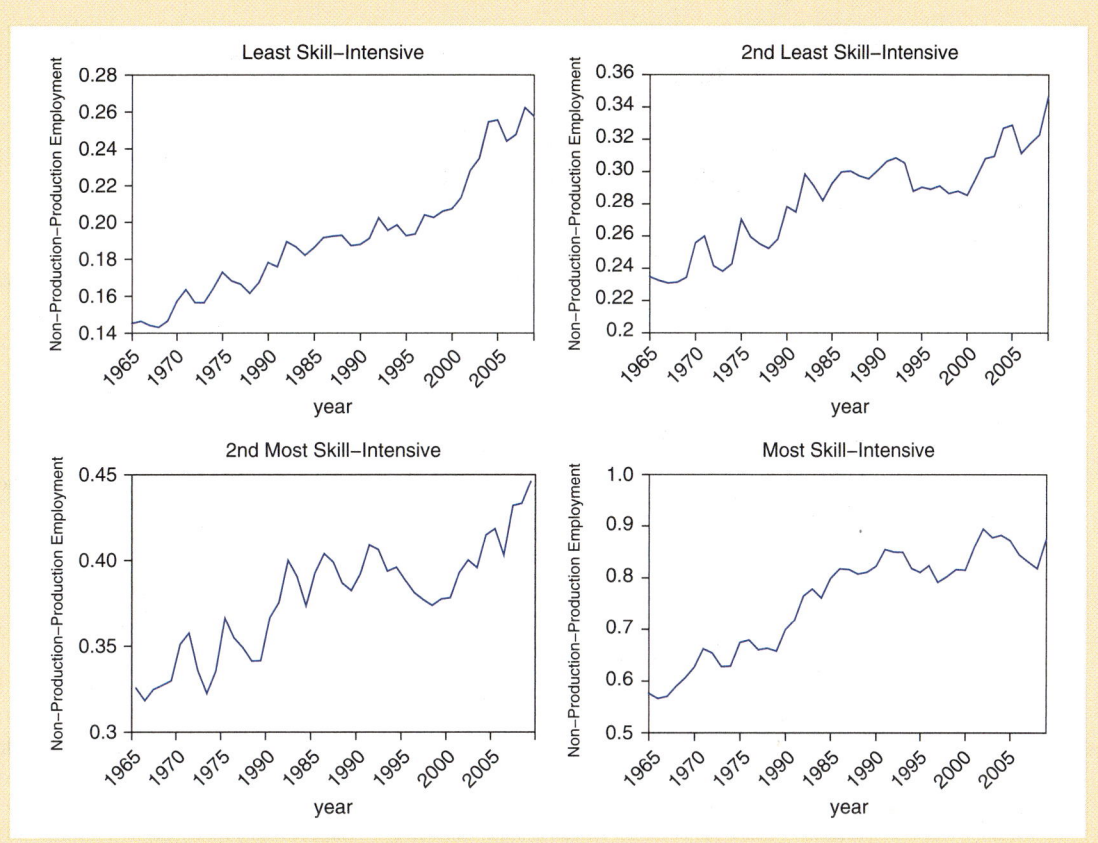

FIGURE 5-11

Evolution of U.S. Non-Production–Production Employment Ratios in Four Groups of Sectors

Sectors are grouped based on their skill intensity. The non-production–production employment ratio has increased over time in all four sector groups.

Source: NBER-CES Manufacturing Productivity Database

technologies. Trade liberalization can then generate widespread technological change by inducing a large proportion of firms to make such technology-upgrade choices.

Another example is related to foreign outsourcing and the liberalization of trade and foreign investment. In particular, the NAFTA treaty (see Chapter 2) between the United States, Canada, and Mexico has made it substantially easier for firms to move different parts of their production processes (research and development, component production, assembly, marketing) across different locations in North America. Because production worker wages are substantially lower in Mexico, U.S. firms have an incentive to move the processes that use production workers more intensively to Mexico (such as component production and assembly). The processes that rely more intensively on higher-skilled, non-production workers (such as research and development and marketing) tend to stay in the United States (or Canada). From the U.S. perspective, this break-up of the production process increases the relative demand for skilled workers and is very similar to skill-biased technological change. One study finds that this outsourcing process from the United States to Mexico can explain

21 to 27 percent of the increase in the wage premium between non-production and production workers.[11]

Thus, some of the observed skill-biased technological change, and its effect on increased wage inequality, can be traced back to increased openness to trade and foreign investment. And, as we have mentioned, increases in wage inequality in advanced economies are a genuine concern. However, the use of trade restrictions targeted at limiting technological innovations—because those innovations favor relatively higher-skilled workers—is particularly problematic: Those innovations also bring substantial aggregate gains (along with the standard gains from trade) that would then be foregone. Consequently, economists favor longer-term policies that ease the skill-acquisition process for all workers so that the gains from the technological innovations can be spread as widely as possible.

---

[11]See Robert Feenstra and Gordon Hanson, "The Impact of Outsourcing and High-Technology Capital on Wages: Estimates for the United States, 1979–1990," *Quarterly Journal of Economics* 144 (August 1999), pp. 907–940.

Factor-Price Equalization

In the absence of trade, labor would earn less in Home than in Foreign, and capital would earn more. Without trade, labor-abundant Home would have a lower relative price of cloth than capital-abundant Foreign, and the difference in relative prices of *goods* implies an even larger difference in the relative prices of *factors*.

When Home and Foreign trade, the relative prices of goods converge. This convergence, in turn, causes convergence of the relative prices of capital and labor. Thus, there is clearly a tendency toward **equalization of factor prices.** How far does this tendency go?

The surprising answer is that in the model, the tendency goes all the way. International trade leads to complete equalization of factor prices. Although Home has a higher ratio of labor to capital than Foreign, once they trade with each other, the wage rate and the capital rent rate are the same in both countries. To see this, refer back to Figure 5-6, which shows that given the prices of cloth and food, we can determine the wage rate and the rental rate without reference to the supplies of capital and labor. If Home and Foreign face the same relative prices of cloth and food, they will also have the same factor prices.

To understand how this equalization occurs, we have to realize that when Home and Foreign trade with each other, more is happening than a simple exchange of goods. In an indirect way, the two countries are in effect trading factors of production. Home lets Foreign use some of its abundant labor, not by selling the labor directly but by trading goods produced with a high ratio of labor to capital for goods produced with a low labor-capital ratio. The goods that Home sells require more labor to produce than the goods it receives in return; that is, more labor is *embodied* in Home's exports than in its imports. Thus Home exports its labor, embodied in its labor-intensive exports. Conversely, since Foreign's exports embody more capital than its imports, Foreign is indirectly exporting its capital. When viewed this way, it is not surprising that trade leads to equalization of the two countries' factor prices.

Although this view of trade is simple and appealing, there is a major problem with it: In the real world, factor prices are *not* equalized. For example, there is an extremely wide range of wage rates across countries (Table 5-1). While some of these differences

TABLE 5-1	Comparative International Wage Rates (United States = 100)
Country	Hourly Compensation of Production Workers, 2011
United States	100
Germany	133
Japan	101
Spain	80
South Korea	53
Brazil	33
Mexico	18
China*	4

*2008

Source: Bureau of Labor Statistics, *Foreign Labor Statistics Home Page.*

may reflect differences in the quality of labor, they are too wide to be explained away on this basis alone.

To understand why the model doesn't give us an accurate prediction, we need to look at its assumptions. Three assumptions crucial to the prediction of factor-price equalization are in reality certainly untrue. These are the assumptions that (1) technologies are the same; (2) costless trade equalizes the prices of goods in the two countries; and (3) both countries produce both goods.

1. The proposition that trade equalizes factor prices will not hold if countries have different technologies of production. For example, a country with superior technology might have both a higher wage rate and a higher rental rate than a country with an inferior technology.

2. Complete factor-price equalization also depends on complete convergence of the prices of goods. In the real world, prices of goods are not fully equalized by international trade. This lack of convergence is due to both natural barriers (such as transportation costs) and barriers to trade such as tariffs, import quotas, and other restrictions.

3. Even if all countries use the same technologies and face the same goods prices, factor price equalization still depends on the assumption that countries produce the same set of goods. We assumed this when we derived the wage and rental rates from the prices of cloth and food in Figure 5-6. However, countries may be induced to specialize in the production of different goods. A country with a very high ratio of labor to capital might produce only cloth, while a country with a very high ratio of capital to labor might produce only food. This implies that factor-price equalization occurs only if the countries involved are sufficiently similar in their relative factor endowments. (A more thorough discussion of this point is given in the appendix to this chapter.) Thus, factor prices need not be equalized between countries with radically different ratios of capital to labor or of skilled to unskilled labor.

Empirical Evidence on the Heckscher-Ohlin Model

The essence of the Heckscher-Ohlin model is that trade is driven by differences in factor abundance across countries. We just saw how this leads to the natural prediction that goods trade is substituting for factor trade, and hence that goods trade across countries should *embody* those factor differences. This prediction, based on the **factor content of trade,** is very powerful and can be tested empirically. However, we will see that the empirical success of this strict test is very limited—mainly due to the same reasons that undermine the prediction for factor-price equalization. Does this mean that differences in factor abundance do *not* help explain the observed patterns of trade across countries? Not at all. First, we will show that relaxing the assumptions generating factor price equalization vastly improves the predictive success for the factor content of trade. Second, we will look directly at the pattern of goods traded between developed and developing countries—and we will see how well they fit with the predictions of the Heckscher-Ohlin model.

Trade in Goods as a Substitute for Trade in Factors: Factor Content of Trade

Tests on U.S. Data Until recently, and to some extent even now, the United States has been a special case among countries. Until a few years ago, the United States was much wealthier than other countries, and U.S. workers visibly worked with more capital per person than their counterparts in other countries. Even now, although some Western European countries and Japan have caught up, the United States continues to be high on the scale of countries as ranked by capital-labor ratios.

One would then expect the United States to be an exporter of capital-intensive goods and an importer of labor-intensive goods. Surprisingly, however, this was not the case in the 25 years after World War II. In a famous study published in 1953, economist Wassily Leontief (winner of the Nobel Prize in 1973) found that U.S. exports were less capital-intensive than U.S. imports.[12] This result is known as the **Leontief paradox.**

Table 5-2 illustrates the Leontief paradox as well as other information about U.S. trade patterns. We compare the factors of production used to produce $1 million worth of 1962 U.S. exports with those used to produce the same value of 1962 U.S. imports. As the first two lines in the table show, Leontief's paradox was still present in that year: U.S. exports were produced with a lower ratio of capital to labor than U.S. imports. As the rest of the table shows, however, other comparisons of imports and exports are more in line with what one might expect. The United States exported products that were more *skilled*-labor-intensive than its imports, as measured by average years of education. We also tended to export products that were

TABLE 5-2	Factor Content of U.S. Exports and Imports for 1962	
	Imports	**Exports**
Capital per million dollars	$2,132,000	$1,876,000
Labor (person-years) per million dollars	119	131
Capital-labor ratio (dollars per worker)	$17,916	$14,321
Average years of education per worker	9.9	10.1
Proportion of engineers and scientists in work force	0.0189	0.0255

Source: Robert Baldwin, "Determinants of the Commodity Structure of U.S. Trade," *American Economic Review* 61 (March 1971), pp. 126–145.

---

[12]See Wassily Leontief, "Domestic Production and Foreign Trade: The American Capital Position Re-Examined," *Proceedings of the American Philosophical Society* 7 (September 1953), pp. 331–349.

"technology-intensive," requiring more scientists and engineers per unit of sales. These observations are consistent with the position of the United States as a high-skill country, with a comparative advantage in sophisticated products. Why then do we observe the Leontief paradox? Is it limited to the United States and/or the types of factors considered? The short answer is no.

Tests on Global Data   A study by Harry P. Bowen, Edward E. Leamer, and Leo Sveikauskas[13] extended Leontief's predictions for the factor content of trade to 27 countries and 12 factors of production. Based on the factor content of a country's exports and imports, they checked whether a country was a net exporter of a factor of production whenever it was relatively abundantly endowed with that factor (and conversely, whether the country was a net importer for the other factors). They assessed factor abundance by comparing a country's endowment of a factor (as a share of the world's supply of that factor) with the country's share of world GDP. For example, the United States has about 25 percent of world income in 2011 but only about 5 percent of the world's workers. This yields Leontief's original prediction that the factor content of U.S. trade should show net imports of labor. Bowen et al., tallied the success/failure of this sign test across the 27 countries and 12 factors in their study. They ended up with a success rate of only 61 percent—not much better than what one would obtain from a random coin toss! In other words, the factor content of trade ran in the opposite direction to the prediction of the factor proportions theory in 39 percent of the cases.

These results confirmed that the Leontief paradox was not an isolated case. However, this negative empirical performance is perhaps not surprising—given that it represents a demanding test of a theory that also predicts factor price equalization (which is clearly at odds with the empirical evidence on cross-country wage differences). As we discussed, the assumption of common technology across countries plays a crucial role in delivering this prediction.

The Case of the Missing Trade   Another indication of large technology differences across countries comes from discrepancies between the observed volumes of trade and those predicted by the Heckscher-Ohlin model. In an influential paper, Daniel Trefler[14] at the University of Toronto pointed out that the Heckscher-Ohlin model can also be used to derive predictions for a country's volume of trade based on differences in that country's factor abundance with that of the rest of the world (since, in this model, trade in goods is substituting for trade in factors). In fact, factor trade turns out to be substantially smaller than the Heckscher-Ohlin model predicts.

A large part of the reason for this disparity comes from a false prediction of large-scale trade in labor between rich and poor nations. Consider our example for the United States in 2011, with 25 percent of world income but only 5 percent of the world's workers. Our simple factor-proportions theory should not only predict that U.S. trade should embody net imports of labor—but that the *volume* of those imported labor services should be huge because they need to account for the United States' very low abundance of labor relative to the rest of the world. In fact, the volume of factor content of trade between labor and capital abundant countries is several orders of magnitude smaller than the volume predicted by the factor proportions theory (based on the observed differences in factor abundance across countries).

---

[13]See Harry P. Bowen, Edward E. Leamer, and Leo Sveikauskas, "Multicountry, Multifactor Tests of the Factor Abundance Theory," *American Economic Review* 77 (December 1987), pp. 791–809.
[14]Daniel Trefler, "The Case of the Missing Trade and Other Mysteries," *American Economic Review* 85 (December 1995), pp. 1029–1046.

TABLE 5-3	Estimated Technological Efficiency, 1983 (United States = 1)
Country	
Bangladesh	0.03
Thailand	0.17
Hong Kong	0.40
Japan	0.70
West Germany	0.78

Source: Daniel Trefler, "The Case of the Missing Trade and Other Mysteries," *American Economic Review* 85 (December 1995), pp. 1029–1046.

Trefler showed that allowing for technology differences across countries helped to resolve the predictive success of both the sign test for the direction of the factor content of trade as well as the missing trade (although there was still plenty of trade left missing). The way this resolution works is roughly as follows: If workers in the United States are much more efficient than the world average, then the "effective" labor supply in the United States is correspondingly larger—and hence the expected volume of imported labor services into the United States is correspondingly lower.

If one makes the working assumption that technological differences between countries take a simple multiplicative form—that is, a given set of inputs in any country produces a multiple or fraction of the output produced in the United States—it is possible to use data on factor trade to estimate the relative efficiency of production in different countries. Table 5-3 shows Trefler's estimates for a sample of countries (the multiplicative constant relative to the United States); they suggest that technological differences are in fact very large.

A Better Empirical Fit for the Factor Content of Trade Subsequently, an important study by Donald Davis and David Weinstein at Columbia University showed that if one relaxes this assumption on common technologies along with the remaining two assumptions underlying factor price equalization (countries produce the same set of goods and costless trade equalizes goods prices), then the predictions for the direction and volume of the factor content of trade line-up substantially better with the empirical evidence—ultimately generating a good fit. Table 5-4 shows the improvement in the empirical fit, measured both by the predictive success for the sign test (the

TABLE 5-4	A Better Empirical Fit for the Factor Content of Trade			
	Assumptions Dropped*			
	None	**Drop (1)**	**Drop (1)–(2)**	**Drop (1)–(3)**
Predictive Success (sign test)	0.32	0.50	0.86	0.91
Missing Trade (observed/ predicted)	0.0005	0.008	0.19	0.69

*Assumptions: (1) common technologies across countries; (2) countries produce the same set of goods; and (3) costless trade equalizes goods prices.

Source: Don R. Davis and David Weinstein, "An Account of Global Factor Trade," *American Economic Review* (2001), pp. 1423–1453.

direction of the factor content of trade) and the missing trade ratio: the ratio of the actual volume of factor content trade to the predicted volume (if one, then there is no missing trade; as the ratio decreases below one, an increasing proportion of predicted trade is missing). For this study, the required data (which included detailed information on the technologies used by each country) was only available for two factors (labor and capital) and 10 countries.

In the first column of Table 5-4, all three assumptions behind factor price equalization are imposed (same technologies across countries, countries produce the same set of goods, and costless trade equalizes goods prices). This test is very similar to the one performed by Bowen et al., though the predictive success for the sign test is substantially worse (32 percent success versus 61 percent reported by Bowen et al.). This is due to the different sample of countries and factors considered, and data cleaning procedures based on the newly available information on production techniques. We also see the extent of the missing trade: virtually all of the predicted volume of factor trade is missing. These results confirm once more that this strict test for the Heckscher-Ohlin model performs very poorly.

The results in the second column were obtained once the assumption of common technologies was dropped, as in the study by Trefler. There is a substantial improvement in both empirical tests, although their overall predictive success is still quite weak. In the third column, the assumption that countries produce the same set of goods is also dropped. We see how this induces a massive improvement for the predictive success of the sign test for the direction of the factor content of trade (up to 86 percent success). The extent of missing trade is also vastly reduced, though the observed trade volume still represents only 19 percent of predicted trade. In the fourth and last column, the assumption of goods price equalization via costless trade is also dropped. The predictive success for the direction of trade increases further to 91 percent. At this point, we can say that the Leontief paradox is relegated to a statistical anomaly. Column four also shows a huge improvement in the extent of missing trade: the observed trade now represents 69 percent of predicted trade.

Overall, Table 5-4 highlights vast differences in the predictive success of the factor-proportions theory for the direction and volume of the factor content of trade. At one end (column one), we find virtually no support for the prediction of the Heckscher-Ohlin model; however, we also see how this failure is driven by particular assumptions built-into our "pure" Heckscher-Ohlin model. When those assumptions are dropped, we can reformulate a model of trade based on differences in factor proportions that fits the observed pattern of factor content of trade quite well (column four).

Patterns of Exports between Developed and Developing Countries

Another way to see how differences in factor proportions shape empirical trade patterns is to contrast the exports of labor-abundant, skill-scarce nations in the developing world with the exports of skill-abundant, labor-scarce nations. In our "2 by 2 by 2" theoretical model (2 goods, 2 countries, 2 factors), we obtained the Heckscher-Ohlin theorem stating that the country abundant in a factor exports the good whose production is intensive in that factor. A paper by John Romalis at the University of Sydney[15] showed how this prediction for the pattern of exports can be extended to multiple countries producing multiple goods: As a country's skill abundance increases, its exports are increasingly concentrated in sectors with higher skill intensity. We now

---

[15]John Romalis, "Factor Proportions and the Structure of Commodity Trade," *American Economic Review* 94 (March 2004), pp. 67–97.

see how this prediction holds when comparing the exports of countries at opposite ends of the skill-abundance spectrum as well as when we compare how exports change when a country such as China grows and becomes relatively more skill-abundant.

Figure 5-12 contrasts the exports of three developing countries (Bangladesh, Cambodia, and Haiti) at the lower-end of the skill-abundance spectrum with the three largest European economics (Germany, France, and United Kingdom) at the upper end of the skill-abundance spectrum. The countries' exports to the United States by sector are partitioned into four groups in increasing order of skill intensity. These are the same four sector groups used in Figure 5-11.[16] Figure 5-12 clearly shows how the exports of the three developing countries to the United States are overwhelmingly concentrated in sectors with the lowest skill-intensity. Their exports in high skill-intensity sectors are virtually nil. The contrast with the export pattern for the three European countries is apparent: The exports to the United States for those skill abundant countries are concentrated in sectors with higher skill intensity.

Changes over time also follow the predictions of the Heckscher-Ohlin model. Consider the experience of China over the last three decades, where high growth (especially in the last decade in a half) has been associated with substantial increases in skill

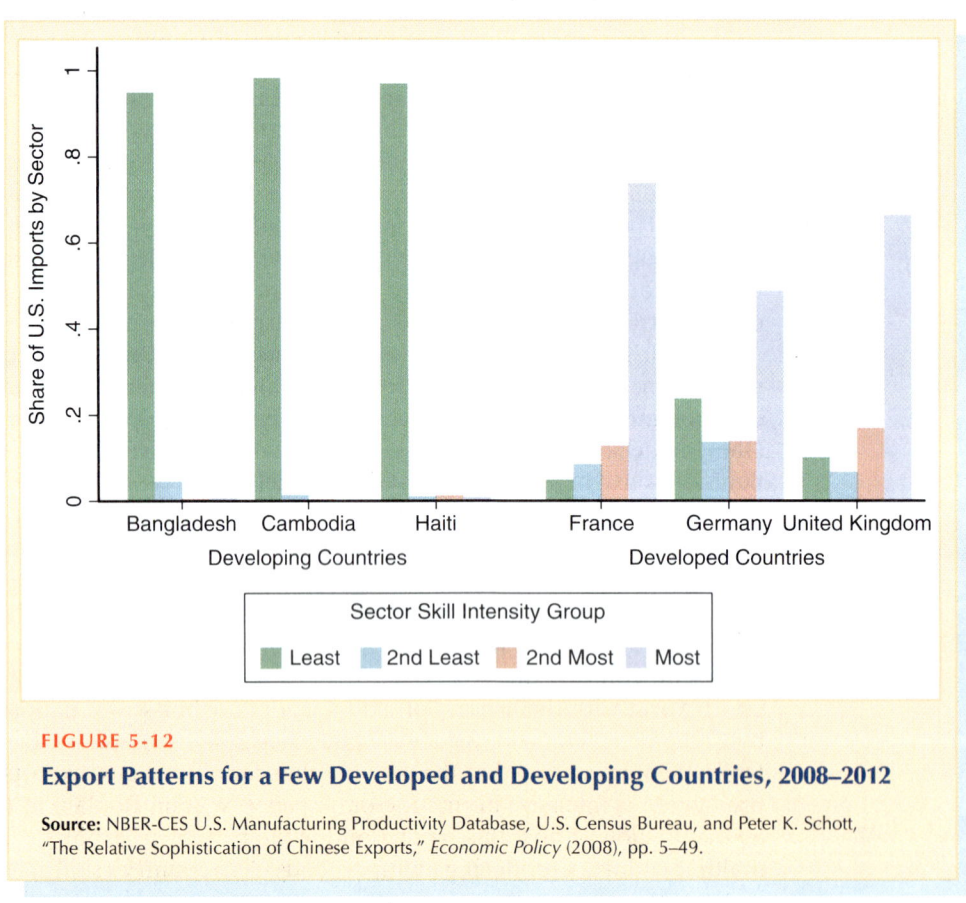

FIGURE 5-12

Export Patterns for a Few Developed and Developing Countries, 2008–2012

Source: NBER-CES U.S. Manufacturing Productivity Database, U.S. Census Bureau, and Peter K. Schott, "The Relative Sophistication of Chinese Exports," *Economic Policy* (2008), pp. 5–49.

---

[16]As previously discussed, a sector's skill intensity is measured by the ratio of non-production to production workers in that sector.

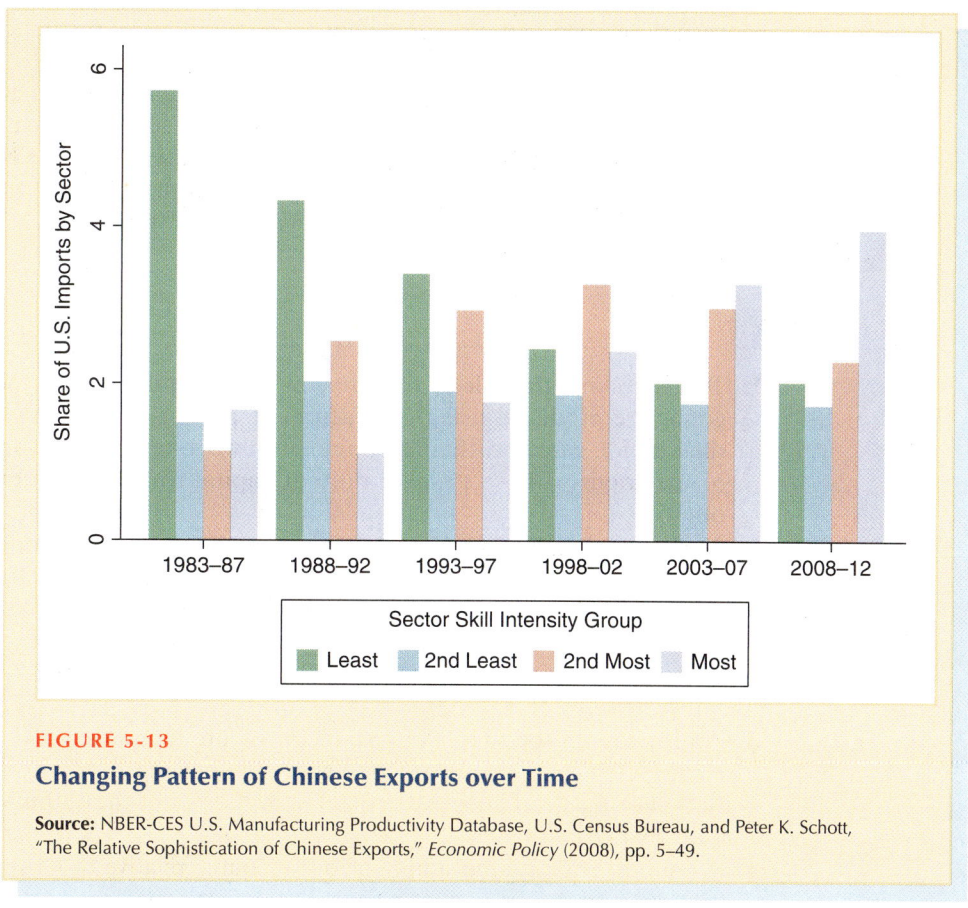

FIGURE 5-13

Changing Pattern of Chinese Exports over Time

Source: NBER-CES U.S. Manufacturing Productivity Database, U.S. Census Bureau, and Peter K. Schott, "The Relative Sophistication of Chinese Exports," *Economic Policy* (2008), pp. 5–49.

abundance. Figure 5-13 shows how the pattern of Chinese exports to the United States by sector has changed over time. Exports are partitioned into the same four groups as Figure 5-12, ordered by the sectors' skill intensity. We clearly see how the pattern of Chinese exports has fundamentally shifted: As predicted by the Chinese change in factor proportions, the concentration of exports in high-skill sectors steadily increases over time. In the most recent years, we see how the greatest share of exports is transacted in the highest skill-intensity sectors—whereas exports were concentrated in the lowest skill-intensity sectors in the earlier years.[17]

Implications of the Tests

We do not observe factor price equalization across countries. When we test the "pure" version of the Heckscher-Ohlin model that maintains all the assumptions behind factor price equalization, we find that a country's factor content of trade bears little resemblance to the theoretical predictions based on that country's factor abundance. However, a less restrictive version of the factor proportions model fits the predicted patterns for the factor content of trade. The pattern of goods trade

---

[17]Comparing Figures 5-12 and 5-13 (latest years), we see that the pattern of Chinese exports to the U.S. is not (yet) as concentrated in high skill-intensity sectors as it is for the three European economies. However, Chinese exports are still remarkably concentrated in high-skill sectors considering China's current GDP per capita. See Peter K. Schott, "The Relative Sophistication of Chinese Exports," *Economic Policy* (2008), pp. 5–49.

between developed and developing countries also fits the predictions of the model quite well.

Lastly, the Heckscher-Ohlin model remains vital for understanding the *effects* of trade, especially on the distribution of income. Indeed, the growth of North-South trade in manufactures—a trade in which the factor intensity of the North's imports is very different from that of its exports—has brought the factor-proportions approach into the center of practical debates over international trade policy.

SUMMARY

1. To understand the role of resources in trade, we develop a model in which two goods are produced using two factors of production. The two goods differ in their *factor intensity*, that is, at any given wage-rental ratio, production of one of the goods will use a higher ratio of capital to labor than production of the other.

2. As long as a country produces both goods, there is a one-to-one relationship between the relative prices of *goods* and the relative prices of *factors* used to produce the goods. A rise in the relative price of the labor-intensive good will shift the distribution of income in favor of labor and will do so very strongly: The real wage of labor will rise in terms of both goods, while the real income of capital owners will fall in terms of both goods.

3. An increase in the supply of one factor of production expands production possibilities, but in a strongly *biased* way: At unchanged relative goods prices, the output of the good intensive in that factor rises while the output of the other good actually falls.

4. A country with a large supply of one resource relative to its supply of other resources is *abundant* in that resource. A country will tend to produce relatively more of goods that use its abundant resources intensively. The result is the basic Heckscher-Ohlin theory of trade: Countries tend to export goods that are intensive in the factors with which they are abundantly supplied.

5. Because changes in relative prices of goods have very strong effects on the relative earnings of resources, and because trade changes relative prices, international trade has strong income distribution effects. The owners of a country's abundant factors gain from trade, but the owners of scarce factors lose. In theory, however, there are still gains from trade, in the limited sense that the winners *could* compensate the losers and everyone would be better off.

6. Increasing trade integration between developed and developing countries could *potentially* explain rising wage inequality in developed countries. However, little empirical evidence supports this direct link. Rather, the empirical evidence suggests that technological change rewarding worker skill has played a much greater role in driving wage inequality.

7. In an idealized model, international trade would actually lead to equalization of the prices of factors such as labor and capital between countries. In reality, complete *factor-price equalization* is not observed because of wide differences in resources, barriers to trade, and international differences in technology.

8. Empirical evidence is mixed on the Heckscher-Ohlin model. Yet, a less restrictive version of the model fits the predicted patterns for the factor content of trade quite well. Also, the Heckscher-Ohlin model does a good job of predicting the pattern of trade between developed and developing countries.

KEY TERMS

abundant factor, p. 120
biased expansion of production
   possibilities, p. 117
equalization of factor prices,
   p. 126
factor abundance, p. 108

factor content of trade, p. 128
factor intensity, p. 108
factor prices, p. 113
factor-proportions theory,
   p. 108
Heckscher-Ohlin theory, p. 108

Leontief paradox, p. 128
scarce factor, p. 120
skill-biased technological
   change, p. 122

PROBLEMS

MyEconLab

1. Go back to the numerical example with no factor substitution that leads to the production possibility frontier in Figure 5-1.
   a. What is the range for the relative price of cloth such that the economy produces both cloth and food? Which good is produced if the relative price is outside of this range?

   For parts (b) through (f), assume the price range is such that both goods are produced.

   b. Write down the unit cost of producing one yard of cloth and one calorie of food as a function of the price of one machine-hour, r, and one work-hour, w. In a competitive market, those costs will be equal to the prices of cloth and food. Solve for the factor prices r and w.
   c. What happens to those factor prices when the price of cloth rises? Who gains and who loses from this change in the price of cloth? Why? Do those changes conform to the changes described for the case with factor substitution?
   d. Now assume the economy's supply of machine-hours increases from 3,000 to 4,000. Derive the new production possibility frontier.
   e. How much cloth and food will the economy produce after this increase in its capital supply?
   f. Describe how the allocation of machine-hours and work-hours between the cloth and food sectors changes. Do those changes conform with the changes described for the case with factor substitution?

2. Suppose in the year 2013, Australia had a population of 45 million and its capital stock is US $90,000 million, and the corresponding figure for Malaysia is 30 million and US $75,000 million. Answer the following, on the basis of this information
   a. Which country is capital abundant and why?
   b. If production of cloth is labor intensive relative to the production of computers, which country would export cloth, if engaged in trade?

3. "The world's poorest countries cannot find anything to export. There is no resource that is abundant—certainly not capital or land, and in small poor nations not even labor is abundant." Discuss.

4. The U.S. labor movement—which mostly represents blue-collar workers rather than professionals and highly educated workers—has traditionally favored limits on imports from less-affluent countries. Is this a shortsighted policy or a rational one in view of the interests of union members? How does the answer depend on the model of trade?

5. Recently, computer programmers in developing countries such as India have begun doing work formerly done in the United States. This shift has undoubtedly led to substantial pay cuts for some programmers in the United States. Answer the following two questions: How is this possible, when the wages of skilled labor

are rising in the United States as a whole? What argument would trade economists make against seeing these wage cuts as a reason to block outsourcing of computer programming?

6. Explain why the Leontief paradox and the more recent Bowen, Leamer, and Sveikauskas results reported in the text contradict the factor-proportions theory.

7. Will free trade and perfect competition lead to an equalization of wage rate internationally? Explain. Why would the wage rate greatly vary between developed and developing countries, in the same sector in a real world situation, even after the adoption of free trade?

FURTHER READINGS

Donald R. Davis and David E. Weinstein. "An Account of Global Factor Trade." *American Economic Review* 91 (December 2001), pp. 1423–1453. This paper confirms the results from earlier studies that the empirical performance of a "pure" Heckscher-Ohlin model is very poor. It then shows how the empirical success of a modified version of the model is vastly improved.

Alan Deardorff. "Testing Trade Theories and Predicting Trade Flows," in Ronald W. Jones and Peter B. Kenen, eds. *Handbook of International Economics.* Vol. 1. Amsterdam: North-Holland, 1984. A survey of empirical evidence on trade theories, especially the factor-proportions theory.

Lawrence Edwards and Robert Z. Lawrence, *Rising Tide: Is Growth in Emerging Economies Good for the United States?* (Peterson Institute for International Economics, 2013). A new book discussing the impact for the United States of increased integration with rapidly growing countries in the develop world.

Gordon Hanson and Ann Harrison. "Trade and Wage Inequality in Mexico." *Industrial and Labor Relations Review* 52 (1999), pp. 271–288. A careful study of the effects of trade on income inequality in our nearest neighbor, showing that factor prices have moved in the opposite direction from what one might have expected from a simple factor-proportions model. The authors also put forward hypotheses about why this may have happened.

Ronald W. Jones. "Factor Proportions and the Heckscher-Ohlin Theorem." *Review of Economic Studies* 24 (1956), pp. 1–10. Extends Samuelson's 1948–1949 analysis (cited on the next page), which focuses primarily on the relationship between trade and income distribution, into an overall model of international trade.

Ronald W. Jones. "The Structure of Simple General Equilibrium Models." *Journal of Political Economy* 73 (December 1965), pp. 557–572. A restatement of the Heckscher-Ohlin-Samuelson model in terms of elegant algebra.

Ronald W. Jones and J. Peter Neary. "The Positive Theory of International Trade," in Ronald W. Jones and Peter B. Kenen, eds. *Handbook of International Economics.* Vol. 1. Amsterdam: North-Holland, 1984. An up-to-date survey of many trade theories, including the factor-proportions theory.

Bertil Ohlin. *Interregional and International Trade.* Cambridge: Harvard University Press, 1933. The original Ohlin book presenting the factor-proportions view of trade remains interesting—its complex and rich view of trade contrasts with the more rigorous and simplified mathematical models that followed.

John Van Reenen. "Wage Inequality, Technology and Trade: 21st Century Evidence." Labour Economics (December 2011), pp. 30–741. A recent survey discussing how trade and new technologies are linked to increases in wage inequality for the United States and the United Kingdom.

John Romalis. "Factor Proportions and the Structure of Commodity Trade." *The American Economic Review* 94 (March 2004), pp. 67–97. A paper showing that a modified version of the Heckscher-Ohlin model has a lot of explanatory power.

Paul Samuelson. "International Trade and the Equalisation of Factor Prices." *Economic Journal* 58 (1948), pp. 163–184; and "International Factor Price Equalisation Once Again." *Economic Journal* 59 (1949), pp. 181–196. The most influential formalizer of Ohlin's ideas is Paul Samuelson (again!), whose two *Economic Journal* papers on the subject are classics.

MyEconLab Can Help You Get a Better Grade

MyEconLab   If your exam were tomorrow, would you be ready? For each chapter, MyEconLab Practice Tests and Study Plans pinpoint sections you have mastered and those you need to study. That way, you are more efficient with your study time, and you are better prepared for your exams.

To see how it works, turn to page 33 and then go to

www.myeconlab.com

Factor Prices, Goods Prices, and Production Decisions

In the main body of this chapter, we made three assertions that are true but not carefully derived. First was the assertion, embodied in Figure 5-5, that the ratio of labor to capital employed in each industry depends on the wage-rental ratio w/r. Second was the assertion, embodied in Figure 5-6, that there is a one-to-one relationship between relative goods prices P_C/P_F and the wage-rental ratio. Third was the assertion that an increase in a country's labor supply (at a given relative goods price P_C/P_F) will lead to movements of both labor and capital from the food sector to the cloth sector (the labor-intensive sector). This appendix briefly demonstrates those three propositions.

Choice of Technique

Figure 5A-1 illustrates again the trade-off between labor and capital input in producing one unit of food—the *unit isoquant* for food production shown in curve *II*. It also, however, illustrates a number of *isocost lines*: combinations of capital and labor input that cost the same amount.

An isocost line may be constructed as follows: The cost of purchasing a given amount of labor L is wL; the cost of renting a given amount of capital K is rK. So if one is able to produce a unit of food using units of labor and units of capital, the total cost of producing that unit, c, is

$$c = wa_{LF} + ra_{KF}.$$

FIGURE 5A-1

Choosing the Optimal Labor-Capital Ratio

To minimize costs, a producer must get to the lowest possible isocost line; this means choosing the point on the unit isoquant (curve *II*) where the slope is equal to minus the wage-rental ratio w/r.

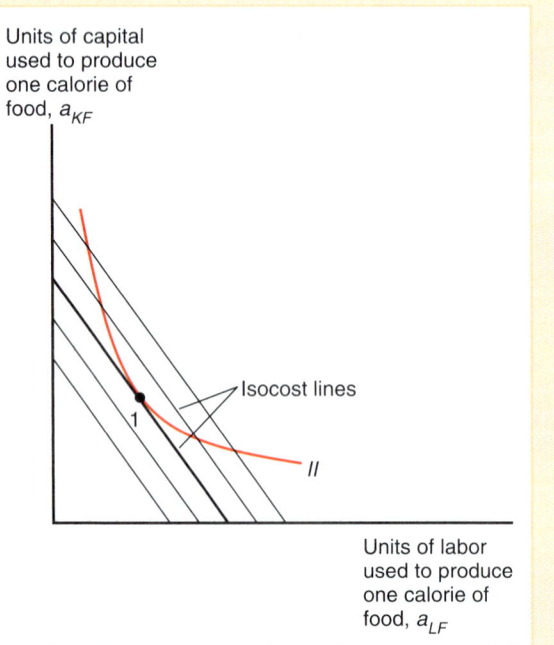

Units of capital used to produce one calorie of food, a_{KF}

Isocost lines

II

Units of labor used to produce one calorie of food, a_{LF}

FIGURE 5A-2

Changing the Wage-Rental Ratio

A rise in w/r shifts the lowest-cost input choice from point 1 to point 2; that is, it leads to the choice of a lower labor-capital ratio.

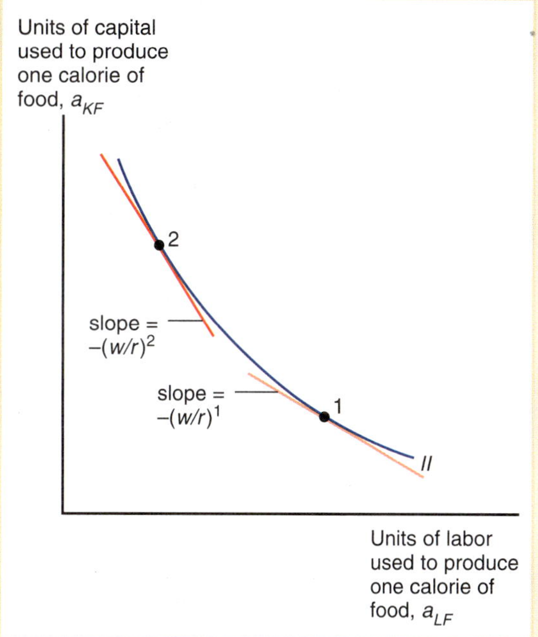

A line showing all combinations of a_{LF} and a_{KF} with the same cost has the equation

$$a_{KF} = (c/r) - (w/r)a_{LF}.$$

That is, it is a straight line with a slope of $-w/r$.

The figure shows a family of such lines, each corresponding to a different level of costs; lines farther from the origin indicate higher total costs. A producer will choose the lowest possible cost given the technological trade-off outlined by curve *II*. Here, this occurs at point 1, where *II* is *tangent* to the isocost line and the slope of *II* equals $-w/r$. (If these results seem reminiscent of the proposition in Figure 4-5 that the economy produces at a point on the production possibility frontier whose slope equals minus P_C/P_F, you are right: The same principle is involved.)

Now compare the choice of labor-capital ratio for two different factor-price ratios. In Figure 5A-2, we show input choices given a low relative price of labor, $(w/r)^1$ and a high relative price of labor $(w/r)^2$. In the former case, the input choice is at 1; in the latter case at 2. That is, the higher relative price of labor leads to the choice of a lower labor-capital ratio, as assumed in Figure 5-5.

Goods Prices and Factor Prices

We now turn to the relationship between goods prices and factor prices. There are several equivalent ways of approaching this problem; here, we follow the analysis introduced by Abba Lerner in the 1930s.

Figure 5A-3 shows capital and labor inputs into both cloth and food production. In previous figures, we have shown the inputs required to produce one unit of a good. In this figure, however, we show the inputs required to produce *one dollar's worth* of each good. (Actually, any dollar amount will do as long as it is the same for both goods.) Thus, the isoquant for cloth, *CC*, shows the possible input combinations for producing $1/P_C$ units of cloth; the isoquant for food, *FF*, shows the possible combinations for

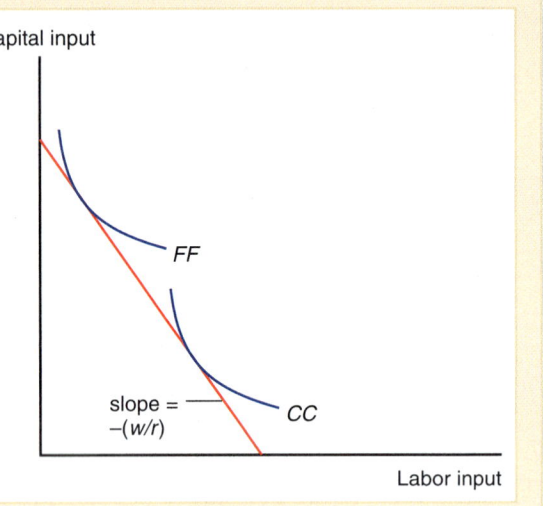

FIGURE 5A-3

Determining the Wage-Rental Ratio

The two isoquants *CC* and *FF* show the inputs necessary to produce *one dollar's worth* of cloth and food, respectively. Since price must equal the cost of production, the inputs into each good must also cost one dollar. This means that the wage-rental ratio must equal minus the slope of a line tangent to both isoquants.

producing $1/P_F$ units of food. Notice that as drawn, cloth production is labor-intensive (and food production is capital-intensive): For any given w/r, cloth production will always use a higher labor-capital ratio than food production.

If the economy produces both goods, then it must be the case that the cost of producing one dollar's worth of each good is, in fact, one dollar. Those two production costs will be equal to one another only if the minimum-cost points of production for both goods lie on the *same* isocost line. Thus, the slope of the line shown, which is just tangent to both isoquants, must equal (minus) the wage-rental ratio w/r.

Finally, now, consider the effects of a rise in the price of cloth on the wage-rental ratio. If the price of cloth rises, it is necessary to produce fewer yards of cloth in order to have one dollar's worth. Thus, the isoquant corresponding to a dollar's worth of cloth shifts inward. In Figure 5A-4, the original isoquant is shown as CC^1, the new isoquant as CC^2.

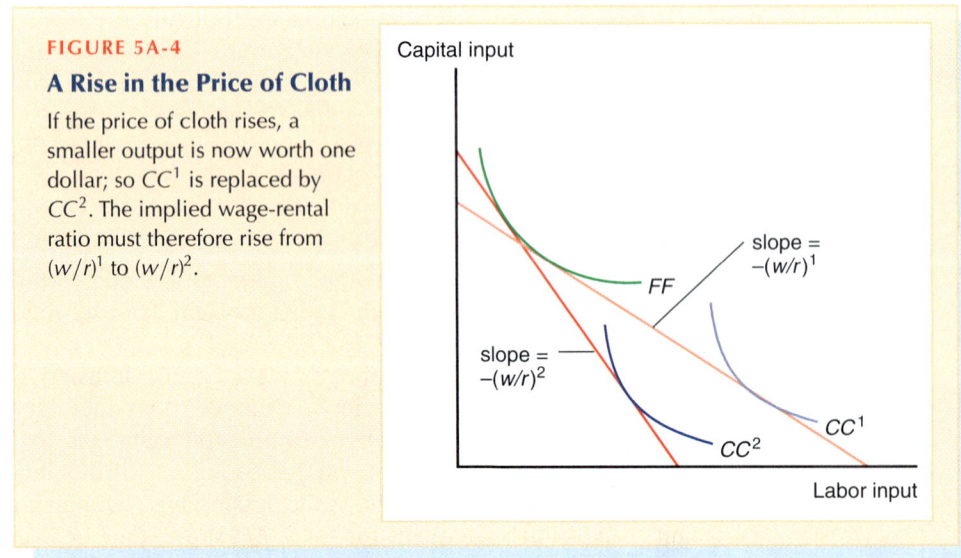

FIGURE 5A-4

A Rise in the Price of Cloth

If the price of cloth rises, a smaller output is now worth one dollar; so CC^1 is replaced by CC^2. The implied wage-rental ratio must therefore rise from $(w/r)^1$ to $(w/r)^2$.

Once again, we must draw a line just tangent to both isoquants; the slope of that line is minus the wage-rental ratio. It is immediately apparent from the increased steepness of the isocost line (slope $= -(w/r)^2$) that the new w/r is higher than the previous one: A higher relative price of cloth implies a higher wage-rental ratio.

More on Resources and Output

We now examine more rigorously how a change in resources—holding the prices of cloth and food constant—affects the allocation of those factors of production across sectors and how it thus affects production responses. The aggregate employment of labor to capital L/K can be written as a weighted average of the labor-capital employed in the cloth sector (L_C/K_C) and in the food sector (L_F/K_F):

$$\frac{L}{K} = \frac{K_C}{K}\frac{L_C}{K_C} + \frac{K_F}{K}\frac{L_F}{K_F} \tag{5A-1}$$

Note that the weights in this average, K_C/K and K_F/K, add up to 1 and are the proportions of capital employed in the cloth and food sectors. We have seen that a given relative price of cloth is associated with a given wage-rental ratio (so long as the economy produces both cloth and food), which in turn is associated with given labor-capital employment levels in both sectors (L_C/K_C and L_F/K_F). Now consider the effects of an increase in the economy's labor supply L at a given relative price of cloth: L/K increases while L_C/K_C and L_F/K_F both remain constant. For equation (5A-1) to hold, the weight on the higher labor-capital ratio, L_C/K_C, must increase. This implies an increase in the weight K_C/K and a corresponding decrease in the weight K_F/K. Thus, capital moves from the food sector to the cloth sector (since the total capital supply K remains constant in this example). Furthermore, since L_F/K_F remains constant, the decrease in K_F must also be associated with a decrease in labor employment L_F in the food sector. This shows that the increase in the labor supply, at a given relative price of cloth, must be associated with movements of *both* labor and capital from the food sector to the cloth sector. The expansion of the economy's production possibility frontier is so biased toward cloth that—at a constant relative price of cloth—the economy produces *less* food.

As the economy's labor supply increases, the economy concentrates more and more of both factors in the labor-intensive cloth sector. If enough labor is added, then the economy specializes in cloth production and no longer produces any food. At that point, the one-to-one relationship between the relative goods price P_C/P_F and the wage-rental ratio w/r is broken; further increases in the labor supply L are then associated with decreases in the wage-rental ratio along the CC curve in Figure 5-7.

A similar process would occur if the economy's capital supply were to increase—again holding the relative goods price P_C/P_F fixed. So long as the economy produces both cloth and food, the economy responds to the increased capital supply by concentrating production in the food sector (which is capital-intensive): Both labor and capital move to the food sector. The economy experiences growth that is strongly biased toward food. At a certain point, the economy completely specializes in the food sector, and the one-to-one relationship between the relative goods price P_C/P_F and the wage-rental ratio w/r is broken once again. Further increases in the capital supply K are then associated with increases in the wage-rental ratio along the FF curve in Figure 5-7.

CHAPTER 6

THE STANDARD TRADE MODEL

Previous chapters developed several different models of international trade, each of which makes different assumptions about the determinants of production possibilities. To bring out important points, each of these models leaves out aspects of reality that the others stress. These models are:

- *The Ricardian model.* Production possibilities are determined by the allocation of a single resource, labor, between sectors. This model conveys the essential idea of comparative advantage but does not allow us to talk about the distribution of income.
- *The specific factors model.* This model includes multiple factors of production, but some are specific to the sectors in which they are employed. It also captures the short-run consequences of trade on the distribution of income.
- *The Heckscher-Ohlin model.* The multiple factors of production in this model can move across sectors. Differences in resources (the availability of those factors at the country level) drive trade patterns. This model also captures the long-run consequences of trade on the distribution of income.

When we analyze real problems, we want to base our insights on a mixture of these models. For example, in the last two decades one of the central changes in world trade was the rapid growth in exports from newly industrializing economies. These countries experienced rapid productivity growth; to discuss the implications of this productivity growth, we may want to apply the Ricardian model of Chapter 3. The changing pattern of trade has differential effects on different groups in the United States; to understand the effects of increased trade on the U.S. income distribution, we may want to apply the specific factors (for the short-run effects) or the Heckscher-Ohlin models (for the long-run effects) of Chapters 4 and 5.

In spite of the differences in their details, our models share a number of features:

1. The productive capacity of an economy can be summarized by its production possibility frontier, and differences in these frontiers give rise to trade.
2. Production possibilities determine a country's relative supply schedule.
3. World equilibrium is determined by world relative demand and a *world* relative supply schedule that lies between the national relative supply schedules.

Because of these common features, the models we have studied may be viewed as special cases of a more general model of a trading world economy. There are many important issues in international economics whose analysis can be conducted in terms of this general model, with only the details depending on which special model you choose. These issues include the effects of shifts in world supply resulting from economic growth and simultaneous shifts in supply and demand resulting from tariffs and export subsidies.

This chapter stresses those insights from international trade theory that are not strongly dependent on the details of the economy's supply side. We develop a standard model of a trading world economy, of which the models of Chapters 3 through 5 can be regarded as special cases, and use this model to ask how a variety of changes in underlying parameters affect the world economy.

LEARNING GOALS

After reading this chapter, you will be able to:

- Understand how the components of the standard trade model, production possibilities frontiers, isovalue lines, and indifference curves fit together to illustrate how trade patterns are established by a combination of supply-side and demand-side factors.
- Recognize how changes in the terms of trade and economic growth affect the welfare of nations engaged in international trade.
- Understand the effects of tariffs and subsidies on trade patterns and the welfare of trading nations and on the distribution of income within countries.
- Relate international borrowing and lending to the standard trade model, where goods are exchanged over time.

A Standard Model of a Trading Economy

The **standard trade model** is built on four key relationships: (1) the relationship between the production possibility frontier and the relative supply curve; (2) the relationship between relative prices and relative demand; (3) the determination of world equilibrium by world relative supply and world relative demand; and (4) the effect of the **terms of trade**—the price of a country's exports divided by the price of its imports—on a nation's welfare.

Production Possibilities and Relative Supply

For the purposes of our standard model, we assume that each country produces two goods, food (F) and cloth (C), and that each country's production possibility frontier is a smooth curve like that illustrated by TT in Figure 6-1.[1] The point on its production possibility frontier at which an economy actually produces depends on the price of cloth relative to food, P_C/P_F. At given market prices, a market economy will choose production levels that maximize the value of its output $P_C Q_C + P_F Q_F$, where Q_C is the quantity of cloth produced and Q_F is the quantity of food produced.

---

[1]We have seen that when there is only one factor of production, as in Chapter 3, the production possibility frontier is a straight line. For most models, however, it will be a smooth curve, and the Ricardian result can be viewed as an extreme case.

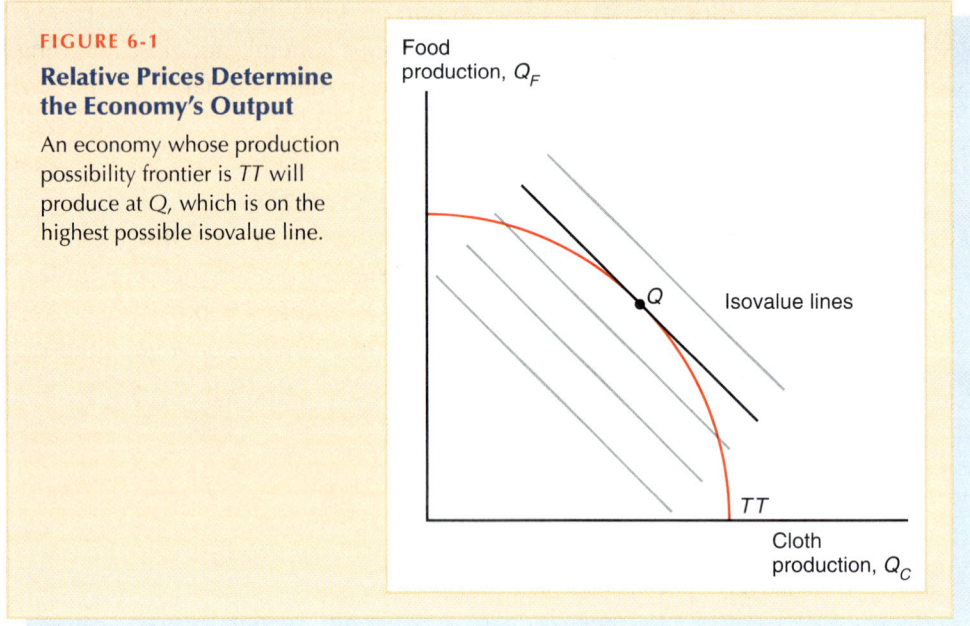

FIGURE 6-1

Relative Prices Determine the Economy's Output

An economy whose production possibility frontier is *TT* will produce at Q, which is on the highest possible isovalue line.

We can indicate the market value of output by drawing a number of **isovalue lines**—that is, lines along which the value of output is constant. Each of these lines is defined by an equation of the form $P_C Q_C + P_F Q_F = V$, or, by rearranging, $Q_F = V/P_F - (P_C/P_F)Q_C$, where V is the value of output. The higher V is, the farther out an isovalue line lies; thus isovalue lines farther from the origin correspond to higher values of output. The slope of an isovalue line is $-P_C/P_F$. In Figure 6-1, the highest value of output is achieved by producing at point Q, where *TT* is just tangent to an isovalue line.

Now suppose that P_C/P_F were to rise (cloth becomes more valuable relative to food). Then the isovalue lines would be steeper than before. In Figure 6-2, the highest isovalue line the economy could reach before the change in P_C/P_F is shown as VV^1; the highest line after the price change is VV^2, the point at which the economy produces shifts from Q^1 to Q^2. Thus, as we might expect, a rise in the relative price of cloth leads the economy to produce more cloth and less food. The relative supply of cloth will therefore rise when the relative price of cloth rises. This relationship between relative prices and relative production is reflected in the economy's relative supply curve shown in Figure 6-2b.

Relative Prices and Demand

Figure 6-3 shows the relationship among production, consumption, and trade in the standard model. As we pointed out in Chapter 5, the value of an economy's consumption equals the value of its production:

$$P_C Q_C + P_F Q_F = P_C D_C + P_F D_F = V,$$

where D_C and D_F are the consumption of cloth and food, respectively. The equation above says that production and consumption must lie on the same isovalue line.

The economy's choice of a point on the isovalue line depends on the tastes of its consumers. For our standard model, we assume the economy's consumption decisions

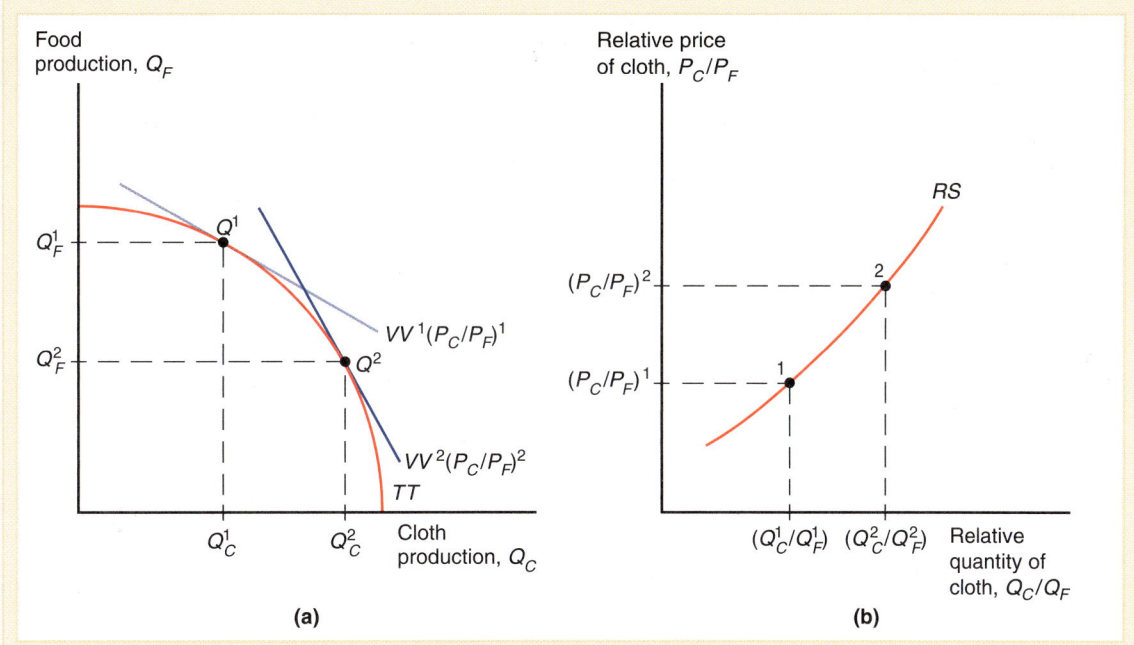

FIGURE 6-2

How an Increase in the Relative Price of Cloth Affects Relative Supply

In panel (a), the isovalue lines become steeper when the relative price of cloth rises from $(P_C/P_F)^1$ to $(P_C/P_F)^2$ (shown by the rotation from VV^1 to VV^2). As a result, the economy produces more cloth and less food and the equilibrium output shifts from Q^1 to Q^2. Panel (b) shows the relative supply curve associated with the production possibilities frontier TT. The rise from $(P_C/P_F)^1$ to $(P_C/P_F)^2$ leads to an increase in the relative production of cloth from $Q_C{}^1/Q_F{}^1$ to $Q_C{}^2/Q_F{}^2$.

may be represented as if they were based on the tastes of a single representative individual.[2]

The tastes of an individual can be represented graphically by a series of **indifference curves.** An indifference curve traces a set of combinations of cloth (C) and food (F) consumption that leave the individual equally well off. As illustrated in Figure 6-3, indifference curves have three properties:

1. They are downward sloping: If an individual is offered less food (F), then to be made equally well off, she must be given more cloth (C).
2. The farther up and to the right an indifference curve lies, the higher the level of welfare to which it corresponds: An individual will prefer having more of both goods to less.
3. Each indifference curve gets flatter as we move to the right (they are bowed-out to the origin): The more C and the less F an individual consumes, the more valuable a unit of F is at the margin compared with a unit of C, so more C will have to be provided to compensate for any further reduction in F.

---

[2]Several sets of circumstances can justify this assumption. One is that all individuals have the same tastes and the same share of all resources. Another is that the government redistributes income so as to maximize its view of overall social welfare. Essentially, the assumption requires that effects of changing income distribution on demand not be too important.

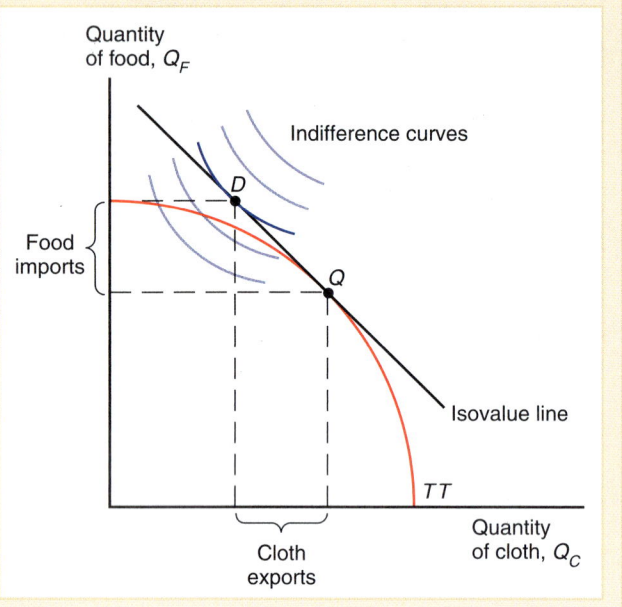

FIGURE 6-3

Production, Consumption, and Trade in the Standard Model

The economy produces at point Q, where the production possibility frontier is tangent to the highest possible isovalue line. It consumes at point D, where that isovalue line is tangent to the highest possible indifference curve. The economy produces more cloth than it consumes and therefore exports cloth; correspondingly, it consumes more food than it produces and therefore imports food.

As you can see in Figure 6-3, the economy will choose to consume at the point on the isovalue line that yields the highest possible welfare. This point is where the isovalue line is tangent to the highest reachable indifference curve, shown here as point D. Notice that at this point, the economy exports cloth (the quantity of cloth produced exceeds the quantity of cloth consumed) and imports food.

Now consider what happens when P_C/P_F increases. Panel (a) in Figure 6-4 shows the effects. First, the economy produces more C and less F, shifting production from Q^1 to Q^2. This shifts, from VV_1^1 to VV_2^2 the isovalue line on which consumption must lie. The economy's consumption choice therefore also shifts, from D^1 to D^2.

The move from D^1 to D^2 reflects two effects of the rise in P_C/P_F. First, the economy has moved to a higher indifference curve, meaning that it is better off. The reason is that this economy is an exporter of cloth. When the relative price of cloth rises, the economy can trade a given amount of cloth for a larger amount of food imports. Thus, the higher relative price of its export good represents an advantage. Second, the change in relative prices leads to a shift along the indifference curve, toward food and away from cloth (since cloth is now relatively more expensive).

These two effects are familiar from basic economic theory. The rise in welfare is an *income effect*; the shift in consumption at any given level of welfare is a *substitution effect*. The income effect tends to increase consumption of both goods, while the substitution effect acts to make the economy consume less C and more F.

Panel (b) in Figure 6-4 shows the relative supply and demand curves associated with the production possibilities frontier and the indifference curves.[3] The graph shows how the increase in the relative price of cloth induces an increase in the relative production of cloth (move from point 1 to 2) as well as a decrease in the relative

---

[3]For general preferences, the relative demand curve will depend on the country's total income. We assume throughout this chapter that the relative demand curve is independent of income. This is the case for a widely used type of preferences called homothetic preferences.

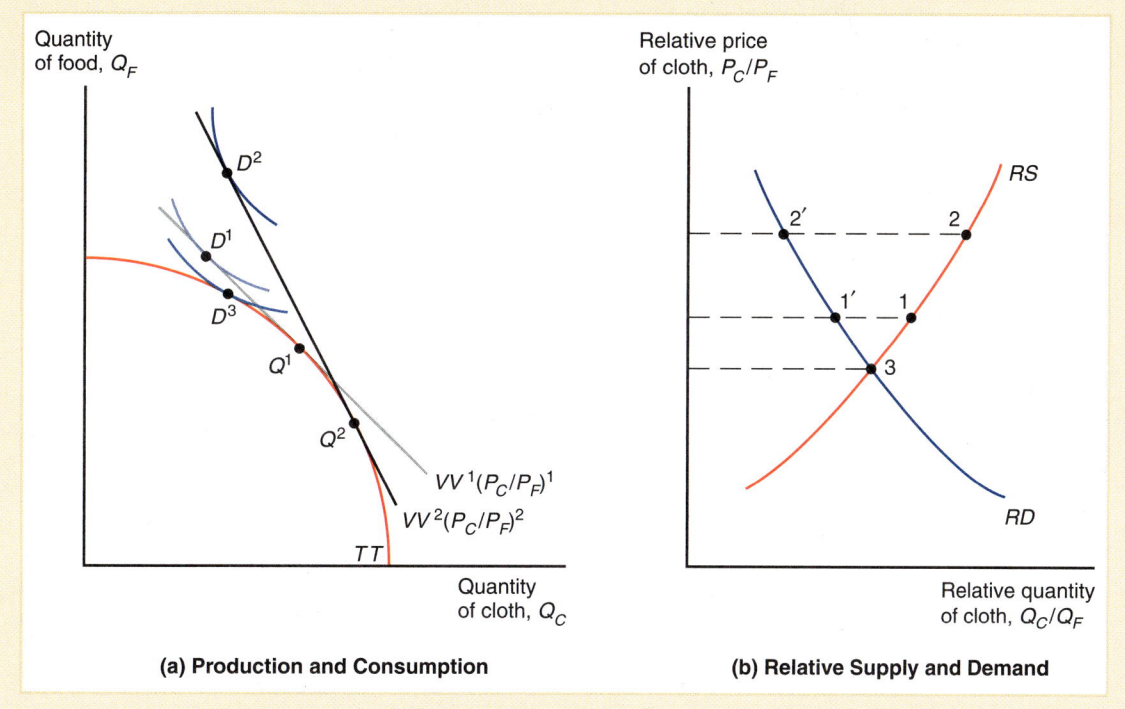

FIGURE 6-4

Effects of a Rise in the Relative Price of Cloth and Gains from Trade

In panel (a), the slope of the isovalue lines is equal to minus the relative price of cloth, P_C/P_F. As a result, when that relative price rises, all isovalue lines become steeper. In particular, the maximum-value line rotates from VV^1 to VV^2. Production shifts from Q^1 to Q^2 and consumption shifts from D^1 to D^2. If the economy cannot trade, then it produces and consumes at point D^3. Panel (b) shows the effects of the rise in the relative price of cloth on relative production (move from 1 to 2) and relative demand (move from 1' to 2'. If the economy cannot trade, then it consumes and produces at point 3.

consumption of cloth (move from point 1' to 2'). This change in relative consumption captures the substitution effect of the price change. If the income effect of the price change were large enough, then consumption levels of both goods could rise (D_C and D_F both increase); but the substitution effect of demand dictates that the *relative* consumption of cloth, D_C/D_F, decrease. If the economy cannot trade, then it consumes and produces at point 3 (associated with the relative price $(P_C/P_F)^3$.

The Welfare Effect of Changes in the Terms of Trade

When P_C/P_F increases, a country that initially exports cloth is made better off, as illustrated by the movement from D^1 to D^2 in panel (a) of Figure 6-4. Conversely, if P_C/P_F were to decline, the country would be made worse off; for example, consumption might move back from D^2 to D^1.

If the country were initially an exporter of food instead of cloth, the direction of this effect would be reversed. An increase in P_C/P_F would mean a fall in P_F/P_C and the country would be worse off: The relative price of the good it exports (food) would drop. We cover all these cases by defining the terms of trade as the price of the good a country initially exports divided by the price of the good it initially imports.

The general statement, then, is that *a rise in the terms of trade increases a country's welfare, while a decline in the terms of trade reduces its welfare.*

Note, however, that changes in a country's terms of trade can never decrease the country's welfare below its welfare level in the absence of trade (represented by consumption at D^3). The gains from trade mentioned in Chapters 3, 4, and 5 still apply to this more general approach. The same disclaimers previously discussed also apply: Aggregate gains are rarely evenly distributed, leading to both gains and losses for individual consumers.

Determining Relative Prices

Let's now suppose that the world economy consists of two countries once again named Home (which exports cloth) and Foreign (which exports food). Home's terms of trade are measured by P_C/P_F while Foreign's are measured by P_C/P_F. We assume these trade patterns are induced by differences in Home's and Foreign's production capabilities, as represented by the associated relative supply curves in panel (a) of Figure 6.5. We also assume the two countries share the same preferences and hence have the same relative demand curve. At any given relative price P_C/P_F, Home will produce quantities of cloth and food Q_C and Q_F, while Foreign produces quantities Q_C^* and Q_F^*, where $Q_C/Q_F > Q_C^*/Q_F^*$. The relative supply for the world is then obtained by summing those production levels for both cloth and food and taking the ratio: $(Q_C + Q_C^*)/(Q_F + Q_F^*)$. By construction, this relative supply curve for the world must lie in between the relative supply curves for both countries.[4] Relative demand for the world also aggregates the demands for cloth and food across the two countries: $(D_C + D_C^*)/(D_F + D_F^*)$. Since there are no differences in preferences across the two countries, the relative demand curve for the world overlaps with the same relative demand curve for each country.

The equilibrium relative price for the world (when Home and Foreign trade) is then given by the intersection of world relative supply and demand at point 1. This relative price determines how many units of Home's cloth exports are exchanged for Foreign's food exports. At the equilibrium relative price, Home's desired exports of cloth, $Q_C - D_C$, match up with Foreign's desired imports of cloth, $D_C^* - Q_C^*$. The food market is also in equilibrium so that Home's desired imports of food, $D_F - Q_F$, match up with Foreign's desired food exports, $Q_F^* - D_F^*$. The production possibility frontiers for Home and Foreign, along with the budget constraints and associated production and consumption choices at the equilibrium relative price $(P_C/P_F)^1$, are illustrated in panel (b).

Now that we know how relative supply, relative demand, the terms of trade, and welfare are determined in the standard model, we can use it to understand a number of important issues in international economics.

Economic Growth: A Shift of the *RS* Curve

The effects of economic growth in a trading world economy are a perennial source of concern and controversy. The debate revolves around two questions. First, is economic growth in other countries good or bad for our nation? Second, is growth in a country more or less valuable when that nation is part of a closely integrated world economy?

In assessing the effects of growth in other countries, commonsense arguments can be made on either side. On one side, economic growth in the rest of the world

---

[4]For any positive numbers X_1, X_2, Y_1, Y_2, if $X_1/Y_1 < X_2/Y_2$, then $X_1/Y_1 < (X_1 + X_2)/(Y_1 + Y_2) < X_2/Y_2$.

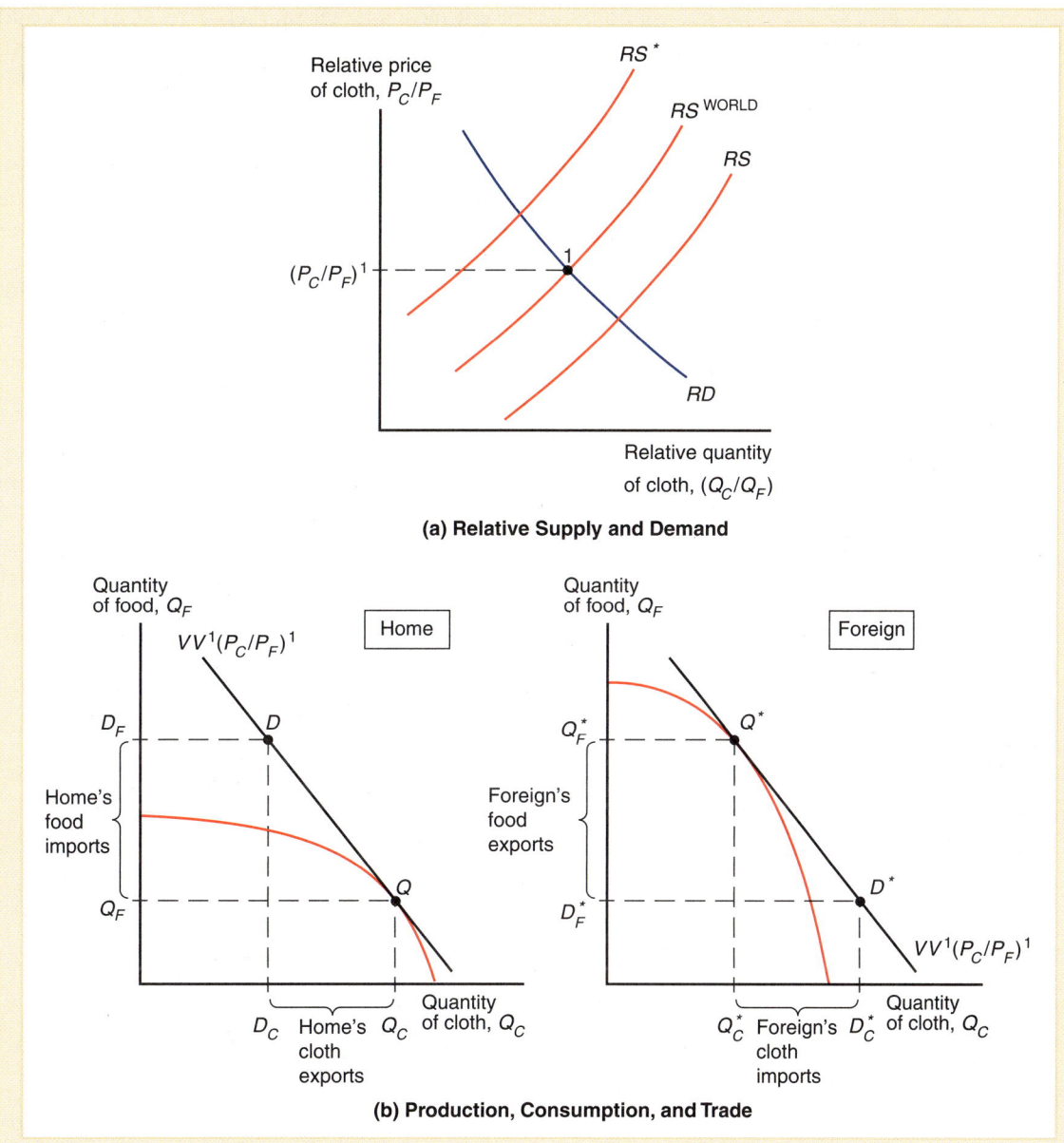

FIGURE 6-5

Equilibrium Relative Price with Trade and Associated Trade Flows

Panel (a) shows the relative supply of cloth in Home (RS), in Foreign (RS*), and for the world. Home and Foreign have the same relative demand, which is also the relative demand for the world. The equilibrium relative price $P_C/P_F)^1$ is determined by the intersection of the world relative supply and demand curves. Panel (b) shows the associated equilibrium trade flows between Home and Foreign. At the equilibrium relative price $(P_C/P_F)^1$, Home's exports of cloth equals Foreign's imports of cloth; and Home's imports of food equals Foreign's exports of food.

may be good for our economy because it means larger markets for our exports and lower prices for our imports. On the other side, growth in other countries may mean increased competition for our exporters and domestic producers, who need to compete with foreign exporters.

We can find similar ambiguities when we look at the effects of growth at Home. On one hand, growth in an economy's production capacity should be more valuable when that country can sell some of its increased production to the world market. On the other hand, the benefits of growth may be passed on to foreigners in the form of lower prices for the country's exports rather than retained at home.

The standard model of trade developed in the last section provides a framework that can cut through these seeming contradictions and clarify the effects of economic growth in a trading world.

Growth and the Production Possibility Frontier

Economic growth means an outward shift of a country's production possibility frontier. This growth can result either from increases in a country's resources or from improvements in the efficiency with which these resources are used.

The international trade effects of growth result from the fact that such growth typically has a *bias*. **Biased growth** takes place when the production possibility frontier shifts out more in one direction than in the other. Panel (a) of Figure 6-6 illustrates growth biased toward cloth (shift from TT^1 to TT^2), while panel (b) shows growth biased toward food (shift from TT^1 to TT^3).

Growth may be biased for two main reasons:

1. The Ricardian model of Chapter 3 showed that technological progress in one sector of the economy will expand the economy's production possibilities in the direction of that sector's output.
2. The Heckscher-Ohlin model of Chapter 5 showed that an increase in a country's supply of a factor of production—say, an increase in the capital stock resulting from saving and investment—will produce biased expansion of production possibilities. The bias will be in the direction of either the good to which the factor is specific or the good whose production is intensive in the factor whose supply has increased. Thus, the same considerations that give rise to international trade will also lead to biased growth in a trading economy.

The biases of growth in panels (a) and (b) are strong. In each case the economy is able to produce more of both goods. However, at an unchanged relative price of cloth, the output of food actually falls in panel (a), while the output of cloth actually falls in panel (b). Although growth is not always as strongly biased as it is in these examples, even growth that is more mildly biased toward cloth will lead, *for any given relative price of cloth*, to a rise in the output of cloth *relative* to that of food. In other words, the country's relative supply curve shifts to the right. This change is represented in panel (c) as the transition from RS^1 to RS^2. When growth is biased toward food, the relative supply curve shifts to the left, as shown by the transition from RS^1 to RS^3.

World Relative Supply and the Terms of Trade

Suppose now that Home experiences growth strongly biased toward cloth, so that its output of cloth rises at any given relative price of cloth, while its output of food declines (as shown in panel (a) of Figure 6-6). Then the output of cloth relative to food will rise at any given price for the world as a whole, and the world relative

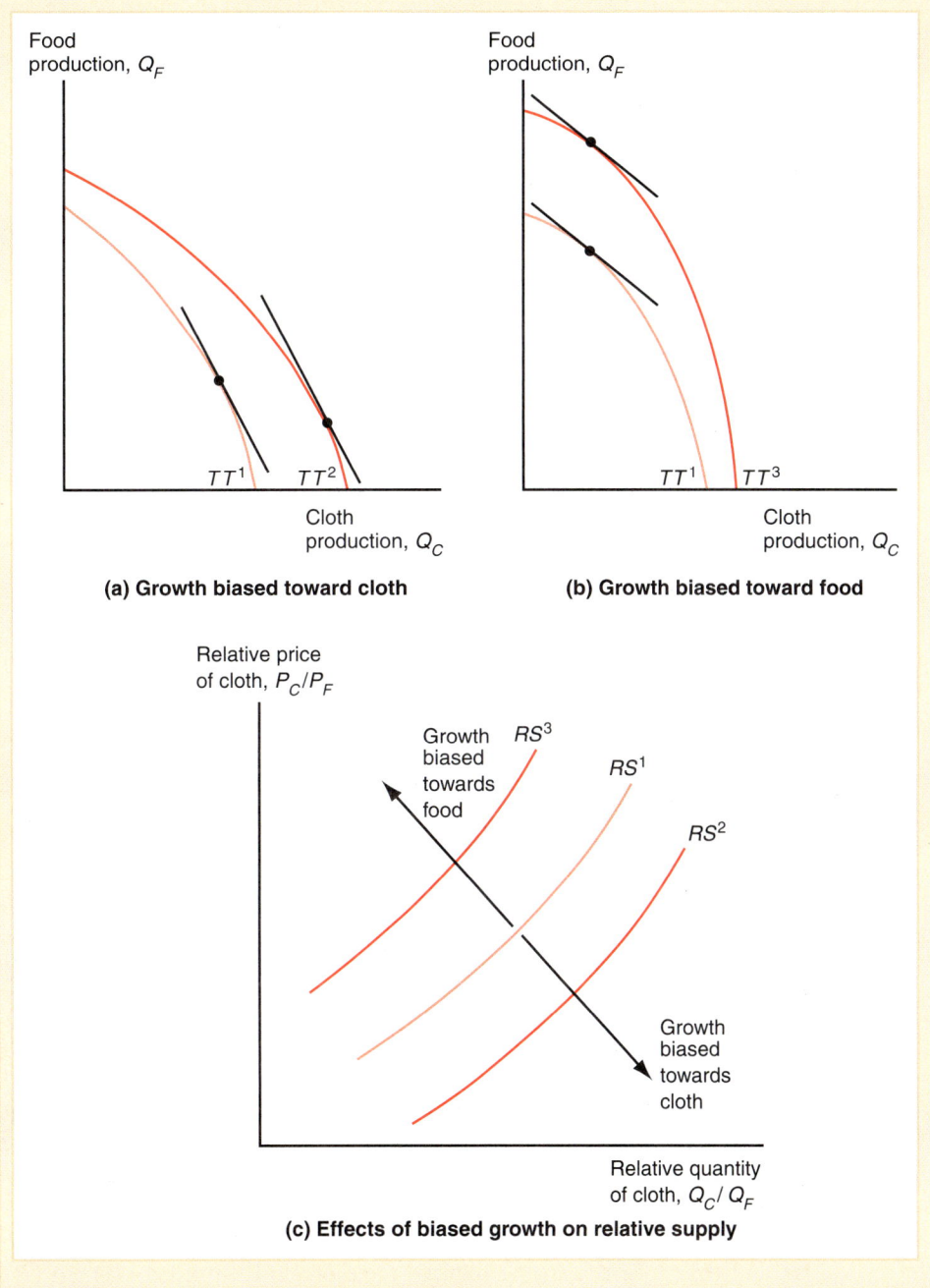

(a) Growth biased toward cloth

(b) Growth biased toward food

(c) Effects of biased growth on relative supply

FIGURE 6-6

Biased Growth

Growth is biased when it shifts production possibilities out more toward one good than toward another. In case (a), growth is biased toward cloth (shift from TT^1 to TT^2), while in case (b), growth is biased toward food (shift from TT^1 to TT^3). The associated shifts in the relative supply curve are shown in panel (c): shift to the right (from RS^1 to RS^2) when growth is biased toward cloth, and shift to the left (from RS^1 to RS^3) when growth is biased toward food.

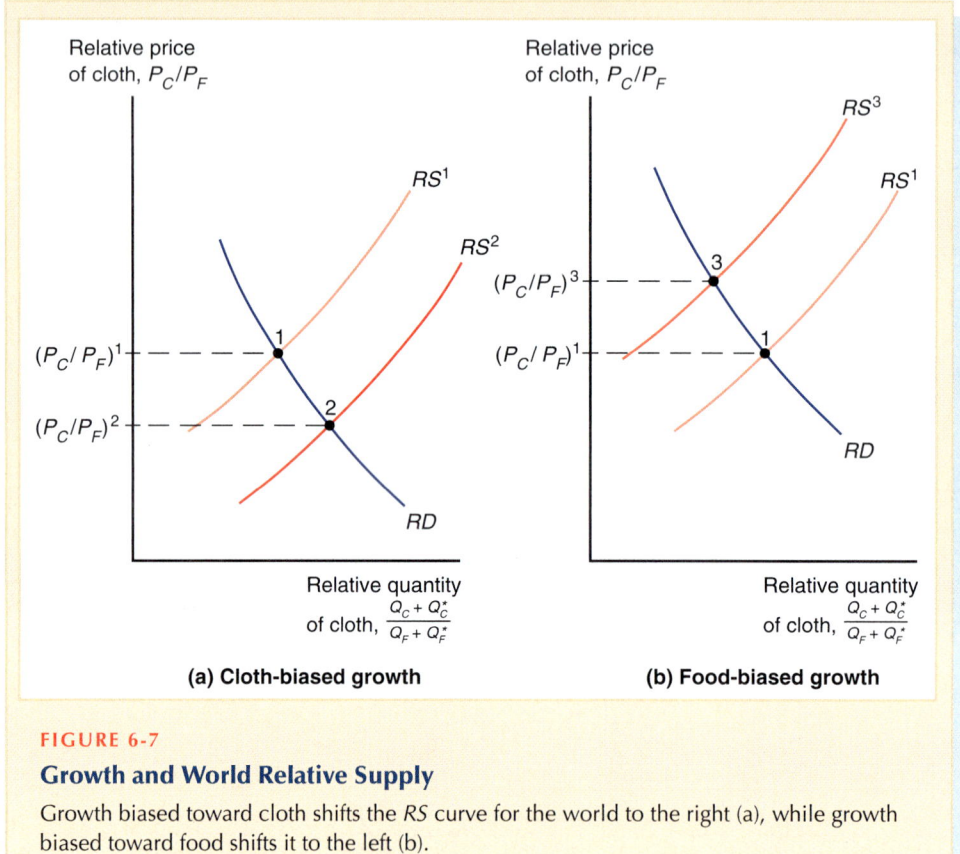

FIGURE 6-7

Growth and World Relative Supply

Growth biased toward cloth shifts the *RS* curve for the world to the right (a), while growth biased toward food shifts it to the left (b).

supply curve will shift to the right, just like the relative supply curve for Home. This shift in the world relative supply is shown in panel (a) of Figure 6-7 as a shift from RS^1 to RS^2. It results in a decrease in the relative price of cloth from $(P_C/P_F)^1$ to $(P_C/P_F)^2$, a worsening of Home's terms of trade and an improvement in Foreign's terms of trade.

Notice that the important consideration here is not *which* economy grows but rather the bias of that growth. If Foreign had experienced growth strongly biased toward cloth, the effect on the world relative supply curve and thus on the terms of trade would have been similar. On the other hand, either Home or Foreign growth strongly biased toward food will lead to a *leftward* shift of the *RS* curve (RS^1 to RS^3) for the *world* and thus to a rise in the relative price of cloth from $(P_C/P_F)^1$ to $(P_C/P_F)^3$ (as shown in panel (b)). This relative price increase is an improvement in Home's terms of trade, but a worsening of Foreign's.

Growth that disproportionately expands a country's production possibilities in the direction of the good it exports (cloth in Home, food in Foreign) is **export-biased growth**. Similarly, growth biased toward the good a country imports is **import-biased growth**. Our analysis leads to the following general principle: *Export-biased growth tends to worsen a growing country's terms of trade, to the benefit of the rest of the world; import-biased growth tends to improve a growing country's terms of trade at the rest of the world's expense.*

International Effects of Growth

Using this principle, we are now in a position to resolve our questions about the international effects of growth. Is growth in the rest of the world good or bad for our country? Does the fact that our country is part of a trading world economy increase or decrease the benefits of growth? In each case the answer depends on the *bias* of the growth. Export-biased growth in the rest of the world is good for us, improving our terms of trade, while import-biased growth abroad worsens our terms of trade. Export-biased growth in our own country worsens our terms of trade, reducing the direct benefits of growth, while import-biased growth leads to an improvement of our terms of trade, a secondary benefit.

During the 1950s, many economists from poorer countries believed that their nations, which primarily exported raw materials, were likely to experience steadily declining terms of trade over time. They believed that growth in the industrial world would be marked by an increasing development of synthetic substitutes for raw materials, while growth in the poorer nations would take the form of a further extension of their capacity to produce what they were already exporting rather than a move toward industrialization. That is, the growth in the industrial world would be import-biased, while that in the less-developed world would be export-biased.

Some analysts even suggested that growth in the poorer nations would actually be self-defeating. They argued that export-biased growth by poor nations would worsen their terms of trade so much that they would be worse off than if they had not grown at all. This situation is known to economists as the case of **immiserizing growth**.

In a famous paper published in 1958, economist Jagdish Bhagwati of Columbia University showed that such perverse effects of growth can in fact arise within a rigorously specified economic model.[5] However, the conditions under which immiserizing growth can occur are extreme: Strongly export-biased growth must be combined with very steep RS and RD curves, so that the change in the terms of trade is large enough to offset the direct favorable effects of an increase in a country's productive capacity. Most economists now regard the concept of immiserizing growth as more a theoretical point than a real-world issue.

While growth at home normally raises our own welfare even in a trading world, this is by no means true of growth abroad. Import-biased growth is not an unlikely possibility, and whenever the rest of the world experiences such growth, it worsens our terms of trade. Indeed, as we point out below, it is possible that the United States has suffered some loss of real income because of foreign growth over the postwar period.

CASE STUDY

Has the Growth of Newly Industrializing Countries Hurt Advanced Nations?

In the early 1990s, many observers began warning that the growth of newly industrializing economies would pose a threat to the prosperity of advanced nations. In the Case Study in Chapter 5 on North-South trade, we addressed one way in which that growth might prove to be a problem: It might aggravate the growing gap in incomes between high-skilled and low-skilled workers in advanced nations. Some alarmists, however,

[5]"Immiserizing Growth: A Geometrical Note," *Review of Economic Studies* 25 (June 1958), pp. 201–205.

believed that the threat was still broader—that the overall real income of advanced nations, as opposed to its distribution, had been or would be reduced by the appearance of new competitors. This view was also held by a majority of respondents to a 2008 CBS poll: When asked "Do you think the recent economic expansion in countries like China and India has been generally good for the U.S. economy, or bad for the U.S. economy, or had no effect on the U.S. economy?" 62 percent said bad.

These concerns appeared to gain some intellectual support from a 2004 paper by Paul Samuelson, who created much of the modern theory of international trade. In that paper, Samuelson, using a Ricardian model, offered an example of how technological progress in developing countries can hurt advanced countries.[6] His analysis was simply a special case of the analysis we have just described: Growth in the rest of the world can hurt you if it takes place in sectors that compete with your exports. Samuelson took this to its logical conclusion: If China becomes sufficiently good at producing goods it currently imports, comparative advantage disappears—and the United States loses the gains from trade.

The popular press seized on this result, treating it as if it were somehow revolutionary. "The central question Samuelson and others raise is whether unfettered trade is always still as good for the U.S. as they have long believed," wrote *BusinessWeek*, which went on to suggest that such results might "completely derail comparative advantage theory."[7] Politicians also weighed-in, using Samuelson's paper and his towering stature within the economics profession to buttress arguments in favor of more protectionist policies.[8]

But the proposition that growth abroad can hurt your economy isn't a new idea, and it says nothing about whether free trade is better than protection. Also, it's an empirical question whether the growth of newly industrializing countries such as China has actually hurt advanced countries. And the facts don't support the claim.

Bear in mind that the channel through which growth abroad can hurt a country is via the terms of trade. So if the claim that competition from newly industrializing countries hurts advanced economies were true, we should see large negative numbers for the terms of trade of advanced countries and large positive numbers for the terms of trade of the new competitors. In the Mathematical Postscript to this chapter, we show that the percentage real income effect of a change in the terms of trade is approximately equal to the percent change in the terms of trade, multiplied by the share of imports in income. Since advanced countries on average spend about 25 percent of their income on imports (the United States' import share of GDP is lower than this average), a 1 percent decline in the terms of trade would reduce real income by only about 0.25 percent. So the terms of trade would have to decline by several percent a year to be a noticeable drag on economic growth.

Figure 6-8 shows the evolution of the terms of trade for both the United States and China over the last 30 years (normalized at 100 in 2000). We see that the magnitude of the yearly fluctuations in the terms of trade for the United States is small, with no clear trend over time. The U.S. terms of trade in 2011 is essentially at the same level as it was in 1980. Thus, there is no evidence that the United States has

---

[6]Paul Samuelson, "Where Ricardo and Mill Rebut and Confirm Arguments of Mainstream Economists Supporting Globalization," *Journal of Economic Perspectives* 18 (Summer 2004), pp. 135–146.
[7]"Shaking up Trade Theory," *BusinessWeek*, December 6, 2004.
[8]See, for example, "Clinton Doubts Benefits of Doha", *Financial Times*, December 3, 2007.

suffered any kind of sustained loss from a long-term deterioration in its terms of trade. Additionally, there is no evidence that China's terms of trade have steadily appreciated as it has become increasingly integrated into the world economy. If anything, its terms of trade have deteriorated over the last decade. This effect was confirmed in a recent paper using much more detail on Chinese industrial production.[9] The authors isolated the effects of Chinese manufacturing productivity growth (from 1995 to 2007) on its trading partners' terms of trade and found that this effect was positive, though small at .7 percent.

FIGURE 6-8

Evolution of the Terms of Trade for the United States and China (1980–2011, 2000 = 100)

One final point: In Samuelson's example, Chinese technological progress makes the United States worse off by eliminating trade between the two countries! Since what we actually see is rapidly growing China–U.S. trade, it's hard to find much of a relationship between the model and today's reality.

Source: World Development Indicators, World Bank.

Most developed countries tend to experience mild swings in their terms of trade, around 1 percent or less a year (on average), as illustrated for the United States in Figure 6-8. However, some developing countries' exports are heavily concentrated in mineral and agricultural sectors. The prices of those goods on world markets are very

---

[9]See Chang-Tai Hsieh and Ralph Ossa, "A Global View of Productivity Growth in China," National Bureau of Economic Research Working Paper 16778 (2011).

volatile, leading to large swings in the terms of trade. These swings in turn translate into substantial changes in welfare (because trade is concentrated in a small number of sectors and represents a substantial percentage of GDP). In fact, some studies show that most of the fluctuations in GDP in several developing countries (where GDP fluctuations are quite large relative to the GDP fluctuations in developed countries) can be attributed to fluctuations in their terms of trade.[10] For example, Argentina suffered a 6 percent deterioration in its terms of trade in 1999 (due to declining agricultural prices), which induced a 1.4 percent drop in GDP. (The actual GDP loss was higher, but other factors contributed to this deterioration.) On the other hand, Ecuador enjoyed an 18 percent increase in its terms of trade in 2000 (due to increases in oil prices), which added 1.6 percent to the GDP growth rate for that year.[11]

Tariffs and Export Subsidies: Simultaneous Shifts in *RS* and *RD*

Import tariffs (taxes levied on imports) and **export subsidies** (payments given to domestic producers who sell a good abroad) are not usually put in place to affect a country's terms of trade. These government interventions in trade usually take place for income distribution, for the promotion of industries thought to be crucial to the economy, or for balance of payments. (Note: We will examine these motivations in Chapters 10, 11, and 12.) Whatever the motive for tariffs and subsidies, however, they *do* have effects on terms of trade that can be understood by using the standard trade model.

The distinctive feature of tariffs and export subsidies is that they create a difference between prices at which goods are traded on the world market and prices at which those goods can be purchased within a country. The direct effect of a tariff is to make imported goods more expensive inside a country than they are outside the country. An export subsidy gives producers an incentive to export. It will therefore be more profitable to sell abroad than at home unless the price at home is higher, so such a subsidy raises the prices of exported goods inside a country. Note that this is very different from the effects of a production subsidy, which also lowers domestic prices for the affected goods (since the production subsidy does not discriminate based on the sales destination of the goods).

When countries are big exporters or importers of a good (relative to the size of the world market), the price changes caused by tariffs and subsidies change both relative supply and relative demand on world markets. The result is a shift in the terms of trade, both of the country imposing the policy change and of the rest of the world.

Relative Demand and Supply Effects of a Tariff

Tariffs and subsidies drive a wedge between the prices at which goods are traded internationally (**external prices**) and the prices at which they are traded within a country (**internal prices**). This means that we have to be careful in defining the terms of trade, which are intended to measure the ratio at which countries exchange goods; for example, how many units of food can Home import for each unit of cloth that it exports? This means that the terms of trade correspond to external, rather than internal, prices.

---

[10]See M. Ayhan Kose, "Explaining Business Cycles in Small Open Economies: 'How Much Do World Prices Matter?'" *Journal of International Economics* 56 (March 2002), pp. 299–327.

[11]See Christian Broda and Cédric Tille, "Coping with Terms-of-Trade Shocks in Developing Countries," *Current Issues in Economics and Finance* 9 (November 2003), pp 1–7.

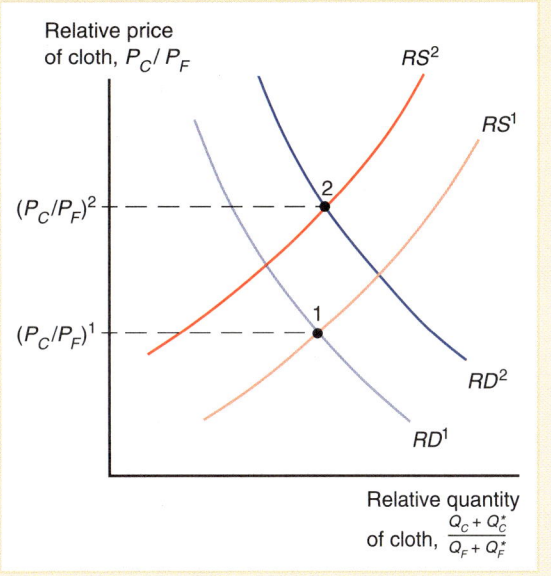

FIGURE 6-9

Effects of a Food Tariff on the Terms of Trade

An import tariff on food imposed by Home both reduces the relative supply of cloth (from RS^1 to RS^2) and increases the relative demand (from RD^1 to RD^2) for the world as a whole. As a result, the relative price of cloth must rise from $(P_C/P_F)^1$ to $(P_C/P_F)^2$.

When analyzing the effects of a tariff or export subsidy, therefore, we want to know how that tariff or subsidy affects relative supply and demand *as a function of external prices.*

If Home imposes a 20 percent tariff on the value of food imports, for example, the internal price of food relative to cloth faced by Home producers and consumers will be 20 percent higher than the external relative price of food on the world market. Equivalently, the internal relative price of cloth on which Home residents base their decisions will be lower than the relative price on the external market.

At any given world relative price of cloth, then, Home producers will face a lower relative cloth price and therefore will produce less cloth and more food. At the same time, Home consumers will shift their consumption toward cloth and away from food. From the point of view of the world as a whole, the relative supply of cloth will fall (from RS^1 to RS^2 in Figure 6-9) while the relative demand for cloth will rise (from RD^1 to RD^2). Clearly, the world relative price of cloth rises from $(P_C/P_F)^1$ to $(P_C/P_F)^2$, and thus Home's terms of trade improve at Foreign's expense.

The extent of this terms of trade effect depends on how large the country imposing the tariff is relative to the rest of the world: If the country is only a small part of the world, it cannot have much effect on world relative supply and demand and therefore cannot have much effect on relative prices. If the United States, a very large country, were to impose a 20 percent tariff, some estimates suggest that the U.S. terms of trade might rise by 15 percent. That is, the price of U.S. imports relative to exports might fall by 15 percent on the world market, while the relative price of imports would rise only 5 percent inside the United States. On the other hand, if Luxembourg or Paraguay were to impose a 20 percent tariff, the terms of trade effect would probably be too small to measure.

Effects of an Export Subsidy

Tariffs and export subsidies are often treated as similar policies, since they both seem to support domestic producers, but they have opposite effects on the terms of trade. Suppose that Home offers a 20 percent subsidy on the value of any cloth

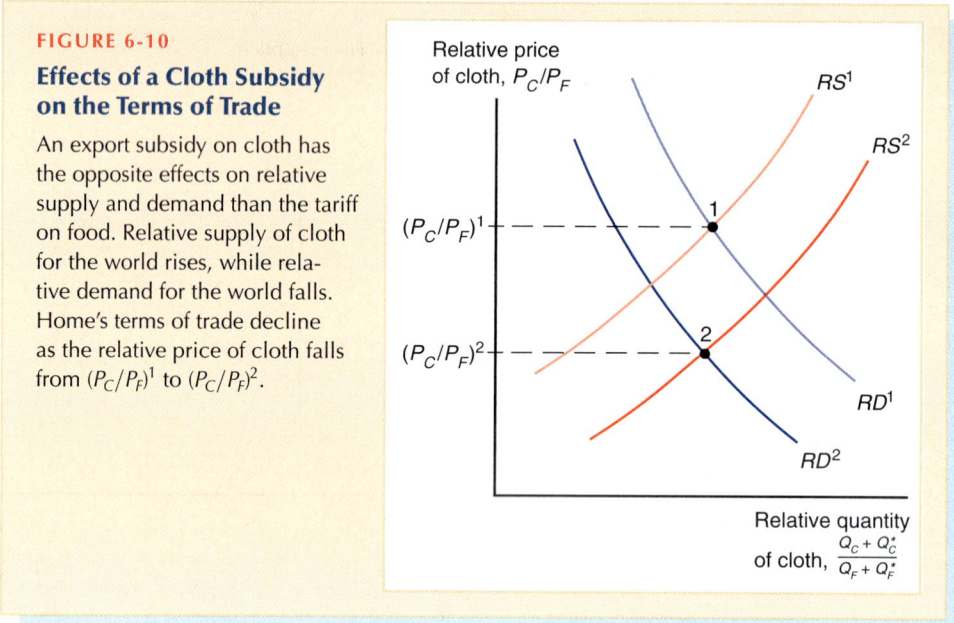

FIGURE 6-10

Effects of a Cloth Subsidy on the Terms of Trade

An export subsidy on cloth has the opposite effects on relative supply and demand than the tariff on food. Relative supply of cloth for the world rises, while relative demand for the world falls. Home's terms of trade decline as the relative price of cloth falls from $(P_C/P_F)^1$ to $(P_C/P_F)^2$.

exported. For any given world prices, this subsidy will raise Home's internal price of cloth relative to that of food by 20 percent. The rise in the relative price of cloth will lead Home producers to produce more cloth and less food, while leading Home consumers to substitute food for cloth. As illustrated in Figure 6-10, the subsidy will increase the world relative supply of cloth (from RS^1 to RS^2) and decrease the world relative demand for cloth (from RD^1 to RD^2), shifting equilibrium from point 1 to point 2. A Home export subsidy worsens Home's terms of trade and improves Foreign's.

Implications of Terms of Trade Effects: Who Gains and Who Loses?

If Home imposes a tariff, it improves its terms of trade at Foreign's expense. Thus, tariffs hurt the rest of the world. The effect on Home's welfare is not quite as clear-cut. The terms of trade improvement benefits Home; however, a tariff also imposes costs by distorting production and consumption incentives within Home's economy (see Chapter 9). The terms of trade gains will outweigh the losses from distortion only as long as the tariff is not too large. We will see later how to define an optimum tariff that maximizes net benefit. (For small countries that cannot have much impact on their terms of trade, the optimum tariff is near zero.)

The effects of an export subsidy are quite clear. Foreign's terms of trade improve at Home's expense, leaving it clearly better off. At the same time, Home loses from terms of trade deterioration *and* from the distorting effects of its policy.

This analysis seems to show that export subsidies never make sense. In fact, it is difficult to come up with situations where export subsidies would serve the national interest. The use of export subsidies as a policy tool usually has more to do with the peculiarities of trade politics than with economic logic.

Are foreign tariffs always bad for a country and foreign export subsidies always beneficial? Not necessarily. Our model is of a two-country world, where the other country exports the good we import and vice versa. In the real, multination world, a foreign government may subsidize the export of a good that competes with U.S. exports; this foreign subsidy will obviously hurt the U.S. terms of trade. A good example of this effect is European subsidies to agricultural exports (see Chapter 9). Alternatively, a country may impose a tariff on something the United States also imports, lowering its price and benefiting the United States. We thus need to qualify our conclusions from a two-country analysis: Subsidies to exports of things *the United States imports* help us, while tariffs *against U.S. exports* hurt us.

The view that subsidized foreign sales to the United States are good for us is not a popular one. When foreign governments are charged with subsidizing sales in the United States, the popular and political reaction is that this is unfair competition. Thus when the Commerce Department determined in 2012 that the Chinese government was subsidizing exports of solar panels to the United States, it responded by imposing a tariff on solar panel imports from China.[12] The standard model tells us that lower prices for solar panels are a good thing for the U.S. economy (which is a net importer of solar panels). On the other hand, some models based on imperfect competition and increasing returns to scale in production point to some potential welfare losses from the Chinese subsidy. Nevertheless, the subsidy's biggest impact falls on the distribution of income within the United States. If China subsidizes exports of solar panels to the United States, most U.S. residents gain from cheaper solar power. However, workers and investors in the U.S. solar panel industry are hurt by the lower import prices.

International Borrowing and Lending

Up to this point, all of the trading relationships we have described were not referenced by a time dimension: One good, say cloth, is exchanged for a different good, say food. In this section, we show how the standard model of trade we have developed can also be used to analyze another very important kind of trade between countries that occurs over time: international borrowing and lending. Any international transaction that occurs over time has a financial aspect, and this aspect is one of the main topics we address in the second half of this book. However, we can also abstract from those financial aspects and think of borrowing and lending as just another kind of trade: Instead of trading one good for another at a point in time, we exchange goods today in return for some goods in the future. This kind of trade is known as **intertemporal trade**; we will have much more to say about it later in this text, but for now we will analyze it using a variant of our standard trade model with a time dimension.[13]

Intertemporal Production Possibilities and Trade

Even in the absence of international capital movements, any economy faces a trade-off between consumption now and consumption in the future. Economies usually do not consume all of their current output; some of their output takes the form of investment in machines, buildings, and other forms of productive capital. The more investment an economy undertakes now, the more it will be able to produce and consume in the future. To invest more, however, an economy must release resources by consuming less (unless there are unemployed resources, a possibility we temporarily disregard). Thus, there is a trade-off between current and future consumption.

---

[12]See "U.S. Will Place Tariffs on Chinese Solar Panels," *New York Times*, October 10, 2012.

[13]See the appendix for additional details and derivations.

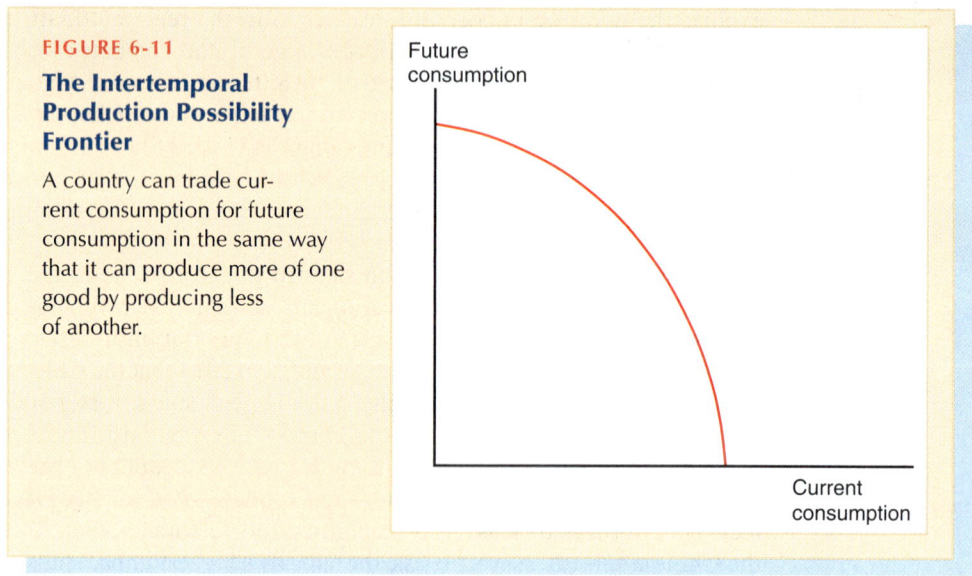

FIGURE 6-11

The Intertemporal Production Possibility Frontier

A country can trade current consumption for future consumption in the same way that it can produce more of one good by producing less of another.

Let's imagine an economy that consumes only one good and will exist for only two periods, which we will call current and future. Then there will be a trade-off between current and future production of the consumption good, which we can summarize by drawing an **intertemporal production possibility frontier**. Such a frontier is illustrated in Figure 6-11. It looks just like the production possibility frontiers between two goods at a point in time that we have been drawing.

The shape of the intertemporal production possibility frontier will differ among countries. Some countries will have production possibilities that are biased toward current output, while others are biased toward future output. We will ask in a moment what real differences these biases correspond to, but first let's simply suppose that there are two countries, Home and Foreign, with different intertemporal production possibilities. Home's possibilities are biased toward current consumption, while Foreign's are biased toward future consumption.

Reasoning by analogy, we already know what to expect. In the absence of international borrowing and lending, we would expect the relative price of future consumption to be higher in Home than in Foreign, and thus if we open the possibility of trade over time, we would expect Home to export current consumption and import future consumption.

This may, however, seem a little puzzling. What is the relative price of future consumption, and how does one trade over time?

The Real Interest Rate

How does a country trade over time? Like an individual, a country can trade over time by borrowing or lending. Consider what happens when an individual borrows: She is initially able to spend more than her income or, in other words, to consume more than her production. Later, however, she must repay the loan with interest, and therefore in the future she consumes *less* than she produces. By borrowing, then, she has in effect traded future consumption for current consumption. The same is true of a borrowing country.

Clearly the price of future consumption in terms of current consumption has something to do with the interest rate. As we will see in the second half of this book, in the real world the interpretation of interest rates is complicated by the possibility of changes in the overall price level. For now, we bypass that problem by supposing that loan contracts are specified in "real" terms: When a country borrows, it gets the right to purchase some quantity of consumption now in return for repayment of some larger quantity in the future. Specifically, the quantity of repayment in the future will be $(1 + r)$ times the quantity borrowed in the present, where r is the **real interest rate** on borrowing. Since the trade-off is one unit of current consumption for $(1 + r)$ units in the future, the relative price of future consumption is $1/(1 + r)$.

When this relative price of future consumption rises (that is, the real interest rate r falls), a country responds by investing more; this increases the supply of future consumption relative to current consumption (a leftward movement along the intertemporal production possibility frontier in Figure 6-11) and implies an upward-sloping relative supply curve for future consumption. We previously saw how a consumer's preferences for cloth and food could be represented by a relative demand curve relating relative consumption to the relative prices of those goods. Similarly, a consumer will also have preferences over time that capture the extent to which she is willing to substitute between current and future consumption. Those substitution effects are also captured by an intertemporal relative demand curve that relates the relative demand for future consumption (the ratio of future consumption to current consumption) to its relative price $1/(1 + r)$.

The parallel with our standard trade model is now complete. If borrowing and lending are allowed, the relative price of future consumption, and thus the world real interest rate, will be determined by the world relative supply and demand for future consumption. The determination of the equilibrium relative price $1/(1 + r^1)$ is shown in Figure 6-12 (notice the parallel with trade in goods and panel (a) of Figure 6-5). The intertemporal relative supply curves for Home and Foreign reflect how Home's production possibilities are biased toward current consumption whereas Foreign's production possibilities are biased toward future consumption. In other words, Foreign's

FIGURE 6-12

Equilibrium Interest Rate with Borrowing and Lending

Home, Foreign, and world supply of future consumption relative to current consumption. Home and Foreign have the same relative demand for future consumption, which is also the relative demand for the world. The equilibrium interest rate $1/(1 + r^1)$ is determined by the intersection of world relative supply and demand.

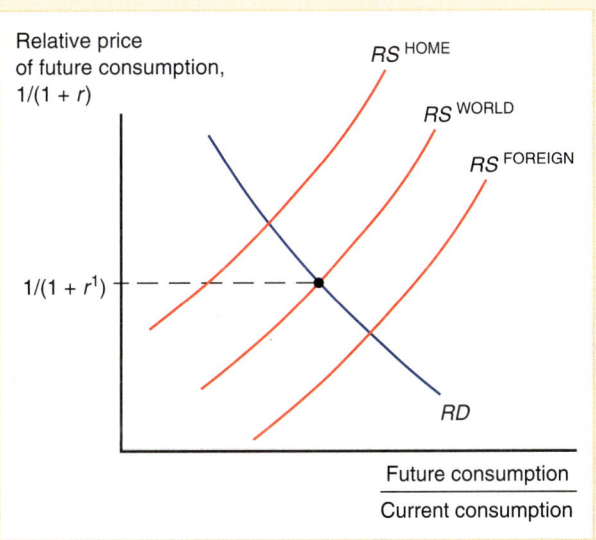

relative supply for future consumption is shifted out relative to Home's relative supply. At the equilibrium real interest rate, Home will export current consumption in return for imports of future consumption. That is, Home will lend to Foreign in the present and receive repayment in the future.

Intertemporal Comparative Advantage

We have assumed that Home's intertemporal production possibilities are biased toward current production. But what does this mean? The sources of intertemporal comparative advantage are somewhat different from those that give rise to ordinary trade.

A country that has a comparative advantage in future production of consumption goods is one that in the absence of international borrowing and lending would have a low relative price of future consumption, that is, a high real interest rate. This high real interest rate corresponds to a high return on investment, that is, a high return to diverting resources from current production of consumption goods to production of capital goods, construction, and other activities that enhance the economy's future ability to produce. So countries that borrow in the international market will be those where highly productive investment opportunities are available relative to current productive capacity, while countries that lend will be those where such opportunities are not available domestically.

SUMMARY

1. The standard trade model derives a world relative supply curve from production possibilities and a world relative demand curve from preferences. The price of exports relative to imports, a country's terms of trade, is determined by the intersection of the world relative supply and demand curves. Other things equal, a rise in a country's terms of trade increases its welfare. Conversely, a decline in a country's terms of trade will leave the country worse off.

2. Economic growth means an outward shift in a country's production possibility frontier. Such growth is usually biased; that is, the production possibility frontier shifts out more in the direction of some goods than in the direction of others. The immediate effect of biased growth is to lead, other things equal, to an increase in the world relative supply of the goods toward which the growth is biased. This shift in the world relative supply curve in turn leads to a change in the growing country's terms of trade, which can go in either direction. If the growing country's terms of trade improve, this improvement reinforces the initial growth at home but hurts the growth in the rest of the world. If the growing country's terms of trade worsen, this decline offsets some of the favorable effects of growth at home but benefits the rest of the world.

3. The direction of the terms of trade effects depends on the nature of the growth. Growth that is export-biased (growth that expands the ability of an economy to produce the goods it was initially exporting more than it expands the economy's ability to produce goods that compete with imports) worsens the terms of trade. Conversely, growth that is import-biased, disproportionately increasing the ability to produce import-competing goods, improves a country's terms of trade. It is possible for import-biased growth abroad to hurt a country.

4. Import tariffs and export subsidies affect both relative supply and relative demand. A tariff raises relative supply of a country's import good while lowering relative demand. A tariff unambiguously improves the country's terms of trade at the rest

of the world's expense. An export subsidy has the reverse effect, increasing the relative supply and reducing the relative demand for the country's export good, and thus worsening the terms of trade. The terms of trade effects of an export subsidy hurt the subsidizing country and benefit the rest of the world, while those of a tariff do the reverse. This suggests that export subsidies do not make sense from a national point of view and that foreign export subsidies should be welcomed rather than countered. Both tariffs and subsidies, however, have strong effects on the distribution of income within countries, and these effects often weigh more heavily on policy than the terms of trade concerns.

5. International borrowing and lending can be viewed as a kind of international trade, but one that involves trade of current consumption for future consumption rather than trade of one good for another. The relative price at which this intertemporal trade takes place is 1 plus the real rate of interest.

KEY TERMS

biased growth, p. 150
export-biased growth, p. 152
export subsidy, p. 156
external price, p. 156
immiserizing growth, p. 153
import-biased growth, p. 152

import tariff, p. 156
indifference curves, p. 145
internal price, p. 156
intertemporal production
    possibility frontier, p. 160
intertemporal trade, p. 159

isovalue lines, p. 144
real interest rate, p. 161
standard trade model, p. 143
terms of trade, p. 143

PROBLEMS

MyEconLab

1. Suppose Indonesia and China are trading partners. Indonesia initially exports palm oil to and imports lubricants from China. Using the standard trade model, explain how an increase in the relative price of palm oil—in relation to lubricant prices—would affect production and consumption of palm oil for Indonesia (assuming that the taste for both goods is the same in both countries). If the income effect of price change of palm oil is greater than the substitution effect, what would happen to palm oil consumption in Indonesia?

2. In the trade scenario in problem 1, due to overfishing, Norway becomes unable to catch the quantity of fish that it could in previous years. This change causes both a reduction in the potential quantity of fish that can be produced in Norway and an increase in the relative world price for fish, P_f/P_a.
   a. Show how the overfishing problem can result in a decline in welfare for Norway.
   b. Also show how it is possible that the overfishing problem could result in an *increase* in welfare for Norway.

3. Imagine the world having two countries producing wheat and cloth, with no difference in preferences across the two countries. If the home country—exporting cloth—experiences a growth strongly biased towards it, what would happen to the home country's terms of trade? How would the terms of trade be affected if the home country's production grows in favor of wheat?

4. The counterpart to immobile factors on the supply side would be lack of substitution on the demand side. Imagine an economy where consumers always buy goods in rigid proportions—for example, one yard of cloth for every pound of

food—regardless of the prices of the two goods. Show that an improvement in the terms of trade benefits this economy as well.

5. Japan primarily exports manufactured goods, while importing raw materials such as food and oil. Analyze the impact on Japan's terms of trade of the following events:

   a. A war in the Middle East disrupts oil supply.
   b. Korea develops the ability to produce automobiles that it can sell in Canada and the United States.
   c. U.S. engineers develop a fusion reactor that replaces fossil fuel electricity plants.
   d. A harvest failure in Russia.
   e. A reduction in Japan's tariffs on imported beef and citrus fruit.

6. The Internet has allowed for increased trade in services such as programming and technical support, a development that has lowered the prices of such services relative to those of manufactured goods. India in particular has been recently viewed as an "exporter" of technology-based services, an area in which the United States had been a major exporter. Using manufacturing and services as tradable goods, create a standard trade model for the U.S. and Indian economies that shows how relative price declines in exportable services that lead to the "outsourcing" of services can reduce welfare in the United States and increase welfare in India.

7. Countries A and B have two factors of production, capital and labor, with which they produce two goods, X and Y. Technology is the same in the two countries. X is capital-intensive; A is capital-abundant.

   Analyze the effects on the terms of trade and on the two countries' welfare of the following:

   a. An increase in A's capital stock.
   b. An increase in A's labor supply.
   c. An increase in B's capital stock.
   d. An increase in B's labor supply.

8. Economic growth is just as likely to worsen a country's terms of trade as it is to improve them. Why, then, do most economists regard immiserizing growth, where growth actually hurts the growing country, as unlikely in practice?

9. From an economic point of view, India and China are somewhat similar: Both are huge, low-wage countries, probably with similar patterns of comparative advantage, which until recently were relatively closed to international trade. China was the first to open up. Now that India is also opening up to world trade, how would you expect this to affect the welfare of China? Of the United States? (Hint: Think of adding a new economy identical to that of China to the world economy.)

10. "In a two country and a two commodity world, an imposition of home country's import tariff increases its terms of trade and export subsidy reduces its terms of trade"—explain. If an import tariff increases the home country's terms of trade, then, at present, why do countries agree to reduce the tariffs under bilateral and multilateral free trade agreements?

11. In a trade-off between current and future consumption, discuss how real interest rates affect the relative price of future consumption.

12. Which of the following countries would you expect to have intertemporal production possibilities biased toward current consumption goods, and which biased toward future consumption goods?

   a. A country like Argentina or Canada in the last century that has only recently been opened for large-scale settlement and is receiving large inflows of immigrants.

b. A country like the United Kingdom in the late 19th century or the United States today that leads the world technologically but is seeing that lead eroded as other countries catch up.

c. A country like Saudi Arabia that has discovered large oil reserves that can be exploited with little new investment.

d. A country that has discovered large oil reserves that can be exploited only with massive investment, such as Norway, whose oil lies under the North Sea.

e. A country like South Korea that has discovered the knack of producing industrial goods and is rapidly gaining on advanced countries.

FURTHER READINGS

Rudiger Dornbusch, Stanley Fischer, and Paul Samuelson. "Comparative Advantage, Trade, and Payments in a Ricardian Model with a Continuum of Goods." *American Economic Review* 67 (1977). This paper, cited in Chapter 3, also gives a clear exposition of the role of nontraded goods in establishing the presumption that a transfer improves the recipient's terms of trade.

Lawrence Edwards and Robert Z. Lawrence, *Rising Tide: Is Growth in Emerging Economies Good for the United States?* (Peterson Institute for International Economics, 2013), Chapter 5. This chapter provides a detailed analysis of the question raised in the case study on the effects of developing country growth on overall U.S. welfare.

Irving Fisher. *The Theory of Interest.* New York: Macmillan, 1930. The "intertemporal" approach described in this chapter owes its origin to Fisher.

J. R. Hicks. "The Long Run Dollar Problem." *Oxford Economic Papers* 2 (1953), pp. 117–135. The modern analysis of growth and trade has its origins in the fears of Europeans, in the early years after World War II, that the United States had an economic lead that could not be overtaken. (This sounds dated today, but many of the same arguments have now resurfaced about Japan.) The paper by Hicks is the most famous exposition.

Harry G. Johnson. "Economic Expansion and International Trade." *Manchester School of Social and Economic Studies* 23 (1955), pp. 95–112. The paper that laid out the crucial distinction between export- and import-biased growth.

Paul Krugman. "Does Third World Growth Hurt First World Prosperity?" *Harvard Business Review* 72 (July–August 1994), pp. 113–121. An analysis that attempts to explain why growth in developing countries need not hurt advanced countries in principle and probably does not do so in practice.

Jeffrey Sachs. "The Current Account and Macroeconomic Adjustment in the 1970s." *Brookings Papers on Economic Activity*, 1981. A study of international capital flows that views such flows as intertemporal trade.

MyEconLab Can Help You Get a Better Grade

MyEconLab   If your exam were tomorrow, would you be ready? For each chapter, MyEconLab Practice Tests and Study Plans pinpoint sections you have mastered and those you need to study. That way, you are more efficient with your study time, and you are better prepared for your exams.

To see how it works, turn to page 33 and then go to

www.myeconlab.com

More on Intertemporal Trade

This appendix contains a more detailed examination of the two-period intertemporal trade model described in the chapter. First consider Home, whose intertemporal production possibility frontier is shown in Figure 6A-1. Recall that the quantities of current and future consumption goods produced at Home depend on the amount of current consumption goods invested to produce future goods. As currently available resources are diverted from current consumption to investment, production of current consumption, Q_P, falls and production of future consumption, Q_F, rises. Increased investment therefore shifts the economy up and to the left along the intertemporal production possibility frontier.

The chapter showed that the price of future consumption in terms of current consumption is $1/(1 + r)$, where r is the real interest rate. Measured in terms of current consumption, the value of the economy's total production over the two periods of its existence is therefore

$$V = Q_C + Q_F/(1 + r).$$

Figure 6A-1 shows the isovalue lines corresponding to the relative price $1/(1 + r)$ for different values of V. These are straight lines with slope $-(1 + r)$ (because future consumption is on the vertical axis). As in the standard trade model, firms' decisions lead to a production pattern that maximizes the value of production at market prices $Q_C + Q_F/(1 + r)$. Production therefore occurs at point Q. The economy invests the amount shown, leaving Q_C available for current consumption and producing an amount Q_F of future consumption when the first-period investment pays off. (Notice the parallel with Figure 6-1 where production levels of cloth and food are chosen for a single period in order to maximize the value of production.)

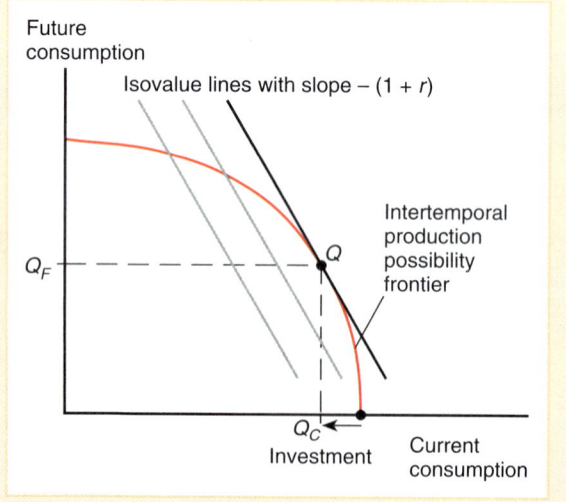

FIGURE 6A-1

Determining Home's Intertemporal Production Pattern

At a world real interest rate of r, Home's investment level maximizes the value of production over the two periods that the economy exists.

FIGURE 6A-2

Determining Home's Intertemporal Consumption Pattern

Home's consumption places it on the highest indifference curve touching its intertemporal budget constraint. The economy exports $Q_C - D_C$ units of current consumption and imports $D_F - Q_F = (1 + r) \times (Q_C - D_C)$ units of future consumption.

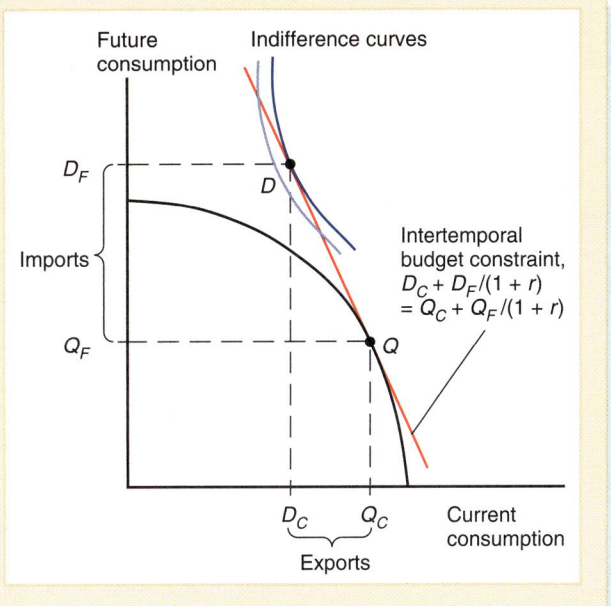

At the chosen production point Q, the extra future consumption that would result from investing an additional unit of current consumption just equals $(1 + r)$. It would be inefficient to push investment beyond point Q because the economy could do better by lending additional current consumption to foreigners instead. Figure 6A-1 implies that a rise in the world real interest rate r, which steepens the isovalue lines, causes investment to fall.

Figure 6A-2 shows how Home's consumption pattern is determined for a given world interest rate. Let D_C and D_F represent the demands for current and future consumption goods, respectively. Since production is at point Q, the economy's consumption possibilities over the two periods are limited by the *intertemporal budget constraint*:

$$D_C + D_F/(1 + r) = Q_C + Q_F/(1 + r).$$

This constraint states that the value of Home's consumption over the two periods (measured in terms of current consumption) equals the value of consumption goods produced in the two periods (also measured in current consumption units). Put another way, production and consumption must lie on the same isovalue line.

Point D, where Home's budget constraint touches the highest attainable indifference curve, shows the current and future consumption levels chosen by the economy. Home's demand for current consumption, D_C, is smaller than its production of current consumption, Q_C, so it exports (that is, lends) $Q_C - D_C$ units of current consumption to Foreigners. Correspondingly, Home imports $D_F - Q_F$ units of future consumption from abroad when its first-period loans are repaid to it with interest. The intertemporal budget constraint implies that $D_F - Q_F = (1 + r) \times (Q_C - D_C)$, so trade is *intertemporally* balanced. (Once again, note the parallel with Figure 6-3, where the economy exports cloth in return for imports of food.)

Figure 6A-3 shows how investment and consumption are determined in Foreign. Foreign is assumed to have a comparative advantage in producing *future* consumption

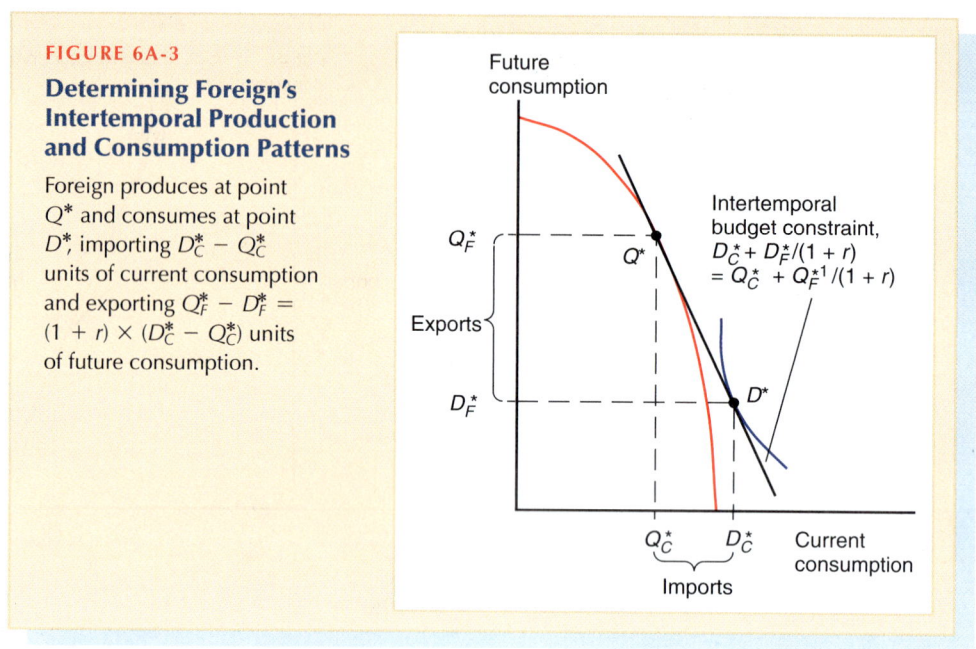

FIGURE 6A-3

Determining Foreign's Intertemporal Production and Consumption Patterns

Foreign produces at point Q^* and consumes at point D^*, importing $D_C^* - Q_C^*$ units of current consumption and exporting $Q_F^* - D_F^* = (1 + r) \times (D_C^* - Q_C^*)$ units of future consumption.

goods. The diagram shows that at a real interest rate of r, Foreign borrows consumption goods in the first period and repays this loan using consumption goods produced in the second period. Because of its relatively rich domestic investment opportunities and its relative preference for current consumption, Foreign is an importer of current consumption and an exporter of future consumption.

The differences between Home and Foreign's production possibility frontiers lead to the differences in the relative supply curves depicted in Figure 6-11. At the equilibrium interest rate $1/(1 + r^1)$, Home's desired export of current consumption equals Foreign's desired import of current consumption. Put another way, at that interest rate, Home's desired first-period lending equals Foreign's desired first-period borrowing. Supply and demand are therefore equal in both periods.

EXTERNAL ECONOMIES OF SCALE AND THE INTERNATIONAL LOCATION OF PRODUCTION

In Chapter 3, we pointed out that there are two reasons why countries specialize and trade. First, countries differ either in their resources or in their technology and specialize in the things they do relatively well; second, economies of scale (or increasing returns) make it advantageous for each country to specialize in the production of only a limited range of goods and services. The past four chapters considered models in which all trade is based on comparative advantage; that is, differences between countries are the only reason for trade. This chapter introduces the role of economies of scale.

The analysis of trade based on economies of scale presents certain problems that we have avoided so far. Until now, we have assumed markets are perfectly competitive, so that all monopoly profits are always competed away. When there are increasing returns, however, large firms may have an advantage over small ones, so that markets tend to be dominated by one firm (monopoly) or, more often, by a few firms (oligopoly). If this happens, our analysis of trade has to take into account the effects of imperfect competition.

However, economies of scale need not lead to imperfect competition if they take the form of *external* economies, which apply at the level of the industry rather than at the level of the individual firm. In this chapter, we will focus on the role of such external economies of scale in trade, reserving the discussion of internal economies for the next chapter.

LEARNING GOALS

After reading this chapter, you will be able to:

- Recognize why international trade often occurs from increasing returns to scale.
- Understand the differences between internal and external economies of scale.
- Discuss the sources of external economies.
- Discuss the roles of external economies and knowledge spillovers in shaping comparative advantage and international trade patterns.

169

Economies of Scale and International Trade: An Overview

The models of comparative advantage already presented were based on the assumption of constant returns to scale. That is, we assumed that if inputs to an industry were doubled, industry output would double as well. In practice, however, many industries are characterized by **economies of scale** (also referred to as increasing returns), so that production is more efficient the larger the scale at which it takes place. Where there are economies of scale, doubling the inputs to an industry will more than double the industry's production.

A simple example can help convey the significance of economies of scale for international trade. Table 7-1 shows the relationship between input and output of a hypothetical industry. Widgets are produced using only one input, labor; the table shows how the amount of labor required depends on the number of widgets produced. To produce 10 widgets, for example, requires 15 hours of labor, while to produce 25 widgets requires 30 hours. The presence of economies of scale may be seen from the fact that doubling the input of labor from 15 to 30 more than doubles the industry's output   in fact, output increases by a factor of 2.5. Equivalently, the existence of economies of scale may be seen by looking at the average amount of labor used to produce each unit of output: If output is only 5 widgets, the average labor input per widget is 2 hours, while if output is 25 units, the average labor input falls to 1.2 hours.

We can use this example to see why economies of scale provide an incentive for international trade. Imagine a world consisting of two countries, the United States and Britain, both of which have the same technology for producing widgets. Suppose each country initially produces 10 widgets. According to the table, this requires 15 hours of labor in each country, so in the world as a whole, 30 hours of labor produce 20 widgets. But now suppose we concentrate world production of widgets in one country, say the United States, and let the United States employ 30 hours of labor in the widget industry. In a single country, these 30 hours of labor can produce 25 widgets. So by concentrating production of widgets in the United States, the world economy can use the same amount of labor to produce 25 percent more widgets.

But where does the United States find the extra labor to produce widgets, and what happens to the labor that was employed in the British widget industry? To get the labor to expand its production of some goods, the United States must decrease or abandon the production of others; these goods will then be produced in Britain instead, using the labor formerly employed in the industries whose production has expanded in the United States. Imagine there are many goods subject to economies of scale in production, and give them numbers 1, 2, 3,.... To take advantage of economies of scale, each

TABLE 7-1	Relationship of Input to Output for a Hypothetical Industry	
Output	**Total Labor Input**	**Average Labor Input**
5	10	2
10	15	1.5
15	20	1.333333
20	25	1.25
25	30	1.2
30	35	1.166667

of the countries must concentrate on producing only a limited number of goods. Thus, for example, the United States might produce goods 1, 3, 5, and so on, while Britain produces 2, 4, 6, and so on. If each country produces only some of the goods, then each good can be produced at a larger scale than would be the case if each country tried to produce everything. As a result, the world economy can produce more of each good.

How does international trade enter the story? Consumers in each country will still want to consume a variety of goods. Suppose industry 1 ends up in the United States and industry 2 ends up in Britain; then American consumers of good 2 will have to buy goods imported from Britain, while British consumers of good 1 will have to import it from the United States. International trade plays a crucial role: It makes it possible for each country to produce a restricted range of goods and to take advantage of economies of scale without sacrificing variety in consumption. Indeed, as we will see in Chapter 8, international trade typically leads to an increase in the variety of goods available.

Our example, then, suggests how mutually beneficial trade can arise as a result of economies of scale. Each country specializes in producing a limited range of products, which enables it to produce these goods more efficiently than if it tried to produce everything for itself; these specialized economies then trade with each other to be able to consume the full range of goods.

Unfortunately, to go from this suggestive story to an explicit model of trade based on economies of scale is not that simple. The reason is that economies of scale may lead to a market structure other than that of perfect competition, and we need to be careful about analyzing this market structure.

Economies of Scale and Market Structure

In the example in Table 7-1, we represented economies of scale by assuming the labor input per unit of production is smaller the more units produced; this implies that at a given wage rate per hour, the average cost of production falls as output rises. We did not say how this production increase was achieved—whether existing firms simply produced more, or whether there was instead an increase in the number of firms. To analyze the effects of economies of scale on market structure, however, one must be clear about what kind of production increase is necessary to reduce average cost. **External economies of scale** occur when the cost per unit depends on the size of the industry but not necessarily on the size of any one firm. **Internal economies of scale** occur when the cost per unit depends on the size of an individual firm but not necessarily on that of the industry.

The distinction between external and internal economies can be illustrated with a hypothetical example. Imagine an industry that initially consists of 10 firms, each producing 100 widgets, for a total industry production of 1,000 widgets. Now consider two cases. First, suppose the industry were to double in size, so that it now consists of 20 firms, each one still producing 100 widgets. It is possible that the costs of each firm will fall as a result of the increased size of the industry; for example, a bigger industry may allow more efficient provision of specialized services or machinery. If this is the case, the industry exhibits external economies of scale. That is, the efficiency of firms is increased by having a larger industry, even though each firm is the same size as before.

Second, suppose the industry's output is held constant at 1,000 widgets, but that the number of firms is cut in half so that each of the remaining five firms produces 200 widgets. If the costs of production fall in this case, then there are internal economies of scale: A firm is more efficient if its output is larger.

External and internal economies of scale have different implications for the structure of industries. An industry where economies of scale are purely external (that is, where there are no advantages to large firms) will typically consist of many small firms and be perfectly competitive. Internal economies of scale, by contrast, give large firms a cost advantage over small firms and lead to an imperfectly competitive market structure.

Both external and internal economies of scale are important causes of international trade. Because they have different implications for market structure, however, it is difficult to discuss both types of scale economy–based trade in the same model. We will therefore deal with them one at a time. In this chapter, we focus on external economies; in the next, on internal economies.

The Theory of External Economies

As we have already pointed out, not all scale economies apply at the level of the individual firm. For a variety of reasons, it is often the case that concentrating production of an industry in one or a few locations reduces the industry's costs even if the individual firms in the industry remain small. When economies of scale apply at the level of the industry rather than at the level of the individual firm, they are called *external economies*. The analysis of external economies goes back more than a century to the British economist Alfred Marshall, who was struck by the phenomenon of "industrial districts"—geographical concentrations of industry that could not be easily explained by natural resources. In Marshall's time, the most famous examples included such concentrations of industry as the cluster of cutlery manufacturers in Sheffield and the cluster of hosiery firms in Northampton.

There are many modern examples of industries where there seem to be powerful external economies. In the United States, these examples include the semiconductor industry, concentrated in California's famous Silicon Valley; the investment banking industry, concentrated in New York; and the entertainment industry, concentrated in Hollywood. In the rising manufacturing industries of developing countries such as China, external economies are pervasive—for example, one town in China accounts for a large share of the world's underwear production; another produces nearly all of the world's cigarette lighters; yet another produces a third of the world's magnetic tape heads; and so on. External economies have also played a key role in India's emergence as a major exporter of information services, with a large part of this industry still clustered in and around the city of Bangalore.

Marshall argued that there are three main reasons why a cluster of firms may be more efficient than an individual firm in isolation: the ability of a cluster to support **specialized suppliers;** the way that a geographically concentrated industry allows **labor market pooling;** and the way that a geographically concentrated industry helps foster **knowledge spillovers.** These same factors continue to be valid today.

Specialized Suppliers

In many industries, the production of goods and services—and to an even greater extent, the development of new products—requires the use of specialized equipment or support services; yet an individual company does not provide a large enough market for these services to keep the suppliers in business. A localized industrial cluster can solve this problem by bringing together many firms that collectively provide a large enough market to support a wide range of specialized suppliers. This phenomenon has been extensively documented in Silicon Valley: A 1994 study recounts how, as the local industry grew, "engineers left established semiconductor companies to start firms that manufactured capital goods such as diffusion ovens, step-and-repeat cameras, and testers, and materials and components such as photomasks, testing jigs, and specialized chemicals.... This independent equipment sector promoted the continuing formation of semiconductor firms by freeing individual producers from the expense of developing capital equipment internally and by spreading the costs of development. It also reinforced the tendency toward industrial localization, as most of these specialized inputs were not available elsewhere in the country."

As the quote suggests, the availability of this dense network of specialized suppliers has given high-technology firms in Silicon Valley some considerable advantages over firms elsewhere. Key inputs are cheaper and more easily available because there are many firms competing to provide them, and firms can concentrate on what they do best, contracting out other aspects of their business. For example, some Silicon Valley firms that specialize in providing highly sophisticated computer chips for particular customers have chosen to become "fabless," that is, they do not have any factories in which chips can be fabricated. Instead, they concentrate on designing the chips, and then hire another firm to actually fabricate them.

A company that tried to enter the industry in another location—for example, in a country that did not have a comparable industrial cluster—would be at an immediate disadvantage because it would lack easy access to Silicon Valley's suppliers and would either have to provide them for itself or be faced with the task of trying to deal with Silicon Valley–based suppliers at long distance.

Labor Market Pooling

A second source of external economies is the way that a cluster of firms can create a pooled market for workers with highly specialized skills. Such a pooled market is to the advantage of both the producers and the workers, as the producers are less likely to suffer from labor shortages and the workers are less likely to become unemployed.

The point can best be made with a simplified example. Imagine there are two companies that both use the same kind of specialized labor, say, two film studios that make use of experts in computer animation. Both employers are, however, uncertain about how many workers they will want to hire: If demand for their product is high, both companies will want to hire 150 workers, but if it is low, they will want to hire only 50. Suppose also that there are 200 workers with this special skill. Now compare two situations: one with both firms and all 200 workers in the same city, the other with the firms, each with 100 workers, in two different cities. It is straightforward to show that both the workers and their employers are better off if everyone is in the same place.

First, consider the situation from the point of view of the companies. If they are in different locations, whenever one of the companies is doing well, it will be confronted with a labor shortage: It will want to hire 150 workers, but only 100 will be available. If the firms are near each other, however, it is at least possible that one will be doing well when the other is doing badly, so both firms may be able to hire as many workers as they want. By locating near each other, the companies increase the likelihood that they will be able to take advantage of business opportunities.

From the workers' point of view, having the industry concentrated in one location is also an advantage. If the industry is divided between two cities, then whenever one of the firms has a low demand for workers, the result will be unemployment: The firm will be willing to hire only 50 of the 100 workers who live nearby. But if the industry is concentrated in a single city, low labor demand from one firm will at least sometimes be offset by high demand from the other. As a result, workers will have a lower risk of unemployment.

Again, these advantages have been documented for Silicon Valley, where it is common both for companies to expand rapidly and for workers to change employers. The same study of Silicon Valley that was quoted previously notes that the concentration of firms in a single location makes it easy to switch employers. One engineer is quoted as saying that "it wasn't that big a catastrophe to quit your job on Friday and have another job on Monday.... You didn't even necessarily have to tell your wife. You just drove off in another direction on Monday morning."[1] This flexibility makes Silicon Valley an attractive location both for highly skilled workers and for the companies that employ them.

Knowledge Spillovers

It is by now a cliché that in the modern economy, knowledge is at least as important an input as are factors of production like labor, capital, and raw materials. This is especially true in highly innovative industries, where being even a few months behind the cutting edge in production techniques or product design can put a company at a major disadvantage.

But where does the specialized knowledge that is crucial to success in innovative industries come from? Companies can acquire technology through their own research and development efforts. They can also try to learn from competitors by studying their products and, in some cases, by taking them apart to "reverse engineer" their design and manufacture. An important source of technical know-how, however, is the informal exchange of information and ideas that takes place at a personal level. And this kind of informal diffusion of knowledge often seems to take place most effectively when an industry is concentrated in a fairly small area, so that employees of different companies mix socially and talk freely about technical issues.

Marshall described this process memorably when he wrote that in a district with many firms in the same industry, "The mysteries of the trade become no mystery, but are as it were in the air.... Good work is rightly appreciated, inventions and improvements in machinery, in processes and the general organization of the business have their merits promptly discussed: If one man starts a new idea, it is taken up by others and combined with suggestions of their own; and thus it becomes the source of further new ideas."

A journalist described how these knowledge spillovers worked during the rise of Silicon Valley (and also gave an excellent sense of the amount of specialized knowledge involved in the industry) as follows: "Every year there was some place, the Wagon Wheel, Chez Yvonne, Rickey's, the Roundhouse, where members of this esoteric fraternity, the young men and women of the semiconductor industry, would head after work to have a drink and gossip and trade war stories about phase jitters, phantom circuits, bubble memories, pulse trains, bounceless contacts, burst modes, leapfrog tests, p-n junctions, sleeping sickness modes, slow-death episodes, RAMs, NAKs, MOSes, PCMs, PROMs, PROM blowers, PROM blasters, and teramagnitudes...."[2] This kind of informal information flow means it is easier for

---

[1]Saxenian, p. 35.
[2]Tom Wolfe, quoted in Saxenian, p. 33.

companies in the Silicon Valley area to stay near the technological frontier than it is for companies elsewhere; indeed, many multinational firms have established research centers and even factories in Silicon Valley simply in order to keep up with the latest technology.

External Economies and Market Equilibrium

As we've just seen, a geographically concentrated industry is able to support specialized suppliers, provide a pooled labor market, and facilitate knowledge spillovers in a way that a geographically dispersed industry cannot. But the strength of these economies presumably depends on the industry's size: Other things equal, a bigger industry will generate stronger external economies. What does this say about the determination of output and prices?

While the details of external economies in practice are often quite subtle and complex (as the example of Silicon Valley shows), it can be useful to abstract from the details and represent external economies simply by assuming that the larger the industry, the lower the industry's costs. If we ignore international trade for the moment, then market equilibrium can be represented with a supply-and-demand diagram like Figure 7-1, which illustrates the market for widgets. In an ordinary picture of market equilibrium, the demand curve is downward sloping, while the supply curve is upward sloping. In the presence of external economies of scale, however, there is a **forward-falling supply curve:** the larger the industry's output, the lower the price at which firms are willing to sell, because their **average cost of production** falls as industry output rises.

In the absence of international trade, the unusual slope of the supply curve in Figure 7-1 doesn't seem to matter much. As in a conventional supply-and-demand analysis, the equilibrium price, P_1, and output, Q_1, are determined by the intersection of the demand curve and the supply curve. As we'll see next, however, external economies of scale make a huge difference to our view of the causes and effects of international trade.

FIGURE 7-1

External Economies and Market Equilibrium

When there are external economies of scale, the average cost of producing a good falls as the quantity produced rises. Given competition among many producers, the downward-sloping average cost curve *AC* can be interpreted as a *forward-falling supply curve*. As in ordinary supply-and-demand analysis, market equilibrium is at point 1, where the supply curve intersects the demand curve, *D*. The equilibrium level of output is Q_1, the equilibrium price P_1.

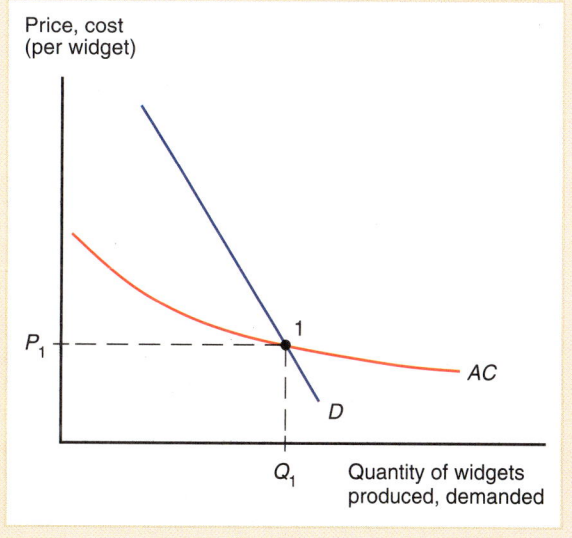

External Economies and International Trade

External economies drive a lot of trade both within and between countries. For example, New York exports financial services to the rest of the United States, largely because external economies in the investment industry have led to a concentration of financial firms in Manhattan. Similarly, Britain exports financial services to the rest of Europe, largely because those same external economies have led to a concentration of financial firms in London. But what are the implications of this kind of trade? We'll look first at the effects of trade on output and prices; then at the determinants of the pattern of trade; and finally at the effects of trade on welfare.

External Economies, Output, and Prices

Imagine, for a moment, we live in a world in which it is impossible to trade buttons across national borders. Assume, also, there are just two countries in this world: China and the United States. Finally, assume button production is subject to external economies of scale, which lead to a forward-falling supply curve for buttons in each country. (As the box on page 179 shows, this is actually true of the button industry.)

In that case, equilibrium in the world button industry would look like the situation shown in Figure 7-2.[3] In both China and the United States, equilibrium prices and output would be at the point where the domestic supply curve intersects the domestic

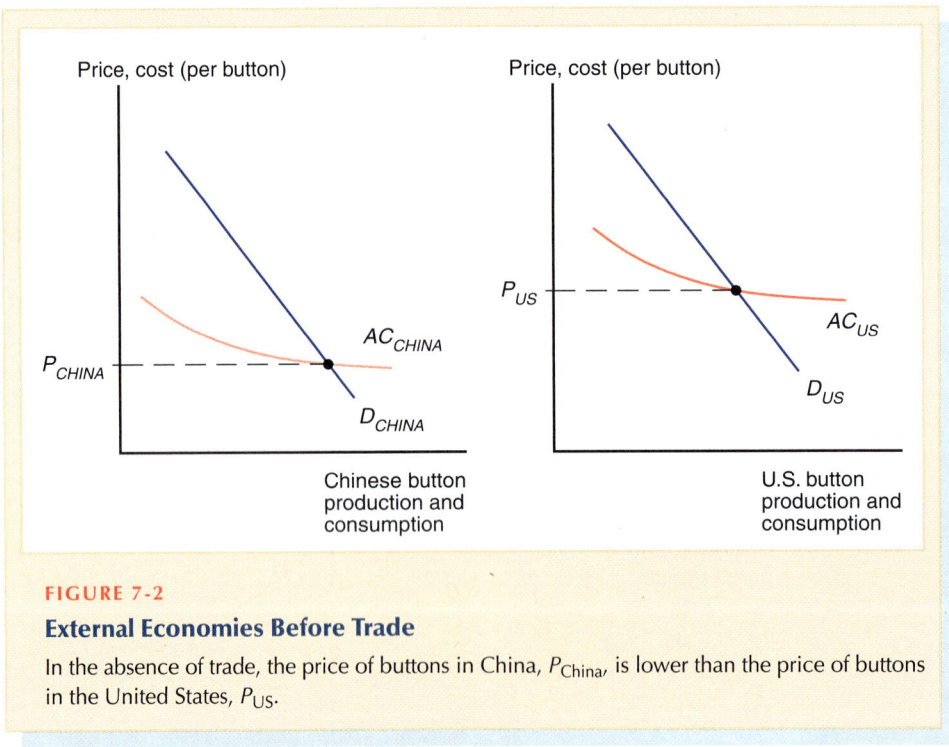

FIGURE 7-2

External Economies Before Trade

In the absence of trade, the price of buttons in China, P_{China}, is lower than the price of buttons in the United States, P_{US}.

---

[3]In this exposition, we focus for simplicity on *partial equilibrium* in the market for buttons, rather than on general equilibrium in the economy as a whole. It is possible, but much more complicated, to carry out the same analysis in terms of general equilibrium.

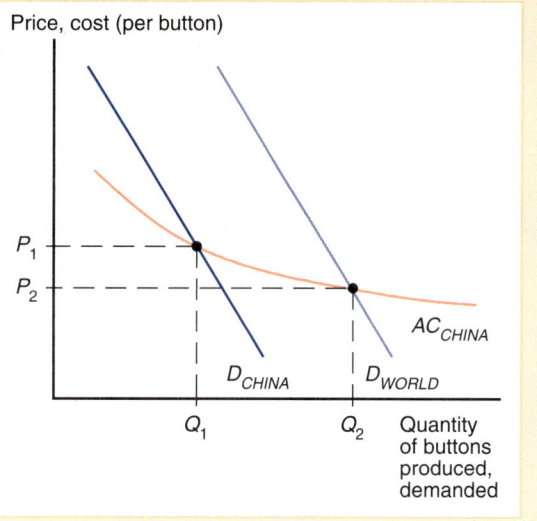

FIGURE 7-3

Trade and Prices

When trade is opened, China ends up producing buttons for the world market, which consists both of its own domestic market and of the U.S. market. Output rises from Q_1 to Q_2, leading to a fall in the price of buttons from P_1 to P_2, which is lower than the price of buttons in either country before trade.

demand curve. In the case shown in Figure 7-2, Chinese button prices in the absence of trade would be lower than U.S. button prices.

Now suppose we open up the potential for trade in buttons. What will happen?

It seems clear that the Chinese button industry will expand, while the U.S. button industry will contract. And this process will feed on itself: As the Chinese industry's output rises, its costs will fall further; as the U.S. industry's output falls, its costs will rise. In the end, we can expect all button production to be concentrated in China.

The effects of this concentration are illustrated in Figure 7-3. Before the opening of trade, China supplied only its own domestic button market. After trade, it supplies the world market, producing buttons for both Chinese and U.S. consumers.

Notice the effects of this concentration of production on prices. Because China's supply curve is forward-falling, increased production as a result of trade leads to a button price that is lower than the price before trade. And bear in mind that Chinese button prices were lower than American button prices before trade. What this tells us is that trade leads to button prices that are lower than the prices in *either* country before trade.

This is very different from the implications of models without increasing returns. In the standard trade model, as developed in Chapter 6, relative prices converge as a result of trade. If cloth is relatively cheap in Home and relatively expensive in Foreign before trade opens, the effect of trade will be to raise cloth prices in Home and reduce them in Foreign. In our button example, by contrast, the effect of trade is to reduce prices everywhere. The reason for this difference is that when there are external economies of scale, international trade makes it possible to concentrate world production in a single location, and therefore to reduce costs by reaping the benefits of even stronger external economies.

External Economies and the Pattern of Trade

In our example of world trade in buttons, we simply assumed the Chinese industry started out with lower production costs than the American industry. What might lead to such an initial advantage?

One possibility is comparative advantage—underlying differences in technology and resources. For example, there's a good reason why Silicon Valley is in California, rather than in Mexico. High-technology industries require a highly skilled work force, and such a work force is much easier to find in the United States, where 40 percent of the working-age population is college-educated, than in Mexico, where the number is below 16 percent. Similarly, there's a good reason why world button production is concentrated in China, rather than in Germany. Button production is a labor-intensive industry, which is best conducted in a country where the average manufacturing worker earns less than a dollar an hour rather than in a country where hourly compensation is among the highest in the world.

However, in industries characterized by external economies of scale, comparative advantage usually provides only a partial explanation of the pattern of trade. It was probably inevitable that most of the world's buttons would be made in a relatively low-wage country, but it's not clear that this country necessarily had to be China, and it certainly wasn't necessary that production be concentrated in any particular location within China.

So what does determine the pattern of specialization and trade in industries with external economies of scale? The answer, often, is historical contingency: Something gives a particular location an initial advantage in a particular industry, and this advantage gets "locked in" by external economies of scale even after the circumstances that created the initial advantage are no longer relevant. The financial centers in London and New York are clear examples. London became Europe's dominant financial center in the 19th century, when Britain was the world's leading economy and the center of a world-spanning empire. It has retained that role even though the empire is long gone and modern Britain is only a middle-sized economic power. New York became America's financial center thanks to the Erie Canal, which made it the nation's leading port. It has retained that role even though the canal currently is used mainly by recreational boats.

Often sheer accident plays a key role in creating an industrial concentration. Geographers like to tell the tale of how a tufted bedspread, crafted as a wedding gift by a 19th-century teenager, gave rise to the cluster of carpet manufacturers around Dalton, Georgia. Silicon Valley's existence may owe a lot to the fact that a couple of Stanford graduates named Hewlett and Packard decided to start a business in a garage in that area. Bangalore might not be what it is today if vagaries of local politics had not led Texas Instruments to choose, back in 1984, to locate an investment project there rather than in another Indian city.

One consequence of the role of history in determining industrial location is that industries aren't always located in the "right" place: Once a country has established an advantage in an industry, it may retain that advantage even if some other country could potentially produce the goods more cheaply.

Figure 7-4, which shows the cost of producing buttons as a function of the number of buttons produced annually, illustrates this point. Two countries are shown: China and Vietnam. The Chinese cost of producing a button is shown as AC_{China}, the Vietnamese cost as $AC_{Vietnam}$. D_{world} represents the world demand for buttons, which we assume can be satisfied either by China or by Vietnam.

Suppose the economies of scale in button production are entirely external to firms. Since there are no economies of scale at the level of the firm, the button industry in each country consists of many small, perfectly competitive firms. Competition therefore drives the price of buttons down to its average cost.

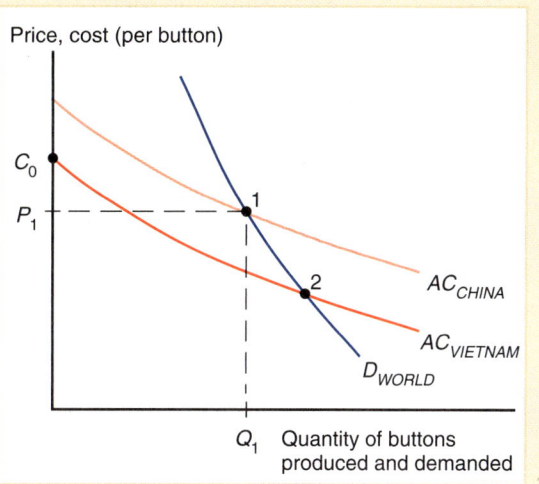

FIGURE 7-4

The Importance of Established Advantage

The average cost curve for Vietnam, $AC_{Vietnam}$, lies below the average cost curve for China, AC_{China}. Thus Vietnam could potentially supply the world market more cheaply than China. If the Chinese industry gets established first, however, it may be able to sell buttons at the price P_1, which is below the cost C_0 that an individual Vietnamese firm would face if it began production on its own. So a pattern of specialization established by historical accident may persist even when new producers could potentially have lower costs.

HOLDING THE WORLD TOGETHER

If you are reading this while fully clothed, the odds are that crucial parts of your outfit—specifically, the parts that protect you from a wardrobe malfunction—came from the Chinese town of Qiaotou, which produces 60 percent of the world's buttons and a large proportion of its zippers.

The Qiaotou fastener industry fits the classic pattern of geographical concentration driven by external economies of scale. The industry's origins lie in historical accident: In 1980, three brothers spotted some discarded buttons in the street, retrieved and sold them, then realized there was money to be made in the button business. There clearly aren't strong internal economies of scale: The town's button and zipper production is carried out by hundreds of small, family-owned firms. Yet there are clearly advantages to each of these small producers in operating in close proximity to the others.

Qiaotou isn't unique. As a fascinating article on the town's industry* put it, in China, "many small towns, not even worthy of a speck on most maps, have also become world-beaters by focusing on labour-intensive niches.... Start at the toothbrush town of Hang Ji, pass the tie mecca of Sheng Zhou, head east to the home of cheap cigarette lighters in Zhang Qi, slip down the coast to the giant shoe factories of Wen Ling, then move back inland to Yiwu, which not only makes more socks than anywhere else on earth, but also sells almost everything under the sun."

At a broad level, China's role as a huge exporter of labor-intensive products reflects comparative advantage: China is clearly labor-abundant compared with advanced economies. Many of those labor-intensive goods, however, are produced by highly localized industries, which benefit strongly from external economies of scale.

---

*"The Tiger's Teeth," *The Guardian*, May 25, 2005.

We assume the Vietnamese cost curve lies below the Chinese curve because, say, Vietnamese wages are lower than Chinese wages. This means that at any given level of production, Vietnam could manufacture buttons more cheaply than China. One might hope that this would always imply that Vietnam will in fact supply the world market. Unfortunately, this need not be the case. Suppose China, for historical reasons, establishes its button industry first. Then, initially, world button equilibrium will be established at point 1 in Figure 7-4, with Chinese production of Q_1 units per year and a price of P_1. Now introduce the possibility of Vietnamese production. If Vietnam could take over the world market, the equilibrium would move to point 2. However, if there is no initial Vietnamese production ($Q = 0$), any individual Vietnamese firm considering manufacture of buttons will face a cost of production of C_0. As we have drawn it, this cost is above the price at which the established Chinese industry can produce buttons. So although the Vietnamese industry could potentially make buttons more cheaply than China's industry, China's head start enables it to hold on to the industry.

As this example shows, external economies potentially give a strong role to historical accident in determining who produces what, and may allow established patterns of specialization to persist even when they run counter to comparative advantage.

Trade and Welfare with External Economies

In general, we can presume that external economies of scale lead to gains from trade over and above those from comparative advantage. The world is more efficient and thus richer because international trade allows nations to specialize in different industries and thus reap the gains from external economies as well as from comparative advantage.

However, there are a few possible qualifications to this presumption. As we saw in Figure 7-4, the importance of established advantage means that there is no guarantee that the right country will produce a good subject to external economies. In fact, it is possible that trade based on external economies may actually leave a country worse off than it would have been in the absence of trade.

An example of how a country can actually be worse off with trade than without is shown in Figure 7-5. In this example, we imagine that Thailand and Switzerland

FIGURE 7-5

External Economies and Losses from Trade

When there are external economies, trade can potentially leave a country worse off than it would be in the absence of trade. In this example, Thailand imports watches from Switzerland, which is able to supply the world market (D_{WORLD}) at a price (P_1) low enough to block entry by Thai producers, who must initially produce the watches at cost C_0. Yet if Thailand were to block all trade in watches, it would be able to supply its domestic market (D_{THAI}) at the lower price, P_2.

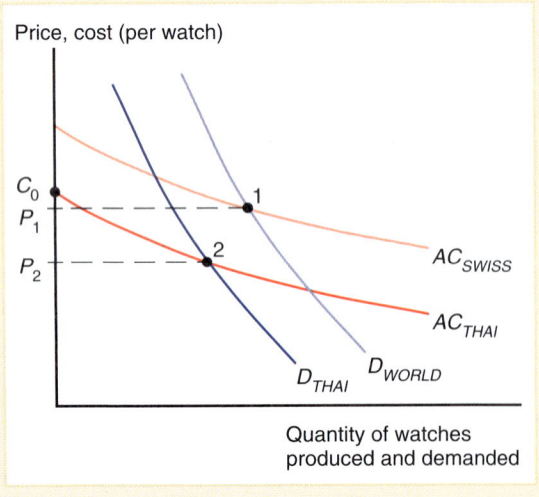

CHAPTER 7 ■ External Economies of Scale and the International Location of Production ___ 181

could both manufacture watches, that Thailand could make them more cheaply, but that Switzerland has gotten there first. D_{WORLD} is the world demand for watches, and, given that Switzerland produces the watches, the equilibrium is at point 1. However, we now add to the figure the Thai demand for watches, D_{THAI}. If no trade in watches were allowed and Thailand were forced to be self-sufficient, then the Thai equilibrium would be at point 2. Because of its lower average cost curve, the price of Thai-made watches at point 2, P_2, is actually lower than the price of Swiss-made watches at point 1, P_1.

We have presented a situation in which the price of a good that Thailand imports would actually be lower if there were no trade and the country were forced to produce the good for itself. Clearly in this situation, trade leaves the country worse off than it would be in the absence of trade.

There is an incentive in this case for Thailand to protect its potential watch industry from foreign competition. Before concluding that this justifies protectionism, however, we should note that in practice, identifying cases like that shown in Figure 7-5 is far from easy. Indeed, as we will emphasize in Chapters 10 and 11, the difficulty of identifying external economies in practice is one of the main arguments against activist government policies toward trade.

It is also worth pointing out that while external economies can sometimes lead to disadvantageous patterns of specialization and trade, it's virtually certain that it is still to the benefit of the *world* economy to take advantage of the gains from concentrating industries. Canada might be better off if Silicon Valley were near Toronto instead of San Francisco; Germany might be better off if the City (London's financial district, which, along with Wall Street, dominates world financial markets) could be moved to Frankfurt. But overall, it's better for the world that each of these industries be concentrated *somewhere*.

Dynamic Increasing Returns

Some of the most important external economies probably arise from the accumulation of knowledge. When an individual firm improves its products or production techniques through experience, other firms are likely to imitate the firm and benefit from its knowledge. This spillover of knowledge gives rise to a situation in which the production costs of individual firms fall as the industry as a whole accumulates experience.

Notice that external economies arising from the accumulation of knowledge differ somewhat from the external economies considered so far, in which industry costs depend on current output. In this alternative situation, industry costs depend on experience, usually measured by the cumulative output of the industry to date. For example, the cost of producing a ton of steel might depend negatively on the total number of tons of steel produced by a country since the industry began. This kind of relationship is often summarized by a **learning curve** that relates unit cost to cumulative output. Such learning curves are illustrated in Figure 7-6. They are downward sloping because of the effect on costs of the experience gained through production. When costs fall with cumulative production over time rather than with the current rate of production, this is referred to as a case of **dynamic increasing returns.**

Like ordinary external economies, dynamic external economies can lock in an initial advantage or head start in an industry. In Figure 7-6, the learning curve L is that of a country that pioneered an industry, while L^* is that of a country that has lower input costs—say, lower wages—but less production experience. Provided the first country has a sufficiently large head start, the potentially lower costs of the second country may not allow the second country to enter the market. For example, suppose

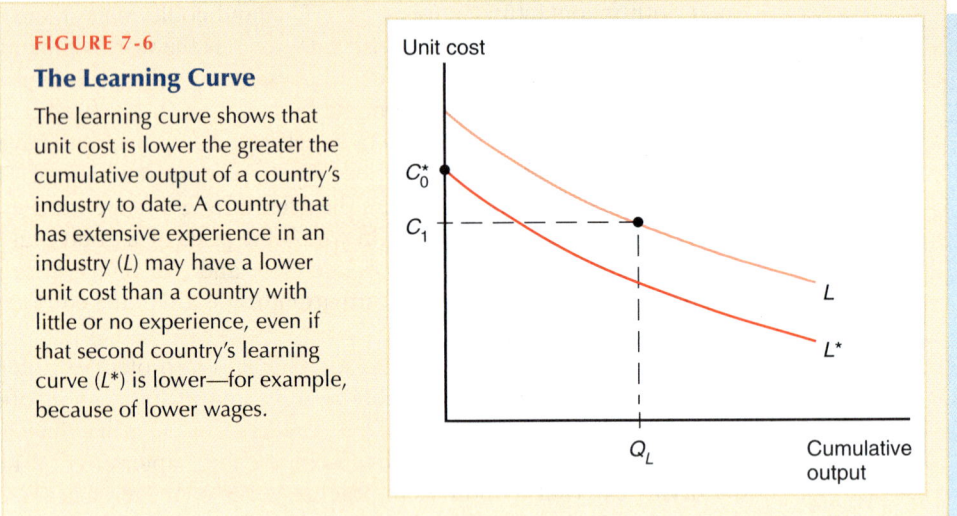

FIGURE 7-6

The Learning Curve

The learning curve shows that unit cost is lower the greater the cumulative output of a country's industry to date. A country that has extensive experience in an industry (L) may have a lower unit cost than a country with little or no experience, even if that second country's learning curve (L^*) is lower—for example, because of lower wages.

the first country has a cumulative output of Q_L units, giving it a unit cost of C_1, while the second country has never produced the good. Then the second country will have an initial start-up cost, C_0^*, that is higher than the current unit cost, C_1, of the established industry.

Dynamic scale economies, like external economies at a point in time, potentially justify protectionism. Suppose a country could have low enough costs to produce a good for export if it had more production experience, but given the current lack of experience, the good cannot be produced competitively. Such a country might increase its long-term welfare either by encouraging the production of the good by a subsidy or by protecting it from foreign competition until the industry can stand on its own feet. The argument for temporary protection of industries to enable them to gain experience is known as the **infant industry argument**; this argument has played an important role in debates over the role of trade policy in economic development. We will discuss the infant industry argument at greater length in Chapter 10, but for now, we simply note that situations like that illustrated in Figure 7-6 are just as hard to identify in practice as those involving nondynamic increasing returns.

Interregional Trade and Economic Geography

External economies play an important role in shaping the pattern of international trade, but they are even more decisive in shaping the pattern of **interregional trade**—trade that takes place between regions *within* countries.

To understand the role of external economies in interregional trade, we first need to discuss the nature of regional economics—that is, how the economies of regions within a nation fit into the national economy. Studies of the location of U.S. industries suggest that more than 60 percent of U.S. workers are employed by industries whose output is nontradable even within the United States—that is, it must be supplied locally. Table 7-2 shows some examples of tradable and nontradable industries. Thus, motion pictures made in Hollywood are shown across the country, and indeed around the world, but newspapers are mainly read in their home cities. Wall Street trades stocks and makes deals for clients across the United States, but savings banks mainly serve local depositors. Scientists at the National Institutes of Health develop

TABLE 7-2	Some Examples of Tradable and Nontradable Industries	
Tradable Industries	**Nontradable Industries**
Motion pictures	Newspaper publishers
Securities, commodities, etc.	Savings institutions
Scientific research	Veterinary services

Source: J. Bradford Jensen and Lori. G. Kletzer, "Tradable Services: Understanding the Scope and Impact of Services Outsourcing," in Lael Brainard and Susan M. Collins, eds., *Brookings Trade Forum 2005: Offshoring White Collar Work* (Washington, D.C.: Brookings Institution, 2005), pp. 75–116.

medical knowledge that is applied across the whole country, but the veterinarian who figures out why your pet is sick has to be near your home.

As you might expect, the share of nontradable industries in employment is pretty much the same across the United States. For example, restaurants employ about 5 percent of the work force in every major U.S. city. On the other hand, tradable industries vary greatly in importance across regions. Manhattan accounts for only about 2 percent of America's total employment, but it accounts for a quarter of those employed in trading stocks and bonds and about one-seventh of employment in the advertising industry.

But what determines the location of tradable industries? In some cases, natural resources play a key role—for example, Houston is a center for the oil industry because east Texas is where the oil is. However, factors of production such as labor and capital play a less decisive role in interregional trade than in international trade, for the simple reason that such factors are highly mobile within countries. As a result, factors tend to move to where the industries are rather than the other way around. For example, California's Silicon Valley, near San Francisco, has a very highly educated labor force, with a high concentration of engineers and computer experts. That's not because California trains lots of engineers; it's because engineers move to Silicon Valley to take jobs in the region's high-tech industry.

Resources, then, play a secondary role in interregional trade. What largely drives specialization and trade, instead, is external economies. Why, for example, are so many advertising agencies located in New York? The answer is because so many *other* advertising agencies are located in New York. As one study put it, "Information sharing and information diffusion are critical to a team and an agency's success.... In cities like New York, agencies group in neighborhood clusters. Clusters promote localized networking, to enhance creativity; agencies share information and ideas and in doing this face-to-face contact is critical."[4] In fact, the evidence suggests the external economies that support the advertising business are *very* localized: To reap the benefits of information spillovers, ad agencies need to be located within about 300 yards of each other!

But if external economies are the main reason for regional specialization and interregional trade, what explains how a particular region develops the external economies that support an industry? The answer, in general, is that accidents of history play a crucial role. As noted earlier, a century and a half ago, New York was America's most important port city because it had access to the Great Lakes via the Erie Canal.

---

[4]J. Vernon Henderson, "What Makes Big Cities Tick? A Look at New York," mimeo, Brown University, 2004.

TINSELTOWN ECONOMICS

What is the United States' most important export sector? The answer depends to some extent on definitions; some people will tell you that it is agriculture, others that it is aircraft. By any measure, however, one of the biggest exporters in the United States is the entertainment sector, movies in particular. In 2011, rental fees generated by exports of films and tape were $14.3 billion, compared with only $10.2 billion in domestic box office receipts. American films dominated ticket sales in much of the world; for example, they accounted for about two-thirds of box office receipts in Europe.

Why is the United States the world's dominant exporter of entertainment? There are important advantages arising from the sheer size of the American market. A film aimed primarily at the French or Italian markets, which are far smaller than that of the United States, cannot justify the huge budgets of many American films. Thus, films from these countries are typically dramas or comedies whose appeal fails to survive dubbing or subtitles. Meanwhile, American films can transcend the language barrier with lavish productions and spectacular special effects.

But an important part of the American dominance in the industry also comes from the external economies created by the immense concentration of entertainment firms in Hollywood. Hollywood clearly generates two of Marshall's types of external economies: specialized suppliers and labor market pooling. While the final product is provided by movie studios and television networks, these in turn draw on a complex web of independent producers, casting and talent agencies, legal firms, special effects experts, and so on. And the need for labor market pooling is obvious to anyone who has ever watched the credits at the end of a movie: Each production requires a huge but temporary army that includes not just cameramen and makeup artists but musicians, stuntmen and women, and mysterious occupations like gaffers and grips (and—oh yes—actors and actresses). Whether it also generates the third kind of external economies—knowledge spillovers—is less certain. After all, as the author Nathaniel West once remarked, the key to understanding the movie business is to realize that "nobody knows anything." Still, if there is any knowledge to spill over, surely it does so better in the intense social environment of Hollywood than it could anywhere else.

An indication of the force of Hollywood's external economies has been its persistent ability to draw talent from outside the United States. From Garbo and von Sternberg to Russell Crowe and Guillermo del Toro, "American" films have often been made by ambitious foreigners who moved to Hollywood—and in the end, reached a larger audience even in their original nations than they could have if they had remained at home.

Is Hollywood unique? No, similar forces have led to the emergence of several other entertainment complexes. In India, whose film market has been protected from American domination partly by government policy and partly by cultural differences, a moviemaking cluster known as "Bollywood" has emerged in Bombay. In recent years, Bollywood films have developed a wide following outside India, and film is rapidly becoming a significant Indian export industry. A substantial film industry catering to Chinese speakers has emerged in Hong Kong; in addition, many U.S.-made action films are strongly influenced by Hong Kong style. A specialty industry producing Spanish-language television programs for all of Latin America, focusing on so-called *telenovelas*, long-running soap operas, has emerged in Caracas, Venezuela. And in recent years a Nigerian film complex—"Nollywood"—has emerged, using digital techniques to produce relatively low-budget films that are exported as direct-to-video entertainment, largely but not entirely to other African nations.

That led to New York's becoming America's financial center; it remains America's financial center today thanks to the external economies the financial industry creates for itself. Los Angeles became the center of the early film industry when films were shot outdoors and needed good weather; it remains the center of the film industry today, even though many films are shot indoors or on location, because of the externalities described in the box on page 184.

A question you might ask is whether the forces driving interregional trade are really all that different from those driving international trade. The answer is that they are not, especially when one looks at trade between closely integrated national economies, such as those of Western Europe. Indeed, London plays a role as Europe's financial capital similar to the role played by New York as America's financial capital. In recent years, there has been a growing movement among economists to model interregional and international trade, as well as such phenomena as the rise of cities, as different aspects of the same phenomenon—economic interaction across space. Such an approach is often referred to as **economic geography**.

SUMMARY

1. Trade need not be the result of comparative advantage. Instead, it can result from increasing returns or economies of scale, that is, from a tendency of unit costs to be lower with larger output. Economies of scale give countries an incentive to specialize and trade even in the absence of differences in resources or technology between countries. Economies of scale can be internal (depending on the size of the firm) or external (depending on the size of the industry).

2. Economies of scale can lead to a breakdown of perfect competition, unless they take the form of external economies, which occur at the level of the industry instead of the firm.

3. External economies give an important role to history and accident in determining the pattern of international trade. When external economies are important, a country starting with a large advantage may retain that advantage even if another country could potentially produce the same goods more cheaply. When external economies are important, countries can conceivably lose from trade.

KEY TERMS

average cost of production,
 p. 175
dynamic increasing returns,
 p. 181
economic geography, p. 185
economies of scale, p. 170
external economies of scale,
 p. 171

forward-falling supply curve,
 p. 175
infant industry argument,
 p. 182
internal economies of scale,
 p. 171
interregional trade, p. 182

knowledge spillovers, p. 172
labor market pooling, p. 172
learning curve, p. 181
specialized suppliers,
 p. 172

PROBLEMS

MyEconLab

1. For each of the following examples, explain whether it is a case of external or internal economies of scale:

   a. A number of firms doing contract research for the drug industry are concentrated in southeastern South Carolina.

   b. All Hondas produced in the United States come from plants in Ohio, Indiana, or Alabama.

    c. All airframes for Airbus, Europe's only producer of large aircraft, are assembled in Toulouse, France.

    d. Cranbury, New Jersey, is the artificial flavor capital of the United States.

2. It is often argued that local knowledge spillover is more feasible for firms existing in clusters. The difficulty in transferring the knowledge lies in the distance. Explain with reference to the situation addressed in the knowledge spillovers section. Give one example of an industry cluster in a developing country.

3. Give two examples of products that are traded on international markets for which there are dynamic increasing returns. In each of your examples, show how innovation and learning-by-doing are important to the dynamic increasing returns in the industry.

4. Evaluate the relative importance of economies of scale and comparative advantage in causing the following:

    a. Most of the world's aluminum is smelted in Norway or Canada.

    b. Half of the world's large jet aircraft are assembled in Seattle.

    c. Most semiconductors are manufactured in either the United States or Japan.

    d. Most Scotch whiskey comes from Scotland.

    e. Much of the world's best wine comes from France.

5. Consider two countries—India and Japan—facing a forward falling supply curve. Both produce two commodities—cloth and radios. India, a labor surplus country, produces cloth using cheap labor. This reduces its domestic price in comparison to Japan. Similarly, Japan being technologically advanced produces radios at a lower cost than India. If both are open to trade, ceteris paribus.

    a. What will happen to the world market price for cloth and radio?

    b. What would you expect of the international trade and who would produce what, if neither India nor Japan has an initial advantage of lower price?

6. It is fairly common for an industrial cluster to break up and for production to move to locations with lower wages when the technology of the industry is no longer rapidly improving—when it is no longer essential to have the absolutely most modern machinery, when the need for highly skilled workers has declined, and when being at the cutting edge of innovation conveys only a small advantage. Explain this tendency of industrial clusters to break up in terms of the theory of external economies.

7. Is it always true that trade increases the welfare of a nation? Under what circumstances would the concentration of industries in one country leave another country worse off when trade resumes between them? Explain with an example.

8. In our discussion of labor market pooling, we stressed the advantages of having two firms in the same location: If one firm is expanding while the other is contracting, it's to the advantage of both workers and firms that they be able to draw on a single labor pool. But it might happen that both firms want to expand or contract at the same time. Does this constitute an argument against geographical concentration? (Think through the numerical example carefully.)

9. Which of the following goods or services would be most likely to be subject to (1) external economies of scale and (2) dynamic increasing returns? Explain your answers.

    a. Software tech-support services

    b. Production of asphalt or concrete

    c. Motion pictures

    d. Cancer research

    e. Timber harvesting

FURTHER READINGS

Frank Graham. "Some Aspects of Protection Further Considered." *Quarterly Journal of Economics* 37 (1923), pp. 199–227. An early warning that international trade may be harmful in the presence of external economies of scale.

Li & Fung Research Centre. *Industrial Cluster Series*, 2006–2010. Li and Fung, a Hong Kong–based trading group, has published a series of reports on rising industrial concentrations in Chinese manufacturing.

Staffan Burenstam Linder. *An Essay on Trade and Transformation.* New York: John Wiley and Sons, 1961. An early and influential statement of the view that trade in manufactures among advanced countries mainly reflects forces other than comparative advantage.

Michael Porter. *The Competitive Advantage of Nations.* New York: Free Press, 1990. A best-selling book that explains national export success as the result of self-reinforcing industrial clusters, that is, external economies.

Annalee Saxenian. *Regional Advantage.* Cambridge: Harvard University Press, 1994. A fascinating comparison of two high-technology industrial districts, California's Silicon Valley and Boston's Route 128.

World Bank. *World Development Report 2009.* A huge survey of the evidence on economic geography, with extensive discussion of industrial clusters in China and other emerging economies.

MyEconLab Can Help You Get a Better Grade

MyEconLab   If your exam were tomorrow, would you be ready? For each chapter, MyEconLab Practice Tests and Study Plans pin-point sections you have mastered and those you need to study. That way, you are more efficient with your study time, and you are better prepared for your exams.

To see how it works, turn to page 33 and then go to

www.myeconlab.com

FIRMS IN THE GLOBAL ECONOMY: EXPORT DECISIONS, OUTSOURCING, AND MULTINATIONAL ENTERPRISES

In this chapter, we continue to explore how economies of scale generate incentives for international specialization and trade. We now focus on economies of scale that are internal to the firm. As mentioned in the previous chapter, this form of increasing returns leads to a market structure that features imperfect competition. **Internal economies of scale** imply that a firm's average cost of production decreases the more output it produces. Perfect competition that drives the price of a good down to marginal cost would imply losses for those firms because they would not be able to recover the higher costs incurred from producing the initial units of output.[1] As a result, perfect competition would force those firms out of the market, and this process would continue until an equilibrium featuring imperfect competition is attained.

Modeling imperfect competition means that we will explicitly consider the behavior of individual firms. This will allow us to introduce two additional characteristics of firms that are prevalent in the real world: (1) In most sectors, firms produce goods that are differentiated from one another. In the case of certain goods (such as bottled water, staples, etc.), those differences across products may be small, while in others (such as cars, cell phones, etc.), the differences are much more significant. (2) Performance measures (such as size and profits) vary widely across firms. We will incorporate this first characteristic (product differentiation) into our analysis throughout this chapter. To ease exposition and build intuition, we will initially consider the case when there are no performance differences between firms. We will thus see how internal economies of scale and product differentiation combine to generate some new sources of gains of trade via economic integration.

---

[1]Whenever average cost is decreasing, the cost of producing one extra unit of output (marginal cost) is lower than the average cost of production (since that average includes the cost of those initial units that were produced at higher unit costs).

We will then introduce differences across firms so that we can analyze how firms respond differently to international forces. We will see how economic integration generates both winners and losers among different types of firms. The better-performing firms thrive and expand, while the worse-performing firms contract. This generates one additional source of gain from trade: As production is concentrated toward better-performing firms, the overall efficiency of the industry improves. Lastly, we will study why those better-performing firms have a greater incentive to engage in the global economy, either by exporting, by outsourcing some of their intermediate production processes abroad, or by becoming multinationals and operating in multiple countries.

LEARNING GOALS

After reading this chapter, you will be able to:

- Understand how internal economies of scale and product differentiation lead to international trade and intra-industry trade.
- Recognize the new types of welfare gains from intra-industry trade.
- Describe how economic integration can lead to both winners and losers among firms in the same industry.
- Explain why economists believe that "dumping" should not be singled out as an unfair trade practice, and why the enforcement of antidumping laws leads to protectionism.
- Explain why firms that engage in the global economy (exporters, outsourcers, multinationals) are substantially larger and perform better than firms that do not interact with foreign markets.
- Understand theories that explain the existence of multinationals and the motivation for foreign direct investment across economies.

The Theory of Imperfect Competition

In a perfectly competitive market—a market in which there are many buyers and sellers, none of whom represents a large part of the market—firms are *price takers*. That is, they are sellers of products who believe they can sell as much as they like at the current price but cannot influence the price they receive for their product. For example, a wheat farmer can sell as much wheat as she likes without worrying that if she tries to sell more wheat, she will depress the market price. The reason she need not worry about the effect of her sales on prices is that any individual wheat grower represents only a tiny fraction of the world market.

When only a few firms produce a good, however, the situation is different. To take perhaps the most dramatic example, the aircraft manufacturing giant Boeing shares the market for large jet aircraft with only one major rival, the European firm Airbus. As a result, Boeing knows that if it produces more aircraft, it will have a significant effect on the total supply of planes in the world and will therefore significantly drive down the price of airplanes. Or to put it another way, Boeing knows that if it wants to sell more airplanes, it can do so only by significantly reducing its price. In **imperfect competition**, then, firms are aware that they can influence the prices of their products and that they can sell more only by reducing their price. This situation occurs in one of two ways: when there are only a few major producers of a particular good, or when each firm produces a good that is differentiated (in the eyes of the consumer) from that of rival firms. As we mentioned in the introduction, this type of competition is an inevitable outcome when there are economies of scale at the level of the firm: The number of surviving firms is forced down to a small number and/or firms must develop products that are clearly differentiated from those produced by their rivals. Under these circumstances, each firm views itself as a *price setter*, choosing the price of its product, rather than a price taker.

When firms are not price takers, it is necessary to develop additional tools to describe how prices and outputs are determined. The simplest imperfectly competitive market structure to examine is that of a **pure monopoly**, a market in which a firm faces no competition; the tools we develop for this structure can then be used to examine more complex market structures.

Monopoly: A Brief Review

Figure 8-1 shows the position of a single monopolistic firm. The firm faces a downward-sloping demand curve, shown in the figure as *D*. The downward slope of *D* indicates that the firm can sell more units of output only if the price of the output falls. As you may recall from basic microeconomics, a **marginal revenue** curve corresponds to the demand curve. Marginal revenue is the extra or marginal revenue the firm gains from selling an additional unit. Marginal revenue for a monopolist is always less than the price because to sell an additional unit, the firm must lower the price of *all* units (not just the marginal one). Thus, for a monopolist, the marginal revenue curve, *MR*, always lies below the demand curve.

Marginal Revenue and Price   For our analysis of the monopolistic competition model later in this section, it is important for us to determine the relationship between the price the monopolist receives per unit and marginal revenue. Marginal revenue is always less than the price—but how much less? The relationship between marginal revenue and price depends on two things. First, it depends on how much output the

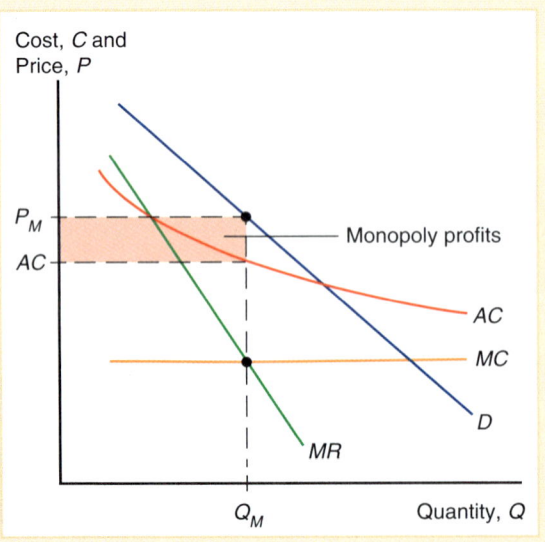

FIGURE 8-1

Monopolistic Pricing and Production Decisions

A monopolistic firm chooses an output at which marginal revenue, the increase in revenue from selling an additional unit, equals marginal cost, the cost of producing an additional unit. This profit-maximizing output is shown as Q_M; the price at which this output is demanded is P_M. The marginal revenue curve *MR* lies below the demand curve *D* because, for a monopoly, marginal revenue is always less than the price. The monopoly's profits are equal to the area of the shaded rectangle, the difference between price and average cost times the amount of output sold.

firm is already selling: A firm not selling very many units will not lose much by cutting the price it receives on those units. Second, the gap between price and marginal revenue depends on the slope of the demand curve, which tells us how much the monopolist has to cut his price to sell one more unit of output. If the curve is very flat, then the monopolist can sell an additional unit with only a small price cut. As a result, he will not have to lower the price by very much on the units he would otherwise have sold, so marginal revenue will be close to the price per unit. On the other hand, if the demand curve is very steep, selling an additional unit will require a large price cut, implying that marginal revenue will be much less than the price.

We can be more specific about the relationship between price and marginal revenue if we assume that the demand curve the firm faces is a straight line. When this is the case, the dependence of the monopolist's total sales on the price it charges can be represented by an equation of the form

$$Q = A - B \times P, \tag{8-1}$$

where Q is the number of units the firm sells, P the price it charges per unit, and A and B are constants. We show in the appendix to this chapter that in this case, marginal revenue is

$$\text{Marginal revenue} = MR = P - Q/B, \tag{8-2}$$

implying that

$$P - MR = Q/B.$$

Equation (8-2) reveals that the gap between price and marginal revenue depends on the initial sales, Q, of the firm and the slope parameter, B, of its demand curve. If sales quantity, Q, is higher, marginal revenue is lower, because the decrease in price required to sell a greater quantity costs the firm more. In other words, the greater is B, the more sales fall for any given increase in price and the closer the marginal revenue is to the price of the good. Equation (8-2) is crucial for our analysis of the monopolistic competition model of trade in the upcoming section.

Average and Marginal Costs   Returning to Figure 8-1, AC represents the firm's **average cost** of production, that is, its total cost divided by its output. The downward slope reflects our assumption that there are economies of scale, so the larger the firm's output, the lower its costs per unit. MC represents the firm's **marginal cost** (the amount it costs the firm to produce one extra unit). In the figure, we assumed the firm's marginal cost is constant (the marginal cost curve is flat). The economies of scale must then come from a fixed cost (unrelated to the scale of production). This fixed cost pushes the average cost above the constant marginal cost of production, though the difference between the two becomes smaller and smaller as the fixed cost is spread over an increasing number of output units.

If we denote c as the firm's marginal cost and F as the fixed cost, then we can write the firm's total cost (C) as

$$C = F + c \times Q, \tag{8-3}$$

where Q is once again the firm's output. Given this linear cost function, the firm's average cost is

$$AC = C/Q = (F/Q) + c. \tag{8-4}$$

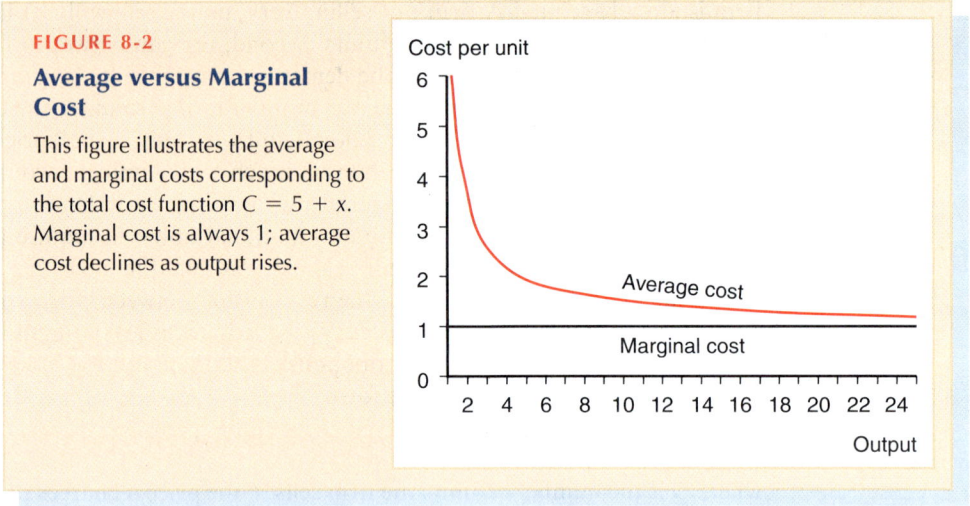

FIGURE 8-2

Average versus Marginal Cost

This figure illustrates the average and marginal costs corresponding to the total cost function $C = 5 + x$. Marginal cost is always 1; average cost declines as output rises.

As we have discussed, this average cost is always greater than the marginal cost c, and declines with output produced Q.

If, for example, $F = 5$ and $c = 1$, the average cost of producing 10 units is $(5/10) + 1 = 1.5$, and the average cost of producing 25 units is $(5/25) + 1 = 1.2$. These numbers may look familiar, because they were used to construct Table 7-1 in the previous chapter. (However, in this case, we assume a unit wage cost for the labor input, and that the technology now applies to a firm instead of an industry.) The marginal and average cost curves for this specific numeric example are plotted in Figure 8-2. Average cost approaches infinity at zero output and approaches marginal cost at very large output.

The profit-maximizing output of a monopolist is that at which marginal revenue (the revenue gained from selling an extra unit) equals marginal cost (the cost of producing an extra unit), that is, at the intersection of the MC and MR curves. In Figure 8-1, we can see that the price at which the profit-maximizing output Q_M is demanded is P_M, which is greater than average cost. When $P > AC$, the monopolist is earning some monopoly profits, as indicated by the shaded box.[2]

Monopolistic Competition

Monopoly profits rarely go uncontested. A firm making high profits normally attracts competitors. Thus, situations of pure monopoly are rare in practice. In most cases, competitors do not sell the same products—either because they cannot (for legal or technological reasons) or because they would rather carve out their own product niche. This leads to a market where competitors sell **differentiated products**. Thus, even when there are many competitors, product differentiation allows firms to remain price setters for their own individual product "variety" or brand. However, more competition implies lower sales for any given firm at any chosen price: Each firm's demand curve shifts in when there are more competitors (we will model this more explicitly in the following sections). Lower demand, in turn, translates into lower profits.

---

[2]The economic definition of *profits* is not the same as that used in conventional accounting, where any revenue over and above labor and material costs is called a profit. A firm that earns a rate of return on its capital less than what that capital could have earned in other industries is not making profits; from an economic point of view, the normal rate of return on capital represents part of the firm's costs, and only returns over and above that normal rate of return represent profits.

The incentive for additional new competitors persists so long as such entry is profitable. Once competition reaches a certain level, additional entry would no longer be profitable and a long-run equilibrium is attained. In some cases, this occurs when there are only a small number of competing firms in the market (such as the market for large jet aircraft). This leads to a market structure called **oligopoly**. In this situation, a single firm has enough market share to influence market aggregates such as total industry output and average industry price.[3] This in turn affects the demand conditions for the other firms. They will therefore have an incentive to adjust their prices in response to the pricing decision of the large firm and vice versa when the other firms are large, too. Thus, pricing decisions of firms are *interdependent* in an oligopoly market structure: Each firm in an oligopoly will consider the expected responses of competitors when setting their price. These responses, however, depend in turn on the competitors' expectations about the firm's behavior—and we are therefore in a complex game in which firms are trying to second-guess each other's strategies. We will briefly discuss an example of an oligopoly model with two firms in Chapter 12.

Let's focus on a much simpler case of imperfect competition known as **monopolistic competition**. This market structure arises when the equilibrium number of competing firms is large and no firm attains a substantial market share. Then, the pricing decision of any given firm will not affect market aggregates and the demand conditions for the other firms, so the pricing decisions of the firms are no longer interrelated. Each firm sets its price given those market aggregates, knowing that the response of any other individual firm would be inconsequential. We next develop such a model of monopolistic competition. We then introduce trade under this market structure in the following section.

Assumptions of the Model   We begin by describing the demand facing a typical monopolistically competitive firm. In general, we would expect a firm to sell more, the larger the total demand for its industry's product and the higher the prices charged by its rivals. On the other hand, we would expect the firm to sell less the greater the number of firms in the industry and the higher its own price. A particular equation for the demand facing a firm that has these properties is[4]

$$Q = S \times [1/n - b \times (P - \overline{P})], \tag{8-5}$$

where Q is the quantity of output demanded, S is the total output of the industry, n is the number of firms in the industry, b is a positive constant term representing the responsiveness of a firm's sales to its price, P is the price charged by the firm itself, and $\overline{P}$ is the average price charged by its competitors. Equation (8-5) may be given the following intuitive justification: If all firms charge the same price, each will have a market share $1/n$. A firm charging more than the average of other firms will have a smaller market share, whereas a firm charging less will have a larger share.[5]

It is helpful to assume that total industry output S is unaffected by the average price $\overline{P}$ charged by firms in the industry. That is, we assume that firms can gain customers only at each other's expense. This is an unrealistic assumption, but it

---

[3]This typically occurs when the fixed cost F is high relative to demand conditions: Each firm must operate at a large scale in order to bring average cost down and be profitable, and the market is not big enough to support many such large firms.
[4]Equation (8-5) can be derived from a model in which consumers have different preferences and firms produce varieties tailored to particular segments of the market. See Stephen Salop, "Monopolistic Competition with Outside Goods," *Bell Journal of Economics* 10 (1979), pp. 141–156, for a development of this approach.
[5]Equation (8-5) may be rewritten as $Q = (S/n) - S \times b \times (P - \overline{P})$. If $P = \overline{P}$, this equation reduces to $Q = S/n$. If $P > \overline{P}$, $Q < S/n$, while if $P < \overline{P}$, $Q > S/n$.

simplifies the analysis and helps us focus on the competition among firms. In particular, it means that S is a measure of the size of the market and that if all firms charge the same price, each sells S/n units.[6]

Next, we turn to the costs of a typical firm. Here we simply assume that total and average costs of a typical firm are described by equations (8-3) and (8-4). Note that in this initial model, we assume all firms are *symmetric* even though they produce differentiated products: They all face the same demand curve (8-5) and have the same cost function (8-3). We will relax this assumption in the next section.

Market Equilibrium   When the individual firms are symmetric, the state of the industry can be described without describing any of the features of individual firms: All we really need to know to describe the industry is how many firms there are and what price the typical firm charges. To analyze the industry—for example, to assess the effects of international trade—we need to determine the number of firms n and the average price they charge $\overline{P}$. Once we have a method for determining n and $\overline{P}$, we can ask how they are affected by international trade.

Our method for determining n and $\overline{P}$ involves three steps. (1) First, we derive a relationship between the number of firms and the *average cost* of a typical firm. We show that this relationship is upward sloping; that is, the more firms there are, the lower the output of each firm—and thus the higher each firm's cost per unit of output. (2) We next show the relationship between the number of firms and the price each firm charges, which must equal $\overline{P}$ in equilibrium. We show that this relationship is downward sloping: The more firms there are, the more intense is the competition among firms, and as a result the lower the prices they charge. (3) Finally, we introduce firm entry and exit decisions based on the profits that each firm earns. When price exceeds average cost, firms earn positive profits and additional firms will enter the industry; conversely, when the price is less than average cost, profits are negative and those losses induce some firms to exit. In the long run, this entry and exit process drives profits to zero. So the price $\overline{P}$ set by each firm must equal the average cost from step (1).

   1. *The number of firms and average cost.* As a first step toward determining n and $\overline{P}$, we ask how the average cost of a typical firm depends on the number of firms in the industry. Since all firms are symmetric in this model, in equilibrium they all will charge the same price. But when all firms charge the same price, so that $P = \overline{P}$, equation (8-5) tells us that $Q = S/n$; that is, each firm's output Q is a $1/n$ share of the total industry sales S. But we saw in equation (8-4) that average cost depends inversely on a firm's output. We therefore conclude that average cost depends on the size of the market and the number of firms in the industry:

$$AC = F/Q + c = (n \times F/S) + c. \tag{8-6}$$

Equation (8-6) tells us that other things equal, *the more firms there are in the industry, the higher is average cost.* The reason is that the more firms there are, the less each firm produces. For example, imagine an industry with total sales of 1 million widgets annually. If there are five firms in the industry, each will sell 200,000 annually. If there are ten firms, each will sell only 100,000, and therefore each firm will have higher average cost. The upward-sloping relationship between n and average cost is shown as CC in Figure 8-3.

---

[6]Even if firms set different prices, the demand equation (8-5) ensures that the sum of Q over firms is always equal to total output S (because the sum of $P - \overline{P}$ over firms must be zero).

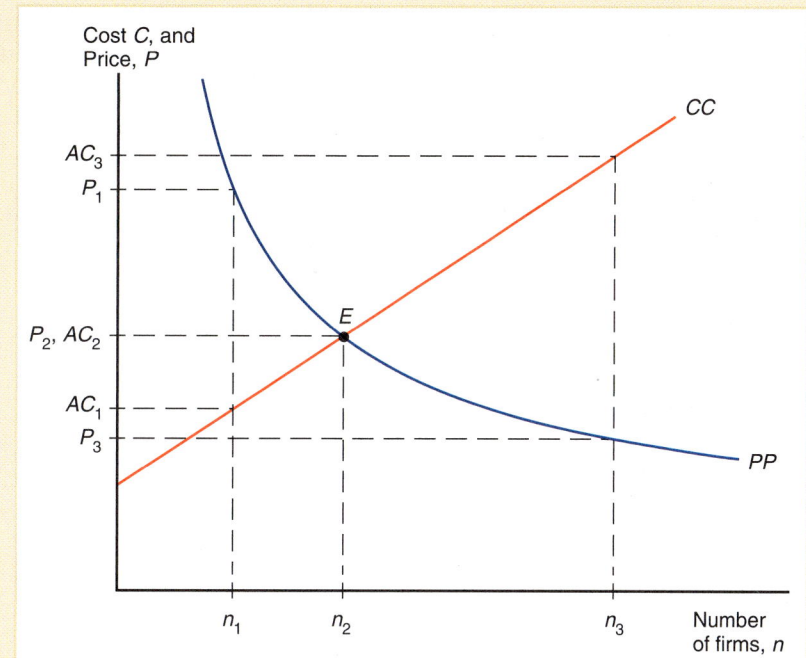

FIGURE 8-3

Equilibrium in a Monopolistically Competitive Market

The number of firms in a monopolistically competitive market, and the prices they charge, are determined by two relationships. On one side, the more firms there are, the more intensely they compete, and hence the lower is the industry price. This relationship is represented by *PP*. On the other side, the more firms there are, the less each firm sells and therefore the higher is the industry's average cost. This relationship is represented by *CC*. If price exceeds average cost (that is, if the *PP* curve is above the *CC* curve), the industry will be making profits and additional firms will enter the industry; if price is less than average cost, the industry will be incurring losses and firms will leave the industry. The equilibrium price and number of firms occurs when price equals average cost, at the intersection of *PP* and *CC*.

2. *The number of firms and the price.* Meanwhile, the price the typical firm charges also depends on the number of firms in the industry. In general, we would expect that the more firms there are, the more intense will be the competition among them, and hence the lower the price. This turns out to be true in this model, but proving it takes a moment. The basic trick is to show that each firm faces a straight-line demand curve of the form we showed in equation (8-1), and then to use equation (8-2) to determine prices.

First recall that in the monopolistic competition model, firms are assumed to take each other's prices as given; that is, each firm ignores the possibility that if it changes its price, other firms will also change theirs. If each firm treats $\overline{P}$ as given, we can rewrite the demand curve (8-5) in the form

$$Q = [(S/n) + S \times b \times \overline{P}] - S \times b \times P, \qquad (8\text{-}7)$$

where b is the parameter in equation (8-5) that measured the sensitivity of each firm's market share to the price it charges. Now this equation is in the same form as (8-1), with $(S/n) + S \times b \times \overline{P}$ in place of the constant term A and $S \times b$ in place of the slope coefficient B. If we plug these values back into the formula for marginal revenue, (8-2), we have a marginal revenue for a typical firm of

$$MR = P - Q/(S \times b). \tag{8-8}$$

Profit-maximizing firms will set marginal revenue equal to their marginal cost, c, so that

$$MR = P - Q/(S \times b) = c,$$

which can be rearranged to give the following equation for the price charged by a typical firm:

$$P = c + Q/(S \times b). \tag{8-9}$$

We have already noted, however, that if all firms charge the same price, each will sell an amount $Q = S/n$. Plugging this back into (8-9) gives us a relationship between the number of firms and the price each firm charges:

$$P = c + 1/(b \times n). \tag{8-10}$$

Equation (8-10) says algebraically that *the more firms there are in an industry, the lower the price each firm will charge.* This is because each firm's **markup over marginal cost**, $P - c = 1/(b \times n)$, decreases with the number of competing firms. Equation (8-10) is shown in Figure 8-3 as the downward-sloping curve PP.

   3. *The equilibrium number of firms.* Let us now ask what Figure 8-3 means. We have summarized an industry by two curves. The downward-sloping curve PP shows that the more firms there are in the industry, the lower the price each firm will charge: The more firms there are, the more competition each firm faces. The upward-sloping curve CC tells us that the more firms there are in the industry, the higher the average cost of each firm: If the number of firms increases, each firm will sell less, so firms will not be able to move as far down their average cost curve.

   The two schedules intersect at point E, corresponding to the number of firms n_2. The significance of n_2 is that it is the *zero-profit* number of firms in the industry. When there are n_2 firms in the industry, their profit-maximizing price is P_2, which is exactly equal to their average cost AC_2. This is the long-run monopolistic competition equilibrium that we previously described.

   To see why, suppose that n were less than n_2, say n_1. Then the price charged by firms would be P_1, while their average cost would be only AC_1. Thus, firms would be earning positive profits.[7] Conversely, suppose that n were greater than n_2, say n_3. Then firms would charge only the price P_3, while their average cost would be AC_3. Firms would be suffering losses (profit is negative). Over time, firms will enter an industry that is profitable and exit one in which they lose money. The number of firms will rise over time if it is less than n_2, fall if it is greater, leading to the equilibrium price P_2 with n_2 firms.[8]

---

[7]Recall that this represents *economic* profit, which nets out all fixed and capital costs—as opposed to *accounting* profit (which does not).

[8]This analysis slips past a slight problem: The number of firms in an industry must, of course, be a whole number like 5 or 8. What if n_2 turns out to equal 6.37? The answer is that there will be six firms in the industry, all earning a small positive profit. That profit is not challenged by new entrants because everyone knows that a seven-firm industry would lose money. In most examples of monopolistic competition, this whole-number or "integer constraint" problem turns out not to be very important, and we ignore it here.

We have just developed a model of a monopolistically competitive industry in which we can determine the equilibrium number of firms and the average price that firms charge. We now use this model to derive some important conclusions about the role of economies of scale in international trade.

Monopolistic Competition and Trade

Underlying the application of the monopolistic competition model to trade is the idea that trade increases market size. In industries where there are economies of scale, both the variety of goods that a country can produce and the scale of its production are constrained by the size of the market. By trading with each other, and therefore forming an integrated world market that is bigger than any individual national market, nations are able to loosen these constraints. Each country can thus specialize in producing a narrower range of products than it would in the absence of trade; yet by buying from other countries the goods that it does not make, each nation can simultaneously increase the variety of goods available to its consumers. As a result, trade offers an opportunity for mutual gain even when countries do not differ in their resources or technology.

Suppose, for example, there are two countries, each with an annual market for 1 million automobiles. By trading with each other, these countries can create a combined market of 2 million autos. In this combined market, more varieties of automobiles can be produced, at lower average costs, than in either market alone.

The monopolistic competition model can be used to show how trade improves the trade-off between scale and variety that individual nations face. We will begin by showing how a larger market leads to both a lower average price and the availability of a greater variety of goods in the monopolistic competition model. Applying this result to international trade, we observe that trade creates a world market larger than any of the national markets that comprise it. Integrating markets through international trade therefore has the same effects as growth of a market within a single country.

The Effects of Increased Market Size

The number of firms in a monopolistically competitive industry and the prices they charge are affected by the size of the market. In larger markets there usually will be both more firms and more sales per firm; consumers in a large market will be offered both lower prices and a greater variety of products than consumers in small markets.

To see this in the context of our model, look again at the CC curve in Figure 8-3, which showed that average costs per firm are higher the more firms there are in the industry. The definition of the CC curve is given by equation (8-6):

$$AC = F/Q + c = n \times F/S + c.$$

Examining this equation, we see that an increase in total industry output S will reduce average costs for any given number of firms n. The reason is that if the market grows while the number of firms is held constant, output per firm will increase and the average cost of each firm will therefore decline. Thus, if we compare two markets, one with higher S than the other, the CC curve in the larger market will be below that in the smaller one.

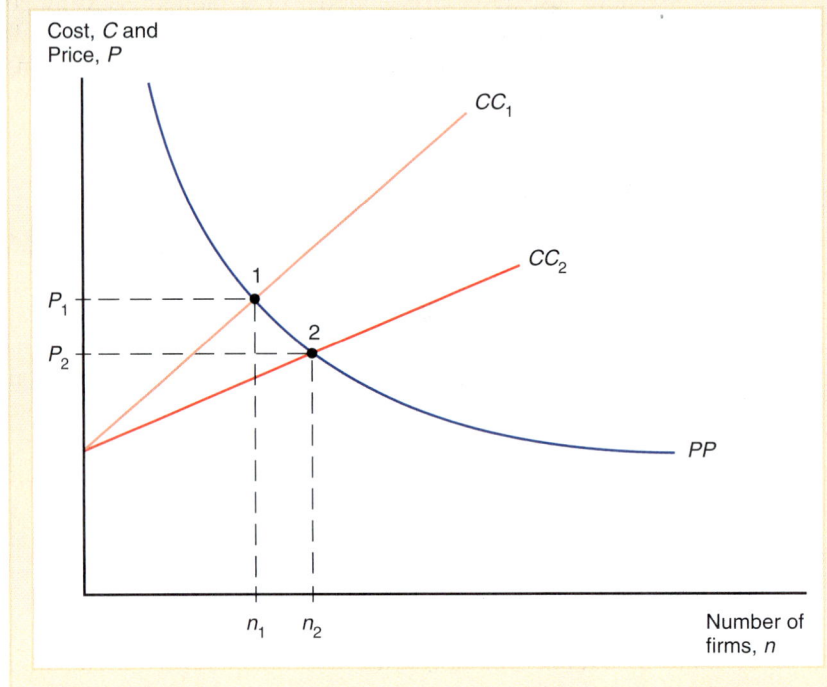

FIGURE 8-4

Effects of a Larger Market

An increase in the size of the market allows each firm, other things equal, to produce more and thus have lower average cost. This is represented by a downward shift from CC_1 to CC_2. The result is a simultaneous increase in the number of firms (and hence in the variety of goods available) and a fall in the price of each.

Meanwhile, the PP curve in Figure 8-3, which relates the price charged by firms to the number of firms, does not shift. The definition of that curve was given in equation (8-10):

$$P = c + 1/(b \times n).$$

The size of the market does not enter into this equation, so an increase in S does not shift the PP curve.

Figure 8-4 uses this information to show the effect of an increase in the size of the market on long-run equilibrium. Initially, equilibrium is at point 1, with a price P_1 and a number of firms n_1. An increase in the size of the market, measured by industry sales S, shifts the CC curve down from CC_1 to CC_2, while it has no effect on the PP curve. The new equilibrium is at point 2: The number of firms increases from n_1 to n_2, while the price falls from P_1 to P_2.

Clearly, consumers would prefer to be part of a large market rather than a small one. At point 2, a greater variety of products is available at a lower price than at point 1.

Gains from an Integrated Market: A Numerical Example

International trade can create a larger market. We can illustrate the effects of trade on prices, scale, and the variety of goods available with a specific numerical example.

Suppose automobiles are produced by a monopolistically competitive industry. The demand curve facing any given producer of automobiles is described by equation (8-5), with $b = 1/30,000$ (this value has no particular significance; it was chosen to make the example come out neatly). Thus, the demand facing any one producer is given by

$$Q = S \times [(1/n) - (1/30,000) \times (P - \overline{P})],$$

where Q is the number of automobiles sold per firm, S is the total number sold for the industry, n is the number of firms, P is the price that a firm charges, and $\overline{P}$ is the average price of other firms. We also assume that the cost function for producing automobiles is described by equation (8-3), with a fixed cost $F = \$750,000,000$ and a marginal cost $c = \$5,000$ per automobile (again, these values were chosen to give nice results). The total cost is

$$C = 750,000,000 + (5,000 \times Q).$$

The average cost curve is therefore

$$AC = (750,000,000/Q) + 5,000.$$

Now suppose there are two countries, Home and Foreign. Home has annual sales of 900,000 automobiles; Foreign has annual sales of 1.6 million. The two countries are assumed, for the moment, to have the same costs of production.

Figure 8-5a shows the *PP* and *CC* curves for the Home auto industry. We find that in the absence of trade, Home would have six automobile firms, selling autos at a price of $10,000 each. (It is also possible to solve for n and P algebraically, as shown in the Mathematical Postscript to this chapter.) To confirm that this is the long-run equilibrium, we need to show that the pricing equation (8-10) is satisfied and that the price equals average cost.

Substituting the actual values of the marginal cost c, the demand parameter b, and the number of Home firms n into equation (8-10), we find

$$P = \$10,000 = c + 1/(b \times n) = \$5,000 + 1/[(1/30,000) \times 6]$$
$$= \$5,000 + \$5,000,$$

so the condition for profit maximization—marginal revenue equaling marginal cost—is satisfied. Each firm sells 900,000 units/6 firms = 150,000 units/firm. Its average cost is therefore

$$AC = (\$750,000,000/150,000) + \$5,000 = \$10,000.$$

Since the average cost of $10,000 per unit is the same as the price, all monopoly profits have been competed away. Thus six firms, selling each unit at a price of $10,000, with each firm producing 150,000 cars, is the long-run equilibrium in the Home market.

What about Foreign? By drawing the *PP* and *CC* curves (panel (b) in Figure 8-5), we find that when the market is for 1.6 million automobiles, the curves intersect at $n = 8$, $P = 8,750$. That is, in the absence of trade, Foreign's market would support eight firms, each producing 200,000 automobiles, and selling them at a price of $8,750. We can again confirm that this solution satisfies the equilibrium conditions:

$$P = \$8,750 = c + 1/(b \times n) = \$5,000 + 1/[(1/30,000) \times 8] = \$5,000 + \$3,750,$$

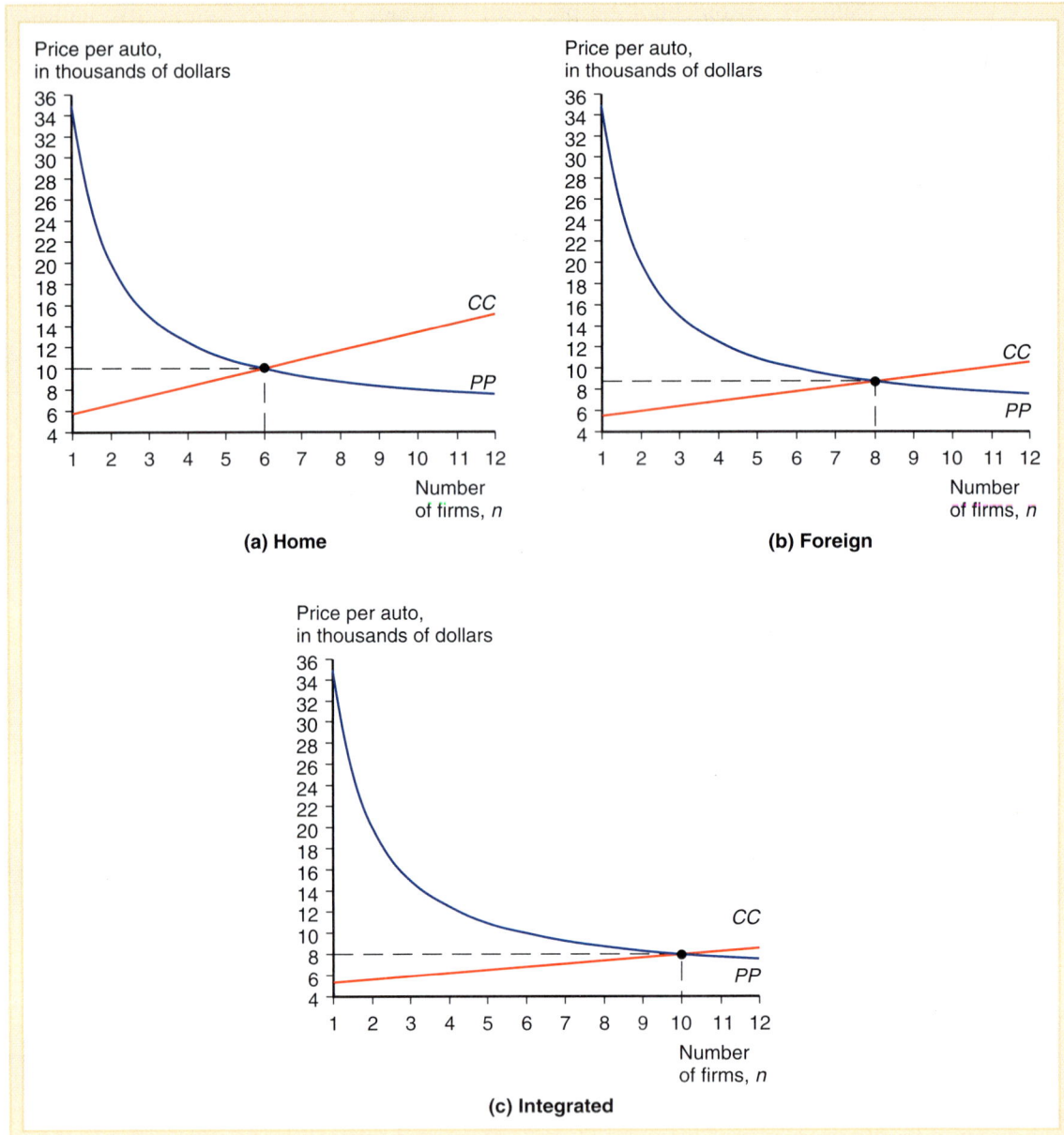

FIGURE 8-5

Equilibrium in the Automobile Market

(a) The Home market: With a market size of 900,000 automobiles, Home's equilibrium, determined by the intersection of the *PP* and *CC* curves, occurs with six firms and an industry price of $10,000 per auto. (b) The Foreign market: With a market size of 1.6 million automobiles, Foreign's equilibrium occurs with eight firms and an industry price of $8,750 per auto. (c) The combined market: Integrating the two markets creates a market for 2.5 million autos. This market supports ten firms, and the price of an auto is only $8,000.

and

$$AC = (\$750{,}000{,}000/200{,}000) + \$5{,}000 = \$8{,}750.$$

Now suppose it is possible for Home and Foreign to trade automobiles costlessly with one another. This creates a new, integrated market (panel (c) in Figure 8-5) with total sales of 2.5 million. By drawing the PP and CC curves one more time, we find that this integrated market will support ten firms, each producing 250,000 cars and selling them at a price of $8,000. The conditions for profit maximization and zero profits are again satisfied:

$$P = 8{,}000 = c + 1/(b \times n) = 5{,}000 + 1/[(1/30{,}000) \times 10]$$
$$= \$5{,}000 + \$3{,}000,$$

and

$$AC = (\$750{,}000{,}000/250{,}000) + \$5{,}000 = \$8{,}000.$$

We summarize the results of creating an integrated market in Table 8-1. The table compares each market alone with the integrated market. The integrated market supports more firms, each producing at a larger scale and selling at a lower price than either national market does on its own.

Clearly everyone is better off as a result of integration. In the larger market, consumers have a wider range of choices, yet each firm produces more and is therefore able to offer its product at a lower price. To realize these gains from integration, the countries must engage in international trade. To achieve economies of scale, each firm must concentrate its production in one country—either Home or Foreign. Yet it must sell its output to customers in both markets. So each product will be produced in only one country and exported to the other.

This numerical example highlights two important new features about trade with monopolistic competition relative to the models of trade based on comparative advantage that we covered in Chapters 3 through 6: (1) First, the example shows how product differentiation and internal economies of scale lead to trade between similar countries with no comparative advantage differences between them. This is a very different kind of trade than the one based on comparative advantage, where each country exports its comparative advantage good. Here, both Home and Foreign export autos to one another. Home pays for the imports of some automobile models (those produced by firms in Foreign) with exports of different types of models (those produced by firms in Home)—and vice versa. This leads to what is called **intra-industry trade:** two-way

TABLE 8-1	Hypothetical Example of Gains from Market Integration		
	Home Market, Before Trade	Foreign Market, Before Trade	Integrated Market, After Trade
Industry output (# of autos)	900,000	1,600,000	2,500,000
Number of firms	6	8	10
Output per firm (# of autos)	150,000	200,000	250,000
Average cost	$10,000	$8,750	$8,000
Price	$10,000	$8,750	$8,000

exchanges of similar goods. (2) Second, the example highlights two new channels for welfare benefits from trade. In the integrated market after trade, both Home and Foreign consumers benefit from a greater variety of automobile models (ten versus six or eight) at a lower price ($8,000 versus $8,750 or $10,000) as firms are able to consolidate their production destined for both locations and take advantage of economies of scale.[9]

Empirically, is intra-industry trade relevant, and do we observe gains from trade in the form of greater product variety and consolidated production at lower average cost? The answer is yes.

The Significance of Intra-Industry Trade

The proportion of intra-industry trade in world trade has steadily grown over the last half-century. The measurement of intra-industry trade relies on an industrial classification system that categorizes goods into different industries. Depending on the coarseness of the industrial classification used (hundreds of different industry classifications versus thousands), intra-industry trade accounts for one-quarter to nearly one-half of all world trade flows. Intra-industry trade plays an even more prominent role in the trade of manufactured goods among advanced industrial nations, which accounts for the majority of world trade.

Table 8-2 shows measures of the importance of intra-industry trade for a number of U.S. manufacturing industries in 2009. The measure shown is intra-industry trade as a proportion of overall trade.[10] The measure ranges from 0.97 for metalworking machinery and inorganic chemicals—industries where U.S. exports and imports are nearly equal—to 0.10 for footwear, an industry in which the United States has large imports but virtually no exports. The measure would be 0 for an industry in which the United States is only an exporter or only an importer, but not both; it would be 1 for an industry in which U.S. exports exactly equal U.S. imports.

Table 8-2 shows that intra-industry trade is a very important component of trade for the United States in many different industries. Those industries tend to be ones that produce sophisticated manufactured goods, such as chemicals, pharmaceuticals, and specialized machinery. These goods are exported principally by advanced nations and are probably subject to important economies of scale in production. At the other end of the scale are the industries with very little intra-industry trade, which typically produce labor-intensive products such as footwear and apparel. These are goods that the United States imports primarily from less-developed countries, where comparative advantage is the primary determinant of U.S. trade with these countries.

---

[9]Also note that Home consumers gain more than Foreign consumers from trade integration. This is a standard feature of trade models with increasing returns and product differentiation: A smaller country stands to gain more from integration than a larger country. This is because the gains from integration are driven by the associated increase in market size; the country that is initially smaller benefits from a bigger increase in market size upon integration.

[10]To be more precise, the standard formula for calculating the importance of intra-industry trade within a given industry is

$$I = \frac{min\{\text{exports, imports}\}}{(\text{exports} + \text{imports})/2},$$

where min{exports, imports} refers to the smallest value between exports and imports. This is the amount of two-way exchanges of goods reflected in *both* exports and imports. This number is measured as a proportion of the average trade flow (average of exports and imports). If trade in an industry flows in only one direction, then $I = 0$ since the smallest trade flow is zero: There is no intra-industry trade. On the other hand, if a country's exports and imports within an industry are equal, we get the opposite extreme of $I = 1$.

TABLE 8-2	Indexes of Intra-Industry Trade for U.S. Industries, 2009
Metalworking Machinery	0.97
Inorganic Chemicals	0.97
Power-Generating Machines	0.86
Medical and Pharmaceutical Products	0.85
Scientific Equipment	0.84
Organic Chemicals	0.79
Iron and Steel	0.76
Road Vehicles	0.70
Office Machines	0.58
Telecommunications Equipment	0.46
Furniture	0.30
Clothing and Apparel	0.11
Footwear	0.10

What about the new types of welfare gains via increased product variety and economies of scale? A recent paper by Christian Broda at Duquesne Capital Management and David Weinstein at Columbia University estimates that the number of available products in U.S. imports tripled in the 30-year time-span from 1972 to 2001. They further estimate that this increased product variety for U.S. consumers represented a welfare gain equal to 2.6 percent of U.S. GDP![11]

Table 8-1 from our numerical example showed that the gains from integration generated by economies of scale were most pronounced for the smaller economy: Prior to integration, production there was particularly inefficient, as the economy could not take advantage of economies of scale in production due to the country's small size. This is exactly what happened when the United States and Canada followed a path of increasing economic integration starting with the North American Auto Pact in 1964 (which did not include Mexico) and culminating in the North American Free Trade Agreement (NAFTA, which does include Mexico). The Case Study that follows describes how this integration led to consolidation and efficiency gains in the automobile sector—particularly on the Canadian side (whose economy is one-tenth the size of the U.S. economy).

Similar gains from trade have also been measured for other real-world examples of closer economic integration. One of the most prominent examples has taken place in Europe over the last half-century. In 1957, the major countries of Western Europe established a free trade area in manufactured goods called the Common Market, or European Economic Community (EEC). (The United Kingdom entered the EEC later, in 1973.) The result was a rapid growth of trade that was dominated by intra-industry trade. Trade within the EEC grew twice as fast as world trade as a whole during the 1960s. This integration slowly expanded into what has become the European Union. When a subset of these countries (mostly, those countries that had formed the EEC) adopted the common euro currency in 1999, intra-industry trade among those countries further increased (even relative to that of the other countries in the European Union). Recent studies have also found that the adoption of the euro has led to a substantial increase in the number of different products that are traded within the Eurozone.

---

[11]See Christian Broda and David E. Weinstein, "Globalization and the Gains from Variety," *Quarterly Journal of Economics* 121 (April 2006), pp. 541–585.

CASE STUDY   The Emergence of the Turkish Automotive Industry

The automotive and automotive spare parts industry is known to be one of the most "open" sectors of a market economy. Mostly dominated by a few large enterprises and transnationals, the sector is often characterized by fierce competition in design and manufacturing, vigorous two-way trade, and significant economies of scale.

The Turkish automotive industry has been one of the fastest expanding export sectors over the 2000s. Currently Turkey is regarded as one of the main automotive producer countries in the world, thanks to its 825,000-vehicle production capacity. As of 2007 (just before the outbreak of the global crisis), the Turkish automotive industry was comprised of 28 firms employing 42,493 people. In addition to the manufacturing of vehicles—which includes the spare parts, accessories, and coachwork segments—motor vehicles trade and repair and maintenance were also a major source of employment. In 2007, motor vehicle-related services (sales, repair and maintenance, gas stations, etc.,) together with land transportation, employed 1,180,000 additional people. The share of the aggregate motor vehicle industry in total manufacturing employment was 4.8 percent, whereas its output and value added shares were almost double, at 9.0 percent. Thus, the industry is about two times more productive than the manufacturing industry as a whole, and pays 60 percent higher wages than the manufacturing average.

Automotive exports increased rapidly in the early 2000s, mainly in response to liberalization of the trade regime starting in 1983. However, the main impetus came in 1996, when Turkey signed a *customs union* agreement with the European Union.

The customs union enabled Turkish manufacturers to import strategic components for the final good duty free, and also to export components of higher value added based on its labor cost advantage. Increased specialization followed, with intensive inter-industry, two-way trading within the sector.

Turkish exports of automotives were only worth US$1,011 million back in 1997.

Imports of automotives totalled US$5,596 million. This gave rise to an export-import ratio of barely 0.18. However, by 2007, exports of Turkish automotives reached US$18,059 million, whereas sectoral imports were US$14,043 million. Thus, within a decade the automotive industry turned into a net exporting sector, with an export-import ratio of 1.28.

Trade expansion fed itself in a self-supporting, synergistic expansion of employment and productivity over the early 2000s. As technology had been improved from imports with high value added content, it became the source of a dynamic advantage in exporting.

The automotive industry in Turkey is expected to grow at a rapid pace in the next decade due to the high income elasticity of domestic as well as international demand and the tendency toward regionalization of motor vehicle production chains in the global economy, especially within the European Union. In other words, the automotive industry is expected to play a crucial role in the development of the Turkish economy in the medium term.

Source: E. Taymaz and K. Yilmaz. "Integration with the Global Economy: The Case of Turkish Automobile and Consumer Electronic Industries." *Commission on Growth and Development Working Papers* No. 37, 2008.

Firm Responses to Trade: Winners, Losers, and Industry Performance

In our numerical example of the auto industry with two countries, we saw how economic integration led to an increase in competition between firms. Of the 14 firms producing autos before trade (6 in Home and 8 in Foreign), only 10 firms "survive" after economic integration; however, each of those firms now produces at a bigger scale (250,000 autos produced per firm versus either 150,000 for Home firms or 200,000 for Foreign firms before trade). In that example, the firms were assumed to be symmetric, so exactly which firms exited and which survived and expanded was inconsequential. In the real world, however, performance varies widely across firms, so the effects of increased competition from trade are far from inconsequential. As one would expect, increased competition tends to hurt the worst-performing firms the hardest because they are the ones who are forced to exit. If the increased competition comes from trade (or economic integration), then it is also associated with sales opportunities in new markets for the surviving firms. Again, as one would expect, it is the best-performing firms that take greatest advantage of those new sales opportunities and expand the most.

These composition changes have a crucial consequence at the level of the industry: When the better-performing firms expand and the worse-performing ones contract or exit, then overall industry performance improves. This means that trade and economic integration can have a direct impact on industry performance: It is as if there was technological growth at the level of the industry. Empirically, these composition changes generate substantial improvements in industry productivity.

Take the example of Canada's closer economic integration with the United States (see the preceding Case Study and the discussion in Chapter 2). We discussed how this integration led the automobile producers to consolidate production in a smaller number of Canadian plants, whose production levels rose dramatically. The Canada–U.S. Free Trade Agreement, which went into effect in 1989, extended the auto pact to most manufacturing sectors. A similar process of consolidation occurred throughout the affected Canadian manufacturing sectors. However, this was also associated with a selection process: The worst-performing producers shut down while the better-performing ones expanded via large increases in exports to the U.S. market. Daniel Trefler at the University of Toronto has studied the effects of this trade agreement in great detail, examining the varied responses of Canadian firms.[12] He found that productivity in the most affected Canadian industries rose by a dramatic 14 to 15 percent (replicated economy-wide, a 1 percent increase in productivity translates into a 1 percent increase in GDP, holding employment constant). On its own, the contraction and exit of the worst-performing firms in response to increased competition from U.S. firms accounted for half of the 15 percent increase in those sectors.

Performance Differences across Producers

We now relax the symmetry assumption we imposed in our previous development of the monopolistic competition model so that we can examine how competition from increased market size affects firms differently.[13] The symmetry assumption meant that all firms had the same cost curve (8-3) and the same demand curve (8-5). Suppose now that firms have different cost curves because they produce with different marginal cost levels c_i. We assume all firms still face the same demand curve. Product-quality differences between firms would lead to very similar predictions for firm performance as the ones we now derive for cost differences.

Figure 8-6 illustrates the performance differences between firms 1 and 2 when $c_1 < c_2$. In panel (a), we have drawn the common demand curve (8-5) as well as its associated marginal revenue curve (8-8). Note that both curves have the same intercept on the vertical axis (plug $Q = 0$ into (8-8) to obtain $MR = P$); this intercept is given by the price P from (8-5) when $Q = 0$, which is the slope of the demand curve is $1/(S \times b)$. As we previously discussed, the marginal revenue curve is steeper than the demand curve. Firms 1 and 2 choose output levels Q_1 and Q_2, respectively, to maximize their profits. This occurs where their respective marginal cost curves intersect the common marginal revenue curve. They set prices P_1 and P_2 that correspond to those output levels on the common demand curve. We immediately see that firm 1 will set a lower price and produce a higher output level than firm 2. Since the marginal revenue curve is steeper than the demand curve, we also see that firm 1 will set a higher markup over marginal cost than firm 2: $P_1 - c_1 > P_2 - c_2$.

The shaded areas represent operating profits for both firms, equal to revenue $P_i \times Q_i$ minus operating costs $c_i \times Q_i$ (for both firms, $i = 1$ and $i = 2$). Here, we have assumed the fixed cost F (assumed to be the same for all firms) cannot be recovered and does not enter into operating profits (that is, it is a sunk cost). Since operating profits can be rewritten as the product of the markup times the number of output units sold, $(P_i - c_i) \times Q_i$, we can determine that firm 1 will earn higher profits than firm 2 (recall that firm 1 sets a higher markup and produces more output than firm 2). We can thus summarize all the relevant performance differences based on marginal cost differences across firms. Compared to a firm with a higher marginal cost, a firm with a lower marginal cost will (1) set a lower price but at a higher markup over marginal cost; (2) produce more output; and (3) earn higher profits.[14]

---

[12]See Daniel Trefler, "The Long and Short of the Canada-U.S. Free Trade Agreement," *American Economic Review* 94 (September 2004), pp. 870–895, and the summary of this work in the *New York Times:* "What Happened When Two Countries Liberalized Trade? Pain, Then Gain" by Virginia Postel (January 27, 2005); and Marc J. Melitz and Daniel Trefler, "Gains from Trade When Firms Matter," *Journal of Economic Perspectives* 26 (2012), pp. 91–118.

[13]A more detailed exposition of this model is presented in Marc J. Melitz and Daniel Trefler, "Gains from Trade When Firms Matter," *Journal of Economic Perspectives* 26 (2012), pp. 91–118.

[14]Recall that we have assumed that all firms face the same nonrecoverable fixed cost F. If a firm earns higher operating profits, then it also earns higher overall profits (that deduct the fixed cost F).

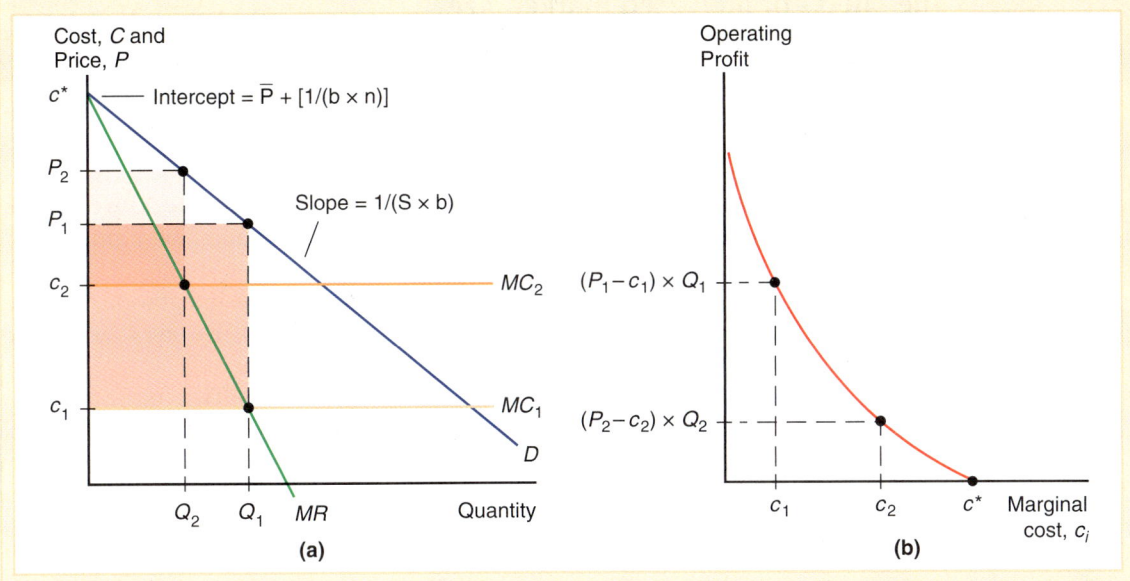

FIGURE 8-6

Performance Differences across Firms

(a) Demand and cost curves for firms 1 and 2. Firm 1 has a lower marginal cost than firm 2: $c_1 < c_2$. Both firms face the same demand curve and marginal revenue curve. Relative to firm 2, firm 1 sets a lower price and produces more output. The shaded areas represent operating profits for both firms (before the fixed cost is deducted). Firm 1 earns higher operating profits than firm 2. (b) Operating profits as a function of a firm's marginal cost c_i. Operating profits decrease as the marginal cost increases. Any firm with marginal cost above c^* cannot operate profitably and shuts down.

Panel (b) in Figure 8-6 shows how a firm's operating profits vary with its marginal cost c_i. As we just mentioned, this will be a decreasing function of marginal cost. Going back to panel (a), we see that a firm can earn a positive operating profit so long as its marginal cost is below the intercept of the demand curve on the vertical axis at $\overline{P} + [1/(b \times n)]$. Let c^* denote this cost cutoff. A firm with a marginal cost c_i above this cutoff is effectively "priced out" of the market and would earn negative operating profits if it were to produce any output. Such a firm would choose to shut down and not produce (incurring an overall profit loss equal to the fixed cost F). Why would such a firm enter in the first place? Clearly, it wouldn't if it knew about its high cost c_i prior to entering and paying the fixed cost F.

We assume that entrants face some randomness about their future production cost c_i. This randomness disappears only *after* F is paid and is sunk. Thus, some firms will regret their entry decision if their overall profit (operating profit minus the fixed cost F) is negative. On the other hand, some firms will discover that their production cost c_i is very low and that they earn high positive overall profit levels. Entry is driven by a similar process as the one we described for the case of symmetric firms. In that previous case, firms entered until profits for all firms were driven to zero. Here, there are profit differences between firms, and entry occurs until *expected* profits across all potential cost levels c_i are driven to zero.

The Effects of Increased Market Size

Panel (b) of Figure 8-6 summarizes the industry equilibrium given a market size S. It tells us which range of firms survive and produce (with cost c_i below c^*), and how their profits will vary with their cost levels c_i. What happens when economies integrate into a single larger market? As was the case with symmetric firms, a larger market can support a larger number of firms than can a smaller market. This leads to more competition in addition to the direct effect of increased market size S. As we will see, these changes will have very different repercussions on firms with different production costs.

Figure 8-7 summarizes those repercussions induced by market integration. In panel (a), we start with the demand curve D faced by each firm. All else equal, we expect increased competition to shift demand in for each firm. On the other hand, we also expect a bigger market size S, on its own, to move demand out. This intuition is correct and leads to the overall change in demand from D to D' shown in panel (a). Notice how the demand curve rotates, inducing an inward shift for the smaller firms (with lower output quantities) as well as an outward shift for the larger firms. In essence, the effects of increased competition dominate for those smaller firms whereas the effects of increased market size are dominant for the larger firms.

We can also analytically characterize the effects of increased competition and market size on the demand curve D. Recall that the vertical intercept of this demand curve is $\bar{P} + [1/(b \times n)]$, while its slope is $1/(S \times b)$. Increased competition (a higher number of firms n) holding market size S constant lowers the vertical intercept for

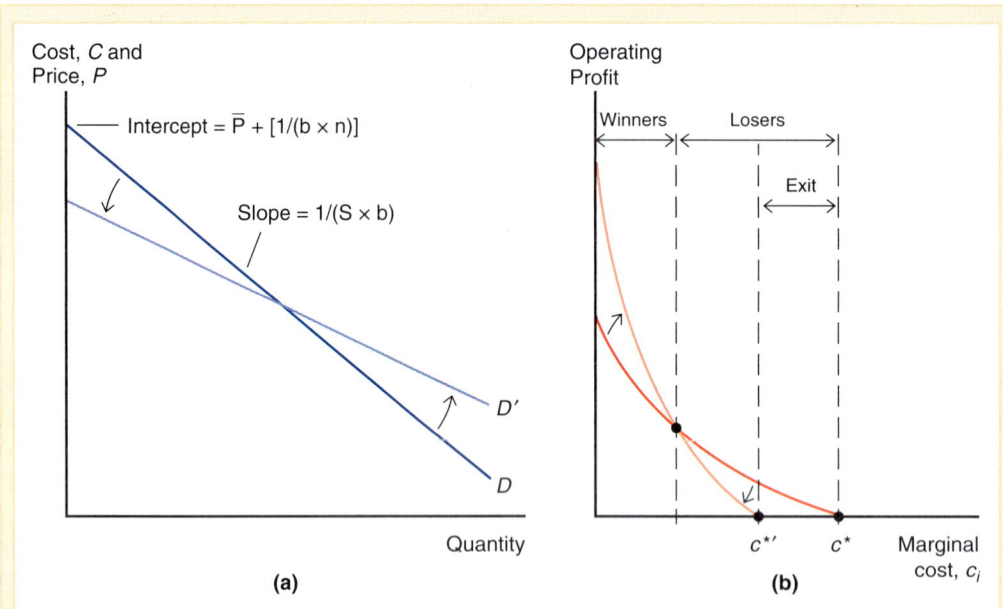

(a)   (b)

FIGURE 8-7

Winners and Losers from Economic Integration

(a) The demand curve for all firms changes from D to D'. It is flatter, and has a lower vertical intercept.
(b) Effects of the shift in demand on the operating profits of firms with different marginal cost c_i. Firms with marginal cost between the old cutoff, c^*, and the new one, $c^{*'}$, are forced to exit. Some firms with the lowest marginal cost levels gain from integration and their profits increase.

demand, leaving its slope unchanged: This is the induced inward shift from more competition.[15] The direct effect of increased market size S flattens the demand curve (lower slope), leaving the intercept unchanged: This generates an outward rotation of demand. Combining these two effects, we obtain the new demand curve D', which has a lower vertical intercept and is flatter than the original demand curve D

Panel (b) of Figure 8-7 shows the consequences of this demand change for the operating profits of firms with different cost levels c_i. The decrease in demand for the smaller firms translates into a new, lower-cost cutoff, $c^{*\prime}$: Some firms with the high cost levels above $c^{*\prime}$ cannot survive the decrease in demand and are forced to exit. On the other hand, the flatter demand curve is advantageous to some firms with low cost levels: They can adapt to the increased competition by lowering their markup (and hence their price) and gain some additional market share.[16] This translates into increased profits for some of the best-performing firms with the lowest cost levels c_i.[17]

Figure 8-7 illustrates how increased market size generates both winners and losers among firms in an industry. The low-cost firms thrive and increase their profits and market shares, while the high-cost firms contract and the highest-cost firms exit. These composition changes imply that overall productivity in the industry is increasing as production is concentrated among the more productive (low-cost) firms. This replicates the findings for Canadian manufacturing following closer integration with U.S. manufacturing, as we previously described. These effects tend to be most pronounced for smaller countries that integrate with larger ones, but it is not limited to those small countries. Even for a big economy such as the United States, increased integration via lower trade costs leads to important composition effects and productivity gains.[18]

Trade Costs and Export Decisions

Up to now, we have modeled economic integration as an increase in market size. This implicitly assumes that this integration occurs to such an extent that a single combined market is formed. In reality, integration rarely goes that far: Trade costs among countries are reduced, but they do not disappear. In Chapter 2, we discussed how these trade costs are manifested even for the case of the two very closely integrated economies of the United States and Canada. We saw how the U.S.–Canada border substantially decreases trade volumes between Canadian provinces and U.S. states.

Trade costs associated with this border crossing are also a salient feature of firm-level trade patterns: Very few firms in the United States reach Canadian customers. In fact, most U.S. firms do not report *any* exporting activity at all (because they sell only to U.S. customers). In 2002, only 18 percent of U.S. manufacturing firms reported undertaking some export sales. Table 8-3 shows the proportion of firms that report some export sales across several different U.S. manufacturing sectors. Even

---

[15]In equilibrium, increased competition also leads to a lower average price $\bar{P}$, which will further decrease the intercept.

[16]Recall that the lower the firm's marginal cost c_i, the higher its markup over marginal cost $P_i - c_i$. High-cost firms are already setting low markups and cannot lower their prices to induce positive demand, as this would mean pricing below their marginal cost of production.

[17]Another way to deduce that profit increases for some firms is to use the entry condition that drives average profits to zero: If profit decreases for some of the high-cost firms, then it must increase for some of the low-cost firms, since the average across all firms must remain equal to zero.

[18]See A. B. Bernard, J. B. Jensen, and P. K. Schott, "Trade Costs, Firms and Productivity," *Journal of Monetary Economics* 53 (July 2006), pp. 917–937.

TABLE 8-3	Proportion of U.S. Firms Reporting Export Sales by Industry, 2002
Printing	5%
Furniture	7%
Apparel	8%
Wood Products	8%
Fabricated Metals	14%
Petroleum and Coal	18%
Transportation Equipment	28%
Machinery	33%
Chemicals	36%
Computer and Electronics	38%
Electrical Equipment and Appliances	38%

Source: A. B. Bernard, J. B. Jensen, S. J. Redding, and P. K. Schott, "Firms in International Trade." *Journal of Economic Perspectives* 21 (Summer 2007), pp. 105–130.

in industries where exports represent a substantial proportion of total production, such as chemicals, machinery, electronics, and transportation, fewer than 40 percent of firms export. In fact, one major reason why trade costs associated with national borders reduce trade so much is that they drastically cut down the number of firms willing or able to reach customers across the border. (The other reason is that the trade costs also reduce the export sales of firms that do reach those customers across the border.)

In our integrated economy without any trade costs, firms were indifferent as to the location of their customers. We now introduce trade costs to explain why firms actually do care about the location of their customers and why so many firms choose not to reach customers in another country. As we will see shortly, this will also allow us to explain important differences between those firms that choose to incur the trade costs and export, and those that do not. Why would some firms choose not to export? Simply put, the trade costs reduce the profitability of exporting for all firms. For some, that reduction in profitability makes exporting unprofitable. We now formalize this argument.

To keep things simple, we will consider the response of firms in a world with two identical countries (Home and Foreign). Let the market size parameter S now reflect the size of each market, so that $2 \times S$ now reflects the size of the world market. We cannot analyze this world market as a single market of size $2 \times S$ because this market is no longer perfectly integrated due to trade costs.

Specifically, assume that a firm must incur an additional cost t for each unit of output that it sells to customers across the border. We now have to keep track of the firms' behavior in each market separately. Due to the trade cost t, firms will set different prices in their export market relative to their domestic market. This will lead to different quantities sold in each market and ultimately to different profit levels earned in each market. As each firm's marginal cost is constant (does not vary with production levels), those decisions regarding pricing and quantity sold in each market can be separated: A decision regarding the domestic market will have no impact on the profitability of different decisions for the export market.

Consider the case of firms located in Home. Their situation regarding their domestic (Home) market is exactly as was illustrated in Figure 8-6, except that all

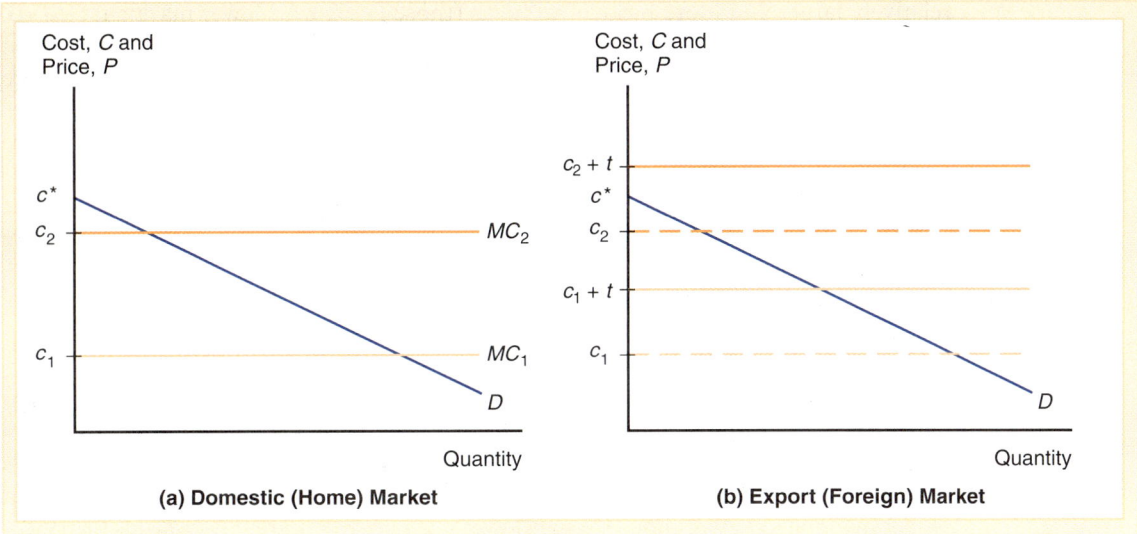

FIGURE 8-8

Export Decisions with Trade Costs

(a) Firms 1 and 2 both operate in their domestic (Home) market. (b) Only firm 1 chooses to export to the Foreign market. It is not profitable for firm 2 to export given the trade cost t.

the outcomes, such as price, output, and profit, relate to the domestic market only.[19] Now consider the decisions of firms 1 and 2 (with marginal costs c_1 and c_2) regarding the export (Foreign) market. They face the same demand curve in Foreign as they do in Home (recall that we assumed the two countries are identical). The only difference is that the firms' marginal cost in the export market is shifted up by the trade cost t. Figure 8-8 shows the situation for the two firms in both markets.

What are the effects of the trade cost on the firms' decisions regarding the export market? We know from our previous analysis that a higher marginal cost induces a firm to raise its price, which leads to a lower output quantity sold and lower profits. We also know that if marginal cost is raised above the threshold level c^*, then a firm cannot profitably operate in that market. This is what happens to firm 2 in Figure 8-8. Firm 2 can profitably operate in its domestic market because its cost there is below the threshold: $c_2 \leq c^*$. However, it cannot profitably operate in the export market because its cost there is above the threshold: $c_2 + t > c^*$. Firm 1, on the other hand, has a low enough cost that it can profitably operate in both the domestic and the export markets: $c_1 + t \leq c^*$. We can extend this prediction to all firms based on their marginal cost c_i. The lowest-cost firms with $c_i \leq c^* - t$ export; the higher-cost firms with $c^* - t < c_i \leq c^*$ still produce for their domestic market but do not export; the highest-cost firms with $c_i > c^*$ cannot profitably operate in either market and thus exit.

We just saw how the modeling of trade costs added two important predictions to our model of monopolistic competition and trade: Those costs explain why only a subset of firms export, and they also explain why this subset of firms will consist of

---

[19] The number of firms n is the total number of firms selling in the Home market. (This includes both firms located in Home as well as the firms located in Foreign that export to Home). $\overline{P}$ is the average price across all those firms selling in Home.

relatively larger and more productive firms (those firms with lower marginal cost c_i). Empirical analyses of firms' export decisions from numerous countries have provided overwhelming support for this prediction that exporting firms are bigger and more productive than firms in the same industry that do not export. In the United States in a typical manufacturing industry, an exporting firm is on average more than twice as large as a firm that does not export. The average exporting firm also produces 11 percent more value added (output minus intermediate inputs) per worker than the average nonexporting firm. These differences across exporters and nonexporters are even larger in many European countries.[20]

Dumping

Adding trade costs to our model of monopolistic competition also added another dimension of realism: Because markets are no longer perfectly integrated through cost-less trade, firms can choose to set different prices in different markets. The trade costs also affect how a firm responds to competition in a market. Recall that a firm with a higher marginal cost will choose to set a lower markup over marginal cost (this firm faces more intense competition due to its lower market share). This means that an exporting firm will respond to the trade cost by lowering its markup for the export market.

Consider the case of firm 1 in Figure 8-8. It faces a higher marginal cost $c_1 + t$ in the Foreign export market. Let P_1^D and P_1^X denote the prices that firm 1 sets on its domestic (Home) market and export (Foreign) market, respectively. Firm 1 sets a lower markup $P_1^X - (c_1 + t)$ on the export market relative to its markup $P_1^D - c_1$ on the domestic market. This in turn implies that $P_1^X - t < P_1^D$ and that firm 1 sets an export price (net of trade costs) lower than its domestic price.

That is considered **dumping** by firm 1 and is regarded by most countries as an "unfair" trade practice. Any firm from Foreign can appeal to its local authorities (in the United States, the Commerce Department and the International Trade Commission are the relevant authorities) and seek punitive damages against firm 1. This usually takes the form of an **antidumping duty** imposed on firm 1 and would usually be scaled to the price difference between P_1^D and $P_1^X - t$.[21]

Dumping is a controversial issue in trade policy; we discuss policy disputes surrounding dumping in Chapter 10. For now, we just note that firm 1 is not behaving any differently than the foreign firms it is competing against in the Foreign market. In that market, firm 1 sets exactly the same markup over marginal cost as Foreign firm 2 with marginal cost $c_2 = c_1 + t$. Firm 2's pricing behavior is perfectly legal, so why is firm 1's export pricing decision considered to represent an "unfair" trade practice? This is one major reason why economists believe that the enforcement of dumping claims is misguided (see the Case Study for a further discussion) and that there is no good economic justification for dumping to be considered particularly harmful.

Our model of monopolistic competition highlighted how trade costs have a natural tendency to induce firms to lower their markups in export markets, where they face

---

[20]See A. B. Bernard, J. B. Jensen, S. J. Redding, and P. K. Schott, "Firms in International Trade," *Journal of Economic Perspectives* 21 (Summer 2007), pp. 105–130; and Thierry Mayer and Gianmarco I. P. Ottaviano, "The Happy Few: The Internationalisation of European Firms: New Facts Based on Firm-Level Evidence," *Intereconomics* 43 (May/June 2008), pp. 135–148.

[21]$P_1^X - t$ is called firm 1's *ex* factory price for the export market (the price at the "factory gate" before the trade costs are incurred). If firm 1 incurred some transport or delivery cost in its domestic market, then those costs would be deducted from its domestic price P_1^D to obtain an *ex factory* price for the domestic market. Antidumping duties are based on differences between a firm's ex factory prices in the domestic and export markets.

more intense competition due to their reduced market share. This makes it relatively easy for domestic firms to file a dumping complaint against exporters in their markets. In practice, those antidumping laws can then be used to erect barriers to trade by discriminating against exporters in a market.

CASE STUDY

Antidumping as Protectionism

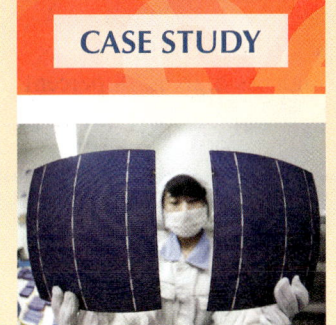

In the United States and a number of other countries, dumping is regarded as an unfair competitive practice. U.S. firms that claim to have been injured by foreign firms that dump their products in the domestic market at low prices can appeal, through a quasi-judicial procedure, to the Commerce Department for relief. If their complaint is ruled valid, an "antidumping duty" is imposed, equal to the calculated difference between the actual and the "fair" price of imports. In practice, the Commerce Department accepts the great majority of complaints by U.S. firms about unfair foreign pricing. The determination that this unfair pricing has actually caused injury, however, is in the hands of a different agency, the International Trade Commission, which rejects about half of its cases.

Economists have never been very happy with the idea of singling out dumping as a prohibited practice. For one thing, setting different prices for different customers is a perfectly legitimate business strategy—like the discounts that airlines offer to students, senior citizens, and travelers who are willing to stay over a weekend. Also, the legal definition of dumping deviates substantially from the economic definition. Since it is often difficult to prove that foreign firms charge higher prices to domestic than to export customers, the United States and other nations instead often try to calculate a supposedly fair price based on estimates of foreign production costs. This "fair price" rule can interfere with perfectly normal business practices: A firm may well be willing to sell a product for a loss while it is lowering its costs through experience or breaking into a new market. Even absent such dynamic considerations, our model highlighted how monopolistically competitive firms have an incentive to lower their markups in export markets due to competition effects associated with trade costs.

In spite of almost universally negative assessments from economists, however, formal complaints about dumping have been filed with growing frequency since about 1970. In the early 1990s, the bulk of anti-dumping complaints were directed at developed countries. But since 1995, developing countries have accounted for the majority of anti-dumping complaints. And among those countries, China has attracted a particularly large number of complaints.

There are two main reasons behind this trend. First and foremost has been China's massive export growth. No firm enjoys facing stiff increases in competition, and anti-dumping laws allow firms to insulate themselves from this competition by raising their competitors' costs. Second, proving unfair pricing by a Chinese firm is relatively easier than for exporters from other countries. Most developed countries (including the United States) facing this surge in Chinese exports have labeled China a "non-market" economy. A *Business Week* story describes the difference that this description makes when a U.S. firm files an anti-dumping complaint against a Chinese exporter: "That means the U.S. can simply ignore Chinese data on costs on the assumption they are distorted by subsidized loans, rigged markets, and the controlled yuan. Instead, the government uses data from other developing nations regarded as market economies. In the TV and furniture cases, the U.S. used India—even though it is not a big exporter of these goods. Since India's production costs were higher, China was ruled guilty of dumping."[22]

As the quote suggests, China has been subject to antidumping duties on TVs and furniture, along with a number of other products including crepe paper, hand trucks, shrimp, ironing tables, plastic shopping bags, steel fence posts, iron pipe fittings, saccharin, and most recently solar panels. These duties are high: as high as 78 percent on color TVs and 330 percent on saccharin.

Multinationals and Outsourcing

When is a corporation multinational? In U.S. statistics, a U.S. company is considered foreign-controlled, and therefore a subsidiary of a foreign-based multinational, if 10 percent or more of its stock is held by a foreign company; the idea is that 10 percent is enough to convey effective control. Similarly, a U.S.-based company is considered multinational if it owns more than 10 percent of a foreign firm. The controlling (owning) firm is called the multinational parent, while the "controlled" firms are called the multinational affiliates.

When a U.S. firm buys more than 10 percent of a foreign firm, or when a U.S. firm builds a new production facility abroad, that investment is considered a U.S. outflow of **foreign direct investment (FDI)**. The latter is called *greenfield* FDI, while the former is called *brownfield* FDI (or cross-border mergers and acquisitions). Conversely, investments by foreign firms in production facilities in the United States are considered U.S. FDI inflows. We describe the worldwide patterns of FDI flows in the Case Study that follows. For now, we focus on the decision of a firm to become a multinational parent. Why would a firm choose to operate an affiliate in a foreign location?

CASE STUDY   **Patterns of Foreign Direct Investment Flows Around the World**

Figure 8-9 shows how the magnitude of worldwide FDI flows has evolved over the last 40 years. We first examine patterns for the world, where FDI flows must be balanced: Hence world inflows are equal to world outflows. We see that there was a massive increase in multinational activity in the mid- to late-1990s, when worldwide FDI flows more than quintupled and then again in the early 2000s. We also see that the growth rate of FDI is very uneven, with huge peaks and troughs. Those peaks and troughs correlate with the gyrations of stock markets worldwide

[22]"Wielding a Heavy Weapon Against China," *BusinessWeek*, June 21, 2004.

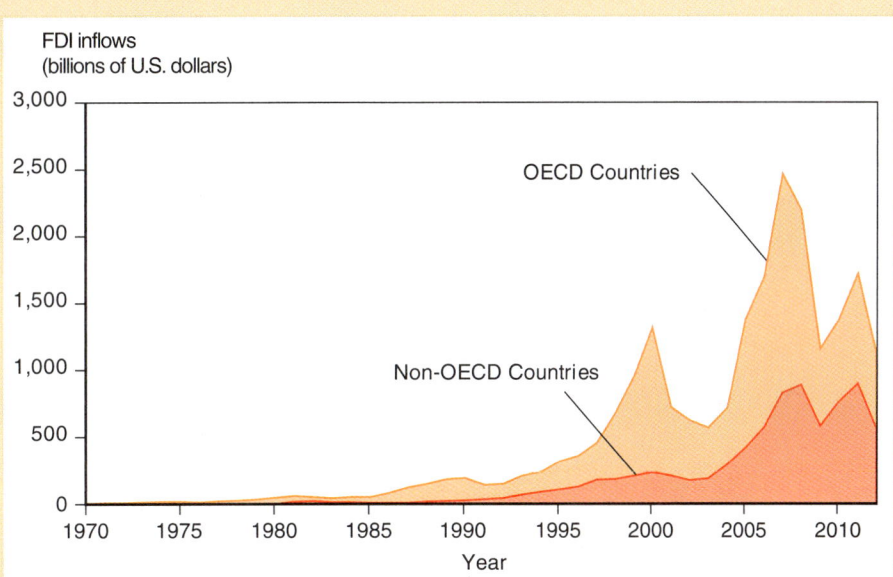

FIGURE 8-9

Inflows of Foreign Direct Investment, 1970–2012 (billions of dollars)

Worldwide flows of FDI have significantly increased since the mid-1990s, though the rates of increase have been very uneven. Historically, most of the inflows of FDI have gone to the developed countries in the OECD. However, the proportion of FDI inflows going to developing and transition economies has steadily increased over time and accounted for over half of worldwide FDI flows since 2009.

Source: World Bank, *World Development Indicators.*

(strongly dominated by fluctuations in the U.S. stock market). The financial collapse in 2000 (the bursting of the dot-com bubble) and the most recent financial crisis in 2007–2009 also induced huge crashes in worldwide FDI flows. Most recently, global FDI flows sharply declined in 2012, even though world GDP grew and the largest stock markets all posted significant gains. (Uncertainty related to the fragility of the economic recovery and political stability played a significant role—as well as the repatriation of profits by multinationals.) Most of those FDI flows related to cross-border mergers and acquisitions, whereas greenfield FDI remained relatively stable.

Looking at the distribution of FDI inflows across groups of countries, we see that historically, the richest OECD countries have been the biggest recipients of inward FDI. However, we also see that those inflows are much more volatile (this is where the FDI related to mergers and acquisitions is concentrated) than the FDI going to the remaining countries with lower incomes. Finally, we also see that there has been a steady expansion in the share of FDI that flows to those countries outside the OECD. This accounted for over half of worldwide FDI flows since 2009. The BRICS countries (Brazil, the Russian Federation, China, India, and South Africa) have accounted for a substantial portion of this increase: FDI flows to those countries increased 20-fold in the past decade.

Figure 8-10 shows the list of the top 25 countries whose firms engage in FDI outflows. Because those flows are very volatile, especially with the recent crisis, they have

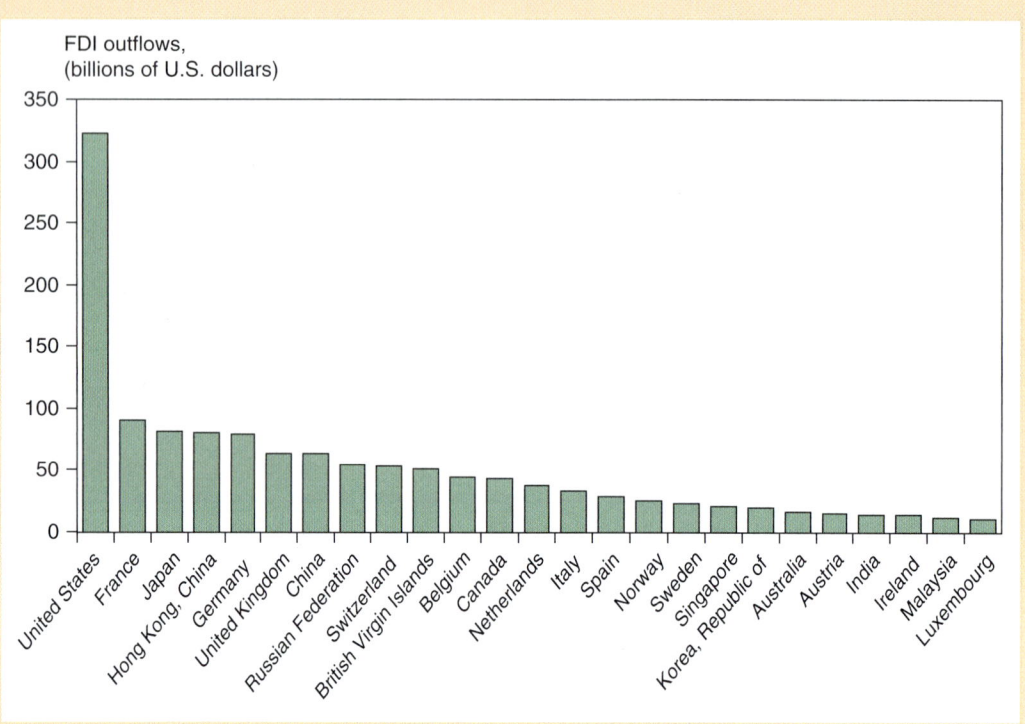

FIGURE 8-10

Outward Foreign Direct Investment for Top 25 Countries, Yearly Average for 2009–2011 (billions of dollars)

Developed countries dominate the list of the top countries whose firms engage in outward FDI. More recently, firms from some big developing countries such as China and India have performed significantly more FDI.

Source: UNCTAD, World Investment Report, 2012.

been averaged over the past three years. We see that FDI outflows are still dominated by the developed economies; but we also see that big developing countries, most notably China (including Hong Kong), are playing an increasingly important role. In fact, one of the fastest-growing FDI segments is flows *from* developing countries *into* other developing countries. Multinationals in both China and India play a prominent role in this relatively new type of FDI. We also see that international tax policies can shape the location of FDI. For example, the British Virgin Islands would not figure in that top-25 list were it not for its status as an international tax haven.[23] Firms from that location that engage in FDI are mainly offshore companies: They are incorporated in the British Virgin Islands, but their productive activities are located elsewhere in the world.

---

[23]The British Virgin Islands is an even bigger recipient of inward FDI: In 2012, it was the fifth largest recipient in the world.

FDI flows are not the only way to measure the presence of multinationals in the world economy. Other measures are based on economic activities such as sales, value added (sales minus purchased intermediate goods), and employment. Sales of FDI affiliates are often used as the benchmark of multinational activity. This provides the relevant benchmark when comparing the activities of multinationals to export volumes. However, the sales of multinationals are also often compared to country GDPs showing, for example, that the big multinationals have higher sales volumes than the GDPs of many countries in the world. For the world as a whole in 2000, the total sales of the largest multinationals (top 200) amounted to more than 27 percent of world GDP.

However striking, this comparison is misleading and overstates the influence of multinationals because country GDP is measured in terms of value added: Intermediate goods used in final production are not double-counted in this GDP measure. On the other hand, the intermediate goods that one multinational sells to another are double-counted in the multinationals' sales totals (once in the sales of the producer of the intermediate goods and another time as part of the final value of the goods sold by the user of the intermediate goods). As a result, the appropriate comparison between multinationals and GDPs should be based on value added. By this metric, the value added produced by the biggest multinationals accounted for 4.3 percent of world GDP in 2000. This is still a big percentage, but not as eye-catching as the 27 percent measure.

The answer depends, in part, on the production activities that the affiliate carries out. These activities fall into two main categories: (1) The affiliate replicates the production process (that the parent firm undertakes in its domestic facilities) elsewhere in the world; and (2) the production chain is broken up, and parts of the production processes are transferred to the affiliate location. Investing in affiliates that do the first type of activities is categorized as **horizontal FDI**. Investing in affiliates that do the second type of activities is categorized as **vertical FDI**.[24]

Vertical FDI is mainly driven by production cost differences between countries (for those parts of the production process that can be performed in another location). What drives those cost differences between countries? This is just the outcome of the theory of comparative advantage that we developed in Chapters 3 through 7. For example, Intel (the world's largest computer chip manufacturer) has broken up the production of chips into wafer fabrication, assembly, and testing. Wafer fabrication and the associated research and development are very skill-intensive, so Intel still performs most of those activities in the United States as well as in Ireland and Israel (where skilled labor is still relatively abundant).[25] On the other hand, chip assembly and testing are labor-intensive, and Intel has moved those production processes to countries where labor is relatively abundant, such as Malaysia, the Philippines, Costa Rica, and China. This type of vertical FDI is one of the fastest-growing types of FDI and is behind the large increase in FDI inflows to developing countries (see Figure 8-9).

---

[24]In reality, the distinctions between horizontal and vertical FDI can be blurred. Some large multinational parents operate large networks of affiliates that replicate parts of the production process, but are also vertically connected to other affiliates in the parent's network. This is referred to as "complex" FDI.

[25]In 2010, Intel opened a new wafer fabrication plant in Dalian, China, where older chip models are produced.

In contrast to vertical FDI, horizontal FDI is dominated by flows between developed countries; that is, both the multinational parent and the affiliates are located in developed countries. The main reason for this type of FDI is to locate production near a firm's large customer bases. Hence, trade and transport costs play a much more important role than production cost differences for these FDI decisions. Consider the example of Toyota, which is the world's largest motor vehicle producer (at least, at the time of writing, though Volkswagen is a closed second). At the start of the 1980s, Toyota produced almost all of its cars and trucks in Japan and exported them throughout the world, but mostly to North America and Europe. High trade costs to those markets (in large part due to trade restrictions; see Chapter 9) and rising demand levels there induced Toyota to slowly expand its production overseas. By 2009, Toyota produced over half of its vehicles in assembly plants abroad. Toyota has replicated the production process for its most popular car model, the Corolla, in assembly plants in Brazil, Canada, China, India, Japan, Pakistan, South Africa, Taiwan, Thailand, Turkey, the United States, the United Kingdom, Vietnam, and Venezuela: This is horizontal FDI in action.

The Firm's Decision Regarding Foreign Direct Investment

We now examine in more detail the firm's decision regarding horizontal FDI. We mentioned that one main driver was high trade costs associated with exporting, which leads to an incentive to locate production near customers. On the other hand, there are also increasing returns to scale in production. As a result, it is not cost effective to replicate the production process too many times and operate facilities that produce too little output to take advantage of those increasing returns. This is called the *proximity-concentration* trade-off for FDI. Empirical evidence on the extent of FDI across sectors strongly confirms the relevance of this trade-off: FDI activity is concentrated in sectors where trade costs are high (such as the automobile industry); however, when increasing returns to scale are important and average plant sizes are large, one observes higher export volumes relative to FDI.

Empirical evidence also shows that there is an even stronger sorting pattern for FDI at the firm level *within* industries: Multinationals tend to be substantially larger and more productive than nonmultinationals in the same country. Even when one compares multinationals to the subset of exporting firms in a country, one still finds a large size and productivity differential in favor of the multinationals. We return to our monopolistic competition model of trade to analyze how firms respond differently to the proximity-concentration trade-off involved with the FDI decision.

The Horizontal FDI Decision   How does the proximity trade-off fit into our model of firms' export decisions captured in Figure 8-8? There, if a firm wants to reach customers in Foreign, it has only one possibility: export and incur the trade cost t per unit exported. Let's now introduce the choice of becoming a multinational via horizontal FDI: A firm could avoid the trade cost t by building a production facility in Foreign. Of course, building this production facility is costly and implies incurring the fixed cost F again for the foreign affiliate. (Note, however, that this additional fixed cost need not equal the fixed cost of building the firm's original production facility in Home; characteristics specific to the individual country will affect this cost.) For simplicity, continue to assume that Home and Foreign are similar countries so that this firm could build a unit of a good at the same marginal cost in this foreign facility. (Recall that horizontal FDI mostly involves developed countries with similar factor prices.)

The firm's export versus FDI choice will then involve a trade-off between the per-unit export cost t and the fixed cost F of setting up an additional production facility. Any such trade-off between a per-unit and a fixed cost boils down to scale. If the firm sells Q units in the foreign market, then it incurs a total trade-related cost $Q \times t$ to export; this is weighed against the alternative of the fixed cost F. If $Q > F/t$, then exporting is more expensive, and FDI is the profit-maximizing choice.

This leads to a scale cutoff for FDI. This cutoff summarizes the proximity-concentration trade-off: Higher trade costs on one hand, and lower fixed production costs on the other hand, both lower the FDI cutoff. The firm's scale, however, depends on its performance measure. A firm with low enough cost c_i will want to sell more than Q units to foreign customers. The most cost-effective way to do this is to build an affiliate in Foreign and become a multinational. Some firms with intermediate cost levels will still want to serve customers in Foreign, but their intended sales Q are low enough that exports, rather than FDI, will be the most cost-effective way to reach those customers.

The Vertical FDI Decision   A firm's decision to break up its production chain and move parts of that chain to a foreign affiliate will also involve a trade-off between per-unit and fixed costs—so the scale of the firm's activity will again be a crucial element determining this outcome. When it comes to vertical FDI, the key cost saving is not related to the shipment of goods across borders; rather, it involves production cost differences for the parts of the production chain that are being moved. As we previously discussed, those cost differences stem mostly from comparative advantage forces.

We will not discuss those cost differences further here, but rather ask why—given those cost differences—all firms do not choose to operate affiliates in low-wage countries to perform the activities that are most labor-intensive and can be performed in a different location. The reason is that, as with the case of horizontal FDI, vertical FDI requires a substantial fixed cost investment in a foreign affiliate in a country with the appropriate characteristics.[26] Again, as with the case of horizontal FDI, there will be a scale cutoff for vertical FDI that depends on the production cost differentials on one hand, and the fixed cost of operating a foreign affiliate on the other hand. Only those firms operating at a scale above that cutoff will choose to perform vertical FDI.

Outsourcing

Our discussion of multinationals up to this point has neglected an important motive. We discussed the **location motive** for production facilities that leads to multinational formation. However, we did not discuss why the parent firm chooses to *own* the affiliate in that location and operate as a single multinational firm. This is known as the **internalization motive**.

As a substitute for horizontal FDI, a parent could license an independent firm to produce and sell its products in a foreign location; as a substitute for vertical FDI, a parent could contract with an independent firm to perform specific parts of the production process in the foreign location with the best cost advantage. This substitute for vertical FDI is known as **foreign outsourcing** (sometimes just referred to as outsourcing, where the foreign location is implied).

---

[26]Clearly, factor prices such as wages are a crucial component, but other country characteristics, such as its transportation/public infrastructure, the quality of its legal institutions, and its tax/regulation policies toward multinationals, can be critical as well.

Offshoring represents the relocation of parts of the production chain abroad and groups together both foreign outsourcing and vertical FDI. Offshoring has increased dramatically in the last decade and is one of the major drivers of the increased world-wide trade in services (such as business and telecommunications services); in manu-facturing, trade in intermediate goods accounted for 40 percent of worldwide trade in 2008. When the intermediate goods are produced within a multinational's affiliate network, the shipments of those intermediate goods are classified as intra-firm trade. Intra-firm trade represents roughly one-third of worldwide trade and over 40 percent of U.S. trade.

What are the key elements that determine this internalization choice? Control over a firm's proprietary technology offers one clear advantage for internalization. Licensing another firm to perform the entire production process in another location (as a sub-stitute for horizontal FDI) often involves a substantial risk of losing some proprietary technology. On the other hand, there are no clear reasons why an independent firm should be able to replicate that production process at a lower cost than the parent firm. This gives internalization a strong advantage, so horizontal FDI is widely favored over the alternative of technology licensing to replicate the production process.

The trade-off between outsourcing and vertical FDI is much less clear-cut. There are many reasons why an independent firm could produce some parts of the pro-duction process at lower cost than the parent firm (in the same location). First and foremost, an independent firm can specialize in exactly that narrow part of the pro-duction process. As a result, it can also benefit from economies of scale if it performs those processes for many different parent firms.[27] Other reasons stress the advantages of local ownership in the alignment and monitoring of managerial incentives at the production facility.

But internalization also provides its own benefits when it comes to vertical integra-tion between a firm and its supplier of a critical input to production: This avoids (or at least lessens) the potential for a costly renegotiation conflict after an initial agree-ment has been reached. Such conflicts can arise regarding many specific attributes of the input that cannot be specified in (or enforced by) a legal contract written at the time of the initial agreement. This can lead to a holdup of production by either party. For example, the buying firm can claim that the quality of the part is not exactly as specified and demand a lower price. The supplying firm can claim that some changes demanded by the buyer led to increased costs and demand a higher price at delivery time.

Much progress has been made in recent research formalizing those trade-offs. This research explains how this important internalization choice is made, by describ-ing when a firm chooses to integrate with its suppliers via vertical FDI and when it chooses an independent contractual relationship with those suppliers abroad. Developing those theories is beyond the scope of this text; ultimately, many of those theories boil down to different trade-offs between production cost savings and the fixed cost of moving parts of the production process abroad.

Describing which types of firms pick one offshoring option versus the other is sen-sitive to the details of the modeling assumptions. Nonetheless, there is one prediction that emerges from almost all of those models with respect to the offshoring option. Relative to no offshoring (not breaking up the production chain and moving parts

---

[27]Companies that provide outsourced goods and services have expanded their list of clients to such an extent that they have now become large multinationals themselves. They specialize in providing a narrow set of services (or parts of the production process), but replicate this many times over for client companies across the globe.

of it abroad), both vertical FDI and foreign outsourcing involve lower production costs combined with a higher fixed cost. As we saw, this implies a scale cutoff for a firm to choose either offshoring option. Thus, only the larger firms will choose either offshoring option and import some of their intermediate inputs.

This sorting scheme for firms to import intermediate goods is similar to the one we described for the firm's export choice: Only a subset of relatively more productive (lower-cost) firms will choose to offshore (import intermediate goods) and export (reach foreign customers)—because those are the firms that operate at sufficiently large scale to favor the trade-off involving higher fixed costs and lower per-unit costs (production- or trade-related).

Empirically, are the firms that offshore and import intermediate goods the same set of firms that also export? The answer is a resounding yes. For the United States in 2000, 92 percent of firms (weighed by employment) that imported intermediate goods also exported. Those importers thus also shared the same characteristics as U.S. exporters: They were substantially larger and more productive than the U.S. firms that did not engage in international trade.

CASE STUDY

"We design them here, but the labor is cheaper in Hell."

©2004 Drew Dernavich/The New Yorker Collection/www.cartoonbank.com

Shipping Jobs Overseas? Offshoring and Unemployment in the United States

When a company offshores part of its production chain abroad, it is then importing an intermediate good or service. For example, a company may import a part, component, or even an entire assembled product; or it may import business services by using accountants and/or call centers located abroad. As we discuss in the next section, the overall effects of trade in such intermediates are very similar to the trade in final goods that we have focused on up to now. Yet, when it comes to the effects of offshoring on employment, there is one additional dimension: the lower price of the imported intermediates not only benefits a firm's owners and their consumers, it also benefits the firm's remaining workers—because the lower price induces firms to increase their purchases of intermediates, which improves the productivity of the remaining workers.[28]

This productivity effect also induces the offshoring firm to hire additional workers dedicated to the remaining parts of the production process. In many cases, the overall employment effect for the offshoring firm is positive: Several studies of U.S. multinationals have found that when they expand their overseas employment, they concurrently also expand their U.S. employment.[29]

What about foreign outsourcers who no longer maintain ownership of their foreign suppliers? A recent study covering the entire U.S. manufacturing sector found that overall, increases in offshoring from 2001–2007 did have a negative impact on

---

[28]This additional dimension of offshoring, and its effects for low-skilled workers, is emphasized in an influential new paper. See Gene M. Grossman and Esteban Rossi-Hansberg. "The Rise of Offshoring: It's Not Wine for Cloth Anymore." *The New Economic Geography: Effects and Policy Implications*, 2006, pp. 59–102.
[29]See Mihir Desai, C. Fritz Foley, and James R Hines. "Domestic Effects of the Foreign Activities of US Multinationals." *American Economic Journal: Economic Policy*, (January 2009).

U.S. manufacturing employment.[30] However, those losses connected to offshoring accounted for only a tiny fraction (2.3%) of the total employment losses during that period. Those total employment losses were indeed substantial: The decrease in U.S. manufacturing employment totaled 2 million (manufacturing employment has been steadily decreasing over the past 30 years); but offshoring played a very minor role in this trend.

This study also found that the productivity effect for the remaining workers played a very important role: The cost benefits from offshoring lead firms to substantially expand their U.S. operations and hire additional workers. Non-production workers benefited most from this increased employment because they were much less likely to directly suffer from the displacement effect of offshoring in the first place. However, production workers also benefited from this expansion effect tied to offshoring: The initial displacement unemployment for those production workers was cut in half by this increased employment response.

Another channel mitigating the worker displacement effects of offshoring is that—just as with trade in final goods—intermediate goods and services are traded in both directions. In the United States, the popular press and many politicians single-out the employment losses associated with offshoring.[31] Of particular concern are the losses of service jobs to offshoring, given the recent technological trends that have vastly expanded the scope of "offshorable" business services (see the discussion in Chapter 2). This has lead to headlines such as "More U.S. service jobs go overseas; Offshoring is expected to grow" in the *USA Today*.[32] Yet, offshoring in one country is *inshoring* in another country: That is, for every import transaction of an intermediate good or service, there is a corresponding export transaction for the country hosting the offshored part of the production process. And it turns out that for the United States, this inshoring of service jobs (exports of intermediate services) is growing even faster than the offshoring of service jobs out of the United States (imports of intermediate services), leading to a surplus; and one that has been growing over time. Figure 8-11 plots all U.S. cross-border trade over time in service categories related to offshoring (financial, insurance, telecommunications, and business services; that is, all traded services other than tourism, transportation, and royalties).[33] Clearly, there is nothing ominous in the time trend of trade in business services for overall U.S. employment.

Given all these facts on the impact of offshoring for U.S. employment, the view that offshoring simply amounts to "shipping jobs overseas" is misleading. True, when a firm based in the United States moves a call center to India, or moves the assembly of its product to China, then some specific jobs that used to be performed in the United States are now performed in India or China. However, the evidence shows that in terms of overall employment, those jobs are replaced

---

[30]See Greg C. Wright, "Revisiting the Employment Impact of Offshoring." *University of Essex*, mimeo, 2013.
[31]Public Citizen reported a sharp increase in political ads condemning offshoring in the 2012 congressional elections (it tracked 90 ads condemning offshoring in campaigns spanning 30 states).
[32]*USA Today*, December 7, 2012.
[33]Those trade flows also include transactions by multinationals with their affiliates abroad. The net balance of exports over imports is positive for the United States, both among multinational transactions, as well as for transactions between unaffiliated parties.

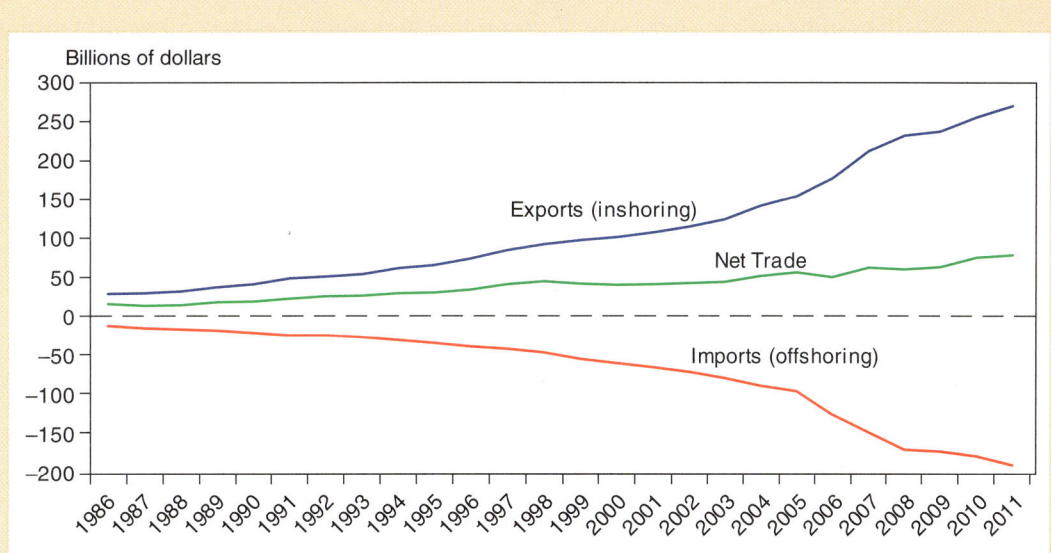

FIGURE 8-11

U.S. International Trade in Business Services (all traded services excluding tourism, transportation, and royalties and license fees), 1986–2011

U.S. service offshoring is captured by U.S. imports of business services. Although service offshoring has dramatically increased over the past decade, U.S. inshoring (exports of business services) has grown even faster. The net balance is positive and has also substantially increased over the past decade.

Source: U.S. Bureau of Economic Analysis.

by other ones in the United States: some related to the expansion effect at the offshoring firms and others by firms providing intermediate goods and services to firms located abroad (inshoring).

Yet, just as with other forms of trade, trade in intermediates has substantial consequences for the distribution of income. Those call center or manufacturing workers displaced by offshoring are often not the ones who are hired by the expanding firms. Their plight is not made any easier by the gains that accrue to other workers. We discuss these overall welfare consequences in the next section.

Consequences of Multinationals and Foreign Outsourcing

Earlier in this chapter, we mentioned that internal economies of scale, product differentiation, and performance differences across firms combined to deliver some new channels for the gains from trade: increased product variety and higher industry performance as firms move down their average cost curve and production is concentrated in the larger, more productive firms. What are the consequences for welfare of the expansion in multinational production and outsourcing?

We just saw how multinationals and firms that outsource take advantage of cost differentials that favor moving production (or parts thereof) to particular locations. In essence, this is very similar to the relocation of production that occurred *across* sectors when opening to trade. As we saw in Chapters 3 through 6, the location of production then shifts to take advantage of cost differences generated by comparative advantage.

We can therefore predict similar welfare consequences for the case of multinationals and outsourcing: Relocating production to take advantage of cost differences leads to overall gains from trade, but it is also likely to induce income distribution effects that leave some people worse off. We discussed one potential long-run consequence of outsourcing for income inequality in developed countries in Chapter 5.

Yet some of the most visible effects of multinationals and offshoring more generally occur in the short run, as some firms expand employment while others reduce employment in response to increased globalization. In Chapter 4, we described the substantial costs associated with involuntary worker displacements linked to inter-industry trade (especially for lower-skilled workers). The costs associated with displacements linked to offshoring are just as severe for workers with similar characteristics. As we argued in Chapter 4, the best policy response to this serious concern is still to provide an adequate safety net to unemployed workers without discriminating based on the economic force that induced their involuntary unemployment. Policies that impede firms' abilities to relocate production and take advantage of these cost differences may prevent these short-run costs for some, but they also forestall the accumulation of long-run economy-wide gains.

SUMMARY

1. Trade need not be the result of comparative advantage. Instead, it can result from increasing returns or economies of scale, that is, from a tendency of unit costs to be lower with larger output. Economies of scale give countries an incentive to specialize and trade even in the absence of differences between countries in their resources or technology. Economies of scale can be internal (depending on the size of the firm) or external (depending on the size of the industry).

2. Economies of scale internal to firms lead to a breakdown of perfect competition; models of imperfect competition must be used instead to analyze the consequences of increasing returns at the level of the firm. An important model of this kind is the monopolistic competition model, which is widely used to analyze models of firms and trade.

3. In monopolistic competition, an industry contains a number of firms producing differentiated products. These firms act as individual monopolists, but additional firms enter a profitable industry until monopoly profits are competed away. Equilibrium is affected by the size of the market: A large market will support a larger number of firms, each producing at a larger scale and thus a lower average cost, than a small market.

4. International trade allows for the creation of an integrated market that is larger than any one country's market. As a result, it is possible to simultaneously offer consumers a greater variety of products and lower prices. The type of trade generated by this model is intra-industry trade.

5. When firms differ in terms of their performance, economic integration generates winners and losers. The more productive (lower-cost) firms thrive and expand, while the less productive (higher-cost) firms contract. The least-productive firms are forced to exit.

6. In the presence of trade costs, markets are no longer perfectly integrated through trade. Firms can set different prices across markets. These prices reflect trade costs as well as the level of competition perceived by the firm. When there are trade costs, only a subset of more productive firms choose to export; the remaining firms serve only their domestic market.

7. Dumping occurs when a firm sets a lower price (net of trade costs) on exports than it charges domestically. A consequence of trade costs is that firms will feel competition more intensely on export markets because the firms have smaller market shares in those export markets. This leads firms to reduce markups for their export sales relative to their domestic sales; this behavior is characterized as dumping. Dumping is viewed as an unfair trade practice, but it arises naturally in a model of monopolistic competition and trade costs where firms from both countries behave in the same way. Policies against dumping are often used to discriminate against foreign firms in a market and erect barriers to trade.

8. Some multinationals replicate their production processes in foreign facilities located near large customer bases. This is categorized as horizontal foreign direct investment (FDI). An alternative is to export to a market instead of operating a foreign affiliate in that market. The trade-off between exports and FDI involves a lower per-unit cost for FDI (no trade cost) but an additional fixed cost associated with the foreign facility. Only firms that operate at a big enough scale will choose the FDI option over exports.

9. Some multinationals break up their production chain and perform some parts of that chain in their foreign facilities. This is categorized as vertical foreign direct investment (FDI). One alternative is to outsource those parts of the production chain to an independent foreign firm. Both of those modes of operation are categorized as offshoring. Relative to the option of no offshoring, offshoring involves lower production costs but an additional fixed cost. Only firms that operate at a big enough scale will choose to offshore.

10. Multinational firms and firms that outsource parts of production to foreign countries take advantage of cost differences across production locations. This is similar to models of comparative advantage where production at the level of the industry is determined by differences in relative costs across countries. The welfare consequences are similar as well: There are aggregate gains from increased multinational production and outsourcing, but also changes in the income distribution that leaves some people worse off.

KEY TERMS

antidumping duty, p. 212
average cost, p. 191
dumping, p. 212
foreign direct investment (FDI), p. 214
foreign outsourcing, p. 219
horizontal FDI, p. 217
imperfect competition, p. 189

internal economies of scale, p. 188
internalization motive, p. 219
intra-industry trade, p. 201
location motive, p. 219
marginal cost, p. 191
marginal revenue, p. 190
markup over marginal cost, p. 196

monopolistic competition, p. 193
offshoring, p. 220
oligopoly, p. 193
product differentiation, 192
pure monopoly, p. 190
vertical FDI, p. 217

PROBLEMS

1. Why do firms prefer being price setters over price takers, even in the absence of monopoly? Explain with an example.

2. Suppose the two countries we considered in the numerical example on pages 198–202 were to integrate their automobile market with a third country, which has an annual market for 3.75 million automobiles. Find the number of firms, the output per firm, and the price per automobile in the new integrated market after trade.

3. Suppose that fixed costs for a firm in the automobile industry (start-up costs of factories, capital equipment, and so on) are $5 billion and that variable costs are equal to $17,000 per finished automobile. Because more firms increase competition in the market, the market price falls as more firms enter an automobile market, or specifically, $P = 17,000 + (150/n)$, where n represents the number of firms in a market. Assume that the initial size of the U.S. and the European automobile markets are 300 million and 533 million people, respectively.

   a. Calculate the equilibrium number of firms in the U.S. and European automobile markets *without* trade.

   b. What is the equilibrium price of automobiles in the United States and Europe if the automobile industry is closed to foreign trade?

   c. Now suppose the United States decides on free trade in automobiles with Europe. The trade agreement with the Europeans adds 533 million consumers to the automobile market, in addition to the 300 million in the United States. How many automobile firms will there be in the United States and Europe combined? What will be the new equilibrium price of automobiles?

   d. Why are prices in the United States different in (c) and (b)? Are consumers better off with free trade? In what ways?

4. Go back to the model with firm performance differences in a single integrated market (pages 206–207). Now assume a new technology becomes available. Any firm can adopt the new technology, but its use requires an additional fixed-cost investment. The benefit of the new technology is that it reduces a firm's marginal cost of production by a given amount.

   a. Could it be profit maximizing for some firms to adopt the new technology but not profit maximizing for other firms to adopt that same technology? Which firms would choose to adopt the new technology? How would they be different from the firms that choose not to adopt it?

   b. Now assume there are also trade costs. In the new equilibrium with both trade costs and technology adoption, firms decide whether to export and also whether to adopt the new technology. Would exporting firms be more or less likely to adopt the new technology relative to nonexporters? Why?

5. In the chapter, we described a situation where dumping occurs between two symmetric countries. Briefly describe how things would change if the two countries had different sizes.

   a. How would the number of firms competing in a particular market affect the likelihood that an exporter to that market would be accused of dumping? (Assume the likelihood of a dumping accusation is related to the firm's price difference between its domestic price and its export price: the higher the price difference, the more likely the dumping accusation.)

   b. Would a firm from a small country be more or less likely to be accused of dumping when it exports to a large country (relative to a firm from the large country exporting to the small country)?

6. Which of the following are direct foreign investments?
   a. A Saudi businessman buys $10 million of IBM stock.
   b. The same businessman buys a New York apartment building.
   c. A French company merges with an American company; stockholders in the U.S. company exchange their stock for shares in the French firm.
   d. An Italian firm builds a plant in Russia and manages the plant as a contractor to the Russian government.

7. FDI's, according to their typology, can be divided into (1) horizontal and vertical; (2) inward and outward; (3) portfolio investments and Greenfield. Classify the following cases according to the above parameters:
   a. Huawei (a Chinese corporation) opens up a factory in Indonesia.
   b. Samsung (a Korean chaebol) acquires a minority stake in Japanese stylus maker Wacom.
   c. Geely (a Chinese multinational auto manufacturer) opens some new dealerships in the UK, after having acquired the Swedish Volvo.
   d. Unilever (an Anglo-Dutch corporation and one of the world's main producers of health-care and food products) builds a new production factory in Thailand to produce for regional markets in ASEAN.

8. Sometimes a company, instead of investing directly in a country, chooses alternatives. Provide an example of substitutes for horizontal and vertical FDI and motivations for such choices.

9. Most firms in the apparel and footwear industries choose to outsource production to countries where labor is abundant (primarily, Southeast Asia and the Caribbean)—but those firms do not integrate with their suppliers there. On the other hand, firms in many capital-intensive industries choose to integrate with their suppliers. What could be some differences between the labor-intensive apparel and footwear industries on the one hand and capital-intensive industries on the other hand that would explain these choices?

10. Consider the example of industries in the previous problem. What would those choices imply for the extent of *intra-firm* trade across industries? That is, in what industries would a greater proportion of trade occur within firms?

FURTHER READINGS

Andrew B. Bernard, J. Bradford Jensen, Stephen J. Redding, and Peter K. Schott. "Firms in International Trade." *Journal of Economic Perspectives* 21 (Summer 2007), pp. 105–130. A nontechnical description of empirical patterns of trade at the firm level that focuses on U.S. firms.

Andrew B. Bernard, J. Bradford Jensen, and Peter K. Schott. "Importers, Exporters, and Multinationals: A Portrait of Firms in the US that Trade Goods," in T. Dunne, J. B. Jensen, and M. J. Roberts, eds. *Producer Dynamics: New Evidence from Micro Data*. Chicago: University of Chicago Press, 2009. A nontechnical description of empirical patterns of trade at the firm level that focuses on U.S. firms and multinationals operating in the United States.

Robert Feenstra. "Integration of Trade and Disintegration of Production in the Global Economy." *Journal of Economic Perspectives* 12 (Fall 1998), pp. 32–50. A description of how the supply chain has been broken up into many processes that are then performed in different locations.

Gordon Hanson, Raymond Mataloni, and Matthew Slaughter. "Vertical Production Networks in Multinational Firms." *Review of Economics and Statistics* 87 (March 2005), pp. 664–678. An empirical description of vertical FDI patterns based on multinationals operating in the United States.

Keith Head. *Elements of Multinational Strategy*. New York: Springer, 2007. A recent textbook focused on multinationals.

Elhanan Helpman. "Trade, FDI, and the Organization of Firms." *Journal of Economic Literature* 44 (September 2006), pp. 589–630. A technical survey of recent research on models that incorporate firm performance differences, and on multinationals and outsourcing.

Elhanan Helpman. *Understanding Global Trade*. Cambridge, MA: Harvard University Press, forthcoming. A nontechnical book that covers both comparative advantage theories of trade and more recent theories of trade based on the firm.

Elhanan Helpman and Paul R. Krugman. *Market Structure and Foreign Trade*. Cambridge: MIT Press, 1985. A technical presentation of monopolistic competition and other models of trade with economies of scale.

J. Bradford Jensen. *Global Trade in Services: Fear, Facts, and Offshoring*. Washington, DC: Peterson Institute for International Economics, 2011. A non-technical book focusing on the effects of increased trade in services for the U.S. economy.

James Markusen. "The Boundaries of Multinational Enterprises and the Theory of International Trade." *Journal of Economic Perspectives* 9 (Spring 1995), pp. 169–189. A nontechnical survey of models of trade and multinationals.

Thierry Mayer and Gianmarco I. P. Ottaviano. "The Happy Few: The Internationalisation of European Firms: New Facts Based on Firm-Level Evidence." *Intereconomics* 43 (May/June 2008), pp. 135–148.

Marc J. Melitz and Daniel Trefler, "Gains from Trade When Firms Matter," *Journal of Economic Perspectives* 26 (2012), pp. 91–118. A non-technical survey that develops the monopolistic competition model with performance differences across firms in greater detail than in this chapter. The paper also contains a detailed description of the associated evidence for Canadian firms following implementation of the Canada-U.S. Free Trade Agreement.

Determining Marginal Revenue

In our exposition of monopoly and monopolistic competition, we found it useful to have an algebraic statement of the marginal revenue faced by a firm given the demand curve it faced. Specifically, we asserted that if a firm faces the demand curve

$$Q = A - B \times P, \tag{8A-1}$$

its marginal revenue is

$$MR = P - (1/B) \times Q. \tag{8A-2}$$

In this appendix, we demonstrate why this is true.

Notice first that the demand curve can be rearranged to state the price as a function of the firm's sales rather than the other way around. By rearranging (8A-1), we get

$$P = (A/B) - (1/B) \times Q. \tag{8A-3}$$

The revenue of a firm is simply the price it receives per unit multiplied by the number of units it sells. Letting R denote the firm's revenue, we have

$$R = P \times Q = [(A/B) - (1/B) \times Q] \times Q. \tag{8A-4}$$

Let us next ask how the revenue of a firm changes if it changes its sales. Suppose the firm decides to increase its sales by a small amount, dX, so that the new level of sales is $Q = Q + dQ$. Then the firm's revenue after the increase in sales, R', will be

$$R' = P' \times Q' = [(A/B) - (1/B) \times (Q + dQ)] \times (Q + dQ) \tag{8A-5}$$
$$= [(A/B) - (1/B) \times Q] \times Q + [(A/B) - (1/B) \times Q] \times dQ$$
$$- (1/B) \times Q \times dQ - (1/B) \times (dQ)^2.$$

Equation (8A-5) can be simplified by substituting in from (8A-1) and (8A-4) to get

$$R' = R + P \times dQ - (1/B) \times Q \times dQ - (1/B) \times (dQ)^2. \tag{8A-6}$$

When the change in sales dQ is small, however, its square $(dQ)^2$ is very small (e.g., the square of 1 is 1, but the square of $1/10$ is $1/100$). So for a small change in Q, the last term in (8A-6) can be ignored. This gives us the result that the *change* in revenue from a small change in sales is

$$R' - R = [(P - (1/B) \times Q)] \times dQ. \tag{8A-7}$$

So the increase in revenue *per unit of additional sales*—which is the definition of marginal revenue—is

$$MR = (R' - R)/dQ = P - (1/B) \times Q,$$

which is just what we asserted in equation (8A-2).

THE INSTRUMENTS OF TRADE POLICY

Previous chapters have answered the question, "Why do nations trade?" by *describing* the causes and effects of international trade and the functioning of a trading world economy. While this question is interesting in itself, its answer is even more interesting if it also helps answer the question, "What should a nation's trade policy be?" For example, should the United States use a tariff or an import quota to protect its automobile industry against competition from Japan and South Korea? Who will benefit and who will lose from an import quota? Will the benefits outweigh the costs?

This chapter examines the policies that governments adopt toward international trade, policies that involve a number of different actions. These actions include taxes on some international transactions, subsidies for other transactions, legal limits on the value or volume of particular imports, and many other measures. The chapter thus provides a framework for understanding the effects of the most important instruments of trade policy.

LEARNING GOALS

After reading this chapter, you will be able to:

- Evaluate the costs and benefits of tariffs, their welfare effects, and winners and losers of tariff policies.
- Discuss what export subsidies and agricultural subsidies are, and explain how they affect trade in agriculture in the United States and the European Union.
- Recognize the effect of voluntary export restraints (VERs) on both importing and exporting countries, and describe how the welfare effects of these VERs compare with tariff and quota policies.

Basic Tariff Analysis

A tariff, the simplest of trade policies, is a tax levied when a good is imported. **Specific tariffs** are levied as a fixed charge for each unit of goods imported (for example, $3 per barrel of oil). **Ad valorem tariffs** are taxes that are levied as a fraction of the value of the imported goods (for example, a 25 percent U.S. tariff on imported trucks—see the following box). In either case, the effect of the tariff is to raise the cost of shipping goods to a country.

Tariffs are the oldest form of trade policy and have traditionally been used as a source of government income. Until the introduction of the income tax, for instance, the U.S. government raised most of its revenue from tariffs. Their true purpose, however, has usually been twofold: to provide revenue and to protect particular domestic sectors. In the early 19th century, for example, the United Kingdom used tariffs (the famous Corn Laws) to protect its agriculture from import competition. In the late 19th century, both Germany and the United States protected their new industrial sectors by imposing tariffs on imports of manufactured goods. The importance of tariffs has declined in modern times because modern governments usually prefer to protect domestic industries through a variety of **nontariff barriers,** such as **import quotas** (limitations on the quantity of imports) and **export restraints** (limitations on the quantity of exports—usually imposed by the exporting country at the importing country's request). Nonetheless, an understanding of the effects of a tariff remains vital for understanding other trade policies.

In developing the theory of trade in Chapters 3 through 8, we adopted a *general equilibrium* perspective. That is, we were keenly aware that events in one part of the economy have repercussions elsewhere. However, in many (though not all) cases, trade policies toward one sector can be reasonably well understood without going into detail about those policies' repercussions on the rest of the economy. For the most part, then, trade policy can be examined in a *partial equilibrium* framework. When the effects on the economy as a whole become crucial, we will refer back to general equilibrium analysis.

Supply, Demand, and Trade in a Single Industry

Let's suppose there are two countries, Home and Foreign, both of which consume and produce wheat, which can be costlessly transported between the countries. In each country, wheat is a simple competitive industry in which the supply and demand curves are functions of the market price. Normally, Home supply and demand will depend on the price in terms of Home currency, and Foreign supply and demand will depend on the price in terms of Foreign currency. However, we assume the exchange rate between the currencies is not affected by whatever trade policy is undertaken in this market. Thus, we quote prices in both markets in terms of Home currency.

Trade will arise in such a market if prices are different in the absence of trade. Suppose that in the absence of trade, the price of wheat is higher in Home than it is in Foreign. Now let's allow foreign trade. Since the price of wheat in Home exceeds the price in Foreign, shippers begin to move wheat from Foreign to Home. The export of wheat raises its price in Foreign and lowers its price in Home until the difference in prices has been eliminated.

To determine the world price and the quantity traded, it is helpful to define two new curves: the Home **import demand curve** and the Foreign **export supply curve**, which are derived from the underlying domestic supply and demand curves. Home import demand is the excess of what Home consumers demand over what Home producers supply; Foreign export supply is the excess of what Foreign producers supply over what Foreign consumers demand.

Figure 9-1 shows how the Home import demand curve is derived. At the price P^1, Home consumers demand D^1, while Home producers supply only S^1. As a result, Home import demand is $D^1 - S^1$. If we raise the price to P^2, Home consumers demand only D^2, while Home producers raise the amount they supply to S^2, so import

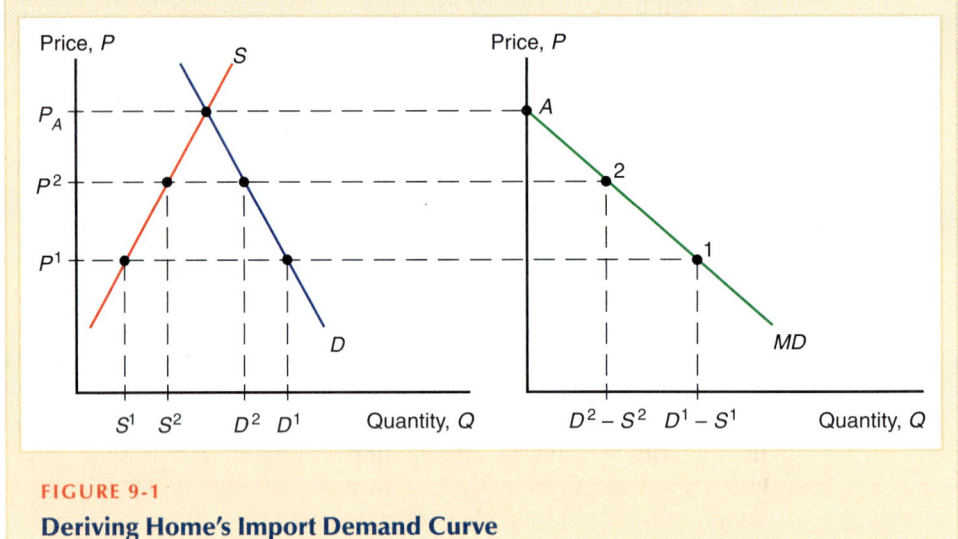

FIGURE 9-1

Deriving Home's Import Demand Curve

As the price of the good increases, Home consumers demand less, while Home producers supply more, so that the demand for imports declines.

demand falls to $D^2 - S^2$. These price-quantity combinations are plotted as points 1 and 2 in the right-hand panel of Figure 9-1. The import demand curve MD is downward sloping because as price increases, the quantity of imports demanded declines. At P_A, Home supply and demand are equal in the absence of trade, so the Home import demand curve intercepts the price axis at P_A (import demand = zero at P_A).

Figure 9-2 shows how the Foreign export supply curve XS is derived. At P^1 Foreign producers supply S^{*1}, while Foreign consumers demand only D^{*1}, so the amount of

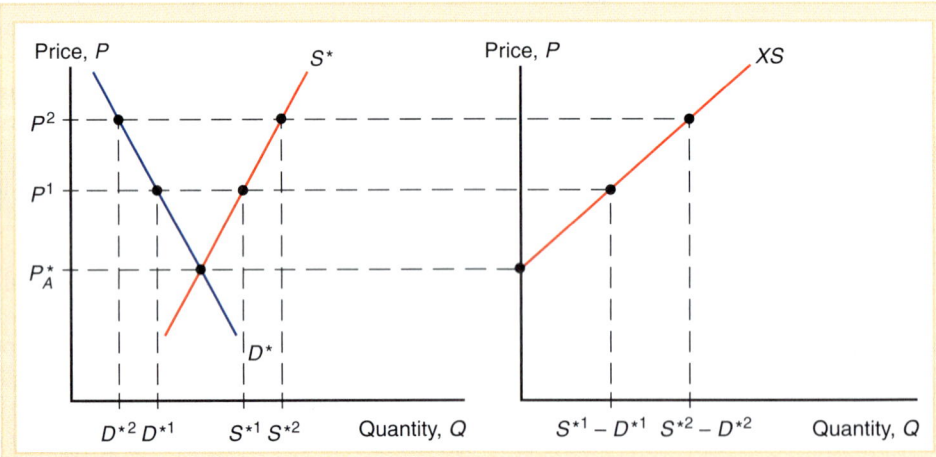

FIGURE 9-2

Deriving Foreign's Export Supply Curve

As the price of the good rises, Foreign producers supply more while Foreign consumers demand less, so that the supply available for export rises.

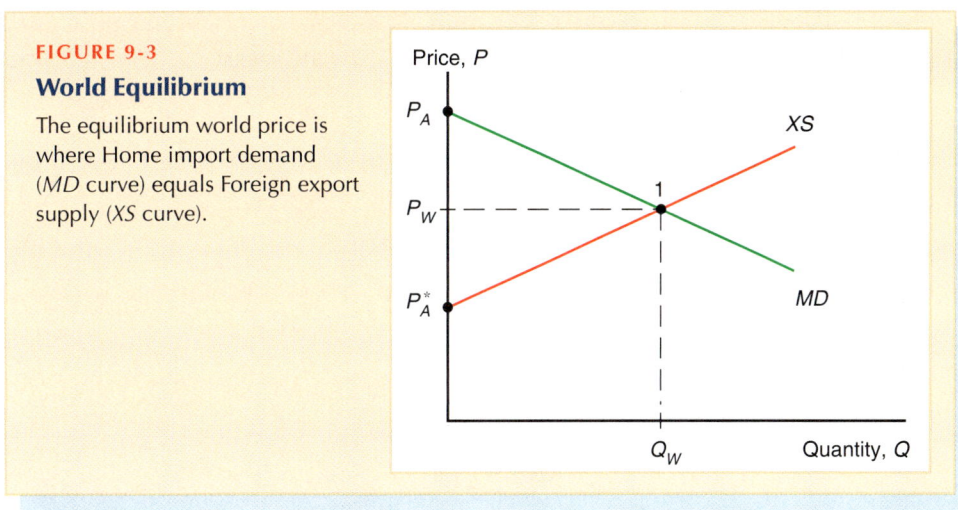

FIGURE 9-3

World Equilibrium

The equilibrium world price is where Home import demand (*MD* curve) equals Foreign export supply (*XS* curve).

the total supply available for export is $S^{*1} - D^{*1}$. At P^2 Foreign producers raise the quantity they supply to S^{*2} and Foreign consumers lower the amount they demand to D^{*2}, so the quantity of the total supply available to export rises to $S^{*2} - D^{*2}$. Because the supply of goods available for export rises as the price rises, the Foreign export supply curve is upward sloping. At P_A^*, supply and demand would be equal in the absence of trade, so the Foreign export supply curve intersects the price axis at P_A^* (export supply = zero at P_A^*).

World equilibrium occurs when Home import demand equals Foreign export supply (Figure 9-3). At the price P_W where the two curves cross, world supply equals world demand. At the equilibrium point 1 in Figure 9-3,

$$\text{Home demand} - \text{Home supply} = \text{Foreign supply} - \text{Foreign demand}.$$

By adding and subtracting from both sides, this equation can be rearranged to say that

$$\text{Home demand} + \text{Foreign demand} = \text{Home supply} + \text{Foreign supply}$$

or, in other words,

$$\text{World demand} = \text{World supply}.$$

Effects of a Tariff

From the point of view of someone shipping goods, a tariff is just like a cost of transportation. If Home imposes a tax of $2 on every bushel of wheat imported, shippers will be unwilling to move the wheat unless the price difference between the two markets is at least $2.

Figure 9-4 illustrates the effects of a specific tariff of t per unit of wheat (shown as t in the figure). In the absence of a tariff, the price of wheat would be equalized at P_W in both Home and Foreign, as seen at point 1 in the middle panel, which illustrates the world market. With the tariff in place, however, shippers are not willing to move wheat from Foreign to Home unless the Home price exceeds the Foreign price by at least t. If no wheat is being shipped, however, there will be an excess demand for wheat in Home and an excess supply in Foreign. Thus, the price in Home will rise and that in Foreign will fall until the price difference is t.

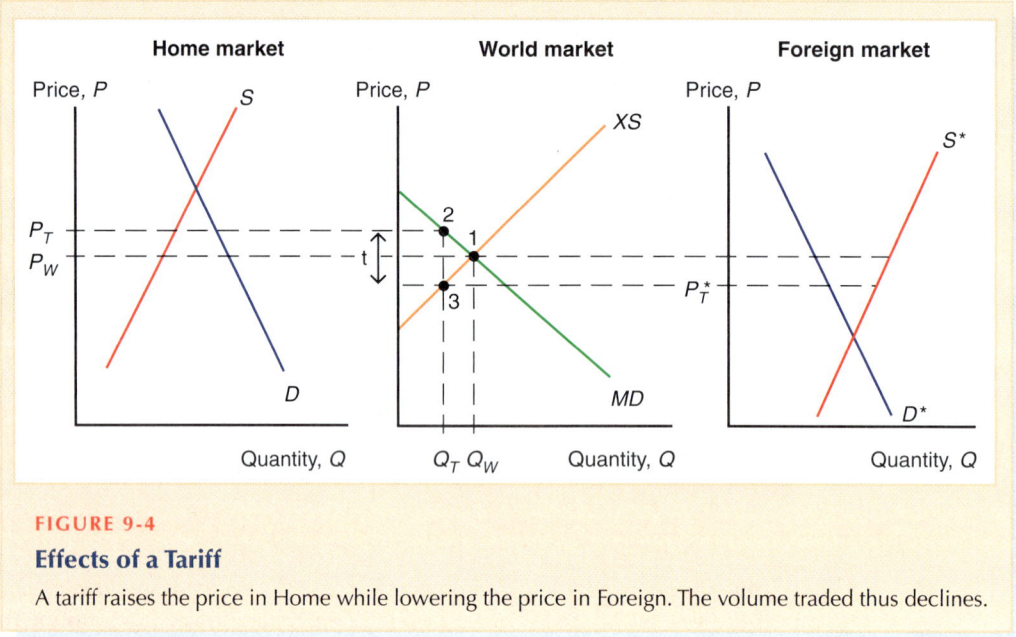

FIGURE 9-4

Effects of a Tariff

A tariff raises the price in Home while lowering the price in Foreign. The volume traded thus declines.

Introducing a tariff, then, drives a wedge between the prices in the two markets. The tariff raises the price in Home to P_T and lowers the price in Foreign to $P_T^* = P_T - t$. In Home, producers supply more at the higher price, while consumers demand less, so that fewer imports are demanded (as you can see in the move from point 1 to point 2 on the MD curve). In Foreign, the lower price leads to reduced supply and increased demand, and thus a smaller export supply (as seen in the move from point 1 to point 3 on the XS curve). Thus, the volume of wheat traded declines from Q_W, the free trade volume, to Q_T, the volume with a tariff. At the trade volume Q_T, Home import demand equals Foreign export supply when $P_T - P_T^* = t$.

The increase in the price in Home, from P_W to P_T, is less than the amount of the tariff because part of the tariff is reflected in a decline in Foreign's export price and thus is not passed on to Home consumers. This is the normal result of a tariff and of any trade policy that limits imports. The size of this effect on the exporters' price, however, is often very small in practice. When a small country imposes a tariff, its share of the world market for the goods it imports is usually minor to begin with, so that its import reduction has very little effect on the world (foreign export) price.

The effects of a tariff in the "small country" case where a country cannot affect foreign export prices are illustrated in Figure 9-5. In this case, a tariff raises the price of the imported good in the country imposing the tariff by the full amount of the tariff, from P_W to $P_W + t$. Production of the imported good rises from S^1 to S^2, while consumption of the good falls from D^1 to D^2. As a result of the tariff, then, imports fall in the country imposing the tariff.

Measuring the Amount of Protection

A tariff on an imported good raises the price received by domestic producers of that good. This effect is often the tariff's principal objective—to *protect* domestic producers from the low prices that would result from import competition. In analyzing trade policy in practice, it is important to ask how much protection a tariff or other trade

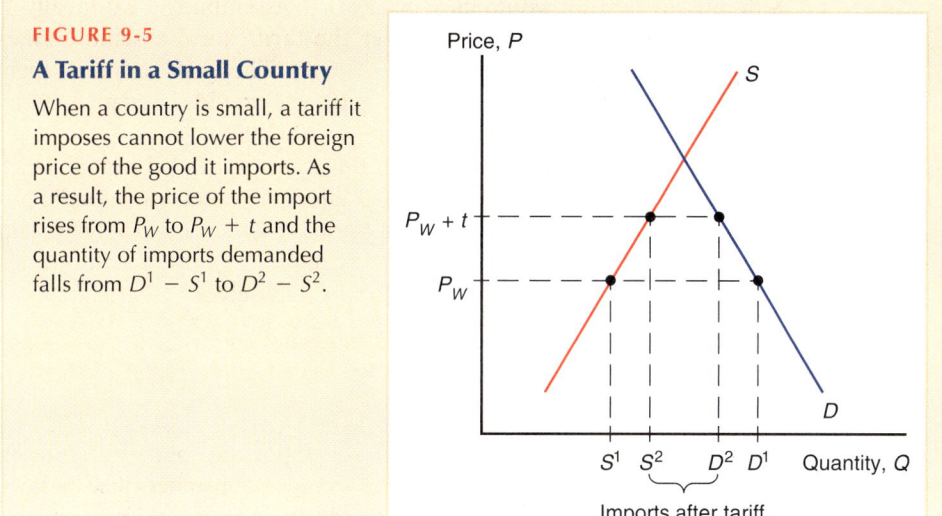

FIGURE 9-5

A Tariff in a Small Country

When a country is small, a tariff it imposes cannot lower the foreign price of the good it imports. As a result, the price of the import rises from P_W to $P_W + t$ and the quantity of imports demanded falls from $D^1 - S^1$ to $D^2 - S^2$.

policy actually provides. The answer is usually expressed as a percentage of the price that would prevail under free trade. An import quota on sugar could, for example, raise the price received by U.S. sugar producers by 35 percent.

Measuring protection would seem to be straightforward in the case of a tariff: If the tariff is an ad valorem tax proportional to the value of the imports, the tariff rate itself should measure the amount of protection; if the tariff is specific, dividing the tariff by the price net of the tariff gives us the ad valorem equivalent.

However, there are two problems with trying to calculate the rate of protection this simply. First, if the small country assumption is not a good approximation, part of the effect of a tariff will be to lower foreign export prices rather than to raise domestic prices. This effect of trade policies on foreign export prices is sometimes significant.

The second problem is that tariffs may have very different effects on different stages of production of a good. A simple example illustrates this point.

Suppose an automobile sells on the world market for $8,000, and the parts out of which that automobile is made sell for $6,000. Let's compare two countries: one that wants to develop an auto assembly industry and one that already has an assembly industry and wants to develop a parts industry.

To encourage a domestic auto industry, the first country places a 25 percent tariff on imported autos, allowing domestic assemblers to charge $10,000 instead of $8,000. In this case, it would be wrong to say that the assemblers receive only 25 percent protection. Before the tariff, domestic assembly would take place only if it could be done for $2,000 (the difference between the $8,000 price of a completed automobile and the $6,000 cost of parts) or less; now it will take place even if it costs as much as $4,000 (the difference between the $10,000 price and the cost of parts). That is, the 25 percent tariff rate provides assemblers with an **effective rate of protection** of 100 percent.

Now suppose the second country, to encourage domestic production of parts, imposes a 10 percent tariff on imported parts, raising the cost of parts of domestic assemblers from $6,000 to $6,600. Even though there is no change in the tariff on assembled automobiles, this policy makes it less advantageous to assemble domestically.

Before the tariff, it would have been worth assembling a car locally if it could be done for $2,000 ($8,000 − $6,000); after the tariff, local assembly takes place only if it can be done for $1,400 ($8,000 − $6,600). The tariff on parts, then, while providing positive protection to parts manufacturers, provides negative effective protection to assembly at the rate of −30 percent (−600/2,000).

Reasoning similar to that seen in this example has led economists to make elaborate calculations to measure the degree of effective protection actually provided to particular industries by tariffs and other trade policies. Trade policies aimed at promoting economic development, for example (Chapter 11), often lead to rates of effective protection much higher than the tariff rates themselves.[1]

Costs and Benefits of a Tariff

A tariff raises the price of a good in the importing country and lowers it in the exporting country. As a result of these price changes, consumers lose in the importing country and gain in the exporting country. Producers gain in the importing country and lose in the exporting country. In addition, the government imposing the tariff gains revenue. To compare these costs and benefits, it is necessary to quantify them. The method for measuring costs and benefits of a tariff depends on two concepts common to much microeconomic analysis: consumer and producer surplus.

Consumer and Producer Surplus

Consumer surplus measures the amount a consumer gains from a purchase by computing the difference between the price he actually pays and the price he would have been willing to pay. If, for example, a consumer would have been willing to pay $8 for a bushel of wheat but the price is only $3, the consumer surplus gained by the purchase is $5.

Consumer surplus can be derived from the market demand curve (Figure 9-6). For example, suppose the maximum price at which consumers will buy 10 units of a good is $10. Then, the 10th unit of the good purchased must be worth $10 to consumers. If it were worth less, they would not purchase it; if it were worth more, they would have been willing to purchase it even if the price were higher. Now suppose that in order to get consumers to buy 11 units, the price must be cut to $9. Then, the 11th unit must be worth only $9 to consumers.

Suppose the price is $9. Then, consumers are willing to purchase only the 11th unit of the good and thus receive no consumer surplus from their purchase of that unit. They would have been willing to pay $10 for the 10th unit, however, and thus receive $1 in consumer surplus from that unit. They would also have been willing to pay $12 for the 9th unit; in that case, they would have received $3 of consumer surplus on that unit, and so on.

---

[1]The effective rate of protection for a sector is formally defined as $(V_T - V_W)/V_W$, where V_W is value added in the sector at world prices, and V_T is value added in the presence of trade policies. In terms of our example, let P_A be the world price of an assembled automobile, P_C the world price of its components, t_A the ad valorem tariff rate on imported autos, and t_C the ad valorem tariff rate on components. You can check that if the tariffs don't affect world prices, they provide assemblers with an effective protection rate of

$$\frac{V_T - V_W}{V_W} = t_A + P_C\left(\frac{t_A - t_C}{P_A - P_C}\right).$$

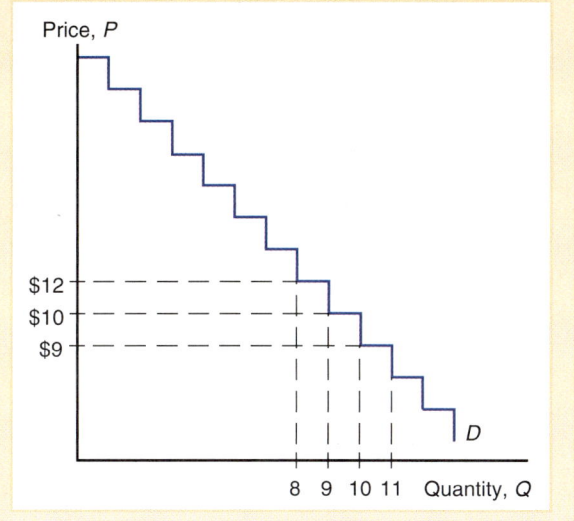

FIGURE 9-6

Deriving Consumer Surplus from the Demand Curve

Consumer surplus on each unit sold is the difference between the actual price and what consumers would have been willing to pay.

Generalizing from this example, if P is the price of a good and Q the quantity demanded at that price, then consumer surplus is calculated by subtracting P times Q from the area under the demand curve up to Q (Figure 9-7). If the price is P^1, the quantity demanded is D^1 and the consumer surplus is measured by the areas labeled a plus b. If the price rises to P^2, the quantity demanded falls to D^2 and consumer surplus falls by b to equal just a.

Producer surplus is an analogous concept. A producer willing to sell a good for $2 but receiving a price of $5 gains a producer surplus of $3. The same procedure used to derive consumer surplus from the demand curve can be used to derive producer surplus from the supply curve. If P is the price and Q the quantity supplied at that price, then producer surplus is P times Q minus the area under the supply curve up to Q

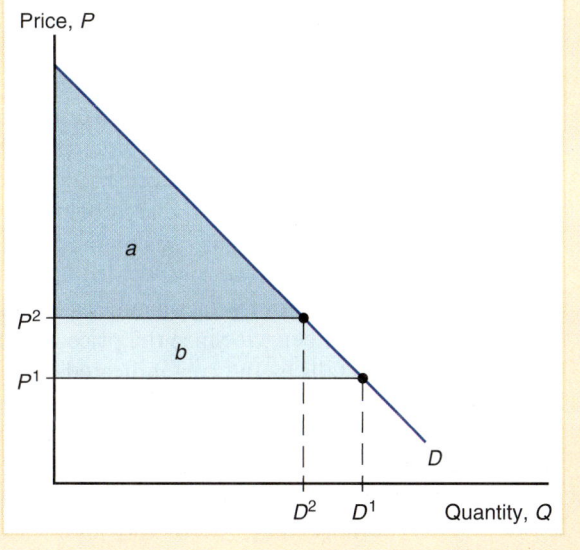

FIGURE 9-7

Geometry of Consumer Surplus

Consumer surplus is equal to the area under the demand curve and above the price.

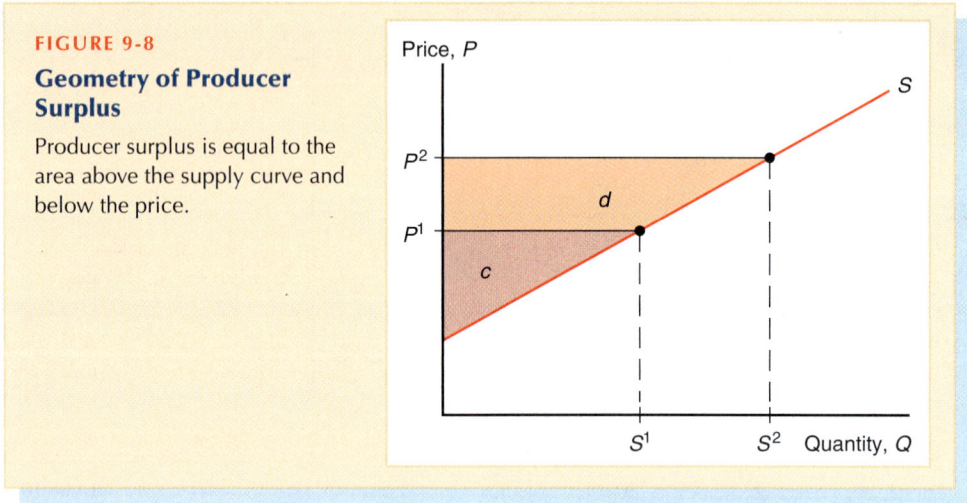

FIGURE 9-8

Geometry of Producer Surplus

Producer surplus is equal to the area above the supply curve and below the price.

(Figure 9-8). If the price is P^1, the quantity supplied will be S^1, and producer surplus is measured by area c. If the price rises to P^2, the quantity supplied rises to S^2, and producer surplus rises to equal c plus the additional area d.

Some of the difficulties related to the concepts of consumer and producer surplus are technical issues of calculation that we can safely disregard. More important is the question of whether the direct gains to producers and consumers in a given market accurately measure the *social* gains. Additional benefits and costs not captured by consumer and producer surplus are at the core of the case for trade policy activism discussed in Chapter 10. For now, however, we will focus on costs and benefits as measured by consumer and producer surplus.

Measuring the Costs and Benefits

Figure 9-9 illustrates the costs and benefits of a tariff for the importing country. The tariff raises the domestic price from P_W to P_T but lowers the foreign export price from P_W to P_T^* (refer back to Figure 9-4). Domestic production rises from S^1 to S^2 while domestic consumption falls from D^1 to D^2. The costs and benefits to different groups can be expressed as sums of the areas of five regions, labeled a, b, c, d, e.

Consider first the gain to domestic producers. They receive a higher price and therefore have higher producer surplus. As we saw in Figure 9-8, producer surplus is equal to the area below the price but above the supply curve. Before the tariff, producer surplus was equal to the area below P_W but above the supply curve; with the price rising to P_T, this surplus rises by the area labeled a. That is, producers gain from the tariff.

Domestic consumers also face a higher price, which makes them worse off. As we saw in Figure 9-7, consumer surplus is equal to the area above the price but below the demand curve. Since the price consumers face rises from P_W to P_T, the consumer surplus falls by the area indicated by $a + b + c + d$. So consumers are hurt by the tariff.

There is a third player here as well: the government. The government gains by collecting tariff revenue. This is equal to the tariff rate t times the volume of imports $Q_T = D^2 - S^2$. Since $t = P_T - P_T^*$, the government's revenue is equal to the sum of the two areas c and e.

Since these gains and losses accrue to different people, the overall cost-benefit evaluation of a tariff depends on how much we value a dollar's worth of benefit to

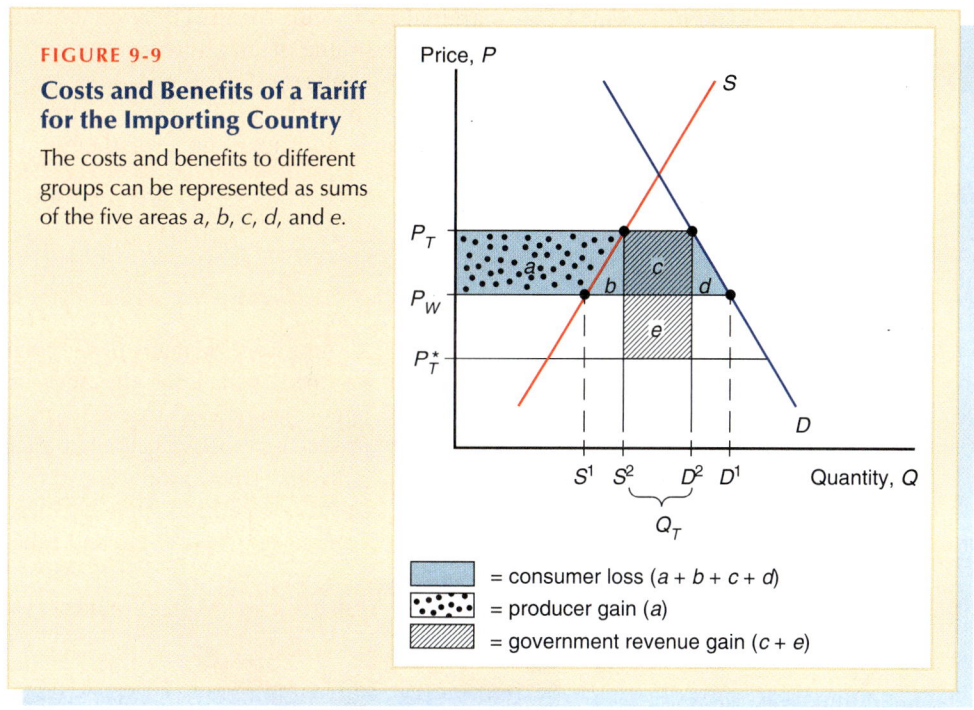

FIGURE 9-9

Costs and Benefits of a Tariff for the Importing Country

The costs and benefits to different groups can be represented as sums of the five areas *a*, *b*, *c*, *d*, and *e*.

each group. If, for example, the producer gain accrues mostly to wealthy owners of resources, while consumers are poorer than average, the tariff will be viewed differently than if the good is a luxury bought by the affluent but produced by low-wage workers. Further ambiguity is introduced by the role of the government: Will it use its revenue to finance vitally needed public services or waste that revenue on $1,000 toilet seats? Despite these problems, it is common for analysts of trade policy to attempt to compute the net effect of a tariff on national welfare by assuming that at the margin, a dollar's worth of gain or loss to each group is of the same social worth.

Let's look, then, at the net effect of a tariff on welfare. The net cost of a tariff is

$$\text{Consumer loss} - \text{producer gain} - \text{government revenue,} \qquad (9\text{-}1)$$

or, replacing these concepts by the areas in Figure 9-9,

$$(a + b + c + d) - a - (c + e) = b + d - e. \qquad (9\text{-}2)$$

That is, there are two "triangles" whose area measures loss to the nation as a whole and a "rectangle" whose area measures an offsetting gain. A useful way to interpret these gains and losses is the following: The triangles represent the **efficiency loss** that arises because a tariff distorts incentives to consume and produce while the rectangle represents the **terms of trade gain** that arise because a tariff lowers foreign export prices.

The gain depends on the ability of the tariff-imposing country to drive down foreign export prices. If the country cannot affect world prices (the "small country" case illustrated in Figure 9-5), region *e*, which represents the terms of trade gain, disappears, and it is clear that the tariff reduces welfare. A tariff distorts the incentives of both producers and consumers by inducing them to act as if imports were more expensive than they actually are. The cost of an additional unit of consumption to the economy is the price of an additional unit of imports, yet because the tariff raises the domestic price above the world price, consumers reduce their consumption to the point at which that marginal unit yields them welfare equal to the tariff-inclusive domestic price. This means that the value of an additional unit of production to the economy is the price of the unit of imports it saves, yet domestic producers expand production to the point at which the marginal cost is equal to the tariff-inclusive price. Thus, the economy produces at home additional units of the good that it could purchase more cheaply abroad.

TARIFFS FOR THE LONG HAUL

We just saw how a tariff can be used to increase producer surplus at the expense of a loss in consumer surplus. There are also many other indirect costs of tariffs: They can lead trading partners to retaliate with their own tariffs (thus hurting exporting producers in the country that first imposed the tariff); they can also be fiendishly hard to remove later on even after economic conditions have completely changed, because they help to politically organize the small group of producers that is protected from foreign competition. (We will discuss this further in Chapter 10.) Finally, large tariffs can induce producers to behave in creative—though ultimately wasteful—ways in order to avoid them.

Before opening production facilities in the United States, Subaru got around the tariff on light commercial trucks by bolting two plastic seats to the open bed of its pickup truck (Subaru BRAT) exported to the United States. Thus, the BRAT was classified as a passenger vehicle thereby avoiding the tariff.

In the case of the tariff known as the "Chicken Tax," the tariff lasted for so long (47 years and counting) that it ended up hurting the same producers that had intensively lobbied to maintain the tariff in the first place!* This tariff got its name because it was a retaliation by U.S. President Lyndon Johnson's administration against a tariff on U.S. chicken exports imposed by Western Europe in the early 1960s. The U.S. retaliation, focusing on Germany (one of the main political forces behind the original chicken tariff), imposed a 25 percent tariff on imports of light commercial truck vehicles. At the time, Volkswagen was a big producer of such vehicles and exported many of them to the United States.

As time went by, many of the original tariffs were dropped, except for the ones on chickens and light commercial trucks. Volkswagen stopped producing those vehicles, but the U.S. "big three" auto and truck producers were then concerned about competition from Japanese truck producers and lobbied to keep the tariff in place. Japanese producers then responded by building those light trucks in the United States (see Chapter 8).

As a result, the latest company to be hit by the consequences of the tariff is Ford, one of those "big three" U.S. producers! Ford produces a small commercial van in Europe, the "Transit Connect," which is designed (with its smaller capacity and ability to navigate old, narrow streets) for European cities. The recent spike in fuel prices sharply increased demand in some U.S. cities for this truck. In 2009, Ford started selling these vehicles in the United States. To get around the 25 percent tariff, Ford installs rear windows, rear seats, and seat belts prior to shipping the vehicles to the United States. These vehicles are no longer classified as commercial trucks but as passenger vehicles, which are subject to the much lower 2.5 percent tariff. Upon arrival in Baltimore, Maryland, the rear seats are promptly removed and the rear windows replaced with metal panels—before delivery to the Ford dealers.

---

*See Matthew Dolan, "To Outfox the Chicken Tax, Ford Strips Its Own Vans," *Wall Street Journal*, September 23, 2009.

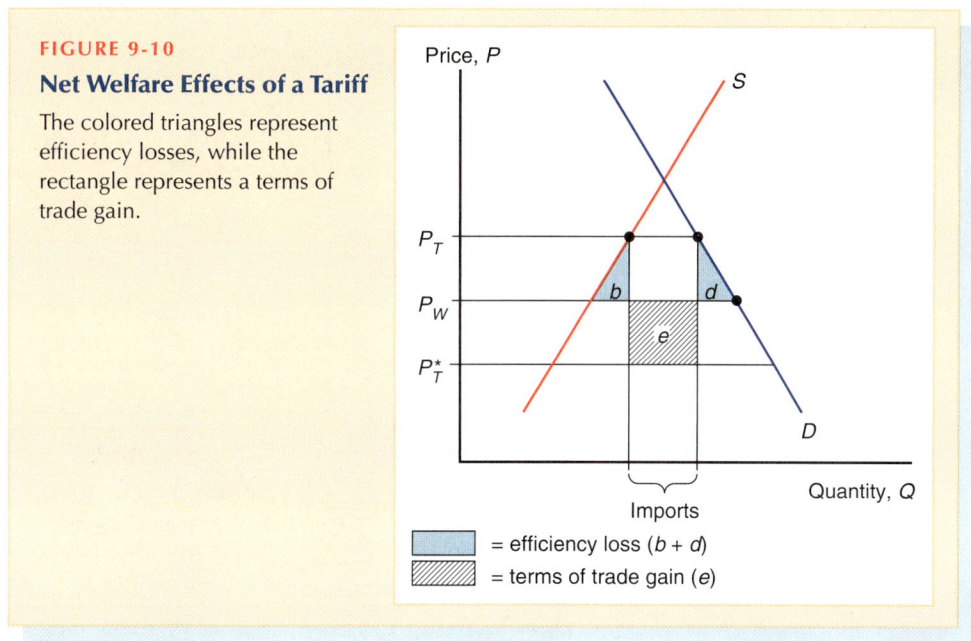

FIGURE 9-10

Net Welfare Effects of a Tariff

The colored triangles represent efficiency losses, while the rectangle represents a terms of trade gain.

= efficiency loss ($b + d$)

= terms of trade gain (e)

The net welfare effects of a tariff are summarized in Figure 9-10. The negative effects consist of the two triangles b and d. The first triangle is the **production distortion loss** resulting from the fact that the tariff leads domestic producers to produce too much of this good. The second triangle is the domestic **consumption distortion loss** resulting from the fact that a tariff leads consumers to consume too little of the good. Against these losses must be set the terms of trade gain measured by the rectangle e, which results from the decline in the foreign export price caused by a tariff. In the important case of a small country that cannot significantly affect foreign prices, this last effect drops out; thus, the costs of a tariff unambiguously exceed its benefits.

Other Instruments of Trade Policy

Tariffs are the simplest trade policies, but in the modern world, most government intervention in international trade takes other forms, such as export subsidies, import quotas, voluntary export restraints, and local content requirements. Fortunately, once we have understood tariffs, it is not too difficult to understand these other trade instruments.

Export Subsidies: Theory

An **export subsidy** is a payment to a firm or individual that ships a good abroad. Like a tariff, an export subsidy can be either specific (a fixed sum per unit) or ad valorem (a proportion of the value exported). When the government offers an export subsidy, shippers will export the good up to the point at which the domestic price exceeds the foreign price by the amount of the subsidy.

The effects of an export subsidy on prices are exactly the reverse of those of a tariff (Figure 9-11). The price in the exporting country rises from P_W to P_S, but because the price in the importing country falls from P_W to P_S^*, the price increase is less than

FIGURE 9-11

Effects of an Export Subsidy

An export subsidy raises prices in the exporting country while lowering them in the importing country.

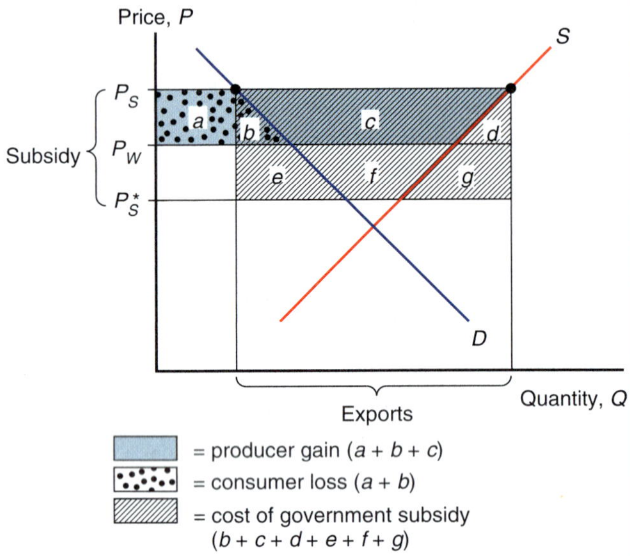

Price, P

P_S

Subsidy

P_W

P_S^*

a b c d

e f g

S

D

Exports

Quantity, Q

= producer gain ($a + b + c$)

= consumer loss ($a + b$)

= cost of government subsidy
($b + c + d + e + f + g$)

the subsidy. In the exporting country, consumers are hurt, producers gain, and the government loses because it must expend money on the subsidy. The consumer loss is the area $a + b$; the producer gain is the area $a + b + c$; the government subsidy (the amount of exports times the amount of the subsidy) is the area $b + c + d + e + f + g$. The net welfare loss is therefore the sum of the areas $b + d + e + f + g$. Of these, b and d represent consumption and production distortion losses of the same kind that a tariff produces. In addition, and in contrast to a tariff, the export subsidy *worsens* the terms of trade because it lowers the price of the export in the foreign market from P_W to P_S^*. This leads to the additional terms of trade loss $e + f + g$, which is equal to $P_W - P_S^*$ times the quantity exported with the subsidy. So an export subsidy unambiguously leads to costs that exceed its benefits.

CASE STUDY

Europe's Common Agricultural Policy

In 1957, six Western European nations—Germany, France, Italy, Belgium, the Netherlands, and Luxembourg—formed the European Economic Community, which has since grown to include most of Europe. Now called the European Union (EU), its two biggest effects are on trade policy. First, the members of the European Union have removed all tariffs with respect to each other, thus creating a customs union (discussed in the next chapter). Second, the agricultural policy of the European Union has developed into a massive export subsidy program.

The European Union's Common Agricultural Policy (CAP) began not as an export subsidy but as an effort to guarantee high prices to European farmers by having the European Union buy agricultural products whenever the prices fell below

FIGURE 9-12

Europe's Common Agricultural Policy

Agricultural prices are fixed not only above world market levels but also above the price that would clear the European market. An export subsidy is used to dispose of the resulting surplus.

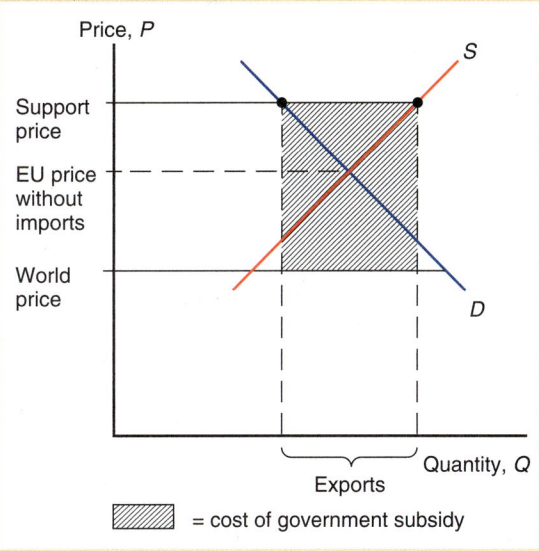

specified support levels. To prevent this policy from drawing in large quantities of imports, it was initially backed by tariffs that offset the difference between European and world agricultural prices.

Since the 1970s, however, the support prices set by the European Union have turned out to be so high that Europe—which, under free trade, would be an importer of most agricultural products—was producing more than consumers were willing to buy. As a result, the European Union found itself obliged to buy and store huge quantities of food. At the end of 1985, for example, European nations had stored

780,000 tons of beef, 1.2 million tons of butter, and 12 million tons of wheat. To avoid unlimited growth in these stockpiles, the European Union turned to a policy of subsidizing exports to dispose of surplus production.

Figure 9-12 shows how the CAP works. It is, of course, exactly like the export subsidy shown in Figure 9-11, except that Europe would actually be an importer under free trade. The support price is set not only above the world price that would prevail in its absence but also above the price that would equate demand and supply even without imports. To export the resulting surplus, an export subsidy is paid that offsets the difference between European and world prices. The subsidized exports themselves tend to depress the world price, increasing the required subsidy. A recent study estimated that the welfare cost to European consumers exceeded the benefits to farm producers by nearly $30 billion (21.5 billion euros) in 2007.[2]

---

[2]See Pierre Boulanger and Patrick Jomini, *Of the Benefits to the EU of Removing the Common Agricultural Policy*, Sciences Politique Policy Brief, 2010.

Despite the considerable net costs of the CAP to European consumers and taxpayers, the political strength of farmers in the EU has been so strong that the program has been difficult to rein in. One source of pressure has come from the United States and other food-exporting nations, which complain that Europe's export subsidies drive down the price of their own exports. The budgetary consequences of the CAP have also posed concerns: In 2013, the CAP cost European taxpayers $78 billion (58 billion euros)—and that figure doesn't include the indirect costs to food consumers. Government subsidies to European farmers are equal to about 22 percent of the value of farm output, more than twice the U.S. figure of 8.6 percent. (U.S. agriculture subsidies are more narrowly targeted on a subset of crops.)

Recent reforms in Europe's agricultural policy represent an effort to reduce the distortion of incentives caused by price support while continuing to provide aid to farmers. If politicians go through with their plans, farmers will increasingly receive direct payments that aren't tied to how much they produce; this should lower agricultural prices and reduce production.

Import Quotas: Theory

An import quota is a direct restriction on the quantity of some good that may be imported. The restriction is usually enforced by issuing licenses to some group of individuals or firms. For example, the United States has a quota on imports of foreign cheese. The only firms allowed to import cheese are certain trading companies, each of which is allocated the right to import a maximum number of pounds of cheese each year; the size of each firm's quota is based on the amount of cheese it imported in the past. In some important cases, notably sugar and apparel, the right to sell in the United States is given directly to the governments of exporting countries.

It is important to avoid having the misconception that import quotas somehow limit imports without raising domestic prices. The truth is that *an import quota always raises the domestic price of the imported good.* When imports are limited, the immediate result is that at the initial price, the demand for the good exceeds domestic supply plus imports. This causes the price to be bid up until the market clears. In the end, an import quota will raise domestic prices by the same amount as a tariff that limits imports to the same level (except in the case of domestic monopoly, in which the quota raises prices more than this; see the appendix to this chapter).

The difference between a quota and a tariff is that with a quota, the government receives no revenue. When a quota instead of a tariff is used to restrict imports, the sum of money that would have appeared with a tariff as government revenue is collected by whoever receives the import licenses. License holders are thus able to buy imports and resell them at a higher price in the domestic market. The profits received by the holders of import licenses are known as **quota rents**. In assessing the costs and benefits of an import quota, it is crucial to determine who gets the rents. When the rights to sell in the domestic market are assigned to governments of exporting countries, as is often the case, the transfer of rents abroad makes the costs of a quota substantially higher than the equivalent tariff.

CASE STUDY

An Import Quota in Practice: U.S. Sugar

The U.S. sugar problem is similar in its origins to the European agricultural problem: A domestic price guarantee by the federal government has led to U.S. prices above world market levels. Unlike the European Union, however, the domestic supply in the United States does not exceed domestic demand. Thus, the United States has been able to keep domestic prices at the target level with an import quota on sugar.

A special feature of the import quota is that the rights to sell sugar in the United States are allocated to foreign governments, which then allocate these rights to their own residents. As a result, rents generated by the sugar quota accrue to foreigners. The quotas restrict the imports of both raw sugar (almost exclusively, sugar cane) as well as refined sugar. Figure 9-13 shows the effect of the U.S. import restrictions on the price of raw sugar in the United States relative to the world price. As we can see, these import restrictions have been quite successful in raising the U.S. domestic price above the world price. When the world sugar price sharply increased in 2010–2011, the import restrictions were eased but not enough to limit sharp increases in the U.S. price—which still remained well above the world price.

We now describe the most recent forecast for the effects of these import restrictions and the associated higher sugar prices.[3] Figure 9-14 shows the raw sugar market equilibrium with and without the quota restriction. Currently, the quota limits imports of raw sugar to $3.4 million tons, while U.S. production totals 8.4 million tons. This leads to a U.S. sugar price that is 34% above the world price. Absent import restrictions, the U.S. price would drop down to the world price level. The figure is drawn assuming the United States is "small" in the world market for raw sugar; that is, removing the quota would not have a significant effect on the world price. According

FIGURE 9-13

U.S. and World Raw Sugar Prices in $ per ton (short ton, raw value), 1989–2011

Source: U.S. Department of Agriculture.

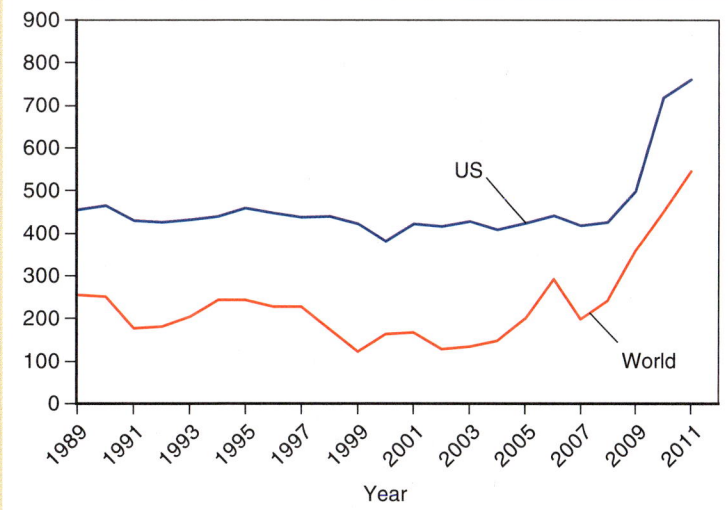

---

[3]These estimates are for 2014, assuming the import restrictions are eliminated in 2013. For further details, see Beghin, John Christopher and Amani Elobeid, "The Impact of the U.S. Sugar Program Redux." *Food and Agricultural Policy Research Institute (FAPRI) Publications*, 2013.

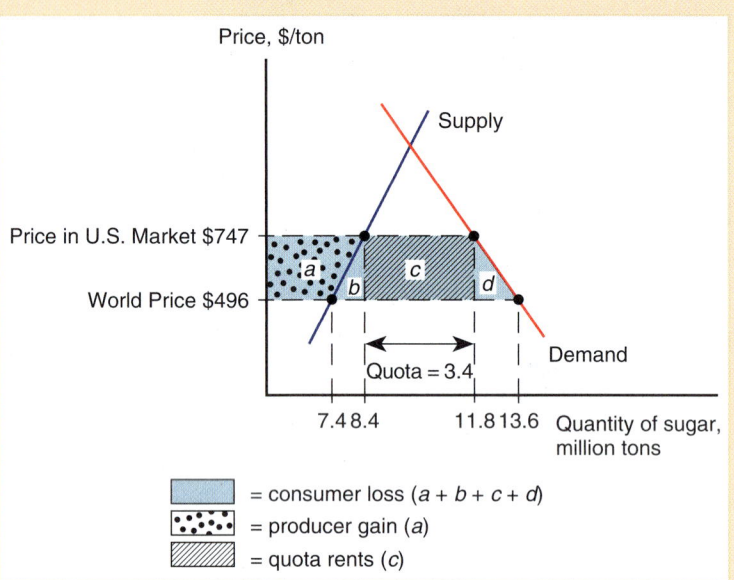

FIGURE 9-14

Effects of the U.S. Import Quota on Sugar

The quota limits imports of raw sugar to 3.4 million tons. Without the quota, imports of sugar would be 84 percent higher, or 6.2 million tons. The result of the quota is that the price of sugar is $747 per ton, versus the $496 price on world markets. This produces a gain for U.S. sugar producers, but a much larger loss for U.S. consumers. There is no offsetting gain in revenue because the quota rents are collected by foreign governments.

to this estimate, free trade would increase sugar imports by 84 percent and an associated 11 percent contraction in domestic production.

The welfare effects of the import quota are indicated by the areas *a, b, c,* and *d*. Consumers lose the surplus *a + b + c + d* associated with the higher price. Part of this consumer loss represents a transfer to U.S. sugar producers, who gain the producer surplus *a*. Part of the loss represents the production distortion *b* and the consumption distortion *d*. The rents to the foreign governments that receive import rights are summarized by area *c*.

In order to put dollar figures on these welfare effects, one must take into account how the higher raw sugar price leads to a higher refined sugar price, which then feeds into higher prices for all food products containing sugar. Even though the ultimate food price increases paid by U.S. consumers are modest—on the order of 0–2 percent—the total consumer surplus losses are massive because those price increases apply to such a large basket of widely consumed goods. The estimated consumer loss for 2014 (relative to a hypothetical outcome where the sugar quota is phased out in 2013) is $3.5 billion! In addition, the higher prices for refined sugar also generate producer surplus losses for the food industry (all food producers who use refined sugar as an ingredient). This adds another $909 million to the consumer losses, for a total cost estimate of $4.4 billion associated with the U.S. sugar quota.

Of course, U.S. sugar producers gain from the higher sugar prices. Their estimated gain for 2014 totals $3.9 billion. (Most of those gains go to sugar processors/refiners, with "only" $486 million going to sugar farmers.) Lastly, foreign sugar exporters who have been allocated the rights to sell sugar into the United States also benefit from those quota rights—as they pocket the difference between the higher U.S. price relative to the world price. (Several of those foreign sugar exporters are owned by large U.S. sugar processors.) This gain makes up most of the differential between the $4.4 billion loss to sugar users (consumers and food producers) and the $3.9 billion gain to sugar producers, as the deadweight losses are relatively minor.

The sugar quota illustrates in an extreme way the tendency of protection to provide benefits to a small group of producers, each of whom receives a large benefit, at the expense of a large number of consumers, each of whom bears only a small cost. In this case, the yearly consumer loss amounts to "only" $11 per capita, or a little under $30 for a typical household. Not surprisingly, the average American voter is unaware that the sugar quota exists, and so there is little effective opposition.

From the point of view of the raw sugar producers (farmers and processors), however, the quota is a life-or-death issue. These producers employ only about 20,000 workers, so the producer gains from the quota represent an implicit subsidy of about $200,000 per worker. It should be no surprise that these sugar producers are very effectively mobilized in defense of their protection. They donated more than $4.5 million in the 2012 congressional races, and the American Sugar Alliance spent an additional $3 million on lobbying expenses in the 12 months period leading up to the 2013 congressional vote on the U.S. farm bill (which reauthorizes the restrictions on U.S. imports of sugar).[4]

Opponents of protection often try to frame their criticism not in terms of consumer and producer surplus but in terms of the cost to consumers of every job "saved" by an import restriction. Clearly, the loss of the $200,000 subsidy per employee indirectly provided by the quota would force sugar producers to contract and reduce their employment. Estimates for this employment contraction vary between 500 and 2000 workers. Even taking this larger employment loss, the sugar quota would still cost the U.S. consumer $1.75 million per job saved. And this cost does not factor in all the job losses that high sugar prices impose on the food industry.

Sugar-using food producers, along with consumers, are hurt by the sugar quota, which artificially raises the price of sugar in the United States. It is estimated that employment in chocolate and confectionary manufacturing would rise by 34 percent if the sugar quota were lifted. Dum Dums are still produced in Ohio, though its producer, Spangler Inc., has moved production of its candy canes to Mexico. A substantial portion of the North American confectionary industry has moved to Canada and Mexico, where sugar prices are substantially lower. Spangler CEO Kirk Vashaw estimates that he could save $15,000 *per day* by moving his production facility from Ohio to Canada.[5]

If the sugar restrictions were lifted, the drop in the refined sugar price would induce a substantial expansion in the sugar-using food industry. We already mentioned the associated $909 million increase in producer surplus for those sectors; but this expansion would also generate 17,000–20,000 new jobs. In fact, the expansion would be big enough to turn the United States from a net importer to a net exporter of sugar-containing foods. Comparing the figures for jobs saved by sugar producers (500–2,000) with the figures for jobs lost in the food sector (17,000–20,000), we see that the employment dimension of protection is no longer that the consumer cost per job saved is astronomically high; rather, it is plainly that jobs are being *lost*, and not saved, by the sugar quota.

---

[4]An amendment to phase out the sugar import restrictions was introduced to the 2013 Farm Bill (Sugar Reform Act of 2013). It was narrowly defeated by votes of 45–54 in the Senate and 206–221 in the House.
[5]See "Farm Bill's Subsidy for Sugar under Pressure" in *Columbia Dispatch*, June 20, 2013.

Voluntary Export Restraints

A variant on the import quota is the **voluntary export restraint (VER)**, also known as a voluntary restraint agreement (VRA). (Welcome to the bureaucratic world of trade policy, where everything has a three-letter symbol!) A VER is a quota on trade imposed from the exporting country's side instead of the importer's. The most famous example is the limitation on auto exports to the United States enforced by Japan after 1981.

Voluntary export restraints are generally imposed at the request of the importer and are agreed to by the exporter to forestall other trade restrictions. As we will see in Chapter 10, certain political and legal advantages have made VERs preferred instruments of trade policy in some cases. From an economic point of view, however, a voluntary export restraint is exactly like an import quota where the licenses are assigned to foreign governments and is therefore very costly to the importing country.

A VER is always more costly to the importing country than a tariff that limits imports by the same amount. The difference is that what would have been revenue under a tariff becomes rents earned by foreigners under the VER, so that the VER clearly produces a loss for the importing country.

A study of the effects of the three major U.S. voluntary export restraints of the 1980s—in textiles and apparel, steel, and automobiles—found that about two-thirds of the cost to consumers of these restraints was accounted for by the rents earned by foreigners.[6] In other words, the bulk of the cost represents a transfer of income rather than a loss of efficiency. This calculation also emphasizes that, from a national point of view, VERs are much more costly than tariffs. Given this fact, the widespread preference of governments for VERs over other trade policy measures requires some careful analysis.

Some voluntary export agreements cover more than one country. The most famous multilateral agreement is the Multi-Fiber Arrangement, which limited textile exports from 22 countries until the beginning of 2005. Such multilateral voluntary restraint agreements are known by yet another three-letter abbreviation: OMA, for "orderly marketing agreement."

CASE STUDY   **A Voluntary Export Restraint in Practice**

JAPANESE AUTOS

For much of the 1960s and 1970s, the U.S. auto industry was largely insulated from import competition by the difference in the kinds of cars bought by U.S. and foreign consumers. U.S. buyers, living in a large country with low gasoline taxes, preferred much larger cars than Europeans and Japanese, and, by and large, foreign firms had chosen not to challenge the United States in the large-car market.

In 1979, however, sharp oil price increases and temporary gasoline shortages caused the U.S. market to shift abruptly toward smaller cars. Japanese producers, whose costs had been falling relative to those of their U.S. competitors in any case, moved in to fill the new demand. As the Japanese market share soared and U.S. output fell, strong political forces in the United States demanded protection for the U.S.

---

[6]See David G. Tarr, *A General Equilibrium Analysis of the Welfare and Employment Effects of U.S. Quotas in Textiles, Autos, and Steel* (Washington, D.C.: Federal Trade Commission, 1989).

industry. Rather than act unilaterally and risk creating a trade war, the U.S. government asked the Japanese government to limit its exports. The Japanese, fearing unilateral U.S. protectionist measures if they did not do so, agreed to limit their sales. The first agreement, in 1981, limited Japanese exports to the United States to 1.68 million automobiles. A revision raised that total to 1.85 million in 1984. In 1985, the agreement was allowed to lapse.

The effects of this voluntary export restraint were complicated by several factors. First, Japanese and U.S. cars were clearly not perfect substitutes. Second, the Japanese industry to some extent responded to the quota by upgrading its quality and selling larger autos with more features. Third, the auto industry is clearly not perfectly competitive. Nonetheless, the basic results were what the discussion of voluntary export restraints earlier would have predicted: The price of Japanese cars in the United States rose, with the rent captured by Japanese firms. The U.S. government estimates the total costs to the United States to be $3.2 billion in 1984, primarily in transfers to Japan rather than efficiency losses.

CHINESE SOLAR PANELS

Although voluntary export restraints are no longer allowed under WTO rules, this only applies to an agreement negotiated by governments and imposed onto exporters. Recently, a European Union–China trade dispute over a surge in Chinese exports of solar panels was resolved by the Chinese producers "agreeing" to limit their exports to EU countries below 7 gigawatts-worth of solar panels per year—along with a minimum price floor for those units. EU solar panel makers were disappointed, as this agreement forestalled the imposition of 47 percent anti-dumping duties on all Chinese solar panel imports (the threat that generated those concessions by Chinese solar panel producers). However, the imposition of the anti-dumping duties would have triggered a significant retaliation from China, whose officials had already drawn up a list of European products—including luxury fashion goods and wines—that would be subjected to stiff import duties into China. Chinese producers were persuaded to agree to the export limit and price floor instead, since this would allow them to keep the higher prices charged in the European Union. The main losers are European consumers, who will pay substantially more for solar power (and the environment).

Local Content Requirements

A **local content requirement** is a regulation that requires some specified fraction of a final good to be produced domestically. In some cases, this fraction is specified in physical units, like the U.S. oil import quota in the 1960s. In other cases, the requirement is stated in value terms by requiring that some minimum share of the price of a good represent domestic value added. Local content laws have been widely used by developing countries trying to shift their manufacturing base from assembly back into intermediate goods. In the United States, a local content bill for automobiles was proposed in 1982 but was never acted on.

From the point of view of the domestic producers of parts, a local content regulation provides protection in the same way an import quota does. From the point of view of the firms that must buy locally, however, the effects are somewhat different. Local content does not place a strict limit on imports. Instead, it allows firms

BRIDGING THE GAP

In Chapter 8, we discussed how trade in intermediate goods—just like trade in final goods—generates aggregate welfare gains (though gains that are far from evenly distributed). In addition, access to cheaper imported intermediate goods generates private gains for firms as they expand their scale of production. It may therefore seem surprising that U.S. government agencies (at the local, state, and federal level) are expressly forbidden to take advantage of such opportunities. The U.S. Buy American Act, originally passed in 1933, requires those government agencies to purchase many specific inputs from U.S. firms—unless the foreign bid for that input is more than 25 percent below the lowest bid from a U.S. firm. This provision was written into the American Recovery and Re-Investment Act of 2009 (ARRA), the $831 billion stimulus package that was passed in the wake of the severe economic recession. Any public work project funded by the ARRA must use iron, steel, and manufactured goods made in the United States (subject to that same 25 percent differential).

The new Bay Bridge connecting San Francisco and Oakland.

Typically, the percentage difference between the U.S. and foreign bids is substantially below 25 percent, so the Buy American provision results in a cost increase well below the 25 percent maximum. However, China is developing unique capabilities in the production of some highly specialized steel products dedicated to very large-scale infrastructure projects (due in large part to the experience generated from the high demand for such projects in China). For those specialized steel products, the cost difference between Chinese producers and the tiny handful of U.S. firms with the required production capacity is approaching that 25 percent maximum—a very large differential, especially given the massive scale of several infrastructure projects.

For the construction of the new Bay Bridge linking San Francisco and Oakland, the 23 percent difference between the Chinese bid and the lone U.S. bid for some key steel components amounted to a $400 million cost difference, which was so large that the state of California was pushed to forego federal funds under the ARRA and rely instead on bonds financed by future tolls. This financing option is not available for many other infrastructure projects, which must then incur the substantially higher costs associated with the Buy American provisions.

Those provisions not only raise the cost to U.S. taxpayers, they also induce substantial delays in some essential projects as managers navigate the administrative paperwork required to show that some key components are entirely unavailable in the United States. This happened to the Department of Homeland Security, which was unable to operate its electronic baggage screening systems until its contractor was allowed to buy some key foreign components needed for integration with the airports' security systems. Lastly, the Buy American provisions have also triggered similar protectionist clauses from other foreign governments, shutting out U.S. firms from those business opportunities.

to import more, provided that they also buy more domestically. This means that the effective price of inputs to the firm is an average of the price of imported and domestically produced inputs.

Consider, for instance, the earlier automobile example in which the cost of imported parts is $6,000. Suppose purchasing the same parts domestically would cost $10,000, but assembly firms are required to use 50 percent domestic parts. Then, they will face an average cost of parts of $8,000 (0.5 × $6,000 + 0.5 × $10,000), which will be reflected in the final price of the car.

The important point is that a local content requirement does not produce either government revenue or quota rents. Instead, the difference between the prices of imports and domestic goods in effect gets averaged in the final price and is passed on to consumers.

An interesting innovation in local content regulations has been to allow firms to satisfy their local content requirement by exporting instead of using parts domestically. This is sometimes important. For example, U.S. auto firms operating in Mexico have chosen to export some components from Mexico to the United States, even though those components could be produced in the United States more cheaply because doing so allows them to use less Mexican content in producing cars in Mexico for Mexico's market.

Other Trade Policy Instruments

Governments influence trade in many other ways. We list some of them briefly.

1. *Export credit subsidies.* This is like an export subsidy except that it takes the form of a subsidized loan to the buyer. The United States, like most other countries, has a government institution, the Export-Import Bank, devoted to providing at least slightly subsidized loans to aid exports.

2. *National procurement.* Purchases by the government or strongly regulated firms can be directed toward domestically produced goods even when these goods are more expensive than imports. The classic example is the European telecommunications industry. The nations of the European Union in principle have free trade with each other. The main purchasers of telecommunications equipment, however, are phone companies—and in Europe, these companies have until recently all been government-owned. These government-owned telephone companies buy from domestic suppliers even when the suppliers charge higher prices than suppliers in other countries. The result is that there is very little trade in telecommunications equipment within Europe.

3. *Red-tape barriers.* Sometimes a government wants to restrict imports without doing so formally. Fortunately or unfortunately, it is easy to twist normal health, safety, and customs procedures in order to place substantial obstacles in the way of trade. The classic example is the French decree in 1982 that all Japanese videocassette recorders had to pass through the tiny customs house at Poitiers (an inland city nowhere near a major port)—effectively limiting the actual imports to a handful.

The Effects of Trade Policy: A Summary

The effects of the major instruments of trade policy are usefully summarized by Table 9-1, which compares the effect of four major kinds of trade policy on the welfare of consumers.

This table certainly does not look like an advertisement for interventionist trade policy. All four trade policies benefit producers and hurt consumers. The effects of the policies on economic welfare are at best ambiguous; two of the policies definitely hurt the nation as a whole, while tariffs and import quotas are potentially beneficial only for large countries that can drive down world prices.

TABLE 9-1	**Effects of Alternative Trade Policies**			
Policy	**Tariff**	**Export Subsidy**	**Import Quota**	**Voluntary Export Restraint**
Producer surplus	Increases	Increases	Increases	Increases
Consumer surplus	Falls	Falls	Falls	Falls
Government revenue	Increases	Falls (government spending rises)	No change (rents to license holders)	No change (rents to foreigners)
Overall national welfare	Ambiguous (falls for small country)	Falls	Ambiguous (falls for small country)	Falls

Why, then, do governments so often act to limit imports or promote exports? We turn to this question in Chapter 10.

SUMMARY

1. In contrast to our earlier analysis, which stressed the general equilibrium interaction of markets, for analysis of trade policy it is usually sufficient to use a partial equilibrium approach.

2. A tariff drives a wedge between foreign and domestic prices, raising the domestic price but by less than the tariff rate. An important and relevant special case, however, is that of a "small" country that cannot have any substantial influence on foreign prices. In the small country case, a tariff is fully reflected in domestic prices.

3. The costs and benefits of a tariff or other trade policy may be measured using the concepts of consumer surplus and producer surplus. Using these concepts, we can show that the domestic producers of a good gain because a tariff raises the price they receive; the domestic consumers lose, for the same reason. There is also a gain in government revenue.

4. If we add together the gains and losses from a tariff, we find that the net effect on national welfare can be separated into two parts: On one hand is an efficiency loss, which results from the distortion in the incentives facing domestic producers and consumers. On the other hand is a terms of trade gain, reflecting the tendency of a tariff to drive down foreign export prices. In the case of a small country that cannot affect foreign prices, the second effect is zero, so that there is an unambiguous loss.

5. The analysis of a tariff can be readily adapted to analyze other trade policy measures, such as export subsidies, import quotas, and voluntary export restraints. An export subsidy causes efficiency losses similar to those of a tariff but compounds these losses by causing a deterioration of the terms of trade. Import quotas and voluntary export restraints differ from tariffs in that the government gets no revenue. Instead, what would have been government revenue accrues as rents to the recipients of import licenses (in the case of a quota) and to foreigners (in the case of a voluntary export restraint).

KEY TERMS

ad valorem tariff, p. 230
consumer surplus, p. 236
consumption distortion loss,
   p. 241
effective rate of protection,
   p. 235
efficiency loss, p. 239
export restraint, p. 231

export subsidy, p. 241
export supply curve, p. 231
import demand curve, p. 231
import quota, p. 231
local content requirement,
   p. 249
nontariff barriers, p. 231
producer surplus, p. 237

production distortion
   loss, p. 241
quota rent, p. 244
specific tariff, p. 230
terms of trade gain, p. 239
voluntary export restraint
   (VER), p. 248

PROBLEMS

MyEconLab

1. Home's demand curve for wheat is

$$D = 100 - 20P.$$

   Its supply curve is

$$S = 20 + 20P.$$

   Derive and graph Home's *import* demand schedule. What would the price of wheat be in the absence of trade?

2. Now add Foreign, which has a demand curve

$$D* = 80 - 20P$$

   and a supply curve

$$S* = 40 + 20P.$$

   a. Derive and graph Foreign's export supply curve and find the price of wheat that would prevail in Foreign in the absence of trade.
   b. Now allow Foreign and Home to trade with each other, at zero transportation cost. Find and graph the equilibrium under free trade. What is the world price? What is the volume of trade?

3. Home imposes a specific tariff of 0.5 on wheat imports.
   a. Determine and graph the effects of the tariff on the following: (1) the price of wheat in each country; (2) the quantity of wheat supplied and demanded in each country; (3) the volume of trade.
   b. Determine the effect of the tariff on the welfare of each of the following groups: (1) Home import-competing producers; (2) Home consumers; (3) the Home government.
   c. Show graphically and calculate the terms of trade gain, the efficiency loss, and the total effect on welfare of the tariff.

4. Suppose Foreign had been a much larger country, with domestic demand

$$D* = 800 - 200P, S* = 400 + 200P.$$

   (Notice that this implies the Foreign price of wheat in the absence of trade would have been the same as in problem 2.)
   Recalculate the free trade equilibrium and the effects of a 0.5 specific tariff by Home. Relate the difference in results to the discussion of the small country case in the text.

5. The recent growth in Chinese industries has enabled them to follow the dumping and anti-dumping activities in the international market. Elucidate how dumping and anti-dumping would affect the bargaining power and market price in the dumped country.

6. In a world having two nations, the imposition of tariff adversely affects the import and export of the country that imposes tariff—evaluate. How would the imposition of protective tariff by the home country affect employment? Do you believe that this may also lead to an increase in unemployment in some other industries of the country, which levies tariff?

7. Return to the example of problem 2. Starting from free trade, assume that Foreign offers exporters a subsidy of 0.5 per unit. Calculate the effects on the price in each country and on welfare, both of individual groups and of the economy as a whole, in both countries.

8. Use your knowledge about trade policy to evaluate each of the following statements:
   a. "An excellent way to reduce unemployment is to enact tariffs on imported goods."
   b. "Tariffs have a more negative effect on welfare in large countries than in small countries."
   c. "Automobile manufacturing jobs are heading to Mexico because wages are so much lower there than they are in the United States. As a result, we should implement tariffs on automobiles equal to the difference between U.S. and Mexican wage rates."

9. The nation of Acirema is "small" and unable to affect world prices. It imports peanuts at the price of $10 per bag. The demand curve is

$$D = 400 - 10P.$$

The supply curve is

$$S = 50 + 5P.$$

Determine the free trade equilibrium. Then calculate and graph the following effects of an import quota that limits imports to 50 bags.
   a. The increase in the domestic price.
   b. The quota rents.
   c. The consumption distortion loss.
   d. The production distortion loss.

10. Suppose Brazil—the largest producer of sugar—provides 20 percent export subsidy to sugar companies. By what extent would the domestic prices and the terms of trade be affected in Brazil? If the export subsidy of Brazil hampers the sugar manufacturers of importing countries, what countervailing action would you suggest to protect the domestic industries and prices of the latter?

11. Suppose workers involved in manufacturing are paid less than all other workers in the economy. What would be the effect on the real income *distribution* within the economy if there were a substantial tariff levied on manufactured goods?

FURTHER READINGS

Jagdish Bhagwati. "On the Equivalence of Tariffs and Quotas," in Robert E. Baldwin et al., eds. *Trade, Growth, and the Balance of Payments.* Chicago: Rand McNally, 1965. The classic comparison of tariffs and quotas under monopoly.

W. M. Corden. *The Theory of Protection.* Oxford: Clarendon Press, 1971. A general survey of the effects of tariffs, quotas, and other trade policies.

Robert W. Crandall. *Regulating the Automobile*. Washington, D.C.: Brookings Institution, 1986. Contains an analysis of the most famous of all voluntary export restraints.

Robert C. Feenstra. "How Costly Is Protectionism?" *Journal of Economic Perspectives* 6 (1992), pp. 159–178. A survey article summarizing the empirical work measuring the costs associated with protectionist policies.

Gary Clyde Hufbauer and Kimberly Ann Elliot. *Measuring the Costs of Protection in the United States*. Washington, D.C.: Institute for International Economics, 1994. An assessment of U.S. trade policies in 21 different sectors.

Kala Krishna. "Trade Restrictions as Facilitating Practices." *Journal of International Economics* 26 (May 1989), pp. 251–270. A pioneering analysis of the effects of import quotas when both foreign and domestic producers have monopoly power, showing that the usual result is an increase in the profits of both groups—at consumers' expense.

Patrick Messerlin. *Measuring the Costs of Protection in Europe: European Commercial Policy in the 2000s*. Washington, D.C.: Institute for International Economics, 2001. A survey of European trade policies and their effects, similar to Hufbauer and Elliot's work for the United States.

D. Rousslang and A. Suomela. "Calculating the Consumer and Net Welfare Costs of Import Relief." U.S. International Trade Commission Staff Research Study 15. Washington, D.C.: International Trade Commission, 1985. An exposition of the framework used in this chapter, with a description of how the framework is applied in practice to real industries.

U.S. International Trade Commission. *The Economic Effects of Significant U.S. Import Restraints*. Washington, D.C., 2009. A regularly updated economic analysis of the effects of protection on the U.S. economy.

MyEconLab Can Help You Get a Better Grade

MyEconLab   If your exam were tomorrow, would you be ready? For each chapter, MyEconLab Practice Tests and Study Plans pinpoint sections you have mastered and those you need to study. That way, you are more efficient with your study time, and you are better prepared for your exams.

To see how it works, turn to page 33 and then go to

www.myeconlab.com

Tariffs and Import Quotas in the Presence of Monopoly

The trade policy analysis in this chapter assumed that markets are perfectly competitive, so that all firms take prices as given. As we argued in Chapter 8, however, many markets for internationally traded goods are imperfectly competitive. The effects of international trade policies can be affected by the nature of the competition in a market.

When we analyze the effects of trade policy in imperfectly competitive markets, a new consideration appears: International trade limits monopoly power, and policies that limit trade may therefore increase monopoly power. Even if a firm is the only producer of a good in a country, it will have little ability to raise prices if there are many foreign suppliers and free trade. If imports are limited by a quota, however, the same firm will be free to raise prices without fear of competition.

The link between trade policy and monopoly power may be understood by examining a model in which a country imports a good and its import-competing production is controlled by only one firm. The country is small on world markets, so the price of the import is unaffected by its trade policy. For this model, we examine and compare the effects of free trade, a tariff, and an import quota.

The Model with Free Trade

Figure 9A-1 shows free trade in a market where a domestic monopolist faces competition from imports. D is the domestic demand curve: demand for the product by domestic residents. P_W is the world price of the good; imports are available in unlimited quantities at that price. The domestic industry is assumed to consist of only a single firm, whose marginal cost curve is MC.

FIGURE 9A-1

A Monopolist under Free Trade

The threat of import competition forces the monopolist to behave like a perfectly competitive industry.

If there were no trade in this market, the domestic firm would behave as an ordinary profit-maximizing monopolist. Corresponding to D is a marginal revenue curve MR, and the firm would choose the monopoly profit-maximizing level of output Q_M and price P_M.

With free trade, however, this monopoly behavior is not possible. If the firm tried to charge P_M, or indeed any price above P_W, nobody would buy its product, because cheaper imports would be available. Thus international trade puts a lid on the monopolist's price at P_W.

Given this limit on its price, the best the monopolist can do is produce up to the point where marginal cost is equal to the world price, at Q_f. At the price P_W, domestic consumers will demand D_f units of the good, so imports will be $D_f - Q_f$. This outcome, however, is exactly what would have happened if the domestic industry had been perfectly competitive. With free trade, then, the fact that the domestic industry is a monopoly does not make any difference in the outcome.

The Model with a Tariff

The effect of a tariff is to raise the maximum price the domestic industry can charge. If a specific tariff t is charged on imports, the domestic industry can now charge $P_W + t$ (Figure 9A-2). The industry still is not free to raise its price all the way to the monopoly price, however, because consumers will still turn to imports if the price rises above the world price plus the tariff. Thus the best the monopolist can do is to set price equal to marginal cost, at Q_t. The tariff raises the domestic price as well as the output of the domestic industry, while demand falls to D_t and thus imports fall. However, the domestic industry still produces the same quantity as if it were perfectly competitive.[7]

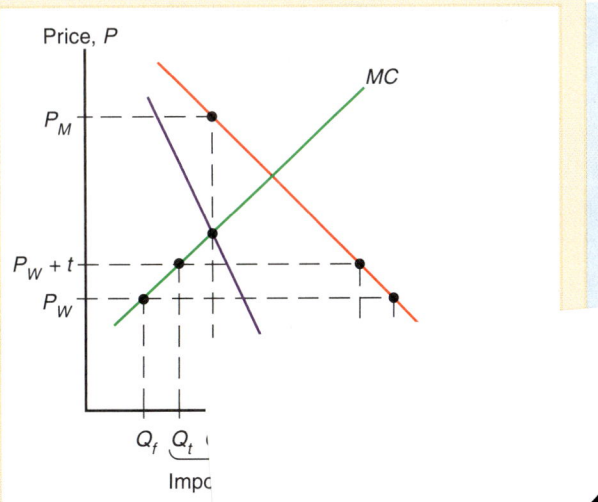

FIGURE 9A-2

A Monopolist Protected by a Tariff

The tariff allows the monopolist to raise its price, but the price is still limited by the threat of imports.

---

[7]There is one case in which a tariff will have different effects on a competitive one. This is the case where a tariff is so high that imp tive tariff). For a competitive industry, once imports have been eli has no effect. A monopolist, however, will be forced to limit its pr imports are zero. Thus, an increase in a prohibitive tariff will allo the profit-maximizing price P_M.

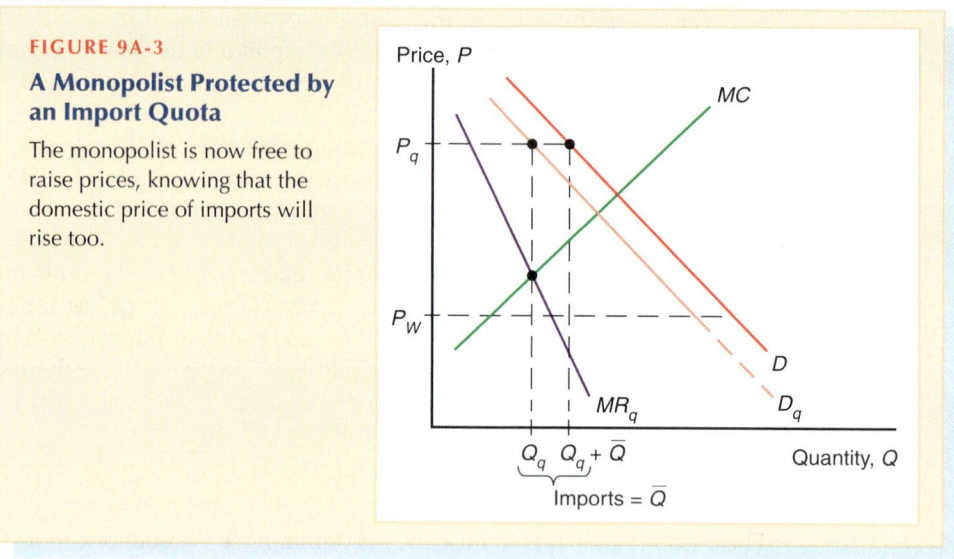

FIGURE 9A-3

A Monopolist Protected by an Import Quota

The monopolist is now free to raise prices, knowing that the domestic price of imports will rise too.

The Model with an Import Quota

Suppose the government imposes a limit on imports, restricting their quantity to a fixed level $\overline{Q}$. Then the monopolist knows that when it charges a price above P_W, it will not lose all its sales. Instead, it will sell whatever domestic demand is at that price, minus the allowed imports $\overline{Q}$. Thus, the demand facing the monopolist will be domestic demand less allowed imports. We define the post-quota demand curve as D_q; it is parallel to the domestic demand curve D but shifted $\overline{Q}$ units to the left (so long as the quota is binding and the domestic price is above the world price P_W, see Figure 9A-3).

Corresponding to D_q is a new marginal revenue curve MR_q. The firm protected by an import quota maximizes profit by setting marginal cost equal to this new marginal revenue, producing Q_q and charging the price P_q. (The license to import one unit of the good will therefore yield a rent of $P_q - P_W$.)

Comparing a Tariff and a Quota

We now ask how the effects of a tariff and a quota compare. To do this, we compare a tariff and a quota that lead to *the same level of imports* (Figure 9A-4). The tariff level t leads to a level of imports $\overline{Q}$; we therefore ask what would happen if instead of a tariff, the government simply limited imports to $\overline{Q}$.

We see from the figure that the results are not the same. The tariff leads to domestic production of Q_t and a domestic price of $P_W + t$. The quota leads to a lower level of domestic production, Q_q, and a higher price, P_q. When protected by a tariff, the monopolistic domestic industry behaves as if it were perfectly competitive; when protected by a quota, it clearly does not.

The reason for this difference is that an import quota creates more monopoly power than a tariff. When monopolistic industries are protected by tariffs, domestic firms know that if they raise their prices too high, they will still be undercut by imports. An import quota, on the other hand, provides absolute protection: No matter how high the domestic price, imports cannot exceed the quota level.

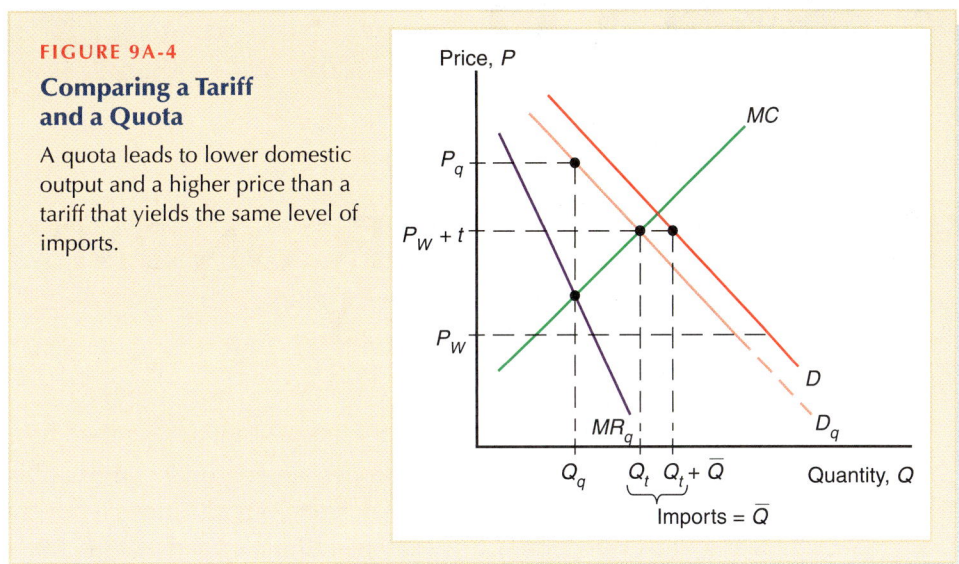

FIGURE 9A-4

Comparing a Tariff and a Quota

A quota leads to lower domestic output and a higher price than a tariff that yields the same level of imports.

This comparison seems to say that if governments are concerned about domestic monopoly power, they should prefer tariffs to quotas as instruments of trade policy. In fact, however, protection has increasingly drifted away from tariffs toward nontariff barriers, including import quotas. To explain this, we need to look at considerations other than economic efficiency that motivate governments.

CHAPTER 10

THE POLITICAL ECONOMY OF TRADE POLICY

O n November 8, 2005, the U.S. government and the government of China signed a memorandum of understanding under which China agreed, under U.S. pressure, to establish quotas on its exports of various types of clothing and textiles to the United States. For example, China agreed that in 2006 it would not ship more than 772.8 million pairs of socks to America. This agreement significantly raised the price of socks and other goods to American consumers. While China was willing to accommodate the United States on this point, however, it balked at U.S. demands that it reduce its own tariffs on manufactured and agricultural goods.

Both the Chinese and the U.S. governments, then, were determined to pursue policies that, according to the cost-benefit analysis developed in Chapter 9, produced more costs than benefits. Clearly, government policies reflect objectives that go beyond simple measures of cost and benefit.

In this chapter, we examine some of the reasons governments either should not or, at any rate, do not base their trade policy on economists' cost-benefit calculations. The examination of the forces motivating trade policy in practice continues in Chapters 11 and 12, which discuss the characteristic trade policy issues facing developing and advanced countries, respectively. The first step toward understanding actual trade policies is to ask what reasons there are for governments *not* to interfere with trade—that is, what is the case for free trade? With this question answered, arguments for intervention can be examined as challenges to the assumptions underlying the case for free trade.

LEARNING GOALS

After reading this chapter, you will be able to:

- Articulate arguments for free trade that go beyond the conventional gains from trade.
- Evaluate national welfare arguments against free trade.
- Relate the theory and evidence behind "political economy" views of trade policy.
- Explain how international negotiations and agreements have promoted world trade.
- Discuss the special issues raised by preferential trade agreements.

The Case for Free Trade

Few countries have anything approaching completely free trade. The city of Hong Kong, which is legally part of China but maintains a separate economic policy, may be the only modern economy with no tariffs or import quotas. Nonetheless, since the time of Adam Smith, economists have advocated free trade as an ideal toward which trade policy should strive. The reasons for this advocacy are not quite as simple as the idea itself. At one level, theoretical models suggest that free trade will avoid the efficiency losses associated with protection. Many economists believe free trade produces additional gains beyond the elimination of production and consumption distortions. Finally, even among economists who believe free trade is a less-than-perfect policy, many believe free trade is usually better than any other policy a government is likely to follow.

Free Trade and Efficiency

The **efficiency case for free trade** is simply the reverse of the cost-benefit analysis of a tariff. Figure 10-1 shows the basic point once again for the case of a small country that cannot influence foreign export prices. A tariff causes a net loss to the economy measured by the area of the two triangles; it does so by distorting the economic incentives of both producers and consumers. Conversely, a move to free trade eliminates these distortions and increases national welfare.

In the modern world, for reasons we will explain later in this chapter, tariff rates are generally low and import quotas relatively rare. As a result, estimates of the total costs of distortions due to tariffs and import quotas tend to be modest in size. Table 10-1 shows one fairly recent estimate of the gains from a move to worldwide free trade, measured as a percentage of GDP. For the world as a whole, according to these estimates, protection costs less than 1 percent of GDP. The gains from free trade are somewhat smaller for advanced economies such as the United States and Europe and somewhat larger for poorer "developing countries."

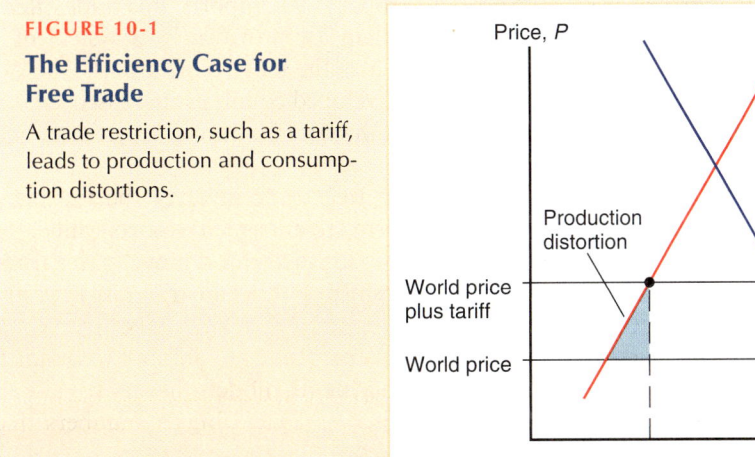

FIGURE 10-1

The Efficiency Case for Free Trade

A trade restriction, such as a tariff, leads to production and consumption distortions.

TABLE 10-1	Benefits of a Move to Worldwide Free Trade (percent of GDP)
United States	0.57
European Union	0.61
Japan	0.85
Developing countries	1.4
World	0.93

Source: William Cline, *Trade Policy and Global Poverty* (Washington, D.C.: Institute for International Economics, 2004), p. 180.

Additional Gains from Free Trade[1]

There is a widespread belief among economists that such calculations, even though they report substantial gains from free trade in some cases, do not represent the whole story. In the case of small countries in general and developing countries in particular, many economists would argue that there are important gains from free trade not accounted for in conventional cost-benefit analysis.

One kind of additional gain involves economies of scale, which were the theme of Chapters 7 and 8. Protected markets limit gains from external economies of scale by inhibiting the concentration of industries; when the economies of scale are internal, they not only fragment production internationally, but by reducing competition and raising profits, they also lead too many firms to enter the protected industry. With a proliferation of firms in narrow domestic markets, the scale of production of each firm becomes inefficient. A good example of how protection leads to inefficient scale is the case of the Argentine automobile industry, which emerged because of import restrictions. An efficient scale assembly plant should make from 80,000 to 200,000 automobiles per year, yet in 1964 the Argentine industry, which produced only 166,000 cars, had no fewer than 13 firms! Some economists argue that the need to deter excessive entry and the resulting inefficient scale of production is a reason for free trade that goes beyond the standard cost-benefit calculations.

Another argument for free trade is that by providing entrepreneurs with an incentive to seek new ways to export or compete with imports, free trade offers more opportunities for learning and innovation than are provided by a system of "managed" trade, where the government largely dictates the pattern of imports and exports. Chapter 11 discusses the experiences of less-developed countries that discovered unexpected export opportunities when they shifted from systems of import quotas and tariffs to more open trade policies.

A related form of gains from free trade involves the tendency, documented in Chapter 8, for more productive firms to engage in exports while less productive firms stay with the domestic market. This suggests that a move to free trade makes the economy as a whole more efficient by shifting the industrial mix toward firms with higher productivity.

These additional arguments for free trade are difficult to quantify, although some economists have tried to do so. In general, models that try to take economies of scale and imperfect competition into account yield bigger numbers than those reported

---

[1]The additional gains from free trade discussed here are sometimes referred to as "dynamic" gains because increased competition and innovation may need more time to take effect than the elimination of production and consumption distortions.

in Table 10-1. However, there is no consensus about just how much bigger the gains from free trade really are. If the additional gains from free trade are as large as some economists believe, the costs of distorting trade with tariffs, quotas, export subsidies, and so on are correspondingly larger than the conventional cost-benefit analysis measures.

Rent Seeking

When imports are restricted with a quota rather than a tariff, the cost is sometimes magnified by a process known as **rent seeking.** Recall from Chapter 9 that to enforce an import quota, a government has to issue import licenses and economic rents accrue to whoever receives these licenses. In some cases, individuals and companies incur substantial costs—in effect, wasting some of the economy's productive resources—in an effort to get import licenses.

A famous example involved India in the 1950s and 1960s. At that time, Indian companies were allocated the right to buy imported inputs in proportion to their installed capacity. This created an incentive to overinvest—for example, a steel company might build more blast furnaces than it expected to need simply because this would give it a larger number of import licenses. The resources used to build this idle capacity represented a cost of protection over and above the costs shown in Figure 10-1.

A more modern and unusual example of rent seeking involves U.S. imports of canned tuna. Tuna is protected by a "tariff-rate quota": A small quantity of tuna (4.8 percent of U.S. consumption) can be imported at a low tariff rate, 6 percent, but any imports beyond that level face a 12.5 percent tariff. For some reason, there are no import licenses; each year, the right to import tuna at the low tariff rate is assigned on a first come, first served basis. The result is a costly race to get tuna into the United States as quickly as possible. Here's how the U.S. International Trade Commission describes the process of rent-seeking:

> Importers attempt to qualify for the largest share of the TRQ [tariff-rate quota] as possible by stockpiling large quantities of canned tuna in Customs-bonded warehouses in late December and releasing the warehoused product as soon as the calendar year begins.

The money importers spend on warehousing lots of tuna in December represents a loss to the U.S. economy over and above the standard costs of protection.

Political Argument for Free Trade

A **political argument for free trade** reflects the fact that a political commitment to free trade may be a good idea in practice even though there may be better policies in principle. Economists often argue that trade policies in practice are dominated by special-interest politics rather than by consideration of national costs and benefits. Economists can sometimes show that in theory, a selective set of tariffs and export subsidies could increase national welfare, but that in reality, any government agency attempting to pursue a sophisticated program of intervention in trade would probably be captured by interest groups and converted into a device for redistributing income to politically influential sectors. If this argument is correct, it may be better to advocate free trade without exceptions even though on purely economic grounds, free trade may not always be the best conceivable policy.

The three arguments outlined in the previous section probably represent the standard view of most international economists, at least those in the United States:

1. The conventionally measured costs of deviating from free trade are large.
2. There are other benefits from free trade that add to the costs of protectionist policies.
3. Any attempt to pursue sophisticated deviations from free trade will be subverted by the political process.

Nonetheless, there are intellectually respectable arguments for deviating from free trade, and these arguments deserve a fair hearing.

CASE STUDY

The Gains from 1992

In 1987, the nations of the European Community (now known as the European Union) agreed on what formally was called the Single European Act, with the intention to create a truly unified European market. Because the act was supposed to go into effect within five years, the measures it embodied came to be known generally as "1992."

The unusual thing about 1992 was that the European Community was already a customs union, that is, there were no tariffs or import quotas on intra-European trade. So, what was left to liberalize? The advocates of 1992 argued that there were still substantial barriers to international trade within Europe. Some of these barriers involved the costs of crossing borders; for example, the mere fact that trucks carrying goods between France and Germany had to stop for legal formalities often resulted in long waits that were costly in time and fuel. Similar costs were imposed on business travelers, who might fly from London to Paris in an hour, then spend another hour waiting to clear immigration and customs. Differences in regulations also had the effect of limiting the integration of markets. For example, because health regulations on food differed among the European nations, one could not simply fill a truck with British goods and take them to France, or vice versa.

Eliminating these subtle obstacles to trade was a very difficult political process. Suppose France decided to allow goods from Germany to enter the country without any checks. What would prevent the French people from being supplied with manufactured goods that did not meet French safety standards, foods that did not meet French health standards, or medicines that had not been approved by French doctors? Thus, the only way that countries can have truly open borders is if they are able to agree on common standards so that a good that meets French requirements is acceptable in Germany and vice versa. The main task of the 1992 negotiations was therefore one of harmonizing regulations in hundreds of areas, negotiations that were often acrimonious because of differences in national cultures.

The most emotional examples involved food. All advanced countries regulate things such as artificial coloring to ensure that consumers are not unknowingly fed chemicals that are carcinogens or otherwise harmful. The initially proposed regulations on artificial coloring would, however, have destroyed the appearance of several traditional British foods: Pink bangers (breakfast sausages) would have become white, golden kippers gray, and mushy peas a drab rather than a brilliant green. Continental consumers did not mind; indeed, they could not understand how the British could eat such things in the first place. But in Britain, the issue became tied up with fear over the loss of national identity, and loosening the proposed regulations became a top priority for the British government, which succeeded in getting the necessary exemptions. On the other hand, Germany was forced to accept imports of beer that do not meet its centuries-old purity laws and Italy to accept pasta made from—horrors!—the wrong kind of wheat.

But why engage in all this difficult negotiating? What were the potential gains from 1992? Attempts to estimate the direct gains have always suggested that they are fairly modest. Costs associated with crossing borders amount to no more than a few percent of the value of the goods shipped; removing these costs adds at best a fraction of a percent to the real income of Europe as a whole. Yet economists at the European Commission (the administrative arm of the European Union) argued that the true gains would be much larger.

Their reasoning relied to a large extent on the view that the unification of the European market would lead to greater competition among firms and to a more efficient scale of production. Much was made of the comparison with the United States, a country whose purchasing power and population are similar to those of the European Union, but that is a borderless, fully integrated market. Commission economists pointed out that in a number of industries, Europe seemed to have markets that were segmented: Instead of treating the whole continent as a single market, firms seemed to have carved it into local zones served by relatively small-scale national producers. The economists argued that with all barriers to trade removed, there would be a consolidation of these producers, with substantial gains in productivity. These putative gains raised the overall estimated benefits from 1992 to several percent of the initial income of European nations. The Commission economists argued further that there would be indirect benefits because the improved efficiency of the European economy would improve the trade-off between inflation unemployment. At the end of a series of calculations, the Commission estimated a gain from 1992 of 7 percent of European income.[2]

While nobody involved in this discussion regarded 7 percent as a particularly reliable number, many economists shared the conviction of the Commission that the gains would be large. There were, however, skeptics who suggested that the segmentation of markets had more to do with culture than with trade policy. For example, Italian consumers wanted washing machines that were quite different from those preferred in Germany. Italians tend to buy relatively few clothes, but those they buy are stylish and expensive, so they prefer slow, gentle washing machines that conserve their clothing investment.

Now that a number of years have passed since 1992, it is clear that both the supporters and the skeptics had valid points. In some cases, there have been notable consolidations of industry; for example, Hoover closed its vacuum cleaner plant in France and concentrated all its production in a more efficient plant in Britain. In other cases, old market segmentations have clearly broken down, and sometimes in surprising ways, like the emergence of British sliced bread as a popular item in France. But in still other cases, markets have shown little sign of merging: Germans have shown little taste for imported beer and Italians none for pasta made with soft wheat.

How large were the economic gains from 1992? By 2003, when the European Commission decided to review the effects of the Single European Act, it came up with more modest estimates than it had before 1992: It put the gains at about 1.8 percent of GDP. If this number is correct, it represents a mild disappointment but hardly a failure.

---

[2]See Michael Emerson, Michel Aujean, Michel Catinat, Philippe Goubet, and Alexis Jacquemin, "The Economics of 1992," *European Economy* 35 (March 1988).

National Welfare Arguments against Free Trade

Most tariffs, import quotas, and other trade policy measures are undertaken primarily to protect the income of particular interest groups. Politicians often claim, however, that the policies are being undertaken in the interest of the nation as a whole, and sometimes they are even telling the truth. Although economists frequently argue that deviations from free trade reduce national welfare, there are some theoretical grounds for believing that activist trade policies can sometimes increase the welfare of the nation as a whole.

The Terms of Trade Argument for a Tariff

One argument for deviating from free trade comes directly out of cost-benefit analysis: For a large country that is able to affect the prices of foreign exporters, a tariff lowers the price of imports and thus generates a terms of trade benefit. This benefit must be set against the costs of the tariff, which arise because the tariff distorts production and consumption incentives. It is possible, however, that in some cases the terms of trade benefits of a tariff outweigh its costs, so there is a **terms of trade argument for a tariff**.

The appendix to this chapter shows that for a sufficiently small tariff, the terms of trade benefits must outweigh the costs. Thus, at small tariff rates, a large country's welfare is higher than with free trade (Figure 10-2). As the tariff rate is increased, however, the costs eventually begin to grow more rapidly than the benefits and the curve relating national welfare to the tariff rate turns down. A tariff rate that completely prohibits trade (t_p in Figure 10-2) leaves the country worse off than with free trade; further increases in the tariff rate beyond t_p have no effect, so the curve flattens out.

At point 1 on the curve in Figure 10-2, corresponding to the tariff rate t_o, national welfare is maximized. The tariff rate t_o that maximizes national welfare is the **optimum tariff**. (By convention, the phrase *optimum tariff* is usually used to refer to the tariff justified by a terms of trade argument rather than to the best tariff given all possible

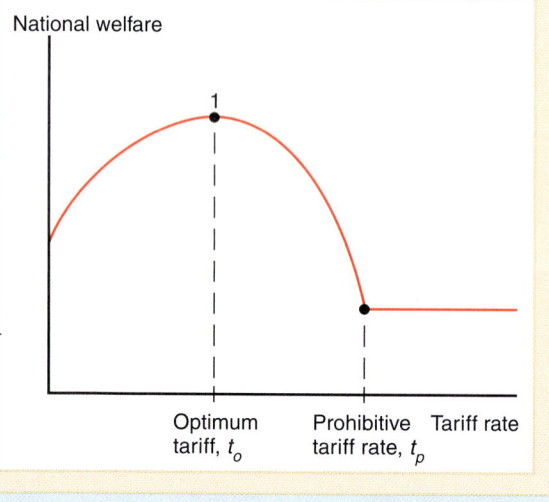

FIGURE 10-2

The Optimum Tariff

For a large country, there is an optimum tariff t_o at which the marginal gain from improved terms of trade just equals the marginal efficiency loss from production and consumption distortion.

considerations.) The optimum tariff rate is always positive but less than the prohibitive rate (t_p) that would eliminate all imports.

What policy would the terms of trade argument dictate for *export* sectors? Since an export subsidy *worsens* the terms of trade, and therefore unambiguously reduces national welfare, the optimal policy in export sectors must be a negative subsidy, that is, a *tax* on exports that raises the price of exports to foreigners. Like the optimum tariff, the optimum export tax is always positive but less than the prohibitive tax that would eliminate exports completely.

The policy of Saudi Arabia and other oil exporters has been to tax their exports of oil, raising the price to the rest of the world. Although oil prices have fluctuated up and down over the years, it is hard to argue that Saudi Arabia would have been better off under free trade.

The terms of trade argument against free trade has some important limitations, however. Most small countries have very little ability to affect the world prices of either their imports or their exports, and thus the terms of trade argument is of little practical importance to them. For big countries like the United States, the problem is that the terms of trade argument amounts to an argument for using national monopoly power to extract gains at other countries' expense. The United States could surely do this to some extent, but such a predatory policy would probably bring retaliation from other large countries. A cycle of retaliatory trade moves would, in turn, undermine the attempts at international trade policy coordination described later in this chapter.

The terms of trade argument against free trade, then, is intellectually impeccable but of doubtful usefulness. In practice, it is more often emphasized by economists as a theoretical proposition than actually used by governments as a justification for trade policy.

The Domestic Market Failure Argument against Free Trade

Leaving aside the issue of the terms of trade, the basic theoretical case for free trade rested on cost-benefit analysis using the concepts of consumer and producer surplus. Many economists have made a case against free trade based on the counterargument that these concepts, producer surplus in particular, do not properly measure costs and benefits.

Why might producer surplus not properly measure the benefits of producing a good? We consider a variety of reasons in the next two chapters: These include the possibility that the labor used in a sector would otherwise be unemployed or underemployed, the existence of defects in the capital or labor markets that prevent resources from being transferred as rapidly as they should be to sectors that yield high returns, and the possibility of technological spillovers from industries that are new or particularly innovative. These can all be classified under the general heading of **domestic market failures**. That is, in each of these examples, some market in the country is not doing its job right—the labor market is not clearing, the capital market is not allocating resources efficiently, and so on.

Suppose, for example, that the production of some good yields experience that will improve the technology of the economy as a whole but that the firms in the sector cannot appropriate this benefit and therefore do not take it into account in deciding how much to produce. Then there is a **marginal social benefit** to additional production that is not captured by the producer surplus measure. This marginal social benefit can serve as a justification for tariffs or other trade policies.

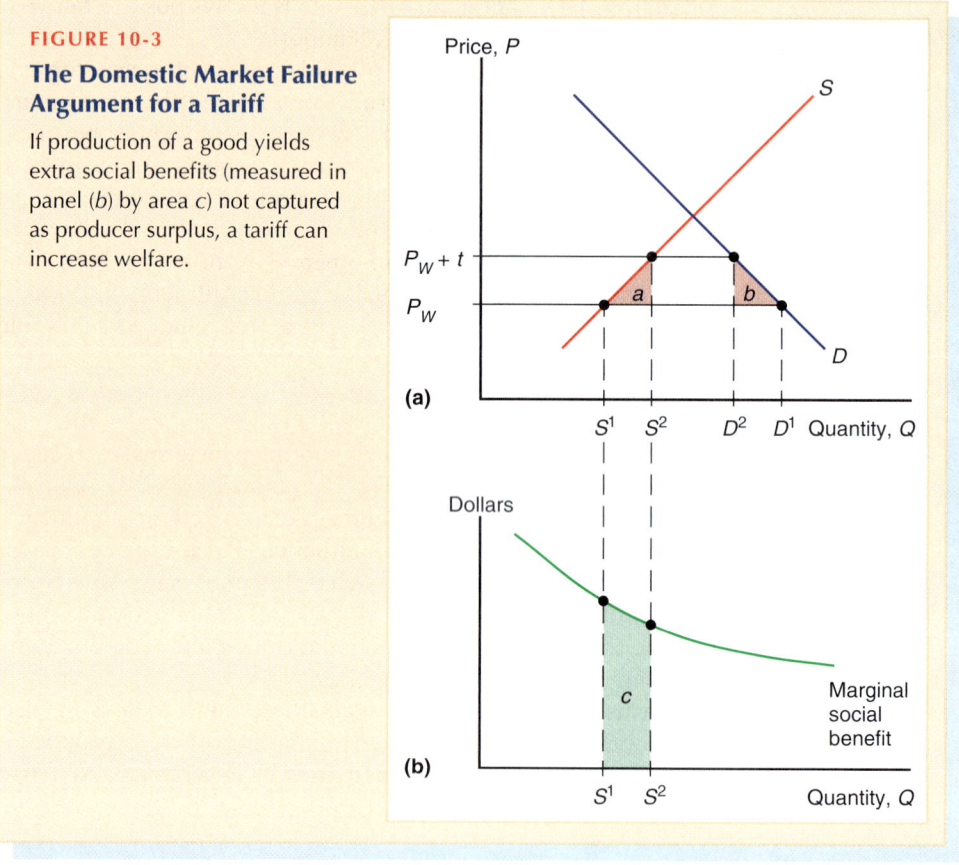

FIGURE 10-3

The Domestic Market Failure Argument for a Tariff

If production of a good yields extra social benefits (measured in panel (b) by area c) not captured as producer surplus, a tariff can increase welfare.

Figure 10-3 illustrates the domestic market failure argument against free trade. Figure 10-3a shows the conventional cost-benefit analysis of a tariff for a small country (which rules out terms of trade effects). Figure 10-3b shows the marginal benefit from production that is not taken account of by the producer surplus measure. The figure shows the effects of a tariff that raises the domestic price from P_W to $P_W + t$. Production rises from S^1 to S^2, with a resulting production distortion indicated by the area labeled a. Consumption falls from D^1 to D^2, with a resulting consumption distortion indicated by the area b. If we considered only consumer and producer surplus, we would find that the costs of the tariff exceed its benefits. Figure 10-3b shows, however, that this calculation overlooks an additional benefit that may make the tariff preferable to free trade. The increase in production yields a social benefit that may be measured by the area under the marginal social benefit curve from S^1 to S^2, indicated by c. In fact, by an argument similar to that in the terms of trade case, we can show that if the tariff is small enough, the area c must always exceed the area $a + b$ and that there is some welfare-maximizing tariff that yields a level of social welfare higher than that of free trade.

The domestic market failure argument against free trade is a particular case of a more general concept known in economics as the **theory of the second best**. This theory states that a hands-off policy is desirable in any one market only if all other markets are working properly. If they are not, a government intervention that appears to distort incentives in one market may actually increase welfare by offsetting the consequences of market failures elsewhere. For example, if the labor market is malfunctioning and fails to deliver full employment, a policy of subsidizing labor-intensive industries, which would be undesirable in a full-employment economy, might turn out to be a good idea. It would be better to fix the labor market by, for example, making wages more flexible, but if for some reason this cannot be done, intervening in other markets may be a "second-best" way of alleviating the problem.

When economists apply the theory of the second best to trade policy, they argue that imperfections in the *internal* functioning of an economy may justify interfering in its external economic relations. This argument accepts that international trade is not the source of the problem but suggests nonetheless that trade policy can provide at least a partial solution.

How Convincing Is the Market Failure Argument?

When they were first proposed, market failure arguments for protection seemed to undermine much of the case for free trade. After all, who would want to argue that the real economies we live in are free from market failures? In poorer nations, in particular, market imperfections seem to be legion. For example, unemployment and massive differences between rural and urban wage rates are present in many less-developed countries (Chapter 11). The evidence that markets work badly is less glaring in advanced countries, but it is easy to develop hypotheses suggesting major market failures there as well—for example, the inability of innovative firms to reap the full rewards of their innovations. How can we defend free trade given the likelihood of interventions that could raise national welfare?

There are two lines of defense for free trade: The first argues that domestic market failures should be corrected by domestic policies aimed directly at the problems' sources; the second argues that economists cannot diagnose market failure well enough to prescribe policy.

The point that domestic market failure calls for domestic policy changes, not international trade policies, can be made by cost-benefit analysis modified to account for any unmeasured marginal social benefits. Figure 10-3 showed that a tariff might raise welfare, despite the production and consumption distortions it causes, because it leads to additional production that yields social benefits. If the same production increase were achieved via a production subsidy rather than a tariff, however, the price to consumers would not increase and the consumption loss *b* would be avoided. In other words, by targeting directly the particular activity we want to encourage, a production subsidy would avoid some of the side costs associated with a tariff.

This example illustrates a general principle when dealing with market failures: It is always preferable to deal with market failures as directly as possible because indirect policy responses lead to unintended distortions of incentives elsewhere in the economy. Thus, trade policies justified by domestic market failure are never the most efficient response; they are always "second-best" rather than "first-best" policies.

This insight has important implications for trade policy makers: Any proposed trade policy should always be compared with a purely domestic policy aimed at correcting the same problem. If the domestic policy appears too costly or has undesirable side effects, the trade policy is almost surely even less desirable—even though the costs are less apparent.

In the United States, for example, an import quota on automobiles has been supported on the grounds that it is necessary to save the jobs of autoworkers. The advocates of an import quota argue that U.S. labor markets are too inflexible for autoworkers to remain employed either by cutting their wages or by finding jobs in other sectors. Now consider a purely domestic policy aimed at the same problem: a subsidy to firms that employ autoworkers. Such a policy would encounter massive political opposition. For one thing, to preserve current levels of employment without protection would require large subsidy payments, which would either increase the federal government's budget deficit or require a tax increase. Furthermore, autoworkers are among the highest-paid workers in the manufacturing sector; the general public would surely object to subsidizing them. It is hard to believe an employment subsidy for autoworkers could pass Congress. Yet an import quota *would be even more expensive* because while it would bring about the same increase in employment, it would also distort consumer choice. The only difference is that the costs would be less visible, taking the form of higher automobile prices rather than direct government outlays.

Critics of the domestic market failure justification for protection argue that this case is typical: Most deviations from free trade are adopted not because their benefits exceed their costs but because the public fails to understand their true costs. Comparing the costs of trade policy with alternative domestic policies is thus a useful way to focus attention on just how large these costs are.

The second defense of free trade is that because market failures are typically hard to identify precisely, it is difficult to be sure what the appropriate policy response should be. For example, suppose there is urban unemployment in a less-developed country; what is the appropriate policy? One hypothesis (examined more closely in Chapter 11) says that a tariff to protect urban industrial sectors will draw the unemployed into productive work and thus generate social benefits that would more than compensate for the tariff's costs. However, another hypothesis says that this policy will encourage so much migration to urban areas that unemployment will, in fact, increase. It is difficult to say which of these hypotheses is right. While economic theory says much about the working of markets that function properly, it provides much less guidance on those that don't; there are many ways in which markets can malfunction, and the choice of a second-best policy depends on the details of the market failure.

The difficulty of ascertaining the correct second-best trade policy to follow reinforces the political argument for free trade mentioned earlier. If trade policy experts are highly uncertain about how policy should deviate from free trade and disagree among themselves, it is all too easy for trade policy to ignore national welfare altogether and become dominated by special-interest politics. If the market failures are not too bad to start with, a commitment to free trade might in the end be a better policy than opening a Pandora's box of a more flexible approach.

This is, however, a judgment about politics rather than about economics. We need to realize that economic theory does *not* provide a dogmatic defense of free trade, even though it is often accused of doing so.

Income Distribution and Trade Policy

The discussion so far has focused on national welfare arguments for and against tariff policy. It is appropriate to start there, both because a distinction between national welfare and the welfare of particular groups helps to clarify the issues and because the advocates of trade policies usually claim that the policies will benefit the nation as a whole. When looking at the actual politics of trade policy, however, it becomes necessary to deal with the reality that there is no such thing as national welfare; there are only the desires of individuals, which get more or less imperfectly reflected in the objectives of government.

How do the preferences of individuals get added up to produce the trade policy we actually see? There is no single, generally accepted answer, but there has been a growing body of economic analysis that explores models in which governments are assumed to be trying to maximize political success rather than an abstract measure of national welfare.

Electoral Competition

Political scientists have long used a simple model of competition among political parties to show how the preferences of voters might be reflected in actual policies.[3] The model runs as follows: Suppose two competing parties are willing to promise whatever will enable each to win the next election, and suppose policy can be described along a single dimension, say, the level of the tariff rate. And finally, suppose voters differ in the policies they prefer. For example, imagine a country exports skill-intensive goods and imports labor-intensive goods. Then voters with high skill levels will favor low tariff rates, but voters with low skills will be better off if the country imposes a high tariff (because of the Stolper-Samuelson effect discussed in Chapter 5). We can therefore think of lining up all the voters in the order of the tariff rate they prefer, with the voters who favor the lowest rate on the left and those who favor the highest rate on the right.

What policies will the two parties then promise to follow? The answer is that they will try to find the middle ground—specifically, both will tend to converge on the tariff rate preferred by the **median voter,** the voter who is exactly halfway up the lineup. To see why, consider Figure 10-4. In the figure, voters are lined up by their preferred tariff rate, which is shown by the hypothetical upward-sloping curve; t_M is the median voter's preferred rate. Now suppose one of the parties has proposed the tariff rate t_A, which is considerably above that preferred by the median voter. Then the other party could propose the slightly lower rate, t_B, and its program would be preferred by almost all voters who want a lower tariff, that is, by a majority. In other words, it would always be in the political interest of a party to undercut any tariff proposal that is higher than what the median voter wants.

FIGURE 10-4

Political Competition

Voters are lined up in order of the tariff rate they prefer. If one party proposes a high tariff of t_A, the other party can win over most of the voters by offering a somewhat lower tariff, t_B. This political competition drives both parties to propose tariffs close to t_M, the tariff preferred by the median voter.

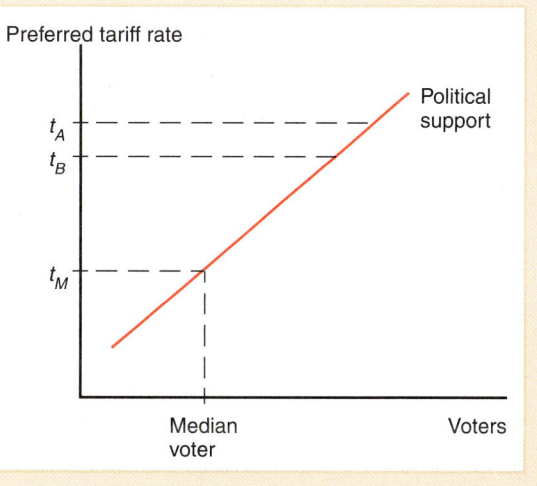

[3]See Anthony Downs, *An Economic Theory of Democracy* (Washington, D.C.: Brookings Institution, 1957).

Similar reasoning shows that self-interested politicians will always want to promise a higher tariff if their opponents propose one that is lower than the tariff the median voter prefers. So both parties end up proposing a tariff close to the one the median voter wants.

Political scientists have modified this simple model in a number of ways. For example, some analysts stress the importance of party activists in getting out the vote; since these activists are often ideologically motivated, the need for their support may prevent parties from being quite as cynical, or adopting platforms quite as indistinguishable, as this model suggests. Nonetheless, the median voter model of electoral competition has been very helpful as a way of thinking about how political decisions get made in the real world, where the effects of policy on income distribution may be more important than their effects on efficiency.

One area in which the median voter model does not seem to work very well, however, is trade policy! In fact, it makes an almost precisely wrong prediction. According to this model, a policy should be chosen on the basis of how many voters it pleases: A policy that inflicts large losses on a few people but benefits a large number of people should be a political winner; a policy that inflicts widespread losses but helps a small group should be a loser. In fact, however, protectionist policies are more likely to fit the latter than the former description. For example, the U.S. dairy industry is protected from foreign competition by an elaborate system of tariffs and quotas. These restrictions impose losses on just about every family in America while providing much smaller benefits to a dairy industry that employs only about 0.1 percent of the nation's work force. How can such a thing happen politically?

Collective Action

In a now famous book, economist Mancur Olson pointed out that political activity on behalf of a group is a public good; that is, the benefits of such activity accrue to all members of the group, not just the individual who performs the activity.[4] Suppose a consumer writes a letter to his congressperson demanding a lower tariff rate on his favorite imported good, and this letter helps change the congressperson's vote so that the lower tariff is approved. Then all consumers who buy the good benefit from lower prices, even if they did not bother to write letters.

This public good character of politics means policies that impose large losses in total—but small losses on any individual—may not face any effective opposition. Again, take the example of dairy protectionism. This policy imposes a cost on a typical American family of approximately $3 per year. Should a consumer lobby his or her congressperson to remove the policy? From the point of view of individual self-interest, surely not. Since one letter has only a marginal effect on the policy, the individual payoff from such a letter is probably not worth the paper it is written on, let alone the postage stamp. (Indeed, it is surely not worth even learning of the policy's existence unless you are interested in such things for their own sake.) And yet, if a million voters were to write demanding an end to dairy protection, it would surely be repealed, bringing benefits to consumers significantly exceeding the costs of sending the letters. In Olson's phrase, there is a problem of **collective action**: While it is in the interests of the group as a whole to press for favorable policies, it is not in any individual's interest to do so.

---

[4]Mancur Olson, *The Logic of Collective Action* (Cambridge: Harvard University Press, 1965).

POLITICIANS FOR SALE: EVIDENCE FROM THE 1990s

As we explain in the text, it's hard to make sense of actual trade policy if you assume governments are genuinely trying to maximize national welfare. On the other hand, actual trade policy does make sense if you assume special-interest groups can buy influence. But is there any direct evidence that politicians really are for sale?

Votes by the U.S. Congress on some crucial trade issues in the 1990s offer useful test cases. The reason is that U.S. campaign finance laws require politicians to reveal the amounts and sources of campaign contributions; this disclosure allows economists and political scientists to look for any relationship between those contributions and actual votes.

A 1998 study by Robert Baldwin and Christopher Magee* focuses on two crucial votes: the 1993 vote on the North American Free Trade Agreement (generally known as NAFTA, and described at greater length below), and the 1994 vote ratifying the latest agreement under the General Agreement on Tariffs and Trade (generally known as the GATT, also described below). Both votes were bitterly fought, largely along business-versus-labor lines—that is, business groups were strongly in favor; labor unions were strongly against. In both cases, the free trade position backed by business won; in the NAFTA vote, the outcome was in doubt until the last minute, and the margin of victory—34 votes in the House of Representatives—was not very large.

Baldwin and Magee estimate an econometric model of congressional votes that controls for such factors as the economic characteristics of members' districts as well as business and labor contributions to the congressional representative. They find a strong impact of money on the voting pattern. One way to assess this impact is to run a series of "counterfactuals": How different would the overall vote had been if there had been no business contributions, no labor contributions, or no contributions of any type at all?

The following table summarizes the results. The first row shows how many representatives

voted in favor of each bill; bear in mind that passage required at least 214 votes. The second row shows the number of votes predicted by Baldwin and Magee's equations: Their model gets it right in the case of NAFTA but overpredicts by a few votes in the case of the GATT. The third row shows how many votes each bill would have received, according to the model, in the absence of labor contributions; the next row shows how many representatives would have voted in favor in the absence of business contributions. The last row shows how many would have voted in favor if both business and labor contributions had been absent.

	Vote for NAFTA	Vote for GATT
Actual	229	283
Predicted by model	229	290
Without labor contributions	291	346
Without business contributions	195	257
Without any contributions	256	323

If these estimates are correct, contributions had big impacts on the vote totals. In the case of NAFTA, labor contributions induced 62 representatives who would otherwise have supported the bill to vote against; business contributions moved 34 representatives the other way. If there had been no business contributions, according to this estimate, NAFTA would have received only 195 votes—not enough for passage.

On the other hand, given that both sides were making contributions, their effects tended to cancel out. Baldwin and Magee's estimates suggest that in the absence of contributions from either labor or business, both NAFTA and the GATT would have passed anyway.

It's probably wrong to emphasize the fact that in these particular cases, contributions from the two sides did not change the final outcome. The really important result is that politicians are, indeed, for sale—which means that theories of trade policy that emphasize special interests are on the right track.

*Robert E. Baldwin and Christopher S. Magee, "Is Trade Policy for Sale? Congressional Voting on Recent Trade Bills," Working Paper 6376, National Bureau of Economic Research, January 1998.

The problem of collective action can best be overcome when a group is small (so that each individual reaps a significant share of the benefits of favorable policies) and/or well organized (so that members of the group can be mobilized to act in their collective interest). The reason that a policy like dairy protection can happen is that dairy producers form a relatively small, well-organized group that is well aware of the size of the implicit subsidy members receive, while dairy consumers are a huge population that does not even perceive itself as an interest group. The problem of collective action, then, can explain why policies that not only seem to produce more costs than benefits but that also seem to hurt far more voters than they help can nonetheless be adopted.

Modeling the Political Process

While the logic of collective action has long been invoked by economists to explain seemingly irrational trade policies, the theory is somewhat vague on the ways in which organized interest groups actually go about influencing policy. A growing body of analysis tries to fill this gap with simplified models of the political process.[5]

The starting point of this analysis is obvious: While politicians may win elections partly because they advocate popular policies, a successful campaign also requires money for advertising, polling, and so on. It may therefore be in the interest of a politician to adopt positions against the interest of the typical voter if the politician is offered a sufficiently large financial contribution to do so; the extra money may be worth more votes than those lost by taking the unpopular position.

Modern models of the political economy of trade policy therefore envision a sort of auction in which interest groups "buy" policies by offering contributions contingent on the policies followed by the government. Politicians will not ignore overall welfare, but they will be willing to trade off some reduction in the welfare of voters in return for a larger campaign fund. As a result, well-organized groups—that is, groups that are able to overcome the problem of collective action—will be able to get policies that favor their interests at the expense of the public as a whole.

Who Gets Protected?

As a practical matter, which industries actually get protected from import competition? Many developing countries traditionally have protected a wide range of manufacturing, in a policy known as import-substituting industrialization. We discuss this policy and the reasons why it has become considerably less popular in recent years in Chapter 11. The range of protectionism in advanced countries is much narrower; indeed, much protectionism is concentrated in just two sectors: agriculture and clothing.

Agriculture   There are not many farmers in modern economies—in the United States, agriculture employs only about 2 million workers out of a labor force of more than 130 million. Farmers are, however, usually a well-organized and politically powerful group that has been able in many cases to achieve very high rates of effective protection. We discussed Europe's Common Agricultural Policy in Chapter 9; the export subsidies in that program mean that a number of agricultural products sell at two or three

---

[5]See, in particular, Gene Grossman and Elhanan Helpman, "Protection for Sale," *American Economic Review* 89 (September 1994), pp. 833–850.

times world prices. In Japan, the government has traditionally banned imports of rice, thus driving up internal prices of the country's staple food to more than five times as high as the world price. This ban was slightly relaxed in the face of bad harvests in the mid-1990s, but in late 1998—over the protests of other nations, including the United States—Japan imposed a 1,000 percent tariff on rice imports.

The United States is generally a food exporter, which means that tariffs or import quotas cannot raise prices. (Sugar and dairy products are exceptions.) While farmers have received considerable subsidies from the federal government, the government's reluctance to pay money out directly (as opposed to imposing more or less hidden costs on consumers) has limited the size of these subsidies. As a result of the government's reluctance, much of the protection in the United States is concentrated on the other major protected sector: the clothing industry.

Clothing   The clothing industry consists of two parts: textiles (spinning and weaving of cloth) and apparel (assembly of cloth into clothing). Both industries, but especially the apparel industry, historically have been protected heavily through both tariffs and import quotas. Until 2005, they were subject to the Multi-Fiber Arrangement (MFA), which set both export and import quotas for a large number of countries.

Apparel production has two key features. It is labor-intensive: A worker needs relatively little capital, in some cases no more than a sewing machine, and can do the job without extensive formal education. And the technology is relatively simple: There is no great difficulty in transferring the technology even to very poor countries. As a result, the apparel industry is one in which low-wage nations have a strong comparative advantage and high-wage countries have a strong comparative disadvantage. It is also traditionally a well-organized sector in advanced countries; for example, many American apparel workers have long been represented by the International Ladies' Garment Worker's Union.

Later in this chapter, we'll describe how trade negotiations work; one of the most important provisions of the Uruguay Round trade agreements, signed in 1994, was the phaseout of the MFA, which took place at the end of 2004. Although import quotas were reimposed on China in 2005, those quotas have since phased out. At this point, trade in clothing no longer faces many restrictions.

Table 10-2 shows just how important clothing used to be in U.S. protectionism, and how much difference the end of the restrictions on clothing makes. In 2002, with the MFA still in effect, clothing restrictions were responsible for more than 80 percent of the overall welfare costs of U.S. protectionism. Because the MFA assigned import licenses to exporting countries, most of the welfare cost to the United States came not from distortion of production and consumption but from the transfer of quota rents to foreigners.

With the expiration of the MFA, the costs of clothing protection and hence the overall costs of U.S. protection fell sharply.

TABLE 10-2	**Welfare Costs of U.S. Protection ($ billion)**	
	2002 Estimate	**2015 Projected**
Total	14.1	2.6
Textiles and apparel	11.8	0.5

Source: U.S. International Trade Commission.

International Negotiations and Trade Policy

Our discussion of the politics of trade policy has not been very encouraging. We have argued that it is difficult to devise trade policies that raise national welfare and that trade policy is often dominated by interest group politics. "Horror stories" of trade policies that produce costs that greatly exceed any conceivable benefits abound; it is thus easy to be highly cynical about the practical side of trade theory.

Yet, in fact, from the mid-1930s until about 1980, the United States and other advanced countries gradually removed tariffs and some other barriers to trade, and by so doing aided a rapid increase in international integration. Figure 10-5 shows the average U.S. tariff rate on dutiable imports from 1891 to 2010; after rising sharply in the early 1930s, the rate has steadily declined.[6] Most economists believe this progressive trade liberalization was highly beneficial. Given what we have said about the politics of trade policy, however, how was this removal of tariffs politically possible?

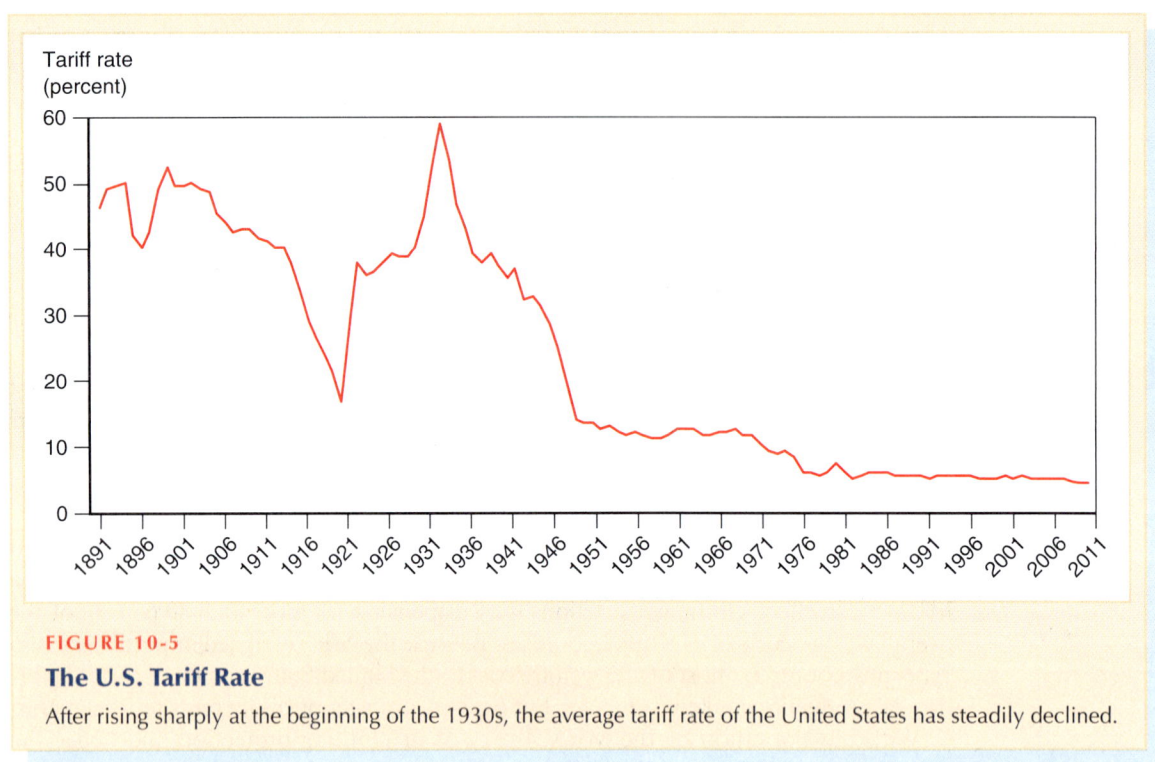

FIGURE 10-5

The U.S. Tariff Rate

After rising sharply at the beginning of the 1930s, the average tariff rate of the United States has steadily declined.

---

[6]Measures of changes in the average rate of protection can be problematic because the composition of imports changes—partly because of tariff rates themselves. Imagine, for example, a country that imposes a tariff on some goods that is so high that it shuts off all imports of these goods. Then the average tariff rate on goods actually imported will be zero! To try to correct for this, the measure we use in Figure 10-5 shows the rate only on "dutiable" imports; that is, it excludes imports that for some reason were exempt from tariffs. At their peak, U.S. tariff rates were so high that goods subject to tariffs accounted for only one-third of imports; by 1975 that share had risen to two-thirds. As a result, the average tariff rate on all goods fell much less than the rate on dutiable goods. The numbers shown in Figure 10-5, however, give a more accurate picture of the major liberalization of trade actually experienced by the United States.

At least part of the answer is that the great postwar liberalization of trade was achieved through **international negotiation**. That is, governments agreed to engage in mutual tariff reduction. These agreements linked reduced protection for each country's import-competing industries to reduced protection by other countries against that country's export industries. Such a linkage, as we will now argue, helps to offset some of the political difficulties that would otherwise prevent countries from adopting good trade policies.

The Advantages of Negotiation

There are at least two reasons why it is easier to lower tariffs as part of a mutual agreement than to do so as a unilateral policy. First, a mutual agreement helps mobilize support for freer trade. Second, negotiated agreements on trade can help governments avoid getting caught in destructive trade wars.

The effect of international negotiations on support for freer trade is straightforward. We have noted that import-competing producers are usually better informed and organized than consumers. International negotiations can bring in domestic exporters as a counterweight. The United States and Japan, for example, could reach an agreement in which the United States refrains from imposing import quotas to protect some of its manufacturers from Japanese competition in return for removal of Japanese barriers against U.S. exports of agricultural or high-technology products to Japan. U.S. consumers might not be effective politically in opposing such import quotas on foreign goods, even though these quotas may be costly to them, but exporters who want access to foreign markets may, through their lobbying for mutual elimination of import quotas, protect consumer interests.

International negotiation can also help to avoid a **trade war**. The concept of a trade war can best be illustrated with a stylized example.

Imagine there are only two countries in the world, the United States and Japan, and these countries have only two policy choices: free trade or protection. Suppose these are unusually clear-headed governments that can assign definite numerical values to their satisfaction with any particular policy outcome (Table 10-3).

The particular values of the payoffs given in the table represent two assumptions. First, we assume that each country's government would choose protection if it could take the other country's policy as given. That is, whichever policy Japan chooses, the U.S. government is better off with protection. This assumption is by no means necessarily true; many economists would argue that free trade is the best policy for the nation, regardless of what other governments do. Governments, however, must act not only in the public interest but also in their own political interest. For the reasons discussed

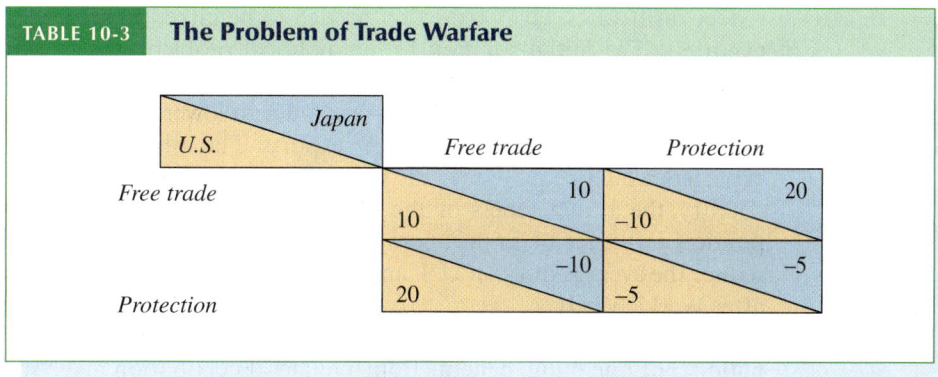

TABLE 10-3   The Problem of Trade Warfare

U.S. \ Japan	Free trade	Protection
Free trade	10 / 10	−10 / 20
Protection	20 / −10	−5 / −5

in the previous section, governments often find it politically difficult to avoid giving protection to some industries.

The second assumption built into Table 10-3 is that even though each government acting individually would be better off with protection, they would both be better off if both chose free trade. That is, the U.S. government has more to gain from an opening of Japanese markets than it has to lose from opening its own markets, and the same is true for Japan. We can justify this assumption simply by appealing to the gains from trade.

To those who have studied game theory, this situation is known as a **Prisoner's dilemma**. Each government, making the best decision for itself, will choose to protect. These choices lead to the outcome in the lower right box of the table. Yet both governments are better off if neither protects: The upper left box of the table yields a payoff that is higher for both countries. By acting unilaterally in what appear to be their best interests, the governments fail to achieve the best outcome possible. If the countries act unilaterally to protect, there is a trade war that leaves both worse off. Trade wars are not as serious as shooting wars, but avoiding them is similar to the problem of avoiding armed conflict or arms races.

Obviously, Japan and the United States need to establish an agreement (such as a treaty) to refrain from protection. Each government will be better off if it limits its own freedom of action, provided the other country limits its freedom of action as well. A treaty can make everyone better off.

This is a highly simplified example. In the real world there are both many countries and many gradations of trade policy between free trade and complete protection against imports. Nonetheless, the example suggests both that there is a need to coordinate trade policies through international agreements and that such agreements can actually make a difference. Indeed, the current system of international trade is built around a series of international agreements.

International Trade Agreements: A Brief History

Internationally coordinated tariff reduction as a trade policy dates back to the 1930s. In 1930, the United States passed a remarkably irresponsible tariff law, the Smoot-Hawley Act. Under this act, tariff rates rose steeply and U.S. trade fell sharply; some economists argue that the Smoot-Hawley Act helped deepen the Great Depression. Within a few years after the act's passage, the U.S. administration concluded that tariffs needed to be reduced, but this posed serious problems of political coalition building. Any tariff reduction would be opposed by those members of Congress whose districts contained firms producing competing goods, while the benefits would be so widely diffused that few in Congress could be mobilized on the other side. To reduce tariff rates, tariff reduction needed to be linked to some concrete benefits for exporters. The initial solution to this political problem was bilateral tariff negotiations. The United States would approach some country that was a major exporter of some good—say, a sugar exporter—and offer to lower tariffs on sugar if that country would lower its tariffs on some U.S. exports. The attractiveness of the deal to U.S. exporters would help counter the political weight of the sugar interest. In the foreign country, the attractiveness of the deal to foreign sugar exporters would balance the political influence of import-competing interests. Such bilateral negotiations helped reduce the average duty on U.S. imports from 59 percent in 1932 to 25 percent shortly after World War II.

Bilateral negotiations, however, do not take full advantage of international coordination. For one thing, benefits from a bilateral negotiation may "spill over" to parties that have not made any concessions. For example, if the United States reduces tariffs on coffee as a result of a deal with Brazil, Colombia will also gain from a higher world coffee price. Furthermore, some advantageous deals may inherently involve more than two partners: The United States sells more to Europe, Europe sells more to Saudi Arabia, Saudi Arabia sells more to Japan, and Japan sells more to the United States. Thus, the next step in international trade liberalization was to proceed to multilateral negotiations involving a number of countries.

Multilateral negotiations began soon after the end of World War II. Originally, diplomats from the victorious Allies imagined such negotiations would take place under the auspices of a proposed body called the International Trade Organization, paralleling the International Monetary Fund and the World Bank (described in the second half of this book). In 1947, unwilling to wait until the ITO was in place, a group of 23 countries began trade negotiations under a provisional set of rules that became known as the **General Agreement on Tariffs and Trade**, or **GATT**. As it turned out, the ITO was never established because it ran into severe political opposition, especially in the United States. So the provisional agreement ended up governing world trade for the next 48 years.

Officially, the GATT was an agreement, not an organization—the countries participating in the agreement were officially designated as "contracting parties," not members. In practice, the GATT did maintain a permanent "secretariat" in Geneva, which everyone referred to as "the GATT." In 1995, the **World Trade Organization**, or **WTO**, was established, finally creating the formal organization envisaged 50 years earlier. However, the GATT rules remain in force, and the basic logic of the system remains the same.

One way to think about the GATT-WTO approach to trade is to use a mechanical analogy: It's like a device designed to push a heavy object, the world economy, gradually up a slope—the path to free trade. To get there requires both "levers" to push the object in the right direction and "ratchets" to prevent backsliding.

The principal ratchet in the system is the process of **binding**. When a tariff rate is "bound," the country imposing the tariff agrees not to raise the rate in the future. At present, almost all tariff rates in developed countries are bound, as are about three-quarters of the rates in developing countries. There is, however, some wiggle room in bound tariffs: A country can raise a tariff if it gets the agreement of other countries, which usually means providing compensation by reducing other tariffs. In practice, binding has been highly effective, with very little backsliding in tariffs over the past half-century.

In addition to binding tariffs, the GATT-WTO system generally tries to prevent non-tariff interventions in trade. Export subsidies are not allowed, with one big exception: Back at the GATT's inception, the United States insisted on a loophole for agricultural exports, which has since been exploited on a large scale by the European Union.

As we pointed out earlier in this chapter, most of the actual cost of protection in the United States comes from import quotas. The GATT-WTO system in effect "grandfathers" existing import quotas, though there has been an ongoing and often successful effort to remove such quotas or convert them to tariffs. New import quotas are generally forbidden except as temporary measures to deal with "market disruption," an undefined phrase usually interpreted to mean surges of imports that threaten to put a domestic sector suddenly out of business.

The lever used to make forward progress is the somewhat stylized process known as a **trade round**, in which a large group of countries get together to negotiate a set of tariff reductions and other measures to liberalize trade. Eight trade rounds have been completed since 1947, the last of which—the Uruguay Round, completed in 1994—established the WTO. In 2001, a meeting in the Persian Gulf city of Doha inaugurated a ninth round, which by 2014 appeared to have failed to achieve an agreement. We'll discuss the reasons for the Doha Round's apparent failure later in this chapter.

The first five trade rounds under the GATT took the form of "parallel" bilateral negotiations, where each country negotiates pairwise with a number of countries at once. For example, if Germany were to offer a tariff reduction that would benefit both France and Italy, it could ask both of them for reciprocal concessions. The ability to make more extensive deals, together with the worldwide economic recovery from the war, helped to permit substantial tariff reductions.

The sixth multilateral trade agreement, known as the Kennedy Round, was completed in 1967. This agreement involved an across-the-board 50 percent reduction in tariffs by the major industrial countries, except for specified industries whose tariffs were left unchanged. The negotiations concerned which industries to exempt rather than the size of the cut for industries not given special treatment. Overall, the Kennedy Round reduced average tariffs by about 35 percent.

The so-called Tokyo Round of trade negotiations (completed in 1979) reduced tariffs by a formula more complex than that of the Kennedy Round. In addition, new codes were established in an effort to control the proliferation of nontariff barriers, such as voluntary export restraints and orderly marketing agreements. Finally, in 1994, an eighth round of negotiations, the so-called Uruguay Round, was completed. The provisions of that round were approved by the U.S. Congress after acrimonious debate; we describe the results of these negotiations below.

The Uruguay Round

Major international trade negotiations invariably open with a ceremony in one exotic locale and conclude with a ceremonial signing in another. The eighth round of global trade negotiations carried out under the GATT began in 1986, with a meeting at the coastal resort of Punta del Este, Uruguay (hence the name Uruguay Round). The participants then repaired to Geneva, where they engaged in years of offers and counteroffers, threats and counterthreats, and, above all, tens of thousands of hours of meetings so boring that even the most experienced diplomat had difficulty staying awake. The round had been scheduled for completion by 1990 but ran into serious political difficulties. In late 1993, the negotiators finally produced a basic document consisting of 400 pages of agreements, together with supplementary documents detailing the specific commitments of member nations with regard to particular markets and products—about 22,000 pages in all. The agreement was signed in Marrakesh, Morocco, in April 1994, and ratified by the major nations—after bitter political controversy in some cases, including in the United States—by the end of that year.

As the length of the document suggests, the end results of the Uruguay Round are not easy to summarize. The most important results, however, may be grouped under two headings, trade liberalization and administrative reforms.

Trade Liberalization

The Uruguay Round, like previous GATT negotiations, cut tariff rates around the world. The numbers can sound impressive: The average tariff imposed by advanced countries fell almost 40 percent as a result of the round. However, tariff rates were already quite low. In fact, the average tariff rate fell only from 6.3 to 3.9 percent, enough to produce only a small increase in world trade.

More important than this overall tariff reduction were the moves to liberalize trade in two important sectors: agriculture and clothing.

World trade in agricultural products has been highly distorted. Japan is notorious for import restrictions that lead to internal prices of rice, beef, and other foods that are several times as high as world market prices; Europe's massive export subsidies under the Common Agricultural Policy were described in Chapter 9. At the beginning of the Uruguay Round, the United States had an ambitious goal: free trade in agricultural products by the year 2000. The actual achievement was far more modest but still significant. The agreement required agricultural exporters to reduce the value of subsidies by 36 percent, and the volume of subsidized exports by 21 percent, over a six-year period. Countries like Japan that protect their farmers with import quotas were required to replace quotas with tariffs, which may not be increased in the future.

World trade in textiles and clothing was also highly distorted by the Multi-Fiber Arrangement, also described in Chapter 9. The Uruguay Round phased out the MFA over a ten-year period, eliminating all quantitative restrictions on trade in textiles and clothing. (Some high tariffs remain in place.) This was a fairly dramatic liberalization—remember, most estimates suggested that protection of clothing imposed a larger cost on U.S. consumers than all other protectionist measures combined. It is worth noting, however, that the formula used in phasing out the MFA was heavily "backloaded": Much of the liberalization was postponed until 2003 and 2004, with the final end of the quotas not taking place until January 1, 2005.

Sure enough, the end of the MFA brought a surge in clothing exports from China. For example, in January 2005, China shipped 27 million pairs of cotton trousers to the United States, up from 1.9 million a year earlier. And there was a fierce political reaction from clothing producers in the United States and Europe. While new restrictions were imposed on Chinese clothing exports, these restrictions were phased out over time; world trade in clothing has, in fact, been largely liberalized. A final important trade action under the Uruguay Round was a new set of rules concerning government procurement, purchases made not by private firms or consumers but by government agencies. Such procurement has long provided protected markets for many kinds of goods, from construction equipment to vehicles. (Recall the box on Hungarian buses in Chapter 9.) The Uruguay Round set new rules that should open up a wide range of government contracts for imported products.

Administrative Reforms: From the GATT to the WTO

Much of the publicity that surrounded the Uruguay Round, and much of the controversy swirling around the world trading system since then, has focused on the round's creation of a new institution, the World Trade Organization. In 1995, this organization replaced the ad hoc secretariat that had administered the GATT. As we'll see in Chapter 12, the WTO has become the organization that opponents of globalization love to hate; it has been accused by both the left and the right of acting as a sort of world government, undermining national sovereignty.

How different is the WTO from the GATT? From a legal point of view, the GATT was a provisional agreement, whereas the WTO is a full-fledged international organization; however, the actual bureaucracy remains small (a staff of 500). An updated version of the original GATT text has been incorporated into the WTO rules. The GATT, however, applied only to trade in goods; world trade in services—that is, intangible things like insurance, consulting, and banking—was not subject to any agreed-upon set of rules. As a result, many countries applied regulations that openly or de facto discriminated against foreign suppliers. The GATT's neglect of trade in services became an increasingly glaring omission, because modern economies have increasingly focused on the production of services rather than physical goods. So the WTO agreement includes rules on trade in services (the General Agreement on Trade in Services, or GATS). In practice, these rules have not yet had much impact on trade in services; their main purpose is to serve as the basis for negotiating future trade rounds.

In addition to a broad shift from producing goods to producing services, advanced countries have also experienced a shift from depending on physical capital to depending on "intellectual property," which is protected by patents and copyrights. (Thirty years ago, General Motors was the quintessential modern corporation; now it's Apple or Google.) Thus, defining the international application of international property rights has also become a major preoccupation. The WTO tries to take on this issue with its Agreement on Trade-Related Aspects of Intellectual Property (TRIPS). The application of TRIPS in the pharmaceutical industry has become a subject of heated debate.

The most important new aspect of the WTO, however, is generally acknowledged to be its "dispute settlement" procedure. A basic problem arises when one country accuses another of violating the rules of the trading system. Suppose, for example, that Canada accuses the United States of unfairly limiting timber imports—and the United States denies the charge. What happens next?

Before the WTO, there were international tribunals in which Canada could press its case, but such proceedings tended to drag on for years, even decades. And even when a ruling had been issued, there was no way to enforce it. This did not mean that the GATT's rules had no force: Neither the United States nor other countries wanted to acquire a reputation as scofflaws, so they made considerable efforts to keep their actions "GATT-legal." But gray-area cases tended to go unresolved.

The WTO contains a much more formal and effective procedure. Panels of experts are selected to hear cases, usually reaching a final conclusion in less than a year; even with appeals, the procedure is not supposed to take more than 15 months.

Suppose the WTO concludes that a nation has, in fact, been violating the rules—and the country nonetheless refuses to change its policy. Then what? The WTO itself has no enforcement powers. What it can do is grant the country that filed the complaint the right to retaliate. To use our Canada–U.S. example, the government of Canada might be given the right to impose restrictions on U.S. exports without being considered in violation of WTO rules. In the case of the banana dispute described in the box on page 290, a WTO ruling found the European Union in violation; when Europe remained recalcitrant, the United States temporarily imposed tariffs on such items as designer handbags.

The hope and expectation is that few disputes will get this far. In many cases, the threat to bring a dispute before the WTO should lead to a settlement; in the great majority of other cases, countries accept the WTO ruling and change their policies.

The following box describes an example of the WTO dispute settlement procedure at work: the U.S.–Venezuela dispute over imported gasoline. As the box explains, this case has also become a prime example for those who accuse the WTO of undermining national sovereignty.

Benefits and Costs

The economic impact of the Uruguay Round is difficult to estimate. If nothing else, think about the logistics: To do an estimate, one must translate an immense document from one impenetrable jargon (legalese) into another (economese), assign numbers to the translation, then feed the whole thing into a computer model of the world economy.

SETTLING A DISPUTE—AND CREATING ONE

The very first application of the WTO's new dispute settlement procedure has also been one of the most controversial. To WTO supporters, it illustrates the new system's effectiveness. To opponents, it shows that the organization stands in the way of important social goals such as protecting the environment.

The case arose out of new U.S. air pollution standards. These standards set rules for the chemical composition of gasoline sold in the United States. A uniform standard would clearly have been legal under WTO rules. However, the new standards included some loopholes: Refineries in the United States, or those selling 75 percent or more of their output in the United States, were given "baselines" that depended on their 1990 pollutant levels. This provision generally set a less strict standard than was set for imported gasoline, and thus in effect introduced a preference for gasoline from domestic refineries.

Venezuela, which ships considerable quantities of gasoline to the United States, brought a complaint against the new pollution rules early in 1995. Venezuela argued that the rules violated the principle of "national treatment," which says that imported goods should be subject to the same regulations as domestic goods (so that regulations are not used as an indirect form of protectionism). A year later, the panel appointed by the WTO ruled in Venezuela's favor; the United States appealed, but the appeal was rejected. The United States and Venezuela then negotiated a revised set of rules.

At one level, this outcome was a demonstration of the WTO doing exactly what it was supposed to do. The United States had introduced measures that pretty clearly violated the letter of its trade agreements; when a smaller, less influential country appealed against those measures, it got fairly quick results.

On the other hand, environmentalists were understandably upset: The WTO ruling, in effect, blocked a measure that would have made the air cleaner. Furthermore, there was little question that the clean-air rules were promulgated in good faith—that is, they were really intended to reduce air pollution, not to exclude exports.

Defenders of the WTO point out that the United States clearly could have written a rule that did not discriminate against imports; the fact that it had not done so was a political concession to the refining industry, which *did* in effect constitute a sort of protectionism. The most you can say is that the WTO's rules made it more difficult for U.S. environmentalists to strike a political deal with the industry.

In the mythology of the anti-globalization movement, which we discuss in Chapter 12, the WTO's intervention against clean-air standards has taken on iconic status: The case is seen as a prime example of how the organization deprives nations of their sovereignty, preventing them from following socially and environmentally responsible policies. The reality of the case, however, is nowhere near that clearcut: If the United States had imposed a "clean" clean-air rule that had not discriminated among sources, the WTO would have had no complaints.

The most widely cited estimates are those of the GATT itself and of the Organization for Economic Cooperation and Development, another international organization (this one consisting only of rich countries and based in Paris). Both estimates suggest a gain to the world economy as a whole of more than $200 billion annually, raising world income by about 1 percent. As always, there are dissenting estimates on both sides. Some economists claim that the estimated gains are exaggerated, particularly because the estimates assume that exports and imports responded strongly to the new liberalizing moves. A probably larger minority of critics argues that these estimates are considerably too low, for the "dynamic" reasons discussed earlier in this chapter.

In any case, it is clear that the usual logic of trade liberalization applies: The costs of the Uruguay Round were felt by concentrated, often well-organized groups, while the benefit accrued to broad, diffuse populations. The progress on agriculture hurt the small but influential populations of farmers in Europe, Japan, and other countries where agricultural prices are far above world levels. These losses were much more than offset by gains to consumers and taxpayers in those countries, but because these benefits were very widely spread, they were little noticed. Similarly, the liberalization of trade in textiles and clothing produced some concentrated pain for workers and companies in those industries, offset by considerably larger but far less visible consumer gains.

Given these strong distributional impacts of the Uruguay Round, it is actually remarkable that an agreement was reached at all. Indeed, after the failure to achieve anything close to agreement by the 1990 target, many commentators began to pronounce the whole trade negotiation process to be dead. That in the end, agreement was achieved, if on a more modest scale than originally hoped, may be attributed to an interlocking set of political calculations. In the United States, the gains to agricultural exporters and the prospective gains to service exporters if the GATT opened the door to substantial liberalization helped offset the complaints of the clothing industry. Many developing countries supported the round because of the new opportunities it would offer to their own textile and clothing exports. Also, some of the "concessions" negotiated under the agreement were an excuse to make policy changes that would eventually have happened anyway. For example, the sheer expense of Europe's Common Agricultural Policy in a time of budget deficits made it ripe for cutting in any case.

An important factor in the final success of the round, however, was fear of what would happen if it failed. By 1993, protectionist currents were evidently running strong in the United States and elsewhere. Trade negotiators in countries that might otherwise have refused to go along with the agreement—such as France, Japan, or South Korea, in all of which powerful farm lobbies angrily opposed trade liberalization—therefore feared that failure to agree would be dangerous. That is, they feared a failed round would not merely mean lack of progress but substantial backsliding on the progress made toward free trade over the previous four decades.

CASE STUDY   The Salmon War

In July 2010, the 20-year-long Salmon War between Norway and Scotland finally came to an end. The dispute dates back to 1989, when the first restrictions on salmon imports from Norway were put into place. Scottish and Irish salmon farmers claimed that Norwegian fish were being exported to the EU at a lower price than the cost of production. At that time the average production cost was 3.7 euros per kilogram in Norway while it was 4.7 euros in Scotland. Later it was shown that the main reason for this difference was a higher rate of wastage in Scottish fish farms.

In response to the claim, the EU Commission proposed a tariff of 11.3 percent on Norwegian salmon. The proposal was repealed after Norway started to freeze and put into storage a large part of its production. In addition, 12 million smolts (young salmons) were destroyed. Both measures were intended to reduce the quantity sent to the market. However, Scottish and Irish fish farmers maintained their complaint, and in 1991 the EU fixed a minimum price on Norwegian salmon; later, a 9.88 percent tariff and an additional 3.8 percent subsidize tax were imposed.

Negotiations in 1997 between Norway and the EU resulted in the "Salmon Agreement." This agreement implied an export tax, a minimum price of 2.9 euros per kilogram, and a cap on the export quantity. Due to economics of scale the most efficient Norwegian salmon producers were able to sell for a price as low as 2.5 euros per kilogram and still make a profit. After an evaluation of Norwegian salmon producers in 2002, the EU scrapped the Salmon Agreement because it found no reason to punish Norway anymore. However, the conflict was not over.

In the spring of 2004, the European Union Salmon Producers Group, a minority group of Irish and Scottish salmon producers, with 20 percent of the EU production, asked for protection from import of salmon to the EU. As a result, a safeguard measurement was imposed in which Norway got an export quota combined with a tariff. The rate of the tariff varied from 6.8 to 24.5 percent. A minimum import price was also fixed. This led to protests from the Danish and French fish-processing industries, which use Norwegian salmon.

In 2006, Norway brought the antidumping measures before the WTO's settlement body. A year later, the WTO stated that the measures were inconsistent with international trade. The European Commission initiated a review of the measures and concluded that there were no grounds for continuing with the measures, as no evidence of dumping had been found. In 2010, the EU Council decided to repeal the antidumping measures on imports of farmed salmon from Norway.

The Doha Disappointment

The ninth major round of world trade negotiations began in 2001 with a ceremony in the Persian Gulf city of Doha. Like previous rounds, this one was marked by difficult negotiation. But as of the summer of 2010, it appeared that something new had happened: For the first time since the creation of the GATT, a round of trade negotiations appeared to have broken down with no agreement in sight.

It's important to understand that the apparent failure of the Doha Round does not undo the progress achieved in previous trade negotiations. Remember that the world trading system is a combination of "levers"—international trade negotiations that push trade liberalization forward—and "ratchets," mainly the practice of binding tariffs, which prevent backsliding. The levers seem to have failed in the latest trade round, but the ratchets are still in place: The reductions in tariff rates that took place in the previous eight rounds remain in effect. As a result, world trade remains much freer than at any previous point in modern history.

In fact, Doha's apparent failure owes a lot to the success of previous trade negotiations. Because previous negotiations had been so successful at reducing trade barriers, the remaining barriers to trade are fairly low, so that the potential gains from further trade liberalization are modest. Indeed, barriers to trade in most manufactured goods other than apparel and textiles are now more or less trivial. Most of the potential gains from a move to freer trade would come from reducing tariffs and export subsidies in agriculture—which has been the last sector to be liberalized because it's the most sensitive sector politically.

Table 10-4 illustrates this point. It shows a World Bank estimate of where the welfare gains from "full liberalization"—that is, the elimination of all remaining barriers to trade and export subsidies—would come from, and how they would be distributed across countries. In the modern world, agricultural goods account for less than 10 percent of total international trade. Nonetheless, according to the World Bank's

TABLE 10-4	**Percentage Distribution of Potential Gains from Free Trade**			
	Full Liberalization of:			
Economy	**Agriculture and Food**	**Textiles and Clothing**	**Other Merchandise**	**All Goods**
Developed	46	6	3	55
Developing	17	8	20	45
All	63	14	23	100

Source: Kym Anderson and Will Martin, "Agricultural Trade Reform and the Doha Agenda," *The World Economy* 28 (September 2005), pp. 1301–1327.

estimate, liberalizing agricultural trade would produce 63 percent of the total world gains from free trade for the world as a whole. And these gains are very hard to get at. As already described, farmers in rich countries are highly effective at getting favors from the political process.

The proposals that came closest to actually getting accepted in the Doha Round in fact fell far short of full liberalization. As a result, the likely gains even from a successful round would have been fairly small. Table 10-5 shows World Bank estimates of the welfare gains, as a percentage of income, under two scenarios of how Doha might have played out: an "ambitious" scenario that would have been very difficult to achieve, and a "less ambitious" scenario in which "sensitive" sectors would have been spared major liberalization. The gains for the world as a whole even in the ambitious scenario would have been only 0.18 percent of GDP; in the more plausible scenario, the gains would have been less than a third as large. For middle- and lower-income countries, the gains would have been even smaller. (Why would China have actually lost? Because, as

DO AGRICULTURAL SUBSIDIES HURT THE THIRD WORLD?

One of the major complaints of developing countries during the Doha negotiations was the continuing existence of large agricultural export and production subsidies in rich countries. The U.S. cotton subsidy, which depresses world cotton prices and therefore hurts cotton growers in West Africa, is the most commonly cited example.

But we learned in Chapter 9 that an export subsidy normally raises the welfare of the importing country, which gets to buy goods more cheaply. So shouldn't export subsidies by rich countries actually help poorer countries?

The answer is that in many cases they do. The estimates shown in Table 10-5 indicate that a successful Doha Round would actually have hurt China. Why? Because China, which exports manufactured goods and imports food and other

agricultural products, would be hurt by the removal of agricultural subsidies.

And it's not just China that may actually benefit from rich-country export subsidies. Some third world farmers are hurt by low prices of subsidized food exports from Europe and the United States—but urban residents in the third world benefit, and so do those farmers producing goods, such as coffee, that don't compete with the subsidized products.

Africa is a case in point. A survey of estimates of the likely effects of the Doha Round on low-income African nations found that, in most cases, African countries would actually be made worse off, because the negative effects of higher food prices would more than offset the gains from higher prices for crops such as cotton.

TABLE 10-5	Percentage Gains in Income under Two Doha Scenarios	
	Ambitious	**Less Ambitious**
High-income	0.20	0.05
Middle-income	0.10	0.00
China	−0.02	−0.05
Low-income	0.05	0.01
World	0.18	0.04

Source: See Table 10-4.

explained in the box above, it would have ended up paying higher prices for imported agricultural goods.)

The smallness of the numbers in Table 10-5 helps explain why the round failed. Poor countries saw little in the proposals for them; they pressed for much bigger concessions from rich countries. The governments of rich countries, in turn, refused to take the political risk of crossing powerful interest groups, especially farmers, without something in return—and poor countries were unwilling to offer the deep cuts in their remaining tariffs that might have been sufficient.

There was a more or less desperate attempt to revive the Doha Round in June 2007 because of the U.S. political calendar. Normally, Congress gives U.S. presidents a special privilege called trade promotion authority, also known informally as fast-track. When trade promotion authority is in effect, the president can send Congress a trade agreement and demand an up-or-down vote—members of Congress can't introduce amendments that, say, give special protection to industries in their home districts. Without this authority, trade agreements tend to get warped beyond recognition.

But President Bush's trade promotion authority was scheduled to expire at the end of July 2007, and a Democratic Congress wasn't going to give new authority to a lame-duck Republican president. Everyone realized, then, that a failure to reach a deal in the summer of 2007 would ensure no deal before well into the next president's administration. So a meeting was held in the German city of Potsdam between the four key players: the United States, the European Union, Brazil, and India (China sat on the sidelines). The result was an impasse. The United States and the European Union blamed Brazil and India for being unwilling to open their markets to manufactured goods, while Brazil and India accused the United States and the European Union of doing too little on agriculture.

There was one more attempt to revive the round, in July 2008. But talks collapsed after only eight days, over disagreements on agricultural trade among the United States, India, and China. At the time of writing, the whole round appeared to be in a state of suspension, with nobody admitting failure but no active negotiations underway.

Preferential Trading Agreements

The international trade agreements that we have described so far all involved a "nondiscriminatory" reduction in tariff rates. For example, when the United States agrees with Germany to lower its tariff on imported machinery, the new tariff rate applies to machinery from any nation rather than just imports from Germany. Such nondiscrimination is normal in most tariffs. Indeed, the United States grants many countries a status known formally as that of "most favored nation" (MFN), a guarantee that their exporters will pay tariffs no higher than that of the nation that pays the lowest. All countries granted MFN status thus pay the same rates. Tariff reductions under the GATT always—with one important exception—are made on an MFN basis.

There are some important cases, however, in which nations establish **preferential trading agreements** under which the tariffs they apply to each other's products are lower than the rates on the same goods coming from other countries. The GATT in general prohibits such agreements but makes a rather strange exception: It is against the rules for country A to have lower tariffs on imports from country B than on those from country C, but it is acceptable if countries B and C agree to have zero tariffs on each other's products. That is, the GATT forbids preferential trading agreements in general, as a violation of the MFN principle, but allows them if they lead to free trade between the agreeing countries.[7]

In general, two or more countries agreeing to establish free trade can do so in one of two ways. They can establish a **free trade area** in which each country's goods can be shipped to the other without tariffs, but in which the countries set tariffs against the outside world independently. Or they can establish a **customs union** in which the countries must agree on tariff rates. The North American Free Trade Agreement—which establishes free trade among Canada, the United States, and Mexico—creates a free trade area: There is no requirement in the agreement that, for example, Canada and Mexico have the same tariff rate on textiles from China. The European Union, on the other hand, is a full customs union. All of the countries must agree to charge the same tariff rate on each imported good. Each system has both advantages and disadvantages; these are discussed in the accompanying box.

Subject to the qualifications mentioned earlier in this chapter, tariff reduction is a good thing that raises economic efficiency. At first, it might seem that preferential tariff reductions are also good, if not as good as reducing tariffs all around. After all, isn't half a loaf better than none?

Perhaps surprisingly, this conclusion is too optimistic. It is possible for a country to make itself worse off by joining a customs union. The reason may be illustrated by a hypothetical example using Britain, France, and the United States. The United States is a low-cost producer of wheat ($4 per bushel), France a medium-cost producer ($6 per bushel), and Britain a high-cost producer ($8 per bushel). Both Britain and France maintain tariffs against all wheat imports. If Britain forms a customs union with France, the tariff against French, but not U.S., wheat will be abolished. Is this good or bad for Britain? To answer this, consider two cases.

First, suppose Britain's initial tariff was high enough to exclude wheat imports from either France or the United States. For example, with a tariff of $5 per bushel, it would cost $9 to import U.S. wheat and $11 to import French wheat, so British consumers would buy $8 British wheat instead. When the tariff on French wheat is eliminated, imports from France will replace British production. From Britain's point of view, this is a gain, because it costs $8 to produce a bushel of wheat domestically, while Britain needs to produce only $6 worth of export goods to pay for a bushel of French wheat.

---

[7]The logic here seems to be legal rather than economic. Nations are allowed to have free trade within their boundaries: Nobody insists that California wine pay the same tariff as French wine when it is shipped to New York. That is, the MFN principle does not apply within political units. But what is a political unit? The GATT sidesteps that potentially thorny question by allowing any group of economies to do what countries do, and establish free trade within some defined boundary.

FREE TRADE AREA VERSUS CUSTOMS UNION

The difference between a free trade area and a customs union is, in brief, that the first is politically straightforward but an administrative headache, while the second is just the opposite.

Consider first the case of a customs union. Once such a union is established, tariff administration is relatively easy: Goods must pay tariffs when they cross the border of the union, but from then on can be shipped freely between countries. A cargo that is unloaded at Marseilles or Rotterdam must pay duties there, but will not face any additional charges if it then goes by truck to Munich. To make this simple system work, however, the countries must agree on tariff rates: The duty must be the same whether the cargo is unloaded at Marseilles, Rotterdam, or, for that matter, Hamburg, because otherwise, importers would choose the point of entry that minimizes their fees. So a customs union requires that Germany, France, the Netherlands, and all the other countries agree to charge the same tariffs. This is not easily done: Countries are, in effect, ceding part of their sovereignty to a supranational entity, the European Union.

This has been possible in Europe for a variety of reasons, including the belief that economic unity would help cement the postwar political alliance between European democracies. (One of the founders of the European Union once joked that it should erect a statue of Joseph Stalin, without whose menace the Union might never have been created.) But elsewhere these conditions are lacking. The three nations that formed NAFTA would find it very difficult to cede control over tariffs to any supranational body; if nothing else, it would be hard to devise any arrangement that would give due weight to U.S. interests without effectively allowing the United States to dictate trade policy to Canada and Mexico. NAFTA, therefore, while it permits Mexican goods to enter the United States without tariffs and vice versa, does not require that Mexico and the United States adopt a common external tariff on goods they import from other countries.

This, however, raises a different problem. Under NAFTA, a shirt made by Mexican workers can be brought into the United States freely. But suppose the United States wants to maintain high tariffs on shirts imported from other countries, while Mexico does not impose similar tariffs. What is to prevent someone from shipping a shirt from, say, Bangladesh to Mexico, then putting it on a truck bound for Chicago?

The answer is that even though the United States and Mexico may have free trade, goods shipped from Mexico to the United States must still pass through a customs inspection. And they can enter the United States without duty only if they have documents proving that they are in fact Mexican goods, not transshipped imports from third countries.

But what is a Mexican shirt? If a shirt comes from Bangladesh, but Mexicans sew on the buttons, does that make it Mexican? Probably not. But if everything except the buttons were made in Mexico, it probably should be considered Mexican. The point is that administering a free trade area that is not a customs union requires not only that the countries continue to check goods at the border, but that they specify an elaborate set of "rules of origin" that determine whether a good is eligible to cross the border without paying a tariff.

As a result, free trade agreements like NAFTA impose a large burden of paperwork, which may be a significant obstacle to trade even when such trade is in principle free.

On the other hand, suppose the tariff was lower, for example, $3 per bushel, so that before joining the customs union, Britain bought its wheat from the United States (at a cost to consumers of $7 per bushel) rather than producing its own wheat. When the customs union is formed, consumers will buy French wheat at $6 rather than U.S. wheat at $7. So imports of wheat from the United States will cease. However,

U.S. wheat is really cheaper than French wheat; the $3 tax that British consumers must pay on U.S. wheat returns to Britain in the form of government revenue and is therefore not a net cost to the British economy. Britain will have to devote more resources to exports to pay for its wheat imports and will be worse off rather than better off.

DO TRADE PREFERENCES HAVE APPEAL?

The European Union has slipped repeatedly into bunches of trouble over the question of trade preferences for bananas.

Most of the world's banana exports come from several small Central American nations—the original "banana republics." Several European nations, however, have traditionally bought their bananas instead from their past or present West Indian colonies in the Caribbean. To protect the island producers, France and the United Kingdom have historically imposed import quotas against the "dollar bananas" of Central America, which are typically about 40 percent cheaper than the West Indian product. Germany, however, which has never had West Indian colonies, allowed free entry to dollar bananas.

With the integration of European markets after 1992, the existing banana regime became impossible to maintain because it was easy to import the cheaper dollar bananas into Germany and then ship them elsewhere in Europe. To prevent this outcome, the European Commission announced plans in 1993 to impose a new common European import quota against dollar bananas. Germany angrily protested the move and even denied its legality: The Germans pointed out that the Treaty of Rome, which established the European Community, contains an explicit guarantee (the "banana protocol") that Germany would be able to import bananas freely.

Why did the Germans go ape about bananas? During the years of communist rule in East Germany, bananas were a rare luxury. The sudden availability of inexpensive bananas after the fall of the Berlin Wall made them a symbol of freedom. So the German government was very unwilling to introduce a policy that would sharply increase banana prices.

In the end, the Germans grudgingly went along with a new, unified system of European trade preferences on bananas. But that did not end the controversy: In 1995, the United States entered the fray, claiming that by monkeying around with the existing system of preferences, the Europeans were hurting the interests not only of Central American nations but also those of a powerful U.S. corporation, the Chiquita Banana Company, whose CEO had donated large sums to both Democratic and Republican politicians.

In 1997, the World Trade Organization found that Europe's banana import regime violated international trade rules. Europe then imposed a somewhat revised regime, but this halfhearted attempt to resolve the banana split proved fruitless. The dispute with the United States escalated, with the United States eventually retaliating by imposing high tariffs on a variety of European goods, including designer handbags and pecorino cheese.

In 2001, Europe and the United States agreed on a plan to phase out the banana import quotas over time. The plan created much distress and alarm in Caribbean nations, which feared dire consequences from their loss of privileged access to the European market. But even then the story wasn't over. In January 2005, the European Union announced it would eliminate import quotas on bananas, but that it would *triple* the tariff on bananas that did not come from the so-called ACP countries (African, Caribbean, and Pacific—essentially, former European colonies). Latin American countries immediately moved to challenge the new tariff, and in December 2007 the WTO ruled that Europe's latest banana regime, like its predecessor, was illegal. (Chiquita's stock price jumped with the news.)

Finally, in December 2009, the European Union reached an agreement with Latin American banana producers. It wouldn't completely eliminate trade preferences, but it would cut tariffs on bananas by a third over a seven-year period.

This possibility of a loss is another example of the theory of the second best. Think of Britain as initially having two policies that distort incentives: a tariff against U.S. wheat and a tariff against French wheat. Although the tariff against French wheat may seem to distort incentives, it may actually help to offset the distortion of incentives resulting from the tariff against the United States by encouraging consumption of the cheaper U.S. wheat. Thus, removing the tariff on French wheat can actually reduce welfare.

Returning to our two cases, notice that Britain gains if the formation of a customs union leads to new trade—French wheat replacing domestic production—while it loses if the trade within the customs union simply replaces trade with countries outside the union. In the analysis of preferential trading arrangements, the first case is referred to as **trade creation**, while the second is **trade diversion**. Whether a customs union is desirable or undesirable depends on whether it mainly leads to trade creation or trade diversion.

CASE STUDY   Trade Diversion in South America

In 1991, four South American nations, Argentina, Brazil, Paraguay, and Uruguay, formed a free trade area known as Mercosur. The pact had an immediate and dramatic effect on trade: Within four years, the value of trade among the nations tripled. Leaders in the region proudly claimed Mercosur as a major success, part of a broader package of economic reform.

But while Mercosur clearly was successful in increasing intraregional trade, the theory of preferential trading areas tells us that this need not be a good thing: If the new trade came at the expense of trade that would otherwise have taken place with the rest of the world—that is, if the pact diverted trade instead of created it—it might actually have reduced welfare. And sure enough, in 1996 a study prepared by the World Bank's chief trade economist concluded that despite Mercosur's success in increasing regional trade—or rather, because that success came at the expense of other trade—the net effects on the economies involved were probably negative.

In essence, the report argued that as a result of Mercosur, consumers in the member countries were being induced to buy expensively produced manufactured goods from their neighbors rather than cheaper but heavily tariffed goods from other countries. In particular, because of Mercosur, Brazil's highly protected and somewhat inefficient auto industry had in effect acquired a captive market in Argentina, thus displacing imports from elsewhere, just like our text example in which French wheat displaces American wheat in the British market. "These findings," concluded the initial draft of the report, "appear to constitute the most convincing, and disturbing, evidence produced thus far concerning the potential adverse effects of regional trade arrangements."

But that is not what the final, published report said. The initial draft was leaked to the press and generated a firestorm of protest from Mercosur governments, Brazil in particular. Under pressure, the World Bank first delayed publication, then eventually released a version that included a number of caveats. Still, even in its published version, the report made a fairly strong case that Mercosur, if not entirely counterproductive, nonetheless has produced a considerable amount of trade diversion.

SUMMARY

1. Although few countries practice free trade, most economists continue to hold up free trade as a desirable policy. This advocacy rests on three lines of argument. First is a formal case for the efficiency gains from free trade that is simply the cost-benefit analysis of trade policy read in reverse. Second, many economists believe that free trade produces additional gains that go beyond this formal analysis. Finally, given the difficulty of translating complex economic analysis into real policies, even those who do not see free trade as the best imaginable policy see it as a useful rule of thumb.

2. There is an intellectually respectable case for deviating from free trade. One argument that is clearly valid in principle is that countries can improve their terms of trade through optimal tariffs and export taxes. This argument is not too important in practice, however. Small countries cannot have much influence on their import or export prices, so they cannot use tariffs or other policies to raise their terms of trade. Large countries, on the other hand, can influence their terms of trade, but in imposing tariffs, they run the risk of disrupting trade agreements and provoking retaliation.

3. The other argument for deviating from free trade rests on domestic market failures. If some domestic market, such as the labor market, fails to function properly, deviating from free trade can sometimes help reduce the consequences of this malfunctioning. The theory of the second best states that if one market fails to work properly, it is no longer optimal for the government to abstain from intervention in other markets. A tariff may raise welfare if there is a marginal social benefit to production of a good that is not captured by producer surplus measures.

4. Although market failures are probably common, the domestic market failure argument should not be applied too freely. First, it is an argument for domestic policies rather than trade policies; tariffs are always an inferior, "second-best" way to offset domestic market failure, which is always best treated at its source. Furthermore, market failure is difficult to analyze well enough to be sure of the appropriate policy recommendation.

5. In practice, trade policy is dominated by considerations of income distribution. No single way of modeling the politics of trade policy exists, but several useful ideas have been proposed. Political scientists often argue that policies are determined by competition among political parties that try to attract as many votes as possible. In the simplest case, this leads to the adoption of policies that serve the interests of the median voter. While useful for thinking about many issues, however, this approach seems to yield unrealistic predictions for trade policies, which typically favor the interest of small, concentrated groups over that of the general public. Economists and political scientists generally explain this by appealing to the problem of collective action. Because individuals may have little incentive to act politically on behalf of groups to which they belong, those groups that are well organized—typically small groups with a lot at stake—are often able to get policies that serve their interests at the expense of the majority.

6. If trade policy were made on a purely domestic basis, progress toward freer trade would be very difficult to achieve. In fact, however, industrial countries have achieved substantial reductions in tariffs through a process of international negotiation. International negotiation helps the cause of tariff reduction in two ways: It helps broaden the constituency for freer trade by giving exporters a direct stake, and it helps governments avoid the mutually disadvantageous trade wars that internationally uncoordinated policies could bring.

7. Although some progress was made in the 1930s toward trade liberalization via bilateral agreements, since World War II international coordination has taken place primarily via multilateral agreements under the auspices of the General Agreement on Tariffs and Trade. The GATT, which comprises both a bureaucracy and a set of rules of conduct, is the central institution of the international trading system. The most recent worldwide GATT agreement also set up a new organization, the World Trade Organization (WTO), to monitor and enforce the agreement.

8. In addition to the overall reductions in tariffs that have taken place through multilateral negotiation, some groups of countries have negotiated preferential trading agreements under which they lower tariffs with respect to each other but not the rest of the world. Two kinds of preferential trading agreements are allowed under the GATT: customs unions, in which the members of the agreement set up common external tariffs, and free trade areas, in which members do not charge tariffs on each other's products but set their own tariff rates against the outside world. Either kind of agreement has ambiguous effects on economic welfare. If joining such an agreement leads to replacement of high-cost domestic production by imports from other members of the agreement—the case of trade creation—a country gains. But if joining leads to the replacement of low-cost imports from outside the zone with higher-cost goods from member nations—the case of trade diversion—a country loses.

KEY TERMS

binding, p. 279
collective action, p. 272
customs union, p. 288
domestic market failures, p. 267
efficiency case for free trade, p. 261
free trade area, p. 288
General Agreement on Tariffs and Trade (GATT), p. 279

international negotiation, p. 277
marginal social benefit, p. 267
median voter, p. 271
optimum tariff, p. 266
political argument for free trade, p. 263
preferential trading agreement, p. 288
Prisoner's dilemma, p. 278
rent seeking, p. 263

terms of trade argument for a tariff, p. 266
theory of the second best, p. 268
trade creation, p. 291
trade diversion, p. 291
trade round, p. 279
trade war, p. 277
World Trade Organization (WTO), p. 279

PROBLEMS

MyEconLab

1. According to the WTO and its MFN principle, all preferential tariffs granted to a member have to be extended to all others. However, there are exceptions to this rule; and this is where all preferential trade agreements originate. The EU, for example, is an exception, even if it is of the most complete kind. List the typologies existing in this area and how would a country select which to belong to? Explain with an example.

2. Which of the following are potentially valid arguments for tariffs or export subsidies, and which are not? Explain your answers.

   a. "The more oil the United States imports, the higher the price of oil will go in the next world shortage."

   b. "The growing exports of off-season fruit from Chile, which now accounts for 80 percent of the U.S. supply of such produce as winter grapes, are contributing to sharply falling prices of these former luxury goods."

c. "U.S. farm exports don't just mean higher incomes for farmers—they mean higher income for everyone who sells goods and services to the U.S. farm sector."

d. "Semiconductors are the crude oil of technology; if we don't produce our own chips, the flow of information that is crucial to every industry that uses micro-electronics will be impaired."

e. "The real price of timber has fallen 40 percent, and thousands of timber workers have been forced to look for other jobs."

3. A small country can import a good at a world price of 10 per unit. The domestic supply curve of the good is

$$S = 20 + 10P$$

The demand curve is

$$D = 400 - 5P$$

In addition, each unit of production yields a marginal social benefit of 10.

a. Calculate the total effect on welfare of a tariff of 5 per unit levied on imports.

b. Calculate the total effect of a production subsidy of 5 per unit.

c. Why does the production subsidy produce a greater gain in welfare than the tariff?

d. What would the optimal production subsidy be?

4. Suppose demand and supply are exactly as described in problem 3, but there is no marginal social benefit to production. However, for political reasons the government counts a dollar's worth of gain to producers as being worth $3 of either consumer gain or government revenue. Calculate the effects *on the government's objective* of a tariff of 5 per unit.

5. Upon Poland's entering the European Union, suppose it is discovered that the cost of automobile production in Poland is €20,000 while it is €30,000 in Germany. Suppose the EU, which has a customs union, has an X percent tariff on automobiles and the costs of production are equal to Y (valued in euros) in Japan. Comment on whether the addition of Poland to the European Union would result in trade *creation* or trade *diversion* under the following scenarios:

a. $X = 50\%$ and $Y = €18,000$

b. $X = 100\%$ and $Y = €18,000$

c. $X = 100\%$ and $Y = €12,000$

6. "There is no point in the United States complaining about trade policies in Japan and Europe. Each country has a right to do whatever is in its own best interest. Instead of complaining about foreign trade policies, the United States should let other countries go their own way, and give up our own prejudices about free trade and follow suit." Discuss both the economics and the political economy of this viewpoint.

7. What is a rent-seeking decision and how is it applied in practice?

8. Free trade is a precise political choice, with arguments for and against it. One of them includes providing incentives to companies to internationalize themselves and export to new countries, thus fostering learning and innovation, which eventually benefits the whole economy and helps competitiveness. Discuss this approach with examples.

9. One argument against free trade is the terms of trade—since an export subsidy worsens the terms, it has to be conceived as a negative one, a tax paid by foreigners. However, the optimum export tax is one that maximizes national gain without harming export. How would it work in the case of a commodity exporting country like Indonesia?

FURTHER READINGS

W. Max Corden. *Trade Policy and Economic Welfare*. Oxford: Clarendon Press, 1974. The classic survey of economic arguments for and against protection.

I. M. Destler. *American Trade Politics*, 4th edition. Washington, D.C.: Peterson Institute for International Economics, 2005. A comprehensive portrait of the real-world process of trade policy making, and its evolution over time.

Gene M. Grossman and Elhanan Helpman. *Interest Groups and Trade Policy*. Princeton: Princeton University Press, 2002. A collection of papers and case studies on modern political economy models of trade policy.

Jeffrey Schott. *The Uruguay Round: An Assessment*. Washington, D.C.: Institute for International Economics, 1994. A mercifully brief and readable survey of the issues and accomplishments of the most recent GATT round, together with a survey of much of the relevant research.

Peter Van den Bossche. *The Law and Policy of the World Trade Organization*. Cambridge: Cambridge University Press, 2008. A comprehensive survey, with texts and other materials, of the legal framework of international trade.

World Trade Organization, *Understanding the WTO*. Geneva: World Trade Organization, 2007. A useful self-survey of the institution's role and history.

MyEconLab Can Help You Get a Better Grade

MyEconLab   If your exam were tomorrow, would you be ready? For each chapter, MyEconLab Practice Tests and Study Plans pinpoint sections you have mastered and those you need to study. That way, you are more efficient with your study time, and you are better prepared for your exams.

To see how it works, turn to page 33 and then go to

www.myeconlab.com

Proving that the Optimum Tariff Is Positive

A tariff always improves the terms of trade of a large country but at the same time distorts production and consumption. This appendix shows that for a sufficiently small tariff, the terms of trade gain is always larger than the distortion loss. Thus, there is always an optimal tariff that is positive.

To make the point, we focus on the case where all demand and supply curves are *linear*, that is, are straight lines.

Demand and Supply

We assume that Home, the importing country, has a demand curve whose equation is

$$D = a - b\widetilde{P}, \tag{10A-1}$$

where $\widetilde{P}$ is the internal price of the good, and a supply curve whose equation is

$$Q = e + f\widetilde{P}. \tag{10A-2}$$

Home's import demand is equal to the difference between domestic demand and supply,

$$D - Q = (a - e) - (b + f)\widetilde{P}. \tag{10A-3}$$

Foreign's export supply is also a straight line,

$$(Q^* - D^*) = g + hP_W, \tag{10A-4}$$

where P_W is the world price. The internal price in Home will exceed the world price by the tariff

$$\widetilde{P} = P_W + t. \tag{10A-5}$$

The Tariff and Prices

A tariff drives a wedge between internal and world prices, driving the internal Home price up and the world price down (Figure 10A-1).

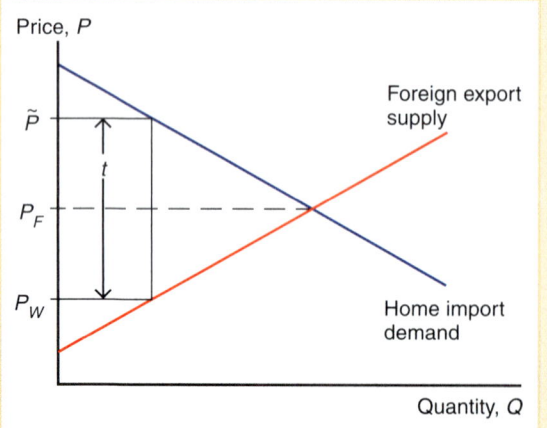

FIGURE 10A-1

Effects of a Tariff on Prices

In a linear model, we can calculate the exact effect of a tariff on prices.

Price, P

$\widetilde{P}$

t

P_F

P_W

Foreign export supply

Home import demand

Quantity, Q

In world equilibrium, Home import demand equals Foreign export supply:

$$(a - e) - (b + f) \times (P_W + t) = g + hP_W. \tag{10A-6}$$

Let P_F be the world price that would prevail if there were no tariff. Then a tariff, t, will raise the internal price to

$$\widetilde{P} = P_F + th/(b + f + h), \tag{10A-7}$$

while lowering the world price to

$$P_W = P_F - t(b + f)/(b + f + h). \tag{10A-8}$$

(For a small country, foreign supply is highly elastic; that is, h is very large. So for a small country, a tariff will have little effect on the world price while raising the domestic price almost one-for-one.)

The Tariff and Domestic Welfare

We now use what we have learned to derive the effects of a tariff on Home's welfare (Figure 10A-2). Q^1 and D^1 represent the free trade levels of consumption and production. With a tariff, the internal price rises, with the result that Q rises to Q^2 and D falls to D^2, where

$$Q^2 = Q^1 + tfh/(b + f + h) \tag{10A-9}$$

and

$$D^2 = D^1 - tbh/(b + f + h). \tag{10A-10}$$

The gain from a lower world price is the area of the rectangle in Figure 10A-2, the fall in the price multiplied by the level of imports after the tariff:

$$\text{Gain} = (D^2 - Q^2) \times t(b + f)/(b + f + h) \tag{10A-11}$$

$$= t \times (D^1 - Q^1) \times (b + f)/(b + f + h) - (t)^2 \times h(b + f)^2/(b + f + h)^2.$$

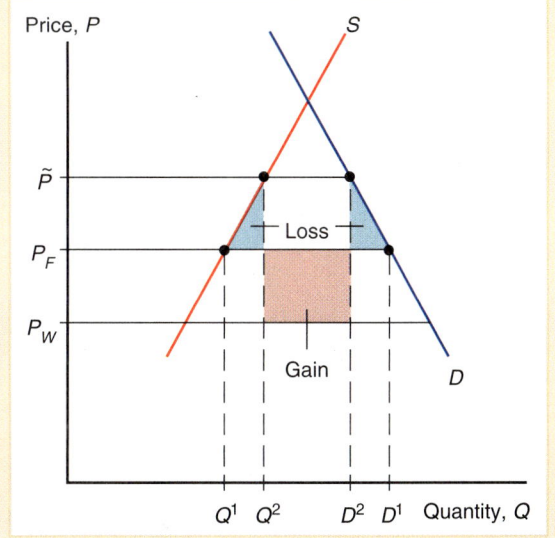

FIGURE 10A-2

Welfare Effects of a Tariff

The net benefit of a tariff is equal to the area of the colored rectangle minus the area of the two shaded triangles.

The loss from distorted consumption is the sum of the areas of the two triangles in Figure 10A-2:

$$\text{Loss} = (1/2) \times (Q^2 - Q^1) \times (\tilde{P} - P_F) + (1/2) \times (D^1 - D^2) \times (\tilde{P} - P_F)$$

$$= (t)^2 \times (b + f) \times (h)^2 / 2(b + f + h)^2. \tag{10A-12}$$

The net effect on welfare, therefore, is

$$\text{Gain} - \text{loss} = t \times U - (t)^2 \times V, \tag{10A-13}$$

where U and V are complicated expressions that are, however, independent of the level of the tariff and positive. That is, the net effect is the sum of a positive number times the tariff rate and a negative number times the *square* of the tariff rate.

We can now see that when the tariff is small enough, the net effect must be positive. The reason is that when we make a number smaller, the square of that number gets smaller faster than the number itself. Suppose a tariff of 20 percent turns out to produce a net loss. Then try a tariff of 10 percent. The positive term in that tariff's effect will be only half as large as with a 20 percent tariff, but the negative part will be only one-quarter as large. If the net effect is still negative, try a 5 percent tariff; this will again reduce the negative effect twice as much as the positive effect. At some sufficiently low tariff, the negative effect will have to be outweighed by the positive effect.

CHAPTER 11

TRADE POLICY IN DEVELOPING COUNTRIES

So far, we have analyzed the instruments of trade policy and its objectives without specifying the context—that is, without saying much about the country undertaking these policies. Each country has its own distinctive history and issues, but in discussing economic policy, one difference between countries becomes obvious: their income levels. As Table 11-1 suggests, nations differ greatly in their per-capita incomes. At one end of the spectrum are the developed or advanced nations, a club whose members include Western Europe, several countries largely settled by Europeans (including the United States), and Japan; these countries have per-capita incomes that in some cases exceed $40,000 per year. Most of the world's population, however, live in nations that are substantially poorer. The income range among these **developing countries**[1] is very wide. Some of these countries, such as South Korea, are now considered members of a group of "newly industrialized" nations with de facto developed-country status, both in terms of official statistics and in the way they think about themselves. Others, such as Bangladesh, remain desperately poor. Nonetheless, for virtually all developing countries, the attempt to close the income gap with more advanced nations has been a central concern of economic policy.

Why are some countries so much poorer than others? Why have some countries that were poor a generation ago succeeded in making dramatic progress, while others have not? These are deeply disputed questions, and to try to answer them—or even to describe at length the answers that economists have proposed over the years—would take us outside the scope of this book. What we can say, however, is that changing views about economic development have had a major role in determining trade policy.

For about 30 years after World War II, trade policies in many developing countries were strongly influenced by the beliefs that the key to economic development was the creation of a strong manufacturing sector, and that the best way to create that manufacturing sector was to protect domestic manufacturers from

---

[1]*Developing country* is a term used by international organizations that has now become standard, even though some "developing" countries have gone through extended periods of declining living standards. A more descriptive but less polite term is *less-developed countries* (LDCs).

MyEconLab Real-time data

TABLE 11-1	Gross Domestic Product Per Capita, 2009 (dollars, adjusted for differences in price levels)
United States	49,428
Germany	40,511
Japan	37,449
South Korea	32,954
Mexico	14,943
China	10,371
Bangladesh	1,929

Source: Conference Board Total Economy Database.

international competition. The first part of this chapter describes the rationale for this strategy of import-substituting industrialization, as well as the critiques of that strategy that became increasingly common after about 1970 and the emergence in the late 1980s of a new conventional wisdom that stressed the virtues of free trade. The second part of the chapter describes the remarkable shift in developing-country trade policy that has taken place since the 1980s.

Finally, while economists have debated the reasons for persistent large income gaps between nations, since the mid-1960s a widening group of Asian nations has astonished the world by achieving spectacular rates of economic growth. The third part of this chapter is devoted to the interpretation of this "Asian miracle" and its (much disputed) implications for international trade policy.

LEARNING GOALS

After reading this chapter, you will be able to:

- Recapitulate the case for protectionism as it has been historically practiced in developing countries and discuss import-substitution-led industrialization and the "infant industry" argument.
- Summarize the basic ideas behind "economic dualism" and its relationship to international trade.
- Discuss the recent economic history of the Asian countries, such as China and India, and detail the relationship between their rapid economic growth and their participation in international trade.

Import-Substituting Industrialization

From World War II until the 1970s, many developing countries attempted to accelerate their development by limiting imports of manufactured goods, in order to foster a manufacturing sector serving the domestic market. This strategy became popular for a number of reasons, but theoretical economic arguments for import substitution played an important role in its rise. Probably the most important of these arguments was the *infant industry argument*, which we mentioned in Chapter 7.

The Infant Industry Argument

According to the infant industry argument, developing countries have a *potential* comparative advantage in manufacturing, but new manufacturing industries in developing countries cannot initially compete with well-established manufacturing in developed countries. To allow manufacturing to get a toehold, then, governments should temporarily support new industries until they have grown strong enough to meet international competition. Thus, it makes sense, according to this argument, to use tariffs or import quotas as temporary measures to get industrialization started. It is a historical fact that some of the world's largest market economies began their industrialization behind trade barriers: The United States had high tariff rates on manufacturing in the 19th century, while Japan had extensive import controls until the 1970s.

Problems with the Infant Industry Argument   The infant industry argument seems highly plausible, and in fact it has been persuasive to many governments. Yet economists have pointed out many pitfalls in the argument, suggesting that it must be used cautiously.

First, it is not always a good idea to try to move today into the industries that will have a comparative advantage in the future. Suppose a country that is currently labor-abundant is in the process of accumulating capital. When it accumulates enough capital, it will have a comparative advantage in capital-intensive industries. However, that does not mean it should try to develop these industries immediately. In the 1980s, for example, South Korea became an exporter of automobiles; it would probably not have been a good idea for South Korea to have tried to develop its auto industry in the 1960s, when capital and skilled labor were still very scarce.

Second, protecting manufacturing does no good unless the protection itself helps make industry competitive. For example, Pakistan and India have protected their manufacturing sectors for decades and have recently begun to develop significant exports of manufactured goods. The goods they export, however, are light manufactures like textiles, not the heavy manufactures that they protected; a good case can be made that they would have developed their manufactured exports even if they had never protected manufacturing. Some economists have warned of the case of the "pseudoinfant industry," in which an industry is initially protected, then becomes competitive for reasons that have nothing to do with the protection. In this case, infant industry protection ends up looking like a success but may actually have been a net cost to the economy.

More generally, the fact that it is costly and time-consuming to build up an industry is not an argument for government intervention unless there is some domestic market failure. If an industry is supposed to be able to earn high enough returns for capital, labor, and other factors of production to be worth developing, then why don't private investors develop the industry without government help? Sometimes, it is argued that private investors take into account only the current returns in an industry and fail to take account of the future prospects, but this argument is not consistent with market behavior. In advanced countries at least, investors often back projects whose returns are uncertain and lie far in the future. (Consider, for example, the U.S. biotechnology industry, which attracted hundreds of millions of dollars of capital years before it made even a single commercial sale.)

Market Failure Justifications for Infant Industry Protection   To justify the infant industry argument, it is necessary to go beyond the plausible but questionable view that industries always need to be sheltered when they are new. Whether infant industry protection is justified depends on an analysis of the kind we discussed in Chapter 10. That is, the argument for protecting an industry in its early growth must be related to some particular set of market failures that prevent private markets from developing the industry as rapidly as they should. Sophisticated proponents of the infant industry argument have identified two market failures as reasons why infant industry protection may be a good idea: **imperfect capital markets** and the problem of **appropriability**.

The *imperfect capital markets justification* for infant industry protection is as follows: If a developing country does not have a set of financial institutions (such as efficient stock markets and banks) that would allow savings from traditional sectors (such as agriculture) to be used to finance investment in new sectors (such as manufacturing), then growth of new industries will be restricted by the ability of firms in these industries to earn current profits. Thus, low initial profits will be an obstacle to investment even if the long-term returns on the investment will be high. The first-best policy is to create a better capital market, but protection of new industries, which would raise profits and thus allow more rapid growth, can be justified as a second-best policy option.

The *appropriability argument* for infant industry protection can take many forms, but all have in common the idea that firms in a new industry generate social benefits for which they are not compensated. For example, the firms that first enter an industry may have to incur "start-up" costs of adapting technology to local circumstances or of opening new markets. If other firms are able to follow their lead without incurring these start-up costs, the pioneers will be prevented from reaping any returns from these outlays. Thus, pioneering firms may, in addition to producing physical output, create intangible benefits (such as knowledge or new markets) in which they are unable to establish property rights. In some cases the social benefits from creation of a new industry will exceed its costs, yet because of the problem of appropriability, no private entrepreneurs will be willing to enter. The first best answer is to compensate firms for their intangible contributions. When this is not possible, however, there is a second-best case for encouraging entry into a new industry by using tariffs or other trade policies.

Both the imperfect capital markets argument and the appropriability case for infant industry protection are clearly special cases of the *market failure* justification for interfering with free trade. The difference is that in this case, the arguments apply specifically to *new* industries rather than to *any* industry. The general problems with the market failure approach remain, however. In practice it is difficult to evaluate which industries really warrant special treatment, and there are risks that a policy intended to promote development will end up being captured by special interests. There are many stories of infant industries that have never grown up and remain dependent on protection.

Promoting Manufacturing Through Protection

Although there are doubts about the infant industry argument, many developing countries have seen this argument as a compelling reason to provide special support for the development of manufacturing industries. In principle, such support could be provided in a variety of ways. For example, countries could provide subsidies to manufacturing production in general, or they could focus their efforts on subsidies for the export of some manufactured goods in which they believe they can develop a comparative advantage. In most developing countries, however, the basic strategy for industrialization has been to develop industries oriented toward the domestic market by using trade restrictions such as tariffs and quotas to encourage the replacement of imported manufactures by domestic products. The strategy of encouraging domestic industry by limiting imports of manufactured goods is known as the strategy of **import-substituting industrialization**.

One might ask why a choice needs to be made. Why not encourage both import substitution and exports? The answer goes back to the general equilibrium analysis of tariffs in Chapter 6: A tariff that reduces imports also necessarily reduces exports. By protecting import-substituting industries, countries draw resources away from actual or potential export sectors. So a country's choice to seek to substitute for imports is also a choice to discourage export growth.

The reasons why import substitution rather than export growth has usually been chosen as an industrialization strategy are a mixture of economics and politics. First, until the 1970s many developing countries were skeptical about the possibility of exporting manufactured goods (although this skepticism also calls into question the infant industry argument for manufacturing protection). They believed that industrialization was necessarily based on a substitution of domestic industry for imports rather than on a growth of manufactured exports. Second, in many cases, import-substituting industrialization policies dovetailed naturally with existing political biases. We have already noted the case of Latin American nations that were compelled to develop substitutes for imports during the 1930s because of the Great Depression and during the first half of the 1940s because of the wartime disruption of trade (Chapter 10). In these countries, import substitution directly benefited powerful, established interest groups, while export promotion had no natural constituency.

It is also worth pointing out that some advocates of a policy of import substitution believed that the world economy was rigged against new entrants—that the advantages of established industrial nations were simply too great to be overcome by newly industrializing economies. Extreme proponents of this view called for a general policy of delinking developing countries from advanced nations; but even among milder advocates of protectionist development strategies, the view that the international economic system systematically works against the interests of developing countries remained common until the 1980s.

The 1950s and 1960s saw the high tide of import-substituting industrialization. Developing countries typically began by protecting final stages of industry, such as food processing and automobile assembly. In the larger developing countries, domestic products almost completely replaced imported consumer goods (although the manufacturing was often carried out by foreign multinational firms). Once the possibilities for replacing consumer goods imports had been exhausted, these countries turned to protection of intermediate goods, such as automobile bodies, steel, and petrochemicals.

In most developing economies, the import-substitution drive stopped short of its logical limit: Sophisticated manufactured goods such as computers, precision machine tools, and so on continued to be imported. Nonetheless, the larger countries pursuing import-substituting industrialization reduced their imports to remarkably low levels. The most extreme case was India: In the early 1970s, India's imports of products other than oil were only about 3 percent of GDP.

As a strategy for encouraging growth of manufacturing, import-substituting industrialization clearly worked. Latin American economies began generating almost as large a share of their output from manufacturing as advanced nations. (India generated less, but only because its poorer population continued to spend a high proportion of its income on food.) For these countries, however, the encouragement of manufacturing was not a goal in itself; rather, it was a means to the end goal of

CASE STUDY

Mexico Abandons Import-Substituting Industrialization

In 1994, Mexico, along with Canada and the United States, signed the North American Free Trade Agreement (NAFTA)—an agreement that, as we explain in Chapter 12, has become highly controversial. But Mexico's turn from import-substituting industrialization to relatively free trade actually began almost a decade before the country joined NAFTA.

Mexico's turn toward free trade reversed a half-century of history. Like many developing countries, Mexico turned protectionist during the Great Depression of the 1930s. After World War II, the policy of industrialization to serve a protected domestic market became explicit. Throughout the 1950s and 1960s, trade barriers were raised higher, as Mexican industry became increasingly self-sufficient. By the 1970s, Mexico had largely restricted imports of manufactured goods to such items as sophisticated machinery that could not be produced domestically except at prohibitive cost.

Mexican industry produced very little for export; the country's foreign earnings came largely from oil and tourism, with the only significant manufacturing exports coming from *maquiladoras*, special factories located near the U.S. border that were exempt from some trade restrictions.

By the late 1970s, however, Mexico was experiencing economic difficulties, including rising inflation and growing foreign debt. The problems came to a head in 1982, when the country found itself unable to make full payments on its foreign debt. This led to a prolonged economic crisis—and to a radical change in policy.

Between 1985 and 1988, Mexico drastically reduced tariffs and removed most of the import quotas that had previously protected its industry. The new policy goal was to make Mexico a major exporter of manufactured goods, closely integrated with the U.S. economy. The coming of NAFTA in the 1990s did little to reduce trade barriers, because Mexico had already done the heavy lifting of trade liberalization in the 1980s. NAFTA did, however, assure investors that the change in policy would not be reversed.

So how did the policy change work? Exports did indeed boom. In 1980, Mexican exports were only 10.7 percent of GDP—and much of that was oil. By 2012, exports were up to 34 percent of GDP, primarily manufactures. Today, Mexican manufacturing, rather than being devoted to serving the small domestic market, is very much part of an integrated North American manufacturing system.

The results for the overall Mexican economy have, however, been somewhat disappointing. Per-capita income has risen over the past 25 years, but the rate of growth has actually been lower than that achieved when Mexico was pursuing a policy of import-substituting industrialization.

Does this mean that trade liberalization was a mistake? Not necessarily. Most (but not all) economists who have looked at Mexican performance blame the relatively low growth on such factors as poor education. But the fact is that Mexico's turn away from import substitution, while highly successful at making Mexico an exporting nation, has not delivered as much as hoped in terms of broader economic progress.

economic development. Did import-substituting industrialization promote economic development? Here serious doubts appeared. Although many economists approved of import-substitution measures in the 1950s and early 1960s, since the 1960s, import-substituting industrialization has come under increasingly harsh criticism. Indeed, much of the focus of economic analysts and of policy makers has shifted from trying to encourage import substitution to trying to correct the damage done by bad import-substitution policies.

Results of Favoring Manufacturing: Problems of Import-Substituting Industrialization

Import-substituting industrialization began to lose favor when it became clear that countries pursuing import substitution were not catching up with advanced countries. In fact, some developing countries lagged further behind advanced countries even as they developed a domestic manufacturing base. India was poorer relative to the United States in 1980 than it had been in 1950, the first year after it achieved independence.

Why didn't import-substituting industrialization work the way it was supposed to? The most important reason seems to be that the infant industry argument is not as universally valid as many people had assumed. A period of protection will not create a competitive manufacturing sector if there are fundamental reasons why a country lacks a comparative advantage in manufacturing. Experience has shown that the reasons for failure to develop often run deeper than a simple lack of experience with manufacturing. Poor countries lack skilled labor, entrepreneurs, and managerial competence and have problems of social organization that make it difficult for these countries to maintain reliable supplies of everything from spare parts to electricity. These problems may not be beyond the reach of economic policy, but they cannot be solved by *trade* policy: An import quota can allow an inefficient manufacturing sector to survive, but it cannot directly make that sector more efficient. The infant industry argument is that, given the temporary shelter of tariffs or quotas, the manufacturing industries of less-developed nations will learn to be efficient. In practice, this is not always, or even usually, true.

With import substitution failing to deliver the promised benefits, attention turned to the costs of the policies used to promote industry. On this issue, a growing body of evidence showed that the protectionist policies of many less-developed countries badly distorted incentives. Part of the problem was that many countries used excessively complex methods to promote their infant industries. That is, they used elaborate and often overlapping import quotas, exchange controls, and domestic content rules instead of simple tariffs. It is often difficult to determine how much protection an administrative regulation is actually providing, and studies show that the degree of protection is often both higher and more variable across industries than the government intended. As Table 11-2 shows, some industries in Latin America and South Asia were protected by regulations that were the equivalent of tariff rates of 200 percent or more. These high rates of effective protection allowed industries to exist even when their cost of production was three or four times the price of the imports they replaced. Even the most enthusiastic advocates of market failure arguments for protection find rates of effective protection that high difficult to defend.

TABLE 11-2	Effective Protection of Manufacturing in Some Developing Countries (percent)
Mexico (1960)	26
Philippines (1965)	61
Brazil (1966)	113
Chile (1961)	182
Pakistan (1963)	271

Source: Bela Balassa, *The Structure of Protection in Developing Countries* (Baltimore: Johns Hopkins Press, 1971), p. 82.

A further cost that has received considerable attention is the tendency of import restrictions to promote production at an inefficiently small scale. The domestic markets of even the largest developing countries are only a small fraction of the size of that of the United States or the European Union. Often, the whole domestic market is not large enough to allow an efficient-scale production facility. Yet, when this small market is protected, say, by an import quota, if only a single firm were to enter the market, it could earn monopoly profits. The competition for these profits typically leads several firms to enter a market that does not really have enough room even for one, and production is carried out at a highly inefficient scale. The answer to the problem of scale for small countries is, as noted in Chapter 8, to specialize in the production and export of a limited range of products and to import other goods. Import-substituting industrialization eliminates this option by focusing industrial production on the domestic market.

Those who criticize import-substituting industrialization also argue that it has aggravated other problems, such as income inequality and unemployment.

By the late 1980s, the critique of import-substituting industrialization had been widely accepted, not only by economists but also by international organizations like the World Bank—and even by policy makers in the developing countries themselves. Statistical evidence appeared to suggest that developing countries that followed relatively free trade policies had, on average, grown more rapidly than those that followed protectionist policies (although this statistical evidence has been challenged by some economists).[2] This intellectual sea change led to a considerable shift in actual policies, as many developing countries removed import quotas and lowered tariff rates.

Trade Liberalization since 1985

Beginning in the mid-1980s, a number of developing countries moved to lower tariff rates and removed import quotas and other restrictions on trade. The shift of developing countries toward freer trade is the big trade policy story of the past two and a half decades.

---

[2]See Francisco Rodriguez and Dani Rodrik, "Trade Policy and Economic Growth: A Skeptic's Guide to the Cross-National Evidence," in Ben Bernanke and Kenneth S. Rogoff, eds., *NBER Macroeconomics Annual 2000*. Cambridge, MA: MIT Press for NBER, 2001.

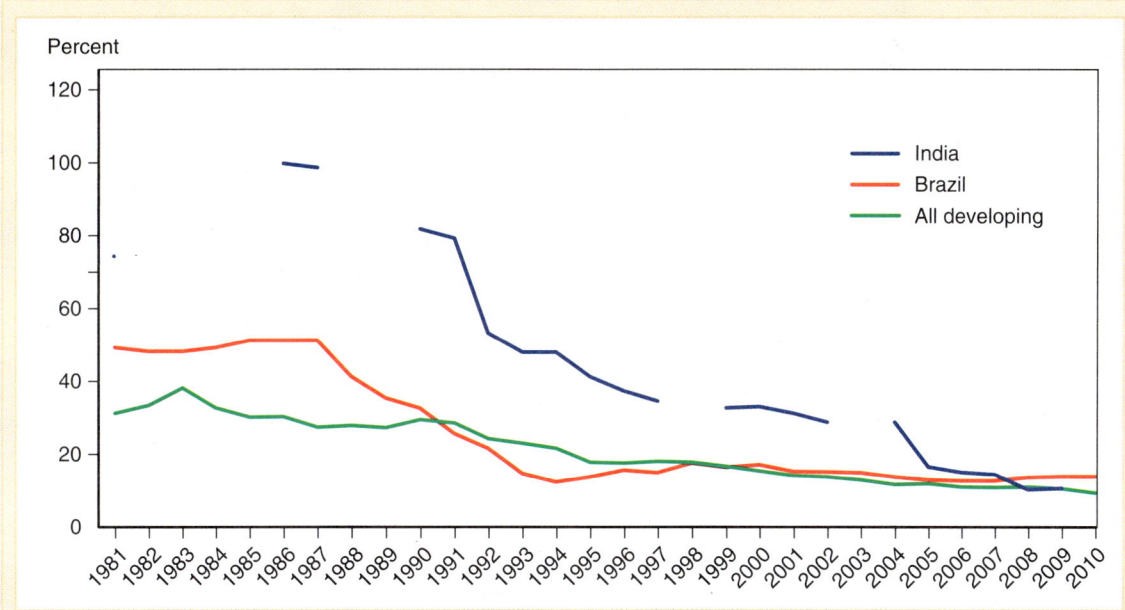

FIGURE 11-1

Tariff Rates in Developing Countries

One measure of the shift away from import-substituting industrialization is the sharp drop in tariff rates in developing countries, which have fallen from an average of more than 30 percent in the early 1980s to only about 10 percent today. Countries that once had especially strong import-substitution policies, like India and Brazil, have also seen the steepest declines in tariff rates.

Source: World Bank.

After 1985, many developing countries reduced tariffs, removed import quotas, and in general opened their economies to import competition. Figure 11-1 shows trends in tariff rates for an average of all developing countries and for two important developing countries, India and Brazil, which once relied heavily on import substitution as a development strategy. As you can see, there has been a dramatic fall in tariff rates in those two countries. Similar if less drastic changes in trade policy took place in many other developing countries.

Trade liberalization in developing countries had two clear effects. One was a dramatic increase in the volume of trade. Figure 11-2 plots exports and imports of developing countries, measured as percentages of GDP, since 1970. As you can see, the share of trade in GDP has tripled over that period, with most of the growth happening after 1985.

The other effect was a change in the nature of trade. Before the change in trade policy, developing countries mainly exported agricultural and mining products. But as we saw in Figure 2-6, that changed after 1980: The share of manufactured goods in developing-country exports surged, coming to dominate the exports of the biggest developing economies.

But trade liberalization, like import substitution, was intended as a means to an end rather than a goal in itself. As we've seen, import substitution fell out of favor as it

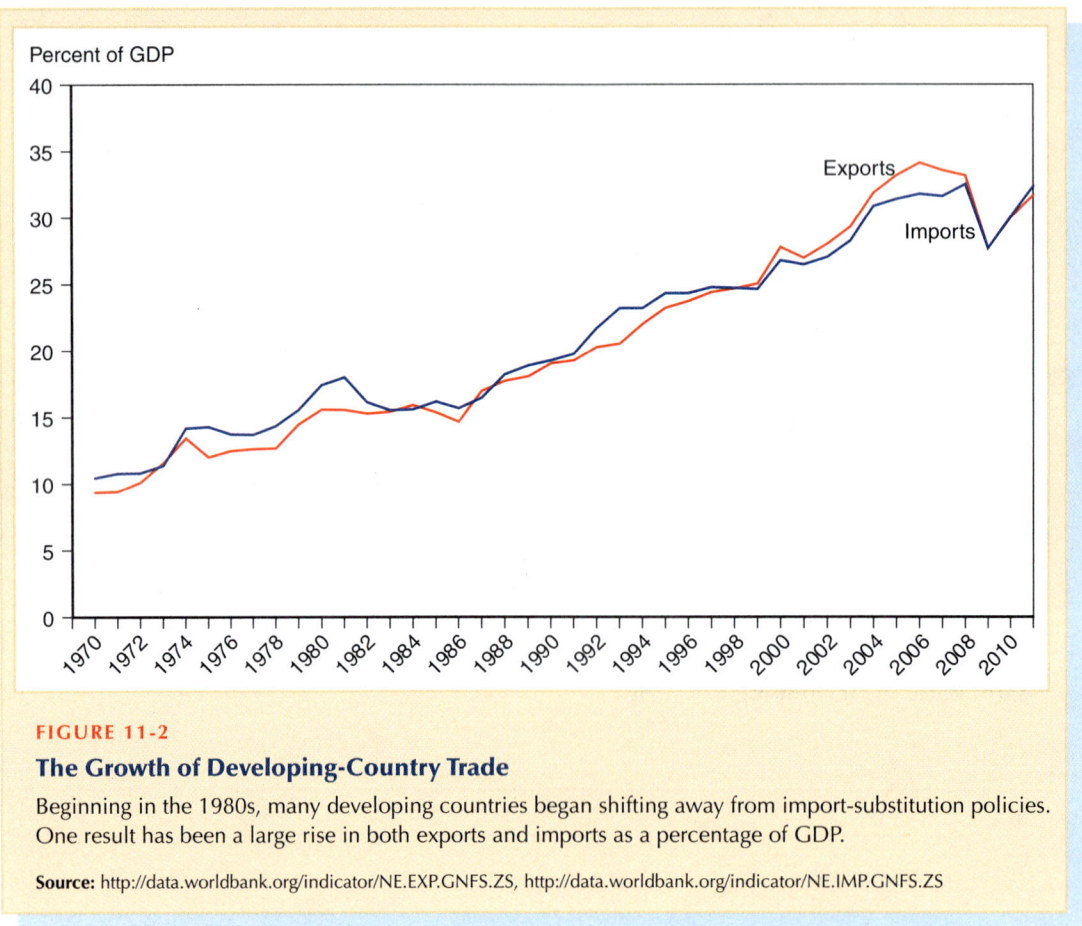

FIGURE 11-2

The Growth of Developing-Country Trade

Beginning in the 1980s, many developing countries began shifting away from import-substitution policies. One result has been a large rise in both exports and imports as a percentage of GDP.

Source: http://data.worldbank.org/indicator/NE.EXP.GNFS.ZS, http://data.worldbank.org/indicator/NE.IMP.GNFS.ZS

became clear that it was not delivering on its promise of rapid economic development. Has the switch to more open trade delivered better results?

The answer is that the picture is mixed. Growth rates in Brazil and other Latin American countries have actually been slower since the trade liberalization of the late 1980s than they were during import-substituting industrialization. India, on the other hand, has experienced an impressive acceleration of growth—but as we'll see in the next section of this chapter, there is intense dispute about how much of that acceleration can be attributed to trade liberalization.

In addition, there is growing concern about rising inequality in developing countries. In Latin America at least, the switch away from import-substituting industrialization seems to have been associated with declining real wages for blue-collar workers, even as earnings of highly skilled workers have risen.

One thing is clear, however: The old view that import substitution is the only path to development has been proved wrong, as a number of developing countries have achieved extraordinary growth while becoming more, not less, open to trade.

Trade and Growth: Takeoff in Asia

As we have seen, by the 1970s there was widespread disillusionment with import-substituting industrialization as a development strategy. But what could take its place?

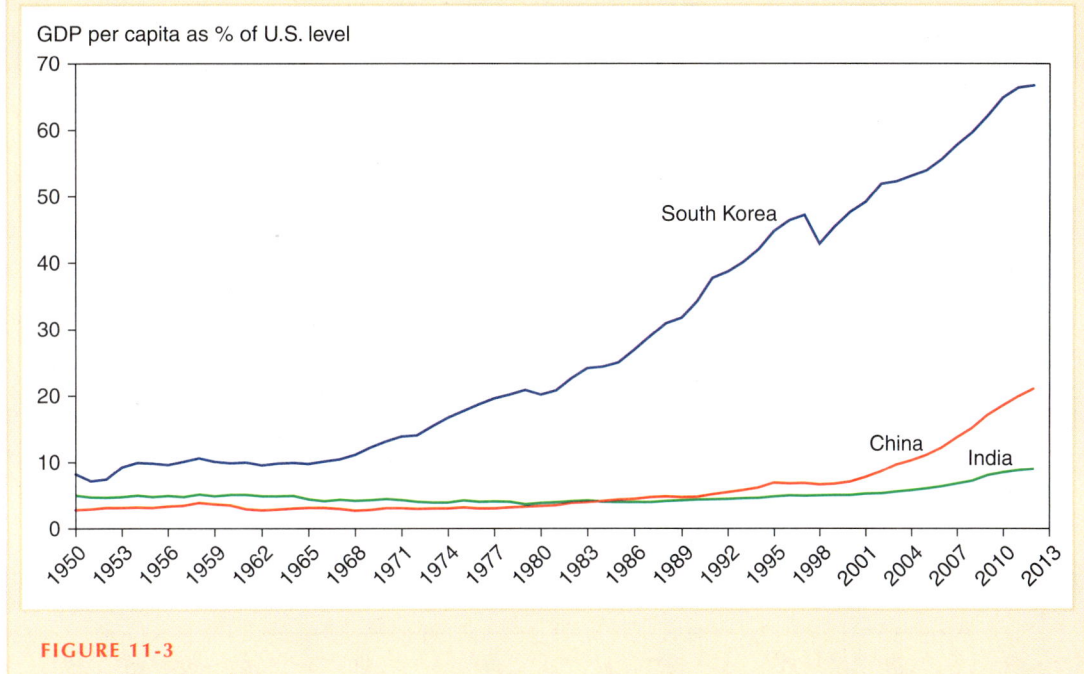

FIGURE 11-3

The Asian Takeoff

Beginning in the 1960s, a series of economies began converging on advanced-country levels of income. Here we show GDP per capita as a percentage of its level in the United States, using a proportional scale to highlight the changes. South Korea began its ascent in the 1960s, China at the end of the 1970s, and India about a decade later.

Source: Total Economy Database.

A possible answer began to emerge as economists and policy makers took note of some surprising success stories in the developing world—cases of economies that experienced a dramatic acceleration in their growth and began to converge on the incomes of advanced nations. At first, these success stories involved a group of relatively small East Asian economies: South Korea, Taiwan, Hong Kong, and Singapore. Over time, however, these successes began to spread; today, the list of countries that have experienced startling economic takeoffs includes the world's two most populous nations, China and India.

Figure 11-3 illustrates the Asian takeoff by showing the experiences of three countries: South Korea, the biggest of the original group of Asian "tigers"; China; and India. In each case, we show per-capita GDP as a percentage of the U.S. level, an indicator that highlights the extent of these nations' economic "catchup." As you can see, South Korea began its economic ascent in the 1960s, China at the end of the 1970s, and India circa 1990.

What caused these economic takeoffs? Each of the countries shown in Figure 11-3 experienced a major change in its economic policy around the time of its takeoff. This new policy involved reduced government regulation in a variety of areas, including a move toward freer trade. The most spectacular change was in China, where Deng Xiaoping, who had taken power in 1978, converted a centrally planned economy into a market economy in which the profit motive had relatively free rein. But as explained in the box on page 311, policy changes in India were dramatic, too.

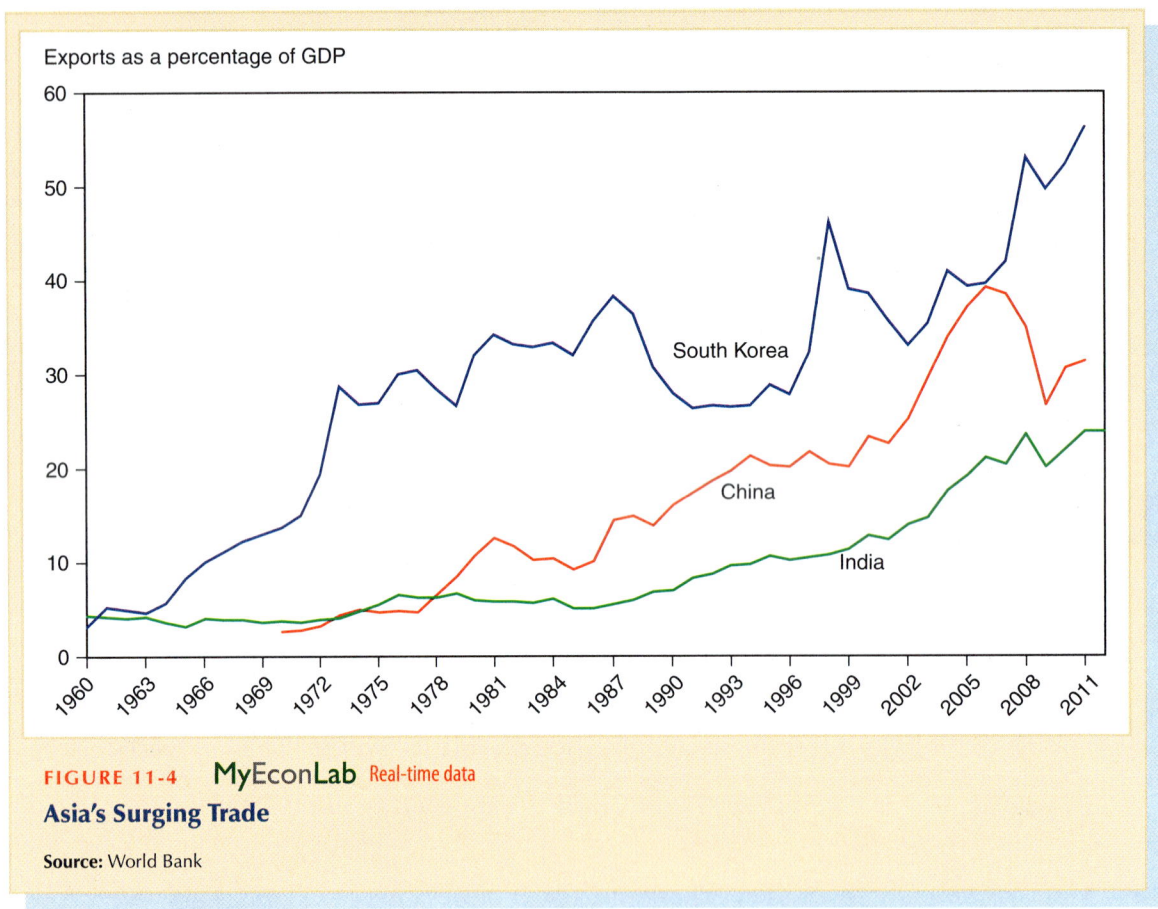

Exports as a percentage of GDP

FIGURE 11-4   MyEconLab Real-time data

Asia's Surging Trade

Source: World Bank

In each case, these policy reforms were followed by a large increase in the economy's openness, as measured by the share of exports in GDP (see Figure 11-4). So it seems fair to say that these Asian success stories demonstrated that the proponents of import-substituting industrialization were wrong: It is possible to achieve development through export-oriented growth.

What is less clear is the extent to which trade liberalization explains these success stories. As we have just pointed out, reductions in tariffs and the lifting of other import restrictions were only part of the economic reforms these nations undertook, which makes it difficult to assess the importance of trade liberalization per se. In addition, Latin American nations like Mexico and Brazil, which also sharply liberalized trade and shifted toward exports, did not see comparable economic take-offs, suggesting at the very least that other factors played a crucial role in the Asian miracle.

So the implications of Asia's economic takeoff remain somewhat controversial. One thing is clear, however: The once widely held view that the world economy is rigged against new entrants and that poor countries cannot become rich have been proved spectacularly wrong. Never before in human history have so many people experienced such a rapid rise in their living standards.

INDIA'S BOOM

India, with a population of more than 1.1 billion people, is the world's second-most-populous country. It's also a growing force in world trade—especially in new forms of trade that involve information rather than physical goods. The Indian city of Bangalore has become famous for its growing role in the global information technology industry.

Yet a generation ago, India was a very minor player in world trade. In part this was because the country's economy performed poorly in general: Until about 1980, India eked out a rate of economic growth—sometimes mocked as the "Hindu rate of growth"—that was only about 1 percentage point higher than population growth.

This slow growth was widely attributed to the stifling effect of bureaucratic restrictions. Observers spoke of a "license Raj": Virtually any kind of business initiative required hard-to-get government permits, which placed a damper on investment and innovation. And India's sluggish economy participated little in world trade. After the country achieved independence in 1948, its leaders adopted a particularly extreme form of import-substituting industrialization as the country's development strategy: India imported almost nothing that it could produce domestically, even if the domestic product was far more expensive and of lower quality than what could

be bought abroad. High costs, in turn, crimped exports. So India was a very "closed" economy. In the 1970s, imports and exports averaged only about 5 percent of GDP, close to the lowest levels of any major nation.

Then everything changed. India's growth accelerated dramatically: GDP per capita, which had risen at an annual rate of only 1.3 percent from 1960 to 1980, has grown at close to 4 percent annually since 1980. And India's participation in world trade surged as tariffs were brought down and import quotas were removed. In short, India has become a high-performance economy. It's still a very poor country, but it is rapidly growing richer and has begun to rival China as a focus of world attention.

The big question, of course, is why India's growth rate has increased so dramatically. That question is the subject of heated debate among economists. Some have argued that trade liberalization, which allowed India to participate in the global economy, was crucial.[*] Others point out that India's growth began accelerating around 1980, whereas the big changes in trade policy didn't occur until the beginning of the 1990s.[†]

Whatever caused the change, India's transition has been a welcome development. More than a billion people now have much greater hope for a decent standard of living.

[*]See Arvind Panagariya, "The Triumph of India's Market Reforms: The Record of the 1980s and 1990s." Policy Analysis 554, Cato Institute, November 2005.
[†]See Dani Rodrik and Arvind Subramanian, "From 'Hindu Growth' to Productivity Surge: The Mystery of the Indian Growth Transition," *IMF Staff Papers* 55 (2, 2005), pp. 193–228.

SUMMARY

1. Trade policy in less-developed countries can be analyzed using the same analytical tools used to discuss advanced countries. However, the particular issues characteristic of *developing countries* are different from those of advanced countries. In particular, trade policy in developing countries is concerned with two objectives: promoting industrialization and coping with the uneven development of the domestic economy.

2. Government policy to promote industrialization has often been justified by the infant industry argument, which says that new industries need a temporary period of protection against competition from established industries in other countries. However, the infant industry argument is valid only if it can be cast as a market failure argument for intervention. Two usual justifications are the existence of *imperfect capital markets* and the problem of *appropriability* of knowledge generated by pioneering firms.

3. Using the infant industry argument as justification, many less-developed countries pursued policies of *import-substituting industrialization* in which domestic industries are created under the protection of tariffs or import quotas. Although these policies succeeded in promoting manufacturing, by and large they did not deliver the expected gains in economic growth and living standards. Many economists are now harshly critical of the results of import substitution, arguing that it fostered high-cost, inefficient production.

4. Beginning about 1985, many developing countries, dissatisfied with the results of import-substitution policies, greatly reduced rates of protection for manufacturing. As a result, developing-country trade grew rapidly, and the share of manufactured goods in exports rose. The results of this policy change in terms of economic development, however, have been, at best, mixed.

5. The view that economic development must take place via import substitution, and the pessimism about economic development that spread as import-substituting industrialization seemed to fail, have been confounded by the rapid economic growth of a number of Asian economies. These Asian economies have grown not via import substitution but via exports. They are characterized both by very high ratios of trade to national income and by extremely high growth rates. The reasons for the success of these economies are highly disputed, with much controversy over the role played by trade liberalization.

KEY TERMS

appropriability, p. 302
developing countries, p. 299

imperfect capital markets,
   p. 302

import-substituting
   industrialization, p. 303

PROBLEMS

MyEconLab

1. Two trade theories have been historically prevalent among developing countries, one being import-substituting industrialization and the other is export-led growth. Which one proved to be more effective?

2. "Japan's experience makes the infant industry case for protection better than any theory. In the early 1950s, Japan was a poor nation that survived by exporting textiles and toys. The Japanese government protected what at first were inefficient, high-cost steel and automobile industries, and those industries came to dominate world markets." Discuss critically.

3. A country currently imports automobiles at $8,000 each. Its government believes that, given time, domestic producers could manufacture autos for only $6,000 but that there would be an initial shakedown period during which autos would cost $10,000 to produce domestically.

   a. Suppose each firm that tries to produce autos must go through the shakedown period of high costs on its own. Under what circumstances would the existence of the initial high costs justify infant industry protection?

   b. Now suppose, on the contrary, that once one firm has borne the costs of learning to produce autos at $6,000 each, other firms can imitate it and do the same. Explain how this can prevent development of a domestic industry and how infant industry protection can help.

4. India and Mexico both followed import-substitution policies after World War II. However, India went much further, producing almost everything for itself, while Mexico continued to rely on imports of capital goods. Why do you think this difference may have emerged?

5. What is export-led growth and why is it so popular? Make an example by referring to the Asian miracle.

FURTHER READINGS

W. Arthur Lewis. *The Theory of Economic Development*. Homewood, IL: Irwin, 1955. A good example of the upbeat view taken of trade policies for economic development during the import-substitution high tide of the 1950s and 1960s.

I. M. D. Little, Tibor Scitovsky, and Maurice Scott. *Industry and Trade in Some Developing Countries*. New York: Oxford University Press, 1970. A key work in the emergence of a more downbeat view of import substitution in the 1970s and 1980s.

Barry Naughton. *The Chinese Economy: Transitions and Growth*. Cambridge: MIT Press, 2007. A good overview of the radical changes in Chinese policy over time.

Dani Rodrik. *One Economics, Many Recipes*. Princeton: Princeton University Press, 2007. Views on trade and development from a leading skeptic of prevailing orthodoxies.

T. N. Srinivasan and Suresh D. Tendulkar. *Reintegrating India with the World Economy*. Washington: Institute for International Economics, 2003. How India shifted away from import substitution and what happened as a result.

CHAPTER 12

CONTROVERSIES IN TRADE POLICY

As we have seen, the theory of international trade policy, like the theory of international trade itself, has a long, intellectual tradition. Experienced international economists tend to have a cynical attitude toward people who come along with "new" issues in trade—the general feeling tends to be that most supposedly new concerns are simply old fallacies in new bottles.

Every once in a while, however, truly new issues do emerge. This chapter describes three controversies over international trade that have arisen over the past quarter-century, each raising issues that previously had not been seriously analyzed by international economists.

First, in the 1980s, a new set of sophisticated arguments for government intervention in trade emerged in advanced countries. These arguments focused on the "high-technology" industries that came to prominence as a result of the rise of the silicon chip. While some of the arguments were closely related to the market failure analysis in Chapter 10, the new theory of **strategic trade policy** was based on different ideas and created a considerable stir. The dispute over high-technology industries and trade subsided for a while in the 1990s, but it has recently made a comeback as new concerns have emerged about U.S. innovation.

Second, in the 1990s, a heated dispute arose over the effects of growing international trade on workers in developing countries—and whether trade agreements should include standards for wage rates and labor conditions. This dispute often widened into a broader debate about the effects of globalization; it was a debate played out not just in academic journals but also, in some cases, in the streets.

More recently, there has been growing concern about the intersection between environmental issues—which increasingly transcend national boundaries—and trade policy, with a serious economic and legal dispute about whether policies such as "carbon tariffs" are appropriate.

LEARNING GOALS

After reading this chapter, you will be able to:

- Summarize the more sophisticated arguments for interventionist trade policy, especially those related to externalities and economies of scale.
- Evaluate the claims of the anti-globalization movement related to trade effects on workers, labor standards, and the environment in light of the counterarguments.
- Discuss the role of the World Trade Organization (WTO) as a forum for resolving trade disputes and the tension between the rulings of the WTO and individual national interests.
- Discuss key issues in the debate over trade policy and the environment.

Sophisticated Arguments for Activist Trade Policy

Nothing in the analytical framework developed in Chapters 9 and 10 rules out the desirability of government intervention in trade. That framework *does* show that activist government policy needs a specific kind of justification; namely, it must offset some preexisting domestic market failure. The problem with many arguments for activist trade policy is precisely that they do not link the case for government intervention to any particular failure of the assumptions on which the case for laissez-faire rests.

The difficulty with market failure arguments for intervention is being able to recognize a market failure when you see one. Economists studying industrial countries have identified two kinds of market failure that seem to be present and relevant to the trade policies of advanced countries: (1) the inability of firms in high-technology industries to capture the benefits of that part of their contribution to knowledge that spills over to other firms and (2) the presence of monopoly profits in highly concentrated oligopolistic industries.

Technology and Externalities

The discussion of the infant industry argument in Chapter 11 noted that there is a potential market failure arising from difficulties of appropriating knowledge. If firms in an industry generate knowledge that other firms can use without paying for it, the industry is in effect producing some extra output—the marginal social benefit of the knowledge—that is not reflected in the incentives of firms. Where such **externalities** (benefits that accrue to parties other than the firms that produce them) can be shown to be important, there is a good case for subsidizing the industry.

At an abstract level, this argument is the same for the infant industries of less-developed countries as it is for the established industries of the advanced countries. In advanced countries, however, the argument has a special edge because in those countries, there are important high-technology industries in which the generation of knowledge is in many ways the central aspect of the enterprise. In high-technology industries, firms devote a great deal of their resources to improving technology, either by explicitly spending on research and development or by being willing to take initial losses on new products and processes to gain experience. Because such activities take place in nearly all industries, there is no sharp line between high-tech and the rest of the economy. There are clear differences in degree, however, and it makes sense to talk of a high-technology sector in which investment in knowledge is the key part of the business.

The point for activist trade policy is that while firms can appropriate some of the benefits of their own investment in knowledge (otherwise they would not be investing!), they usually cannot appropriate them fully. Some of the benefits accrue to other firms that can imitate the ideas and techniques of the leaders. In electronics, for example, it is not uncommon for firms to "reverse engineer" their rivals' designs, taking their products apart to figure out how they work and how they were made. Because patent laws provide only weak protection for innovators, one can reasonably presume that under laissez-faire, high-technology firms do not receive as strong an incentive to innovate as they should.

The Case for Government Support of High-Technology Industries   Should the U.S. government subsidize high-technology industries? While there is a pretty good case for such a subsidy, we need to exercise some caution. Two questions in particular arise: (1) Can the government target the right industries or activities? and (2) How important, quantitatively, would the gains be from such targeting?

Although high-technology industries probably produce extra social benefits because of the knowledge they generate, much of what goes on even in those industries has nothing to do with generating knowledge. There is no reason to subsidize the employment of capital or nontechnical workers in high-technology industries; on the other hand, innovation and technological spillovers happen to some extent even in industries that are not at all high-tech. A general principle is that trade and industrial policy should be targeted specifically on the activity in which the market failure occurs. Thus, policy should seek to subsidize the generation of knowledge that firms cannot appropriate. The problem, however, is that it is not always easy to identify that knowledge generation; as we'll see shortly, industry practitioners often argue that focusing only on activities specifically labeled "research" is taking far too narrow a view of the problem.

The Rise, Fall, and Rise of High-Tech Worries   Arguments that the United States in particular should have a deliberate policy of promoting high-technology industries and helping them compete against foreign rivals have a curious history. Such arguments gained widespread attention and popularity in the 1980s and early 1990s, then fell from favor, only to experience a strong revival in recent years.

The high-technology discussions of the 1980s and early 1990s were driven in large part by the rise of Japanese firms in some prominent high-tech sectors that had previously been dominated by U.S. producers. Most notably, between 1978 and 1986, the U.S. share of world production of dynamic random access memory chips—a key component of many electronic devices—plunged from about 70 percent to 20 percent, while Japan's share rose from under 30 percent to 75 percent. There was widespread concern that other high-technology products might suffer the same fate. But as described in the box on page 321, the fear that Japan's dominance of the semiconductor memory market would translate into a broader dominance of computers and related technologies proved to be unfounded. Furthermore, Japan's overall growth sputtered in the 1990s, while the United States surged into a renewed period of technological dominance, taking the lead in Internet applications and other information industries.

More recently, however, concerns about the status of U.S. high-technology industries have reemerged. A central factor in these concerns has been the decline in U.S. employment in so-called advanced technology—ATP—products. As Figure 12-1 shows, the United States has moved into a large trade deficit in ICT goods, while as Figure 12-2

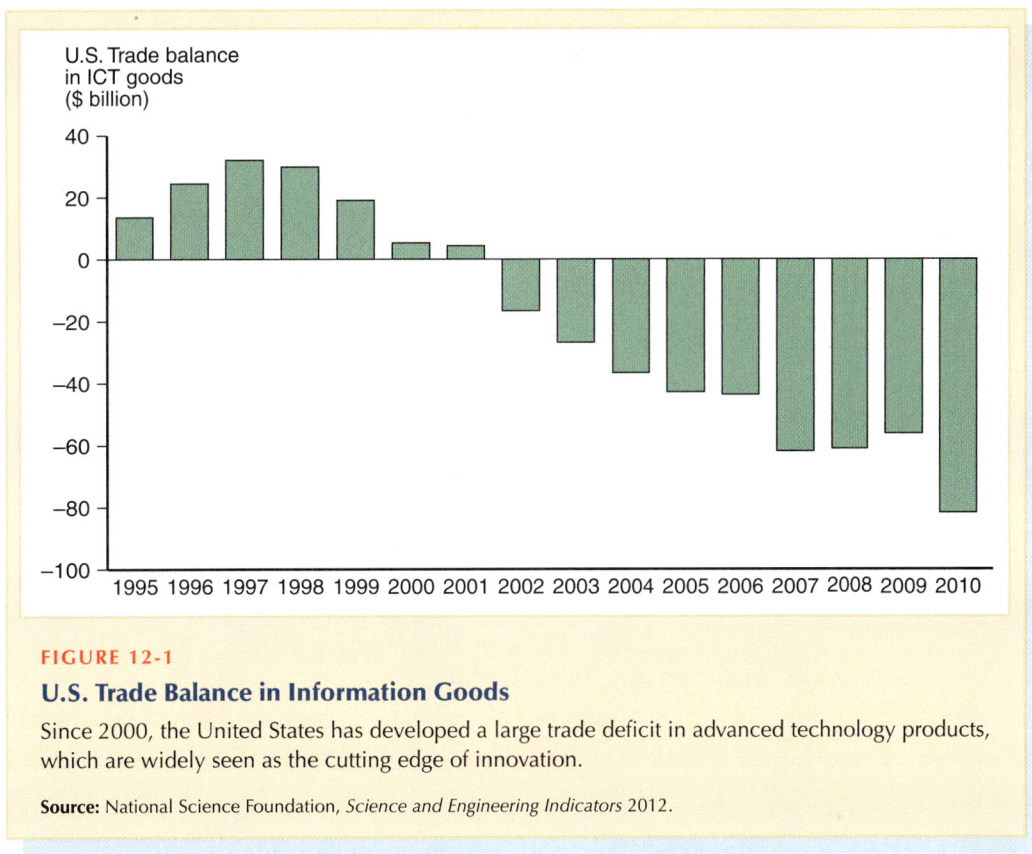

FIGURE 12-1

U.S. Trade Balance in Information Goods

Since 2000, the United States has developed a large trade deficit in advanced technology products, which are widely seen as the cutting edge of innovation.

Source: National Science Foundation, *Science and Engineering Indicators* 2012.

shows U.S. employment in the production of computers and related goods has plunged since 2000, falling substantially faster than overall manufacturing employment.

Does this matter? The United States could, arguably, continue to be at the cutting edge of innovation in information technology while outsourcing much of the actual production of high-technology goods to factories overseas. However, as explained in the box on page 320, some influential voices warn that innovation can't thrive unless the innovators are close, physically and in business terms, to the people who turn those innovations into physical goods.

It's a difficult debate to settle, in large part because it's not at all clear how to put numbers to these concerns. It seems likely, however, that the debate over whether or not high-technology industries need special consideration will grow increasingly intense in the years ahead.

Imperfect Competition and Strategic Trade Policy

During the 1980s, a new argument for industrial targeting received substantial theoretical attention. Originally proposed by economists Barbara Spencer and James Brander of the University of British Columbia, this argument identifies the market failure that justifies government intervention as the lack of perfect competition. In some industries, they point out, there are only a few firms in effective competition. Because of the small number of firms, the assumptions of perfect competition do not apply. In particular, there will typically be **excess returns**; that is, firms will make

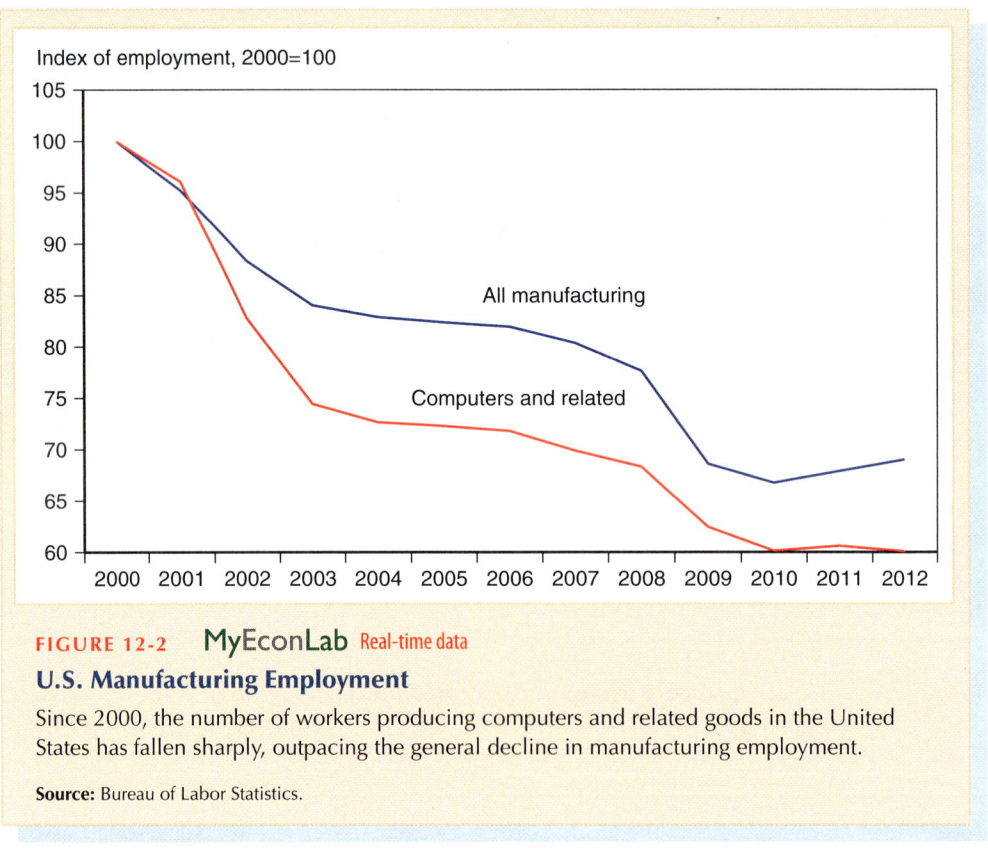

Index of employment, 2000=100

FIGURE 12-2   MyEconLab Real-time data
U.S. Manufacturing Employment

Since 2000, the number of workers producing computers and related goods in the United States has fallen sharply, outpacing the general decline in manufacturing employment.

Source: Bureau of Labor Statistics.

profits above what equally risky investments elsewhere in the economy can earn. There will thus be an international competition over who gets these profits.

Spencer and Brander noticed that, in this case, it is possible in principle for a government to alter the rules of the game to shift these excess returns from foreign to domestic firms. In the simplest case, a subsidy to domestic firms, by deterring investment and production by foreign competitors, can raise the profits of domestic firms by more than the amount of the subsidy. Setting aside the effects on consumers—for example, when firms are selling only in foreign markets—this capture of profits from foreign competitors would mean the subsidy raises national income at other countries' expense.

The Brander-Spencer Analysis: An Example   The **Brander-Spencer analysis** can be illustrated with a simple example in which only two firms compete, each from a different country. Bearing in mind that any resemblance to actual events may be coincidental, let's call the firms Boeing and Airbus and the countries the United States and Europe. Suppose there is a new product, a superjumbo aircraft, that both firms are capable of making. For simplicity, assume each firm can make only a yes/no decision: either to produce superjumbo aircraft or not.

Table 12-1 illustrates how the profits earned by the two firms might depend on their decisions. (The setup is similar to the one we used to examine the interaction of different countries' trade policies in Chapter 10.) Each row corresponds to a particular decision by Boeing; each column corresponds to a decision by Airbus. In each box are two entries: The entry on the lower left represents the profits of Boeing, while that on the upper right represents the profits of Airbus.

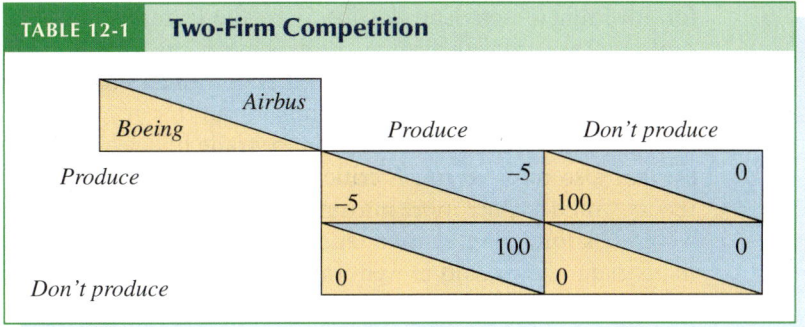

TABLE 12-1   Two-Firm Competition

As set up, the table reflects the following assumption: Either firm alone could earn profits making superjumbo aircraft, but if both firms try to produce them, both will incur losses. Which firm will actually get the profits? This depends on who gets there first. Suppose Boeing is able to get a small head start and commits itself to produce superjumbo aircraft before Airbus can get going. Airbus will find that it has no incentive to enter. The outcome will be in the upper right of the table, with Boeing earning profits.

Now comes the Brander-Spencer point: The European government can reverse this situation. Suppose the European government commits itself to pay its firm a subsidy of 25 if it enters. The result will be to change the table of payoffs to that represented in Table 12-2. In this case, it will be profitable for Airbus to produce superjumbo aircraft whatever Boeing does.

Let's work through the implications of this shift. Boeing now knows that whatever it does, it will have to compete with Airbus and will therefore lose money if it chooses to produce. So now it is Boeing that will be deterred from entering. In effect, the government subsidy has removed the advantage of a head start that we assumed was Boeing's and has conferred it on Airbus instead.

The end result is that the equilibrium shifts from the upper right of Table 12-1 to the lower left of Table 12-2. Airbus ends up with profits of 125 instead of 0, profits that arise because of a government subsidy of only 25. That is, the subsidy raises profits by more than the amount of the subsidy itself, because of its deterrent effect on foreign competition. The subsidy has this effect because it creates an advantage for Airbus comparable with the *strategic* advantage Airbus would have had if it, not Boeing, had had a head start in the industry.

Problems with the Brander-Spencer Analysis   This hypothetical example might seem to indicate that this strategic trade policy argument provides a compelling case

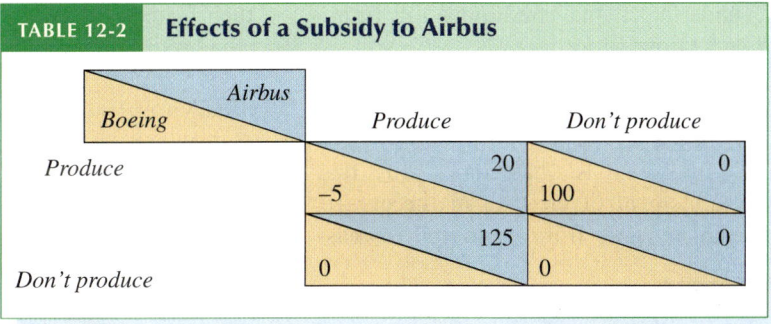

TABLE 12-2   Effects of a Subsidy to Airbus

for government activism. A subsidy by the European government sharply raises the profits of a European firm at the expense of its foreign rivals. Leaving aside the interest of consumers, this seems clearly to raise European welfare (and reduce U.S. welfare). Shouldn't the U.S. government put this argument into practice?

In fact, this strategic justification for trade policy, while it has attracted much interest, has also received much criticism. Critics argue that making practical use of the theory would require more information than is likely to be available, that such policies would risk foreign retaliation, and that in any case, the domestic politics of trade and industrial policy would prevent the use of such subtle analytical tools.

The problem of insufficient information has two aspects. The first is that even when looking at an industry in isolation, it may be difficult to fill in the entries in a table like Table 12-1 with any confidence. And if the government gets it wrong, a subsidy policy may turn out to be a costly misjudgment. Suppose, for example, that Boeing has some underlying advantage—maybe a better technology—so that even if Airbus enters, Boeing will still find it profitable to produce. Airbus, however, cannot produce profitably if Boeing enters.

In the absence of a subsidy, the outcome will be that Boeing produces and Airbus does not. Now suppose that, as in the previous case, the European government provides a subsidy sufficient to induce Airbus to produce. In this case, however, because of Boeing's underlying advantage, the subsidy won't act as a deterrent to Boeing, and the profits of Airbus will fall short of the subsidy's value—in short, the policy will turn out to have been a costly mistake.

The point is that even though the two cases might look very similar, in one case a subsidy looks like a good idea, while in the other case it looks like a terrible idea. It seems that the desirability of strategic trade policies depends on an exact reading

A WARNING FROM INTEL'S FOUNDER

When Andy Grove speaks about technology, people listen. In 1968, he co-founded Intel, which invented the microprocessor—the chip that drives your computer—and dominated the semiconductor business for decades.

So many people took notice in 2010 when Grove issued a stark warning about the fate of U.S. high technology: The erosion of manufacturing employment in technology industries, he argued, undermines the conditions for future innovation.* Grove wrote:

> Startups are a wonderful thing, but they cannot by themselves increase tech employment. Equally important is what comes after that mythical moment of creation in the garage, as technology goes from prototype to mass

production. This is the phase where companies scale up. They work out design details, figure out how to make things affordably, build factories, and hire people by the thousands. Scaling is hard work but necessary to make innovation matter.

> The scaling process is no longer happening in the U.S. And as long as that's the case, plowing capital into young companies that build their factories elsewhere will continue to yield a bad return in terms of American jobs.

In effect, Grove was arguing that technological spillovers require more than researchers; they require the presence of large numbers of workers putting new ideas to work. If he's right, his assertion constitutes a strong argument for industrial targeting.

*Andy Grove, "How to Make an American Job Before It's Too Late," Bloomberg.com, July 1, 2010.

of the situation. This leads some economists to ask whether we are ever likely to have enough information to use the theory effectively.

The information requirement is complicated because we cannot consider industries in isolation. If one industry is subsidized, it will draw resources from other industries and lead to increases in their costs. Thus, even a policy that succeeds in giving U.S. firms a strategic advantage in one industry will tend to cause strategic disadvantage elsewhere. To ask whether the policy is justified, the U.S. government would need to weigh these offsetting effects. Even if the government has a precise understanding of one industry, this is not enough because it also needs an equally precise understanding of those industries with which that industry competes for resources.

If a proposed strategic trade policy can overcome these criticisms, it still faces the problem of foreign retaliation, essentially the same problem faced when considering the use of a tariff to improve the terms of trade (Chapter 10). Strategic policies are **beggar-thy-neighbor policies** that increase our welfare at other countries' expense. These policies therefore risk a trade war that leaves everyone worse off. Few economists would advocate that the United States be the initiator of such policies. Instead, the furthest that most economists are willing to go is to argue that the United States should be prepared to retaliate when other countries appear to be using strategic policies aggressively.

Finally, can theories like this ever be used in a political context? We discussed this issue in Chapter 10, where the reasons for skepticism were placed in the context of a political skeptic's case for free trade.

CASE STUDY

When the Chips Were Up

During the years when arguments about the effectiveness of strategic trade policy were at their height, advocates of a more interventionist trade policy on the part of the United States often claimed that Japan had prospered by deliberately promoting key industries. By the early 1990s, one example in particular—that of semiconductor chips—had become exhibit A in the case that promoting key industries "works." Indeed, when author James Fallows published a series of articles in 1994 attacking free trade ideology and alleging the superiority of Japanese-style interventionism, he began with a piece titled "The Parable of the Chips." By the end of the 1990s, however, the example of semiconductors had come to seem an object lesson in the pitfalls of activist trade policy.

A semiconductor chip is a small piece of silicon on which complex circuits have been etched. As we saw on page 320, the industry began in the United States when the U.S. firm Intel introduced the first microprocessor, the brains of a computer on a chip. Since then, the industry has experienced rapid yet peculiarly predictable technological change: Roughly every 18 months, the number of circuits that can be etched on a chip doubles, a rule known as Moore's Law. This progress underlies much of the information technology revolution of the last three decades.

Japan broke into the semiconductor market in the late 1970s. The industry was definitely targeted by the Japanese government, which supported a research effort that helped build domestic technological capacity. The sums involved in this subsidy, however, were fairly small. The main component of Japan's activist trade policy, according to U.S. critics, was tacit protectionism. Although Japan had few formal tariffs or other barriers to imports, U.S. firms found that once Japan was able to manufacture a given type of semiconductor chip, few U.S. products were sold in that country. Critics alleged that there was a tacit understanding by Japanese firms in such industries as consumer electronics, in which Japan was already a leading producer, that they should buy domestic semiconductors, even if the price was higher or the quality lower than that for competing U.S. products. Was this assertion true? The facts of the case are in dispute to this day.

Observers also alleged that the protected Japanese market—if that was indeed what it was—indirectly promoted Japan's ability to export semiconductors. The argument went like this: Semiconductor production is characterized by a steep learning curve (recall the discussion of dynamic scale economies in Chapter 7). Guaranteed a large domestic market, Japanese semiconductor producers were certain they would be able to work their way down the learning curve, which meant they were willing to invest in new plants that could also produce for export.

It remains unclear to what extent these policies led to Japan's success in taking a large share of the semiconductor market. Some features of the Japanese industrial system may have given the country a "natural" comparative advantage in semiconductor production, where quality control is a crucial concern. During the 1970s and 1980s, Japanese factories developed a new approach to manufacturing based on, among other things, setting acceptable levels of defects much lower than those that had been standard in the United States.

In any case, by the mid-1980s Japan had surpassed the United States in sales of one type of semiconductor, which was widely regarded as crucial to industry success: random access memories, or RAMs. The argument that RAM production was the key to dominating the whole semiconductor industry rested on the belief that it would yield both strong technological externalities and excess returns. RAMs were the largest-volume form of semiconductors; industry experts asserted that the know-how acquired in RAM production was essential to a nation's ability to keep up with advancing technology in other semiconductors, such as microprocessors. So it was widely predicted that Japan's dominance in RAMs would soon translate into dominance in the production of semiconductors generally—and that this supremacy, in turn, would give Japan an advantage in the production of many other goods that used semiconductors.

It was also widely believed that although the manufacture of RAMs had not been a highly profitable business before 1990, it would eventually become an industry characterized by excess returns. The reason was that the number of firms producing RAMs had steadily fallen: In each successive generation of chips, some producers had exited the sector, with no new entrants. Eventually, many observers thought, there would be only two or three highly profitable RAM producers left.

During the decade of the 1990s, however, both justifications for targeting RAMs—technological externalities and excess returns—apparently failed to materialize. On one side, Japan's lead in RAMs ultimately did not translate into an advantage in other types of semiconductors: For example, American firms retained a secure lead in microprocessors. On the other side, instead of continuing to shrink, the number of RAM producers began to rise again, with the main new entrants from South Korea and other newly industrializing economies. By the end of the 1990s, RAM production was regarded as a "commodity" business: Many people could make RAMs, and there was nothing especially strategic about the sector.

The important lesson seems to be how hard it is to select industries to promote. The semiconductor industry appeared, on its face, to have all the attributes of a sector suitable for activist trade policy. But in the end, it yielded neither strong externalities nor excess returns.

Globalization and Low-Wage Labor

It's a good bet that most of the clothing you are wearing as you read this came from a country far poorer than the United States. The rise of manufactured exports from developing countries has been one of the major shifts in the world economy over the last generation; even a desperately poor nation like Bangladesh, with a per-capita GDP less than 5 percent that of the United States, now relies more on exports of manufactured goods than on exports of traditional agricultural or mineral products. (A government official in a developing country remarked to one of the authors, "We are not a banana republic—we are a pajama republic.")

It should come as no surprise that the workers who produce manufactured goods for export in developing countries are paid very little by advanced-country standards—often less than $1 per hour, sometimes less than $0.50. After all, the workers have few good alternatives in such generally poor economies. Nor should it come as any surprise that the conditions of work are also very bad in many cases—sometimes lethal, as explained in the case study on page 321.

Should low wages and poor working conditions be a cause for concern? Many people think so. In the 1990s, the anti-globalization movement attracted many adherents in advanced countries, especially on college campuses. Outrage over low wages and poor working conditions in developing-country export industries was a large part of the movement's appeal, although other concerns (discussed below) were also part of the story.

It's fair to say that most economists have viewed the anti-globalization movement as, at best, misguided. The standard analysis of comparative advantage suggests that trade is mutually beneficial to the countries that engage in it; it suggests, furthermore, that when labor-abundant countries export labor-intensive manufactured goods like clothing, not only should their national incomes rise but the distribution of income should also shift in favor of labor. But is the anti-globalization movement entirely off base?

The Anti-Globalization Movement

Before 1995, most complaints about international trade made by citizens of advanced countries targeted its effects on people who were also citizens of advanced countries. In the United States, most critics of free trade in the 1980s focused on the alleged threat of competition from Japan; in the early 1990s, there was substantial concern in both the United States and Europe over the effects of imports from low-wage countries on the wages of less-skilled workers at home.

In the second half of the 1990s, however, a rapidly growing movement—drawing considerable support from college students—began stressing the alleged harm that world trade was doing to workers in the developing countries. Activists pointed to the low wages and poor working conditions in third world factories that produced goods for Western markets. A crystallizing event was the discovery in 1996 that clothes sold at Wal-Mart, and endorsed by television personality Kathie Lee Gifford, were produced by very poorly paid workers in Honduras.

The anti-globalization movement grabbed world headlines in November 1999, when a major meeting of the World Trade Organization took place in Seattle. The purpose of the meeting was to start another trade round, following on the Uruguay Round described in Chapter 10. Thousands of activists converged on Seattle, motivated by the belief that the WTO was riding roughshod over national independence and imposing free trade ideas that hurt workers. Despite ample warnings, the police were ill prepared, and the demonstrations brought considerable disruption to the meetings. In any case, negotiations were not going well: Nations had failed to agree on an agenda in advance, and it soon became clear that there was not sufficient agreement on the direction of a new trade round to get one started.

In the end, the meeting was regarded as a failure. Most experts on trade policy believe the meeting would have failed even in the absence of the demonstrations, but the anti-globalization movement had achieved at least the appearance of disrupting an important international conference. Over the next two years, large demonstrations also rocked meetings of the International Monetary Fund and the World Bank in Washington as well as a summit meeting of major economic powers in Genoa; at the latter event, Italian police killed one activist.

In other words, the anti-globalization movement had become a highly visible presence in a relatively short period of time. But what was the movement's goal—and was it right?

Trade and Wages Revisited

One strand of the opposition to globalization is familiar from the analysis in Chapter 3. Activists pointed to the very low wages earned by many workers in developing-country export industries. These critics argued that the low wages (and the associated poor working conditions) showed that, contrary to the claims of free trade advocates, globalization was not helping workers in developing countries.

For example, some activists pointed to the example of Mexico's *maquiladoras*, factories near the U.S. border that had expanded rapidly, roughly doubling in employment, in the five years following the signing of the North American Free Trade Agreement. Wages in those factories were in some cases below $5 per day, and conditions were appalling by U.S. standards. Opponents of the free trade agreement argued that by making it easier for employers to replace high-wage workers in the United States with lower-paid workers in Mexico, the agreement had hurt labor on both sides of the border.

The standard economist's answer to this argument goes back to our analysis in Chapter 3 of the misconceptions about comparative advantage. We saw that it is a common misconception that trade must involve the exploitation of workers if they earn much lower wages than their counterparts in a richer country.

Table 12-3 repeats that analysis briefly. In this case, we assume that there are two countries, the United States and Mexico, and two industries, high-tech and low-tech. We also assume that labor is the only factor of production, and that U.S. labor is more productive than Mexican labor in all industries. Specifically, it takes only one hour of U.S. labor to produce a unit of output in either industry; it takes two hours of Mexican labor to produce a unit of low-tech output and eight hours to produce a unit of high-tech output. The upper part of the table shows the real wages of workers in each country in terms of each good in the absence of trade: The real wage in each case is simply the quantity of each good that a worker could produce in one hour.

Now suppose that trade is opened. In the equilibrium after trade, the relative wage rates of U.S. and Mexican workers would be somewhere between the relative productivity of workers in the two industries—for example, U.S. wages might be four times Mexican wages. Thus, it would be cheaper to produce low-tech goods in Mexico and high-tech goods in the United States.

A critic of globalization might look at this trading equilibrium and conclude that trade works against the interest of workers. First of all, in low-tech industries, highly paid jobs in the United States are replaced with lower-paid jobs in Mexico. Moreover, you could make a plausible case that the Mexican workers are underpaid: Although

TABLE 12-3	Real Wages	
(A) Before Trade		
	High-Tech Goods/Hour	**Low-Tech Goods/Hour**
United States	1	1
Mexico	1/8	1/2
(B) After Trade		
	High-Tech Goods/Hour	**Low-Tech Goods/Hour**
United States	1	2
Mexico	1/4	1/2

they are half as productive in low-tech manufacturing as the U.S. workers they replace, their wage rate is only $1/4$ (not $1/2$) that of U.S. workers.

But as shown in the lower half of Table 12-3, in this example the purchasing power of wages has actually increased in both countries. U.S. workers, all of whom are now employed in high-tech, can purchase more low-tech goods than before: two units per hour of work versus one. Mexican workers, all of whom are now employed in low-tech, find that they can purchase more high-tech goods with an hour's labor than before: $1/4$ instead of $1/8$. Because of trade, the price of each country's imported good in terms of that country's wage rate has fallen.

The point of this example is not to reproduce the real situation in any exact way; it is to show that the evidence usually cited as proof that globalization hurts workers in developing countries is exactly what you would expect to see even if the world were well described by a model that says that trade actually benefits workers in both advanced and developing countries.

One might argue that this model is misleading because it assumes that labor is the only factor of production. It is true that if one turns from the Ricardian model to the factor-proportions model discussed in Chapter 5, it becomes possible that trade hurts workers in the labor-scarce, high-wage country—that is, the United States in this example. But this does not help the claim that trade hurts workers in developing countries. On the contrary, the case for believing that trade is beneficial to workers in the low-wage country actually becomes stronger: Standard economic analysis says that while workers in a capital-abundant nation like the United States might be hurt by trade with a labor-abundant country like Mexico, the workers in the labor-abundant country should benefit from a shift in the distribution of income in their favor.

In the specific case of the *maquiladoras*, economists argue that while wages in the *maquiladoras* are very low compared with wages in the United States, that situation is inevitable because of the lack of other opportunities in Mexico, which has far lower overall productivity. And it follows that while wages and working conditions in the *maquiladoras* may appear terrible, they represent an improvement over the alternatives available in Mexico. Indeed, the rapid rise of employment in those factories indicated that workers preferred the jobs they could find there to the alternatives. (Many of the new workers in the *maquiladoras* are in fact peasants from remote and desperately poor areas of Mexico. One could say that they have moved from intense but invisible poverty to less severe but conspicuous poverty, simultaneously achieving an improvement in their lives and becoming a source of guilt for U.S. residents unaware of their former plight.)

The standard economist's argument, in other words, is that despite the low wages earned by workers in developing countries, those workers are better off than they would have been if globalization had not taken place. Some activists do not accept this argument—they maintain that increased trade makes workers in both advanced and developing countries worse off. It is hard, however, to find a clear statement of the channels through which this is supposed to happen. Perhaps the most popular argument is that capital is mobile internationally, while labor is not; and that this mobility gives capitalists a bargaining advantage. As we saw in Chapter 4, however, international factor mobility is similar in its effects to international trade.

Labor Standards and Trade Negotiations

Free trade proponents and anti-globalization activists may debate the big questions such as, is globalization good for workers or not? Narrower practical policy issues are at stake, however: whether and to what extent international trade agreements should also contain provisions aimed at improving wages and working conditions in poor countries.

The most modest proposals have come from economists who argue for a system that monitors wages and working conditions and makes the results of this monitoring available to consumers. Their argument is a version of the market failure analysis in Chapter 10. Suppose, they suggest, that consumers in advanced countries feel better about buying manufactured goods that they know were produced by decently paid workers. Then a system that allows these consumers to know, without expending large efforts on information gathering, whether the workers were indeed decently paid offers an opportunity for mutual gain. (Kimberly Ann Elliott, cited in the Further Readings list at the end of the chapter, quotes a teenager: "Look, I don't have time to be some kind of major political activist every time I go to the mall. Just tell me what kinds of shoes are okay to buy, okay?") Because consumers can choose to buy only "certified" goods, they are better off because they feel better about their purchases. Meanwhile, workers in the certified factories gain a better standard of living than they otherwise would have had.

Proponents of such a system admit that it would not have a large impact on the standard of living in developing countries, mainly because it would affect only the wages of workers in export factories, who are a small minority of the work force even in highly export-oriented economies. But they argue that it would do some good and little harm.

A stronger step would be to include formal labor standards—that is, conditions that export industries are supposed to meet—as part of trade agreements. Such standards have considerable political support in advanced countries; indeed, President Bill Clinton spoke in favor of such standards at the disastrous Seattle meeting described previously.

The economic argument in favor of labor standards in trade agreements is similar to the argument in favor of a minimum wage rate for domestic workers: While economic theory suggests that the minimum wage reduces the number of low-skill jobs available, some (though by no means all!) reasonable economists argue that such effects are small and are outweighed by the effect of the minimum wage in raising the income of the workers who remain employed.

Labor standards in trade, however, are strongly opposed by most developing countries, which believe that the standards would inevitably be used as a protectionist tool: Politicians in advanced countries would set standards at levels that developing countries could not meet, in effect pricing their goods out of world markets. A particular concern—in fact, it was one of the concerns that led to the collapse of the talks in

Seattle—is that labor standards would be used as the basis for private lawsuits against foreign companies, similar to the way antidumping legislation has been used by private companies to harass foreign competitors.

Environmental and Cultural Issues

Complaints against globalization go beyond labor issues. Many critics argue that globalization is bad for the environment. It is unmistakably true that environmental standards in developing-country export industries are much lower than in advanced-country industries. It is also true that in a number of cases, substantial environmental damage has been and is being done in order to provide goods to advanced-country markets. A notable example is the heavy logging of Southeast Asian forests carried out to produce forest products for sale to Japanese and Western markets.

On the other hand, there are at least as many cases of environmental damage that has occurred in the name of "inward-looking" policies of countries reluctant to integrate with the global economy. A notable example is the destruction of many square miles of rain forest in Brazil, the consequence partly of a domestic policy that subsidizes development in the interior. This policy has nothing to do with exports and in fact began during the years that Brazil was attempting to pursue inward-looking development.

As in the case of labor standards, there is debate over whether trade agreements should include environmental standards. On one side, proponents argue that such agreements can lead to at least modest improvements in the environment, benefiting all concerned. On the other side, opponents insist that attaching environmental standards to trade agreements will in effect shut down potential export industries in poor countries, which cannot afford to maintain anything like Western standards.

An even trickier issue involves the effect of globalization on local and national cultures. It is unmistakably true that the growing integration of markets has led to a homogenization of cultures around the world. People worldwide increasingly tend to wear the same clothing, eat the same food, listen to the same music, and watch the same films and TV shows.

Much but not all of this homogenization is also Americanization. For example, McDonald's is now found almost everywhere, but so is sushi. Hollywood action films dominate the global box office, but stylized fight scenes in Hollywood blockbusters like *The Matrix* are based on the conventions of Hong Kong martial arts films.

It is hard to deny that something is lost as a result of this cultural homogenization. One can therefore make a market failure argument on behalf of policies that attempt to preserve national cultural differences by, for example, limiting the number of American films that can be shown in theaters, or the fraction of TV time that can be taken up with programming from overseas.

As soon as one advances this argument, however, it becomes clear that another principle is involved: the right of individuals in free societies to entertain themselves as they like. How would you feel if someone denied you the right to listen to the Rolling Stones or watch Jackie Chan movies, on the grounds that American cultural independence must be safeguarded?

The WTO and National Independence

One recurrent theme in the anti-globalization movement is that the drive for free trade and free flow of capital has undermined national sovereignty. In the extreme versions of this complaint, the World Trade Organization is characterized as a supranational power able to prevent national governments from pursuing policies in their own interests. How much substance is there to this charge?

The short answer is that the WTO does not look anything like a world government; its authority is basically limited to that of requiring countries to live up to their international trade agreements. However, the small grain of truth in the view of the WTO as a supranational authority is that its mandate allows it to monitor not only the traditional instruments of trade policy—tariffs, export subsidies, and quantitative restrictions—but also domestic policies that are de facto trade policies. And since the line between legitimate domestic policies and de facto protectionism is fuzzy, there have been cases in which the WTO has seemed to some observers to be interfering in domestic policy.

On page 327, we described a well-known example that illustrates the ambiguity of the issue. As we saw, the United States amended its Clean Air Act to require imported gasoline to be no more polluting than the average of gasoline supplied by domestic refineries. The WTO ruled that this requirement was a violation of existing trade agreements. To critics of the WTO, this ruling exemplified how the institution could frustrate an attempt by a democratically elected government to improve the environment.

As defenders of the WTO pointed out, however, the ruling was based on the fact that the United States was applying different standards to imports and to domestic production. After all, some U.S. refineries supply gasoline that is more polluting than the average, yet they are allowed to remain in operation. So the rule in effect prevented the sale of polluting gasoline from Venezuela in U.S. markets but permitted the sale of equally polluting gasoline from a domestic refinery. If the new rule had applied the same standards to domestic and foreign gasoline, it would have been acceptable to the WTO.

CASE STUDY   A Tragedy in Bangladesh

Bangladesh is a very poor country. According to World Bank estimates, in 2010 some 77 percent of Bangladeshis were living on the equivalent of less than $2 a day, and 43 percent were living on less than $1.25 a day. Incredibly, however, these numbers reflected a major improvement from the not-so-distant past: In 1992, 93 percent of the population lived on less than $2 a day in today's dollars, 67 percent on less than $1.25.

This decline in poverty was the byproduct of two decades of impressive economic growth that doubled the nation's GDP per capita. Bangladeshi growth, in turn, relied crucially on rising exports, specifically, exports of apparel. As we noted in Chapter 11, the Bangladeshi clothing industry is a classic case of comparative advantage: It has relatively low productivity, even compared with other developing countries, but Bangladesh has even lower relative productivity in other industries, so it has become a clothing export powerhouse.

Bangladeshi competitiveness in clothing depends, however, on low wages and poor working conditions. How poor? On April 24, 2013, the world was shocked by news that an eight-story building in Bangladesh, containing a number of garment factories, had collapsed, killing more than 1,200 people. Inquiries revealed that cracks had appeared in the building the day before, but garment workers had been ordered back to work anyway. It also appeared that the building was structurally unsuited for manufacturing work and may have had extra stories added without a permit.

And who was buying the clothing made under these unsafe conditions? We were: The factories in the building were supplying clothing to a number of popular Western clothing brands.

Clearly, Bangladesh needs to take steps to protect its workers, starting by enforcing its own building and worker-safety laws. But how should consumers in wealthy nations—that means, among other people, you—respond?

An immediate, instinctive response is that we shouldn't buy goods produced in countries where workers are treated so badly. Yet as we've just seen, Bangladesh desperately needs to keep exporting clothing, and it can only do so if its workers receive very low wages by Western standards. Indeed, it needs to pay less even than China, whose apparel industry has higher productivity. And low wages and poor working conditions tend, whatever we might like, to go together.

Does this mean that nothing can be done to help Bangladeshi workers that won't end up hurting them instead? No. One can imagine trying, either by law or simply through consumer pressure, some basic standards for working conditions that apply not just to Bangladesh but to its competitors. Provided that they're not too ambitious, such standards could make life better for Bangladeshi workers without destroying the exports the country relies on.

But it won't be easy, and one shouldn't expect too much from such measures. For the foreseeable future, two uncomfortable facts will continue to be true when it comes to trade with poor countries: Workers in those countries will suffer from worse wages and working conditions than Westerners can easily imagine, yet refusing to buy what those workers produce would make them much worse off.

Globalization and the Environment

Concerns about human impacts on the environment are growing in much of the world. In turn, these concerns are playing a growing role in domestic politics. For example, in November 2007, the government of Australian Prime Minister John Howard was voted out of office; most political analysts believed the ruling party's decisive defeat had a lot to do with public perceptions that Australia's Liberal Party (which is actually conservative—Labor is on the left) was unwilling to act against environmental threats.

Inevitably, then, environmental issues are playing a growing role in disputes about international trade as well. Some anti-globalization activists claim that growing international trade automatically harms the environment; some also claim that international trade agreements—and the role of the World Trade Organization in particular—have the effect of blocking environmental action. Most international economists view the first claim as simplistic and disagree with the second. That is, they deny that there is a simple relationship between globalization and environmental damage and do not believe that trade agreements prevent countries from having enlightened environmental policies. Nonetheless, the intersection of trade and the environment does raise a number of important issues.

Globalization, Growth, and Pollution

Both production and consumption often lead, as a byproduct, to environmental damage. Factories emit pollution into the air and sometimes dump effluent into rivers; farmers use fertilizer and pesticides that end up in water; consumers drive pollution-emitting cars. As a result—other things equal—economic growth, which increases both production and consumption, leads to greater environmental damage.

However, other things are not equal. For one thing, countries change the mix of their production and consumption as they grow richer, to some extent in ways that tend to reduce the environmental impact. For example, as the U.S. economy becomes increasingly devoted to the production of services rather than goods, it tends to use less energy and raw material per dollar of GDP.

In addition, growing wealth tends to lead to growing political demands for environmental quality. As a result, rich countries generally impose stricter regulations to ensure clean air and water than poorer countries—a difference that is apparent to anyone who has gone back and forth between a major city in the United States or Europe and one in a developing country, and taken a deep breath in both places.

In the early 1990s, Princeton economists Gene Grossman and Alan Krueger, studying the relationship between national income levels and pollutants such as sulfur dioxide, found that these offsetting effects of economic growth lead to a distinctive "inverted U" relationship between per-capita income and environmental damage known as the **environmental Kuznets curve**.[1] This concept, whose relevance has been confirmed by a great deal of further research, is illustrated schematically in Figure 12-3.

The idea is that as a country's income per capita rises due to economic growth, the initial effect is growing damage to the environment. Thus, China, whose economy has surged in recent decades, is in effect moving from point A to point B: As the country burns more coal in its power plants and produces more goods in its factories, it emits more sulfur dioxide into the air and dumps more effluent into its rivers.

FIGURE 12-3

The Environmental Kuznets Curve

Empirical evidence suggests that as economies grow, they initially do increasing environmental damage—but they become more environmentally friendly once they become sufficiently rich. China, where the environment is deteriorating as the economy expands, is in effect moving from A to B. Richer countries may be moving from C to D, using some of their growth to improve the environment.

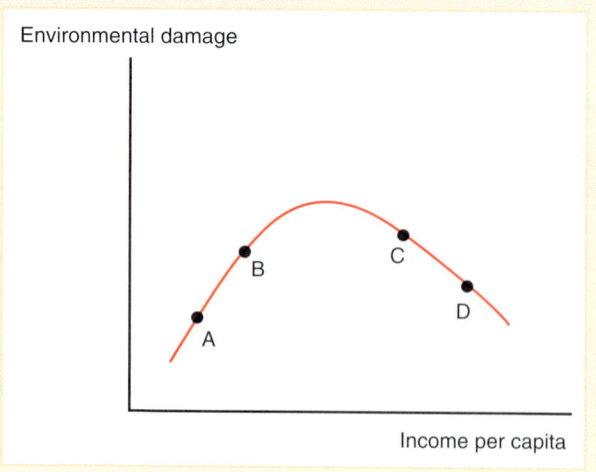

[1]Gene Grossman and Alan Krueger, "Environmental Effects of a North American Free Trade Agreement," in Peter Garber, ed., *The U.S. Mexico Free Trade Agreement*. MIT Press, 1994.

But when a country gets sufficiently rich, it can afford to take action to protect the environment. As the United States has grown richer in recent decades, it has also moved to limit pollution. For example, cars are required to have catalytic converters that reduce smog, and a government-licensing scheme limits emissions of sulfur dioxide from power plants. In terms of Figure 12-3, the United States has on some fronts, such as local air pollution, moved from C to D: growing richer and doing less damage to the environment.

What does this have to do with international trade? Trade liberalization is often advocated on the grounds that it will promote economic growth. To the extent that it succeeds in accomplishing this end, it will raise per-capita income. Will this improve or worsen environmental quality? It depends which side of the environmental Kuznets curve an economy is on. In their original paper, which was in part a response to critics of the North American Free Trade Agreement who argued that the agreement would be environmentally harmful, Grossman and Krueger suggested that Mexico might be on the right side of the curve—that is, to the extent that NAFTA raises Mexican income, it might actually lead to a reduction in environmental damage.

However, the environmental Kuznets curve does not, by any means, necessarily imply that globalization is good for the environment. In fact, it's fairly easy to make the argument that at a world level, globalization has indeed harmed the environment—at least so far.

This argument would run as follows: The biggest single beneficiary of globalization has arguably been China, whose export-led economy has experienced incredible growth since 1980. Meanwhile, the single biggest environmental issue is surely climate change: There is broad scientific consensus that emissions of carbon dioxide and other greenhouse gases are leading to a rise in the Earth's average temperature.

China's boom has been associated with a huge increase in its emissions of carbon dioxide. Figure 12-4 shows carbon dioxide emissions of the United States, Europe, and China from 1980 to 2011. In 1980, China was a minor factor in global warming; by 2008, it was, by a substantial margin, the world's leading emitter of greenhouse gases.

It's important to realize, though, that the problem here isn't globalization per se—it's China's economic success, which has to some extent come as a result of globalization. And despite environmental concerns, it's difficult to argue that China's growth, which has raised hundreds of millions of people out of dire poverty, is a bad thing.

The Problem of "Pollution Havens"

When ships get too old to continue operating, they are disassembled to recover their scrap metal and other materials. One way to look at "shipbreaking" is that it is a form of recycling: Instead of leaving a ship to rust, a shipbreaking firm extracts and reuses its components. Ultimately, this salvaging means that less iron ore needs to be mined, less oil extracted, and so on. One might expect shipbreaking to be good for the environment. The task itself, however, can be environmentally hazardous: Everything from the residual oil in a ship's tanks to the plastic in its chairs and interior fittings, if not handled carefully, can be toxic to the local environment.

As a result, shipbreaking in advanced countries is subject to close environmental regulation. When a ship is taken apart in Baltimore or Rotterdam, great care is taken to avoid environmental harm. But these days, shipbreaking rarely takes place in advanced countries. Instead, it's done in places like the Indian shipbreaking center of Alang, where ships are run aground on a beach and then dismantled by men with blowtorches, who leave a lot of pollution in their wake.

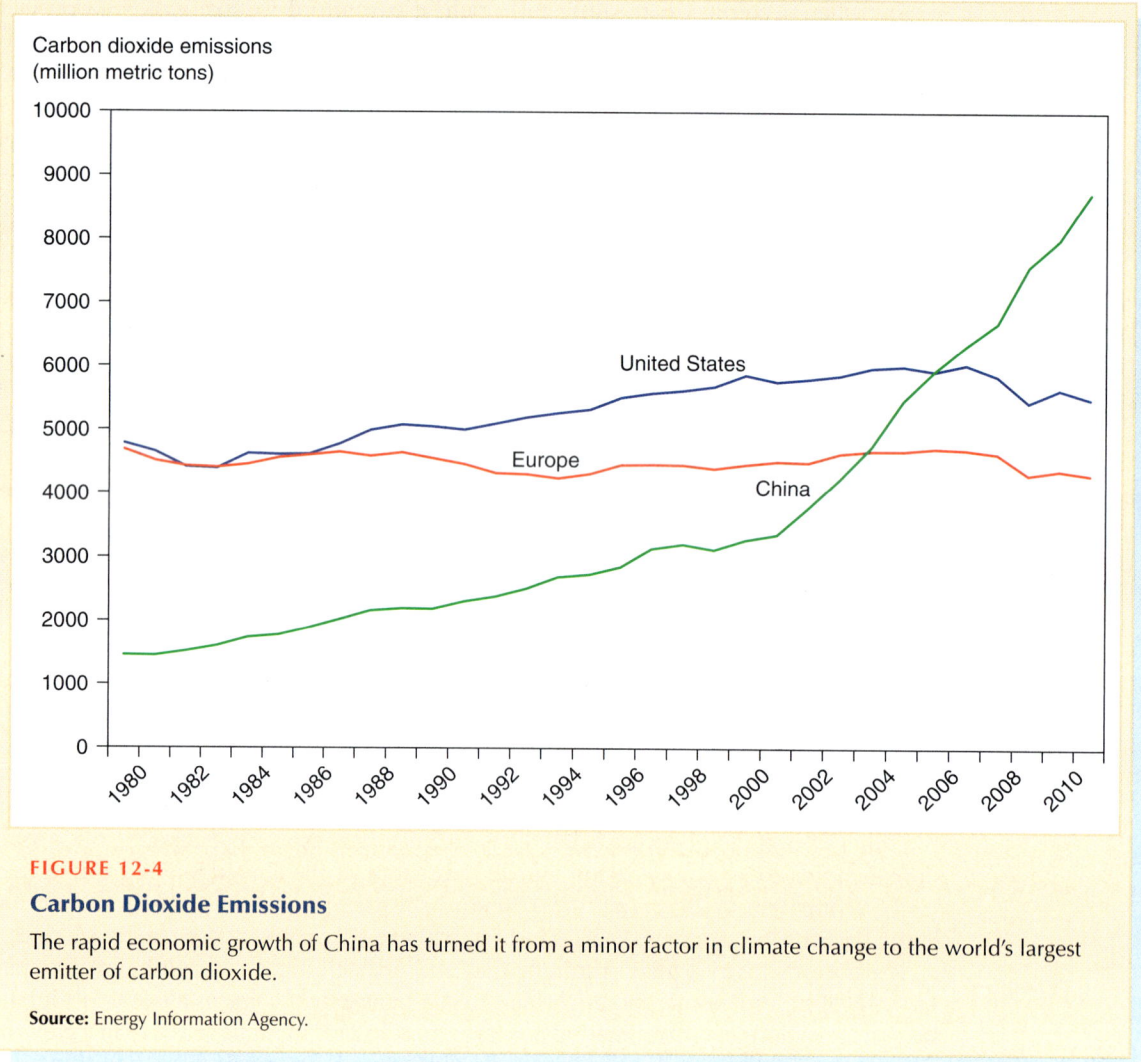

FIGURE 12-4

Carbon Dioxide Emissions

The rapid economic growth of China has turned it from a minor factor in climate change to the world's largest emitter of carbon dioxide.

Source: Energy Information Agency.

In effect, Alang has become a **pollution haven:** Thanks to international trade, an economic activity subject to strong environmental controls in some countries can take place in other countries with less strict regulation. Some activist groups are very concerned about the problem of pollution havens. Indeed, the environmental group Greenpeace made a *cause celebre* out of Alang, demanding that higher environmental standards be imposed. There are really two questions about pollution havens: (1) Are they really an important factor? and (2) Do they deserve to be a subject of international negotiation?

On the first question, most empirical research suggests that the pollution haven effect on international trade is relatively small. That is, there is not much evidence that "dirty" industries move to countries with lax environmental regulation.[2] Even in the case of the

---

[2]See, for example, Josh Ederington, Arik Levinson, and Jenny Minier, "Trade Liberalization and Pollution Havens," Working Paper 10585, National Bureau of Economic Research, June 2004.

shipbreaking industry, India's low wages seem to have been more of a lure than its loose environmental restrictions.

Second, do nations have a legitimate interest in each other's environmental policies? That turns out to depend on the nature of the environmental problem.

Pollution is the classic example of a negative externality—a cost that individuals impose on others but don't pay for. That's why pollution is a valid reason for government intervention. However, different forms of pollution have very different geographical reach—and only those that extend across national boundaries obviously justify international concern.

Thus, to the extent that Indian shipbreaking pollutes the local environment at Alang, this is a problem for India; it's less clear that it is a problem for other countries. Similarly, air pollution in Mexico City is a problem for Mexico; it's not clear why it's a valid U.S. interest. On the other hand, emissions of carbon dioxide affect the future climate for all countries: They're an international externality and deserve to be the subject of international negotiation.

At this point, it's hard to come up with major examples of industries in which the pollution haven phenomenon, to the extent that it occurs, leads to international negative externalities. That situation may change dramatically, however, if some but not all major economies adopt strong policies to limit climate change.

The Carbon Tariff Dispute

In 2009, the U.S. House of Representatives passed a bill that would have created a cap-and-trade system for greenhouse gases—that is, a system under which a limited number of emissions licenses are issued and firms are required to buy enough licenses to cover their actual emissions, in effect putting a price on carbon dioxide and other gases. The Senate failed to pass any comparable bill, so climate-change legislation is on hold for the time being. Nonetheless, there was a key trade provision in the House bill that may represent the shape of things to come: It imposed **carbon tariffs** on imports from countries that fail to enact similar policies.

What was that about? One question that has been raised about climate-change legislation is whether it can be effective if only some countries take action. The United States accounts for only part of the world's emission of greenhouse gases—in fact, as we saw in Figure 12-4, it's not even the largest emitter. So a unilateral reduction in emissions by the United States would have only a limited effect on global emissions, and hence on future climate change. Furthermore, policies that put a high price on carbon might make the pollution haven effect much larger than it has been so far, leading to "carbon leakage" as emissions-intensive industries relocate to countries without strong climate-change policies.

The obvious answer to these concerns is to make the initiative global, to have all major economies adopt similar policies. But there's no guarantee that such an agreement would be forthcoming, especially when some countries like China feel that they deserve the right to have laxer environmental policies than rich countries that have already achieved a high standard of living.

So what's the answer? The idea behind carbon tariffs is to charge importers of goods from countries without climate-change policies an amount proportional to the carbon dioxide emitted in the production of those goods. The charge per ton of emissions would be equal to the price of carbon dioxide emission licenses in the domestic market. This would give overseas producers an incentive to limit their carbon emissions and would remove the incentive to shift production to countries with lax regulation. In addition, it would, possibly, give countries with lax regulations an incentive to adopt climate-change policies of their own.

Critics of carbon tariffs argue that they would be protectionist, and also violate international trade rules, which prohibit discrimination between domestic and foreign products. Supporters argue that they would simply place producers of imported goods and domestic producers on a level playing field when selling to domestic consumers, with both required to pay for their greenhouse gas emissions. And because carbon tariffs create a level playing field, they argue, such tariffs—carefully applied—should also be legal under existing trade rules.

At this point, the issue of carbon tariffs is hypothetical, since no major economy has yet placed a significant price on greenhouse gas emissions. Correspondingly, the WTO hasn't issued any rulings on the legality of such tariffs, and probably won't until or unless a real case emerges. But if climate-change legislation makes a comeback—and it is a good bet that it will sooner or later—it will clearly lead to some major new issues in trade policy.

SUMMARY

1. Some new arguments for government intervention in trade have emerged over the past quarter-century: The theory of *strategic trade policy* offered reasons why countries might gain from promoting particular industries. In the 1990s a new critique of globalization emerged that focused on the effects of globalization on workers in developing countries. And possible action on climate change has raised some major trade issues, including that of the desirability and legality of *carbon tariffs*.

2. Activist trade policy arguments rest on two ideas. One is the argument that governments should promote industries that yield technological *externalities*. The other, which represents a greater departure from standard market failure arguments, is the *Brander-Spencer analysis*, which suggests that strategic intervention can enable nations to capture *excess returns*. These arguments are theoretically persuasive; however, many economists worry that they are too subtle and require too much information to be useful in practice.

3. With the rise of manufactured exports from developing countries, a new movement opposed to globalization has emerged. The central concern of this movement is with the low wages paid to export workers, although there are other themes as well. The response of most economists is that developing-country workers may earn low wages by Western standards, but that trade allows them to earn more than they otherwise would.

4. An examination of cases suggests how difficult the discussion of globalization really is, especially when one tries to view it as a moral issue; it is all too easy for people to do harm when they are trying to do good. The causes most favored by activists, such as labor standards, are feared by developing countries, which believe the standards will be used as protectionist devices.

5. To the extent that globalization promotes economic growth, it has ambiguous effects on the environment. The *environmental Kuznets curve* says that economic growth initially tends to increase environmental damage as a country grows richer but that beyond a certain point, growth is actually good for the environment. Unfortunately, some of the world's fastest-growing economies are still relatively poor and on the "wrong" side of the curve.

6. There is growing concern that globalization may allow highly polluting industries to move to *pollution havens*, where regulation is looser. There is little evidence that

this is a major factor in actual location decisions, at least so far. But that may change if serious climate-change policies are implemented; in that case, there is a strong case for *carbon tariffs*, but also strong criticism of the concept.

KEY TERMS

beggar-thy-neighbor policies, p. 321
Brander-Spencer analysis, p. 318

carbon tariffs, p. 333
environmental Kuznets curve, p. 330
excess returns, p. 317

externalities, p. 315
pollution haven, p. 332
strategic trade policy, p. 314

PROBLEMS

MyEconLab

1. What are the main arguments in favor of an interventionist trade policy? Provide one example of each.

2. Globalization has often attracted a lot of criticism, especially from emerging countries. Taking the analysis made in this chapter into consideration, state your conclusions.

3. If the United States had its way, it would demand that Japan spend more money on basic research in science and less on applied research into industrial applications. Explain why in terms of the analysis of appropriability.

4. Why do strategic trade policies normally attract trade retaliation actions from other countries? Examine a case-study of your choice and analyze its implication.

5. Suppose the European Commission asked you to develop a brief on behalf of subsidizing European development of software for smartphones—bearing in mind that this industry is currently dominated by U.S. firms, notably Apple and Google (whose Android system is used on many phones and tablets). What arguments would you use? What are the weaknesses in those arguments?

6. What is the main critique against the WTO with respect to environmental protection? How does the WTO justify its position on trade disputes that involve environmental issues?

7. France, in addition to its occasional stabs at strategic trade policy, pursues an active nationalist *cultural* policy that promotes French art, music, fashion, cuisine, and so on. This may be primarily a matter of attempting to preserve a national identity in an increasingly homogeneous world, but some French officials also defend this policy on economic grounds. In what sense could some features of such a policy be defended as a kind of strategic trade policy?

8. "The fundamental problem with any attempt to limit climate change is that the countries whose growth poses the greatest threat to the planet are also the countries that can least afford to pay the price of environmental activism." Explain in terms of the environmental Kuznets curve.

9. Many countries have value-added taxes—taxes that are paid by producers, but are intended to fall on consumers. (They're basically just an indirect way of imposing sales taxes.) Such value-added taxes are always accompanied by an equal tax on imports; such import taxes are considered legal because like the value-added tax, they're really an indirect way of taxing all consumer purchases at the same rate. Compare this situation to the argument over carbon tariffs. Why might defenders argue that such tariffs are legal? What objections can you think of?

FURTHER READINGS

James A. Brander and Barbara J. Spencer. "Export Subsidies and International Market Share Rivalry." *Journal of International Economics* 16 (1985), pp. 83–100. A basic reference on the potential role of subsidies as a tool of strategic trade policy.

Kimberly Ann Elliott. *Can Labor Standards Improve Under Globalization?* Washington, D.C.: Institute for International Economics, 2001. A survey of the issues by an economist sympathetic to the cause of the activists.

Edward M. Graham. *Fighting the Wrong Enemy: Antiglobalization Activists and Multinational Corporations.* Washington, D.C.: Institute for International Economics, 2001. A survey of the issues by an economist less sympathetic to the activists.

Elhanan Helpman and Paul Krugman. *Trade Policy and Market Structure.* Cambridge: MIT Press, 1989. A survey and synthesis of the literature on strategic trade policy and related topics.

William Langewiesche. "The Shipbreakers." *The Atlantic Monthly* (August 2000). A fascinating description of the shipbreaking industry of Alang and the dispute it has generated.

Hearing on Trade Aspects of Climate Change Legislation, Before the Subcommittee on Trade, 112th Cong. (March 24 2009) (statement of Joost Pauwelyn). A clear, concise discussion by a trade lawyer of the issues surrounding carbon tariffs, in which he argues that if done carefully, they would be legal under existing agreements.

The Factor-Proportions Model

In this postscript we set out a formal mathematical treatment for the factor-proportions model of production explained in Chapter 5. The mathematical treatment is useful in deepening your understanding of the model.

Factor Prices and Costs

Consider the production of some good that requires capital and labor as factors of production. Provided the good is produced with constant returns to scale, the technology of production may be summarized in terms of the *unit isoquant* (*II* in Figure 5P-1), a curve showing all the combinations of capital and labor that can be used to produce one unit of the good. Curve *II* shows that there is a trade-off between the quantity of capital used per unit of output, a_K, and the quantity of labor per unit of output, a_L. The curvature of the unit isoquant reflects the assumption that it becomes increasingly difficult to substitute capital for labor as the capital-labor ratio increases, and vice-versa.

In a competitive market economy, producers will choose the capital-labor ratio in production that minimizes their cost. Such a cost-minimizing production choice is shown in Figure 5P-1 as point E, the point at which the unit isoquant *II* is tangent to a line whose slope is equal to minus the ratio of the price of labor, w, to the price of capital, r.

The actual cost of production is equal to the sum of the cost of capital and labor inputs,

$$c = a_K r + a_L w, \tag{5P-1}$$

where the input coefficients, a_K and a_L, have been chosen to minimize c.

Because the capital-labor ratio has been chosen to minimize costs, it follows that a change in that ratio cannot reduce costs. Costs cannot be reduced by increasing a_K while reducing a_L, nor conversely. It follows that an infinitesimal change in the capital-labor ratio from the cost-minimizing choice must have no effect on cost. Let da_K, da_L be small changes from the optimal input choices. Then

$$r\,da_K + w\,da_L = 0 \tag{5P-2}$$

for any movement along the unit isoquant.

Consider next what happens if the factor prices r and w change. This will have two effects: It will change the choice of a_K and a_L, and it will change the cost of production.

First, consider the effect on the relative quantities of capital and labor used to produce one unit of output. The cost-minimizing labor-capital ratio depends on the ratio of the price of labor to that of capital:

$$\frac{a_K}{a_L} = \Phi\!\left(\frac{w}{r}\right). \tag{5P-3}$$

337

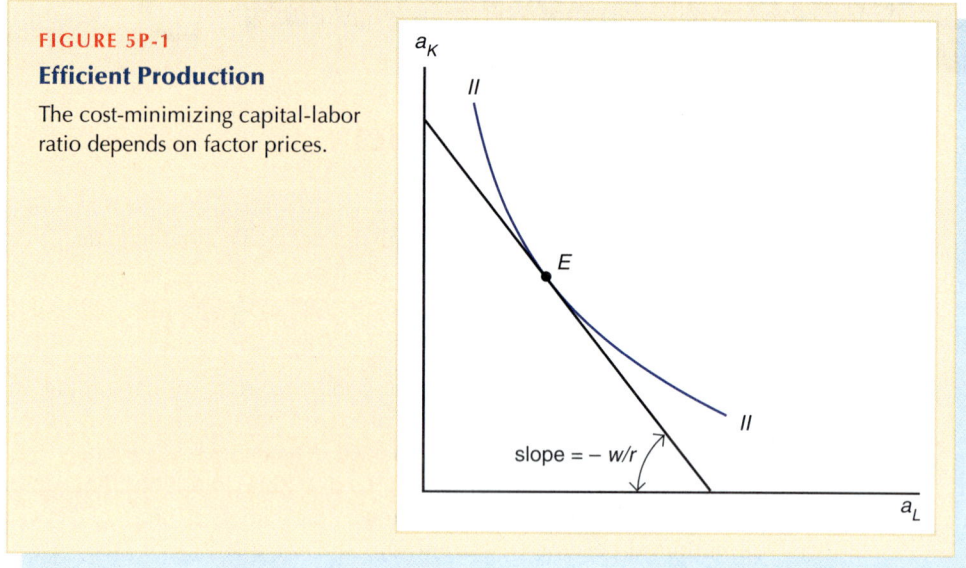

FIGURE 5P-1

Efficient Production

The cost-minimizing capital-labor ratio depends on factor prices.

The cost of production will also change. For small changes in factor prices dr and dw, the change in production cost is

$$dc = a_K dr + a_L dw + r da_K + w da_L. \tag{5P-4}$$

From equation (5P-2), however, we already know that the last two terms of equation (5P-4) sum to zero. Hence the effect of factor prices on cost may be written

$$dc = a_K dr + a_L dw. \tag{5P-4'}$$

It turns out to be very convenient to derive a somewhat different equation from equation (5P-4'). Dividing and multiplying some of the elements of the equation leads to the following new equation:

$$\frac{dc}{c} = \left(\frac{a_K r}{c}\right)\left(\frac{dr}{r}\right) + \left(\frac{a_L w}{c}\right)\left(\frac{dw}{w}\right). \tag{5P-5}$$

The term dc/c may be interpreted as the *percentage change* in c, and may conveniently be designated as $\hat{c}$; similarly, let $dr/r = \hat{r}$ and $dw/w = \hat{w}$. The term $a_K r/c$ may be interpreted as the *share of capital in total production costs*; it may be conveniently designated θ_K. Thus equation (5P-5) can be compactly written

$$\hat{c} = \theta_K \hat{r} + \theta_L \hat{w}, \tag{5P-5'}$$

where

$$\theta_K + \theta_L = 1.$$

This is an example of "hat algebra," an extremely useful way to express mathematical relationships in international economics.

The Basic Equations in the Factor-Proportions Model

Suppose a country produces two goods, cloth C and food F, using two factors of production, capital and labor. Assume that food production is capital-intensive. The price of each good must equal its production cost:

$$P_F = a_{KF}r + a_{LF}w, \tag{5P-6}$$

$$P_C = a_{KC}r + a_{LC}w, \tag{5P-7}$$

where $a_{KF}, a_{LF}, a_{KC}, a_{LC}$ are the cost-minimizing input choices given the price of capital, r and labor, w.

Also, the economy's factors of production must be fully employed:

$$a_{KF}Q_F + a_{KC}Q_C = K, \tag{5P-8}$$

$$a_{LF}Q_F + a_{LC}Q_C = L, \tag{5P-9}$$

where K, L are the total supplies of capital and labor.

The factor-price equations (5P-6) and (5P-7) imply equations for the rate of change for factor prices.

$$\hat{P}_F = \theta_{KF}\hat{r} + \theta_{LF}\hat{w}, \tag{5P-10}$$

$$\hat{P}_C = \theta_{KC}\hat{r} + \theta_{LC}\hat{w}, \tag{5P-11}$$

where θ_{KF} is the share of capital in production cost of F, etc., $\theta_{KF} > \theta_{KC}$ and $\theta_{LF} < \theta_{LC}$ because F is more capital-intensive than C.

The quantity equations (5P-8) and (5P-9) must be treated more carefully. The unit inputs a_{KF}, etc., can change if factor prices change. If goods prices are held constant, however, then factor prices will not change. Thus for *given* prices of F and C, it is also possible to write hat equations in terms of factor supplies and outputs:

$$\alpha_{KF}\hat{Q}_F + \alpha_{KC}\hat{Q}_C = \hat{K}, \tag{5P-12}$$

$$\alpha_{LF}\hat{Q}_F + \alpha_{LC}\hat{Q}_C = \hat{L}, \tag{5P-13}$$

where α_{KF} is the share of the economy's capital supply that is used in production of F, etc. $\alpha_{KF} > \alpha_{LF}$ and $\alpha_{KC} < \alpha_{LC}$ because of the greater capital intensity of F production.

Goods Prices and Factor Prices

The factor-price equations (5P-10) and (5P-11) may be solved together to express factor prices as the outcome of goods prices (these solutions make use of the fact that $\theta_{LF} = 1 - \theta_{KF}$ and $\theta_{LC} = 1 - \theta_{KC}$):

$$\hat{r} = \left(\frac{1}{D}\right)[(1 - \theta_{KC})\hat{P}_F - \theta_{LF}\hat{P}_C], \tag{5P-14}$$

$$\hat{w} = \left(\frac{1}{D}\right)[\theta_{KF}\hat{P}_C - \theta_{KC}\hat{P}_F], \tag{5P-15}$$

where $D = \theta_{KF} - \theta_{KC}$ (implying that $D > 0$). These may be arranged in the form

$$\hat{r} = \hat{P}_F + \left(\frac{\theta_{LF}}{D}\right)(\hat{P}_F - \hat{P}_C), \tag{5P-14'}$$

$$\hat{w} = \hat{P}_C + \left(\frac{\theta_{KC}}{D}\right)(\hat{P}_F - \hat{P}_C). \tag{5P-15'}$$

Suppose that the price of F rises relative to the price of C, so that $\hat{P}_F > \hat{P}_C$. Then it follows that

$$\hat{r} > \hat{P}_F > \hat{P}_C > \hat{w}. \tag{5P-16}$$

That is, the real price of capital rises in terms of both goods, while the real price of labor falls in terms of both goods. In particular, if the price of F were to rise with no change in the price of C, the wage rate would actually fall.

Factor Supplies and Outputs

As long as goods prices may be taken as given, equations (5P-12) and (5P-13) can be solved, using the fact that $\alpha_{KC} = 1 - \alpha_{KF}$ and $\alpha_{LC} = 1 - \alpha_{LF}$, to express the change in output of each good as the outcome of changes in factor supplies:

$$\hat{Q}_F = \left(\frac{1}{\Delta}\right)[\alpha_{LC}\hat{K} - \alpha_{KC}\hat{L}], \tag{5P-17}$$

$$\hat{Q}_C = \left(\frac{1}{\Delta}\right)[-\alpha_{LF}\hat{K} + \alpha_{KF}\hat{L}], \tag{5P-18}$$

where $\Delta = \alpha_{KF} - \alpha_{LF}$, $\Delta > 0$.

These equations may be rewritten

$$\hat{Q}_F = \hat{K} + \left(\frac{\alpha_{KC}}{\Delta}\right)(\hat{K} - \hat{L}), \tag{5P-17'}$$

$$\hat{Q}_F = \hat{L} - \left(\frac{\alpha_{LF}}{\Delta}\right)(\hat{K} - \hat{L}). \tag{5P-18'}$$

Suppose that P_F and P_C remain constant, while the supply of capital rises relative to the supply of labor—$\hat{K} > \hat{L}$. Then it is immediately apparent that

$$\hat{Q}_F > \hat{K} > \hat{L} > \hat{Q}_C. \tag{5P-19}$$

In particular, if K rises with L remaining constant, output of F will rise more than in proportion while output of C will actually fall.

The Trading World Economy

Supply, Demand, and Equilibrium

World Equilibrium

Although for graphical purposes it is easiest to express world equilibrium as an equality between relative supply and relative demand, for a mathematical treatment, it is preferable to use an alternative formulation. This approach focuses on the conditions of equality between supply and demand of either one of the two goods, cloth and food. It does not matter which good is chosen because equilibrium in the cloth market implies equilibrium in the food market and vice versa.

To see this condition, let Q_C, Q_C^* be the output of cloth in Home and Foreign, respectively; D_C, D_C^* the quantity demanded in each country; and corresponding variables with an F subscript the food market. Also, let p be the price of cloth relative to that of food.

In all cases, world expenditure will be equal to world income. World income is the sum of income earned from sales of cloth and sales of food; world expenditure is the sum of purchases of cloth and purchases of food. Thus the equality of income and expenditure may be written

$$p(Q_C + Q_C^*) + Q_F + Q_F^* = p(D_C + D_C^*) + D_F + D_F^*. \tag{6P-1}$$

Now suppose that the world market for cloth is in equilibrium; that is,

$$Q_C + Q_C^* = D_C + D_C^*. \tag{6P-2}$$

Then from equation (6P-1), it follows that

$$Q_F + Q_F^* = D_F + D_F^*. \tag{6P-3}$$

That is, the market for food must be in equilibrium as well. Clearly the converse is also true: If the market for food is in equilibrium, so too is the market for cloth.

It is therefore sufficient to focus on the market for cloth to determine the equilibrium relative price.

Production and Income

Each country has a production possibility frontier along which it can trade off between producing cloth and producing food. The economy chooses the point on the frontier that maximizes the value of output at the given relative price of cloth. This value may be written

$$V = pQ_C + Q_F. \tag{6P-4}$$

As in the cost-minimization cases described in the earlier postscript, the fact that the output mix chosen maximizes value implies that a small shift in production along the production possibility frontier away from the optimal mix has no effect on the value of output:

$$pdQ_C + dQ_F = 0. \tag{6P-5}$$

A change in the relative price of cloth will lead to both a change in the output mix and a change in the value of output. The change in the value of output is

$$dV = Q_C dp + p dQ_C + dQ_F. \tag{6P-6}$$

However, because the last two terms are, by equation (6P-5), equal to zero, this expression reduces to

$$dV = Q_C dp. \tag{6P-6$'$}$$

Similarly, in Foreign,

$$dV^* = Q_C^* dp. \tag{6P-7}$$

Income, Prices, and Utility

Each country is treated as if it were one individual. The tastes of the country can be represented by a utility function depending on consumption of cloth and food:

$$U = U(D_C, D_F). \tag{6P-8}$$

Suppose a country has an income I in terms of food. Its total expenditure must be equal to this income, so that

$$p D_C + D_F = I. \tag{6P-9}$$

Consumers will maximize utility given their income and the prices they face. Let MU_C, MU_F be the marginal utility that consumers derive from cloth and food; then the change in utility that results from any change in consumption is

$$dU = MU_C dD_C + MU_F dD_F. \tag{6P-10}$$

Because consumers are maximizing utility given income and prices, there cannot be any affordable change in consumption that makes them better off. This condition implies that at the optimum,

$$\frac{MU_C}{MU_F} = p. \tag{6P-11}$$

Now consider the effect on utility of changing income and prices. Differentiating equation (6P-9) yields

$$p dD_C + dD_F = dI - D_C dp. \tag{6P-12}$$

But from equations (6P-10) and (6P-11),

$$dU = MU_F[p dD_C + dD_F]. \tag{6P-13}$$

Thus,

$$dU = MU_F[dI - D_C dp]. \tag{6P-14}$$

It is convenient to introduce now a new definition: The change in utility divided by the marginal utility of food, which is the commodity in which income is measured, may be defined as the change in *real income*, and indicated by the symbol dy:

$$dy = \frac{dU}{MU_F} = dI - D_C dp. \tag{6P-15}$$

For the economy as a whole, income equals the value of output: $I = V$. Thus the effect of a change in the relative price of cloth on the economy's real income is

$$dy = [Q_C - D_C]dp. \tag{6P-16}$$

The quantity $Q_C - D_C$ is the economy's exports of cloth. A rise in the relative price of cloth, then, will benefit an economy that exports cloth; it is thus an improvement in that economy's terms of trade. It is instructive to restate this idea in a slightly different way:

$$dy = [p(Q_C - D_C)]\left(\frac{dp}{p}\right). \tag{6P-17}$$

The term in brackets is the value of exports; the term in parentheses is the percentage change in the terms of trade. The expression therefore says that the real income gain from a given percentage in terms of trade change is equal to the percentage change in the terms of trade multiplied by the initial value of exports. If a country is initially exporting \$100 billion and its terms of trade improve by 10 percent, the gain is equivalent to a gain in national income of \$10 billion.

Supply, Demand, and the Stability of Equilibrium

In the market for cloth, a change in the relative price will induce changes in both supply and demand.

On the supply side, a rise in p will lead both Home and Foreign to produce more cloth. We will denote this supply response as in Home and Foreign, respectively, so that

$$dQ_C = s\,dp, \tag{6P-18}$$

$$dQ_C^* = s^*\,dp. \tag{6P-19}$$

The demand side is more complex. A change in p will lead to both *income* and *substitution* effects. These effects are illustrated in Figure 6P-1. The figure shows an economy that initially faces a relative price indicated by the slope of the line VV^0.

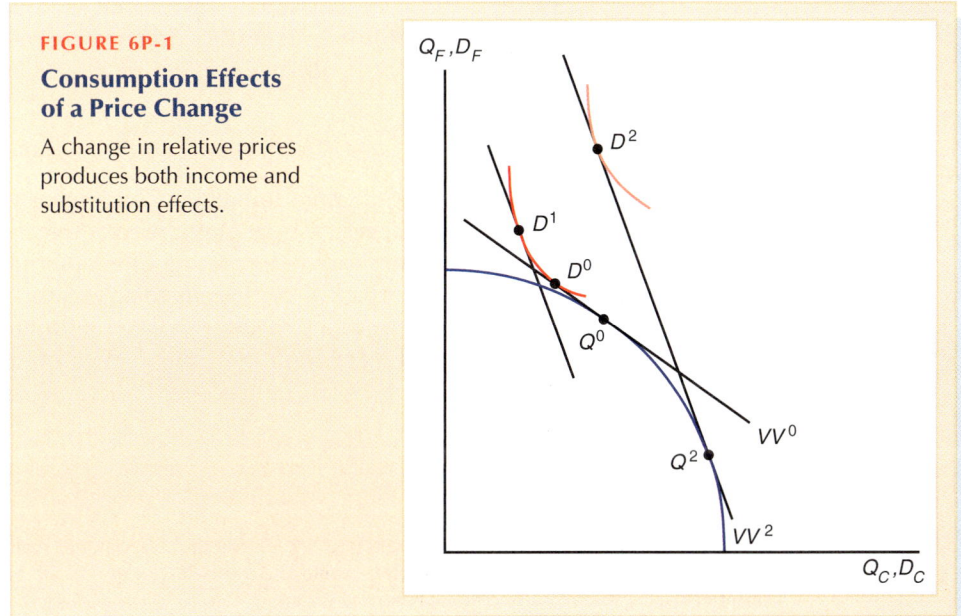

FIGURE 6P-1

Consumption Effects of a Price Change

A change in relative prices produces both income and substitution effects.

Given this relative price, the economy produces at point Q^0 and consumes at point D^0. Now suppose the relative price of cloth rises to the level indicated by the slope of VV^2. If there were no increase in utility, consumption would shift to D^1, which would involve an unambiguous fall in consumption of cloth. There is also, however, a change in the economy's real income; in this case, because the economy is initially a net exporter of cloth, real income rises. This change leads to consumption at D^2 rather than D^1, and this income effect tends to raise consumption of cloth. Analyzing the effect of change in p on demand requires taking account of both the substitution effect, which is the change in consumption that would take place if real income were held constant, and the income effect, which is the additional change in consumption that is the consequence of the fact that real income changes.

Let the substitution effect be denoted by $-e\,dp$; it is always negative. Also, let the income effect be denoted by $n\,dy$; as long as cloth is a normal good for which demand rises with real income, it is positive if the country is a net exporter of cloth, negative if it is a net importer.[1] Then the total effect of a change in p on Home's demand for cloth is

$$dD_C = -e\,dp + n\,dy$$

$$= [-e + n(Q_C - D_C)]dp. \qquad (6P\text{-}20)$$

The effect on Foreign's demand similarly is

$$dD_C^* = [-e^* + n^*(Q_C^* - D_C^*)]dp. \qquad (6P\text{-}21)$$

Because $Q_C^* - D_C^*$ is negative, the income effect in Foreign is negative.

The demand and supply effect can now be put together to get the overall effect of a change in p on the market for cloth. The *excess supply* of cloth is the difference between desired world production and consumption:

$$ES_C = Q_C + Q_C^* - D_C - D_C^* . \qquad (6P\text{-}22)$$

The effect of a change in p on world excess supply is

$$dES_C = [s + s^* + e + e^* - n(Q_C - D_C) - n^*(Q_C^* - D_C^*)]dp. \qquad (6P\text{-}23)$$

If the market is initially in equilibrium, however, Home's exports equal Foreign's imports, so that $Q_C^* - D_C^* = -(Q_C - D_C)$; the effect of p on excess supply may therefore be written

$$dES_C = [s + s^* + e + e^* - (n - n^*)(Q_C - D_C)]dp. \qquad (6P\text{-}23')$$

Suppose the relative price of cloth were initially a little higher than its equilibrium level. If the result were an excess supply of cloth, market forces would push the relative price of cloth down and thus lead to restoration of equilibrium. On the other hand, if an excessively high relative price of cloth leads to an excess *demand* for cloth, the price will rise further, leading the economy away from equilibrium. Thus equilibrium will be *stable* only if a small increase in the relative price of cloth leads to an excess supply of cloth; that is, if

$$\frac{dES_C}{dp} > 0. \qquad (6P\text{-}24)$$

---

[1] If food is also a normal good, n must be less than $1/p$. To see this effect, notice that if I were to rise by dI without any change in p, spending on cloth would rise by $np\,dI$. Unless $n < 1/p$, then, more than 100 percent of the increase in income would be spent on cloth.

Inspection of equation (6P-23′) reveals the factors determining whether or not equilibrium is stable. Both supply effects and substitution effects in demand work toward stability. The only possible source of instability lies in income effects. The net income effect is of ambiguous sign: It depends on whether $n > n^*$; that is, on whether Home has a higher marginal propensity to consume cloth when its real income increases than Foreign does. If $n > n^*$, the income effect works against stability, while if $n < n^*$, it reinforces the other reasons for stability. The income effects can lead to equilibrium instability because they can generate a relative demand curve for the world that is upward sloping.

In what follows, it will be assumed that equation (6P-24) holds, so that the equilibrium of the world economy is in fact stable.

Effects of Changes in Supply and Demand

The Method of Comparative Statics

To evaluate the effects of changes in the world economy, a method known as *comparative statics* is applied. In each of the cases considered in the text, the world economy is subjected to some change that will lead to a change in the world relative price of cloth. The first step in the method of comparative statics is to calculate the effect of the change in the world economy on the excess supply of cloth *at the original p*. This change is denoted by $dES|_p$. Then the change in the relative price needed to restore equilibrium is calculated by

$$dp = \frac{-dES|_p}{(dES/dp)}, \tag{6P-25}$$

where dES/dp reflects the supply, income, and substitution effects described earlier.

The effects of a given change on national welfare can be calculated in two stages. First there is whatever direct effect the change has on real income, which we can denote by $dy|_p$; then there is the indirect effect of the resulting change in the terms of trade, which can be calculated using equation (6P-16). Thus the total effect on welfare is

$$dy = dy|_p + (Q_C - D_C)dp. \tag{6P-26}$$

Economic Growth

Consider the effect of growth in the Home economy. As pointed out in the text, by growth we mean an outward shift in the production possibility frontier. This change will lead to changes in both cloth and food output at the initial relative price p; let dQ_C, dQ_F be these changes in output. If growth is strongly biased, one or the other of these changes may be negative, but because production possibilities have expanded, the value of output at the initial p must rise:

$$dV = p\,dQ_C + dQ_F = dy|_p > 0. \tag{6P-27}$$

At the initial p, the supply of cloth will rise by the amount dQ_C. The demand for cloth will also rise, by an amount $n\,dy|_p$. The net effect on world excess supply of cloth will therefore be

$$dES|_p = dQ_C - n(p\,dQ_C + dQ_F). \tag{6P-28}$$

This expression can have either sign. Suppose first that growth is biased toward cloth, so that while $dQ_C > 0$, $dQ_F \le 0$. Then demand for cloth will rise by

$$dD_C = n(p\,dQ_C + dQ_F) \le np\,dQ_C > dQ_C.$$

(See footnote 1.)

Thus the overall effect on excess supply will be

$$dES|_p = dQ_C - dD_C > 0.$$

As a result, $dp = -dES|_p/(dES/dp) < 0$: Home's terms of trade worsen.

On the other hand, suppose that growth is strongly biased toward food, so that $dQ_C \leq 0$, $dQ_F > 0$. Then the effect on the supply of cloth at the initial p is negative, but the effect on the demand for cloth remains positive. It follows that

$$dES|_p = dQ_C - dD_C < 0,$$

so that $dp > 0$. Home's terms of trade improve.

Growth that is less strongly biased can move p either way, depending on the strength of the bias compared with the way Home divides its income at the margin.

Turning next to the welfare effects, the effect on Foreign depends only on the terms of trade. The effect on Home, however, depends on the combination of the initial income change and the subsequent change in the terms of trade, as shown in equation (6P-26). If growth turns the terms of trade against Home, this condition will oppose the immediate favorable effect of growth.

But can growth worsen the terms of trade sufficiently to make the growing country actually worse off? To see that it can, consider first the case of a country that experiences a biased shift in its production possibilities that raises Q_C and lowers Q_F while leaving the value of its output unchanged at initial relative prices. (This change would not necessarily be considered growth, because it violates the assumption of equation (6P-27), but it is a useful reference point.) Then there would be no change in demand at the initial p, whereas the supply of cloth rises; hence p must fall. The change in real income is $dy|_p - (Q_C - D_C)dp$; by construction, however, this is a case in which $dy|_p = 0$, so dy is certainly negative.

Now, this country did not grow, in the usual sense, because the value of output at initial prices did not rise. By allowing the output of either good to rise slightly more, however, we would have a case in which the definition of growth is satisfied. If the extra growth is sufficiently small, however, it will not outweigh the welfare loss from the fall in p. Therefore, sufficiently biased growth can leave the growing country worse off.

A Transfer of Income

We now describe how a transfer of income (say as foreign aid) affects the terms of trade.[2] Suppose Home makes a transfer of some of its income to Foreign. Let the amount of the transfer, measured in terms of food, be da. What effect does this aid have on the terms of trade?

At unchanged relative prices, there is no effect on supply. The only effect is on demand. Home's income is reduced by da, while Foreign's is raised by the same amount. This adjustment leads to a decline in D_C by $-n\,da$, while D_C^* rises by n^*da. Thus,

$$dES|_p = (n - n^*)da \tag{6P-29}$$

and the change in the terms of trade is

$$dp = -da\frac{(n - n^*)}{(dES/dp)}. \tag{6P-30}$$

---

[2]In the online appendix to Chapter 6, we discuss an important historical example of a large income transfer and its implications for the terms of trade of the donor and recipient countries.

Home's terms of trade will worsen if $n > n^*$, which is widely regarded as the normal case; they will, however, improve if $n^* > n$.

The effect on Home's real income combines a direct negative effect from the transfer and an indirect terms of trade effect that can go either way. Is it possible for a favorable terms of trade effect to outweigh the income loss? In this model it is not.

To see the reason, notice that

$$
\begin{aligned}
dy &= dy|_n + (Q_C - D_C)dp \\
&= -da + (Q_C - D_C)dp \\
&= -da\left\{1 + \frac{(n - n^*)(Q_C - D_C)}{s + s^* + e + e^* - (n - n^*)(Q_C - D_C)}\right\} \\
&= -da\frac{(s + s^* + e + e^*)}{[s + s^* + e + e^* - (n - n^*)(Q_C - D_C)]} < 0.
\end{aligned}
\tag{6P-31}
$$

Similar algebra will reveal correspondingly that a transfer cannot make the recipient worse off.

An intuitive explanation of this result is the following. Suppose p were to rise sufficiently to leave Home as well off as it would be if it made no transfer and to leave Foreign no better off as a result of the transfer. Then there would be no income effects on demand in the world economy. But the rise in price would produce both increased output of cloth and substitution in demand away from cloth, leading to an excess supply that would drive down the price. This result demonstrates that a p sufficiently high to reverse the direct welfare effects of a transfer is above the equilibrium p.

A Tariff

Suppose Home places a tariff on imports, imposing a tax equal to the fraction t of the price. Then for a given world relative price of cloth p, Home consumers and producers will face an internal relative price $\bar{p} = p/(1 + t)$. If the tariff is sufficiently small, the internal relative price will be approximately equal to

$$
\bar{p} = p - p.
\tag{6P-32}
$$

In addition to affecting p, a tariff will raise revenue, which will be assumed to be redistributed to the rest of the economy.

At the initial terms of trade, a tariff will influence the excess supply of cloth in two ways. First, the fall in relative price of cloth inside Home will lower production of cloth and induce consumers to substitute away from food toward cloth. Second, the tariff may affect Home's real income, with resulting income effects on demand. If Home starts with no tariff and imposes a small tariff, however, the problem may be simplified, because the tariff will have a negligible effect on real income. To see this relation, recall that

$$
dy = p\,dD_C + dD_F.
$$

The value of output and the value of consumption must always be equal at world prices, so that

$$
p\,dD_C + dD_F = p\,dQ_C + dQ_F
$$

at the initial terms of trade. But because the economy was maximizing the value of output before the tariff was imposed,

$$
p\,dQ_C + dQ_F = 0.
$$

Because there is no income effect, only the substitution effect is left. The fall in the internal relative price $\bar{p}$ induces a decline in production and a rise in consumption:

$$dQ_C = -sp\ dt, \tag{6P-33}$$

$$dD_C = ep\ dt, \tag{6P-34}$$

where dt is the tariff increase. Hence,

$$dES|_p = -(s+e)p\ dt < 0, \tag{6P-35}$$

implying

$$dp = \frac{-dES|_p}{(dES/dp)}$$

$$= \frac{p\ dt(s+e)}{[s+s^* + e + e^* - (n-n^*)(Q_C - D_C)]} > 0. \tag{6P-36}$$

This expression shows that a tariff unambiguously improves the terms of trade of the country that imposes it.

The Monopolistic Competition Model

We want to consider the effects of changes in the size of the market on equilibrium in a monopolistically competitive industry. Each firm has the total cost relationship

$$C = F + cX, \tag{8P-1}$$

where c is marginal cost, F a fixed cost, and X the firm's output. This implies an average cost curve of the form

$$AC = C/X = F/X + c. \tag{8P-2}$$

Also, each firm faces a demand curve of the form

$$X = S[1/n - b(P - \overline{P})], \tag{8P-3}$$

where S is total industry sales (taken as given), n is the number of firms, and $\overline{P}$ is the average price charged by other firms (which each firm is assumed to take as given).

Each firm chooses its price to maximize profits. Profits of a typical firm are

$$\pi = PX - C = PS[1/n - b(P - \overline{P})] - F - cS[1/n - b(P - \overline{P})]. \tag{8P-4}$$

To maximize profits, a firm sets the derivative $d\pi/dP = 0$. This implies

$$X - SbP + Sbc = 0. \tag{8P-5}$$

Since all firms are symmetric, however, in equilibrium, $P = \overline{P}$ and $X = S/n$. Thus (8P-5) implies

$$P = 1/bn + c, \tag{8P-6}$$

which is the relationship derived in the text.

Since $X = S/n$, average cost is a function of S and n,

$$AC = Fn/S + c. \tag{8P-7}$$

In zero-profit equilibrium, however, the price charged by a typical firm must also equal its average cost. So we must have

$$1/bn + c = Fn/S + c, \tag{8P-8}$$

which in turn implies

$$n = \sqrt{S/bF}. \tag{8P-9}$$

This shows that an increase in the size of the market, S, will lead to an increase in the number of firms, n, but not in proportion—for example, a doubling of the size of the market will increase the number of firms by a factor of approximately 1.4.

The price charged by the representative firm is

$$P = 1/bn + c = c + \sqrt{F/Sb}, \tag{8P-10}$$

which shows that an increase in the size of the market leads to lower prices.

Finally, notice that the sales per firm, X, equal

$$X = S/n = \sqrt{SbF}. \tag{8P-11}$$

This shows that the scale of each individual firm also increases with the size of the market.

CREDITS

Chapter 3   p. 57: AP Images; p. 60: North Wind/ North Wind Picture Archives

Chapter 4   p. 96: Library of Congress Prints and Photographs Division [LC-D4-12683]

Chapter 8   p. 213: Si Wei/Color China Photo/AP Images; p. 221: © 2004 Drew Dernavich/ The New Yorker Collection/www. cartoonbank.com

Chapter 9   p. 240: Courtesy of Subaru of America, Inc.; p. 243: Jockel Finck/AP Images; p. 247: Rachel Youdelman/Pearson Education, Inc.; p. 250: McClatchy-Tribune Information Services/Alamy

Gross National Product per Capita (in 2011 dollars)

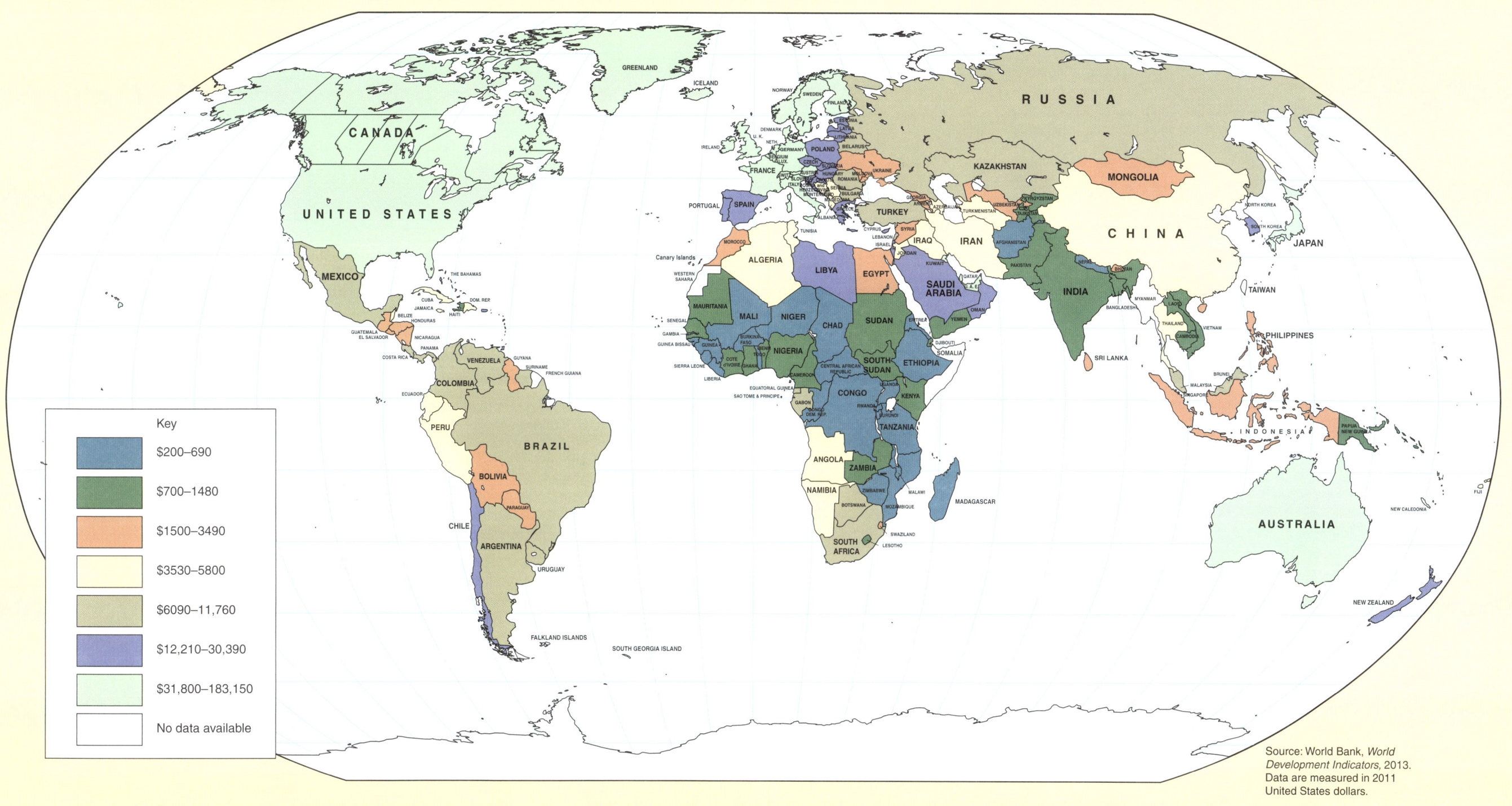

Key

- $200–690
- $700–1480
- $1500–3490
- $3530–5800
- $6090–11,760
- $12,210–30,390
- $31,800–183,150
- No data available

Source: World Bank, *World Development Indicators*, 2013. Data are measured in 2011 United States dollars.